book is to be retu
the last date st

1992
1993

2012

AMERICAN CERAMICS

1876 to the Present

AMERICAN CERAMICS

1876 to the Present

GARTH CLARK

BOOTH−CLIBBORN EDITIONS•LONDON

Editor: Libby W. Seaberg

Copy Editor: Bitite Vinklers

Designer: Joel Avirom

Production Manager: Dana Cole

Library of Congress Cataloging-in-Publication Data
Clark, Garth, 1947–
American ceramics, 1876 to the present.

Rev. ed. of: A century of ceramics in the United States, 1878–1978.
c1979.
Bibliography: p.
Includes index.
1. Pottery, American. 2. Pottery—19th century—United States.
3. Pottery—20th century—United States. 4. Porcelain, American.
5. Porcelain—19th century—United States. 6. Porcelain—20th
century—United States. 7. Potters—United States—Biography.
I. Clark, G. Garth, 1947–   . Century of ceramics in the United
States, 1878–1978. II. Title.
NK4007.C56 1987   738'.0973   87-1177
ISBN 0-904866-59-9

———

FRONTISPIECE: **Roy Lichtenstein** Ceramic Sculpture #11, 1965.
See page 130.

PHOTOGRAPH ON PAGE 8: **Toshiko Takaezu** Closed Form, 1980.
Porcelain, height 6". Collection Daniel Jacobs.

CONTENTS

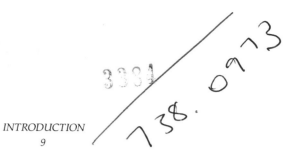

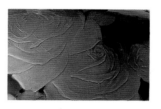

ACKNOWLEDGMENTS

This book is the result of shared knowledge and passion on the part of many friends and colleagues. I have attempted to thank those individuals who provided special assistance, but if I have omitted any names it is just my inefficiency and does not reflect a lack of gratitude. First, I wish to thank Margie Hughto and Ronald Kuchta, director of the Everson Museum of Art, for encouraging me to write *A Century of Ceramics in the United States* ten years ago, the book on which this volume is based. In many ways that book and the exhibition it accompanied changed my professional life, and I am grateful for Hughto's initiative and Kuchta's support and trust over the years. As far as the present project is concerned, I wish to thank my editor, Amy Walsh, for enduring my confusing bicoastal communications, computer glitches, missing discs, and electronic "anomalies." She worked energetically under great pressure. Abbeville Press has been a flexible and understanding partner. In particular the professionalism and cheerful encouragement of Abbeville's Sharon Gallagher and Libby Seaberg's attention to detail and matters of scholarship have made this project a pleasure to work on.

Many museum curators and directors have assisted in gathering the photographic material, and in particular I wish to thank Marjorie Beebe (Galleries of the Claremont Colleges), Ulysses Dietz (The Newark Museum), Suzann Dunaway (Mills College Art Gallery), Susan Harkavy (American Craft Museum), Philip Johnston (Museum of Art, Carnegie Institute), Martha Lynne (Los Angeles County Museum of Art), David McFadden (Cooper-Hewitt Museum), the indefatigable Barbara Perry (Everson Museum of Art), Kevin Stayton (The Brooklyn Museum), Davira Taragin (The Detroit Institute of Arts), John L. Vanco (Erie Art Museum), and Oliver Watson (Victoria and Albert Museum). The cooperation of all the artists and their galleries is enormously appreciated, and although I am loath to single out any individuals, the friendly assistance of Asher/Faure, Allan Frumkin and his gallery staff, Fuller/Goldeen, Barbara Gladstone, and the Jordan-Volpe Gallery was considerable.

I am grateful to all the collectors for helping to arrange photography and for access to their collections. Betty Asher, Martin Davidson and Dawn Bennett, Gwen Laurie Smits, the Jedermann Collection, and Hope and Jay Yampol were most generous with their time. A special thanks must go to Daniel Jacobs for making his impressive and scholarly archives available to me and for allowing so many examples from his collection to be reproduced—the time and energy he expended on this project were considerable and have enhanced the quality of this book. The talents of many photographers (past and present) have been assembled in this book, but in particular I wish to thank Courtney Frisse, Tony Cunha, and the magical John White for their efficient and creative support. In addition my thanks to Joel Avirom for his sensitive design of the book.

In order to write this book I have had to take off five months from my gallery duties. It was my staff and partners, Alice Hohenberg, Wayne Kuwada, and Mark Del Vecchio, who filled in for me. I wish to thank both Wayne and Alice for assisting in organizing the photography. My greatest debt is to Mark for the freedom he provided me during this frenetic time by taking on so much work and for the thankless task of keeping my spirits high. Without him the book could not have been completed in so short a period of time. Lynne Wagner also provided valuable assistance, being a seasoned veteran from the *Century* book.

My sons Kelly and Mark exercised a restraint and maturity beyond their years over the past five months and were charmingly supportive and inquisitive as the project progressed. Last, my thanks to my parents, Reg and Babs Clark, whose visit to this country coincided *again* with my work on the book, and when required they uncomplainingly took a back seat to the bank of clattering Kaypro word processors.

This book is dedicated to Mark Del Vecchio and the creative individuals whose spirit and achievement ennoble these pages.

INTRODUCTION

A decade has passed since I began to work on the book *A Century of Ceramics in the United States 1878–1978*. Much has changed in that relatively brief period of time. Contemporary American ceramics has progressed from the anonymity of the craft shop to the critical spotlight of the museum and the art gallery. Its aesthetic concerns have become the focus of serious scholarly attention. The politics of patronage have dramatically altered from an academic system dominated by educational institutions to free-market support from corporate and private collectors. American art pottery has come out of the attics and into the feverish arena of the auction houses and specialty dealers. It seemed that by 1980 ceramics had, almost overnight, acquired a large and influential audience—a development in which the *Century* book played a role.

The book became the catalogue for an exhibition of the same title, which I co-curated with Margie Hughto and which was organized by the Everson Museum of Art. The timing of the exhibition was perfect—igniting a massive interest in the media. It traveled through the United States from 1979 to 1981, drawing unusually large audiences and enthusiastic support from the art critics. Part of the fascination with the exhibition was in the excitement of discovery. This was the first time that the modern history of American ceramic art had been assembled and presented in an art context.

Most viewers did not realize that ceramics had enjoyed such a cohesive, complex, and provocative tradition. It also became apparent from this exhibition that while the medium was responsive to other visual arts, it also revealed a tough independence, dealing with issues, visual languages, and metaphors that were unique to the medium. In addition, it was also evident that from the 1950s onward American ceramics had taken on a radical leadership role in the ceramics world—a position that it still retains today despite energetic competition from Europe and Japan.

The importance of ceramics in the broader art fabric of the United States has been acknowledged since 1979 by many museums. In the past few years major surveys confirming the originality and importance of American ceramics have taken place at the Victoria and Albert Museum, London; Stedelijk Museum, Amsterdam; Museum of Fine Arts, Boston; Whitney Museum of American Art, New York; Los Angeles County Museum of Art; Nelson-Atkins Museum of Art, Kansas City, Missouri; San Francisco Museum of Modern Art; and many other institutions.

All of these developments have altered the structure of the medium, and with the emergence of a new generation of actively exhibiting ceramists, it was necessary to update and enlarge the *Century* book. The project began as such projects often do—with modest ambitions. In fact, the text has grown by forty percent, and many of the chapters were rewritten, as were most of the biographical essays. In addition, new photography was commissioned. Surprisingly, few of my opinions have altered over the decade. Indeed, I believe that many of the viewpoints, particularly some of the more controversial issues, have been vindicated with time. However, upon rereading the text I found many statements to be too generalized and I have tried to refine definitions and judgments and make them much more specific.

The other difference between this book and its predecessor is that this revision has essentially grown into two books. The first part is a historical narrative organized by decade. The second part constitutes a very substantial body of "back matter." All of the artists in the book are described and discussed in the biography section. Some entries give only a brief introduction to the artist, while most of the entries on the more seminal figures have evolved into detailed and major essays. I would suggest that the narrative be read in tandem with the biographies.

The second part of the book includes a selected listing of ceramics exhibitions since 1876 and a 1,200-entry bibliography, together with a subject and artist index to the bibliography. This provides a substantial resource for scholars and for those who wish to research American ceramics beyond the limits of this overview.

Last, I wish to apologize to the many talented artists whose work I have not been able to include in this study. American ceramics has grown into a massive activity and it will take many books in the future to give this medium all the exposure and credit that is its due. I trust, however, that those artists who have been included will be effective ambassadors for the field at large and represent the complementary mix of tradition and innovation that has characterized the ceramics movement in the United States and maintained its vanguardist role internationally.

AMERICAN CERAMICS
1876 to the Present

Karl Müller *Union Porcelain Works, Greenpoint, New York.
Century Vase, 1876. Porcelain, height 22½". The Brooklyn
Museum. Gift of Carll and Franklin Chace in Memory of Pastora
Forest Smith Chace.*

The Centennial Exposition of 1876 in Philadelphia provided little indication of the brewing revolution in ceramic art. Indeed, the opposite seemed to be true. Isaac Clarke criticized American ceramics, stating that "American attempts at artistic decoration were such as to make the judicious grieve . . . [there was] nothing to approach even the lower grades of European ware."[1] Yet underlying the poor design at the Centennial were the seeds of an American aesthetic that could be seen in Karl Müller's *Century Vase* and Isaac Broome's *Baseball Vase*. The latter was of particular interest because it drew from indigenous experience, resulting in an original, if slightly incongruous, form.

Also at the Centennial was a little-noticed display of painted china by a group of women artists from Cincinnati. Their work was not remarkable in itself, but it represented the first sign of a spirit of invention and achievement that was beginning to surface in this affluent Ohio city, and that was to lead in the next four years to the founding of the art pottery movement in the United States. More importantly, their work set the ceramist on a course that was to lead, eighty years later, to the preeminence of the United States in the world of ceramic art and to the redefinition of the medium's role in the fine and decorative arts.

The first phase of the art pottery movement in the United States lasted from 1878 to 1889. This seminal period covers three important developments: the development of what was later to become known as Cincinnati faience; the founding of the Rookwood Pottery in 1880; and, in 1889, the first international recognition of American art pottery. These achievements were largely the result of the efforts of two socially prominent women, Mary Louise McLaughlin and Maria Longworth Nichols. Both women were central figures in the women's art movement in Cincinnati, "a group of unusually talented and energetic ladies [in] an expanding Midwestern community yearning for culture, refinement and recognition equal to that of the older

CHAPTER ONE

1876

cities along the Eastern Seaboard."[2]

Both McLaughlin and Nichols became involved in pottery decoration through their interest in china painting. Karl Langenbeck, a glaze chemist who had received a set of German china paints as a gift, introduced Nichols to the "Devil's art" in 1873. In the following year, McLaughlin took instruction in china painting from Marie Eggers as part of Benn Pitman's course in wood carving at the Cincinnati School of Design.[3] The course was a popular success, although Ms. Eggers knew little more of the technique than did her students. Excited by the overglaze techniques, the students formed a committee to select china-painted wares for the Centennial in 1876. They raised funds for the city's participation in the Centennial by holding a Martha Washington tea party and auctioning china cups that had been painted at the School of Design. The cups fetched as much as $25 each, and the sale raised $385.

The painted china selected for the Centennial was exhibited alongside carved wood, needlework, and watercolors in the Cincinnati Room of the Woman's Pavilion. Although these china objects lacked formal accomplishment—and at times showed unfortunate lapses of taste—they represented one of the earliest attempts in the United States to employ ceramics as an independent art medium. The sensation of the Centennial, however, was the Japanese ceramics display and the slip-painted *procès barbotine*[4] wares of Haviland Auteuil, which were also exhibited in the French court. First introduced by the French artist-potter Ernest Chaplet, barbotine wares are characterized by their rich, Rembrandtesque underglaze surfaces in tones of brown, ocher, and blue. Writing about what he called the Limoges faience, R. H. Soden Smith of the South Kensington Museum (later known as the Victoria and Albert Museum) hailed the artistic excellence of the work and suggested that "it is not impossible that it will have an art influence on our time."[5] The words were indeed prophetic. For a time, barbotine was the rage of Europe and was extensively imitated. The interest in Europe was short-lived, however, while in the United States the variants of this technique were the basis for the early pioneering work of McLaughlin, Charles Volkmar, Hugh Robertson, and the Rookwood Pottery. Barbotine became the dominant technique in American art pottery, a position it maintained until the early twentieth century.

Soon after the Centennial McLaughlin began to experiment at the Patrick L. Coultry Pottery,

attempting to reproduce the barbotine wares. At first she made the common error of painting underglaze with pure oxides. Then, in 1877, she realized that the depth and richness of the barbotine palette came from mixing the oxides with slip to form an engobe. She applied the engobes to the pots while unfired and leather-hard. In her first firing, in October 1877, she applied the slips too thinly, and the yellow color of the body showed through, marring the effect. But, by January 1878, she had drawn the first technically successful piece from the kiln—a pilgrim bottle. The first exhibition of these wares took place in May, under the auspices of the Women's Art Museum Association. The

Mary Louise McLaughlin Patrick L. Coultry Pottery, Cincinnati. Pilgrim Jar, 1876. Slip-painted, glazed earthenware, height 10⅜". Cincinnati Art Museum.

pieces were later shown in New York and Paris, receiving an honorable mention at the Exposition Universelle.[6]

McLaughlin's achievement was considerable. She had stumbled upon a technique that Chaplet had taken years to perfect, and she rapidly achieved a mature creative use of its potential. The press gave enthusiastic coverage to McLaughlin's success. Part of the media's enthusiasm, however, came from a misunderstanding; the press confused the term "Limoges faience" with "Limoges enamel."[7] The latter technique had been discontinued in the eighteenth century and good examples were enormously expensive.

The extensive media coverage of McLaughlin's achievement sparked a wide interest in Cincinnati in all forms of pottery decoration. Attracted by the publicity, many young women sought instruction from the Coultry Pottery, which took advantage of the popular interest and had begun to offer lessons. McLaughlin remembered this development with mixed emotions. Although she had no part in the instruction, her own pioneering efforts made her feel partly responsible for the work that emerged. Her recollections of this work are both amusing and revealing, for they show McLaughlin's distance from those who treated pottery as merely a dilettante pursuit:

> It may be imagined with what abandon the women of that time, whose efforts had been directed to the making of antimacassars or woolen Afghans, threw themselves into the fascinating occupation of working in wet clay. The potters imparted to them various tricks of the trade and some fearful and wonderful things were produced. Not long ago the proud possessor of some of these treasures showed me a pair of vases with characteristic decoration of the period. While still wet they had been rolled or otherwise peppered with fragments of dry clay until their surfaces were of the texture of nutmeg graters, while all over had been hung realistically colored bunches of fruit. For a time, it was a wild ceramic orgy during which much perfectly good clay was spoiled and numerous freaks created.[8]

In order to set a standard in this overenthu-siastic popular response to ceramics, McLaughlin founded the Cincinnati Pottery Club in 1879. She presided over the club's activities first for a short period at the Coultry Pottery and later at the Frederick Dallas Pottery. The Pottery Club's purpose was "to uphold the standard of good craftsmanship of the best workers in the different branches of pottery."[9] It was the first club of its kind and served as the model for pottery associations in Chicago and New York and in other parts of the country. More broadly, it contributed to the growth of the nascent women's art movement. Invitations to join the club were sent out to fifteen artists in Cincinnati; inadvertently the invitation to Marie Longworth Nichols was not delivered. Although attempts were later made to correct the omission, the imperious Nichols rejected all reconciliatory efforts, sowing the seeds of a long feud between herself and McLaughlin. Nichols started working on her own, first at the Dallas Pottery and then in 1880 at her own studio, the Rookwood Pottery, at 207 Eastern Avenue.

The Cincinnati Pottery Club held its first Annual Reception and Exhibition on May 29, 1880. The event was a considerable success; enough work was sold to balance the budget of the club for a year. Clara Chipman Newton, the secretary of the club and an early china decorator, recalled the event:

> The whitewashed walls were hung with rugs as a background to the masses of dogwood and other fresh blooms. Throughout the appointed hours, crowds surged up and down the old wooden stairway and in and out of the kiln sheds which were also in gala array. In the middle of the afternoon Mr. Dallas, full of excitement, came to a small group of us to tell us that carriages were standing as far as you could see up and down the street and way around the corner. Those carriages were to him the outer and visible expression of reward and spiritual grace he had previously doubted the members of the club possessing.[10]

An artist representing *Harper's Weekly* attended the event and published his wood engraving of the show in the May 29 issue of the magazine.

This was the first national acknowledgment of the growing ceramics movement in Cincinnati. The activities of the club were threatened, however, on October 7, when Thomas J. Wheatley served the club with an injunction restraining both McLaughlin and Nichols at the Rookwood Pottery from producing slip-painted underglaze. Wheatley had applied for a patent on the process earlier in the year and had been granted patent number 232,791 on September 28. The restraining order was eventually thrown out of court but not before the Cincinnati press had turned the tussle into a cause célèbre, reporting the claim with headlines such as "War Among Potters, T. J. Wheatley Secures a Patent on American Limoges."

In the journalistic investigation it became apparent that McLaughlin was the true originator of Cincinnati faience. Even Nichols rallied to her side, remarking in an interview that McLaughlin had produced the wares "before Wheatley even thought of such a thing." Later, however, Nichols reneged on this statement and tried to claim authorship of the technique for Rookwood.[11] The publicity generated by the dispute served only to heighten the interest in Cincinnati as a ceramics center. By 1881 women were coming from New York and Michigan to study and work in Cincinnati. At the Coultry Pottery alone, the work of more than two hundred amateur artists was being regularly fired. The club eventually moved to the Rookwood Pottery, remaining there until its eviction in 1883. Unable to find a new pottery, the members returned to painting on commercial china blanks, the process with which the club had originally been involved. McLaughlin turned to other materials, concentrating on decorative metalwork.

The focus of Cincinnati faience now turned to the Rookwood Pottery. Nichols had drawn her first firing at Rookwood on Thanksgiving Day in 1880. One of her *Aladdin* vases was purchased by Tiffany and Company in New York, and her pottery was shown during a lecture by Edward Atkinson in Boston. The pottery received critical attention in the fall of 1882, when Oscar Wilde visited Rook-

wood. Clara Chipman Newton remembers meeting "the fashionable Disciple of the Aesthetic":

> I was not even at that time, when the newspaper contained accounts of his vagaries, prepared for the callalily leaf overcoat and the shrimp pink necktie of the individual who was shuddering visibly over a vase which he was pronouncing 'too branchy' as I entered the room. I did not claim the vase which heretofore appeared to my unenlightened eyes to be a very good and desirable piece of work. The next day in his lecture Mr. Wilde scored the pottery to the intense amusement of Mrs. Nichols who has a sense of humour and fully appreciated that artistically we had much to learn.[12]

At this point it is necessary to explain the contribution of the Arts and Crafts Movement (of which Wilde was a disciple) and its impact on the time. The movement began in England and was social, political, and reformist in nature. Its founders were John Ruskin and William Morris, who felt a need to counter the decay in taste that was caused by the Industrial Revolution and the commercializing of the decorative arts. Its flashpoint was the *Great Exhibition* of 1851, which Morris denounced as a "death register of design." The movement fostered the ideal (although it rarely practiced it) of equality between artist and craftsman. It also originated the notion of "truth to materials" and established a "style" of structural naturalism that was later emulated by certain potteries.

TOP: *Wood engraving of works in the first Annual Reception and Exhibition of the Cincinnati Pottery Club at the Frederick Dallas Pottery, Cincinnati, 1880. Reproduced from* Harper's Weekly, *May 29, 1880.*

RIGHT: **Maria Longworth Nichols** *Rookwood Pottery, Cincinatti. Vase, 1883. Earthenware, gilt stampwork, slip painting, height 20½". The Newark Museum, Newark, New Jersey. Purchase 1985, Mathilde Oestrich Bequest Fund and Eva Walter Kuhn Bequest Fund.*

FAR RIGHT: **Clara Chipman Newton** *Teapot, 1882. Earthenware with slip painting and overglaze, height 8⅝". Cooper-Hewitt Museum, Smithsonian Institution/Art Resources, New York. Gift of Marcia and William Goodman.*

Charles Volkmar *Greenpoint, New York.* Handled Vases, *1879–81. Earthenware, slip painting under clear glaze, height 12½". The Brooklyn Museum. Gift of Leon Volkmar.*

LEFT: ***Mary Louise McLaughlin*** *Frederick Dallas Pottery, Cincinnati.* Ali Baba Vase, *1880. Earthenware, slip-painted under a clear glaze, height 36½". Cincinnati Art Museum. Gift of Rookwood Pottery.*

Matthew A. Daly Rookwood Pottery, Cincinnati. Vase, 1886. *Earthenware, slip painting under clear glaze, height 20¼". Private collection.*

The Arts and Crafts Movement had little effect on the aesthetics of Rookwood, but it had an impact in other ways. Rookwood was to adopt many of the progressive attitudes of the movement, including the employment of women decorators and the liberal treatment of its "artists." The attention and publicity that the Arts and Crafts Movement was receiving in England provided both a validation and a spur for similar activities in the United States. The art pottery movement in the United States did not, however, have the hard, anti-industry ideological stance of its counterpart in England. Whereas the English movement was socialistic in character, its American version was capitalistic. The art potteries, and in particular Rookwood, were very much at ease with the marriage of industry, art, and craft. Profit was held to be as sacred as aesthetics.

Nichols began to employ decorators at Rookwood. Gradually the pottery developed purpose,

becoming an art pottery in the true sense, concentrating on unique pieces while still producing some transfer wares. An important figure in Rookwood's success story was Benn Pitman, the founder of the Cincinnati School of Design. Most of the earliest, and ultimately some of the most influential, of Rookwood's decorators graduated from Pitman's school. Albert R. Valentien (né Valentine) was Rookwood's first decorator, joining the pottery in September 1881 after graduating from the School of Design. In 1881 and 1882 the pottery engaged new decorators: Alfred L. Brennan, Laura A. Fry, Clara Chipman Newton, Harriet ("Nettie") Wenderoth, Matthew A. Daly, Joseph N. Hirschfield, and William P. MacDonald. All but Brennan were students of Pitman.

Pitman had originally come to the United States from England to promote his brother's invention— shorthand—but he remained to head the School of Design. He was a "progressive" educator and a disciple of John Ruskin and William Morris. In particular, he was passionate in his advocacy of nature as the source of ornament. This was not a unique position. It had been advocated in the influential writings of Owen Jones (*Grammar of Ornament*, 1856) and of Christopher Dresser (*Studies in Design*, 1876). However, the style Pitman advocated relied less on the stylized forms preferred by the Arts and Crafts Movement and more on the clear, balanced, restrained forms of the Beaux-Arts Movement. Pitman's interest in flowers and plants was not just a matter of theoretical or intellectual pursuit; the late nineteenth century was characterized by a populist fascination with nature:

> Perhaps no other century was so taken with flowers and plants as was the nineteenth. Indeed the century's cultural preoccupation with nature is deserving of thorough study. Flowers and plants surrounded the daily lives of people in the past century: through interior designs in wallpaper, carpets and textiles, in cut arrangements, in gardens and parks, in illustrations in popular magazines. Long associated with rituals of courtship and courtesy and invested with profound iconographical religious meaning, flowers became the element of a complicated

"language" developed to permit the wordless expression of sentiment. Through Kate Greenaway and other nineteenth century writers and illustrators the "language of flowers" entered popular culture.[13]

In 1883 Nichols appointed William Watts Taylor as manager and from then on took an ever-diminishing role in the pottery's affairs. Taylor proved to be a shrewd manager, and although Newton never approved of Taylor personally, she rightly credited him with being responsible for the financial and artistic success of the pottery, saying that he was "due the honor of carrying the pottery up from the mud banks of the river to the heights of Mt. Adams."[14]

Taylor's first changes were to cease all transferware production and to evict the Pottery Club (with Nichols's consent), as he did not enjoy nurturing what he saw as a future competitor on the premises. Although businesslike in his handling of affairs, Taylor recognized that the independence of the artists and the encouragement of experiment were important. Thus, he organized lectures on art for his staff and assisted them in their studies and researches. He was careful, however, to allow the production only of wares that were of a conservative nature and astutely avoided the bizarre and exotic. This meant eradicating the remaining grotesque qualities of Nichols's *japonisme*, on which the early style of the pottery had been based,[15] and modifying the Japanese style with that of the more formal Beaux-Arts. Rookwood had been trying since 1881 to enlist a Japanese decorator and finally succeeded, in 1887, in hiring a talented young artist, Kataro Shirayamadani, who introduced a new elegance and purpose to the Rookwood style. The marriage of Japanese art to Pitman's naturalism remained the most vital force acting upon the Rookwood style.

The introduction of significant technical innovations altered the mawkishness of the wares produced during the first three years at Rookwood, giving way to a more accomplished and safe style of slip painting. In 1883 Laura Anne Fry had adapted

a throat atomizer to apply the slips on greenware, a technique she later patented at the suggestion of Taylor.[16] Aware of the need to have greater control of the ceramic processes, Taylor employed Karl Langenbeck in 1884 as the first glaze chemist in the nation. About the time of Langenbeck's arrival, the distinctive tiger's-eye, a crystalline aventurine glaze, was accidentally discovered at Rookwood. European factories, including Sèvres and Meissen, were intrigued by these early innovations in Cincinnati and produced their own imitations.

The Cincinnati art pottery movement came of age in 1889, when Rookwood received a coveted gold medal in competition with Europe's finest potteries at the Exposition Universelle in Paris. The exposition was a double triumph for Cincinnati, since a silver medal was awarded to McLaughlin for her overglaze decoration with metallic effects. This brought to an end what might be termed the movement's period of innocence. Through sheer

Laura Anne Fry *Cincinnati Pottery Club. Plaque, 1881. Slip-painted earthenware under clear glaze, diameter 14¾". The Saint Louis Art Museum. Gift of the artist.*

naiveté and empiric experiment, the movement's leaders had stumbled on a number of significant decorative techniques and glazes. A period of difficult sophistication, in both intent and aesthetics, lay ahead.

The East Coast played only a minor role in art pottery until the late 1890s. Two of the early pioneers, Hugh Cornwall Robertson and Charles Volkmar, were involved, however, in the production of barbotine wares before this date. Soon after the Centennial, Robertson produced Bourg-la-Reine

wares at the Chelsea Keramik Art Works, his family pottery, founded in 1872 in Boston. He named the wares in honor of the town where Chaplet had revived the barbotine process. Volkmar had learned of the process while working with the *maître faïencier* Theodore Deck in Paris.[17] The wares that Volkmar produced on his return to the United States in 1879 were termed ''Volkmar faience'' and were the closest in style and technique to the original barbotine wares. Working on Long Island, Volkmar became known for the bucolic landscapes in the style of the Barbizon school that he painted onto forms derived from Classical Greek models.

Both Robertson and Volkmar eventually turned from the slip-painted wares to Oriental techniques and glazes. Robertson's obsession was with the *flambé rouge* and *sang de boeuf* glazes; unfortunately, he became so preoccupied with these glazes that he neglected the management of the pottery, which closed in 1888. In 1891, with a group of wealthy Bostonians as backers, Robertson established the Chelsea Pottery and continued his experiments. Volkmar meanwhile moved his kilns first to Corona, Long Island, and then to Metuchen, New Jersey. Despite their importance historically—Robertson for his glaze science and Volkmar as a teacher— neither was an artist of consequence, and their achievements fade in comparison to those of their contemporaries in Cincinnati.

Isaac Broome Ott and Brewer Co., Trenton, New Jersey. Baseball Vase, 1876. Parian ware, height 35". New Jersey State Museum, Trenton.

RIGHT: *Maria Longworth Nichols* Vase, 1879. Press-molded earthenware, blue underglaze painting and gilt overglaze, height 6". Cincinnati Art Museum.

During the 1890s the interest in the Arts and Crafts Movement became more sophisticated and better organized. Between 1896 and 1915, when the movement's membership peaked in the United States, thousands of groups were organized to bring together amateur and professional craft workers; Boston and Chicago formed exhibiting societies for the arts and crafts in 1897. Collectively these new craft groups sought to change both public taste and the role of the craftsman in an industrial world.[1] They were influenced by the writings and works of William Morris, founder of the English crafts movement. Several leaders of the English movement visited the United States: Oscar Wilde in 1882, Walter Crane in 1891–92, and Charles R. Ashbee in 1896. A further measure of the new sophistication in the field is the number of new periodicals that began to be published during these years, including *House Beautiful* (1896); *Common Clay* and *Ornamental Iron* (1893); *International Studio* (1897); *Brush and Pencil* (1898); and *Keramik Studio* and *Fine Arts Journal* (1899).

The decorative arts were becoming part of mainstream American culture. As public awareness grew, a profitable market opened up for what the Victorians had euphemistically termed "art manufacture." Ceramics seemed to be one of the most promising activities. During the 1890s a number of new potteries opened, and several existing functional potteries began to turn their attention to decorative wares. For the first part of the decade, Rookwood continued to dominate. But the competition of new potteries, such as the Lonhuda Pottery in Steubenville, Ohio (founded 1892), and the introduction of imitations of so-called Standard Rookwood (with its basic brown palette of slip painting) by Samuel A. Weller and J. B. Owens in Zanesville, Ohio, led to a proliferation of slip-painted wares. The importance of these Beaux-Arts pots began to recede in favor of the simple forms and monochrome glazes that would find favor during the latter part of the decade.

CHAPTER TWO

1890

The major event for American decorative art during the formative years of the 1890s was the 1893 World's Columbian Exposition in Chicago. It was there that William Grueby saw the *flambé rouge* and mat-glazed pots of Auguste Delaherche and Ernest Chaplet, two of France's leading artist-potters, which would later lead to a revolution in pottery tastes. The exposition also exhibited the proto–Art Nouveau ceramics of the brilliant Dutch ceramist Theodoor A. C. Colenbrander.[2] The women's movement still dominated much of the activity in American ceramics. The Cincinnati Pottery Club was re-formed for the exposition, and it exhibited wares in the Cincinnati Room of the Woman's Building. The exhibition of this work marked the end of an era in ceramics, as male, entrepreneurial ceramists began to dominate. Newton called the exposition "a fitting port in which to anchor the good ship, 'Cincinnati Pottery Club' . . . the ripples that vessel made broadened into a great and far-reaching circle which had more influence than we realized possible over the ceramic art of the country."[3]

Susan Goodrich Frackelton, another major figure in the early china-painting movement, received a gold award at the Columbian Exposition for her salt-glazed stonewares.[4] The following year her Frackelton Dry Colors (gold and bronzes) were awarded medals by Leopold II, King of the Belgians, at a competition in Antwerp. She also gained prominence in the field through other activities. In 1892 she had sought to improve communications within the burgeoning china-painting movement and formed the National League of Mineral Painters. In 1895 her book *Tried by Fire*, the bible of the china painters, was published in its third and enlarged edition.

The last major venture into painted decoration came in 1895, with the opening of the Newcomb Pottery in New Orleans. The pottery was a part of Sophie Newcomb Memorial College for Women (today a division of Tulane University) and was conceived as a practical training ground for women pottery decorators.[5] Mary G. Sheerer, a graduate of the Cincinnati Art Academy, joined the pottery at its inception to teach underglaze slip and china painting. At first there was an attempt to emulate Standard Rookwood, but the technique proved difficult to control. About 1897 a new style emerged. Designs were incised into wet clay and painted with oxides after the first firing. The wares were then glazed with a transparent high-gloss glaze. Newcomb was to be associated with this technique until 1910, when it changed to mat glazes under Paul E. Cox.

Newcomb wares, with their distinctive palette of blue, green, yellow, and black, are the most original and freshly inventive of the later painted wares. The choice of color and subject reflected the idyllic setting of the pottery, the Garden District of New Orleans above Canal Street, surrounded by magnolias and huge, spreading oaks. In order to give the pottery a unique character, all motifs and landscapes used in decoration were drawn from the flora and fauna of New Orleans and the surrounding bayou country. The forms were either chosen from the "damp room" or designed by the decorators and thrown by Joseph Fortune Meyer, a gifted and intuitive potter. None of the designs was ever repeated (unless requested by the purchaser), so they retained their lively character, winning numerous honors between 1900 and 1915.[6] The first decorators were undergraduate students, but the later, permanent employees represented a changing nucleus of four to five women who had graduated from the college. In addition to the accomplished decorator Mary G. Sheerer, another important early decorator was Mazie T. Ryan. Her decorations are self-contained within the three-dimensional frame they occupy and have a particular spontaneity and invention. Later stalwarts of the decorating team at the Newcomb Pottery were Sadie Irvine, Anna Frances ("Fannie") Simpson, and Henrietta Bailey.

Decorative tastes began to change in the late 1890s, and a demand for simpler form and limited decoration began to replace the cluttered eclecticism of late Victorianism. This was a victory for the Arts and Crafts Movement purists such as Elbert Hubbard, Gustav Stickley, and Frank Lloyd Wright. In responding to new fashions, American ceramics drew from the simplicity of Chinese and Japanese ceramics as interpreted by the French artist-potters, such as Chaplet and Delaherche. Inspiration also came directly from the growing interest in collecting Oriental ceramics among American museums and private collectors.[7] A number of ceramists, notably Robertson and Volkmar, began to work in imitation of the Chinese potters, but their achievements were uneven and their production limited. Robertson was best known for his Dedham Pottery crackle wares, with their blue framing of rabbit, whale, butterfly, and floral motifs.[8]

The work of William Grueby in Boston[9] was the most significant breakthrough in the modern aesthetic. Grueby concentrated on the relationship between form and the unpainted texture and color of the surface. After seeing the works of Delaherche at the World's Columbian Exposition in Chicago in 1893, Grueby began experimenting to produce a natural mat glaze that did not require bathing the glazed surface with acid, an artificial means of achieving mat surfaces at the time. He accomplished this feat in 1897–98, producing a superb range of intense mat glazes in greens, yellows, ochers, and browns. The most successful glaze was the distinctive "Grueby green," which responded well to the relief-decorated form. The glaze broke to a lighter tone on the raised surfaces, and an overall veined effect, resembling a watermelon rind, enlivened the surface. The character of the glazes was unlike any other in use at the time. Grueby's glazes represented a major breakthrough for the empiric art pottery movement in the United States. The surface of these wares was extremely seductive and, as Jervis wrote in his *Encyclopedia of Ceramics* (1902), it was a glaze "so soft, beautiful, so perfectly glossless, that at one bound it leapt into public favor."[10]

Unlike the glazes, which were an original development, Grueby's early forms relied heavily upon a paraphrasing of the pottery of Delaherche.[11] The early Grueby forms (1898–1901) were designed by George Prentiss Kendrick and show the same climactic use of the shoulder and the massive, monumental neck as are found in the works of Delaherche. Some of the translations, however, were original and inspired, notably Kendrick's adaptation of a multihandled vase, in which the use of clay was lively and less imitative of Delaherche.

In part, the aesthetic character of the ware was conditioned by technical issues. The center of the kilns became too hot for tiles and so Grueby decided to fill this space with vessels. The semiporcelain clay body that was created out of the tile clay to withstand the higher temperatures, in turn, played its role in the "look" of Grueby:

> Some of the heft of a Grueby pot's massiveness is due to natural causes, as the grainy clay was basically the same as that used for Grueby tiles and it necessitated *heavy* potting. However we may see the heavy potting and thick glaze as emblematic of the handcraft revival and the revolt from slickness. The slight irregularities in the relief lend the vibrant quality that art lovers under Ruskin's guidance had come to value. The glaze was temperamentally congenial to the pots and moved with deliberation down their sturdy walls, and in some cases developed a surface as uneven as sculpture slowly patted up over an armature.[12]

The final product had a crispness because no molds were used, even though the designs were reproduced in quantity. Each form was thrown by an elderly potter, and then the relief decoration was applied by young girls culled from the local art

TOP: **Mary Given Sheerer, decorator, and Joseph F. Meyer, potter** *Newcomb Pottery, New Orleans. Vase and Stand, 1898. Earthenware with incised and underglaze decoration, height 12". Cincinnati Art Museum. Gift of Miss Mary Sheerer.*

Grueby Pottery *Grueby Faience Company, Boston. Vase, c. 1898–1902. Earthenware, mat green glaze, height 12½". Courtesy Jordan-Volpe Gallery, New York.*

OPPOSITE: **Albert R. Valentien** Rookwood Pottery, Cincinnati. Vase, 1893. Slip painting under clear glaze, earthenware, height 12½". Private collection.

Matthew A. Daly Rookwood Pottery, Cincinnati. Vase, 1899. Standard glaze on earthenware with slip painting, height 14". Courtesy Jordan-Volpe Gallery, New York.

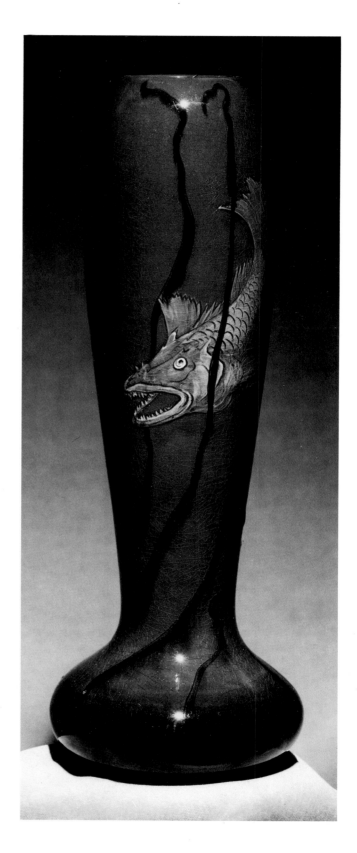

schools.[13] The wares were an immediate success and were given the all-important endorsement of Gustav Stickley, who had emerged as the leader of the Arts and Crafts Movement in the United States, incorporating Grueby wares into his interiors.

Grueby won numerous awards both at home and abroad and was given the signal honor of being represented in Paris by Maison Bing l'Art Nouveau. It is possibly this association that led to Grueby's being linked to the French Art Nouveau style that had emerged in the mid-1890s and had become so popular in Paris. Although Grueby's designs do use stylized, organic shapes, the wares lack other characteristics of French Art Nouveau: the whiplash line in decoration, the symbolic use of the female form, and what the historian Tschudi Madsen calls the "linear thrall" of the forms. There is a slight affinity between Grueby's wares and Jugendstil, the German variant of Art Nouveau, which is more structural and abstract than its French antecedent. In essence, the wares produced by Grueby were a Mission-style adaptation of Delaherche's classic forms. The semantics of Grueby's aesthetic lineage were of little concern to the art pottery movement, which now became involved in a scramble to copy the "eternal matt green with which every potter is trying to outdistance Grueby and win fame and fortune."[14]

Two other noteworthy pioneers were active at the same time as Grueby: Mary Louise McLaughlin and a Biloxian, George E. Ohr. McLaughlin returned to ceramics in 1895 after a long hiatus, remarking, "One who has experienced the fascination of working in wet clay is never safe from its lure, and after a while I was again dreaming of the possibility of carrying out another venture, this time of a much larger scope."[15] At the Brockman Pottery she worked in earthenware and developed a technique for inlaid decoration, which she patented, having learned her lesson from the Wheatley debacle. She was dissatisfied with these wares, however, since they had to be produced with the assistance of a potter. She was eager to have a

more intimate contact with her material and began to experiment with porcelain in 1898. After an arduous period of trial and error, involving eighteen clay bodies and forty-six glazes, she perfected her first new works in 1899.

These "Losantiwares," as she termed them, were small ovoid forms with a delicate carved decoration that was alive with the curvilinear energy and rhythm of Art Nouveau. Ironically, McLaughlin was one of the most outspoken critics of this style, warning that it could not be "followed without reason or moderation except to the detriment and

Mary Louise McLaughlin Losanti Vase, c. 1899. Glazed, once-fired porcelain, height 4½". National Museum of American History, Smithsonian Institution, Washington, D.C.

degradation of the beautiful."[16] A group of twenty-seven Losantiwares was shown in 1901 at the Pan-American Exposition in Buffalo, where they received a bronze medal. At about the same time Adelaide Alsop Robineau wrote that it would take a generation before a new aesthetic in porcelain would arrive.[17] McLaughlin countered with a note pointing out her own achievements. Robineau printed the note in the July 1901 issue of *Keramic Studio*, and invited McLaughlin to contribute an article on her work for the December issue. Once again McLaughlin had emerged in the vanguard of the art pottery movement, this time as one of the first artists to work in the self-sufficient manner of the studio potter. After 1906 her interest waned, although she continued intermittent production of her porcelains until 1914.

The work of George E. Ohr is difficult to categorize. Working in Biloxi, Mississippi, where he ran the Biloxi Art Pottery, he was the maverick of American ceramists and produced the most original work of his day. He was an extremely conspicuous member of the art pottery movement. He often accompanied his work to the major fairs and expositions, where, with his resplendent twenty-inch-long mustache tucked into his shirt or combed into a bizarre shape, he gave demonstrations on potting. Ohr developed extraordinary skill on the potter's wheel, to which he responded "like a wild duck in water,"[18] and threw vulnerable earthenware forms to the point of collapse. He would then fold, ruffle, twist, and pummel the thin vessels and add sinuous, intricate handles. Of Ohr's throwing skills, Paul E. Cox wrote: "It is said that Ohr could work on the wheel whichever way it turned. Certainly he could throw wares of considerable size with walls much thinner than any potter ever has accomplished. It is quite probable that George Ohr, rated simply as a mechanic, was the most expert thrower the craft has ever known."[19]

The manner in which Ohr worked with clay was not entirely without precedent. The ruffling of forms was popular in Victorian glass; both Emile Gallé and the Danish craftsman-designer Theobald

Bindesboll had produced pummeled and ruffled pots in the 1880s. These were effetely decorative, however, whereas the work of Ohr was furiously gestural. It is most likely that Ohr developed this style from the Southern folk pottery wares, of which he must have been well aware and in which this kind of vocabulary, employed more crudely than by Ohr, was common.

Ohr's glazes ranged from livid, mottled pinks and startling polychromes to somber browns and metallic finishes. Few of his contemporaries could appreciate his sense of form, most were impressed and even intimidated by his skill in creating glazes. The opinion of the ceramics historian Edwin Atlee Barber that "the principal beauty of his ware lies in the richness of the glazes" infuriated Ohr. Ohr often made pieces that were deliberately left in the bisque state as completed wares. Once, to underscore this point, he scribbled a legend around a photograph of a group of unglazed pots: "Color and quality counts [*sic*] nothing in my creations. . . . God put no color or quality in souls."

Ohr, who began working about 1879, was chronologically the first of the American studio potters and also the first to achieve stylistic inde-

George E. Ohr Biloxi Art Pottery, Biloxi, Mississippi. Bank, c. 1898. Earthenware, length 3½". Collection Martin and Estelle Shack.

pendence from Europe. He led the assault on the boundaries of applied and fine art, blurring the definition of what the critic John Coplans so succinctly terms "the hierarchy of media." This is implicit in his turning away from the controlled surface concerns of Victorian decorative art and plunging into the aesthetics of risk. Early in his career, Ohr insisted on seeking out the unique and became obsessed with the slogan "no two alike." He pushed to the limit the expressionist qualities of the material, dealt with form on a level of poetic anthropomorphism, and played a capricious game with function. Ohr was able to sidestep the limitations of European formalism with which others, such as Adelaide Robineau and Charles Fergus Binns, became embroiled. Ohr's work expresses the vision of his time. He was the true prophet of American ceramics, anticipating the expressionism, the verbal-visual art, and the surrealism that were to become mainstream concerns in the 1950s and 1960s.[20]

George E. Ohr Vase, c. 1898. Glazed earthenware, height 6⅛" Collection Irving Blum.

LEFT: *George E. Ohr* Three-Handled Mug, c. 1898. Glazed earthenware, height 8". Collection Jasper Johns.

RIGHT: *George E. Ohr* Teapot, 1899–1904. Glazed earthenware, height 8". Jedermann N. A. Collection.

Current-day judgment views Ohr as a great American artist,[21] but only a few appreciated Ohr in his own time. Their distinction, however, makes up for their paucity in numbers: Cox, Barber, and William King. In an address in Buffalo, King made one of the most telling contemporary judgments of Ohr's work: "Ohr is an American potter who stands in a class by himself, both in personality and in his pottery. Sometimes he is referred to as the 'mad potter of Biloxi.' He calls himself the 'second Palissy'; issues a challenge to all potters

of the world to compete with him in making shapes and producing colors. . . . While much of Mr. Ohr's work will not meet the requirements of accepted standards . . . there is art, real art—in this Biloxian's pottery."[22]

The majority of Ohr's contemporaries took a harsher view of his achievement. Most could appreciate his skills but not his aesthetic, so provocative and passionate that it was at odds with the genteel, static style of the Arts and Crafts Movement. Frederick Rhead, a potter and self-elected spokesperson for the field, wrote of Ohr: "Ohr, really a most skillful thrower . . . who was concerned only with regard to his personal reputation. Entirely without art training and altogether lacking in taste, he deliberately distorted every pot he made in order to be violently different from any other potter."[23]

The two important words in the critique are "training" and "taste," the cornerstones of the Arts and Crafts Movement and its prime defenses later against the forces of change and the avantgarde. Ohr, the son of a blacksmith, was not educated in the arts in the formal sense of the term, nor was he concerned with pandering to notions of taste. Indeed, much of his work was a deliberate assault on accepted taste. But, in terms of a ceramic literacy, Ohr was the most sophisticated practitioner of his day. His sources were apparently quite eclectic, ranging from Southern folk wares to the pottery of Bernard Palissy. After a period of apprenticeship to the potter Joseph Fortune Meyer in New Orleans, Ohr left on a sixteen-state, two-year trip, during which he "sized up every potter and pottery . . . and never missed a window, illustration or literary dab on ceramics since that time, 1881."[24]

About the turn of the century, Ohr began to withdraw his major work from sale, selling only fair trinkets and "gimcracks." The reason was that Ohr believed himself to be a genius and that he wished his works to be "purchased entire" by the nation. In fact, the hoard of over six thousand pots that he set aside—the major part of Ohr's art

production—remained in the Ohr family warehouse until 1972, when a New York antiques dealer purchased them for resale.

Ohr's impact on his own time was limited, partly the result of his decision not to sell his art pieces after 1900, partly the result of his incompatibility with the arts and crafts elite. About 1906 he ceased potting and, despite successes at the Pan-American and Saint Louis fairs, disappeared from the American ceramics arena. Aware that he could not compete in the drawing-room atmosphere in which most of his contemporaries operated, Ohr set up his own world of pranks and outrageous behavior, which only led to his being dismissed as a Southern eccentric. There is good reason to believe, however, that he used his bizarre behavior as a defense against the rejection he received as an artist. A clue can be found in an extremely poignant interview described in a letter from Paul Cox to Robert Blasberg: "He sat on the edge of the bed blinking his black eyes at me. Finally he said, 'You think I am crazy don't you?' I replied that Meyer had told me about him and that I did not think he was crazy (I still don't). With that George stopped his act and remarked, 'I found out a long time ago that it paid me to act this way.' "[25]

The letter offers an intimate glimpse of the artist and the mask he wore. This country buffoon was the same man who had the artistic integrity to refuse to sell his work in his lifetime, knowing that his vision would be better appreciated in another time, one more sophisticated in the issues of art. He was a sensitive and committed artist, who played the role of jester to counter the feelings of hurt and frustration at being rejected and misunderstood. He left us a wonderful legacy. Compared to the perfect but sterile works of some of his contemporaries, Ohr showed us that a tour de force of craftsmanship has no value by itself: it must be matched by an equal tour de force of spirit.

Hugh Cornwall Robertson *Dedham Pottery. Dedham, Massachusetts. Three vases, c. 1893. Glazed stoneware, height 5", 8⅞", 6". Cooper-Hewitt Museum, Smithsonian Institution/Art Resources, New York.*

Kataro Shirayamadani *Rookwood Pottery, Cincinnati. Vase,
1900. Earthenware, slip painting in light relief under clear
glaze, height 17⅜". Philadelphia Museum of Art. Gift of John
T. Morris.*

The first decade of the twentieth century was a period of significant growth and expansion for the ceramics movement. During these years the art potteries produced some of their most mature work, a nascent studio pottery movement took hold, and the "art tile" industry expanded. Sculptural issues now entered into the creation of the vessel, while the university emerged as the dominant patron of the ceramic arts.

The 1900 Exposition Universelle proved to be a major victory for American ceramics, confirming the promise that America's art pottery had made on the same platform eleven years earlier. Rookwood showed exceptional wares by Kataro Shirayamadani, Artus Van Briggle, William P. McDonald, Sara Sax, Carl Schmidt, John Wareham, and Harriet Wilcox, and won a Grand Prix. Grueby received one silver and two gold medals and, with Auguste Delaherche, justly won another Grand Prix. Medals also went to the Newcomb Pottery. Nichols (by then Mrs. Bellamy Storer), McLaughlin, and Frackelton were also represented in the exposition. Grueby was particularly popular, and its booth was sold three or four times over. The success of the American ceramists was confirmed when many of Europe's leading museums purchased American wares for their collections of decorative art.[1] Rookwood and Grueby went on to receive major awards at the Exposition Internationale de Céramique et Verrière in Saint Petersburg, Russia (1901), and at the International Exposition of Modern Decorative Art in Turin, Italy (1902).

The excellent reception of American ceramics at these pivotal world's fairs brought new confidence. From 1900 onward a spirited independence began to enter American ceramics. Artists no longer worked with one eye toward recognition in Europe. This was largely due to a series of important expositions that were held in the United States and redirected the interest of the American decorative arts. At the expositions in Buffalo in 1901 and in Saint Louis in 1904, American ceramists began to

CHAPTER THREE

1900

compete with each other rather than European potteries.

The already weakened importance of Rookwood declined further during the first years of the twentieth century, although various attempts were made to sustain its leadership. Following poor sales at the Saint Louis fair, Rookwood tried to develop mail-order sales, but the relatively high prices (from $20 to $250) proved to be unsuitable for merchandising in that manner. New techniques and glazes, notably the mat, vellum glaze, were introduced by a new glaze chemist. The slip-painting technique was improved to include cooler colors, under a brilliant, clear glaze. The Philadelphia Museum of Art owns a masterwork of this style, a vase by Shirayamadani, by far the most talented and skilled of Rookwood's decorators. The shoulder of the pot is wrapped in a swath of roses and painted in a trompe l'oeil manner with a delicate green slip. The brilliant, clear glaze responded to the light relief of the painting, crackling slightly to enhance the illusionary depth of the work. In the end, however, Rookwood suffered because the public had tired of painted pottery, regardless of the skills presented. Artists who worked in a more sculptural manner now began to dominate.

Yet, despite Rookwood's gradual fall from commercial favor, the Arts and Crafts Movement continued to regard it as an ideal. Oscar Lovell Triggs, founder of Chicago's Industrial Arts League, hailed the pottery as the perfect modern workshop:

> The pottery is not merely a workshop; it is in a sense a school of handicraft, an industrial art museum and a social center. The craftsmen, creating and initiating on their own ground, constantly improve in skill and character. . . . A portion of the building is now devoted to exhibition. By means of lectures and other entertainments at the pottery, the public participates in some degree in the enterprise, and by reaction shapes the project. Here are all the elements needed for an ideal workshop—a self-directing workshop, an incidental school of craft, and an associative public.[2]

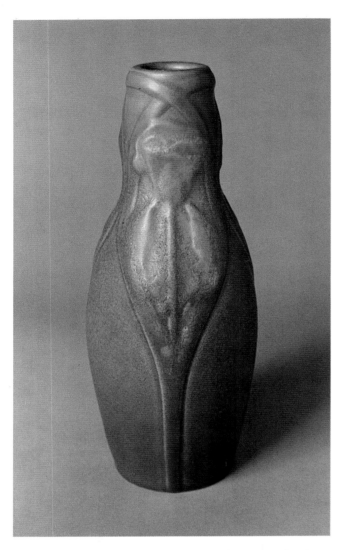

Artus Van Briggle Vase, 1903. Glazed earthenware, height 9". National Museum of History and Technology, Smithsonian Institution, Washington, D.C.

Rookwood was very much a business enterprise. The creation of vases from 1883 onward was based upon the industrial division of labor—a Rookwood vase went through twenty-one hands before completion. Working conditions at Rookwood were difficult. Rookwood's decorators were presented as artists, yet they received salaries as low or lower than other craftsmen in the ceramic industry: Rookwood's male decorators were paid marginally more than their counterparts in other potteries, while the women were paid the same wages as women who performed unskilled chores in the ceramic industry. Decorators were fined for misnumbering vases or for other infringements of the management code. Furthermore, every piece made at Rookwood belonged to the factory. One of the devices the decorators employed to get pieces of their own work that they wanted to retain was to designate the works as seconds, which would allow them to be acquired at a substantial reduction. William Watts Taylor, the manager, was nevertheless also careful to nourish the egos of his creative staff by providing them with perks, such as trips to major expositions and time to make holiday presents to balance their low wages.

Rookwood responded cautiously to the international fascination with Art Nouveau. American interest in this style was unenthusiastic and short-lived—the nation's avant-garde preferred the more austere structuralism of the English Arts and Crafts Movement. William McDonald and Anna Valentien, however, produced figurative wares in a mild Art Nouveau style. Valentien's works showed the influence of her studies in France with, among others, the French sculptor Auguste Rodin. Mary Chase Perry also worked on carved, sculpted forms that were somewhat irregular in shape. Basically, however, she kept to floral relief decoration, and her work was closer in essence to that of Delaherche and Grueby.

The two artists who dominated the sculptural approach to the vessel were Artus Van Briggle and Louis Comfort Tiffany. Van Briggle's work of this style dates from 1900, when he moved for health reasons from Rookwood to Colorado Springs. There, with the assistance of William H. Strieby, a chemist at Colorado College, he adapted the local materials to his needs and established the Van Briggle Pottery. At the Paris Salon in 1903, Van Briggle held the first exhibition of his major works, including *Lorelei* and *Despondency*. The critical and commercial success of this showing was followed in 1904 by the response to his wares at the Louisiana Purchase International Exposition in

Saint Louis, where the wares received two gold, one silver, and two bronze medals. Van Briggle was denied the Grand Prix only because of a rule prohibiting its award to first-time entrants.[3] Van Briggle died while the exposition was in progress, and his exhibition cases were draped in black. He had modeled a large number of works between 1900 and 1904, and in a short period had managed to achieve his objective of "getting ceramics away from glass coating and let the pot itself carry its own beauty."[4] After his death, the Van Briggle Pottery was continued by his wife, Anne Gregory Van Briggle.

Tiffany Studios (Corona, Long Island) introduced Favrile pottery in 1904 at the exposition in Saint Louis and offered it for sale for the first time the following year. It is not known to what extent Louis Comfort Tiffany was directly involved in the

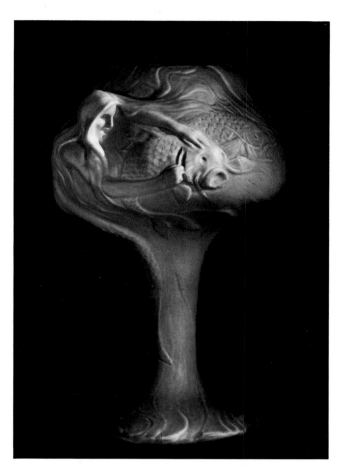

RIGHT: **Artus Van Briggle** Toast Cup, 1901. *Glazed earthenware, height 11". Courtesy Jordan-Volpe Gallery, New York.*

Anna Marie Valentien *Rookwood Pottery, Cincinnati. Bowl, 1901. Glazed earthenware, diameter 10½". Private collection.*

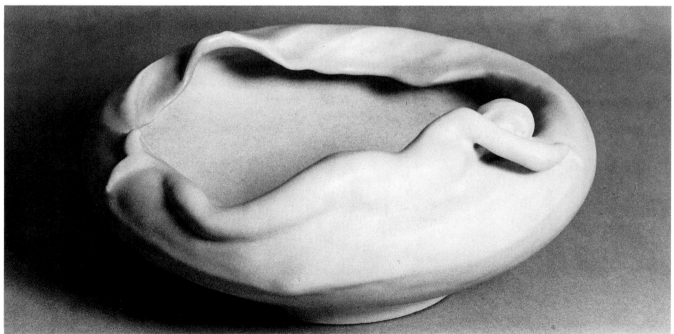

Carl Schmidt *Rookwood Pottery, Cincinnati. Vase with Peacock Feather, 1905. Slip painting under glaze, height 10". The Metropolitan Museum of Art, New York. Purchase 1969, Edward C. Moore Fund.*

BELOW: **Marie de Hoa Le Blanc** *Newcomb Pottery, New Orleans. Three-Handled Vase, c. 1901. Glazed earthenware, height 16⅜". Cooper-Hewitt Museum, Smithsonian Institution/Art Resources, New York. Gift of Marcia and William Goodman.*

RIGHT: **Sarah Elizabeth Coyne** *Rookwood Pottery, Cincinnati. Iris Vase, 1907. Slip painting under clear glaze, height 9". Collection Mark Del Vecchio.*

creation of Favrile pottery.[5] Although the works of Tiffany Studios were produced by anonymous craftsmen from Louis Tiffany's designs, the pottery reflects his intuitive sensitivity to the materials and his clear compositional style. In placing this work stylistically, we have traditionally referred to the pieces as Art Nouveau. However, as pointed out by Martin Eidelberg, the work only occasionally shows the use of the Art Nouveau grammar. The relief modeling is elegant but static. It resembles most closely the Parian wares that were produced by the Bennington Pottery about 1850; it has the same tautness of line, the rhythmic growth of the stalks from the base of the pots, and the formal integration of the floral motifs and form.[6] This work by Tiffany, in common with many other "Art Nouveau" wares, by Fulper, Grueby, and Weller, belongs most properly to a category that Kirsten Keen identifies in her catalogue *American Art Pottery* as "structural naturalism."[7]

Louis Comfort Tiffany *Tiffany Pottery, Corona, New York. Vase, c. 1905–14. Glazed earthenware, height 9". The Newark Museum, Newark, New Jersey. Purchase 1975, Wallace M. Scudder Bequest Fund.*

The studio pottery movement, beginning some thirty years after art pottery, was little involved in the notion of the painted pot. This comment from a 1905 article by William Burton summarizes the central concern and direction of the studio potters:

> In the presence of wonderful examples of the Chinese single color flambé glazes, so perfect in their beauty, so decorative in their appearance, and so entirely free from any effect except those proper to clay and glaze, the Western potter could not but ask himself questions as to the artistic value of his own productions. . . . At the commencement of the twentieth century, therefore, we find that reaction against the elaborately painted pottery of the previous century and a half has reached the position of an international movement, which seems designed to bring pottery once again in harmony with its qualities.[8]

Charles Fergus Binns was a key figure in the development of a support structure for studio pottery in America. Just prior to his move to America in 1897, Binns was the superintendent of the Royal Worcester Porcelain Works and was being groomed to replace his father as director. His wealth of knowledge in ceramic science found an excellent outlet in 1899 through the American Ceramic Society, which he was instrumental in founding. His influence was most important, however, at the New York School of Clayworking and Ceramics in Alfred, New York. Binns directed the school from its inception in 1900 until his retirement in 1931.[9] The school was the second of its kind in the country, and under Binns's astute direction, it rapidly established itself as the premier ceramics school in the nation.[10] Binns advocated a perfectionist aesthetic of restraint based upon Oriental classicism, which was actively propagated and continued by his students and his students' students. The aesthetic grew out of Binns's fondness for the quieter periods of Chinese and Korean pottery.

The "classic Alfred vessel," as it is colloquially known in ceramic circles, is distinguished by a sophisticated use of materials, clean and simple form, little or no ornament, and a strongly classical inspiration. This style brought about a welcome sophistication in craftsmanship and other formal values. But these were won at the expense of expressionist qualities in clay. In many ways, the Binns legacy was inhibiting artistically, and it was not until the 1950s that Alfred began to demonstrate its freedom from this "less is more" regime.

By contrast, Mary Chase Perry was an adventurous artist with a love of color, experiment, and the chance generosity of the kiln. Together with her close friend Adelaide Robineau, Perry was a leading member of the National League of Mineral Painters until 1903, when both artists gave up overglaze decoration. Robineau turned to porcelains, and Perry, in partnership with her intimate friend and business associate Horace J. Caulkins, established the Pewabic Pottery as an art pottery in Detroit. Together, Perry and Caulkins developed the Revelation kiln, a portable, kerosene-burning, muffle kiln that became the standard for the china-painting movement and was used by many of the leading art potteries. In her workshop, Perry adopted an open, modern approach to processes. She installed an electric kiln within a few months of opening the pottery and continued to involve herself with innovative kiln design and clay-handling techniques. Her craft ethic was, however, staunchly anti-industry. She stated that it was not the aim of a pottery to become an "enlarged, systematized, commercial manufactory" but "to solve progressively the various ceramic problems that arise and [to work] out the results and artistic effects that may remain as memorials, or at least to stamp a generation as one that brought about a revival of ceramic art."[11]

In her work, Perry chose not to deal with what she saw as purely mechanistic concerns and never learned to throw. Rather, she had the potter Joseph Herrick produce forms from her drawings while she busied herself with her first love, glaze chemistry. Because she adopted this nineteenth-century "white-collar" approach to pottery, the forms lacked the evolution and continuity of the works of Binns and Robineau. Nonetheless, she produced a few masterpieces, whose beauty derives largely from

Mary Chase Perry *Pewabic Pottery, Detroit. Vase, 1909–11. Earthenware with iridescent glaze, height 18". The Detroit Institute of Arts. Gift of Charles L. Freer.*

her range of extraordinary glazes—from elusive, iridescent glazes to cloudy, rich in-glaze lusters. Her real contribution as an artist can be found in her architectural commissions, which will be discussed later in this chapter.

Although each of these figures has an important position in the history of this decade, it is Adelaide Alsop Robineau who was the most formidable figure. She was the influential editor of the leading ceramics journal, *Keramik Studio;* a dedicated teacher; and the one American studio potter whose work was ranked, without qualification, alongside that of Europe's greatest masters. She was an inspirational example as an artist both for ceramics in general and for the women's art movement in particular. Moreover, through the pages of *Keramik Studio,* she was responsible for introducing ceramists around the nation to the finest work of artists at home and abroad. She encouraged an intelligent use of ceramic processes and materials and herself

provided a standard of artistry and skill.

In 1899, the date of the first publication of *Keramik Studio* by her husband, Samuel Robineau, and an associate, Adelaide Robineau was still involved with the Beaux-Arts style of the china painter's movement, in which she was one of the most prominent decorators. Her work at this point was concerned with the painting of overglaze on commercially produced blanks, which her contemporary Frederick Rhead described as a "veritable riot of gold and color."[12] The seeds of her conversion to a more intimate use of the materials were just discernible in her editorial for the first issue of *Keramik Studio,* in which she called for higher ideals and remarked that the ceramic arts had grown beyond the china-painted "stereotyped spray of flowers and the inevitable butterfly."[13]

Until recently it has been accepted that the French ceramist Taxile Doat was the crucial force in Robineau's conversion from china painter to studio potter. But Martin Eidelberg's probing examination of Robineau's early work in *Adelaide Alsop Robineau: Glory in Porcelain* has revealed a much more complex process of change.[14] Instead of beginning "cold," in 1903, we find that Robineau had actually been quietly planning her move for two years. Robineau made her first pot in 1901, at the studio of Charles Volkmar in New York. It was a crude, lumpish object but decorated somewhat prophetically with a scarab or beetle clutching a disk in its feelers, the motif she would use for her *Scarab Vase* in 1910–11.[15] It seems likely that she later also took lessons in throwing from Volkmar. Eidelberg's research also indicates that Robineau attended Charles F. Binns's Alfred summer school in 1902, rather than 1903, as is generally cited.[16]

Eidelberg argues convincingly that the die was cast in 1901 and not 1903, as Robineau's husband was later to claim. Her earlier involvement is supported by the mood of the time. Robineau herself

---

Frederick Hurten Rhead Roseville Pottery, Roseville, Ohio. Della Robbia Vase, c. 1904. Glazed earthenware, height 10½". Erie Art Museum, Erie, Pennsylvania.

wrote in 1901 that there was a "spreading tendency to go into Keramic work from clay to finish."[17] Speaking at the National League of Mineral Painters, Susan Frackelton reminded her audience that women were civilization's first potters and that this tradition should be revived.[18] Frackelton, a doyenne of the china painters, had already been making salt-fired wares for some time.

In 1902 *Keramic Studio* published an article by William P. Jervis on Doat and illustrated his fecund gourd forms with their luminous mat glazes. Intrigued by his work, the Robineaus obtained a treatise by Doat on high-fired porcelains that they published as a series in the magazine during 1903 and 1904, and in 1905 as a handbook, the first on its subject in the English language. Even though Robineau obviously admired Doat's work, she was only slightly interested in his technique of *pâte-sur-pâte*. Instead, she turned to incising and carving, an interest that can be traced back to July 1901 and a review by Robineau of the porcelains of Bing and Grondahl. In this article, which reads more like a personal manifesto for her future work than a review, Robineau warns against naturalism and does a volte-face on the works of the Danish pottery Royal Copenhagen Porcelain:

> The artists of the Royal Manufactory are painters. Bing and Grondahl are modellers and sculptors. Here the paste is everywhere incised, broken by open work decoration, thrown in powerful and striking shapes, and the color is only used to complete the decoration, while in the Royal Manufactory works the color is the whole decoration. The latter's wares give the impression of charm and refinement, the Bing & Grondahl wares that of strength.[19]

Equipped with what she learned from her studies with Volkmar, from Doat's thesis, and from three weeks of study with Charles Fergus Binns at Alfred, Robineau built her first kiln on a hillside overlooking Syracuse, New York, in 1903. Her ceramic study had been sporadic, and she was still very much an amateur with minimal skills. At first she employed assistants, but the attempt to commercialize her talent was "a dismal fail-

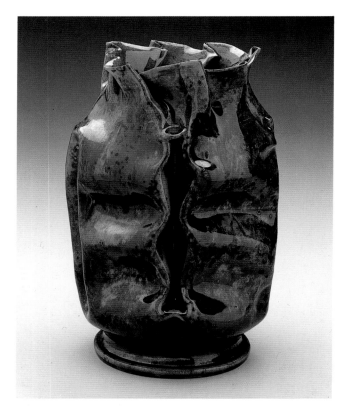

George E. Ohr Vase, c. 1900–1904. Earthenware, height 8".
Jedermann N. A. Collection.

BELOW: *George E. Ohr* Three double-handled vases, c. 1900.
Glazed earthenware, height 11½", 9½", 12". Collection Martin
and Estelle Shack.

RIGHT: *Ruth Erickson* Grueby Pottery, Grueby Faience Company,
Boston. Vase, c. 1900. Earthenware with green mat glaze,
height 16⅜". Cooper-Hewitt Museum, Smithsonian Institution/
Art Resources, New York.

ure . . . she did not like the casting process and even shapes thrown on the wheel by professional throwers from designs, however accurate they were, lacked that finishing touch that she alone could give them."[20] The early porcelains were undecorated, molded, crystalline-glazed bottles and vases, "many of which have disappeared, for the museums were not interested and sales were difficult . . . most people, not understanding high fire porcelain work, objected to the price, which was around $30.00 or $35.00"[21]

In 1905 Robineau began to perfect the technique with which she was to become most closely associated, the carving and excising of dry but unfired porcelain. During the next five years she produced some of her most economical and finely resolved pieces, including the *Viking* (1905), *Monogram* (1905), and *Crab* (1908) vases now in the collection of the Everson Museum of Art, Syracuse, New York. Although bearing a relationship to carved Chinese porcelains, Robineau's interpretation was personal and progressive. Certain pieces were vaguely reminiscent of Doat's early work, of Art Nouveau, proto–Art Deco, and other styles in vogue at the time. The works are expressions of Robineau's eclecticism, given their character and uniqueness through the artist's individual and personal response to a material, its process, and its traditions.

This unique quality was won at high cost, for the techniques employed by Robineau were remorseless, and any error of judgment or skill could result in failure. Once Samuel Robineau, seething with frustration and rage, wrote: "I have never felt so disgusted and discouraged in my life . . . every one of the new pieces is warped and blistered . . . anybody who is foolish enough to do cone 9 porcelains ought to be shut up in an insane asylum."[22] But the Robineaus persevered despite the vagaries of the kiln and the indifference of the public. Their triumph finally came in 1911.

As the first decade of the twentieth century drew to a close, the studio potters began to reject direct mainstream influences such as Art Nouveau and turned their backs on painting and sculpture.

Adelaide Alsop Robineau Monogram Vase, *1905. Thrown form, glazed porcelain, height 12⅜". Everson Museum of Art, Syracuse, New York.*

Adelaide Alsop Robineau Crab Vase, 1908. Glazed and incised porcelain, height 7⅜". Everson Museum of Art, Syracuse, New York.

The independent spirits, such as Charles Fergus Binns, Mary Chase Perry, Henry Chapman Mercer, and last, but most significant, Adelaide Alsop Robineau, developed strong, personal aesthetics based on the interpretation and imitation of the monuments of ceramic history. This development was a mixed blessing. On the one hand, it resulted in an identity for ceramics based on its *own* roots and not a second-hand interpretation in clay of painting or sculpture. But this hermeticism meant that the revolutionary changes in concepts of surface and form that were beginning to emerge in the modern art movement had no influence on the potter. Anyone looking for influence from the Cubists, Fauves, or Constructivists in studio pottery in the first quarter of the century would come away empty-handed. As a result, for several decades the vessel tradition remained an anachronistic pursuit, related to the objet d'art aesthetic, with all its overtones of preciousness, bourgeois materialism, and pedantic craftsmanship. Nonetheless this period, with its unabashed sybaritism, has a lasting charm, despite, or possibly because of, its distance from the stylistic changes that were beginning to sweep American art.

During this decade another development in American ceramics began to peak. Known in the nineteenth century as "art" tiles, they were produced between 1870 and 1930, the "only period when tiles played a significant role in the decorative arts of the [United States]."[23] The achievements of American tilemakers during this time were among the finest of the Arts and Crafts Movement. Until the early 1870s most tiles had been imported from England. After the Centennial Exposition in Philadelphia awakened American ceramists to the "full realization of their insignificance in this field,"[24] several large industrial potteries were established: American Encaustic Tile (1875), United States Encaustic Tile (1877), Low Art Tile (1878), and others.

Most potteries maintained some level of tile production, as interest among the more progressive architects in architectural detailing of fireplaces, custom-designed tiled floors, and doorway frames grew under the influence of the Arts and Crafts Movement. Some potteries produced only architectural ceramics. Among these were the Moravian Pottery and Tile Works and Ernest Batchelder, whose first tile plant opened in Pasadena, California, in 1909. Some tile producers, such as Grueby and Fulper, however, later moved into art pottery. For the purposes of this study, only the tiles produced by the art potteries are of interest. The work of Mary Chase Perry and of one of the Arts and Crafts Movement's most enigmatic and complex figures, Henry Chapman Mercer, will be examined more closely.

The involvement of Perry and her Pewabic Pottery in tile production began when Charles Lang Freer, a leading art connoisseur and patron of the pottery, introduced Perry to the architect Ralph Adams Cram. Cram was in the process of designing Saint Paul's Cathedral in Detroit, and incorporated Perry's tiles as a feature of the building. The commission was completed in 1908 and executed in a glowing palette of blues and deep, lustrous gold. The success of the installation drew the attention of many of the nation's leading architects and commissions from Cass Gilbert, Greene and Greene, Bryant Fleming, and others.[25] Until the 1930s the creative concerns of the pottery were dominated by massive projects that took up to eight years to complete, as in the case of the National Shrine of the Immaculate Conception in Washington, D.C. Perry later directed her energies toward teaching and continued to be involved in the management of Pewabic until her death in 1961, at the age of ninety-four.

Henry Chapman Mercer was a lawyer-turned-archaeologist-turned-potter, and the Moravian Pottery and Tile Works, which he established in Doylestown, Pennsylvania, in 1901, represents one man's mission to preserve and eulogize the craft achievements that he believed constituted the genius of civilization. He undertook this task with the contradictory qualities of visionary and retrogressive romantic, which so often characterized the makeup of the Victorian Arts and Crafts leaders.

On the one hand, he decried the progress of mechanization, and on the other he designed and erected three of the first reinforced-concrete buildings in the country and devised ingenious equipment to reproduce his tiles.

Mercer had at first intended to make pottery to reestablish the tradition of the Pennsylvania German potter, which to his dismay had died out. The clay, however, proved intractable and suitable only for tiles. The first designs came from the cast-iron Moravian stove plates that he collected. From these relief-modeled surfaces, Mercer, a rapacious eclectic, derived ideas and images from which to develop his narrative tile panels. He employed bright primary colors in his glazes, as well as clay stains, and often left his designs unglazed to highlight the free and unbounded values of his local red clay. Mercer's work was in great demand. Like Perry, he was associated with many architects of the Arts and Crafts Movement. He died in 1930, leaving behind a vast legacy that is only now being fully explored.[26]

Henry Chapman Mercer Moravian Tile Works, Doylestown, Pennsylvania. Installation, *c. 1909.*

LEFT: *Arthur Eugene Baggs* Marblehead Pottery, Marblehead, Massachusetts. Vase, *c. 1908. Mat-glazed earthenware, height 5¼". Private collection.*

Adelaide Alsop Robineau Poppy Vase, 1910. Porcelain with
incised decoration of poppies, inlaid slip and crystalline glaze.
Height 6¼". Everson Museum of Art, Syracuse, New York.

By 1910 the foundations for the modern movement in ceramics had been laid. Ceramic art now had its own schools, active exhibiting societies, publications, and some artists of consequence. The preceding decade had greatly enlarged the technical vocabulary of ceramics, the secrets of high fire had become known, and more new glazes were introduced during that time than during any other decade before or since. This technical knowledge was rapidly expanding as ceramics became a more international pursuit. The decade is distinguished by Robineau's successes in Europe and America, the founding of the University City Pottery, and a decline in the importance of the art pottery industry in favor of the studio potter. Aesthetically the potter moved slightly to the right, drawing upon an Oriental historicism as the major inspiration. What the decade lacked, however, was aesthetic direction. Craftsmanship and decorating skills were advanced to a high level of proficiency, but no new vision emerged to give the medium direction.

Unquestionably, the establishment of the University City Pottery was the event of the decade. As the potter Frederick Hurten Rhead later wrote:

> This venture is unique in the history of American ceramics because it is the only one of which I have any knowledge where hundreds of thousands of dollars were lavishly expended for no other purpose than to create and produce beautiful pots. Kings, princes and potentates in other countries have done this sort of thing and some governments are still doing it, but I know of no other instance where a group of potters were assembled together and permitted to run amock regardless of cost and monetary returns.[1]

In 1910 the School of Ceramic Art was opened as part of the Fine Art Academy at the People's University in University City, a suburb of Saint Louis. The school was part of a project by Edward Gardner Lewis, publisher of the *Saint Louis Star*, to create a center for culture in the Midwest. Lewis built his empire on the American Women's League,

CHAPTER FOUR

1910

which he had established in 1907, and on the magazine subscription marketing system on which its fortunes depended—league members (mainly living in remote rural areas) sold magazine subscriptions from which Lewis received a 50-percent commission. Soon these women, whose desire for education Lewis so profitably exploited, were bringing him a staggering income of $40,000 a day. In return, the women were offered free education by correspondence through the People's University. Their response was immediate and overwhelming: over fifty thousand women registered for courses. The best of these were invited as honors students to study at the Fine Art Academy.

The academy was built as part of an ornate square-mile development on the outskirts of Saint Louis that incorporated commercial and residential areas as well as the university. The academy was designed in the Italian style, providing excellent facilities for ceramics, sculpture, and painting. Lewis had assembled a strong faculty, with the sculptor George Julian Zolnay at its head. He hired Taxile Doat to be director of the ceramics school. Doat was then one of the preeminent ceramists in Europe, and his appointment was a coup for Lewis. Doat was paid a magnificent salary, $10,000 a year, and was allowed to bring with him (at the league's cost) the former foreman of a Paris pottery, Eugène Labarrière, and Emile Diffloth, the art director from the Boch Frères Pottery in Belgium. Robineau was appointed instructor of pottery; Frederick Rhead and Kathryn E. Cherry, a Saint Louis china painter, completed the faculty.

Although the venture was short-lived—the Lewis empire foundered and collapsed in 1911—during the year and a half of its existence, the pottery had unlimited resources and aesthetic freedom. The academy sought to foster an atmosphere of creativity and experimentation; there were funds available to encourage investigation into every facet of ceramics. In the chemistry department, thousands of samples of American clayware were tested, and many were evaluated as being superior to European clays.[2] The working conditions at the academy proved, however, to be less than ideal. In particular, the atmosphere was poisoned by Diffloth, a bitter obstructionist who caused numerous problems and isolated Doat from the American potters. Diffloth denied the faculty access to most of Doat's technical information, and their contact with him was disappointingly sporadic.

The ceramists worked in a circuslike atmosphere, for Lewis constantly guided visiting dignitaries through the studios to meet the world-famous Doat. Every opening of the kiln was an opportunity for the publicity-conscious Lewis (himself a dabbler in clay) to call a press conference. The firing of Doat's *University City Vase* was one such occasion:

> About everyone except the chief of police and the president of the United States was invited to peep through the spy-holes while [the kiln] was under fire. Photographers were dragged in and everyone and everything was photographed every ten minutes in all manner of

positions. The opening of the kiln was a breathtaking affair. So many people were in the kiln room that it was hardly possible to open the kiln door. Doat in a cutaway coat was there in all his glory; Diffloth, his first assistant, on one side; Labarrière, chief porter, on the other, with photographers snapping hither and yon. It was most impressive.

Lewis would even bring complete conventions to tour the studios; on one occasion Rhead recalls that the entire ceramics faculty had to stand in line for two hours and shake hands with a "visiting aggregation of over seven thousand people."

This atmosphere of a continuing media event had an impact on the production of art at the pottery. The artists felt a pressure to make a showy pièce de résistance. Doat set out to make his *University City Vase* and Robineau accepted a commission from the league to make the *Scarab Vase*, one of the most famous pieces of American ceramic art. The vase was titled *Apotheosis of the Toiler* (1910) and reputedly took one thousand hours to incise. For Robineau it was literally and figuratively a monument to the Protestant work ethic. She, however, incorrectly described it as depicting a beetle or scarab pushing a ball of food and noted that this symbolized the toiler and his work. She apparently misunderstood the scarab's use of the ball of dung to enclose its eggs. The scarab hardens the dung in the sun and then buries it in the ground; from it the larva later emerges. But the issue is less one of the accuracy of natural history than of the artist's personal symbolism of the imagery she was using.

It is difficult to understand the commitment that this vase represented without some knowledge of the technique employed by Robineau. Rhead was present during its making and recorded the detailed process involved:

> It is a definite fact that carving or excising is the most risky process of all. The carving cannot

Taxile Doat University City Pottery, University City, Missouri. Gourd Vase, 1912. Glazed earthenware, height 9". Private collection.

be well done until the piece is dry, and it is impossible to cut with the freedom possible in wood and ivory. The material is so short and brittle that any undue pressure will chip the surface. A line or excised surface of any depth must be extremely carefully scraped away bit by bit, gradually going deeper. A slight difference in the pressure of the tool, and considerable work, if not an entire piece can be ruined. I have seen the Scarab vase in all its stages of construction. Many times Mrs. Robineau would work all day, and on an otherwise clean floor there would be enough dry porcelain dust to cover a dollar piece and half an inch more carving on the vase.[3]

While Rhead might have dutifully recorded its creation, he did not approve of the final work. He felt that it had several of the failings of Doat's *University City Vase*. In later writings he referred to the *Scarab Vase* as a "monstrosity . . . the sort of thing that a criminal condemned for life would whittle to pass the time."

Modern judgment tends to support Rhead's view. Eidelberg writes of the *Scarab Vase* that it represents a significant "turn away from 'modern' design" and a return to historicism. The form was that of the so-called Chinese ginger jar, the glaze a traditional celadon, and the motif of a scarab holding the sun disk was drawn from Racinet's *Polychromatic Ornament*, the textbook for her earlier forays into historicism. The theme of the scarab was also a return to the subject of her first hand-made pot in 1901.[4] Certainly works such as the masterful *Poppy Vase* (1910), *Wind* (1913), and the *Cloudland Vase* (1914) are more substantial works.

Most of the faculty of the Fine Art Academy departed in 1911, when the Lewis empire began to crumble. The pottery, however, was carried on under the indomitable Doat, and in 1912 was re-organized on more spartan lines. It continued to produce exceptional porcelains until 1915, when

Adelaide Alsop Robineau Apotheosis of the Toiler *(also known as the* Scarab Vase *or the* Thousand Hour Vase *), 1911. Excised and carved, glazed porcelain, height 16⅝". Everson Museum of Art, Syracuse, New York.*

Doat returned permanently to France. Whatever its failings, the University City Pottery proved to be a significant venture. It was through the American Women's League that Robineau assembled a group of fifty-five of her own porcelains and submitted them to the Turin Exposition in 1911.[5] The group, including the *Scarab Vase*, was awarded the grand prize, the highest award at the exposition. Because of a rule preventing the presentation of the grand prize to an individual, the award was formally given to the league while Robineau herself was given the Diploma della Benemerenza, adjudging her porcelains the finest in the world. The award was a signal honor, achieved in the face of competition from Sèvres, Meissen, and other major porcelain factories in Europe. What they achieved through skilled teams of artisans and artists, Robineau, with the support of dutiful Samuel, had matched and surpassed. She was invited to exhibit in the following year at both the Paris Salon and the Musée des Arts Décoratifs. While in Paris, she demonstrated her throwing skills at the Sèvres manufactory to prove that the forms were not cast and that porcelain could be used to throw with precision.[6]

Frederick Rhead probably gained the most from the University City experiment. It enabled him to work closely with Robineau, who was generous in sharing her knowledge. He seemed to enjoy the steamy political atmosphere of the ceramics school, as well as the considerable personal publicity he received during his short stay. Rhead was now emerging as an important presence in American ceramics. Like Binns, he had come from a long line of British potters. He had arrived in the United States in 1902 to manage Vance/Avon, a small, six-kiln pottery in Tiltonville, Ohio. Rhead became a competent designer (if lacking in originality), an educator, and a critic. Above all, Rhead was one of the most enthusiastic promoters of American ceramic art and design.

In mid-1911 Rhead left University City and set up the Arequipa Pottery for Dr. Philip King Brown's tuberculosis sanatorium in Marin County, north of San Francisco. Dr. Brown only wanted to have the pottery for therapeutic purposes, but the ambitious Rhead saw it as an opportunity to set up a major commercial pottery. His wares proved popular, and within a year the pottery was self-supporting. But Rhead became overambitious and soon had a falling-out with Dr. Brown. In 1914 he set up the Rhead Pottery in Santa Barbara, California, where he also founded a magazine, the *Potter*, in 1916. The magazine and the pottery were both short-lived; the magazine lasted for only three issues, and the pottery closed in 1917. During this short period, however, Rhead produced some strong pottery and perfected his famous "mirror black" glaze. The *Potter* was adventurous for its day and presented a sophisticated and critical view of the ceramic arts. After 1917, when Rhead went to work for the American Encaustic Tiling Company, his importance as a potter declined in favor of a highly successful career as a designer. He remained, however, an impassioned voice for the ceramic arts and wrote extensively on the potter's art.[7]

As we look back on this decade, the *Scarab Vase*, with all its failings, characterizes the aesthetic direction of the decade. Robineau's lapses into historicism and her search for perfection and control were repeated in the work of the Binns school. For instance, Binns would throw his forms, even small vases, in three sections. He would then turn them on a lathe to the desired thinness and the exact shape he required; finally he would reassemble them. An indication of his artistic credo can be gleaned from the following excerpt from an article titled "In Defense of Fire": "Glazes must acknowledge the artistic restraint by which the whole work is controlled. Not an ear drop of molten glaze must pass the limit. At the bottom of every piece is a tiny rim of dead ground, a bisque line of demarcation. This far the fluid glaze can come but not further."[8] This formalism, which both Robineau and Binns represented in different ways, continued to be an influence for many decades. The American potter, having obtained a tangible success in technical and design terms, was reluctant

Adelaide Alsop Robineau Indian Vase, 1913. Porcelain, black bronze glaze, height 14½". The Detroit Institute of Arts. Gift of George G. Booth.

Frederick Hurten Rhead Rhead Pottery, Santa Barbara, California. Bowl, c. 1915. Glazed earthenware, diameter 7½". Collection Bob Schmid. Courtesy Erie Art Museum, Erie, Pennsylvania.

to leave the safety of these disciplines and take on the aesthetic of risk and invention.

The decade ended prematurely, in art terms, at the 1915 Panama-Pacific International Exposition in San Francisco. From then on, the harsh reality of World War I dominated life in America. The first phase of the American Arts and Crafts Movement had come to an end:

> After 1915, when Elbert Hubbard was lost with the *Lusitania* and Gustav Stickley went bankrupt, the arts and crafts movement came to a symbolic end. The original crusading impulse had been incorporated into the middle-class outlook and style; as a motif for home or office or leisure activity—rather than a new way of life or a more humane form of work—arts and crafts easily succumbed to the latest decorating fad or popular pastime. Arts and crafts still promised to relieve the body politic by providing an alternative to industrialization and its discontents, but the initial partnership of art and labor was nearly lost, buried under handicraft stands in national parks and a proliferation of do it yourself kits.[9]

In assessing the achievement of American art pottery over the previous four decades, Martin Eidelberg wrote, "Although the movement originated in response to the growing threat of nineteenth century industrialization, it did not successfully resolve the relation of the individual ceramist to an industrialized society."[10] Ironically, many pots that today are classed as "art pottery" were actually industrially produced, ersatz renderings of the craft idiom. These sold well, while those of the studio potter did not. When World War I ended, the ceramists and potters found that the energies that had given impetus to the Arts and Crafts Movement had been spent. Much of the popular public support had been lost; industry began to turn its back as art pottery became less profitable. In their search for patronage, the potters drew closer to the educational establishment and more remote from the art marketplace and art criticism. This created a dilemma, "whose repercussions were felt throughout the present century."[11]

Albert R. Valentien *Valentien Pottery, San Diego, California. Vase, c. 1915. Glazed earthenware, height 11¾". Collection Michiko and Alfred Nobel.*

BELOW: **Charles Fergus Binns** *Three vases, c. 1919. Glazed stoneware, height, 9"–11⅞". The Detroit Institute of Arts. Gift of George G. Booth.*

RIGHT: **Fulper Pottery** *Flemington, New Jersey. Vase, 1914. Glazed stoneware, height 12⅛". The Newark Museum, Newark, New Jersey. Gift of the Fulper Pottery, 1915.*

LEFT: **R. Guy Cowan** *Cowan Pottery Studio, Cleveland. Ginger Jar, 1917. Earthenware, luster with black running glaze, height 14". Cowan Pottery Museum, Rocky River Public Library, Rocky River, Ohio.*

ABOVE: **Anna Frances Simpson** *Plaque, c. 1915. Glazed earthenware, height 5". Private collection. Courtesy Jordan-Volpe Gallery, New York.*

RIGHT: **Fulper Pottery** *Flemington, New Jersey. Vase, 1915. Glazed stoneware, height 12½". Cooper-Hewitt Museum, Smithsonian Institution/Art Resources, New York. Gift of Marcia and William Goodman.*

Waylande Gregory *Cowan Pottery Studio, Cleveland. Burlesque Dancer, c. 1929–30. Porcelain, height 18". Cowan Pottery
Museum, Rocky River Public Library, Rocky River, Ohio. Produced in limited edition of 50.*

After the First World War the art establishment turned against the romantic craftsmanship of the previous decade, and "modernism" became de rigueur in art and design. In 1920 the Arts and Crafts style was considered passé, even embarrassing, and objects of this period were consigned to the attic and basement. Before modernism began to affect taste and style in the United States, there was a return to the classic simplicity of early American furniture and artifacts. It was the decade that began the uneasy marriage between art and industry (never to be fully consummated) and that found its expression in the machine-art exhibitions held annually at the Museum of Modern Art, New York. Through this involvement the museum conceived its curious policy that functional ceramics made by industry could be art, whereas vessels made by a potter with a wealth of intuition were craft and, by implication, of lesser importance.[1] American studio ceramics produced very little that conformed to the cultist machine-age ethic. The small cadre of potters in America were in the process of discovering their past and were little concerned with the present, much less the future, represented by the vanguard art movements. The vessels produced during the 1920s were contemporary interpretations of the Tang and Song dynasties, as well as of the ancient works of Egypt and Persia. The strongest contemporary influence came from the Art Deco potters of France, largely as a result of the publicity given to these artists at the 1925 Paris Exposition Internationale. The French potters were themselves involved in a somewhat decadent rephrasing of past styles.

The ceramists, in search of an aesthetic identity but uninterested in the modern fine-art movements, turned, with uneven results, to contemporary European decorative arts. The 1920s was one of the weakest decades for American ceramics, so it is not surprising that Frank Lloyd Wright wrote pessimistically of ceramics in the United States: "We have little or nothing to say in the clay figure or

CHAPTER FIVE

1920

pottery as a concrete expression of the ideal of beauty that is our own. No sense of form has developed among us that can be called creative—adapted to that material. And it may never come. The life that flowed into this channel in ancient times apparently now goes somewhere else."[2] What Wright and others did not recognize were the foundations that the 1920s were building for later achievement.

The decade has a few important highlights. In 1928 the American Federation of Arts organized the *International Exhibition of Ceramic Art*. It opened in New York at the Metropolitan Museum of Art and subsequently traveled to seven other museums in the United States, attracting considerable attention from the daily press and from art magazines. The best American pottery of the time—painted earthenware by Henry Varnum Poor, Hunt Diederich, and Carl Walters, and the spartan later works of Robineau—was arrayed alongside the work of Europe's best ceramists and potters: Bernard Leach, Michael Cardew, William Staite Murray, Emile Decoeur, Emile Lenoble, Susi Singer, Vally Wieselthier, Hertha Bucher, and others. The comparison was instructive and showed that although the American potters could equal the technical achievements of their European counterparts, the genre as a whole lacked direction. The naiveté of the American potter at that time can be gleaned from Arthur Baggs's delight in discovering the plastic qualities "of the potter's thumbprint" in 1929, after twenty-four years as a practicing potter.[3]

The American potter learned the lessons slowly, as he tried to outgrow the bias of the Alfred school, which tended to treat vessel making as a means of solving design problems rather than as an art of expression. The studio potter wavered between sterile design and vacuous decoration. Of course, there were a few exceptions, notably Henry Varnum Poor.

The lack of vitality in pottery was compensated for by evident signs of growth in ceramic sculpture. Until the 1920s the sculptural treatment of clay in

America had been either confined to the pompous nineteenth-century art porcelains of Ott and Brewer in Trenton, New Jersey, or incorporated into the vessel format, as in the work of Anna Valentien, Artus Van Briggle, and others. The development and acceptance of ceramics as an independent, decorative sculptural genre owed much to the formative role of two artists, Carl Walters and R. Guy Cowan. Walters was the first artist of consequence to use the material sculpturally, and Cowan set about orchestrating the institutions and instruments of power needed to establish the medium as a separate and valid art genre.

Walters was a successful painter when he decided to move to ceramics. His first efforts, in 1921, resulted in painted pottery, but from 1922 on, with the setting up of his kilns in Woodstock, New York, Walters began to produce a body of figurative work. His first showing was in 1924 at the Whitney Studio Club; from this exhibition the Whitney Museum of American Art, New York, later acquired Walters's piece *The Stallion*. Walters dealt almost exclusively with animal subjects, although he did do a few human figures. One of the best of these is the circus fat lady *Ella* (1927, The Museum of Modern Art, New York), a voluptuous figure that threatens to overwhelm the spidery, wrought-iron boudoir stool on which she sits.

Stylistically, Walters's work is difficult to place. It has affinities with what has been termed *folk realism* in paintings of the period. One also finds some of the whimsy in his pieces that later became a stamp of American ceramic sculpture. In Walters's work, however, it is presented without the sentimentality of the Ohio schools. Walters was clearly American in his boldness, verve, and ingenuity of technique, yet, as William Homer commented in his memorial tribute:

> It is difficult to associate him with a native style in ceramics. Because the United States depended heavily on European examples until the present century and because of our insistence on pottery as a utilitarian art, no unified American style had emerged when Walters appeared on the scene. He shared the general spirit of American work in this medium but his main sources were ancient Egypt, Persia and China. By turning to the masters of this art in the distant past, he recaptured the dignity of the medium—and in so doing restored glazed pottery as a sculptural material.[4]

R. Guy Cowan began to campaign actively for the cause of modern ceramic art in 1925. His interest stemmed from his production of limited-edition figurines at the Cowan Pottery Studio in Rocky River, a suburb of Cleveland. The aesthetic level of the early figures was uneven, and the term *ceramic sculpture*, so often used in descriptions of his work, can be applied only loosely. From 1927 on, however, his standards improved markedly. Several talented designers worked with Cowan, including Alexander Blazys and Waylande DeSantis Gregory. The group of Russian peasant figures by

LEFT: **Carl Walters** The Stallion, 1921. *Glazed earthenware, height 10". Whitney Museum of American Art, New York.*

TOP: **Alexander Blazys** *Cowan Pottery Studio, Cleveland.* Dancer *from* Russian Peasants, 1927. *Glazed porcelain, height 10". Cowan Pottery Museum, Rocky River Public Library, Rocky River, Ohio.*

Hunt Diederich Cowboy Mounting Horse, *c. 1926. Glazed earthenware, diameter 15". The Metropolitan Museum of Art, New York. Gift of Mrs. Hunt Slater.*

LEFT: **Adelaide Alsop Robineau** Foxes and Grapes, 1922. *Glazed porcelain with incised decoration, height 7¼". Courtesy Jordan-Volpe Gallery, New York.*

UPPER RIGHT: **Adelaide Alsop Robineau** Vase, 1924. *Crackle glaze on porcelain, height 12¾". The Newark Museum, Newark, New Jersey. Purchase, 1926.*

Mary Chase Perry *Pewabic Pottery, Detroit. Vase, c. 1920. Glazed stoneware, height 12". Courtesy Thomas Brunk.*

Blazys was given the first prize to be awarded for ceramic sculpture as a separate category at the 1927 Annual Exhibition of Work by Cleveland Artists and Craftsmen—also known as the May Show.

This success was a double victory for Cowan, for not only was the prize-winning piece from his studio, but also the creation of the award was the direct result of his shrewd lobbying in Cleveland art circles. The director of the museum, William M. Milliken, became an enthusiastic patron of ceramics, and "all the prestige of the Cleveland Museum was thrown behind the ceramic artists so as to encourage the creative."[5] Milliken joined with the Cleveland School of Art and Cowan Pottery to encourage ceramic sculpture. Cowan taught at the school and employed the students at his pottery, while Milliken provided a platform for their work at the May Shows. Yet, while Milliken was no doubt a valuable friend to the Cleveland ceramist, his friendship was not without its drawbacks, as is pointed out in the Everson Museum's exhibition catalogue *Diversions of Keramos: American Clay Sculpture 1925–1950*:

> Unlike most museum directors in large cities who embraced an elitist "art for art's sake" attitude in their administrative policies, Milliken felt the museum should address itself to broader social interests in the community. Firmly convinced of the commercial applicability of the visual arts, he felt that the competitive display of commercial products in a Museum setting could raise the standards of design in local industries. To make the field of art more accessible to a broader public, he actively refuted the idea that artists were "different" . . . but normal members of society who contributed to the public welfare, and who like everyone else, needed a job. Such an attitude was not without its humanitarian nobility and practicality in terms of financial support [but] it also cast an undeserved populist pallor over the objects themselves, as if they owed their existence to the efforts of good hearted bureaucrats and their desire to please a broad unknowledgeable public.[6]

The tendency toward commercialization was encouraged by Cowan. From 1928 on, an "experimental" laboratory in ceramic sculpture was run at the school by Cowan, Baggs (for a short period), and Mrs. A. R. Dyer. It was experimental in the least dynamic sense of the word, for Cowan was seeking marketable figurines and not avant-garde works of art. This initial class produced most of the future luminaries of the movement: Viktor Schreckengost, Thelma Frazier, Edward Winter, Paul Bogatay, Russell Aitken, and Edris Eckhardt.

In 1930 the Cowan Pottery Studio went into receivership, a victim of the Depression, and Cowan moved to Syracuse, New York. He had been a successful catalyst, and the momentum that he had built up accelerated in the 1930s. Cowan continued to play a central role in the growth of ceramic sculpture and in the Ceramic Nationals that would be initiated during the 1930s. But the commercializing influence of Milliken and Cowan took its toll in a tendency toward the most sentimental and vacuous of works, totally unresponsive to the mainstream of sculpture.

Finally, a major influence on the direction that sculptural-figurative ceramics was to take in the coming years in the United States came from Austrian ceramics. The 1925 Exposition Internationale des Arts Décoratifs et Industriels Modernes in Paris reawakened interest in European ceramics. A series of ten articles written by Adelaide Robineau and published in *Design–Keramik Studio* gave saturation coverage to the works in this exhibition. The American potters were at first attracted by the example of the French Art Deco pottery. Gradually, however, their interests turned to the Austrian ceramists working with the Wiener Werkstätte.[7] The exhibition of works by the Wiener Werkstätte excited much controversy at the highly publicized 1928 *International Exhibition of Ceramic Art* at the Metropolitan Museum of Art. The critic Helen Appleton Read denounced their "careless technique and frivolity"[8] as being tired and vulgar. What most critics failed to perceive was that the "modern style of sobriety and dignity" that they demanded had already been explored by the Viennese ceramists at the beginning of the century, in the seminal

Sezessionstil aesthetic. The artists of the twenties were, in fact, rebelling against the colder, architectonic use of clay by their elders, replacing it with a witty, expressionist approach, liberating the material's potential as a medium for making polychrome figurative imagery.

The "Wiener Werkstätte style," as it was termed, had an immediate impact on the American ceramic arts despite its mixed critical reception. Several artists, including Russell Aitken, Viktor Schreckengost, and Ruth Randall, went to study in Vienna under Michael Powolny at the Kunstgewerbeschule. The influence of the Wiener Werkstätte lessened the sugary aspect of American ceramic sculpture and gave it a tougher, more satiric sense of the decorative. In addition, two of Vienna's most celebrated ceramists, Vally Wieselthier and Susi Singer, moved to the United States. Although neither produced work in the United States to rival the quality of the Viennese period, both were influential in a broader sense. Wieselthier arrived in New York in 1929, joined the decorative-arts group Contempora, and exhibited at the Art Center with Rockwell Kent and Lucien Bernhard. Wieselthier proved to be a strong influence and an articulate spokesperson for a particular school of decorative sculpture. Writing soon after her arrival in the United States, she explained the raison d'être behind her work:

> There are arts which have no deep message to give the world save that of their own beauty and the artist's joy in making intimate arts that make life gayer, and yet have all the seriousness of a thing that is felt intensely and worked out with the utmost care. Of these, pottery is the chief. . . . Good pottery has the feeling of its purpose always in it; it expresses attitudes and moments of life which to the great poet or prophet may seem almost superficial but are, for the ordinary people, of the very stuff of life itself, the delight of the true "Lebenskünstler."[9]

Henry Varnum Poor's entry into pottery was the result of both aesthetic attraction and economic pragmatism. Poor was a painter, but at the beginning of the 1920s he found himself drawn to the applied arts because he genuinely believed "that the natural development of modern art lies in a closer application to things more related to everyday usage."[10] He also felt, however, that potentially he could make a greater income from the applied arts than he was receiving for his paintings. In her excellent essay for the catalogue of a Poor retrospective, Linda Steigleder described his move toward pottery: "Sometime in 1920 Poor surveyed New York galleries and shops to familiarize himself with the state of the ceramic arts. He disliked contemporary products, particularly those with overglaze painted decoration. Poor deduced that no innovative potters were working in America, and he was convinced that the field desperately needed rejuvenation."[11]

Poor received a Revelation kiln as a gift. Undaunted by his lack of skills and knowledge, he set up a makeshift pottery studio at his home, Crow House, in Rockland County, New York. His first works were sold at the Bel Maison Gallery of Wanamaker's department store in New York. Originally, he intended to continue the tradition of making anonymous, utilitarian pottery in the style of the eighteenth- and nineteenth-century Hudson River kilns, but the demand became overwhelming, and rather than develop a production workshop, he decided to limit his production, make unique pieces, and increase his prices. He was taken on in mid-1922 by the dealer Newman Emmerson Montross, an eminent figure in the New York art world and one of the few champions of modern art. Poor's first one-person show at Montross took place in December of that year and was entitled *Decorated Pottery, Paintings and Drawings by H. Varnum Poor*. The exhibition was a considerable success, and the Metropolitan Museum of Art acquired a handsome plate, *Portrait of a Woman*.

Montross and Poor enjoyed an affectionate relationship. Poor recalled his frequent visits to the city, with his Model T Ford stacked with wicker baskets full of pottery: "[Montross] would stand and watch while I unwrapped everything and would teeter back and forth on his heels and say,

'Well Henry! Let's see what merchandise you have now.' . . . It was sort of a joke between us that this pottery was merchandise and he sold it like merchandise too. . . . My prices . . . were very low, and I sold everything I could [make]."[12]

For the next ten years Poor worked almost exclusively on ceramics and design projects. He received several large commissions, including the domed ceiling of the Union Dime Savings Bank in New York in 1927 (demolished in 1956), and in 1928 a mural, *Sports*, for the Hotel Shelton in New York. In the fall of 1928, encouraged by the apparent interest in the decorative arts, Poor and a group of fourteen other artists founded the American Designers' Gallery, Incorporated, drawing upon the model of French design studios such as Maison Bing l'Art Nouveau, Maison Moderne, Primavera, and others.[13] The first exhibition of the American Designers' Gallery took place in October on Fifty-seventh Street in New York. The show included, among other works, a large, ambitious bathroom

with painted tile that featured a life-size tile panel of a nude in the "modern manner." The life of the gallery was brief, and the showroom was closed just before the stock market crashed in October 1929.

Poor continued to make pots and to show them at the Montross Gallery. He became more proficient at his craft, although this had only a small impact upon his work, the most noticeable being a slight increase in scale. Poor was never a perfectionist in terms of pottery technique. Later in his life he was asked by Senator William Benton about a warped plate and he replied: "My work has never been notable for technical perfection. In my first show of pottery at Montross Gallery . . . I enraged the potters by showing warped and even kiln cracked plates because I considered them as works of art. Luckily the critics agreed; the show sold out and played some part in bringing American ceramics to life."[14]

Poor did indeed bring life to American ceramics of his time and was one of the most significant ceramists of the period between the two world wars. Poor attracted a large audience for his work, including Helen Hayes (for whom he created a ceramic fountain that is now in the collection of the Museum of Art, Pennsylvania State University, University Park), Burgess Meredith, Theodore Dreiser, and numerous museums. He also played a significant role as a critic and theorist for his field. He carried American ceramics into the thirties with his mixture of simple, direct craftsmanship and an evolved and sophisticated sense of the decorative.

*TOP LEFT: **Edward T. Hurley** Rookwood Pottery, Cincinnati. Covered Jar, 1928. Earthenware with mottled glaze, height 19". Courtesy Jordan-Volpe Gallery, New York.*

*RIGHT: **Henry Varnum Poor** Portrait of a Woman, plate, 1926. Glazed earthenware, diameter 6½". Courtesy Poor Estate and Garth Clark.*

Elie Nadelman Woman with Poodle, 1934–35.
Glazed earthenware, height 9″. Private collection.
Courtesy Zabriskie Gallery, New York.

CHAPTER SIX

1930

The 1930s produced a number of developments: the beginning of a challenging vessel aesthetic, the growth of a decorative ceramic-sculpture movement, and, most significantly, the founding of the Ceramic Nationals in Syracuse—the annuals were to become the major platform for the ceramic arts for the next forty years. All this activity took place under the cloud of the Great Depression. The austerity of the decade had an indelible influence on the decorative arts, introducing humor to ceramic sculpture, encouraging the use of inexpensive materials and processes, and causing many of the ceramists and potters to acquire a sense of ideological mission.

Recalling the reaction to the 1930s, Mary Chase Perry remembered how the flow of cheaply produced industrial bric-a-brac offended the craftsmen of the day: "We had been given a flood of the commonplace, the crude and the unlovely. That is why it was important for the individual craftsman to keep working and to keep his place in the community, to train our eyes to recognize the fine things. That is one reason why hand-made pottery will always be needed and why the craftsman's studio will always have a place in the scheme of things."[1]

Perry's view was somewhat simplistic but did provide a necessary purpose and idealism. In retrospect, only a few craftsmen provided the bulwark against ugliness; many created as much unlovely bric-a-brac as industry. Some of the most superb examples of clay vessels during this period actually came from industry. The most notable examples are the powerful, sleek forms of the so-called refrigerator ware produced by Hall and Company in East Liverpool, Ohio, as giveaways and premium offers for the refrigerator manufacturers; the bright "California monochromes" from the Bauer Pottery; and Rhead's imitative "Fiesta" wares for Homer Laughlin.

The Depression proved to be a double-edged sword for ceramics. On the one hand, it did staunch any experimental or avant-garde inclinations, but it also promoted a sense of whimsy and humor as a visual antidote to the harsh realities of day-to-day life. This ideally suited polychrome figurative sculpture. What proved to be salable were classical vessels and jocular, amusing sculpture. The austerity of the period gave attention to and encouraged the use of cheaper materials, which introduced several "visitors" to the medium, such as Alexander Archipenko, Reuben Nakian, Isamu Noguchi, and Elie Nadelman.[2] Even Jackson Pollock was attracted to ceramics; encouraged by Thomas Hart Benton, Pollock worked with china paints while he lived in Kansas City.

Until 1930 Nadelman had worked mainly on large, monumental figures, but with the decline of his fortunes and the loss of his home and studio, he turned to experimenting with plaster, papier-mâché, and ceramics in the hope that "room-size statuary, mass produced in inexpensive materials could channel a residual interest in free standing figures."[3] His respect for the more common materials was an outgrowth of his consuming interest in folk art. The figures he formed from clay and glazed simply in white, grays, yellows, and blacks have the directness of the objects he respected and collected, the toys of the Central European folk artists, and the baked clay figures of Tanagra and Taranto. The commanding elegance in these ceramics in 1934–35 gave way to a fragmented and cursory modeling. After Nadelman's death in 1946, hundreds of small plaster and ceramic figures were found in his studio; they represent his last body of work. The figures are bloated and disfigured, yet they are strangely compelling and erotic. Nadelman was happy with his works in clay and believed that he had "achieved what he wanted" in these works.[4] They remain some of the most enigmatic pieces of American sculpture and, to a great extent, they defy categorization: "These strange creatures, the last objects from Nadelman's hands, are reminiscent of nearly everything from ancient cult figures, Kewpie dolls and Mae West to circus performers, burlesque queens and chorus girls. Despite numerous interpretations the figurines remain totally mystifying, the baffling culmination of a lifetime in sculpture."[5]

The Depression also gave birth to the Welfare Art Program of the Works Progress Administration, which was the solution offered by Roosevelt's New Deal brain trust to maintain the professional artist and, thus, the cultural momentum of the nation. The WAP/WPA invited artists to work on projects for a subsistence wage of about $97 a month. Because the program was biased toward populist forms of expression, ceramics fared well. Ceramic sculpture was produced in various parts of the country—some of the better works coming from Tony Rosenthal and Emmanuel Viviano in Chicago and Sargent Johnston in San Francisco. In addition, a Ceramic Sculpture Division was set up under the aegis of the WAP in Cleveland—reinforcing the importance of Ohio as a ceramic-arts center during the 1930s. The division was directed by Edris Eckhardt, and under her pragmatic guidance it undertook a number of projects: figures from children's literature were created for display in the libraries throughout the nation, murals and garden ornaments were produced for estates around Cleveland, and murals were painted for public buildings.[6]

The preference for public rather than for private artworks through WAP/WPA patronage resulted in an ambitious approach to scale, as ceramists sought to rival the monumental outdoor works produced in bronze. One of the most successful artists in this regard was Waylande DeSantis Gregory. In 1938 he completed his largest work, *The Fountain of Atoms*, arguably the largest single work in modern ceramic sculpture. Created for the World's Fair in New York in 1939–40, it comprised twelve colossal earthenware figures, each weighing over a ton: *Fire*, *Earth*, *Air*, *Water*, and the eight *Electrons*. They were an extraordinary technical achievement. Gregory developed a honeycomb method of building up the pieces in the same

Waylande Gregory Water, *from the* Fountain of Atoms, *1938. Stoneware, height 72". Courtesy the Estate of Yolande Gregory and Everson Museum of Art, Syracuse, New York.*

manner as the wasp builds up its nest of mud: what he termed "inner modeling."[7] The work was returned to Gregory's New Jersey studio in 1941 and not publicly exhibited again until 1983, when it was shown at the Everson Museum's exhibition *Diversions of Keramos*. As E. W. Watson wrote, it was an ambitious, sybaritic work: "In the 'water' a sculptured male swimmer of warm terra cotta descends through swirling, watery forms of green-blue glass, accompanied by maroon fish and lemon bubbles. The fire figure is covered in tongues of reddish glaze and reflected areas of faint blue and

Waylande Gregory Factory/Farm Worker, *1938. Stoneware, height 70". Private collection. Courtesy Everson Museum of Art, Syracuse, New York.*

green. The color tone [is] being handled so as to give the sense of being viewed through fumes."[8]

Gregory also received a commission from General Motors at the World's Fair—a sculptural group entitled *American Imports and Exports*:

> In contrast to the exuberant and somewhat flashy style he favored for the fountain, this work reflects the artist in a more sober mood. Eschewing the bright glazes and animated poses of his fountain figures, Gregory here applied the clay so that its texture remained somewhat rough, and he maintained its natural color. The centerpiece for the display was a Janus-like fig-

ure, *Factory/Farm Worker*, a suitable paean to American labor. Almost life-size, the figure conveyed a sense of quiet responsibility and dignity, very much in keeping with the images of idealized workers found in paintings of this period.[9]

Gregory's success at the World's Fair resulted in another large commission, an eighty-foot mural for the Municipal Center in Washington, D.C., that depicted the services of the police and firemen.

The success enjoyed by Gregory and other ceramists in the 1930s was also the result of the attention drawn to the medium by the annual Ceramic National,[10] which was inaugurated in 1932 as a memorial to Adelaide Robineau by Anna Olmsted, the director of the Syracuse [New York] Museum of Art (later known as the Everson Museum of Art). In the first year, entries were restricted to artists from New York State and no funds were available for either a catalogue or proper installation. The objects were set out on sateen-covered folding banquet tables borrowed from the YMCA. In 1933 the annual was declared "open to potters of the United States." Writing to Carlton Atherton, professor of art at Ohio State University, who had assisted in the first annual, Olmsted remarked that the city had again cut the museum budget and that the exhibition's allocation for the full year was now $419. "Perhaps it is rather mad to consider a *national* exhibition just now," she concluded, "but with no other national exhibition devoted exclusively to ceramics in the country this might truly be the chance of a lifetime, and the museum ought to be put on the art map thereby."[11] These were prophetic words.

The second annual, which included 199 pieces representing seventy-two ceramists from eleven states, was accompanied by a simple catalogue. A period of hand-to-mouth improvisation followed, and the annual survived only as a result of Olmsted's indefatigable energy and optimism and, later, through R. Guy Cowan's efforts in obtaining corporate support. Among the many credits for assistance in the early years was a regular and curious entry, the Marcellus Casket Company. Olmsted had discovered that the casket manufacturer had a large stock of boxes, in which the caskets were shipped. These, covered in sateen, lined the walls of the annual for several years, with smaller crates, used for infants' caskets, serving as pedestals. The installation for each annual began with the arrival of the Marcellus truck with its macabre cargo. This seemingly irrelevant "exposé" of the poverty of the museum rather amused the Rockefeller Foundation. It was also instrumental in obtaining financial assistance from the foundation for one of the annual's major achievements of the decade, the first exhibition of American ceramics to tour abroad.[12]

In 1937 an exhibition of 133 pieces of American ceramics from the Ceramic National went to Helsinki; Göteborg, Sweden; and Copenhagen. On its return, it was engaged for an unscheduled showing at the Hanley Museum in Stoke-on-Trent, England, before coming back in triumph to the Whitney Museum of American Art in New York. The tour and the exhibition at the Whitney received enthusiastic notices in the American press and art magazines. One of the most instructive was an article in *Fortune* magazine entitled "The Art with the Inferiority Complex." In this special portfolio, with eight pages of color illustrations, the anonymous writer remarked that America had yet to produce its Wedgwoods, Böttgers, or a Wiener Keramik and that, by comparison with Europe and the East, "has lacked even a high point from which to decline." For this reason, the writer concluded, the interest and growth in ceramics in the 1930s was more portentous than simply a passing fashionable fad, and that the boisterous, mocking heroic figures of Russell Aitken, the speckled bulls of Carl Walters, and the terra-cotta horses of Waylande Gregory represented a breakthrough:

> The stodgier collectors of pottery, with one eye cocked on ancient China and the other on price, may damn such pieces as miniature giraffes and small shiny ruminating hippopotamuses as expensive bric-a-brac. But ceramic enthusiasts see them as signs of the vitality of a growing American art, and if they are true collectors,

treasure them in the way that the homeowners of Rome probably treasured their collections of unterrifying, homely, familiar little household gods. American ceramic art is beginning to show signs of life.[13]

The signs of life were not as evident in the vessel aesthetic—dressed in its less theatrical forms and glazes—but they were nonetheless there. The 1930s showed signs of strong maturity in the work of Charles Harder, Arthur Baggs, Glen Lukens, and others who exhibited regularly in the Ceramic Nationals. European artists also began to play an influential role: the Swiss potter Paul Bonifas, Maija Grotell from Finland, Gertrud and Otto Natzler

Elie Nadelman Two Women, c. 1935–36. *Glazed earthenware, height 16¾". Courtesy Zabriskie Gallery, New York.*

RIGHT: **Russell Barnett Aitken** Futility of a Well-Ordered Life, 1935. *Glazed earthenware, height 18½". The Museum of Modern Art, New York. Anonymous gift.*

Viktor Schreckengost The Dictator, *1939. Glazed earthenware, height 13". Everson Museum of Art, Syracuse, New York. Gift of the artist.*

LEFT: *Alexander Archipenko* Walking Woman, *1937. Earthenware, height 23". Courtesy Zabriskie Gallery, New York.*

RIGHT: *Edris Eckhardt* Mid-Day, *1938. Glazed earthenware, height 12". Private collection. Exhibited at the seventh Ceramic National, Everson Museum of Art, Syracuse, New York.*

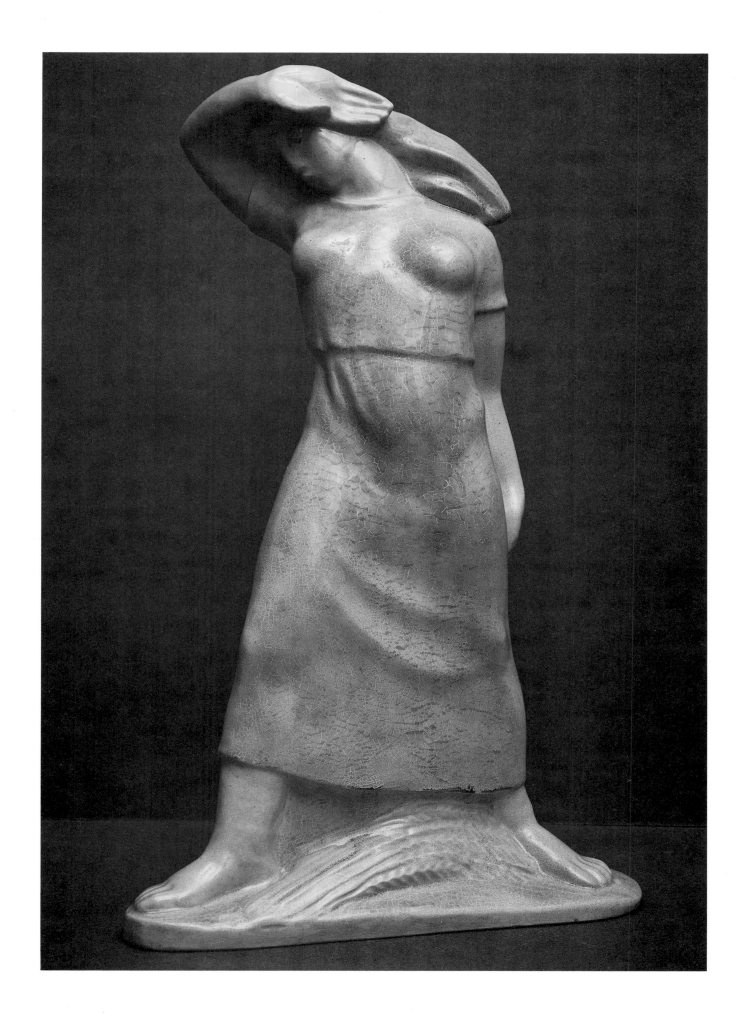

from Austria, and the Bauhaus-trained Marguerite Wildenhain. All made important contributions. Bonifas taught at the University of Washington, Seattle, promoting a purist concept of pottery that had been developed in collaboration with his close friend the French purist Ozenfant. Grotell and the Natzlers concentrated on decorative pottery, and Wildenhain introduced an aesthetic and ideology for the modern functional potter. The latter provided a welcome alternative to the often self-indulgent and arbitrary form of purely decorative pottery.

During this decade the work of the American potters became more sophisticated and was shown abroad at several exhibitions, with Charles Harder taking one of the gold medals at the 1937 Exposition in Paris. Baggs showed new energy with his salt-glazed wares. In these he realized his ambition, declared earlier, to emphasize in his work "clay's fundamental characteristics, plasticity and the beautiful qualities of surface."[14] In 1938 he produced one of the classics of the period, the "definitive" *Cookie Jar*, which won the pottery prize at the 1938 Ceramic National. However, although both Harder's and Baggs's work had improved enormously, neither was able to exorcise fully the "designerly" approach that Binns had inbred during their early

FAR LEFT: **Arthur Eugene Baggs** Cookie Jar, 1938. Salt-glazed stoneware, height 11¾". Everson Museum of Art, Syracuse, New York. Exhibited at the seventh Ceramic National. Awarded first prize for pottery.

TOP LEFT: **Maija Grotell** Vase, c. 1938. Glazed stoneware, height 13". Collection Robert Cugno.

BOTTOM LEFT: **Glen Lukens** Bowl, c. 1936. Glazed earthenware, diameter 11⅝". Everson Museum of Art, Syracuse, New York. Gift of the artist.

ABOVE: **Charles M. Harder** Vase, 1935. Stoneware, sgraffito and slip decoration, height 9½". Private collection.

Viktor Schreckengost *Cowan Pottery Studio, Cleveland.* Jazz
Bowl, 1931. *Porcelain with sgraffito decoration, height 11".
Cowan Pottery Museum, Rocky River Public Library, Rocky
River, Ohio.*

Maija Grotell Vase, 1939. *Glazed stoneware, height 15½".
The Metropolitan Museum of Art, New York. Purchase, Edward
C. Moore, Jr., Gift.*

Carl Walters Cat in Tall Grass, *c. 1939. Glazed earthenware,
height 15½". The Metropolitan Museum of Art, New York.
Rogers Fund, 1942.*

education.

The same situation was evident in the ceramic education of the time. Ceramics was not taught as a discipline in itself but as a convenient tool of art education. Clay was a simple, plastic, and above all, cheap, material with which teacher trainees could learn about surface, texture, color, and form. The interest in ceramic education grew and the medium became more popular, but it was at high cost. The "art education" approach did not acknowledge that the material had its own specific and long-standing tradition as an art form. Literature proliferated, but it was of the simplistic "twenty ways to make a clay horse" variety—an amateur-art bandwagon that later attracted even the usually discerning Museum of Modern Art in New York. The entire emphasis was now placed on the "how-to" aspect of the art. There were, however, a few exceptions: Baggs, Harder, and Lukens. But in terms of creating a sense of professionalism and self-esteem as potters and artists, it was the Natzlers who set a particularly impressive example.

The Natzlers gave lessons for three years after their arrival in the United States in 1939 and played an important, informal role in the education of Beatrice Wood and Laura Andreson. Their major contribution was not, however, as teachers. They were cautious, even secretive, in sharing their information. Their importance to the history of American ceramics was in providing a model for professionalism and for high, formal, aesthetic standards. Their sensibility was new to the United States, where chunky, thick-walled vessels (sometimes due to a lack of skill in forming the vessels) were the order of the day. Gertrud Natzler threw elegant, paper-thin forms. She was arguably the most refined thrower to work in the United States. Otto Natzler created the glazes.

The Natzlers perceived themselves as artists and spoke with pride and authority of pottery as an art form. They defined themselves as purists and held clear and strong views on the character of good pottery form, views that were not unlike those espoused by Binns in "In Defense of Fire" or by the French artist-potter Auguste Delaherche:

> The form of a pot is the main part of its spiritual substance. Its outline, its proportions, the fingermarks impressed on its wall, are the simple statement of its creator, spontaneous and personal as his handwriting. The same pot does not happen twice. . . . A pot is four-dimensional: One can think of it as sculpture in three dimensions with the important inside added as a fourth. The inside, while not identical with the outline of the pot, must relate to it. Only when the pot breaks will it reveal itself, like a tree that reveals much of the marvellous structure of its growth only in death and decay.[15]

The refinement that gave the work its distinction was, however, out of step with the growing movement toward a more expressionist vocabulary. The European ideal of achieving the sublime was being replaced by a search for raw energy. Skilled at marketing, Otto Natzler organized many exhibitions and published several excellent, but highly romantic, catalogues of their work. Although the achievement of the Natzler partnership was extraordinary, it remains strangely out of step with American ceramics and needs to be evaluated on its own terms, isolated like a small, exotic island from the growing storm that was developing on the "mainland" of contemporary pottery.

It was Lukens who spoke most prophetically for the coming changes, changes that would de-emphasize craftsmanship as the standard of quality. The course that Lukens taught at the University of California at Los Angeles from 1934 onward was established initially with structured, art-educational purposes. Lukens succeeded in introducing a sensitivity to the materials and a respect for the potter's traditions. He achieved this by advocating a gentle, monistic view of creativity that anticipated the attitude Bernard Leach was to propose in 1940 in his classic *A Potter's Book*. Lukens had at first been taught to believe, as had most of his contemporaries, that cleverness was the aim in art. Through a close friend, he discovered that this approach simply externalized the creative process, and that to escape this self-consciousness, the potter must sublimate his ego to the material and explore a more inward experience: "There in New Mexico among the priceless remains of a magnificent pre-Civilization, I was taught to study the self-expression of a race of people who for more than a thousand years trained the mechanism of the consciousness so that what they now do takes place independently of the conscious intelligence. The only approach to a sound philosophy of life. The one sure approach to creativity in art."[16]

Lukens was influential because his works matched his rhetoric. He succeeded in the difficult task of making an almost primitive statement without seeming to be what the French term *faux naïf*. His forms went beyond simplicity and can best be termed "primal shapes," with their thick, viscous glazes developed from local raw materials. These glazes in strong yellows, turquoises, and greens were, in the words of R. Guy Cowan, "as luscious as ripe fruit." Lukens was an inspiration to his fellow artists on the West Coast. He was also instrumental in getting the ceramics movement there under way in 1938, when the first all-California ceramic-art exposition was held. "This exhibition," he announced, "means that the Pacific Coast ceramic child is able to walk alone."[17] Lukens lived into the 1960s and was able to see the fruits of that first step, as California began to play the central role in the growth of the ceramic arts.[18]

Isamu Noguchi The Queen, 1931. Terra-cotta, height 45½". *Whitney Museum of American Art, New York. Gift of the artist.*

Louise Nevelson Moving—Static—Moving Figures, *1945.*
Earthenware, height 60". Whitney Museum of American Art,
New York. Gift of the artist.

The 1940s saw new concerns emerge in the sculpture of David Smith, Alexander Calder, Joseph Cornell, and others. These artists pointed the direction that sculpture was to follow for the next three decades: found objects, assemblage, and the fabrication of metal began to replace the traditional craft of the sculptor and his skills of modeling and carving. Sculptors now sought a different "sculptural unity," which allowed the use of totally disparate and discordant elements. This freedom had grown out of early modern art movements—primarily collage, Constructivism, and Suprematism, which had developed in Russia and Europe in the late teens and early twenties. This "constructivist" tendency had a strong impact on the way in which sculptors, and fine artists in general, began to view materials and processes: "To create sculpture by assembling parts that had been fabricated originally for quite a different context did not necessarily involve new technology. But it did mean a change in sculptural practice, for it raised the possibility that making sculpture might involve a conceptual rather than a physical transformation of the material from which it is composed."[1]

This thinking was the death knell of the first ceramic-sculpture movement in the United States. The sculptors working in the medium had, with a few exceptions, based their aesthetic on the ideals of middle-class connoisseurship and on an intimate artist-material relationship in which the subtle nuances of the firing and glazes were all-important. The ceramic sculptors also found that public interest in figurative sculpture was on the wane and that a nation facing the specter of world conflict for the second time in less than twenty-five years was not in a mood for supercilious ceramic humor.

Except for the work of Viktor Schreckengost, the Ohio school declined rapidly, unable to outgrow the cloying whimsy of the early work. Schreckengost retained his playful style of clay handling and the brash comic-book palette of colors, but the content of his works changed markedly. During the 1930s

CHAPTER SEVEN

1940

his work had reflected the influence of the Viennese school, dealing with decorative surfaces and elegant visual puns. Then, in 1939–40, he turned to political satire, which was surprisingly well-suited to his style. In 1939 he completed *The Dictator*, a masterwork from the Ohio school, representing Stalin, Hitler, Mussolini, and Hirohito gamboling in the robes of a corpulent Caesar. A starker quality can be seen in *Apocalypse* (1942), where three of the leaders are mounted on a frenzied horse—striking a disturbing balance between humor and horror.[2]

Although the momentum was lost in ceramic sculpture during the forties, there was some activity of note. Louise Nevelson worked successfully in terra-cotta, creating the constructivist work *Moving—Static—Moving Figures* (1945), which consisted of a group of fifteen assembled clay forms with brusque drawing on the surfaces. The Kansan sculptor Bernard Frazier produced work of a different character in a series of ash-glazed horse sculptures. Two of these, *Prairie Combat* (1941) and *Untamed* (1948), are in the collection of the Everson Museum of Art, Syracuse, New York, having been acquired at the tenth and thirteenth Ceramic Nationals. The style was distinctive and fully employed the plasticity of the material. Frazier massed and distorted elements of the forms so as to direct the viewer's eye and create an almost brutal and explosive sense of strength.

These high points in ceramic sculpture were few, however, as the focus of the medium began to return to the vessel aesthetic. The potters prospered despite the inclement climate in the fine arts because, unlike sculptors, they had little need of the patronage of museums and major galleries. Pottery was a popular and intimate art form that could reach a wide public because of its low price. For two decades pottery had existed outside the mainstream of fine art and had built up an independent structure of patronage and exhibiting platforms. Far from attempting to match developments in painting and sculpture, the potters in many cases consciously saw themselves as providing an alternative—retaining the traditions of craftsmanship against the onslaughts of modernism.

The decade saw a strong group of potters emerge in the United States, many having come to the country in the 1920s and 1930s as already established artists. Although they shared certain characteristics and a common volumetric discipline, the potters were a diverse group, philosophically and intellectually. Some, such as Wildenhain, adhered to a stern functionalist view. This attitude, based on repetition and production ware, was anathema to Beatrice Wood, Maija Grotell, and others who worked with the same intent as painters and sculptors. Between the two poles of thought were the potters who took a vocational view of the art, based on a romantic, traditionalist conception of pottery as a cooperative workshop. This view was reflected in the number of potteries run by husband-and-wife teams, such as Gertrud and Otto Natzler, Edwin and Mary Scheier, and Vivika and Otto Heino.

Of the potters of this decade, Maija Grotell,

Maija Grotell Vase, 1949. Glazed stoneware with slip, height 24". Courtesy Fifty/50, New York.

both as a teacher and as an artist, was the most outstanding figure. Grotell arrived in New York from Helsinki in 1927 and worked first at the Inwood Pottery and then at the Henry Street Settlement House in New York City. In 1936 she joined Rutgers University, New Brunswick, New Jersey. Her early style, with painted Art Deco motifs on simple ovoid or cylindrical forms, was popular and won awards at the 1929 Barcelona and 1937 Paris world's fairs. In 1938 she was appointed the head of the ceramics department at the Cranbrook Academy of Art in Bloomfield Hills, Michigan.

The Cranbrook Academy of Art was part of a complex of small private schools established by the newspaper publisher and art connoisseur George C. Booth. The project began in 1904, when he purchased one hundred acres of rolling Michigan farmland. At first his interest in arts and crafts was restricted to purchases of objects for his home and as gifts for the Detroit Institute of Arts. During the forties, Booth was the most active patron of

Mary and Edwin Scheier Bowl, c. 1949. Glazed earthenware, height 6¼". University Art Museum, University of Minnesota, Minneapolis. Ione and Hudson Walker Collection.

the work of both Robineau and Perry. The inspiration for Cranbrook had come in the 1920s, when Booth had conceived of a plan for an ideal artists' community, where practicing artists could live, work, and teach in a stimulating, pedagogical environment. He found an active supporter of these ideas in the architect Eliel Saarinen, who designed a complex of buildings for the schools and the academy and also enlisted artists for the faculty. The setting was superb, with large sculptures in manicured gardens, custom-designed furnishings and fabrics, and the very best in Art Deco lamps and accessories. Booth's tastes in ceramics changed, and he began to collect the work of the French *moderne* potters, such as André Metthey, Emile Lenoble, René Buthaud, Georges Serré, and others. Waylande Gregory was the first to teach ceramics at Cranbrook, in 1932, but his stay was brief and ended in an acrimonious lawsuit. The sculptor Marshall Fredericks supposedly taught pottery thereafter, but, in fact, there was no real program of ceramics until Grotell's arrival in 1938, joining an all-European faculty: Eliel and Loja Saarinen from Finland, the Finnish weaver Marianne Stren-

Viktor Schreckengost Spring, *1941. Glazed earthenware, height 15". Everson Museum of Art, Syracuse, New York. Gift of IBM, Inc., tenth Ceramic National.*

gel, and the Swedish sculptor Carl Milles.

The work at Cranbrook soon began to change and to assume a monumental quality. This quality had little to do, however, with the scale of the pieces, which ranged from shallow bowls to four-foot-high thrown vases. The presence of Grotell's work derived from the strength, gravity, and simplicity of her forms. For most of her career, Grotell concentrated on only two types of forms. She had come to understand most thoroughly the dynamics of enclosing space, but she did so without any search for elegance or lightness. Her pots "sit" quite heavily on their truncated feet. At times this gives the work a brooding, stoic quality. In other pieces the feet are poorly resolved and her pots end too abruptly.

Grotell developed a palette of direct colors—deep turquoises, reds, and burnt oranges—with which she could draw on her forms emphatic motifs that show a carefully considered relationship to the thrust, lines, and proportions of the host vessel.

Bernard ("Poco") Frazier Untamed, *c. 1948. Stoneware, height 26". Everson Museum of Art, Syracuse, New York. Gift of IBM, Inc., thirteenth Ceramic National.*

LEFT: **Susi Singer** Oriental Woman with Child, 1946. *Glazed earthenware, height 14". Scripps College, Claremont, California.*

RIGHT: **Laura Andreson** Untitled Bowl, 1941. *Glazed earthenware, height 6¾". Private collection.*

BELOW: **Henry Varnum Poor** Man Seated, 1947. *Earthenware with slip painting and sgrafitto under glaze, diameter 12½". Museum of Art, Carnegie Institute, Pittsburgh, Pennsylvania.*

Later she became known for distinctive, craterous glazes, which she obtained by painting a clear Bristol glaze over Albany slip. The results were uneven. Grotell was never content to play safely within accessible decorative limits; she was constantly experimenting, saying, ''Discovering new ways of doing interests me most. . . . Once I have mastered a form, a glaze, an idea, I lose interest and move onto something else . . . this helps as a teacher but not as an exhibitor.''[3]

Grotell was also an unorthodox teacher. She rejected the structured, doctrinaire methods employed by Myrtle French, Arthur Baggs, and others, and taught by example of spirit rather than by example of work. She disliked imitation of her pots and encouraged self-reliance among her students, assisting them in discovering their most truthful responses to the medium. As a result, by 1950 the Cranbrook Academy of Art had developed into one of the most important institutions in ceramic art education in this country, rivaling in reputation the huge school at Alfred University. Several of Grotell's post–World War II students are included in this study: Toshiko Takaezu, Richard DeVore, John Glick, and Susanne and John Stephenson. Under the leadership of DeVore and, subsequently, Graham Marks, the tradition has continued.[4] The legacy that Grotell left through her students and in her vessels was an aesthetic not based on conventional object d'art virtues of beauty. Instead of pleasing in the simplistic sense, Grotell's work challenges and confronts the viewer with its bluntness, its toughness, and its honesty.

Another artist of importance working at Cranbrook in the late 1940s was Leza McVey, who taught summer school at Cranbrook in 1948 at Grotell's invitation. McVey was somewhat radical in her approach. Wheel-thrown symmetry bored her. She preferred asymmetrical forms with strong and unusual silhouettes, to which she very often gave the formal climax of a small, sculpted stopper. Her work received considerable recognition, and in 1951 a black vase with a stopper received the first prize for pottery at the Ceramic National.

The same striving to extend the vocabulary of the medium can be seen in the work of one of the major catalysts of the decade, Thomas Samuel (''Sam'') Haile. Haile's indelible influence on American pottery is surprising, considering his short stay in the country. He came to the United States in 1939, shortly after having graduated from the Royal College of Art in London, where he had studied under one of Europe's finest artist-potters, William Staite Murray. Haile was first and foremost a painter; he stumbled upon ceramics only through force of circumstance. Yet, although he brought to the medium certain painterly qualities—as well

*ABOVE: **Gertrud and Otto Natzler** Pilgrim Bottle, 1949–50. Earthenware with crater glaze, height 17". Los Angeles County Museum of Art. Gift of Howard and Gwen Laurie Smits.*

*RIGHT: **T. Samuel Haile** Chichén Itzá Vase, 1942. Stoneware, glazed, height 15". The Detroit Institute of Arts. Founders Society Purchase, General Membership Fund.*

TOP FAR LEFT: **Antonio Prieto** Pitcher, c. 1948. Ceramic with salt glaze and engobe, height 12". The Metropolitan Museum of Art, New York. Purchase, Edward C. Moore, Jr., Gift.

BOTTOM LEFT: **Marguerite Wildenhain** Tea Service, c. 1946. Glazed stoneware, height of pot, 5". Everson Museum of Art, Syracuse, New York. Recipient of the Richard B. Gump Award and purchase prize, eleventh Ceramic National.

TOP LEFT: **F. Carlton Ball** Teapot Form, 1947. Glazed earthenware, height 14". (Made at Mills College Workshop, Oakland, California.) Collection Jack Lenor Larsen. Courtesy Fifty/50, New York.

ABOVE: **Carl Walters** Caterpillar, 1945. Glazed earthenware, length 16½". The Detroit Institute of Arts. Gift of Mrs. Lillian Henkel Haass.

as his strong Surrealist affinities—Haile always acknowledged ceramics as an independent discipline that required an approach altogether different from that of paint and canvas.

After his arrival in New York, Haile exhibited extensively but did only odd jobs until invited by Charles Harder to study and teach at Alfred University. At Alfred he found glazes being compounded in science laboratories from a highly academic viewpoint. Haile challenged this practice, insisting that "all that craft separated the artist from his instincts and visions."[5] He advocated, instead, simple glazes compounded from two or three readily available materials, and a creative use of the kiln in obtaining variations of color. This refreshing view found a sympathetic ear among the young potters of the time, who had grown weary of Alfred's pedantic use of materials. Harder had plans to groom Haile as his successor, but Haile's restless spirit was not easily tamed, and he moved to Ann Arbor, Michigan. There he taught at the University of Michigan until his induction into the United States Army in 1944; he returned to England after the war.

Haile's work, although figurative, showed many of the same instincts that were to resurface in the so-called Abstract Expressionist ceramics of the mid-1950s. One of the most distinctive qualities was the manner in which Haile dealt with the vessel as format. Unlike many of the potters of the day, who decorated passively within the frame of the vessel, Haile disregarded the defining line on his vessels. His carefully conceived, but freely executed, painting gave depth and purpose to the form. Sometimes his painting quietly conformed to the shape of the vessel, as in *Orpheus* (1941). In other pieces, however, the strong movement of line around the form would break down the outer edge of his bowls, vases, or pitchers so that the interaction of form and painting became complex. One of the finest examples of the latter technique, *Cern Abbas Giant* (1938), has unfortunately been lost, but other masterworks, such as the *Chichén Itzá Vase* (1942) and *Cretan Feast* (1939), have found their

way into American public collections.

Haile died in an automobile accident in England in 1948. As a tribute to an artist who had contributed richly to a more progressive view of the vessel as an art form in America, the Institute of Contemporary Arts (Washington, D.C.) held a well-publicized memorial exhibition of his work in the United States. Robert Richman, the director of the institute, praised Haile's work for demonstrating "belief in the principle that art is a way of thinking, meeting art and function at their foundations by making for use yet transcending it."[6] Speaking more specifically of Haile's influence in this country, Richman added:

> To Americans conditioned to ceramic trivia— fish, gazelles and earrings—the work of Haile is a fresh wind. Here is pottery that is not only perfection in form, and glazes controlled miraculously, but with decorations like those in Etruscan and Greek pots. And always a simple statement: this is a pot, this is a dish, this is a jug. Haile could throw stoneware to the absolute limit of its yield point, achieving thereby a rhythmic tension quite [of] the same essence as sculpture.[7]

The pottery of Beatrice Wood during the forties was similar in spirit to that of Haile. Wood was as unimpressed with notions of perfectionist craftsmanship as he, arguing that "knowing what one was about to take out of the kiln is as exciting as being married to a boring and predictable man." Freely admitting to being a "terrible" craftswoman, Wood looked at ceramics with a sensibility very different from that of most of her contemporaries. Her early involvement in art had come through her membership in Duchamp's Dada circle in New York,[8] so her expectations of ceramics were different from those who had entered the field via the crafts or decorative arts. Wood had dabbled with pottery figures and other ceramics since the early 1930s, but in the late forties began to concentrate on luster glazes. Working out of a small studio/home in Ojai, California, she explored a nonformalist approach to form and materials. Her remarkable success with her glazes soon earned her an international reputation, but because of her laissez-faire approach to craftsmanship, the generally conservative world of ceramics viewed her efforts with suspicion and dismay. However, the livelier spirits, such as Peter Voulkos, saw her work as valid, unique, and radical.

Wood was not interested in luster for its preciousness but for its manipulation of light and color. Indeed, her approach to luster was unique and cannot be directly compared to any lusterwares within the ceramic tradition, with the exception of Mary Chase Perry, who similarly used simple forms and rich surfaces. The surfaces and the soft, informal shapes of Wood's work have a far closer affinity, in fact, to the shimmering patina of Roman glass. Up until the time of Beatrice Wood, the use of luster glazes had always been decorative, as in the work of William De Morgan, one of the leading nineteenth-century potters in the British Arts and Crafts Movement. More commonly, luster was used as an on-glaze technique associated with the vulgar excesses of the china-painting fraternity. Wood's

pots, in contrast, have the surfaces of vessels that have been buried for centuries and have acquired a pitted patina of polychromatic iridescence. The primal forms, at times verging on crudeness, provided the perfect canvas for the glowing surfaces.

Wood attracted a small coterie of admirers, including the writer Anaïs Nin, who wrote of her work in a review for *Artforum*: "People sometimes look wistfully at pieces of ancient ceramics in Museums as if such beauty were part of a lost and buried past. But Beatrice Wood is a modern ceramist creating objects today that would enhance your life. The colors, textures and forms are at once vivid and subtle. Her colors are molded with light. Some have tiny craters, as if formed by the evolutions, contractions and expansions of the earth itself. Some seem made of shells or pearls, others are iridescent and smokey, like trailways left by satellites."[9] With her spirit of freedom and experiment, Wood provided an avant-garde bridge between the 1940s and the revolution in vessel aesthetic that was to take place in Los Angeles in the 1950s.

Beatrice Wood Plate, 1947. Glazed earthenware, diameter 18". Courtesy Garth Clark.

Glen Lukens Bowl, c. 1940. Glazed earthenware, diameter 12". Collection Howard and Gwen Laurie Smits.

Gertrud and Otto Natzler Elliptical Bowl, 1958. *Earthenware with tiger's-eye glaze, height 10". Collection Richard Schroeder.*

The 1950s was the decade of liberation. The American potter finally cut loose the shackles that had bound him for so long to the manners and values of European art and design. That is not to say that Europe ceased to be an influence. On the contrary, Constructivism and the example of artists such as Miró and Picasso, who worked in ceramics during the early 1950s, were crucial to the development of American ceramics. These influences were, however, interpreted, digested, and applied to a new style, a new "machismo," and a new ambitiousness that was distinctively American. Very soon, the tables would be turned, and Europe and Japan would look to the United States for leadership in this ancient art.

The beginnings of the decade were inauspicious, with little indication of the revolution to come. Henry Varnum Poor viewed the activities of the day cynically, pronouncing that "hygienic hotelware" was the true American ceramic aesthetic. Ceramics, together with the other craft media, was experiencing a surge of interest. Popular magazines exhorted housewives to take to macramé, pottery, and weaving in search of the cultural opiate, self-expression. Others, early members of the counterculture movement and ex-GIs, came to the crafts in search of a gentle, romantic life-style.

Out of this interest grew a number of dedicated artists who set aside the romantic traditions of the material and began to establish a contemporary vocabulary. This group included those artists who gathered around Peter Voulkos at the Otis Art Institute (formerly the Los Angeles County Art Institute) during the mid-1950s. Many influences contributed to the breakthrough in the vessel aesthetic in the Otis group: the growing appreciation of jazz, the beat poets, the developments in American art, and, most broadly, the general climate of urgency and release that followed World War II. In purely visual terms, three influences dominated: the Zen pottery of Japan, the surface energies of Abstract Expressionist painting, and the Con-

CHAPTER EIGHT

1950

structivists' freedoms of form.

The dominant influence on American ceramics during the 1950s came from Japanese pottery and the Zen Buddhist theories that accompanied it. The artists on the West Coast were particularly sympathetic to Oriental philosophy. Under the leadership of such scholars as Alan Watts in San Francisco, a popular interest in Zen was growing. In his study on Zen in Japanese culture, Daisetz Suzuki explains part of the Oriental concept of beauty:

> Evidently beauty does not necessarily spell perfection of form. This has been one of the favorite tricks of Japanese artists—to embody beauty in a form of imperfection or even ugliness. When this beauty of imperfection is accompanied by antiquity or primitive uncouthness, we have a glimpse of *sabi*, so prized by Japanese connoisseurs. Antiquity and primitiveness may not be an actuality. If an object of art suggests even superficially the feeling of historical period there is *sabi* in it. *Sabi* consists in rustic unpretentiousness, apparent simplicity of effortlessness in execution, and, lastly, it contains inexplicable elements that raise the object in question to a rank of artistic production.[1]

Zen concepts of beauty appealed to the American potter for a number of reasons. Japanese pottery offered the potter aesthetic values different from those of the West.[2] Above all, Zen was the key to breaking with the formalist regime of European objecthood and its demands for perfectionist craftsmanship. Through Japanese pottery the California potters glimpsed a new value, based on risk and expression. They saw new forms of expression in the subtle asymmetry, in the simplicity, and in the often random, abstract decoration of the wares of the tea ceremony. The earlier works of Japan, particularly the architectonic structure of prehistoric Jomon pottery, inspired curiously weighted proportions and tension between surface and form.

For most American potters the first contact with Oriental philosophy came through Bernard

Leach. In 1940 this English potter wrote *A Potter's Book*, one of the classics of ceramic literature. In the opening chapter, "Towards a Standard," Leach proposed a meeting of East and West that he was later to define as "Bauhaus over Sung." This interest in the bridging of cultures had been a popular crusade among artists and intellectuals during the 1930s and 1940s, when Leach had been a member of an elite group of intellectuals that had assembled at Dartington Hall, a progressive school in Devon, England. The group included Mark Tobey, Ravi Shankar, Aldous Huxley, and Pearl Buck, all of whom were interested in exposing the West to the monistic sensibilities of Eastern philosophy and culture.

In late 1949 Leach visited the United States and toured from coast to coast, drawing large and appreciative audiences. Leach, who was awarded the Binns Medal in 1950 by the American Ceramic Society, had a strong impact on American ceramics. He did, however, slightly sully his reception by pointing out that American ceramics was without a taproot and, by implication, without any sense of direction.[3] It is ironic that the society that Leach had declared to be rootless was the first to achieve his ideal. Earlier Leach had emphasized that "because a potter belongs to our time and aspires to the position of creative artist he is divided in his allegiance between the contemporary movements in our own art and his challenge from the classic periods of the East."[4] The answer, he felt, lay in balance and integration. These qualities were not achieved in Leach's work, nor in that of his contemporaries in England, who remained staunchly traditionalist. The fusion of East and West was to occur in the following years in the United States.

Leach returned to America in 1952. This time he brought with him two close friends, the potter Shoji Hamada and the founder of the Mingei craft movement and director of the National Folk Museum of Japan, Soetsu Yanagi. They had just come from the first International Conference of Potters and Weavers, at Dartington Hall, and were to begin a tour of the United States, speaking on the

issues and concerns raised at that conference. The tour was organized by Alix MacKenzie. The trio (Bernard Leach, Shoji Hamada, and Soetsu Yanagi) drew large audiences wherever they spoke. In Los Angeles more than a thousand people packed a hall to hear them. Hundreds of others were turned away. Leach spoke persuasively of what the Orient had to offer the West; Yanagi explained the mystical principles of Zen Buddhist aesthetics; and Hamada demonstrated throwing and painting pots. For those

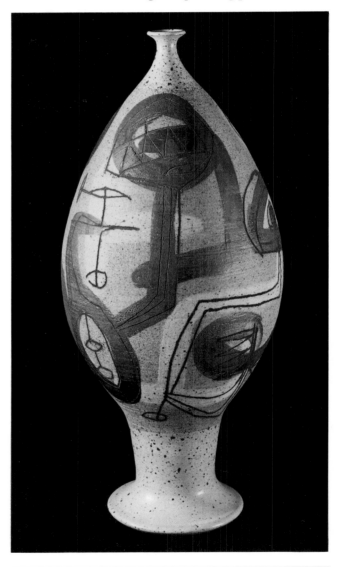

Antonio Prieto Vase, 1958. Glazed stoneware, height 18". Mills College, Oakland, California.

who participated in the various seminars, lectures, and symposia, the tour proved to be a rich and challenging event. The seminars at the Archie Bray Foundation in Montana and at Black Mountain College in North Carolina proved to be particularly far-reaching.

Other visitors provided a different view of Japanese ceramics. In 1954 the perspicacious Rosanjin toured the country, exhibiting at the Museum of Modern Art and at the Grace Borgenicht Gallery, both in New York. Rosanjin was one of the most important ambassadors of the Oriental aesthetic. At one time, he had been a most respected gourmet restaurateur in Japan. When he required certain pottery for his restaurant and was unable to find it from practicing potters, he began to work himself. His approach was audacious. Sidney Cardozo affectionately termed him "the supreme amateur and dilettante,"[5] for he imitated and paraphrased all the great periods, styles, and masters in Japanese ceramics. The results, nonetheless, were distinctly the works of Rosanjin, and his brushwork—so brusque and economical—spoke of his years of studying calligraphy.

To Western eyes, at least, Rosanjin was the embodiment of *sabi*, a mixture of sophistry and savagery. His mercurial temper was legendary, and his progress through the United States was peppered with incidents. Following a heated exchange at Mills College (Oakland, California) with Antonio Prieto, head of the ceramics department, Rosanjin closed his exhibition after only twenty-four hours. Rosanjin had told Prieto that he did not think that his fat, bulbous forms with miniature necks and spouts were the last word in elegance. Prieto responded by calling Rosanjin's pots "turds and kiln shelves." Rosanjin took his pottery from the Mills exhibition to the ceramics department at the California College of Arts and Crafts, where students—including Manuel Neri, Viola Frey, and others—had free access to the pieces for several months.

While in San Francisco, Rosanjin gave a memorable lecture. In contrast to the paternalism of Leach, he spoke enthusiastically of American ceramics and prophesied that the nation would make a great and unique contribution to the ceramic arts in the coming years. In his address, he also dealt with the more spiritual concerns of the potter, insisting that pottery was not an art of technical expertise—machines and soulless craftsmanship, he said, were "reckless tools"—but that ceramics was an art of the mind, "dependent solely upon the beauty of the mind":

> I am learning by trying to produce pottery as fine art, in accordance with art for art's sake principles. Work done by machines is after all, work *by* machines. A work is of no value unless it moves the human mind and the human spirit. As for pottery of daily use, which should of necessity be of moderate price, I think there is nothing wrong with manufacturing it by mechanized methods. *But* once a man wishes to become an artist with the determination to dedicate his mind to the creation of first class art he must disregard the advantages of the machine. In other words, the fine arts are all activities of the intuitive mind and are not affected by the development or advancement of our knowledge, intelligence, or reason alone.[6]

Rosanjin was followed to the United States by the Bizen master Toyo Kaneshige, who gave extraordinary demonstrations. He would swiftly pummel his thrown form and, after a moment's contemplation, declare it good or bad and so consign it to either the kiln or to the soak bin.

The first reaction in American ceramics to the heady influences from Japan was imitation. Many potters made pilgrimages to Japan to learn how to copy Japanese wares, while others, less concerned with purity, simply copied from the examples represented in books and museums. Quasi-Oriental wares proliferated, and potters working outside this tradition found difficulty in being shown at fairs and exhibitions. An archaeologist digging in the future through the shard piles of the mid-1950s could be excused if he deduced that during this time the United States was overrun by an army of fourth-rate potters from China, Korea, and Japan. As more and more Oriental pottery of quality became available and was shown in public collections, however, a greater understanding of the nature of the objects and their beauty began to emerge, and the quality of the pieces produced in America improved.

From a fine-arts point of view two influences were significant for the fifties, Abstract Expressionism and Constructivism. The influence of Constructivism and the idea of collage that grew out of the Dada movement has already been briefly discussed. Although its overall significance has been greatly exaggerated, Abstract Expressionism was important to the American ceramist for several reasons. It was the first major art movement originating in the United States. American ceramists, trying to establish an identity separate from that of their European counterparts, felt considerable kinship with painters such as Jackson Pollock, Clyfford Still, Franz Kline, and others.

The movement began to take shape in the 1940s, but it was not until the 1950s that it began to attract wide attention and recognition. Also named the "New York school," after the city that became its headquarters, the movement involved several ideas with which the ceramist could identify. The critic Harold Rosenberg coined the term "action painting" to describe the creative process of certain painters in the movement, notably Pollock. The term implied a macho physicality and a one-to-one contact between the artist and his materials that had a certain similarity of spirit to that of the Zen potter. The notion of *nonobjective* art—of using color, form, and texture rather than recognizable subject matter as content—was one with which the vessel maker in particular was familiar, albeit from a more traditional vantage point.

Yet, in spite of certain affinities, ceramics, traditionally a conservative art form, was moving ahead much more slowly than painting. The revolutionary spirit that had so transformed American painting in the forties was not to reach the ceramics movement until a decade later. And when it did touch ceramic art, it was greatly modified by the ceramists' interest in their own traditions and roots.

The revolutionary force for ceramics in the fifties was to be Peter Voulkos, a young, dashingly handsome, and precociously talented painter-turned-potter, who provided crucial leadership for a medium in the throes of redefinition. Voulkos had a unique ability to blend the influences from Eastern ceramics with Western art. He had originally studied to be a painter but changed his major to ceramics. He was obsessed with the wheel. While studying for his B.F.A. he had refused to create forms by any other technique. Only when threatened with the withholding of his degree did he consent to work briefly with hand-building techniques. Voulkos received his M.F.A. in 1952 from the California College of Arts and Crafts in Oakland. At the time, he was producing strong, full-formed, but conventional vessels. In a short time, Voulkos established himself as a nationally known potter. Before leaving graduate school, he had won

Peter Voulkos Lidded Bird Vessel, *1956. Glazed stoneware, height 20″. Private collection.*

Peter Voulkos Lidded Jar, *1954. Glazed stoneware, height 17". The Newark Museum, Newark, New Jersey.*

In 1954 Voulkos moved to Los Angeles, where he set up the ceramics facility at the Otis Art Institute and, together with Harrison McIntosh, ran the department. For the first few months, there was little sign of a revolution brewing. Voulkos was then concentrating on functional wares. Slowly, however, the pace toward a new aesthetic began to develop: the students challenged his work; at the same time, Voulkos experienced something of a revelation through a period of studying music.[8] The ceramic work of the European artists Miró, Chagall, Léger, Fontana, and Picasso also began to inspire and excite the American ceramic world. The tempo of experiment built up, and soon Otis was producing the most radical ceramics in the country. The word got around Venice, California, the art enclave for Los Angeles, that "something was happening at Otis," and artists drifted in and

Peter Voulkos Vessel with Slab Surface, *1957. Glazed stoneware, height 22". Collection Howard and Gwen Laurie Smits.*

several prizes from the Ceramic Nationals at Syracuse and had begun to win prizes in international shows as well.

After receiving his M.F.A., Voulkos worked with Rudy Autio at the Archie Bray Foundation as one of the foundation's first artists in residence. The Archie Bray Foundation in Helena, Montana, had been established as a creative workshop by Archie Bray (1886–1953). Bray was the owner of Helena's Western Clay Manufacturing Works, a brick and pipe factory for which Autio also produced large murals. Bray wished to leave the foundation as a memorial, "a fine place to work for all who are sincerely and seriously interested in any branch of creative ceramics."[7] Under the leadership of various artists who succeeded Autio, including Ken Ferguson and David Shaner, the foundation has continued to fulfill Bray's vision.

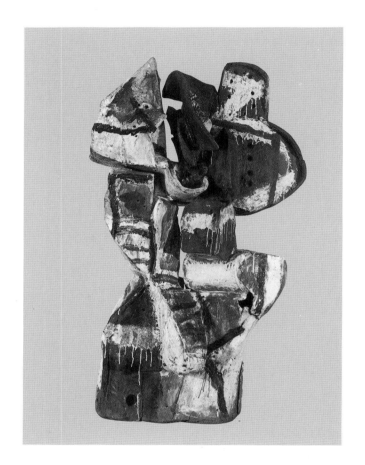

LEFT: **Peter Voulkos** Untitled, 1957. Glazed stoneware, height 62". Private collection. Courtesy Braunstein Gallery, San Francisco.

RIGHT: **Peter Voulkos** Rocking Pot, 1956. Glazed stoneware, cut and assembled from thrown and slab elements, height 19". Jedermann N. A. Collection.

FAR RIGHT: **Isamu Noguchi** Lonely Tower, 1951. Unglazed stoneware, height 28". Collection the artist.

joined the department; among these were Paul Soldner, Kenneth Price, John Mason, Billy Al Bengston, Henry Takemoto, Malcolm McClain, and Jerry Rothman. Artists from other media also became interested in the energies being generated at Otis. Robert Irwin and Craig Kauffman each titled a painting *Black Raku* in recognition of the ceramists' achievements.

There was no common style or ideology at Otis—other than the tacit agreement not to have any common style or ideology. The group was freely, almost purposely, eclectic. They drew from a myriad of sources: Haniwa terra-cottas; Wotruba's sculpture; Pollock's paintings; music; poetry; and the brash, inelegant Los Angeles environment. Books were the major "museum" of the group. Voulkos, in particular, was a ravenous consumer of ceramic literature. The photographs were marvelously abstracting. Soldner recalls a case when Voulkos was inspired to imitate what he saw as the gigantic scale of a Scandinavian pot that he had seen illustrated. Later, however, he discovered that the pot was a mere six inches in height.

The environment celebrated the individual. There were, however, common qualities that linked an otherwise diverse group of artists. One of the first students, Mac McClain (McCloud) recalls the atmosphere that existed: "It became quickly evident that all of us would be 'sharing a studio' with each involved at their own independent level. Pete radiated an overwhelming individuality, a relaxed and humorous charm, radical creative initiative and an enjoyable mix of down home earthiness and aesthetic brilliance. We were all roughly the same age, part of the Post-World-War II generation of young artists searching for a place to make things."[9] The manner in which they handled the clay was looser and more informal than ever before, and there was generally a unifying sense of incompleteness in the seemingly cursory finish of

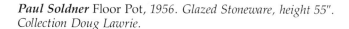

Paul Soldner Floor Pot, 1956. Glazed Stoneware, height 55".
Collection Doug Lawrie.

the works. What was taking place was a broad-ranging experiment that caused the critic Harold Rosenberg to propose that craft represented the ideal in contemporary art—an unfocused play with materials.

In explaining the motivations of the group, the critic John Coplans was later to write that the artists "were totally uninterested in exhibiting. What they needed was time to mature as artists, to seek their own path free from external pressures. The pot, they felt, was no more than an idiom." They were keenly aware of what was taking place in the art world, particularly in San Francisco and New York, but no one in the art world (apart from Rose Slivka, editor of *Craft Horizons*, and Fred Marer, who had collected their work from the outset) was aware of what was taking place, and "this suited their purposes at the time."[10]

The central figure of the decade was undoubtedly Voulkos, but he was not, as recent critics have attempted to suggest, solely responsible for the breakthrough in American ceramics. Voulkos was involved in a dynamic relationship with his stu-

Kenneth Price Plate, 1958. Glazed stoneware, height 11½". Collection Happy Price.

RIGHT: *John Mason* Vase, 1958. Glazed stoneware, height 23¾". Marer Collection, Scripps College, Claremont, California.

and the students would work seven days a week, sometimes through the night, firing hundreds of pots a week. Voulkos influenced students by example; if he had any message or doctrine, it was that the artist must first trust intuition:

> When you are experimenting on the wheel there are a lot of things you cannot explain. You just say to yourself, ''the form will find its way''— it always does. That's what makes it exciting. The minute you begin to feel you understand what you are doing it loses that searching quality. You reach a point where you are no longer concerned with keeping this blob of clay centered on the wheel and up in the air. Your emotions take over and what happens just happens. Pottery has to be more than an exercise in facility— the human element, expression, is usually badly neglected. [13]

In the work of Voulkos at Otis, three devel-

Jerry Rothman B, 1957. Ceramic and metal, height 120". Awarded National Prize, Wichita National.

Malcolm McClain Chamber of Spheres, 1959–60. Stoneware, height 27". Jedermann N. A. Collection.

dents; Otis's victory was really the victory of a highly competitive environment where the participants functioned as ''independent contestants.''[11] Jim Melchert, who had worked with Voulkos since 1958, wrote that working with him gave one the feeling of being onto something big and real:

> At the same time it was unforgettably disturbing. To build confidence in your own authority you had to keep surpassing your preconceptions and expectations. Having Voulkos for a teacher was the most demanding situation that I had encountered. To him a person's notion of existing limitations was largely imaginary. He constantly cautioned against underestimating the artist. If the persons working with him broke with the standard conceptions of formal structure they also managed to get around technical obstacles. [12]

Voulkos set an intimidating example, producing fifteen pots to everyone else's one. Frequently he opments emerged. First, by imitating the ceramics of Picasso, Voulkos came to the same realization as the master painter, that the overall painting of the pot surface destroys the sense of three-dimensionality.[14] At the same time, it allows the artist to rebuild the form, using line and color, and so to distribute the climactic aspects of the form. Second, Voulkos began to assemble his vessels with separate elements. Instead of a fluid, compositional unity, the pots became fragmented, as one part competed for attention with the others. Later, Voulkos and Soldner were to remember the exact point at which this breakthrough was made:

Paul Soldner: Do you remember when, probably for the first time, you broke with the symmetry of the bottle? Some good looking girls came in from Chouinard Art School and asked if you would throw a big pot for them. You threw the pot, and they were impressed. I remember you kept looking at the pot. And then after they left you went over and cut the top off. Then you threw four or five spouts and started sticking them around the rim. And that didn't seem to work, because it was still the same old bottle lip. Then you pared that off. The pot was still soft. Then you recentered it on the wheel and gouged three huge definitions, the top third, the center third and the bottom third. In one afternoon you went from one kind of thinking to something completely different.

Peter Voulkos: I remember it.

Paul Soldner: Do you remember the name of the pot?

Peter Voulkos: Yeah, *Love Is a Many-Splendored Thing.* I showed it at my show at the Felix Landau Gallery in 1956, and it was sold. . . . Pottery at this point began to be noticed by painters and sculptors.[15]

The third development in Voulkos's work at Otis was in his treatment of form. Voulkos began to deal less and less with the pot as volume—a contained space—and more with the pot as mass. The forms were made from almost solid pieces of clay. The traditional components—foot, main form, and neck—remained, but the vessel now became more *sculptural* and constructivist. The claim that Voulkos "turned ceramics into sculpture" is, how-

Michael Frimkess Pot, 1959. Earthenware, height 19½." Marer Collection, Scripps College, Claremont, California.

ever, a misconception. For no matter how sculptural his works became, they remained patently part of the tradition of pottery rather than of sculpture. In reviewing the exhibition *Otis Clay—The Revolutionary Years*, the critic Christopher Knight wrote: "While it cannot be denied that a good deal of ceramic work was created with a concern for sculptural values and with an awareness of contemporaneous developments in Abstract Expressionist painting, the 'revolution' which occurred in Otis in the late 1950s is not found in ceramics attempting to mimic the conventions—long held or newly held—of either sculpture or painting. Rather, it was revolution within the tradition of pottery itself."[16]

Voulkos also began to produce clay sculptures toward the end of the Otis period and after his move in 1958 to the University of California, Berkeley. Some of his forms have a brooding presence.

Generally speaking, however, this was Voulkos's most uneven and unsuccessful period of work. In 1962 he turned to metal as his sculptural medium.

About 1957 the Otis students began to show a more assertive independence. In many cases their exploration of the medium took them in directions different from that of Voulkos. Kenneth Price concentrated on the play of line and color, deemphasizing mass and even volume as he satirically dealt with the counterpoints of two- and three-dimensionality. This has been a continuing theme in his work. John Mason and Malcolm McClain were more intellectually involved in the medium. Their works from this period are clearly constructivist, usually produced out of carefully placed and even modules. Mason also went through a phase of Abstract Expressionist work, when he

created huge wall pieces by trailing long slabs of clay over one another, in a random manner. But his interests became more and more geometrically formal, as he progressed toward Minimalism and Conceptualism.

Henry Takemoto dealt largely with the pot as a canvas, covering his plates and fecund pot forms with energetic calligraphic drawing that was loosely inspired by the work of Miró. Billy Al Bengston worked for a while as the technical assistant to Voulkos, signing his work "Moondog." He did not graduate much beyond the level of inspired dabbler, and his involvement was short-lived and ended when he left ceramics to become a successful painter. Paul Soldner remained a functional potter; Michael Frimkess dealt with the material in an iconographic manner; and Jerry Rothman, the

Harrison McIntosh Bottle Vase, *c. 1959. Glazed stoneware, height 13½". Everson Museum of Art, Syracuse, New York. Purchase, twenty-first Ceramic National.*

LEFT: *Karen Karnes* Demitasse Set, *c. 1958. Glazed stoneware, coffee pot, height 8½". Everson Museum of Art, Syracuse, New York. Purchase, twentieth Ceramic National.*

maverick of the group, flirted at first with Constructivism, creating twelve-foot-high clay and metal sculptures for the Ferus Gallery in 1958. Thereafter, he moved on to more expressionist works, such as his serenely sensual *Sky Pots* of the early sixties.

What took place at Otis was by any standard a major event. The students in that group have gone on to become the leading artists, teachers, and designers in ceramics today. But the momentum did not stop at Otis. In Berkeley a new group assembled around Voulkos—Ron Nagle, Jim Melchert, Stephen DeStaebler, and others—giving rise to a body of strong sculpture in the 1960s and some interesting refinements of the vessel aesthetic. The activities attracted visitors, notably Manuel Neri, who had been working sporadically in clay since 1954, when he had first come in contact with

Voulkos at Archie Bray; and Harold Paris, who worked on mammoth ceramic walls. The peak of the so-called Abstract Expressionist development came between 1957 and 1960. Later developments were to lead away from abstract concerns to figurative imagery, but the effect of the early years of the experiment, as Coplans has noted, has been "to totally revolutionize the approach to ceramics. . . . What was done in those days is now mainstream ceramics."[17]

On the East Coast and in the Midwest, a quieter revolution was taking place. The seeds planted there in the 1950s took a longer time to grow, but the achievements of this time should not be discounted. Alfred University was for the first time producing students with an adventurous approach to their material. Most remained respectful of the functional disciplines of the art but thrived within its limitations, producing a generation of strong potters: Bob Turner, Karen Karnes, Val Cushing, Ken Ferguson. Other students were more experimental. David Weinrib began to produce structured slab pots before moving into a successful career as an internationally known sculptor. Daniel Rhodes developed techniques of combining fiberglass and clay to create sculptural forms that had previously been technically impossible. Rhodes was also to be one of the most influential educators of the post–World War II period through his series of books on clays, glazes, kilns, and recently, potter's form.

Black Mountain College, near Asheville, North Carolina, a progressive community that included at various times such diverse figures as Josef Albers, Clement Greenberg, and Robert Rauschenberg, was a magnet for the Alfred artists. Robert Turner worked there in 1952, building an immaculate and imaginative pottery. When he left, he was replaced by Karen Karnes and her husband, David Weinrib. Their reception was hostile. The dominant radical element in the school looked upon "the crafts" as being insupportably bourgeois. Weinrib was at least experimental, but the down-to-earth functional ware of Karnes was adjudged "not real or grubby

Leza McVey Ceramic Forms, 1950. Glazed stoneware, height
16" and 10⅜". Everson Museum of Art, Syracuse, New York.
Gift of Harshaw Chemical Company, sixteenth Ceramic National.

TOP: **Maria and Popovi Martinez** Bowl with Feather Design, 1956. Burnished earthenware, diameter 12½″. American Craft Museum, New York. Gift of Johnson Wax.

BOTTOM: **Maija Grotell** Bowl, 1956. Glazed stoneware, height 14″. Syracuse University, Syracuse, New York.

enough," and above all she committed the cardinal sin of "actually selling in commercial outlets."[18] On one occasion, the students demonstrated their dislike of the pottery by piling dinner scraps on Karnes's pots. But after the ten-day International Ceramics Symposium at Black Mountain in 1953, with Bernard Leach, Shoji Hamada, Soetsu Yanagi, and the host, Marguerite Wildenhain, the community began to reassess the pottery. At the symposium held in the following year, the embattled resident potters were given official billing with Rhodes and Warren MacKenzie, one of the most influential of Leach's American apprentices. Weinrib recalled that the community finally saw the pottery as a "measurable" achievement and that the more conservative members began to question the depth of students who became "too instantly hip" on reading Rimbaud and Proust, welcoming the potters' contrasting practicality as a counter to the overly libertine elements of the school.[19]

What took place at Black Mountain was a dramatization of what was happening throughout the country. A popular interest in the medium was resulting in the introduction of ceramics programs in art schools, colleges, and universities. The medium, however, was not accepted by the influential postmodernists, who were beginning to take over the academic art institutions and devalue the importance of both craft and object. Furthermore, ceramics still carried the aura of being a tool of art education, and critics and media found it difficult to treat ceramics as a serious medium. Those in the Otis group, for instance, found that once they attempted to engage an audience with their work they were arbitrarily consigned "to what they considered to be a twilight world, that of the crafts, which caused considerable misgivings, even anguish."[20] In the decade that followed, the most determined assault on the boundaries of fine arts took place, during which the American ceramist was finally to establish an artistic beachhead for the medium.

FAR LEFT: **Frans Wildenhain** Coffee Service, 1951. Stoneware, height 8". Private collection.

TOP LEFT: **Toshiko Takaezu** Bottle, 1958. Stoneware, glazed, height 13½". The Detroit Institute of Arts. Winner of the Founders Society Purchase Prize of Michigan Artist-Craftsmen Exhibition, 1958.

BOTTOM LEFT: **Rudolf Staffel** Oval Bowl, 1951. Glazed earthenware, height 8". Los Angeles County Museum of Art. Gift of Howard and Gwen Laurie Smits.

BELOW: **Beatrice Wood** Three bowls, 1958–60. Luster-glazed earthenware, height 7⅛", 3¾", 6". Private collection.

Peter Voulkos Bottle, 1961. Thrown and altered stoneware, glazed, height 18". Collection Mr. and Mrs. Monte Factor.

The sixties was the second decade of revolution for American ceramics. Whereas the previous decade had established a new vision for the vessel in contemporary art, the sixties would prove to be the most formative period for ceramic sculpture. In this decade we see the emergence of the Funk movement, which would dominate ceramic sculpture into the seventies, and also the beginnings of a high-crafted, trompe l'oeil style of still life/object making that I have entitled the "Super-Object." Most of this activity took place in San Francisco and in the adjoining Bay Area. Seattle was the center for a similar movement in painted ceramic sculpture, while in Los Angeles a quieter and less strident change took place, within the region's so-called fetish-finish style in painting and sculpture. The East Coast continued to produce strong work during this period, but it did not contribute meaningfully to the innovative thrust of the medium. Rather, it was the West Coast (California and Washington State) that dominated this decade.

Before a discussion of these new movements, it is necessary to examine the impact of Voulkos and the Otis school during the early 1960s. Up until this point knowledge of the work being done by Voulkos and his followers in Los Angeles and later at Berkeley was limited to the immediate sphere of the participants. Some work had been seen around the country, but the full consequence of what was taking place had not yet been appreciated. It was Rose Slivka's article in the July–August 1961 issue of *Craft Horizons*, titled "The New Ceramic Presence," that brought the new aesthetic into the national forum.

Slivka had been in contact with Voulkos and his students since 1958 and had, in turn, introduced Voulkos to her friends in New York, including Willem de Kooning and others of the New York school. Her article caused a furor, despite her having taken great pains to be nonpartisan and to present as merely *one* approach to the medium the works of Voulkos, Mason, Takemoto, Rothman, and a young

CHAPTER NINE
1960

potter named Robert Arneson. The largely conservative membership of the magazine's parent, today called the American Craft Council, felt confused, angered, and threatened. A debate opened as letters poured in, and it continued for some years. In the long run, the reaction proved to be a healthy one, as the ceramics community began to question and to reject its own entrenched criteria.

Slivka wrote the article from a painterly rather than from a ceramic viewpoint. Thus, while she acknowledged the importance of Japanese pottery for these artists, she did not explore the depth of its influence. What she did not understand was that the primary experience for the potter of the 1950s had been the recognition of the complexity of the Japanese ceramic aesthetic. The pouring of colored pigments one over another, gestural painting, a random use of color, and pure abstraction—developments new to painting—had been consciously explored in a highly sophisticated manner by Japanese potters for centuries. Abstract Expressionism modified the experience of Japanese pottery and gave it a new contemporary context. For the first time in the twentieth century, ceramic tradition and the fine-arts mainstream were involved in parallel ideas and sensibilities.

One of the most insightful comments in Slivka's article had nothing to do with painting—it was Slivka's linking of the new ceramics with jazz, thereby implying the greater importance of the act of making the object than of the object itself. Until the 1950s potters had tended to observe the European approach that viewed process simply as means. In jazz, means and end become one:

> Spontaneity, as the creative manifestation of this intimate knowledge of tools and their use on materials in the pursuit of art, has been dramatically an American identity in the art of jazz, the one medium that was born here. Always seeking to break through unexpected patterns, the jazzman makes it while he is playing it. With superb mastery of his instrument and intimate identification with it, the

instrumentalist creates at the same time as he performs; the entire process is there for the listener to hear—he witnesses the acts of creation at the time when they are happening and shares with the performer the elation of the creative act.[1]

A second explanation of the changes wrought during the 1950s came in 1966, when John Coplans, an art critic who had been pioneering the importance of contemporary ceramics for some years, organized the exhibition *Abstract Expressionist Ceramics* at the Art Gallery of the University of California, Irvine. The exhibition was one of the most important single events in American ceramics history, bringing the ceramics "revolution" to a broader audience than before and, to some extent, legitimizing the body of work within the art world. For numerous ceramists working today it was a turning point in their careers, introducing a new and more challenging vocabulary for ceramics in general and for the vessel in particular.

The selection of works was excellent, pinpointing some of the early masterpieces by Voulkos and his group. What was assembled, however, was *not* Abstract Expressionist ceramics, but for the first time it was identifiably American. The exhibition catalogue was in great demand and ran to three printings. Coplans's catalogue essay is one of the more important statements in contemporary American ceramics. But, in common with Slivka's earlier article, it viewed the work as an experiment in painting—"the most ingenious regional adaptation of . . . Abstract Expressionism . . . yet"—rather than as an independent achievement of a distinct and different discipline—ceramics.[2] Furthermore, the links with Abstract Expressionism were hardly strong enough to justify the title, since Constructivism was patently a more central influence for many works in the exhibition. Even Coplans later admitted that the title was not an effective umbrella, but that "it seemed convenient at the time."[3]

The collector Fred Marer was involved with the project from the beginning, having literally stumbled into the pottery at Otis soon after Voul-

kos's arrival. Marer was fascinated with the group and became its earliest supporter, patron, and collector. Marer feels that the Abstract Expressionist element has consistently been overexploited and overromanticized. Apart from other considerations, there was an underlying element of figurative expression that was freely explored at Otis. Even when Voulkos began to reject the figure about 1957, it proved difficult to exclude. In a letter to the author in January 1977, Marer commented, "I watched Voulkos making his six-seven feet high sculptures, fighting desperately to subdue the figurative formations that seemed to creep out." Interestingly, although Voulkos first met with some of the major figures of the New York school in 1953, there is no mention of any influence from this group until after his 1958 visit to New York, by which time his signature style had already emerged.

Another exhibition, titled *Funk Art* and held at the University of California, Berkeley, in 1967, pinpointed a major new energy and direction. Organized by Peter Selz, the exhibition contained objects in every medium, but it was the clay objects that seemed closest to the aesthetic Selz suggested in his catalogue essay. In fact, the exhibition proved to be far less a definition of Funk than a survey of West Coast art that lacked stylistic labels (the cool egg forms of Kenneth Price and the clean polychrome metal sculptures of Robert Hudson clearly did not belong to the title). The exhibition was nonetheless extremely important, drawing attention to broad Funk concerns in art and providing a showcase for some of the ceramic talents in this area—David Gilhooly, Robert Arneson, and others.

Harold Paris, in an article titled "Sweet Land of Funk," had earlier pinpointed the context out of which the "style" had grown. It was less an identifiably visual expression than an attitude. Each artist interpreted it in a different manner, but when Bay Area artists spoke of Funk, each knew what the other meant. Funk was, in a sense, protest (unspecific) coming out of a feeling (equally unspecific) of being betrayed by traditional forms and ideas in society: "Artists of the current generation have turned inward. Rejecting collective ideas and moral judgment they are hypersensitive to their own elemental feelings and processes. What is felt is real and tangible; what is thought to be is distrusted. Intuitive perception is desirable. The residue, or the by-product, is more interesting and provocative than the intellectual process that creates it. In essence, 'It's a groove to stick your finger down your throat and see what comes up,' this is funk."[4]

Funk originated with the Rat Bastard Protective Association, a group of artists who in 1951 mounted the exhibition *Common Art Accumulations*, at the Place Bar in San Francisco. Bruce Conner, Joan Brown, and others put together ephemeral conglomerations combining all kinds of uncombinable things, "called them Funk and didn't care what happened to them."[5] The term "Funk" was taken from the term "bagless funk," describing a free, improvised, earthy street jazz and also used in Cajun patois to describe the musk smell of a woman's groin.

On the West Coast, the early Funk art had its roots in Dada and Surrealism. The artists were drawn to the blend of insouciance, poetic juxtaposition of found or common objects, and rejection of establishment values in the fine arts. More importantly, Dada and Surrealist objects proposed a new type of sculpture, the "art object." Marcel Duchamp's readymade *The Fountain* (1917), a urinal signed by R. Mutt; Man Ray's *Gift* (1921), an iron with nails attached to the flat surface; and later, Meret Oppenheim's fur-lined teacup and Salvador Dalí's lobster telephone from the exposition *Objets Surréalistes* at the Galerie Charles Ratton, Paris, in 1936, all have one thing in common. Unlike traditional or even most modernist sculpture, which is primarily concerned with form, these objects are equally involved with context. The judgment of good or bad form becomes suspended by the provocative and contextual elements in the art object. Even the participants in the Dada-Surrealist movement agreed that their objects were "Objects of Symbolic function. . . . They depend solely upon our amorous imagination and are extra plastic."[6] The use of found objects and their composition caused a growing involvement with concepts of collage, where "the very conditions of the activity forced the artist to make decisions of a purely pictorial order."[7] As a result, much of ceramic Funk art has tended toward a type of three-dimensional illustration.

Funk continued in spirit through the 1960s at the ceramic department of the University of California at Davis. There, under the leadership of Robert Arneson, a group of students began to explore Funk as an alternative both to the cool,

Robert Arneson No Return, *1961. Glazed ceramic, height 10¾". Collection Mr. and Mrs. Paul C. Mills.*

mannered Pop art and to the so-called Abstract Expressionist ceramics. The latter were then already considered passé by the younger students, who derogatorily referred to them as "the blood-and-guts school." In the mid-sixties Davis produced a body of Funk work that Suzanne Foley described as "expressionist, surrealist and offensive."[8]

The Davis faculty attracted individualists; in addition to Arneson, Wayne Thiebaud, William T. Wiley, Manuel Neri, and Roy De Forest taught there. The art department was established in the early 1960s. Therefore there was, in the words of Arneson, "no academic hierarchy . . . no worshipful old-timers whose word was law. There was no academic infighting. Above all, there was no one to say this is the right way, that is the wrong way, and everybody could work as they saw fit."[9]

Arneson's radicalism had begun to surface long before he joined the Davis faculty. At the California State Fair in the summer of 1961, he had placed a ceramic cap on a "handsomely thrown" bottle and marked it "no return."[10] Until then Arneson had been a potter, making vessels and winning prizes at decorative-art shows such as the Wichita National.

Robert Arneson Herinal, *1965. Glazed earthenware with colored epoxy, height 25½". Private collection. Courtesy Fuller Goldeen Gallery, San Francisco.*

The gesture was not unlike that of Jasper Johns a year earlier, when—in response to Willem de Kooning's remark that Leo Castelli could sell anything, even beer cans—he had made a bronze out of two Ballantine ale cans, titling it *Painted Bronze (Ale Cans)*.

In his catalogue of Arneson's 1986 retrospective, Neal Benezra describes this moment at the State Fair as the beginning of Arneson's "estrangement" from the ceramic establishment.[11] But, on the contrary, *No Return* signaled one of the first salvos in a palace revolution that would place a new California elite in control of American ceramics and Arneson firmly entrenched as the doyen of ceramic sculpture. Arneson's stance vis-à-vis the ceramics world was not "revulsion," as Benezra states, but "ambivalence."

It took another two years before the gesture in *No Return* was to be matched. In 1963 Arneson was invited to participate in the exhibition *California Sculpture*, which took place on the roof of the Kaiser Center in Oakland. Curated by Walter Hopps, Paul Mills, and John Coplans, the exhibition included thirty-two sculptors, including Voulkos, Mason, Edward Kienholz, Simon Rodia, and others. This was the final break for Arneson with both traditional ceramics and with his play with organic, Prieto-esque, Miró-esque sculpture:

> I could see myself, Bob Arneson, between John Mason and Peter Voulkos and would I just be the junior version of those two? I really put my mind together and reflected back on my heritage as a ceramist—somebody who dealt in reproduction. I really thought about the ultimate ceramics in Western culture . . . so I made a toilet and cut loose and let every scatological notation in my mind freely flow across the surface of that toilet.[12]

The finished piece was, in the artist's opinion, his first mature work. He had finally "made a Bob Arneson."[13] Entitled *Funk John*, the piece remained on exhibition for one day, after which a Kaiser Center official, offended by both the subject and its "ceramic emblems" of excrement, had the work removed. In a sense, the gesture was a reenactment of Duchamp's placement of *The Fountain* in the 1917 Indépendants Salon. While the sensibility of the two artists was totally different, their determination to declare independence and to provoke a cause célèbre was indeed similar.

An important change in *Funk John* was the move from stoneware, a clay body that was de rigueur for the Abstract Expressionist, to whiteware, a white earthernware associated with hobbyists and industry. Jim Melchert and Ron Nagle had begun to work intermittently with whiteware at the San Francisco Art Institute in 1961, experimenting with bright, low-fire glazes and later with photographic decals. This provided Arneson with a neutral white ground to paint and removed any of the rustic, "truth to materials" romance from his work.

During the next two years Arneson produced additional works in the *John* series: *John with Art* (1964) and the anthropomorphic and deliciously vulgar work *Herinal* (1965). At the same time a new style was emerging. It was nourished, like that associated with Otis, by the loose, unstructured teaching environment at Davis, which promoted student-teacher interaction. In the fall of 1966, an important exhibition took place at the San Francisco gallery of the American Craft Council.[14] Arneson exhibited alongside seven of his undergraduates: Margaret Dodd, David Gilhooly, Stephen Kaltenbach, Richard Shaw, Peter Vandenberge, Chris Unterseher, and Gerald Walburg.

Arneson's work from the mid-1960s can be seen in two periods. In the first stage he was, in the words of Dennis Adrian, "a fringe Pop Gangster." His early objects from the mid-1960s have become classics but are not his most important works. These early objects—such as the group of eight Seven-up bottles; *Toasties* (1965); *Typewriter* (1966), with red-lacquered fingernails replacing the keys; and the visual puns in *Call Girl* (1967), a telephone with breasts—are amusing and seditious, but they are less confrontational today than they were at the time of their first exhibition. These works are important historically, however, for they

Robert Arneson Typewriter, 1966. Glazed earthenware, length 12". Courtesy Allan Stone Gallery, New York.

show the manner in which the early ceramic Funk artists were working out of a Dadaesque inversion of Pop art. The icons were common to both—typewriters, toilets, canned foods. The difference between the two is a matter of degree rather than kind. Peter Plagens succinctly defined it as the dirty and the clean. Pop reflected the clean: cool, lobotomized images, as in Claes Oldenburg's soft toilets. In Arneson's *John* series, in contrast, the toilets were made out of genitals and were left splendidly unflushed.

In 1967–68 a new phase of Arneson's work began to emerge. His pieces were now less art objects à la Dada and more sculptural. His seminal work *Alice House Wall* (1967), made up of modules, was particularly important in Arneson's growth as a sculptor. It allowed him to work on a larger scale, culminating in works such as *Fragments of Western Civilization* (1972), *Swimming Pool* (1977), and *Mountain and Lake* (1978).

The growth of the verbal-visual in Arneson's work became more considered and less of a one-liner. The wordplay with objects began early in Arneson's work. Among his students, such as Gilhooly, it has continued and spread into non-Funk art, becoming one of the identifying characteristics of contemporary object making in American ceramics. At its best, Arneson's use of the pun evokes a complex and often emotional response from the viewer. In a penetrating study of Arneson's work, Dennis Adrian emphasizes this aspect:

> The catch is of course that to an English/speaking/thinking audience, the pun is usually interpreted as simplistically humorous on a fairly low level, so statements of double meaning in art—as elsewhere—tend to elicit giggles, and not much more. Yet as any scholar of Joyce or Japanese poetry will wearily insist, the primary function of any kind of pun is the expansion of meaning, within discrete form, into at least two simultaneous modes of thought. This is the key to a large area of art which concerns itself seriously with the truly comic; but, because of the fluky nature of the pun in English, intrepretation in that language frequently thrusts aside or misconstrues such art as ignoble.[15]

Apart from a distinguishing use of humorous titles and images among the Funk artists, there is also a common approach to the material. When Alfred Frankenstein said that Arneson had gone one better than Dada, that he had produced the "ready-made home-made,"[16] he touched the essence of the Funk aesthetic. The sloppy use of the material was carefully sustained, linking the objects with the hobby-craft aesthetic of thick, oozing, and virulently colored glazes over complacent whiteware. In this sense the Funk ceramists shared another similarity with the Pop artists: both used craft techniques that were considered outside the boundaries of high art—Pop art drew from commercial art and poster painting, and Funk from the hobbyist. Arneson's realization of this quality in the work is substantiated by his bumper sticker, "Ceramics is the world's most fascinating hobby," and by the works that play on simplistic pottery making, such as *Pottery Lessons* (1967) and *How to Make the Big Dish Plate* (1967).

The Funk artists were also shamelessly eclectic, drawing from many sources and changing directions and subject matter from one exhibition to the next. This catholicism is evident in Gilhooly's frog-world misanthropy. Gilhooly began by producing facetious animal-related objects, such as the *Elephant Ottoman* (1966), but, influenced by Maija Peeples, turned to frogs. Gilhooly's invented culture has allowed him a platform from which to playfully satirize all society and particularly its art.

The last of the Funk artists to be discussed here is Clayton Bailey. Bailey is ceramics' most insistent raconteur. His aesthetic credo can be summed up simply from a statement he once made about his work: "Anyone can do things in poor taste—it takes an artist to be truly gross."[17] Certainly the critics agree that Bailey is beyond poor taste. In his article for the March 1970 issue of *Art and Artists*, David Zack called his work "as gross and phallic as a draught horse's mating equipment." It is a measure of his anarchistic approach that Bailey most treasures reviews that denigrate his work. One of his favorite and most quoted reviews came from Cynthia Barlow, a reviewer for the *Saint Louis Globe Democrat*, who denounced his exhibition at the Craft Alliance Gallery as "a show that is tasteless, obscene and barely above the level of bathroom humor. Dismembered and disfigured fingers, lips and other portions of the human anatomy make up a large part of the objects presented. Even the titles are unpleasant—*Nite Pot*, *Kissing Pot*. The pieces are crudely done, carefully painted to the point of lewdity."[18]

Bailey's works, Arneson's penis teapots and genital trophies, Gilhooly's frogs fornicating with vegetables, and—outside the Bay Area school—the phallic cameras of Fred Bauer constitute the second exorcism for American ceramics. More irreverent than the Otis group and its assault on the vessel, they dealt with the preciousness of the figurative ceramic objects. They broke completely with the role of the ceramist as the producer of tasteful, overly crafted bric-a-brac for middle-class sideboards and mantelpieces. Until then the ceramist had been associated with the conceited and refined court figurines from eighteenth-century Europe; the sentimental figures of Royal Copenhagen; the highly priced limited-edition porcelains of Boehm and Cybis; and, by contrast, the vulgar,

Robert Arneson Call Girl, 1967. *Glazed earthenware and sculp-metal, height 18". Collection Diana Fuller. Courtesy Fuller Goldeen Gallery, San Francisco.*

Kenneth Price M. Green, *1961. Lacquer and acrylic on stoneware, height 10". Collection Betty Asher.*

mass-produced ornaments of the gift shops, with their gilding and lace draping.

The impact of the Funk movement was considerable, but ceramics students misunderstood the complex cultural statement that was developing. Funk was imitated mindlessly throughout the United States and even in Scandinavia and in England (particularly at the Wolverhampton Polytechnic, which became the center for the peculiarly English style of "gentlemanly Funk"). Funk became *the* ceramic buzzword. It seemed that overnight everything was Funk: colors, glazes, images, attitudes. But by 1975, as suddenly as it had become vogue, the Funk movement had fizzled out, leaving behind an embarrassing surfeit of objects that were vulgar, banal, and formless. In retrospect, only a small cadre of artists had produced credible work by 1975; most progressed to a more mature expression in which Funk was not the "style" but only

an element. Within the space of fifteen years, it had moved from being avant-garde to a dated, "historical" style. Yet it had served its purpose as a purgative, flushing out the last vestiges of formalism in ceramics and adding the second indigenous "school" to the American mainstream of ceramic art within a decade.

The protest inherent in Funk ceramics was by no means an isolated activity, unique to the medium. It was taking place close to the Haight-Ashbury district of San Francisco, the spiritual center of the Hippie movement. Draft dodgers were burning their draft cards, feminists were burning their bras. America's youth was "dropping out" of society and rejecting its parents' values and life-styles. In this context it seems appropriate that the Bay Area ceramists should so rudely have turned their backs on the expectations of ceramics as a refined, nonrevolutionary and bourgeois art form.

The true ceramic Funk was never transplanted outside the Bay Area, where those who succeeded in applying the style all lived. Funk, therefore, grew very much out of regional energies and concerns. In describing Funk, the artist Harold Paris emphasized this regionalism: "The casual insincere, irreverent California atmosphere with its absurd elements—weather, clothes, skinny-dipping, hobby craft, sun drenched metality, Doggie Diner, perfumed toilet tissue, do-it-yourself—all this drives the artist's vision inward. This is the land of Funk."[19]

In contrast to the "dirty" aspect of Funk, the art of the clean was growing apace. In the early sixties this was centered primarily in the Los Angeles area and in what was termed the "fetish-finish" style. This was not a single style so much as it was a sensibility that the Los Angeles artists seemed to share. Gradually a taste began to grow in Los Angeles for finely crafted art as a counterpoint to both the rawness of Funk and the macho casualness of the Abstract Expressionists. This can be seen in the ceramics of Kenneth Price, the elegant Minimalism of Robert Irwin, Ron Davis's linoleum-like splatter paintings, Craig Kauffman's serene Plexiglas works, and Bengston's meticulous air-brushed paintings. Price's biomorphic egg forms from the early 1960s placed him among the leaders of this group. Unlike the work in the Bay Area, which was authentically regional, Price's sculpture showed a debt to European abstractionists—in particular the biomorphism of Jean Arp. It was immaculately crafted, with a purist use of form, line, and acidic colors. "Like the geometric redness of the Black Widow's belly or the burning rings of the Coral snake," Henry Hopkins wrote, "these objects proclaim their intent to survive."[20]

John Mason moved away from his earlier involvement with pottery and turned to sculpture, working on a memorable series of monoliths that were up to six feet in height. The first and most successful of these were produced in 1962–63. They were heroic and moving. Mason then worked in a Minimalist format, building up geometric, hard-edged forms with what were intended to be flat, monochrome-glazed surfaces. Elaborate systems of drying the large forms were devised, but, despite the care, the forms warped and cracked, and colors flowed into a rich and busy surface. These and the earlier sculptures were shown in

1966 at the Los Angeles County Museum of Art, proving that the modernist ethos (with slight modification for the clay medium) could be successfully expressed in ceramics. In addition, Mason was working on a series of masterful walls that revealed the formal modularity that in the 1970s was to take him inevitably into Conceptual sculpture and installations of fire brick.

The work of Michael Frimkess from the late 1960s reflects a similar approach. Working in Venice, California, he threw incredibly thin forms that were readily identifiable as cultural "stereotypes": Chinese ginger jars, Greek amphorae, Zuñi bowls. He then covered these with tight, linear, cartoon drawings that dealt with the artist's visions of a utopian society. Although they were different from most of the art of Los Angeles because they dealt with "issues" and not abstraction, in terms of their execution they were nonetheless part of an emerging "look" in the city's art.

Jerry Rothman worked at the same time to

John Mason Wall X, 1965. Ceramic, length 14½'. Courtesy the artist.

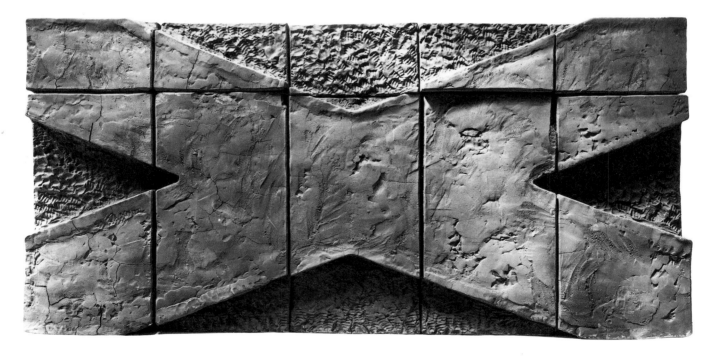

enlarge the scope of the material and overcome the limitations of ceramics that made it unsuitable for the sculptural ambitions of the time. However, Rothman, always the maverick, worked very much outside the ruling style of Los Angeles art. He began to assemble huge triptychs consisting of very erotic figures and dealing with birth and other issues that understandably caused problems in the arena of public art. On one occasion, a 1974 exhibition of his work at the Oakland Museum was removed because of a public outcry over the subject matter.

The sixties also saw the creation of another aesthetic in Los Angeles ceramics, tied to the fetish-finish school but, at the same time, more closely tied to traditional ceramics. It came out of the Chouinard Art Institute, under the chairmanship in 1963–72 of one of its graduates, Ralph Bacerra.

Jerry Rothman Sky Pot, 1960. *Sand-glazed stoneware, thrown and slabbed forms, altered and assembled, height 29". Marer Collection, Scripps College, Claremont, California.*

Howard Kottler Bunny Hop Pot, 1969–70. *Earthenware with decals, glaze, and overglaze luster, height 21". Collection Daniel Jacobs.*

At Chouinard the training was more formalized and more rooted in technique than at Otis. But, given Bacerra's passion for technical virtuosity, this took on a lively quality, and technique began to emerge in this group as an "edge" to be pushed to the point that it became content in itself. The impact of the group would not be strongly felt until the late seventies and early eighties, when Bacerra's pupils—Adrian Saxe, Mineo Mizuno, Peter Shire, Elsa Rady, and Don Pilcher—would emerge as an important group of artists. These artists began to exhibit their work more extensively during the mid-1970s, particularly through the American Hand in Washington. In the 1980s the Jan Turner Gallery in Los Angeles would also begin to exhibit the work of Rady, Mizuno, and Shire. Early in the sixties, the dominant style at Chouinard was what is termed "brown bread pottery"—rustic,

Ron Nagle Bottle with Stopper, *1960. Earthenware with glaze and china paint, height 23¼". Marer Collection, Scripps College, Claremont, California.*

functional wares. But by the end of the decade, all of the Chouinard "school" was beginning to experiment with color, decorative systems, and cultural contexts.

Ron Nagle, a developing artist in the Bay Area, was strongly influenced by Price and by the Los Angeles art scene in general, finding himself temperamentally removed from what he disdainfully labeled "the banana hand" school of figurative painting in the Bay Area and the "yuk-yuk" ceramics of verbal/visual gags in the Funk movement. Nagle was excited to find Price "making these little Grandma wares with bright colors on them . . . a little goofier, a little less macho—totally left field," with a different aesthetic, the whole "finish-fetish intimate-object-oriented thing."[21]

Nagle's interest in china painting was influenced by his mother, who had been involved in

the technique, and by photo-decal decoration. At first, Nagle used china paints to introduce elements of bright color into his palette in such works as *Bottle with Stopper* (1960), one of the ceramic masterpieces of the decade. But later, when he and Melchert introduced whiteware to the ceramics department at the San Francisco Art Institute, he began to explore the possibilities of china paints in a more intense and innovative manner. He built rich, layered surfaces by firing layer after layer of china paints onto his vessels. He was inspired to some extent by the abstraction and jewel-like palette of Japanese Momoyama wares. At an early point, he adopted the cup as a vehicle for his work, following the example of Price's long fascination with this form. Nagle first exhibited his cups in 1963 in *Works in Clay by Six Artists* (Jim Melchert, Manuel Neri, Anne Stockton, Ricardo Gomez, and

Michael Frimkess Covered Jar, *1968. Glazed ceramic with china paint, height 23¾". Marer Collection, Scripps College, Claremont, California.*

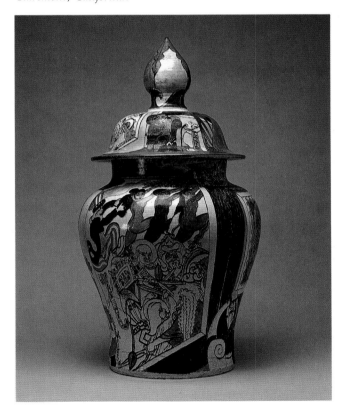

Stephen DeStaebler) at the San Francisco Art Institute.[22]

This exhibition proved to be significant because it provided the first view of the mature work of Jim Melchert. In 1964 Melchert held a one-man show, *Ghostwares*, at the Hansen Fuller Gallery in San Francisco. By this date Melchert had changed from the stoneware of 1962 (such as his seminal *Legpots*) to molded, figurative, china-painted whitewares. His use of these materials became increasingly refined, culminating in his *Games* series and *a* series. Melchert provided a valuable balance in the mix of Bay Area ceramists, being one of the few who, despite the lush and rich ceramic surfaces, was primarily analytical and conceptual in his approach.

In September 1965 the exhibition *New Ceramic Forms*, which was held at the Museum of Contemporary Crafts in New York, finally acknowledged the new thrust in ceramics. All the objects on exhibition came from the whiteware, china-painted tradition.[23] At first, the polarities of the "school" were indistinct and the division of dirty and clean was less apparent. But from 1966 on, a new finesse

was established, as a group of artists began to exhibit pristine, immaculate craftsmanship. An early masterwork in this genre is Richard Shaw's *Ocean Liner Sinking into a Sofa* (1966), from his *Sofa* series. This high-craft approach, belonging to the Super-Object tradition in ceramics, now began to grow rapidly, with a Surrealist base for its imagery. The Bay Area dominated for some time, but many others were also working in this style: Jack Earl in Toledo, Ohio; Victor Spinski and Ka-Kwong Hui in New York. Although Hui worked with abstract form, the accent on refinement, the touch of preciousness, and the hard-edged painting were nonetheless in harmony with the Super-Object's high-craft aesthetic.

In 1966 Hui collaborated with the Pop artist Roy Lichtenstein and assembled a body of work—piles of cups, teapots, and molded heads—that was exhibited at the Leo Castelli Gallery in New York. These works, much like the Super-Objects that were developed elsewhere, were consciously dealing with interaction between the reality of the three-dimensional form and the illusion of painting; Lichtenstein was interested "in putting two di-

Jim Melchert Leg Pot 1, 1962. *Stoneware with cloth inlay, assembled from slab and thrown forms, length 32½". American Craft Museum, New York. Gift of Johnson Wax.*

mensional symbols on a three dimensional object."[24] More broadly, Lichtenstein's aesthetic credo is very much a summary of that of the Super-Object makers: "Lichtenstein conceals the process from an object to art . . . disguising the genuine aesthetic concern in apparent anti-sensibility and his painstaking craftmanship in the appearance of mass-production."[25]

At the same time that Lichtenstein was showing his assembled cup sculptures and benday-dot–decorated mannequin heads, another exhibition, *The Object Transformed*, was taking place at the Museum of Modern Art, New York. The show emphasized the growing interest in the art object as an alternative to either painting or sculpture. Mildred Constantine, the exhibition's organizer, welcomed the art object as "the new still life of the twentieth century." In a review of the exhibition, Alice Adams wrote that, unlike the still lifes of Cézanne, Picasso, and Braque, where the object becomes universalized through successive analysis, the transformed object is unique and personal in concept:

> Objects from the environment, things that were made for specific use, have now entered a realm of artist's media. Along with the altering of images through collage has come the actual disassemblage, shrouding, melting down or otherwise altering ordinary objects so that they resolidify into another form. Usually retaining a ghost of the original, their transformation forces a parallel change in the observer's preconceived notion of what he knows. The world of dreams and fantasies congeals before his eyes, and he must deal with it as reality.[26]

A second school of ceramists working with these aspirations began to develop in Seattle, at the University of Washington, with leadership coming from Howard Kottler, Fred Bauer, and Patti Warashina. Kottler turned from making lumpish stoneware weed pots to making collages from store-bought decals that he fired onto commercial porcelain blanks. As the supreme irony, he would then encase his plates in luxurious, custom-made containers, lavishing more attention on the wrap-

Fred Bauer Steam Drill–Slot Pump, *1967. Painted earthenware, height 65". American Craft Museum, New York. Gift of Johnson Wax.*

pings than on the "art objects" they contained. Bauer worked on the cusp of the Funk–Super-Object border. His imagery was frequently close to that of the Funk artist (cameras with penis lenses, for instance), but he defused the potential vulgarity of the concept with an elegance of craftsmanship, carefully modeling and glazing with slick, lustered surfaces. The Super-Object was beginning to come of age.

The decade ended on a high note with the exhibition *Objects: USA*, organized by Lee Nordness, of the Johnson Wax collection of contemporary crafts.[27] Nordness had managed to capture the mood of the decade and had acquired for the collection many works that are now among the key ceramic monuments of the decade, including Melchert's *Leg Pot # 1*, Rudy Autio's *Button Pot*, Fred Bauer's *Funk Pump*, and others. The exhibition succeeded in revealing both the innocence of the earlier part of the decade and the growing refinement and self-consciousness of the later period, which was to grow and continue into the 1970s.

Roy Lichtenstein Ceramic Sculpture #11, 1965. *Glazed earthenware with overglazes, height 7½". Collection Betty Asher.*

ABOVE: **Jim Melchert** Plate with Muffin Tin, c. 1964. Black glazed stoneware, diameter 24". Jedermann N. A. Collection.

RIGHT: **Roy Lichtenstein** Blonde I, 1965. Glazed earthenware with overglaze, height 15". Collection Mr. and Mrs. Roger Davidson. Courtesy Leo Castelli Gallery, New York.

BELOW: **Ka-Kwong Hui** Ceramic Form, 1967. Stoneware, thrown and assembled, glazed with on-glaze painting, height 22". Everson Museum of Art, Syracuse, New York.

BOTTOM RIGHT: **Ralph Bacerra** Orange Form, 1968. Earthenware vessel with orange slips and chrome overglaze, height 9". American Craft Museum, New York. Gift of Johnson Wax.

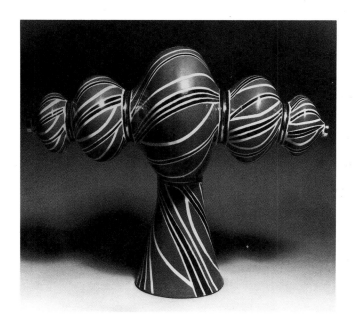

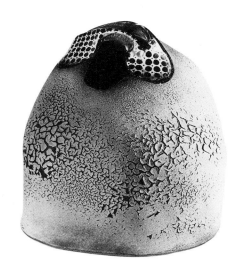

FAR LEFT: **Manuel Neri** Loops No. 2, 1961. *Glazed ceramic, height 18½". Private collection.*

NEAR LEFT: **Reuben Nakian** Europa Theme, 1960. *Terracotta, height 11". Hirshhorn Museum and Sculpture Garden, Smithsonian Institution, Washington, D.C.*

BELOW LEFT: **Peter Voulkos** Untitled Plate, 1963. *Glazed stoneware, length 19". Private collection.*

RIGHT: **Daniel Rhodes** Form, c. 1962. *Stoneware, height 47". Everson Museum of Art, Syracuse, New York.*

BELOW RIGHT: **John Mason** Vertical Sculpture, 1962. *Glazed stoneware, height 64". Jedermann N. A. Collection.*

TOP LEFT: **Betty and George Woodman** Pitcher, 1966. Earthenware, raku glazed, height 14". Private collection.

BOTTOM LEFT: **Paul Soldner** Bottle, 1963. Raku-fired earthenware, height 11". Everson Museum of Art, Syracuse, New York.

Warren MacKenzie Fruit Bowl, 1965. Glazed stoneware, diameter 13". University Art Museum, University of Minnesota, Minneapolis.

RIGHT: **Peter Voulkos** Stack Pot, 1964. Stoneware, glazed, pierced, and assembled from thrown sections, height 30". The Detroit Institute of Arts, Founders Society Purchase.

Kenneth Price California Snail Cup, 1967. Glazed earthenware, height 3½". Private collection.

Robert C. Turner Storage Jar, 1965. Glazed stoneware, height 11". Everson Museum of Art, Syracuse, New York.

BOTTOM LEFT: **William Wyman** Terrace Bottle, 1960. Coiled and thrown, stoneware with slips, height 20". Everson Museum of Art, Syracuse, New York.

BELOW: **Beatrice Wood** Chalice, 1963. Earthenware with blue luster, height 8". Collection Daniel Jacobs.

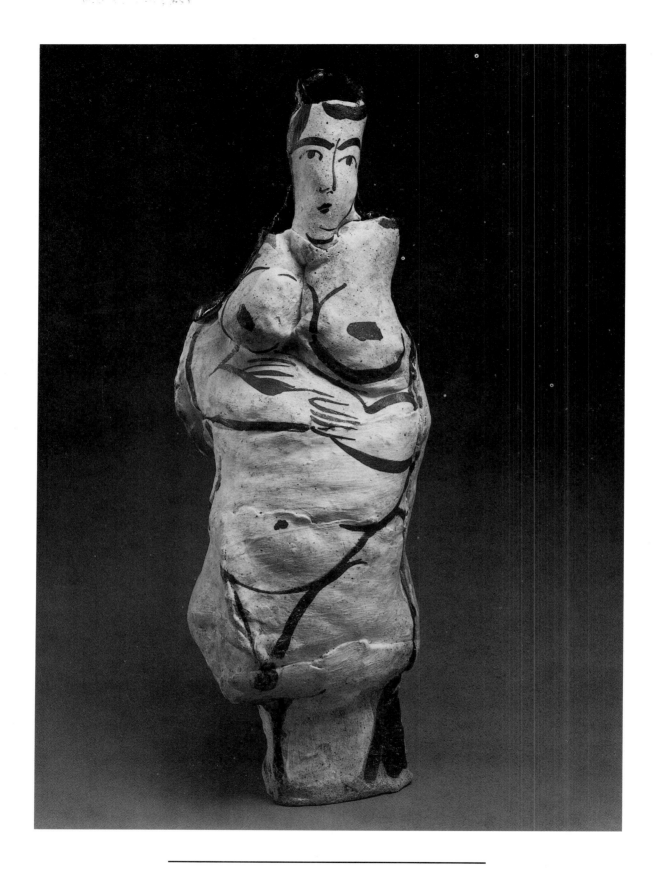

Rudy Autio Double Lady, 1964. Stoneware with black and white slips, height 28½". Everson Museum of Art, Syracuse, New York.

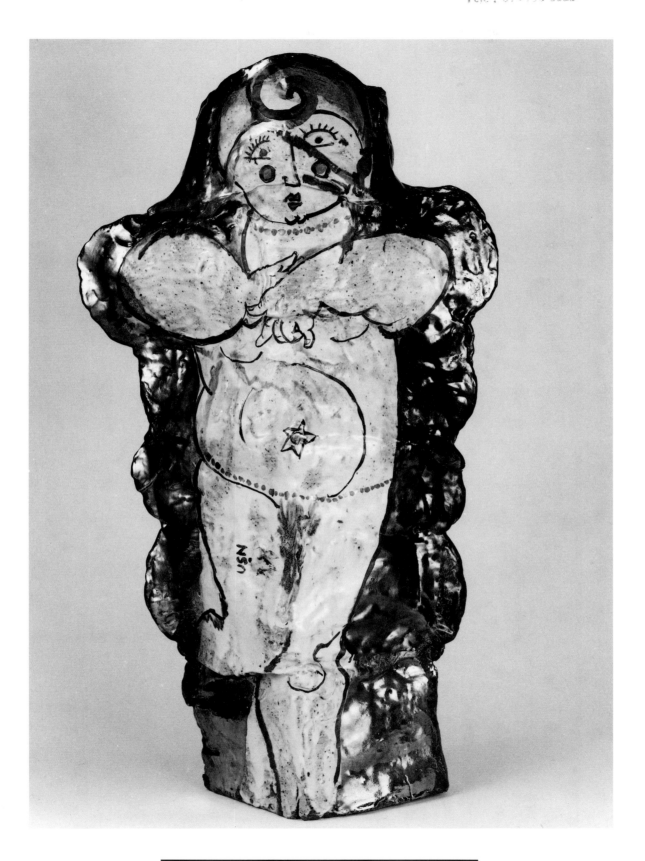

Rudy Autio *Kewpie Doll, 1968. Glazed stoneware with luster,
height 31½". Marer Collection, Scripps College, Claremont,
California.*

Robert Hudson Untitled #60, 1973. *Porcelain, height 9¾".*
Collection Daniel Jacobs.

CHAPTER TEN
1970

The seventies began with an important event, or, to be more accurate, a nonevent: the twenty-seventh Ceramic National, scheduled to take place in 1972 at the Everson Museum, Syracuse. For forty years the Ceramic National provided the major platform for the ceramic artist in the United States. Over the years the Ceramic Nationals had traveled to more than fifty museums, from the Whitney Museum of American Art in New York to small-town museums in dozens of states, and had generated thousands of articles, reviews, and publicity pieces.

By 1972 the Ceramic National had grown to unmanageable proportions—more than 4,500 slide entries were submitted for consideration. Although the standard of submissions was uneven, the upcoming National was anticipated with some optimism. James Harithas, then director of the Everson Museum, declared that the Ceramic National would now become "a basis for reevaluation of what ceramics is . . . a starting point for the presentation of a new aesthetic."[1] But the jurors, Peter Voulkos, Robert Turner, and Jeff Schlanger, decided that the new aesthetic was not present.

Entrants were surprised to receive a letter stating that the Ceramic National would not take place because the jurors had found slides to be an unsuitable means of review. In place of the Ceramic National, the Everson Museum presented a mish-mash, two-part invitational. The first part was an almost all-male section (except for Toshiko Takaezu) of fourteen contemporary and predictable "names." The second part was a group of old-school stalwarts selected by Anna Olmsted from previous Ceramic Nationals, combined with a slide showing of the better entries to the rejected National, and an exhibition of Robineau pots from the Everson's permanent collection. It was a compromised and inglorious end to the medium's most faithful institution, the Ceramic National.

Donna Nicholas recorded the diverse reactions to the announcement of the demise of the National in her detailed investigation into the controversial decision: "There was excitement, all right. Incomprehension. Lots of unanswered questions. Mutterings heard from amongst the clay bags. Many felt the jurors' action to be some sort of Olympian hoax, perpetrated by larger-than-life ceramic figures pointing a collective finger and causing a whole show to disappear. A giant power trip? A gesture of courage? Despair? Indifference? Hope?"[2]

In retrospect, the action seems indefensibly cavalier, as ceramics had so few supportive institutions. Selection by slides is, of course, a compromise, but one with which all juried shows have learned to live. On the other hand, it is argued that the timing of the decision was perfect, that the Ceramic Nationals would only have declined further and in so doing would have diminished the esteem of the medium. It is also possible that significant exhibitions that followed at the Everson Museum, such as Margie Hughto's *New Works in Clay by Contemporary Painters and Sculptors* and *A Century of Ceramics in the United States 1878–1978*, might not have taken place but for the courage of the jurors who canceled the National and thus left the museum open for other exhibitions.

The cancellation of the National was a particularly severe blow for younger artists, for whom it was an important springboard in gaining recognition. Another blow to the field came in 1972, with the closing of a second major juried show, the Wichita National Decorative Arts Competitive Exhibit, founded in 1946. After 1971 the *Young Americans* exhibitions at the Museum of Contemporary Crafts to some extent filled the void left by these cancellations. However, the Annual Ceramics Invitational at Scripps College, initiated in 1945 by William Manker, became the most important annual survey for the field and remains so today. The closure of the Ceramic National sent a very clear message out to the ceramist: a palace revolution had taken place, and a new and more radical leadership was in control. The signal was clear—

the 1970s were to be a decade of change.

Ceramists now no longer saw themselves as part of a polyglot community joined by the commonality of clay. The divisions between the separate disciplines of sculpture and the vessel also became clearer. In looking first at sculpture, one finds that the decade produced great diversity. Funk was no longer rampant and had splintered into a number of more personal and less aggressive styles. The Super-Object came into its own, peaking and declining within the decade.

Some ceramists rejected the notion of a permanent object altogether. They became involved in the avant-garde aspects of the sixties and the "dematerialization" of the art object through process art, installation pieces, conceptual works, and Happenings. Some ceramists dutifully attempted to do away with the kiln, and for a short time a

Jim Melchert Changes, *a performance with drying slip, Amsterdam, August 22, 1972.*

"mud 'n dust" school claimed intellectual domination of the field. In terms of creative exercises, the use of unfired clay was liberating. The first event of importance was the 1970 *Unfired Clay* exhibition at Southern Illinois University (Carbondale), which included the object makers Gilhooly, Arneson, and Victor Cikansky, as well as those more conceptually inclined, such as Jim Melchert. Commenting on the pertinence of the event, Evert Johnson suggested that the concept of making objects that were left outdoors to return to the earth had merits above the concepts of more traditional exhibitions:

> There is something spiritually appropriate in the implication of the pot returning to the earth, of artists participating physically in the installation of their own exhibit, and of creative man being, for a short time at least, really at one with his work, the earth from which it was made and elements that besiege both. The whole idea was a joyful denial of the notion that art is a precious commodity. . . . It was instead a positive affirmation that the most important element in art is man.[3]

This notion now began to be enthusiastically explored. In 1972 Melchert produced a videotape event titled *Changes*, in which the participants dunked their heads in slip and were seated in a room that was cool at one end and hot at the other. The camera recorded the uneven return of the slip to its dry state and, at the same time and more subtly, the altering interpersonal reactions of the participants. In this way, the participants could experience the "lived surface" of a ceramic piece.

In 1973 and 1974 in Los Angeles, Sharon Hare, Doug Humble, Joe Soldate, and others formed a small avant-garde group of ceramists. Humble covered his entire home, even the car in the driveway, in slip. Hare set up installation shows in the deserts outside Los Angeles. Soldate worked with wet and dry clay in structural, installation situations. These energies came to a head in 1974 in the exhibition *Clay Images*, organized by Ed Forde and Soldate at California State University, Los Angeles.

Similar experiments with unfired clay took place elsewhere. In Colorado, Mark Boulding set up his *Forest Firing*. Through careful scientific analysis of the fire risk in the state forests, he selected a site that theoretically had the highest fire risk in the state. Twenty clay spheroids were placed in the area awaiting a wood firing that statistically should occur within the next two hundred years. The final event of this phase of ceramics history was *Clayworks in Progress*, which took place in 1975 at the Los Angeles Institute of Contemporary Art. It was described as "an exhibition of five artists whose work concerns the natural effect of time on clay; forces not at rest or in equilibrium."[4] This exhibition seemed finally to exhaust the play with unfired clay. The concerns were continued to a limited extent in the clay and latex works of Bill Farrell and his students at the Art Institute of Chicago,

but the issues raised by the refusal to make clay permanent through fire no longer seemed quite so relevant or important. Except as a personal learning process, one could argue that this work, with a few exceptions such as that by Melchert, was never pertinent to the art world at large, trailing after the main thrust of Conceptual sculpture. At best, the period can be seen as a time of soft-core Conceptualism, which hopefully had the effect of liberalizing the ceramist's conceptual boundaries and conservative tendencies.

In 1976 the opposite pole of thought to that of the Conceptualists was presented at the Everson Museum of Art's *New Works in Clay by Contemporary Painters and Sculptors*. Curated by Margie Hughto, the exhibition brought together ten mainstream artists. In collaboration with Hughto and her artist friends and students from Syracuse University, the painters and sculptors produced a body of ceramic sculptures. The project involved Billy Al Bengston, Stanley Boxer, Anthony Caro, Friedel Dzubas, Helen Frankenthaler, Michael Hall, Dorothy Hood, Jules

Roger Sweet Untitled works in progress, *August 6, 1975.* Clayworks in Progress, *Los Angeles Institute of Contemporary Art.*

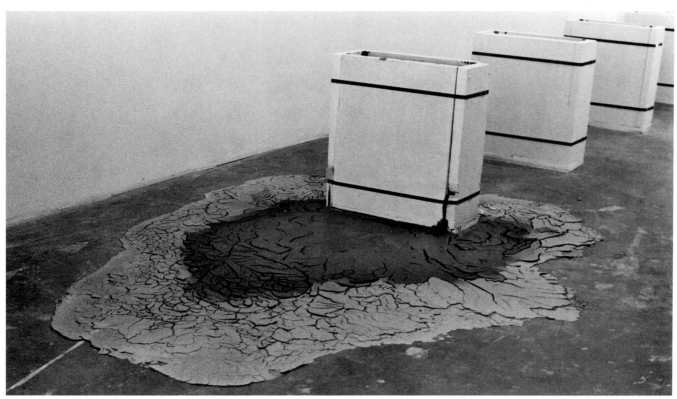

Olitski, Larry Poons, and Michael Steiner. In addition, the ceramics of David Smith were exhibited posthumously alongside these new works. The exhibition caused the ceramics establishment to seethe with controversy and discontent. They argued that there would never be an exhibition of ''paintings by potters,'' and that this project was a waste of resources that could otherwise be applied to the specialists in the medium. But they missed the point; the purpose of the exhibition was simply to introduce a group of active, professional *artists* to a material that was not their day-to-day medium in order to bring a different perspective and, it was hoped, a fresh view to the sculptural use of clay.

In reviewing the impact of the exhibition over the distance of a decade, it has proved to be an important event for the participants, many of whom made substantial changes in their art as a result of their involvement in this project. For the ceramics world, the exhibition did not prove to be of major consequence in aesthetic terms. It did not trigger any new directions in ceramic sculpture or even in the larger world of sculpture. Viewed politically, however, *New Works* takes on significance. The controversy it generated within and without the ceramics world and the publicity it attracted played a substantial role in a growing momentum for redefining ceramic art in the United States.

Together with the Syracuse Clay Institute, a joint venture of Syracuse University and the Everson Museum of Art, Hughto went on to present two more *New Works in Clay* exhibitions. *New Works II* was shown at the Lowe Art Gallery, Syracuse University, in 1978, and *New Works III* at the Everson Museum in 1981. Excellent catalogues were pub-

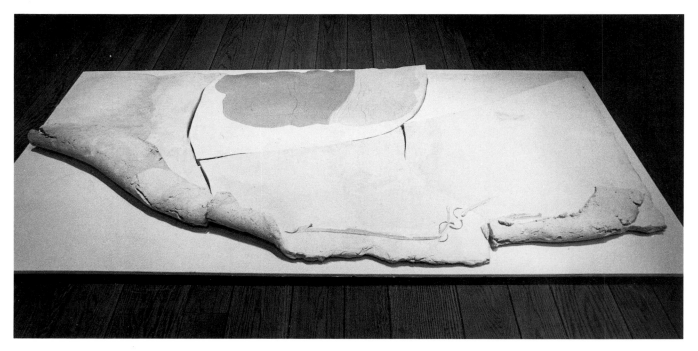

Helen Frankenthaler Mattress II, *1975. Stoneware, slips, length 75". Private collection.*

LEFT: **Doug Humble** Slip environment, *Los Angeles, 1973.*

---

lished for each of the *New Works* exhibitions. The artists who participated in these exhibitions were now a mix of ceramists and nonceramists; the list includes Kenneth Noland, Miriam Schapiro, John Glick, Stephen DeStaebler, George Mason, Mary Frank, and others.

The Syracuse Clay Institute was housed in a huge industrial building owned by the Continental Can Company. The projects were directed toward providing the artists with assistants, resources, and equipment to create experimental works on a more ambitious scale than they could attempt in their own studios. In addition, the institute invited scholars to lecture and monitor proceedings. Students from the ceramics program at the university were invited to work with the artists as their assistants. From an educational point of view, the projects proved to be a considerable success. It was not the first of such projects to be held in the United States; *Art in America* had initiated a similar project as early as 1964, and in 1974 Susan Peterson established an artist-in-residence program at Hunter College in New York.[5]

The *New Works* exhibitions had a limited impact on the ceramics community, because they dealt mainly with Abstract Expressionism at a time when the so-called new figurative movement was being welcomed in painting and sculpture. The same trend was taking place in ceramic sculpture, where figurative work was emerging as the cutting edge for the medium, providing both the freshest ideas and, at the same time, the most convincing work sculpturally. In particular, there were four artists during the seventies whose work most dramatically exhibited the renewed vigor of figurative ceramic sculpture: Mary Frank, Robert Arneson, Stephen DeStaebler, and Viola Frey. Writing of Frank in the *New York Times*, Hilton Kramer acknowledged that she was a magnificent anomaly among sculptors: "While so many expend their energies on making sculpture a language of cerebration, securely quarantined against direct expressions of feeling, Frank insists on making it a language of passion. The result is an oeuvre unlike any other on the

current scene—an oeuvre in which imagery of great inwardness and intimacy is combined with an earthy articulation of emotion."[6]

Although speaking specifically of Frank, Kramer was also suggesting an aesthetic niche for clay. Emphasis on the cerebral had proved in the 1960s to be a poor bedfellow for the ceramic medium, outside the vessel tradition. Again praising the figurative mode, Kramer commented in a later review on the works of Robert Arneson that were on show at the Allan Frumkin Gallery in New York. The review was titled "Sculpture—From the Boring to the Brilliant": the boring contributed by Carl Andre, and the brilliant, a series of large-

scale portraits by Arneson. Kramer praised the "stunning mastery of characterization" in Arneson's work and welcomed the use of color in sculpture. Arneson's work, he pointed out, "reminds us that there is something of a revival of polychrome ceramic sculpture . . . in recent years that New York has never quite caught up on. Perhaps the

Stephen DeStaebler Seating Sculpture, 1970. *Stoneware, height 5". University Art Museum, University of California, Berkeley.*

RIGHT: *Mary Frank* Lovers, 1973–74. *Earthenware, length 62". Private collection. Courtesy Zabriskie Gallery, New York.*

Clayton Bailey La Guillotine, 1973. Wood, glazed earthenware, length 20". Private collection.

BELOW: **Robert Arneson** George and Mona in the Baths of Coloma, 1976. Glazed earthenware, length 57". Stedelijk Museum, Amsterdam.

TOP RIGHT: **Stephen DeStaebler** Standing Man and Woman, 1975. Stoneware, height 96". Private collection.

BOTTOM RIGHT: **Robert Arneson** Cocks Fighting over Art, 1970. Glaze porcelain, length 6". Collection Susan and Stephen D. Paine.

time has come for some museum to bring us up to date on this interesting and unexpected development."[7] Arneson was now showing portraits, first of himself and later of artist friends from the Bay Area, media figures such as Elvis Presley, and iconic artists such as Duchamp, Dürer, van Gogh, and others.

The mock-heroic stance remained, but the works were now anything but one-liners; the satire had now become complex, layered, and drawn from the world of art history. A particularly important exhibition for Arneson during the seventies was entitled *Heroes and Clowns,* at the Allan Frumkin Gallery in New York. In the accompanying catalogue essay, Michael McTwigan explained one of the works, *Rrose Sélavy* (1978):

> Both Robert Arneson and Marcel Duchamp have adopted poses as part of their strategy toward art. Two are shown here: Duchamp as his alter ego *Rrose Sélavy* and Arneson as *Klown.* Wearing masks, these artists can dare to do things they might not normally do and they can reveal something of themselves while claiming that it is just a game. Arneson portrays *Rrose Sélavy* according to two possible readings of Duchamp's pseudonym: Life is pink; eros *c'est la vie.* And so Duchamp is completely covered in a rose pink glaze. As for eros, the pedestal is signed "lovingly Rrose Sélavy," as in the well known photograph of Duchamp dressed as Rrose, taken in 1921 by Man Ray. The fur collar surrounding Duchamp's head is heart shaped (it also resembles a huge pair of lips), a heart is pinned to his hat, and three chocolate Kisses rest on the pedestal. A fine feature of the bust is the step pattern that spirals around the pedestal—no doubt the staircase that Duchamp's *Nude* descends.[8]

McTwigan notes that Arneson has made Duchamp much more masculine in appearance than he appears in Man Ray's photograph. In doing this to Duchamp, the subtle, androgynous ambiguities of Man Ray's *Rrose* are dismissed. Instead, Duchamp is made to appear more absurd—an obvious and awkward drag queen, a figure of derision. McTwigan cites Octavio Paz, who wrote, "Like all of the very limited number of men who have dared

LEFT: **David Gilhooly** Tantric Frog Buddha, 1979. *Gold-glazed earthenware, height 18". Collection Donna Schneier.*

RIGHT: **Richard Notkin** Demons of the Intellect: Professing to Be Wise They Became Fools, 1979. *Molded porcelain, height 11½". Collection Garth Clark/Mark Del Vecchio.*

BELOW: **Michael Frimkess** Ecology Krater II, 1976. *Stoneware, glazed, overglaze painting, height 26". Collection Daniel Jacobs.*

to be free, Duchamp is a clown"—a sentiment that applies as well to Arneson.

The work of Stephen DeStaebler differs totally in mood from that of Arneson. Although both sculptors developed in the Bay Area and were equally influenced by Voulkos and Company, De-Staebler's work is reverential, almost religious, in its solemn qualities, reflecting the spiritual nature of the artist and, no doubt, DeStaebler's theological studies at Princeton:

> The biblical analogy of man and clay is given graphic validity in his work that is neither trite nor forced. Within the context of human participation in the universe, the reemergence of man from earth and his ultimate return to it in the symbolic cycle of life is an absorbing concept. De Staebler's figurative imagery appears to be suspended somewhere in the transformation process. The imprecise features of the faces, the amorphous bodies and the fragments of torsos and limbs seem merely transient rather than distorted or decayed.[9]

Although through the seventies and into the eighties DeStaebler increasingly concentrated on the figure, he did not work only in the figurative mode. One of his masterpieces, *Seating Sculpture* (1970), is a massive grouping of stoneware thrones and stools commissioned by the University Art Museum; University of California, Berkeley. DeStaebler also created what he termed "landscapes."

The most surprising sculptural talent of the 1970s was Viola Frey. She emerged phoenixlike in 1979 after having completely withdrawn from all public activity for over five years, a deliberate move so that she might work without any commercial or exhibiting pressures. Prior to her disappearance from the public scene, she had been developing a local reputation as an artist in California but was not known outside the state. Her first national exposure of any consequence came in 1979, at the exhibition *A Century of Ceramics in the United States*, where she attracted more attention and comment than almost any other of the 160 artists in the exhibition.

The real excitement was not about the suddenness of her appearance; it was about the provocative and original quality of her large, brightly colored figures of humans and animals, which, for all their surface appeal and apparent familiarity of subject, exude a strange undercurrent of menace and unease. Many of her works were assemblages of cast and molded objects (some coming from her massive collection of dime store figurines). Others, such as her *Desert Toys*, a series of figurines, were of her own invention—raw, brutal-looking dolls that seemed to have survived some form of fiery holocaust (or at least seem more than capable of doing so).

Robert Arneson Rrose Sélavy, *1978. Glazed ceramic, height 41". Collection the Honorable Steven D. Robinson. Courtesy Allan Frumkin Gallery, New York.*

Yet, despite the dark side of her work, Frey sees her pieces as placing "an accent on the element of clay," particularly seen in her use of painting to manipulate light and shade on her sculpture—constructing and deconstructing her form. The play of images is more complex: "Clues in the sculpture will lead eventually to a variety of meanings. Hats, shoes and wheels, masks, geese, to mention a few, are all clues. They are used as contemporary symbols that are instantly recognized for what they are by their form, but may have many different meanings depending upon their inflection, size, distortion and association. My completed works are three-dimensional puzzles

Viola Frey Desert Fawn, *1973. Glazed earthenware, height 36". Private collection.*

where parts fit together."[10]

During the seventies Frey was greatly influenced by Claude Lévi-Strauss's notion of the *bricoleur*, which literally means "junk man" or "handyman," although Lévi-Strauss's interpretation has stronger, shamanistic overtones.[11] The concept of the *bricoleur* is linked to mythic thought (prior science), which is in itself a form of intellectual *bricolage*, "building ideological castles out of the debris of what was once social discourse."[12] Similarly, *bricolage* is constructed from what the French term *"des bribes et des morceaux,"* the "debris of events." The *bricoleur* picks up odds and ends from his time; works with all materials at hand; is adept at performing diverse tasks and exploring diverse themes. This notion of the junk man as artist propelled Frey through the late seventies and into the eighties, when a new focus began to emerge in her work.

The most popular genre of ceramic sculpture in the 1970s was not the highly personal explorations of Frank, Arneson, DeStaebler, and Frey, but rather the seductive, glitzy world of the Super-Object, which was to dominate ceramics education and exhibitions through most of the seventies. The origins of the Super-Object are closely tied to the move from stoneware to whitewares and to the use of photographically processed decals, china-painting, on-glaze commercial lusters, and even paint—all processes considered unacceptable within the more purist and traditional areas of the ceramics world.

Development of the Super-Object can be traced through the sixties in the work of Kottler, Melchert, Price, Nagle, and others. The Super-Object in the seventies was identified by an elaborate, almost obsessive concern with craft; the use of trompe l'oeil as the primary stylistic device, and with simplistic references to assemblage and collage and to the art object in Dada and Surrealism. Form was approached as a kind of three-dimensional illustration, mostly through found objects that had been cast in clay. Interest in the Super-Object was based on the West Coast (mainly Seattle, San Francisco, and Los Angeles) but soon spread like

Jack Earl Dogs Are Nice, *1971. Glazed porcelain, height 17".*
American Craft Museum, New York. Gift of Karen Johnson
Boyd.

LEFT: **Karen Breschi** The Bath, *1971–72. Clay, arcylic paint,*
bones, resin, and wood, length 54". Private collection. Courtesy
Braunstein Gallery, San Francisco.

an epidemic of ceramic *faux* across the United States. Clay was produced in every conceivable disguise: cardboard, denim, leather, wood, metal, burlap, paper. The cast ceramic boot, faithfully glazed to look like "real" leather, became the ultimate cliché of the decade (just as the brown Japanesque stoneware bowl had been a decade before) and could be found in just about every ceramics department in the country by the mid-1970s.

The Super-Object has a long-standing, noble tradition in ceramics, reaching its apex during the eighteenth century. In France and Germany it was the vogue to create massive dinner services painted to look like wood, with the illusion of etchings and posters peeling off the surfaces. The works in this style by the Niderviller factory are partic-

ularly distinguished. The development of commercial lusters in England led to the imitation of silver tea and coffee pots, what was known as "poor man's Sheffield." Josiah Wedgwood, having created a particularly rich green glaze and looking for a way to use it to its best advantage, created a series of creamware cauliflower vessels in which the green leaves were set off in perfect complement to the cream of cauliflower. In China the Yixing wares included superrealist peanuts, gnarled pieces of wood, and bamboo shoots being eaten away by worms. Later this led to the imitation of ivory, metal, and other materials in clay, under the rule of Qianlong (1736–95).

Two very fine exhibitions stimulated contemporary interest in this style. The first was *Sharp-Focus Realism*, a multimedia exhibition that took place in 1972 at the Sidney Janis Gallery in New York. The exhibition included the virtuoso work

Kenneth Price Untitled Two-Part Geometric, 1974. Glazed porcelain, height 5". Courtesy Willard Gallery, New York.

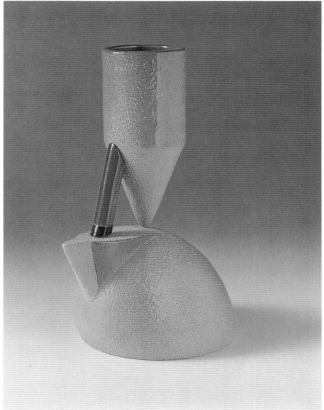

of the ceramist Marilyn Levine, whose stoneware pieces faithfully echoed leather objects: suitcases, leather jackets, and boots. Harold Rosenberg called her works "translations of objects into a different substance without altering the appearance." Although Levine did produce objects, Rosenberg pointed out that this "was essentially a conceptual art, that brings to the eye nothing not present in nature but instructs the spectators that things may not be what they seem."[13] The Super-Object provided an area where the ceramist could indulge in technical matters without the means overpowering the end. In this case the craft *is* the message. As the critic Kim Levin noted, "Old time illusionistic art has collided with the future becoming as literal as minimal forms . . . form has redissolved into content—Pygmalion is back in business."[14]

The second exhibition of importance to the development of the genre of the Super-Object was a joint show of works in porcelain by Richard Shaw and Robert Hudson in 1973 at the San Francisco Museum of Art. It was one of the most important exhibitions of the decade, with superbly conceived, genuinely poetic compositions in porcelain. The exhibition set the stage for a style of Super-Object assemblage of disparate elements that was to be widely emulated throughout the seventies. The craft was not as obsessive as the Super-Object was later to become, and the painting, although frequently suggesting another material, was still somewhat expressionistic. Hudson, a sculptor known for his polychrome metal sculpture, collaborated with Shaw. Although they made separate works, they did use common molds and techniques, and Hudson was dependent upon Shaw for technical assistance.

TOP: **Howard Kottler** The Old Bag Next Door Is Nuts, *1977. Earthenware, glazes, and Plexiglas, height 13". Collection Judith and Martin Schwartz.*

Ron Nagle Cup, *1978. Earthenware with glaze and china paint, height 8". Private collection.*

The collaboration lasted from 1972 to 1973, after which Hudson returned to metal and Shaw continued to explore trompe l'oeil surfaces, as in *Cardboard Tea Set* (1975), with its ceramic decals. Shaw's interest in photolithographic, four-color decals brought true trompe l'oeil illusionism into his work. This led Shaw further from the inventive, painterly incongruities of his earlier works, such as *Ocean Liner Sinking into a Sofa*. Shaw's work now was tied to the conceits of a superrealist tradition in ceramics. As this exploration continued through the decade, his skills increased. In the late seventies he created pieces that were almost nostalgic—assemblages of books, pipes, spent matches, and technically stunning "houses" of stacked playing cards, work that he jokingly termed "den art."

By the mid-seventies the work of Levine and Shaw was being slavishly imitated in almost every ceramics department. In a matter of a few years this style of working had become its own overpopulated genre. In 1977 the Laguna Beach Museum of Art organized the exhibition *Illusionistic Realism as Defined in Contemporary Ceramic Sculpture*, in an attempt to define this new obsession of the

ceramics world. In the catalogue essay,[15] Lukman Glasgow grasped at everything from Surrealism to Gestalt in order to impose fine-arts respectability. But it was sadly apparent that most of the Super-Object makers were not dealing with the ironies of Dada or the poetry and eroticism of Surrealism. Instead, what emerged is a style that can be termed "Hollywood Magritte," a debased and decorative use of Surrealism that completely lacked the passion, the wit, and the visual literacy necessary to give the objects validity.

ABOVE: **Robert Hudson** Ashtray #13, 1973. Porcelain, height 11¾". Courtesy Fuller Goldeen Gallery, San Francisco.

LEFT: **Richard Shaw** Cardboard Tea Set, 1975. Glazed porcelain with ceramic decals, height 7". Private collection.

RIGHT: **Mark Burns** Magician's Dinnerware, 1974–75. Earthenware and paint, height 12½". Everson Museum of Art, Syracuse, New York. Gift of Coy Ludwig.

In 1979 works of the Super-Object school dominated a similar exhibition, *Northern California Clay Routes*, which took place at the San Francisco Museum of Modern Art. The late Thomas Albright, astute art critic of the *San Francisco Chronicle*, reviewed the exhibition and noted that the dilemma facing all art in the postmodernist, pluralistic, anything-goes era was to somehow "maintain distance between the museum . . . and the overwhelming preponderance of hip, cute, clever objects that are only a step or less away from the main floor at Gump's, the Cannery or Ghirardelli Square."[16] This, he noted, was a particularly delicate issue for ceramics, with its roots in the craft shop. Albright pinpointed clearly the failure of the Super-Object genre, while admitting the quality of work by a few of the artists: "The ultimate impression is of superficiality and slickness—that is, craft at its most obvious, vulgarly ostentatious level. This is largely the old ceramic Funk from a decade ago, adapted to the era of High Tech. Eccentricity is not the same as originality. It is a measure of the difference that so much eccentricity can add up to so much sameness."

On the East Coast, Rose Slivka had approached the subject of the art object, examined its context, and come up with a viewpoint that brought more dignity to the activity. In 1976, drawing on the notion of the Surrealist objects of the 1930s, Slivka coordinated *The Object as Poet* at the Renwick Gallery in Washington, D.C. The exhibition brought together the most valid of the art-object makers and suggested a union of spirit and intent that linked Levine's bags, Shaw's assemblages, Melchert's delicately lustered *Precious a* (1970), and Lucian Octavius Pompili's fragile multimedia works.

Their use of material, their selection of images, and their elegance of composition were used to create visual poetry with all the freedom and depth of personal expression that that idea implies:

> The reality of the object—poem and material thing—suggests other realities. Other metaphors in the form of things and poems that interact in the old root way before specialization

divided us from ourselves and each other. The power of these objects to take us into their orbit and beget energy is endless. This is the magic. The Shamanist vision yields multiple mnemonic clues to the enigma of life through intuitive forms invented or found ready made in the touch of each individual maker.[17]

In essence, Slivka's comment is a plea for pure objecthood. Whether utilitarian or not, the concept of the object maker as a visual poet removes the circular debate on the boundaries of art and craft as a consideration. The viewer is thus able to confront the collage, fetish, or assemblage works that have come out of the contemporary crafts movement and deal with them beyond their more obvious virtues of craftsmanship. Slivka's view suggested a different language of appreciation, based upon a more emotional relationship and a very delicate, subtle sensibility in the use of materials, metaphors, associations, and context—a complex visual language of syntax, rhythm, and free association.

The high profile of the ceramic-sculpture movement in both the sixties and the seventies tended to obscure the fact that the vessel maker was making considerable progress, albeit in a quieter and less dramatic manner. The potter was still suffering from a condition of inferiority. Many ceramics departments did not allow students to make pots, only sculpture. Potters responded by not referring to their work as pots or pottery, developing a number of interesting and amusing euphemisms. In the seventies, however, the potters decided to reclaim an equal place for their work, alongside that of ceramic sculpture.

The first step was to return to a sense of identity and purpose. Potters such as Betty Woodman, Richard DeVore, and Bill Daley insisted that their work be described as pottery and be seen, simultaneously, as part of the millennia-old tradition of vessel making *and* as a contribution to contemporary art. Not surprisingly, many critics applauded the return to categorical clarity. The following comment by Kenneth W. Jones, in response to an exhibition of DeVore's pots at the Helen Drutt Gallery in

Marilyn Levine Two-Tone Bag, 1974. *Stoneware, height 9". Los Angeles County Museum of Art. Gift of Howard and Gwen Laurie Smits.*

BELOW: *Jim Melchert* Precious a, 1970. *Earthenware, glaze, luster, height 6". Collection Susan and Stephen D. Paine.*

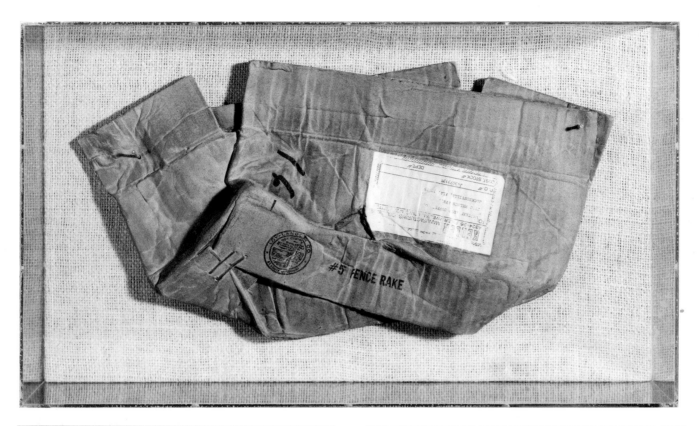

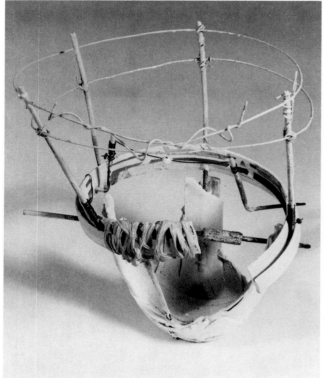

Robert Rauschenberg Tampa Piece #4, 1972. Earthenware, length 15". University of South Florida, Tampa. Courtesy Graphic Studio.

LEFT: **Thom R. Bohnert** Untitled, 1977. Ceramic and wire, height 12". Private collection.

RIGHT: **Rudolf Staffel** Untitled Vessel, 1975. Porcelain, height 7¼". Collection Daniel Jacobs.

Patti Warashina Who Said I Couldn't Fly, *1979. Porcelain, height 21¼". Collection Daniel Jacobs.*

LEFT: ***Jerry Rothman*** Fish Tureen, *1979. Glazed stoneware, height 14". Collection Dawn Bennett and Martin Davidson.*

RIGHT: ***Karen Karnes*** Untitled Vase*, 1971. Salt-glazed stoneware, height 14". Collection Reed Walden.*

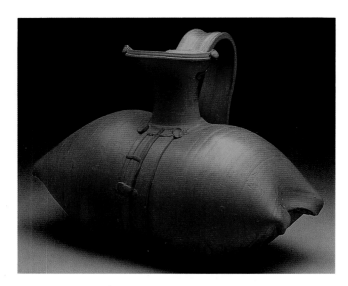

Betty Woodman Pillow Pitcher, *1978–79. Earthenware with terra-sigillata surface, height 17". Collection Daniel Jacobs.*

ward the infinite. So in the final analysis, *feelings*—both emotional and tactile—become the final message."[19]

But achieving this level of sensitivity toward the pot required an understanding of the potter's new sophistication that simply did not exist in the art world at that time. This was highlighted by comments made by Edy de Wilde, the past director of the Stedelijk Museum in Amsterdam. Few museum directors in Europe have had greater perceptivity about contemporary art than de Wilde, yet his remarks about Voulkos in a 1979 catalogue, *West Coast Ceramics*, reveal how little the fine arts understood the pottery revolution that had taken place in the United States. De Wilde warns that Voulkos's pieces "look" like pots but that we should not be deceived, "for their sole purpose appeared to be the visualization of volume and form—

1977, is of particular interest:

> Convulsing from the perplexities of his or her placement in the hierarchy of art, the ceramist has often rejected both the utilitarian aspect of pottery as well as its history as an art. Denying a chain of events can in itself be useful and even produce a new event, but too often repeated it becomes dogma based on a false or nonexistent foundation. As a solution to the problem many ceramists view their art as a sort of mini-sculpture; in consciously rejecting their own discipline, however, they have attached themselves to another. The resultant breakdown in communication creates bewilderment in the audience and frustration in the artist.[18]

A year earlier Andy Nasisse wrote that it was time to acknowledge that the pot was, in a sense, its own subject matter, much as a painting was *about* painting: "In this extensive analysis of a pot's form one becomes aware that many of the aesthetic conclusions are unique to the idea of the vessel, and the vessel itself has the potential for becoming a major metaphor, with complex, sensuous analogies. One also becomes aware of the fallibility of a language which is intrinsically tied to logic . . . to describe these vessels' imponderable tendency to-

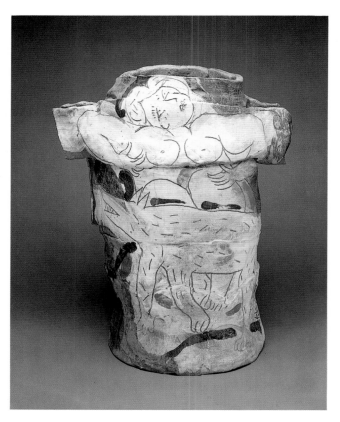

Rudy Autio Two Ladies: Two Dogs, *1979. Slab-built stoneware with slips and glazes, height 25". Collection Mark Del Vecchio.*

Ruth Duckworth Untitled Vessel, *1977. Stoneware, porcelain, height 6¼". Collection Daniel Jacobs.*

Ruth Duckworth Untitled Vessel, *1977. Stoneware, porcelain, height 6¼". Collection Daniel Jacobs.*

sculpture in other words."[20] Volume is no longer the central issue of the sculptor, whereas it has never ceased to be the central, aesthetic dynamic of the potter. De Wilde, despite his good intentions, was suffering from a classic case of ceramic illiteracy.

The seventies produced fine work by potters, despite the problems of context and identity. New artists, such as Richard DeVore and Adrian Saxe, surfaced in the pottery mainstream, while others, who were already well established in the field, now began to produce innovative and surprising work. Among these were Betty Woodman, Robert Turner, Ken Ferguson, Ken Price, and Rudy Autio. It was a time when the potter came of age and established a new aesthetic confidence.

One of the high points of the decade was undoubtedly the Voulkos retrospective. Organized in 1978 by the Museum of Contemporary Crafts

in New York, this touring exhibition opened at the San Francisco Museum of Modern Art. It both celebrated Voulkos's earlier achievement in the fifties and sixties and, in a sense, welcomed him back to ceramics as his primary medium. The problem of an overcrowded installation did little to mar the excitement of the exhibition, nor did it detract from Voulkos's extraordinary achievement in leading the liberation of the American potter from European formalism. Yet, the exhibition signaled the passing of an era. Many of the students and younger potters appreciated the exhibition but now felt distanced from the aesthetic and the ideals that the work represented. The freedoms that Voulkos and his students had striven so hard to gain were now almost taken for granted. The baton had been passed on.

Voulkos had returned to ceramics after a decade of working as a metal sculptor. He now began to concentrate on two forms: platters and massive, three-tiered "stack pots." Interestingly, these tiers, although more radical in their application, were the same divisions that had been made by the formalist Bernard Leach in most of his pots and by Korean and Chinese potters, many centuries

Richard DeVore Untitled, *1979. Stoneware, height 11". Collection Garth Clark.*

FAR LEFT: **Rick Dillingham** Globe Form #79-2, 1979. Raku-fired earthenware, glazed, height 5½". Collection Daniel Jacobs.

LEFT: **Jane Ford Aebersold** Pompey's Pillar, 1979. Stoneware with on-glaze luster, height 18". Private collection.

BOTTOM LEFT: **Val Cushing** Acorn Roll Jar, 1979–80. Thrown and glazed stoneware, height 17". Private collection.

BELOW: **Paul Soldner** VOCO, 1978. Raku, height 11". Collection Lynne Wagner.

RIGHT: **Peter Voulkos** Plate, 1977. *Stoneware with porcelain pellets, gas fired, diameter 23½". Victoria and Albert Museum, London. Gift of Fred and Estelle Marer.*

Peter Voulkos Stack Pot, 1975–82. *Stoneware, assembled from thrown elements, wood fired, height 39½". Courtesy Garth Clark.*

FAR RIGHT: **Robert Turner** Chimney Jar, 1971. *Glazed stoneware, height 14½". Collection Daniel Jacobs.*

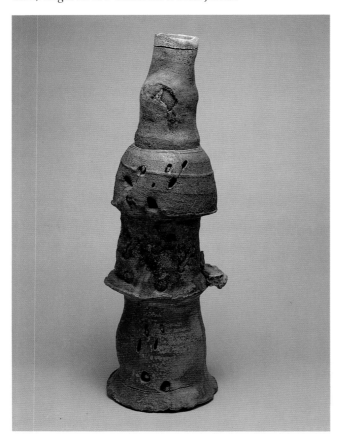

before, to emphasize the "structure" of the vessel. While these divisions were used to emphasize the "wholeness" of the traditional vessel, in Voulkos's hands the same divisions indicate the the contrary— a sense of taking apart, of deconstruction and releasing the parts from the tyranny of the whole.

The best of the platter forms were made between 1977 and 1979 and were fired in a gas kiln with a commercial glaze that produced an ersatz wood-fired look. Their liveliness derived from the energetic drawing on the surface that combined punctured surfaces, deeply incised lines, and porcelain pellets that were inserted into the surface. Reminiscent of the work of the Italian artist Lucio Fontana, they dealt with elements of space, light, and color that were at once primitive in their execution and complex in their formal content. The beginnings of this work can be traced back to a series of five black plates that Voulkos made in 1968 on one of his occasional returns to clay making. Later, in 1979, Voulkos began to fire the plates in a Japanese-style wood-fired *anagama* kiln and produced a few masterpieces, but these pieces were generally retrogressive in their aesthetic, too dependent upon the generosity of the kiln and too imitative of Bizen, Seto, and other traditional Japanese kilns.

While Voulkos's influence on younger potters was beginning to diminish, he continued to have a strong influence and, in a sense, present a *standard* for those who had passed through the fifties and sixties with him. This was particularly evident in the work of Bob Turner, a leading functional potter of about the same age as Voulkos. The seventies saw the production of Turner's finest work to date and his emergence as a leading maker of the "art" pot. Turner had worked as a maker of utilitarian pots since the late forties, encouraged by a belief in the Arts and Crafts ideal that personalized design could be a regenerative force in society. In the 1960s he began to change from making the orthodox "Alfred vessel" to creating contemplative works, what Ed Lebow calls his "decorative" pots.[21] The

influence from Voulkos can be plainly seen in Turner's most distinctive form, a circle cut in half and surmounted by a square tower. Voulkos developed this form in the early sixties but did not play with contradictory geometry, leaving his tower circular. Turner was inspired by Voulkos and drew his new vocabulary from Voulkos's innovations, but what he produced with this vocabulary was not imitative. As Lebow states:

> Cylinders narrowed to cones or widened to hemispheres. Hemispheres opened to cubes. Domes were joined to tapering cylinders. The combination of volumes in these pots moved and shifted in fluid translation. Their geometry was simple. Form still followed function, but now the function was visual and contemplative. Turner no longer disconnected the currents of memory and spontaneity from his hands on the wheel but used them to "Alfredize" the Otis pot. The result was a kind of artistic pacifism, lyrical rather than muscular, cerebral rather than visceral.[22]

The issues of organic geometry and abstraction can be viewed as the primary concern for the vessel maker in this decade. However, in contrast to the fevered physicality of the previous decades, it was now applied on a more conscious and analytical level. This can be seen in the work of Richard DeVore, Ruth Duckworth, Susanne Stephenson, Toshiko Takaezu, Bill Daley, and others. DeVore's gentle and sexually ambiguous pots seem warm and emotional but, in fact, this disguises the colder, analytical geometry that guided their creation. DeVore's pots are also a warning not to read organic work as the result of feeling rather than of intellect. Indeed, this cerebral aspect of the pot's development is so intense that it caused George Woodman to label DeVore and Daley "conceptualists of the vessel."[23] Susanne Stephenson also employed organic abstraction in her work, taking it to a radical edge in which the twisted feet of her pots stand like gnarled wood or fragments of animal skeletons that one might find in the desert. But the interest in the organic was not to continue with the same momentum in the next

LEFT: **David Shaner** Untitled Vessel #27, 1979–80. Stoneware, height 13". Collection Daniel Jacobs.

BOTTOM LEFT: **Adrian Saxe** Untitled Antelope Jar, 1979. Porcelain and stoneware, height 16". Private collection.

BELOW: **John Glick** Plate, 1979. Porcelain, slips, glaze, diameter 11". Private collection.

Ralph Bacerra Soup Tureen, *1978. Blue decoration on porcelain, height 15". Los Angeles County Museum of Art. Gift of Howard and Gwen Laurie Smits.*

decade, when pictorial issues were to resurface strongly.

Also within the realm of the vessel are those works that were, to quote Ken Price, "not pottery so much as being *about* pottery."[24] The distinction may seem purely semantic but in fact it is an important one. Although one could argue that Price is more of a potter than he admits, there *are* certain bodies of work that deal with the notion of pottery as subject matter without the artist's trying to make an important pot *per se*. An example of this use of the vessel as a symbol can be found in one of the key exhibitions of the decade, Price's *Happy's Curios*, an installation at the Los Angeles County Museum of Art in 1978. In this case the impact of the installation as a whole was far greater than the quality of any of its parts.

Happy's Curios proved to be one of the most popular ceramics exhibitions of the decade, the

show being extended three times. The exhibition generated healthy, informal debate among artists, viewers, and even the Hispanic museum guards, who entered into the fray, denouncing the works (particularly those on which were painted Mexicans dozing under their sombreros) as racist. Unfortunately, the printed critiques were less lively and tended to trivialize the work as cartoons based on New Mexico folk and tourist art.[25] Other critics sentimentally suggested that the exhibition represented an "homage to Mexican pottery."

Price's exhibition actually had very little to say about a specific culture beyond the use of the Mexican motif. It was an homage to decorative painting, its vitality, and its pertinence today, a

---

Judy Chicago The Dinner Party, 1979. Mixed media, length 47'. Courtesy ACA Galleries, New York.

message made all the more effective by the use of ceramics—a decorative-arts medium. The statement was about the hierarchy in art—any art. It was a formidable treatment of the "decorative" in art— the element that so disturbs the intellectual establishment. Price was taking pottery as "low art" at its most debased level—the curio shop—and painting the cliché images and forms with such skill and dash that the viewer has to respect, and so reevaluate, what he sees. Furthermore, the exhibition had to do with painting and not form. Indeed, Price did not even make many of the pots, but used painted blanks purchased from Mexican folk potters. Several of the pots that he did make were uncharacteristically flaccid and heavy. None of this mattered much in the overall context, however. As a project it proved to be so open-ended that it became physically, emotionally, and financially draining on Price. In an interview with Joan Simon, then the editor of *Art in America*, Price remarked, "I did what we did in Vietnam at the end—I called it a victory and got the hell out."[26]

Another major exhibition of this type, Judy Chicago's *The Dinner Party*, took place in 1979. It was a grand event—ambitious, controversial, and an important rallying point for feminist opinion. In this exhibition, as in Price's, pottery played a symbolic role. Chicago presented oversized dinner plates not simply for their aesthetic worth as individual artworks, but as key components within a massive five-year installation/collaborative art piece. *The Dinner Party* consisted of thirty-nine elaborate, hand-painted dinner plates placed on a large, triangular table, each with a corresponding embroidered runner. The table stood on "The Heritage Floor," which was made up of 2,300 porcelain tiles. Each dinner plate was dedicated to a "guest," a major figure (mystical or real) in the history of women. The plates were painted and modeled with symbols (centered on the form of the vagina) that were appropriate to the woman being honored. Another 999 names of "women of attainment" were inscribed on the tiles. The piece was the product of over 130 women volunteers who worked on the project. Chicago used the dinner party, an event that women plan and for which they cook but often cannot even attend, as a symbol of sexual inequality and exploitation. What Chicago was attempting to do was to create an event too large to be dismissed. "My dream is that I will make a piece so far beyond judgment that it will enter the cultural pool and never be erased from history as women's work has been erased before."[27]

The Dinner Party opened on March 16 at the San Francisco Museum of Modern Art. The exhibition attracted large audiences but, at least from the art establishment, very poor reviews. What received particular criticism was Chicago's accompanying book/catalogue. In this she attempted a revisionist view of women's history, without any of the tools of scholarship or any attempt to back up her claims with factual data, causing one critic to write, "For God's sake Judy . . . you said you were going to write a history book, instead you wrote a bible."[28] Others questioned whether Chicago hadn't herself exploited women, in creating an exhibition in which they did the work and Chicago took the glory. The ceramists were upset by the inept use of china paint and uneven ceramic techniques. Critics complained about the painting on the plates from a formalist point of view and their morbid, gynecological appearance.

Formalist criticism really had little place for *The Dinner Party*. It was not an artwork about politics. It was a political piece that *used* the vernacular of the art world and its access to large audiences. It was too didactic a work to scale the heights of aesthetic genius. With commendable candor and pragmatism, Chicago comments in her book: "No matter what people say, it is not enough to be supported by those who are powerless. It is in forcing the powerful people to accept one's ideas as significant and important that ultimately one is assured of having those ideas accepted in the world."[29]

Laurel Reuter picked up this aspect and remarked that there is a long history of women giving dinner parties to obtain access to such influence and that this locates the focus of *The Dinner Party*—"it is about power."[30] As such, it only partially achieved its ends. In denying the exhibition its aesthetic endorsement, the art world has, at least for the time being, withheld the most powerful aspect of all—cultural enshrinement. Yet, it remains one of the most remarkable community events in women's art since the china-painting craze of the turn of the century.

The decade closed with a historical exhibition, *A Century of Ceramics in the United States 1878–1978*, curated by Margie Hughto and the author. The exhibition, which opened at the Everson Museum of Art in Syracuse on May 5, 1979, comprised 450 pieces. It was the largest exhibition of its type assembled and the first historical survey of twentieth-century American ceramics, accompanied by the first edition of this book, which functioned as its catalogue. A somewhat reduced traveling version of the show was circulated for three years through the generous support of the Philip Morris Corporation. The exhibition was shown at the Smithsonian Institution's Renwick Gallery of the National Collection of Fine Arts in Washington, D.C., and Cooper-Hewitt Museum in New York; and at other institutions. It generated reams of printed publicity as well as considerable coverage on radio and television; the Philip Morris Corporation was so taken with the exhibition that it produced a film, *Earth, Fire and Water: A Century of Ceramics in the United States* (narrated by Orson Welles), which was extensively shown on public television.

The time had finally arrived when contemporary ceramics had become too large and too energetic to be dismissed as commercial stuff for the craft fairs. There was a growing curiosity in the art world about ceramics and its modern history, particularly among the more adventurous collectors. Second, young ceramists had reached a point where they were curious about, and wanted to embrace, their own roots.

Suddenly critics from the fine arts were looking at ceramics in a new light, not as an orphan but as an independent discipline, coming to terms with its history. John Ashbery wrote, "The show is an important one, for it not only documents but virtually creates a continuing tradition in American ceramics over the last century, which few of us have been aware of."[31] Many ceramists, poorly schooled in their history, enjoyed the same experience. The exhibition set off a wave of collecting (both contemporary ceramics and art pottery) that has continued unabated. The exhibition suffered from many of the flaws of a pioneering study, but in spite of these it opened a new art-historical perspective for ceramics. Writing about the exhibition in *Art in America*, Donald Kuspit commented:

> It is a rare exhibition that can make us question firmly held aesthetic prejudices and help overthrow fixed, unanalyzed positions. Yet this is precisely what *A Century of Ceramics in the United States 1878–1978* has accomplished. By overturning the deeply rooted negative attitude that ceramics is inherently trivial, this exhibition shatters the presumed hierarchy of the arts. . . . A democratic material in which sublime yet personal statements can be made, clay is susceptible to a variety of treatments while retaining its own Protean character. Ceramics may thus be the most truly universal art: its material is highly responsive to aspirations, while the final product is as risky and difficult to achieve as any human individuality.[32]

In conjunction with this exhibition, a symposium on the history and criticism of ceramics, sponsored by the Institute for Ceramic History (founded by the author), was held at the Everson Museum.[33] Its aim was to satisfy the need for a platform to discuss and encourage ceramic criticism and history. At that time the annual conferences of the National Council on Education for the Ceramic Arts (NCECA), which attracted thousands of participants, dealt mainly with technical issues, job hunting, and "hands-on" demonstrations. This annual event was socially exciting but did not address the scholarly needs of the field.[34] In contrast, the three-day symposium held at the Everson Museum (June 1–3), coordinated by Anne Mortimer, was strictly academic. The program attracted five hundred delegates and fifty speakers—mainly historians, curators, and writers. This was an important moment for ceramics—it set a new tone for future conferences and provided an ongoing forum for scholarship. The keynote address was delivered by the critic Clement Greenberg, whose prioritizing of values set the tone for the conference and the decade that followed it:

> Well, is ceramics getting or going to get, as photography has, the benefit of this recent leveling of status? The question requires two different answers. The one has to do with opinion, the other with actual achievement, with aesthetic results. . . . I say that the second is far the more important question, just as it's been with photography. Are ceramists to bother about being put down as potters or hailed as sculptors? Should they, and we, care about nomenclature? Opinion changes, achievement stays. Achievement also erases the difference between utilitarian [the vessels] and fine art [sculpture]. Once again, results, experienced not discussed or debated—are all that count when it comes to art as art. . . . But let the vessel maker not despair. There's nothing to say that a great pot can't match a great statue in value. Let the vessel maker show us that. There are no rules or prescriptions or laid-down-in-advance categories in art.[35]

Kenneth Price Town Unit, *1972–77. Wood and ceramic, height 84". Private collection. Courtesy James Corcoran Gallery, Los Angeles.*

Viola Frey Man with Figurine, *1985–86. Glazed earthenware,
height 35½". Collection Dr. Stanley Josephs. Courtesy Asher/
Faure Gallery, Los Angeles.*

The eighties have delivered to a surprised but excited ceramics world much of what had seemed only vaguely possible in the seventies. The acquisition of ceramic works by museums has risen dramatically in this decade, as has the number of serious exhibitions. The decade has seen major retrospectives for Arneson, Autio, Frey, Wood, Turner, Andreson, Wildenhain, and others. There has also been an increase in the number of historical exhibitions, including scholarly surveys of the work of Grueby, Rookwood, Lukens, Rhead, Fulper, Ohr, Robineau, and Newcomb. The Everson Museum's exhibition *Diversions of Keramos* presented a detailed survey of ceramic sculpture from the thirties and forties. The overall level of scholarship (once a nonissue in the field) has surged ahead. The Institute for Ceramic History holds symposia every two years, while the annual conference of the National Council on Education for the Ceramic Arts has lessened its technical bias to include greater discussion of aesthetic, philosophical, and historical issues.

For the first time, contemporary ceramics has begun to draw the consistent attention of art critics. There were a few critics in the past (notably John Coplans) who took an interest in ceramics, but during the eighties many of the toughest and most independent art writers, including Donald Kuspit, Jeff Perrone, John Perreault, Peter Schjeldahl, Christopher Knight, and Thomas Albright, have been attracted to the field. Other writers, such as Ed Lebow, Jeff Kelley, Michael Dunas, Sarah Bodine, Mac McCloud, though also involved in other media, have become specialists in ceramics, refining their knowledge and authority in the field. In addition, some ceramists, notably Jack Troy and Wayne Higby, have taken to the pen as well. These writers have found fine-arts and crafts journals receptive to critical appraisals of ceramic art. In addition, *American Ceramics*, a quarterly journal devoted solely to ceramics as an art form, was introduced in 1982.

CHAPTER ELEVEN

1980

During the seventies most ceramists (particularly those who made vessels) had sold through the commercial outlet of the craft shop. There were also a few pioneering specialist galleries, such as the American Hand in Washington, D.C., Quay in San Francisco, Helen Drutt in Philadelphia, Alice Westphal's Exhibit A in Chicago, and the Hadler/Rodriguez Gallery and Art Latitude in New York. A handful of fine-arts galleries had also shown ceramics in the seventies, notably Allan Stone and Allan Frumkin in New York. But in the eighties the interest expanded rapidly. In New York—a market once hostile to the notion of ceramic art—Stone and Frumkin were joined by some of the most respected dealers in the city: Charles Cowles, Irving Blum, Max Protetch, André Emmerich, Leo Castelli, Deborah Sharpe, Nancy Hoffman, Grace Borgenicht, Barbara Gladstone, and others. In addition, several new specialist galleries in the medium opened in New York, Chicago, San Francisco, Los Angeles, Saint Louis, and elsewhere, playing a crucial role in developing an educated group of collectors.

This growth and opportunity have not been without their cost. New tensions and pressures have emerged in the eighties, much of them stemming from a fast-changing economic structure. Until this decade the primary patron for ceramics was the university and other educational institutions that employed most of the active, exhibiting ceramic "artists." This world was expanding throughout the seventies and could be counted on to absorb most of the more talented and/or ambitious younger ceramists. During the eighties this trend has begun to reverse itself, as student enrollments decline in the studio arts. Ceramics departments have closed and faculties have shrunk. Ceramists no longer have a choice of secure teaching appointments. Furthermore, the "middle" market for functional wares has also begun to soften.

Yet, for the first time, art gallery sales are substantial enough to match and sometimes exceed

LEFT: **Joyce Kozloff** New England Decorative Arts, 1985–86. *Tile mural for Harvard Square Subway Station, Cambridge, Massachusetts. Courtesy Barbara Gladstone Gallery, New York.*

ABOVE: **Phillip Maberry** Paradise Fountain, 1983. *Installation at 1983 Biennial, Whitney Museum of American Art, New York.*

RIGHT: **Margie Hughto** Seasons, 1985. *Colored stoneware clay, glaze and slips, 32' × 28'. Niagara Frontier Transit Authority, Utica Street Station, Buffalo, New York.*

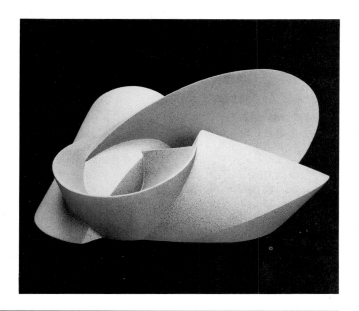

LEFT: **John Roloff** Collision/Lava Ship/Trellis Ship, *1984. Ceramic blanket, wire, length 36'. Phase one firing of* Lava Ship *at Falkirk Community Center, San Rafael, California. Courtesy Fuller Goldeen Gallery, San Francisco.*

RIGHT: **Anne Currier** Untitled, *1987. Ceramic, height 11 inches. Courtesy Helen Drutt Gallery, Philadelphia.*

BELOW: **Bob Sperry** Untitled #625, *1985. White slip over black glaze on kiln shelves, height 128". King County Administration Building, Seattle, Washington.*

teaching incomes. This has begun to reform the character of ceramics radically, as power has gradually been transferred from the educational institution to the private patron. This change of patrons has proved to be stimulating, giving the ceramist a broader and more critical audience than before. But this is balanced by the fact that the gallery system is small, highly selective, and elitist; what is a decade of success and recognition for a few is also a decade of exclusion for many.

In examining this decade it is possible to survey only a few of its formative moments and to provide an overview. A few artists have been selected and featured because the issues raised by their work are representative of changes and concerns in the field at large. It is recommended that the reader refer to the individual biographies to gain a broader knowledge of the artists whose work is illustrated in this chapter.

First, one finds that the division between sculpture and vessel making has grown more distinct. Few ceramists now work in both disciplines. Ceramic sculpture is at a crucial and important phase in its development. On the one hand it is still a "movement" of its own. Its focus and style are different from mainstream sculpture, although its artists frequently exhibit together, and it also has certain common aesthetic characteristics. On the other hand, it seems poised and ready to be more fully integrated into the sculpture world at large. This integration will have the effect of lessening the association to the traditions of ceramic art.

The number of sculptors working in ceramics has declined during the eighties, but the level of energy and achievement has increased. With the demise of the Super-Object craze and the departure of the more excessive hangovers from the Funk movement, the field has taken on a clarity of purpose and statement. It has also become more "serious"—not only in the literal sense of the word but in the level of commitment of the artists. Humor has not departed from ceramic sculpture, but it has taken on a drier, subtler quality. Quite simply—

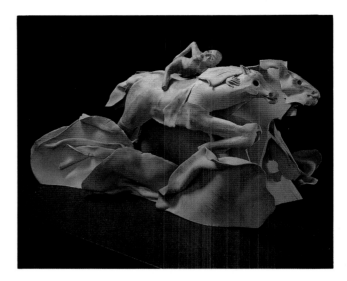

Mary Frank Horse and Rider, *1982. Stoneware, length 48".* *Everson Museum of Art, Syracuse, New York.*

for better or worse—the field has grown up.

However, many of its characteristics from the sixties remain and ceramic sculpture is still very much dominated by the West Coast.[1] Judy Moonelis, Jack Earl, and Mary Frank are among the few ceramic sculptors who did not receive their education in the milieu of northern California or Washington State, the two major centers for ceramic sculpture. While there is no stylistic unity among the West Coast sculptors, there certainly are common sensibilities in the work: the blurring of lines between painting and sculpture, an adventurous use of color, a preference for the eccentric over the classic, and an interest in the iconoclastic and confrontational rather than the sublime. A further unifying factor in the movement is an overwhelming interest in the figure. The use of ceramics in abstract sculpture has greatly declined as the medium has reverted to its traditional sculptural role as a modeling material.

There are a few distinguished exceptions. John Roloff has continued the young tradition of conceptual and process art into the eighties, with his dramatic kiln firings in large 36-foot "kiln-ships" built from steel and ceramic-fiber blankets. In terms of more traditional abstract sculpture, Graham

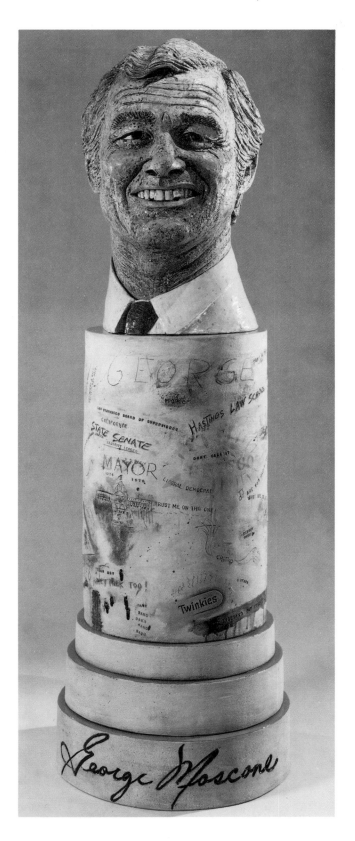

Marks has continued his exploration of large "pod" forms, and Anne Currier has developed her exploration of pure minimalist forms. In addition there has been an increasing interest in large-scale environmental and architectural sculpture, with particularly fine work being done by Joyce Kozloff, Rudy Autio, Phillip Maberry, Margie Hughto, Robert Rauschenberg, and others.

The eighties has been a busy period for ceramic sculptors. It is a decade of controversy, dominated by attempts to legitimize the ceramic-sculpture movement as fine art, and enlivened by the emergence of several important young artists. Of these events it is undoubtedly the Arneson/Moscone fracas that was the most publicized, most controversial, and, arguably, the most instructive event in ceramic sculpture during the first half of the eighties. The controversy over Arneson's portrait of George Moscone dramatized many of the changes that have already been noted, but most of all it showed that ceramic sculpture had passed out of a period of innocence and was now being seen as an increasingly integral part of the fine arts—subject to the same scrutiny, criticism, and social expectations.

In 1978 Mayor Moscone and his colleague, the gay-rights activist Harvey Milk, were gunned down in their offices in San Francisco City Hall by former Supervisor Dan White. The murder occurred just two weeks after nine hundred members of the People's Temple of Guyana had died in a mass suicide. The cult had been founded in San Francisco and most of the dead were connected to the city. San Francisco was in shock. Then, in 1979, Dan White received a reduced sentence, for voluntary manslaughter. His lawyers had built up the so-called Twinkie defense, saying that White had eaten too much junk food and that the resulting hypoglycemia had brought on temporary insanity. The response of the gay community to the verdict was angry and violent. That night a riot at City Hall

Robert Arneson Portrait of George, *1981. Glazed ceramic, height 94". Collection Foster/Goldstrom.*

Robert Arneson California Artist, *1982. Ceramic, glaze, height 78". Courtesy Allan Frumkin Gallery, New York.*

resulted in 119 injuries and over one million dollars in damage.

In 1981, against this powder keg of emotionalism, pain, and unresolved bitterness, Arneson and thirty other artists were invited to provide proposals for public art in the new George Moscone Convention Center, which was then nearing completion. Arneson submitted a drawing of Moscone's bust on a plain pedestal. His proposal was approved. The portrait of Moscone was certainly not offensive, nor was it vintage Arneson. The proposed portrait was oversized, workmanlike, but somehow sculpturally anemic. By Arneson's own standards of invention it was a surprisingly ordinary caricature. But what the drawing did not reveal was the artist's intentions for the pedestal. Arneson embellished the base with graffiti that were biographical in nature but that included references to Moscone's killer—"Smith and Wesson," "Twinkies," and "Harvey Milk, too."

The selection committee was a little alarmed by the piece when completed. Arneson also began to sense the problems in the work and, concerned that it might cause Moscone's widow some anguish, suggested that she might not want to unveil the piece. Mrs. Moscone was indeed upset by the pedestal and requested that the pedestal be covered during her official unveiling of the portrait. The media picked up the story at this point and an issue erupted, spreading from a local story to the news broadcasts of the national networks. The city was in no mood for Arneson's facetiousness. As Mayor Feinstein commented: "On memorials to Lincoln or the Kennedys or Martin Luther King or other fallen leaders it has never been expected or thought necessary to make reference to their killers."[2]

Within the art world Arneson was seen as a martyr and the city of San Francisco as a reactionary villain. But in reality, the situation was much more complex. Inviting Arneson to submit his proposal to the selection committee was perhaps foolish, given the artist's well-known taste for the seditious. However, in defense of the committee, the proposal Arneson presented seemed harmless enough and the committee had acted in good faith. It is Arneson's role that is more troublesome. Arneson professed a certain innocence throughout but could not be naive enough to believe that this piece—so explosively linked to damaged city pride, issues of sexuality, human rights, and the abuse of justice—could have been placed in public without outrage. Perhaps Arneson sought to stir the pot just a little but did not realize just how violently it would overflow. As the critic William Wilson wrote, "It's hard to see how the artist could avoid knowing he was asking for trouble with that base . . . both sides had equal opportunity to see this one coming and either work it out, or scrub the project."[3]

The effect of the controversy was not entirely negative. It placed Arneson in a national spotlight, increased his celebrity in the art world, and conferred the status of masterpiece on one of his more mundane works. It also caused Arneson to begin to question the direction that his sculpture had taken, an investigation that was further propelled by a withering critique by Hilton Kramer in the *New York Times*—just thirteen days after his portrait of Moscone had been rejected by San Francisco.

In 1977 Kramer had termed Arneson's work "brilliant" and "a mastery of characterization that is quite stunning."[4] By 1981, however, his view had changed, and, responding to the exhibition *Ceramic Sculpture: Six Artists* at the Whitney Museum, he wrote: "Mr. Arneson is obviously a star, yet his sensibility—dominated by a gruesome combination of bluster, facetiousness and exhibitionism—places a fatal limitation on what his gifts allow him to accomplish, or even to conceive. It is, I'm afraid, the sensibility of a provincial whose outlook has been decisively shaped by the art department gags of the university campus."[5]

According to Neal Benezra, the author of Arneson's retrospective catalogue, these two rejections of his work caused Arneson to reappraise his stance and to search for a less personal, less self-indulgent focus for his art. In 1984 Allan Frumkin held an exhibition of Arneson's work. Entitled *War Heads and Others,* it was a response both to his critics and to his search for a new expression. In place of the amusing and witty figures from the legerdemain of art history was a new cast of players. They were large works—with distorted, incinerated, lesion-covered faces—

Robert Rauschenberg Pneumonia Lisa, *Japanese Recreational Clayworks, 1986. Porcelain tiles with decals, height 32½". Courtesy Leo Castelli Gallery, New York.*

monumental mutants from the nuclear holocaust. These heads were placed on pedestals as obscene war memorials. Those who came seeking Arneson's humor were surprised and disoriented. Yet, although there was apparently a major shift in style and content, these works were not as much of a break as they seemed; they are neatly linked to the Moscone portrait.

Until Moscone, Arneson's formula of the hero/clown had proved to be the perfect foil for his art—using the comedy to balance the distasteful and disturbing elements in the works. But this formula could not work with Moscone. The slain mayor was neither a hero nor a clown. He was simply and tragically a victim, a condition reinforced rather than ameliorated by the sadly inappropriate smile in his portrait. War memorials are also portraits of victims. Violence exists in other works by Arneson, but it is always "self-inflicted" and made to seem foolish and nonthreatening. With Arneson's *War Heads* the violence was beyond the subject's control. This shift to the victim and the withdrawal of any comedic possibilities seemed to have both animated and confused Arneson. It is difficult to decide at this point whether his *War Heads* are an authentic expression of the artist, a sudden flush of guilt for his years of low-brow humor, or an attempt to prove the critics wrong by creating socially responsible work. Most likely they are a mixture of all three.

In an interview Arneson discussed the problems of working with humor, explaining both his nuclear work and, indirectly, the reactions to the Moscone portrait:

> The nuclear issue, the implication of the holocaust, and the final solution to all mankind—that's a serious issue. I would hope that I could also have some of my natural humor get into that. . . . But humor is a problem in art. The Greeks could deal with it. The two senses of drama were humor and tragedy: The humor was real raw; the tragedy was very basic. Something has happened since the time of the Greeks; it seems like humor has become threatening or debasing. Whenever you get involved with humor people take it personally and become offended. But you can't *not* offend anyone in dealing with tragedy. I am willing to do it, and take a lot of horseshit from the critics for doing it. Yes, it's sophomoric. But I'm sure much of our young culture [is] sophomoric. Should I be beyond that? [6]

The only reminder of Arneson's earlier work in the Frumkin exhibition was a self-portrait, *California Artist* (1982), a self-portrait that stood in the entrance to the gallery. In this piece Arneson made fun of the East Coast critics' vision of the West Coast artist as a provincial and irresponsible figure by dressing himself in a denim jacket and placing it on a pedestal emblazoned with sensemilla leaves and other stereotypes of the sun-bleached California life-style.

Arneson shifted position again in 1986, showing the works from the latter part of that year in an exhibition at Frumkin. Some pieces, such as the "TV" portraits of Ronald Reagan, attempt to reengage the humorous, but they are neither witty enough nor black enough to be more than merely diverting. What was of greater interest in the exhibition were his "straight" portraits of Jackson Pollock. These are now moving toward heroic portraiture, with surfaces that exploit the beauty, texture, and ceramic qualities of the medium without apology or humor. One sees in these a more radical change from the *War Heads,* which, with their cartoonish images, still maintained a link to the Arneson style of caricature.

The new pieces seek to work aesthetically without the trappings of theatricality that have adorned all his previous work. Large, imposing, and brooding, they are obviously contenders as "serious" sculpture in the literal, indeed even classical, sense of the term. Arneson's iconoclasm, his perceptive intelligence and constant movement in subject, scale, content, and now, even style, have kept him in the forefront as one of the most intriguing and inventive artists in contemporary American sculpture. He also unquestionably still remains the leader in the more hermetic world of ceramic sculpture.

Robert Arneson Head-Mined, *1982–83. Glazed ceramic,
height 78". Allan Frumkin Gallery, New York.*

At the same time as the Moscone debate, another controversy was beginning to develop—critical response to the Whitney Museum's exhibition *Ceramic Sculpture: Six Artists.* The exhibition was curated by Suzanne Foley and Richard Marshall and featured the work of Arneson, Voulkos, Price, Mason, Shaw, and Gilhooly. Its opening was one of the most crowded and enthusiastic of the season. The reviews, however, did not support the opening night euphoria. Kramer denounced the exhibition as "defiant provincialism" that left him "brooding about the thinness and the spiritual impoverishment of the cultural life that has sustained this movement."[7] Robert Hughes, the *Time* magazine critic, said that "no antidote has yet been found to the bite of the state's most annoying insect, the California cute-fly. . . . Quaintness, a whiff of sensemilla, weakness of the bone structure, a pervasive reek of the petted ego—such are the signs of the attack coupled with hermetic babblings which on that coastal paradise of the half-blown mind stand in for Imagination."[8]

The irony was that, although the exhibition was a failure on many levels, few of the critics were really criticizing the exhibition itself. What emerged was a bout of slightly hysterical California-bashing. The real questions that the event posed were left unanswered by all but a few. Among the writings that did address these issues were Jeff Kelley's perceptive and balanced review and John Perreault's plain-talking commentary, "Fear of Clay," in *Artforum.*[9] Perreault not only explained the exhibition's considerable failings and the overall dilemma of ceramics in the art world, but he also analyzed and placed in context the hostility with which the exhibition had been greeted.

The exhibition basically lacked both a clear curatorial vision and scholarly foundations. First, the selection of artists was not particularly perceptive, and omissions, such as DeStaebler, Frimkess, and Nagle, are difficult to justify. Second, the omission of women artists (Frey and Marilyn Levine were qualified contenders) made a pointed statement about the macho bias in the early years of the West Coast ceramics movement, but was certainly not a failing that the curators should have perpetuated. As Perreault stated, the exhibition would have been more accurately titled "Two Generations of California Male Artists working in Clay."[10]

Third, the exhibition was only partly about sculpture; it was also about pottery, an issue that the cautious curators decided to sidestep. This is possibly the reason they left out Voulkos's work with the plate—a central format (and the primary one for his drawing) since the 1950s. The problem was not that the curators tried to sanctify Voulkos's stack pots and Ken Price's cups as sculpture, but that they *denied* them their equal identity as pots.

Peter Vandenberge The Bird Watcher, *1981. Stoneware, slips, height 35". Collection Daniel Jacobs.*

In trying to present this medium as a newborn art form and ignoring its controversial and subversive roots in utility and craft, they missed the opportunity to make a truly radical statement.

Last, the selection and installation of work posed major problems. Each artist's work was selected according to a different set of criteria. As a result, the exhibition seemed fragmented beyond the incompatibility of aesthetics. The art ranged from Minimalism through Abstract Expressionism, Superrealism, and three-dimensional cartooning. Price's drawings and prints were shown, but the curators refused the same privilege to Arneson—arguably one of the finer draftsmen of our time. The installation was a set piece in misunderstanding the objects and also in curatorial bias. Ken Price's small objects seemed to occupy a third of the space, while the monumental works of Voulkos and Mason were compressed into a small, claustrophobic area directly in front of the elevators. It was painfully apparent that the simplistic notion of "clay as art" was not enough to meld these artists into a convincing exhibition.

In the final analysis, however, *Ceramic Sculpture: Six Artists* has the distinction of being a paradox—an unsuccessful exhibition, but, by default, a most successful event. It achieved a high level of coverage from critics who, for better or worse, had not considered ceramic sculpture before, nor written about it. The exhibition also excited a period of critical evaluation in the field that went on for months, as the issues, reviews, and selections were considered. It even spawned reviews of the reviews.[11] Ceramics emerged scarred but wiser, and many collectors, critics, museums, and galleries were encouraged to pick up the ceramics baton.

It is to the credit of the Whitney Museum that it did not back away totally from the field. In July 1984, at the urging of Patterson Sims, associate curator of the permanent collection, Viola Frey was given her first one-person exhibition on the East Coast. The exhibition was poorly received critically, but, as with the previous exhibition, the reviews seemed to use Frey's work as a club with

which to attack the museum on other issues.

Again installation proved to be a major hurdle. A group of ten glazed ceramic figures, ranging in height from seven to ten feet, were shown in a tight, curving arc. They stood shoulder to shoulder and were lit only from the front. As a result, they were reduced to becoming a two-dimensional wall and lost their individual character. But the carping of the critics did not slow down the growing fascination with ceramic sculpture. The Whitney acquired one of Frey's large figures as a gift to the museum. Frey was taken on by the Nancy Hoffman Gallery, and she attracted support from some of New York's more adventurous collectors. Both of the Whitney's sorties into ceramic sculpture had been, in a sense, confrontational, if for different reasons. They had awakened the art capital to the realization that ceramics was contributing to con-

Jack Earl NOW I WILL SING TO MY WELL BELOVED A SONG OF MY BELOVED TOUCHING HIS VINEYARD. MY WELL BELOVED HATH A VINEYARD IN A VERY FRUITFUL HILL, *1985. Painted earthenware, height 33". Collection Daniel Jacobs.*

temporary sculpture in a way that was fresh, original, and significant.

The exhibition that perhaps best surveyed this new energy within the sculptural movement was *In the Eye of the Beholder: A Portrait of Our Time.* The exhibition was curated by Michael McTwigan in 1985 at the College Art Gallery, State University of New York, College at New Paltz, New York. Unfortunately, tucked away in upstate New York, it did not attract high attendance. It was, nonetheless, an important statement. McTwigan's catalogue essay tended to give the exhibition a darkly morbid pallor: "We live in a frightening world that offers no grounds for faith, no promise for the future. . . . At the most superficial level, the tortured faces, twisted bodies, and empty lives portrayed in this seem to corroborate the verdict."[12] But, in fact, there was a far lighter edge to the exhibition and an overwhelmingly more optimistic one than McTwigan acknowledged. In a similar way, McTwigan's attribution of labyrinthian psychological constructs to the works completely overwhelmed the often simple and direct visual messages that they contained.

If one puts McTwigan's essay aside, however, and examines the exhibition itself, it was a superbly perceptive assembly of work with that rare sense of symbiosis that brings survey exhibitions to life. The exhibition included eight artists: seven sculptors (Robert Arneson, Viola Frey, Arthur González, Jan Holcomb, Judy Moonelis, Patrick Siler, and Daisy Youngblood) and one potter (Akio Takamori). As always occurs in any survey, there were omissions, such as Michael Lucero and Jack Earl, but McTwigan did a good job of bringing together a mix of masters and exciting young sculptors.

The exhibition also clearly stated the two issues with which contemporary ceramic sculpture is primarily concerned—modeling and painting. Color has always been one of the attractions of ceramic sculpture. The term "painting," however, is used here quite distinctly and separately from color. In previous decades, color was used mainly in a sculptural sense. At times it became more or less

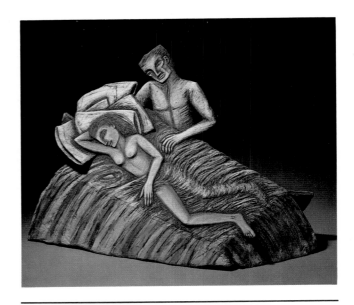

Judy Moonelis Untitled, 1986. Ceramic with painted slip, length 29". Collection Daniel Jacobs.

Arthur González Time Traveler, 1984. Metal, clay, slips, height 28". Collection Hope and Jay Yampol.

Jan Holcomb The Voyagers, *1984–85.*
Stoneware, paint, and underglaze, length 32".
Collection Dawn Bennett and Martin Davidson.

Viola Frey Untitled (Man in Blue I), *1983. Glazed earthenware, height 108". Collection Betty Asher.*

painterly in its application, but primarily it was used sculpturally—as a structural device to serve the form. In this exhibition only one of the artists, Youngblood, did not use painted surfaces. For the rest of the artists, however, the relative relationship of form and surface became intriguing and ambiguous. It was not apparent whether the works were paintings *about* sculpture or sculptures *about* painting. In some cases, such as that of Moonelis, the thickly encrusted slip surfaces even had the feel of heavily applied paint. Holcomb's relief sculptures were meticulously painted with acrylic, completely painting out the host material.

The exhibition dramatized the extent to which ceramics has turned its back on the modernist sculptural notion of "pure form." At one point in the recent history of ceramic sculpture, some ceramists seemed intent upon taking on the modernist sculptors. Some fine work was made, but ceramics ultimately proved to be a poor fabricating material for abstract sculpture. It was too expressionistic, resistant to large-scale use, and without the passive objectivity of metal. Today's ceramic sculptors have largely abandoned modernist sculpture and seem more intent on occupying a no-man's-land between sculpture and painting. In addition, the younger sculptors show little commitment to the moralistic nineteenth-century notion of "truth to materials," getting on with the objective business of making sculpture rather than the more romantic activity of making ceramics.

Of the artists in this exhibition it is Frey who requires further examination. Together with Arneson, she has been one of the formative influences on the direction of ceramic sculpture in the eighties. This decade has seen Frey's most dramatic and monumental work. Frey's figures have rapidly grown from modest, life-size portraits, slightly over five feet in height, to hulking figures over ten feet tall. The painting evolved from careful use of local color to the strongly abstracted use of primary

Viola Frey Untitled, 1983. Glazed earthenware, height 98½".
Collection Garth Clark/Mark Del Vecchio.

color. As a body of work they are among the most remarkable clay figures ever made. In his review of her exhibition in 1986 at the Asher/Faure Gallery in Los Angeles, the *Los Angeles Times* critic William Wilson commented on the figures and their meaning:

> The Bay Area sculptor has concocted an exhibition that will surely stand among the most interesting of the year. It treats the modern corporate Everyman on a par with the Pharaohs of Egypt, the heroes of the Iliad and the Shamans of the primitive tribes. This is the most openly sophisticated group of works I have seen her make. It might have been inspired by the County Museum of Art's masterful "German Expressionist Sculpture" exhibition, with a few dollops of Léger and Dubuffet thrown in for spice. But it doesn't look derivative because it isn't. Frey continues to convince us that her work is her own. She persuades us never again to snigger at the guy in the Hush Puppies taking the family to Sea World. He is Hector, she is Helen and they are the fates in adolescence.[13]

Frey was beginning to find that the scale of the ten-foot-high standing figures was posing a problem. The figurative gesture was losing its presence, and bulk was preying on articulation. The men in particular were becoming awkwardly humpbacked. Some figures seemed to be grappling less with notions of art than with the complexity of engineering and laws of gravity. Frey has solved this quite simply by working with reclining figures, where the sense of structure is less apparent and less physically threatening. Her figures can now continue to grow in scale. Also, the figures have now shed their floral dresses, blue suits, and red "power" ties for a comic, classical repose in the nude. Frey has also begun again to make smaller figures—about three feet in height. These objects and figures are assembled into intriguing and devious arrangements—reminiscent of her earlier china-painted tableaux of the seventies, but much

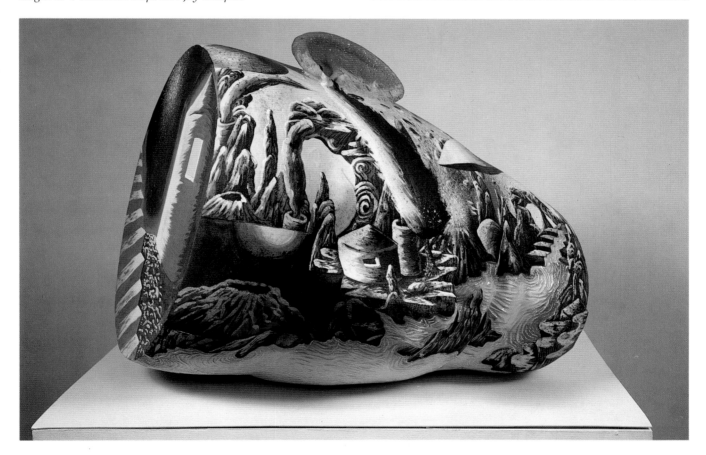

LEFT: **Robert Brady** Eva, 1984. Ceramic, metal, height 52½".
Collection Daniel Jacobs.

RIGHT: **Howard Kottler** Waiting for Master, 1986. Earthenware,
simulated gold leaf and paint, height 15".

Michael Lucero Lunar Life Dreamer, 1984. Glazed ceramic,
height 19". Collection Hope and Jay Yampol.

Tom Rippon An Artist and His Work, *1985. Porcelain, height 15". Courtesy Rena Bransten Gallery, San Francisco.*

his work any connection to ceramic tradition, a growing trend among ceramic sculptors. Earl has consistently been one of the most independent and innovative of ceramic sculptors, playing with a droll, highly personal sense of the narrative. His vision is a curious mixture of the country sage and the literate intellectual.

Michael Lucero works with the same "paint-in-the-round" approach as Earl, although his subject matter and style are unrelated to Earl's realism and folkish narrative. Lucero's interest in painting has evolved through the decade, beginning with his works from 1980—remarkable hanging figures with heads made from pots, and bodies consisting of wire and shards. With his *Dreamers* series in 1984–85, the balance of form over surface began to shift. Large heads became the canvas for the actualization of a dream landscape, where dry surfaces were mixed with liquid pools of reflecting

Richard Shaw Seated Figure with Gray Head, *1984. Porcelain, height 33". Courtesy Allan Frumkin Gallery, New York.*

more spartan and with color employed as a structural element. The use of painting to invoke the artist's own sense of light and shade (i.e., "modeling" the surface) remains a connection between these and earlier works.

In his new work, Jack Earl uses tableaux in a completely different manner than Frey. Frey's work is about action and fragments of events, whereas Earl's work is narrative. His sculpture is supported by titles that can be ten lines or more in length and amplify the narrative, investigative quality of his work. The sculpture is presented in a "pictorial," illustrative format. The works are like a very detailed painting or illustration that has suddenly been transformed into two-and-a-half–dimensional reality. The 1980s have also seen the gradual removal of any material qualities of ceramics. In the seventies Earl used glazes and porcelain, inspired by the example of eighteenth-century figures. Now the clay is painted over with oil paint, removing from glaze. In these the painting began to overcome the form with noses, chins, and brows acceding to the images that covered them. As Mark Shannon comments: "Vision and flesh, eye and land, waking and dream run fluidly into one another where we wander among mountains, rippled pools, pagodas, cliffs and canyons. . . . We feel at home in their worlds; their beauty, unlike the landscape of Surrealism, is not convulsive."[14] In the newest work the painted surface has become even more assertive, with a bright palette on large, complex insect forms.

Lucero has also begun to work concurrently in bronze, and his exhibition at the Charles Cowles Gallery in 1984 included some excellent works in this medium. Working in bronze has become something of a vogue among ceramists. Arneson, Frey, DeStaebler, and others have worked in the medium. Even potters are becoming involved, and Voulkos has recently begun to cast his pots in

Elaine Carhartt The Wizard and Imaginary Beings, *1985. Painted ceramic, height 48" and 24". Courtesy Asher/Faure Gallery, Los Angeles.*

Beverly Mayeri Under Scrutiny, *1984. Clay, acrylic paint, height 15". Private collection.*

bronze. This reflects a healthy interest for a pluralism in materials, but, given the cost of working in bronze, it also reflects a newfound confidence in the talents of these sculptors. The results of these extensions into bronze, however, have been uneven. Arneson's bronzes are flat and lifeless compared to his ceramics. Only Lucero and Frey (who paints her bronzes) have been particularly successful in using the medium with the same energy as their ceramics.

The dominant influence among the younger sculptors has been Surrealism, a romance that continues unabated since the sixties. In some cases the homage is deliberate and specific, as in Tom Rippon's reference to the proto-Surrealist paintings of Giorgio de Chirico or in Richard Shaw's porcelain figures that are assembled much in the style and mood of Miró's Surrealist assemblages from the mid-1930s. Other artists use the vocabulary of

Raymon Elozua Ceramics for Sale, 1981. Ceramic, acrylic, height 15". Collection Daniel Jacobs.

Mel Rubin Phil's Diner, 1984. Earthenware, acrylic paint, length 53". Private collection. Courtesy Jan Baum Gallery, Los Angeles.

Surrealism more informally and personally. Beverly Mayeri and Elaine Carhartt both use painted surfaces on their figurative sculpture, evenly colored and without a touch of expressionism or surface emotion, creating an eerie visual silence that surrounds the work—the distinct feeling of a calm before the storm. In other sculptors' work ceramics continues to provide a vehicle for realism, as in Raymon Elozua's constructions of abandoned mines and dilapidated billboards. In *Ceramics for Sale* he makes a witty connection between his own medium and his interest in structure and decay. Mel Rubin, on the other hand, also uses a degree of realism, à la Hopper, to create affectionate and at times almost nostalgic evocations of architectural fragments in the urban culture.

In reviewing the interest and success achieved

by such young artists as Lucero, Moonelis, González, and others, one should bear in mind that the change in status for ceramic sculpture from a regional curiosity to a real contender in the sculpture world has been recent. Even in the late seventies ceramic sculpture was very much the in-joke, shown mainly to other ceramists in the university gallery, largely free of critical reaction, and, with a few exceptions, without serious collectors among either museums or private patrons. It was a cozy and supportive environment, very different from the tough, open market that exists today. In what remains of the decade, one will see further changes. As much as ceramic sculpture is riding a crest of interest and popularity, it is still very much a genre in flux, defining and redefining its role within the context of American sculpture.

In turning to the vessel, one finds perhaps less controversy, but certainly as much progress. Pottery has gradually acquired its independent identity as an art form. The assertion of the Seattle critic Matthew Kangas, that "most American art critics who have written about clay have never accepted the assumptions [of importance] about the vessel,"[15] could hardly be more inaccurate. Indeed, the list of writers from the fine arts who have written on the autonomy of the vessel in the eighties is long and distinguished; it includes Schjeldahl, Perrone, Knight, Perreault, Gerry Nordland, and many others. This acceptance is not an attempt to place the vessel in a superior position to other works in clay, but simply to accept and explore its unique character and identity.

The concept of the pot as art has been actively argued throughout this century, but in the mid-seventies it began to be energetically promoted by a few writers. The potters became involved as well, and many, including Betty Woodman, Richard DeVore, Wayne Higby, and Bill Daley, discarded the notion of pottery being a subcategory of sculpture. In his 1980 review of the exhibition *A Century of Ceramics in the United States*, Perreault (then the senior art critic for the *Soho News* [New York]) made a plea for the vessel to retain its uniqueness

and warned against its total assimilation into the fine arts:

> Sacrificing the tactile and kinesthetic directness of the utilitarian vessel—the pot—for sculpture may cut ceramics off from its historical, cultural, popular *and* aesthetic roots. I am all for arts/crafts interface. I am all for sculpture in clay. But a real pot, vase or plate . . . can be beautiful and even a moving thing. And pots are no more limiting as formats than those rectangular shapes the paint-on-canvas painters use. The vessel is a discipline sorely needed.[16]

The impact of the British critic and historian Philip Rawson and his book *Ceramics* has been important in outlining the theory of the pottery aesthetic. Although Rawson wrote his book primarily about historical pottery, the lessons in the formal, aesthetic constituents of a vessel, in the principles of surface painting and decoration, and in the exploration of "content" through the polarities of conceit versus metaphor are as meaningful and relevant in judging contemporary pottery.

Ceramics was published in 1971 but it was not until 1980 that it was "discovered" in the United States, rapidly becoming something of a cult classic. This sudden popularity of the book prompted the University of Pennsylvania Press to republish it in 1984. Rawson's visits to the United States to deliver keynote addresses (twice for the Institute for Ceramic History symposia and once for the NCECA) have enlarged the dialogue on the aesthetic autonomy of pottery. Rawson argues that beyond a certain innocent love of the medium, there can be little growth without "ceramic literacy." Speaking at the *Echoes* conference in Kansas City, Missouri, in 1983, Rawson expanded on his literacy theme:

> To people who do not possess writing, a book is a mere, mysteriously pointless object. They may have practical uses for its leaves unconnected with what is written on them; though that was not the reason for its existence. In a similar way a pot object can only be a thing, that may have its uses, to people who know how to read *its* signs and symbols. The comparison is not totally exact, I know. But I think

Ralph Bacerra Untitled Platter, 1986. Earthenware with underglaze, glaze and overglaze painting, diameter 23". Collection Dawn Bennett and Martin Davidson.

LEFT: **Nancy Carman** Desperate, 1983. Glazed porcelain, height 12". Collection Hope and Jay Yampol.

ABOVE: **Graham Marks** Stillings, 1984. *Earthenware clay, coil construction with sand-blasted surface, height 31". Collection Karen Johnson Boyd.*

RIGHT TOP: **Susanne G. Stephenson** Water Rock Vase, 1986. *Earthenware with slips and glazes, height 17". Everson Museum of Art, Syracuse, New York.*

RIGHT CENTER: **William Daley** To Josiah W., 1983. *Unglazed stoneware, height 19". Victoria and Albert Museum, London. Gift of Mr. and Mrs. John Pickett.*

RIGHT BOTTOM: **Beatrice Wood** Spiral Bottle Vase, 1984. *Earthenware, luster glaze, height 16½". Private collection.*

we can accept that however skillfully a potter worked, he can only speak to people who know how to read what he has done in modifying his mother-substances. The potter needs a ceramically literate public.[17]

But this literacy has been difficult to achieve outside the ceramics world, due to an uneasiness that the humble pot seems to stir, particularly within the art world. Perreault characterizes this as

> a fear of clay . . . mainly the fear that the utilitarian and the esthetic could once again *truly* be united. It is a fear of pots, a fear of objects that don't fit neatly into given categories, of objects that can mean more than one thing at once. A pot can be utilitarian *and* esthetic; there is a long history of this that we are supposed to know but for the most part we remain ethnocentric, sexist and full of class bias. A pot can be art *and* craft; sculpture *and* painting; masculine *and* feminine.[18]

One sees this fear in the writings of several critics and, interestingly, even in those who claim a partisan interest in ceramics. Both Neal Benezra and Matthew Kangas show the classic symptoms. In their writing they rejoice over every injury done to the tradition of pottery, as though this act somehow places the antagonist (and the critics who witness the event) in a higher moral and aesthetic order. Yet, as much as the potter might bemoan the difficulties of acceptance, there has been no time in the West when the potter's art has achieved greater status and autonomy. Our progress into a post-Craft culture in the United States has been followed with some envy in Europe, where pottery's status is a full generation behind that of the United States. In the eighties there has been more serious criticism of American pottery (contemporary and historical), its traditions, and its aesthetic ambition than in all the preceding decades combined. In terms of art, this decade shows a diversity and richness of achievement in vessel making that is unequaled in a modern society. After two decades of being the stepchild of the ceramics movement,

the humble pot has emerged from the condition that Stravinsky once characterized as "protective neglect." Much like sculpture, it is now in a high-profile public arena, subject to critical interrogation. It has also become more expensive, and, as a result, is subject to the pressures and manipulations of the marketplace.

In order to explain the newly recognized ambitions of pottery, the critical language has had to be expanded. In this area there has been some original writing and criticism by writers such as Ed Lebow and Jeff Perrone. In particular, Perrone's essay "Some Sherds on Pottery" is a step forward in seeking a revisionist view of the pot as art, breaking away from the classical viewpoint of the vessel as a unified and centered form and seeking to address it as a fragment—a sherd.[19] Perrone's thesis is at times opaquely stated, but his concept has flashes of provocative clarity, replacing the traditional "essence" and "center" with "a very evasive structure, a structure of hide and seek, of inside-and-outside, of the 'complete' fragment—[that] insinuates itself in any ceramic construction where the violence of synthesis and the domination of the center do not overthrow and repress difference."[20]

This strong improvement in scholarship, criticism, and theory is not solely the triumph of the writers. It reflects the growing sophistication of the makers whom they serve. In examining this achievement, it is again beyond the scope of this survey to discuss all the work of consequence. Instead, the issues facing the vessel maker will be explored through four artists: Betty Woodman, Rudy Autio, Adrian Saxe, and Andrew Lord. They have been chosen not as the only artists of importance but, in a sense, as ambassadors for the eighties. Their work brings to the surface issues of content and context that apply to the field at large. As with the discussion of sculpture, the examination of vessel making in the eighties can

Betty Woodman Ostia, Vase and Stand, *1986. Glazed earthenware, height 26". Courtesy Greenberg Gallery, Saint Louis.*

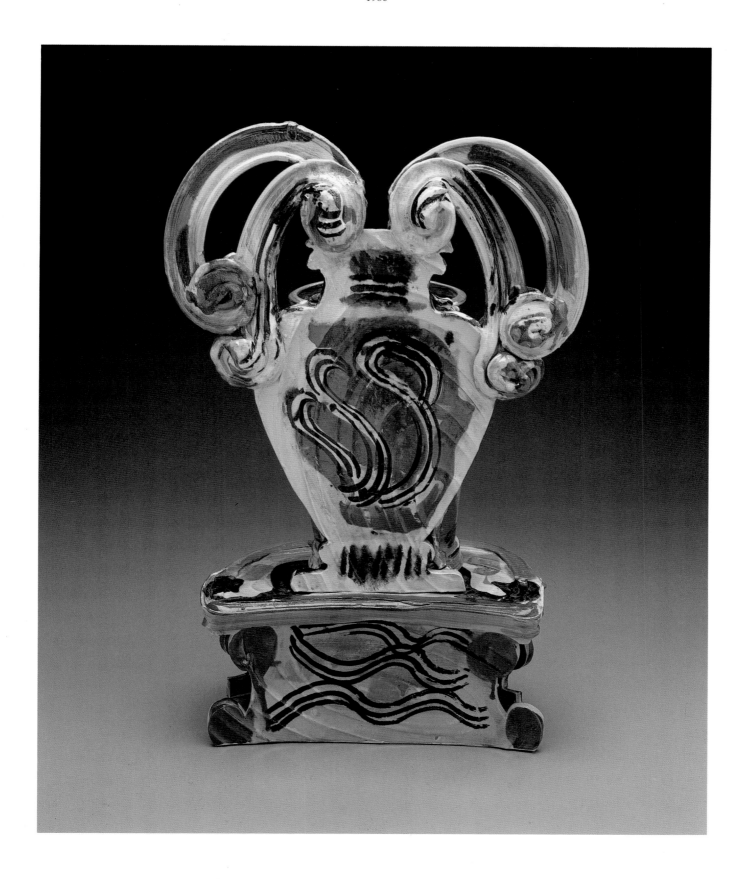

be expanded by consulting the biographies of the other artists illustrated in this chapter.

Perhaps the most noticeable shift in the eighties has been a move from the interest in reductive, organic abstraction that dominated the previous decade (Bob Turner, Richard DeVore, Ruth Duckworth, Toshiko Takaezu, Bill Daley, Rudolf Staffel, and others) toward a more pluralistic menu of options: the pattern and decoration movement (P&D); figurative and other imagery; the use of "cultural" assemblage, a postmodernist "cut and paste" approach to history; and the literal expression of ideas about politics and other issues. By this I do not mean that the work of the organic abstractionists is less valid in this decade, but simply that *taste* has shifted to new concerns, allowing for a different set of aesthetic ideas to be introduced. Indeed, Ruth Duckworth's small groupings of ves-

Ruth Duckworth Two Forms, *1985. Unglazed porcelain, height 7". Victoria and Albert Museum, London. Gift of Helen Drutt and Ruth Duckworth.*

sels, with their inserted "keys" or abstracted lids, are among the most distinctive and moving works to emerge in the eighties. New talents, such as Chris Gustin, are contributing fresh ideas to the "organic" pot. But even though fine work is being done, this type of content is not currently occupying center stage.

This shift in interest from the organic and the reductive is most clearly seen in the interest in the P&D movement, with its accent on craft techniques, its decorative-arts vocabulary, and its sympathy for arts traditionally practiced by women (quilt making, china painting, etc.). P&D has served to legitimize issues that ceramics has been dealing with throughout the century and to place these in the contemporary visual-arts arena. In a prophetic address at the first Ceramics Symposium of the Institute for Ceramic History in 1979, George Woodman told his audience that ceramics should not give up what he termed the "New Decorative Vessel" in favor of modernism's more spartan ideals:

> There is an influential and subversive movement in American art today ready to reconsider the whole relationship between decorative art and so-called fine or serious art. The future, we hope for ceramics, then, may not consist of bubbling up through the aesthetic soup to the top little bit of scum where the "fine" arts are, but in fact the whole thing may be about to turn over. There are artists all over the country who are interested in and concerned about the decorative stance. For clay artists to jump out of that ship now, would be the worst case of timing ever witnessed.[21]

P&D had begun to form as a movement in 1974–75, when some painters who had independently taken up this style of working began to meet informally. This was often under the guidance of the late Amy Goldin, a critic who had a formative influence on the development and definition of the movement. It was nonhierarchal, nonsexist, and nonformalist. Apart from the tile works of Joyce Kozloff, ceramics played a very small role in the movement until 1980, when the potter Betty Woodman became more involved with the P&D

group. By then the group had lost some of its early innocence and had, to some extent, "arrived" in the art world. P&D had already developed its "stars"—Cynthia Carlson, Joyce Kozloff, Ned Smyth, Miriam Schapiro, Robert Zakanitch, Kim MacConnel, and Robert Kushner—and its influential dealers—Holly Solomon, Pam Adler, Robert Miller. But it provided little structure, fewer rules, endless possibility for experiment, and an open, nonjudgmental acceptance of materials and processes from the crafts.

In 1981 Woodman and Kozloff worked on a collaboration for the Tibor de Nagy Gallery in New York. The exhibition, consisting of pots made by Woodman and painted by Kozloff, raised eyebrows. The pots were seen as subversive "because they [were] beautiful."[22] In the following year, Woodman, with Cynthia Carlson, took on a highly ambitious project entitled *An Interior Exchanged* at the Shirley Goodman Resource Center of the Fashion Institute of Technology in New York. Carlson made paintings of Woodman's pots. Woodman made responses in clay to Carlson's system of "relief wallpaper." Except for the paintings and the pots, which were clearly identifiable as those, respectively, of Carlson and Woodman, the issue of who did what in the decorated, L-shaped gallery was deliberately left ambiguous so that it became a true collaboration.

At this point Woodman, always a prodigious producer, began to move fast, working on room-sized installation pieces and beginning to reexamine the vernacular of the pot. In the following four years there was an extraordinary amount of activity and work. Her style is a dynamic mix of boundless energy, invention, and ambition. When the three are in harmony, they are overwhelmingly exciting. When they get out of balance, as they occasionally do, the work becomes arbitrary and empty. A case in point was Woodman's installation piece in 1985 for the exhibition *Ceramic Sculpture: Eight Concepts,* where the ambitious scale of the work completely outgrew its content.

But Woodman's ambition has also made her one of the most experimental and innovative potters working today. Woodman has been something of a leader in expanding the potter's activity into other media, creating multimedia installations, working on fabric, presenting art events around her work, and producing handsome monoprints of vessels. In her use of the ceramic vessel she has been eclectic. She has "appropriated" (to use the patois of the postmodernists) surfaces, forms, handles, spouts, lids, silhouettes, symbols, shapes, clays, and textures from many cultures and periods—predominantly from the Chinese and the

Chris Gustin Untitled Vessel, *1984. Glazed and sand-blasted stoneware, height 30". Collection Dawn Bennett and Martin Davidson.*

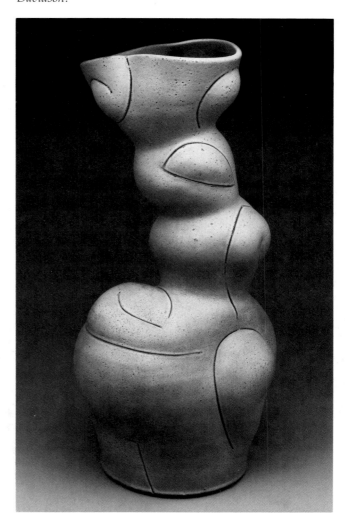

Mediterranean pottery traditions. Many of these are used with clear reference, indeed even a deeply felt homage, to their original source. But they are assembled with witty and playful incongruity—what Perrone terms "Woodman's ever changing constellation of ceramic styles";[23] for instance, a handle from a Greek krater is attached to a plump pillow pitcher drawn from Mediterranean pottery, while the surface is covered in a wash of glaze colors reminiscent of Momoyama wares.

More radically, Woodman has raised an important question in her work. What constitutes a pot? Is it a full, round, volumetric container, or can just the two-dimensional "shape" or image of the vessel suffice? Recently Woodman has been making frontal works, cutting out the silhouette of a vessel from a slab of clay and attaching it to a tall cylinder—the vase behind the vase. This cylinder can be used to hold flowers but also serves the structural role of presenting the silhouette. This is then placed on a base that either stands on a surface or is attached to the wall. This silhouette is treated just like any other pot; it can be lidded,

it is decorated, handles are added, and, if the outline happens to be a teapot, a spout is attached as well.

In addition to the pot having now been moved from a volumetric to a pictorial plane, another issue is raised. The slabs from which the outlines are cut have a spiral in light relief on the surface, the result of Woodman's technique in forming the slabs. This presents a second center for her pots. Perrone has discussed the notion of two centers in Woodman's work under the heading of "doubleness/asymmetry," but his writing deals with her full, volumetric forms. The first of the centers in her silhouette pots comes from the traditional center of the pot—that is, the vertical axis, even though this is implied rather than real. The second center is horizontal, piercing the pot from the point at which the spiral commences. Thus, two intersecting foci cross and interrelate in her work.

Woodman took this spatial play a step forward

Mark Pharis Soy Bottles, *1985. Stoneware, height 8½". Collection Dan Jacobs.*

Philip Cornelius Aspen Teapot, 1983. *Porcelain, slab built, height 13½". Collection Daniel Jacobs.*

in her exhibition in 1986 at the Max Protetch Gallery in New York. Woodman removed the handles from her outlines and pinned them against the wall, thereby creating a third spatial element in the work. She had done this previously, with her shadow pots, but adding the shadow was a less potent gesture than physically detaching an *integral* part of the vessel.

This two-dimensional aspect of Woodman's work has been dealt with in some detail because it raises a current issue, which could be termed the "pictorialization" of the vessel. It is an important and innovative direction that is appearing in the work of many potters, and while Woodman was not its originator, she is certainly one of its most adventurous exponents. Simply, what is developing is a mixture of ideas that are pictorial visions of

the vessel (i.e., what one might do if one drew or painted a pot) and a modified, nominally three-dimensional reality.

The idea has been around for centuries in one form or another, but it has not generally involved the same distortion of form that is now taking place. Its modern pioneer is the British potter Elizabeth Fritsch, who in 1971 began to make extraordinary vessels that appear from a distance to be fat, round pots. But on closer inspection, one finds, in fact, that the pots are actually flattened, oval shapes and that the foot and the rim have only been "drawn" to suggest their fullness. Fritsch influenced a number of potters who began to play with this new illusory, trompe l'oeil space.

In America this illusory volume has taken a wide variety of expression, from Harris Deller's compressed teapots to Akio Takamori's erotic envelope pots with their drawn rims of men, women, and animals. Phil Cornelius has done much the same thing with his paper-thin teapots, reducing the volume on his long, flat forms to a minimum and playing with the silhouette of the pot, which in turn takes on the shape of World War I tanks, airplanes, and battleships. Mark Pharis is the surprising entrant to this field—surprising only in that his roots are traditional, the utilitarian enclave of the Minnesota potters. In his work Pharis takes simple functional forms (mainly the teapot and the sauce bottle) and treats them as three-dimensional drawings. Some teapots are reduced to narrow, flat forms that emphasize the defining edge over volume; other pots are slightly distorted and off center, as though "drawn" from a perspective of looking down at the vessel at a sharp angle. Emerging as it does from the traditional lineage of Leach and MacKenzie, Pharis's work is optimistic and regenerative, pointing to a quiet but growing revolution among America's finest functional potters.

The issue of the pot as a drawing takes on a different significance in the work of Andrew Lord, a British potter who has recently moved to the United States via Amsterdam. Lord's arrival has

Judith Salomon Slab Vase, 1984. Glazed earthenware, height 16". Private collection.

BELOW: **Andrea Gill** Teapot and Cup, 1984–85. Tin-glazed earthenware, height 27". Collection Betty Asher.

BELOW RIGHT: **Roseline Delisle** Série Pneumatique 10, 1986. Porcelain, height 11". Collection Laddie J. Dill.

FAR RIGHT: **Jerry Rothman** Ritual Tureen, 1982. Glazed stoneware, thrown and hand-built elements, height 22". Private collection.

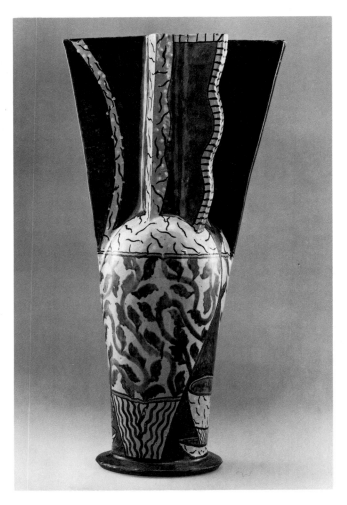

TOP LEFT: **Art Nelson** Meta Vessel, 1984. Glazed earthenware, height 17". Collection Hope and Jay Yampol.

LEFT: **Jeff Oestreich** Vase, 1986. Glazed stoneware, height 14". Private collection.

ABOVE: **Kenneth Price** Gomo, 1985. Acrylic and metallic paint on earthenware, height 10½". Courtesy Willard Gallery, New York.

RIGHT: ***Irvin Tepper*** Daniel's Cup, 1982. Porcelain; cup, height 5½"; saucer, diameter 8". Collection Dan Jacobs.

BELOW: ***James D. Makins*** Cup/Saucer, 1983. Black porcelain, height 7". Courtesy the artist.

Andrew Lord Coffee Service, 1985. *Painted stoneware, height 3⅞″–7⅝″. Courtesy BlumHelman, New York.*

ruffled the feathers of the hermetic ceramics world. This was the result of several factors—a touch of xenophobia, a degree of envy and distrust surrounding Lord's instant celebrity in the United States, and a healthy dose of irritation from the art press's uninformed claims of historical innovation in Lord's work. Although Lord had been exhibiting actively in England and Europe since the early seventies, his first exhibition in the United States took place in 1981, at the BlumHelman gallery. The *New York Times* critic John Russell called it "the most original show of the month,"[24] while

Roberta Smith wrote in the *Village Voice* of the lack of alignment of form and surface as "unusual for ceramics and [something that] makes the work seem poised, ready for action."[25] The claims about the unique use of the vessel and the "break" with ceramic tradition in Lord's work were certainly spurious. Lord's visual vocabulary was at least twenty-five years old by American standards and a good deal older if one takes into account the work of the Italian Futurist "Aeroceramisti" from the twenties. Whereas the Futurists had produced forms similar to Lord's, the Otis group had advanced the idea of breaking up surface and form into a more dynamic relationship. It was probably with this in mind that Michael McTwigan denounced Lord's work as "some kind of disfigured ceramic," noting that "the brilliance of the gallery spotlights certainly aided Lord. . . . I would suspect these [pots] would look rather dull in the light of day. They certainly would in the light of a little history."[26]

But, although Lord's work was not unique in terms of content, it was fresh and innovative in style. As with the work of Pharis, Lord's pots were also drawings—monochrome extractions of pots from the still lifes of Cubist painting. Because they drew from the two-dimensional realm, Lord's pots did not have to "behave" like conventional pots. They were disfigured because they were being constructed with the freedom of a modernist draftsman more than the modern potter. In evaluating Lord's place in the eighties, it is important to distance oneself from the distorting adulation that has been heaped on his work and to examine the real contribution, which is, nonetheless, substantial and impressive.

Examined individually the pots are mute and strangely uninteresting. But to analyze them in this traditional context is incorrect. Lord's pots function only within the idea of a still life, working in groupings of anything from three to fifty-five pieces. Christopher Knight calls these "pictures that have been pushed, pulled, coaxed and cajoled into volumetric space."[27] Some works, where the vessel is flattened, are certainly less volumetric than others, but even in these the tease between two-dimensional origins and three-dimensional realities remained.

What is exciting in Lord's work is that it has consistently grown and expanded. The vocabulary remains limited to a few forms, some of which Lord has been using since his student years, but the level of articulation of his ideas constantly increases, as does his shrewd play with the modern still life. This was particularly apparent in his 1986 exhibition at the Margo Leavin Gallery in Los Angeles, which arguably included his finest work to date. The works show many cracks and fissures to indicate an indifference to the formal concerns

of craft. Some are left exposed. Other cracks are "healed" with a gold resin. In early pieces this use of gold was subtle, filling a crack or two as a highlight. But in this exhibition it was expanded into an impressive, painterly statement. In his newer work Lord dapples the entire surfaces of his bigger still-life groupings with gold "flashes," playing brilliant light against flat, receding darkness. In his geometric still lifes one sees considerable progress as well. The play of line between the two or three vessels making up the group has become more sophisticated and kinetic, resulting in complex relationships of real and implied space.

Whether the work belongs properly to the realm of the vessel or to that of sculpture is possibly more a question of marketing than of the work's true location in art. It could be argued that Lord belongs to both. And yet, Knight is incorrect in stating that Lord's pots have "little if anything to do with the traditions of pottery and crafts."[28] Certainly the making of a traditional pot is not the raison d'être for his work, but Lord is no more

Andrew Lord Jug, Vase, and Dish, Geometry, 1986. Stoneware painted with oxide, height 4"–10". Courtesy Margo Leavin Gallery, Los Angeles.

free from connections to the tradition of pottery than a painter can ever be free of the traditions of painting. It is not his *freedom* from this tradition that matters, but his *relationship* to the tradition.

Lord's work is filled with references to pottery. The use of pitcher forms, bowls, and lidded jars is specific, and, as a result, the association with utility lies just under the surface. It is subconsciously and unavoidably part of the content of the work, even though it is patently not the intent. Lord's forms reveal quite specific and identifiable connections to the history of pottery, particularly to the coarse, satisfying shapes of English medieval wares and to the lidded "ginger jars" of Delft. The cracks and fissures that "would lead any self-respecting potter to consign the [pot] to the scrapheap"[29] in fact have a distinguished precedent from the sixteenth century to the present in Japanese Bizen ware and its aesthetic of the perfect imperfection. In addition, the mending of the cracks in Lord's pots with gold—while functioning superbly for him on an aesthetic level—also has its precedent in ceramic tradition.

In Japan the collector has for centuries had the more valuable pots obviously restored with gold lacquer. This is a symbolic act, placing the aesthetic value of the vessel above that of precious metal. These connections to the potter's tradition are not drawn in order to reduce Lord's work to the level of a craft object but simply to place the claims of innovation in perspective and to illustrate the complexity of his relationship to the sustaining tradition of pottery.

The pictorialization of the vessel extends beyond the abstraction of Woodman, Pharis, and Lord. It is also concerned with more traditional applications of the pictorial—that is, drawing *on* the pot rather than making the pot itself the subject of a drawing. It is only within the last ten years that placing images on vessels has again become fully respectable. In the sixties and for a good part of the seventies the use of pictorial elements on a pot was considered decoration and, by definition, trivial. This was the result of the general dominance

of post-1950s American art by the Abstract Expressionist/Minimalist aesthetics. During this time most ceramists considered even the finest painted maiolica and Greek vases irredeemably decadent. Potters were either exploring the more rugged "truth-to-materials" aesthetic of Japanese pottery or the purity of organic abstraction. Consequently, an undecorated pot was held to be a more pure and serious object.

The current master of this genre of the painted pot is unquestionably Rudy Autio. His appearance in this text has been delayed until the eighties because, much as with Woodman, it is only after thirty years of work that contemporary taste and Autio's art have connected. In addition, the eighties have been Autio's most prolific and accomplished

Rudy Autio Sacrifice of Iphigenia on Her Wedding Day, *1983. Porcelain, glazed, slab built, height 40". Museum of Art, Carnegie Institute, Pittsburgh, Pennsylvania. Decorative Arts Purchase Fund.*

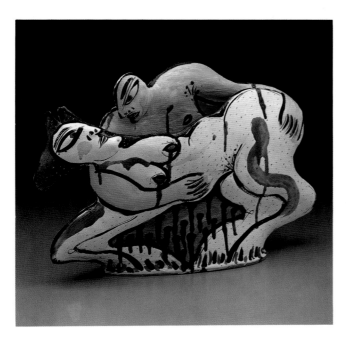

Akio Takamori Man with Dog/Woman, 1983. *Stoneware with glaze and slips, height 17". Collection Hope and Jay Yampol.*

period of work. Autio works on large, vaguely anthropomorphic vessel forms, on which he paints a floating and complex landscape of figures with a style drawn loosely from Matisse, Chagall, and others. Although the appearance of the work is unquestionably contemporary, the concept of the work is centuries old and connects Autio with the tradition of the figural painted vessel. Writing of this continuity, Autio has commented that his situation was not unique:

> Images can lose a sense of proportion even though they may seem graphically correct if viewed from any given face of the vessel. I can imagine an early Greek master in sixth century B.C. working on his pots in the agora, turning the amphora around and around, wondering as he painted how the space would work on the other side. "How will I complete the image? What should I put on the other side to make it work? I have to keep the spirit and the design the same, or nearly like the one on this side and yet it has to be different." A Zuñi potter setting down the geometric patterns of his tradition has the same thoughts. . . . An age-old problem for the potter.[30]

This age-old problem is nonetheless constantly a fresh challenge. Certainly Autio has given the idea new life and a warm, fecund sexuality. There are differences between Autio's use of the pot's pictorial space, or what Rawson prefers to call "potter's" space, and that of the potters of ancient Greece. The Greek pot painter worked within the specific "frame" of the pot and did not involve himself that deeply with the form. The relationship of image to form was complementary but passive. In Autio's work the surface/form relationship becomes active and dynamic. Writing about this relationship, Edward Lebow notes that in Autio's early figurative works the forms were explicitly

Akio Takamori Self-Portrait, 1985. *Salt-glazed stoneware, height 28". Collection Richard Schroeder.*

Richard Notkin Heart Teapot: Sharpesville, *1986. Unglazed stoneware, height 6". Collection Dawn Bennett and Martin Davidson.*

RIGHT: *Richard Notkin* Cooling Towers Teapot #3B, *1983. Stoneware, height 6". Collection Daniel Jacobs.*

Wayne Higby Sun Rim Canyon, *1984. Glazed earthenware, raku fired, height 10½". Collection Daniel Jacobs.*

Lidya Buzio Roofscape Vessel, *1986. Earthenware, slab built and burnished and painted with underglazes, height 16". Collection Betty Asher.*

torsos, but that this anthropomorphism has now become abstracted and liberated, and that his pots are now slab-built into irregular cruciform shapes:

> Not a precise and well formed cross, but crooked, asymmetric, schematic—apparent only after some consideration. By drawing the eye to its irregular but simple volumetric profile it establishes the terms of our experience of the pot. Certainly, Autio must have realized this, for he appears to have begun using these volumetric outlines to waken rather than merely to accommodate the linear power and sensuosity of the surface drawings. He began to *draw* the hollow shapes more completely. . . . Like the animals that primeval man incised and painted on the outcropping walls of caves, Autio's drawings appeared to bring out the innate forms of the underlying clay. This wasn't simply a matter of the surfaces illustrating what their forms already conveyed—though in weaker works this does occur—but one of empathy between their effects.[31]

Younger potters have entered the field of figural vessels and have produced some new "perspec-

tives''—in both the figurative and literal sense of the word. Akio Takamori combines drawing *on* his pots and the notion of the pot *as* a drawing. He has released the rim of the pot to become a free form, a fluid line with which he can draw the outlines of animals, figures, or heads. The image on the vessel and the shape of the pot merge to become one. In addition, the tight, compressed, envelope-shaped forms create the ideal visual tension for Takamori's erotic exploration of sexual ambiguity. In the work of Anne Kraus we find a set of informally molded vases, cups, saucers, teapots, and compotes that draw from familiar shapes in eighteenth-century Meissen and Sèvres pottery as well as from the more vulgar excesses of the nineteenth century. At first the pots seem disarmingly decorative, but closer inspection of the drawings and legends in the reserved panels reveals the subject matter is both contemporary and disturbingly personal—dealing with doubt, alienation, despair, and a collection of moments of disappointment and self-doubt.

As the illustrations to this chapter attest, there are many more artists working on this aspect of the decorative vessel. Among the works by these artists are Wayne Higby's bowls, with their elusive play with perspective and the marrying of inside and outside. Using the dry, transparent manner of fresco, Lidya Buzio paints the sensual, burnished surfaces of her tensely curving pots with a beehive of "inner" architectural volumes. Her literal subject matter is the SoHo roofscape, but her real interest is in creating the effect of plunging deep into the pictorial interior of the vessel by painting architectural perspectives on curved surfaces. Christina Bertoni's constellation bowls appear like latter-day Mimbres pots in their dramatic use of positive and negative. They seem to serve a similar symbolic function in trying to locate man between the tangible and the universal. Richard Notkin's teapots use another aspect of pictorialism. The teapots become representational images of other things. Drawing from the tradition of late–Ming Yixing teapots, he has created a series of provocative works that deal with political issues. The *Cooling Towers Teapot* functions with symbolic clarity. The thought of steaming tea pouring from this object is an image of immediate potency.

The pottery of Adrian Saxe does not fall into the category of either the "new decorative vessel" or the pictorialization of the vessel. Even though the pots are highly decorative and employ pictorial elements, Saxe's work is about something else altogether—a kind of supermannerist collaging of style, cultural appropriation, and witty irony. With Saxe this becomes a confusing combination in which, within a single piece, one decorative device appears simply for its aesthetic appeal (i.e., its beauty), while other elements are suffused with symbolism, literal meanings, and sharp satire. Peter Schjeldahl sees this mixture of beauty and content as making Saxe's pots "glamorous and untrustworthy, like a pedigreed dog that has been known to bite."[32]

A case in point is the *Untitled Jar* (1985) that was exhibited in Los Angeles. In the review of the exhibition in the *Los Angeles Herald Examiner,* Knight remarked on the symbolism in the work and how Saxe was able to incorporate a sybaritic enjoyment of Sèvres pottery into a social and political matrix: "One of the finest pieces is a luxurious royal blue vessel decorated with a golden fleur-de-lis and crowned by a spherical bomb with a gaily upturned fuse. The crazed lust for Sèvres porcelain by the French monarchy—and the subsequent economic chaos brought on by overindulgence of monumental

TOP RIGHT: **Anne Kraus** I'm Always Here Teapot, *1986. Glazed earthenware, height 10". Collection Hope and Jay Yampol.*

BOTTOM RIGHT: **Anne Kraus** Patience/Ambition Vase, *1986. Glazed earthenware, height 9". Private collection.*

Adrian Saxe Untitled Jar, 1985. *Porcelain and stoneware with glazes and overglaze, height 22". Collection Gary McCloy.*

proportions—has long been recognized as one of the primary matches that lit the fuse of the French Revolution."[33]

Certainly the identification of Sèvres porcelain as one of the more *visible* aspects of France's social irresponsibility does give a subtle political edge and unease to Saxe's use of Sèvres—and other court porcelains—as one of his primary motifs. The use of gold luster, remarkably beautiful silver and platinum tracings, and jewel-like glazes is deliberately subversive. Saxe enjoys these surfaces for their decadence while at the same time is happy with the fact that their opulence will set many teeth on edge and raise social issues. This is part of their inherent tension.

In examining Saxe's work Schjeldahl came up with the term "the smart pot." His comments are primarily directed toward the work of Saxe but they are broadly instructive and point the direction in which the vessels of the eighties are already beginning to move:

> The smart pot is an academic object positing an imaginary academy, the brains of an all-embracing civilization. The smart pot is so removed from innocence, so thoroughly implicated in every received notion of nature and culture, so promiscuous in its means and open in its ends, that it's almost innocent all over again—like Magellan leaving by the front door and circumnavigating the globe to come in the back. The smart pot is tantalizing rather than pleasing. It hangs fire. It is not "art." The smart pot X-rays the hoary art/craft distinction to reveal its confusion of values: values of prestige fouling up values of use. . . . The smart pot accepts the semiotic fate of everything made by human beings, the present wisdom that every such thing is consciously or unconsciously *a sign*. Given the choice, the smart pot opts to be conscious. It represses no meaning, however disturbing.[34]

TOP RIGHT: **Adrian Saxe** Untitled Bowl, 1983. Porcelain and raku, height 18". Collection Al and Mary Shands.

BOTTOM RIGHT: **Adrian Saxe** Teapot, 1983. Porcelain, glaze, overglaze, height 10". Collection George and Dorothy Saxe.

BELOW: **Ron Nagle** Blue Waltz, 1985. *Earthenware with china paint, height 3". Collection Daniel Jacobs.*

FAR LEFT TOP: **John Gill** Ewer #9, 1986. *Stoneware, height 12½". Courtesy Grace Borgenicht Gallery, New York.*

FAR LEFT BOTTOM: **Anna Silver** Untitled Vessel, 1985. *Glazed earthenware, height 18". Private collection.*

LEFT TOP: **Patrick Loughran** Untitled Plate, 1987. *Glazed terra-cotta, height 3½". Collection the artist.*

LEFT BOTTOM: **James Lawton** Oval Jar with Bowl, 1985. *Raku, height 13". Private collection.*

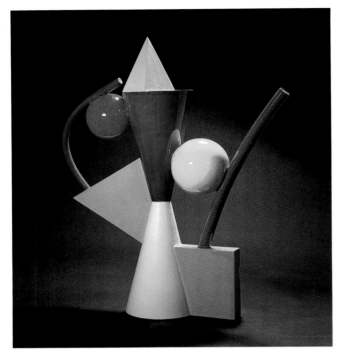

LEFT: **Peter Shire** Hourglass, 1983. Glazed earthenware, height 23". Courtesy Saxon Lee Gallery, Los Angeles.

BELOW: **Dorothy Hafner** Round about Punch Bowl with Ladle, 1986. Slab built, hand-painted porcelain, height 8½". Collection the artist.

RIGHT: **Kenneth Ferguson** Rabbit Basket, 1986. Black stoneware, salt fired, height 18". Collection Connie and Adrian Saxe.

With the increasing sense of the vessel as a separate and distinct art format has come the idea that the ideal home for the potter in the eighties is *not* the fine arts but the decorative arts. To some potters, after years of trying to win over the fine arts (and having achieved a little success), this seems to be a form of heresy—a retrogressive view. But, in fact, it has many benefits. As both Perreault and Schjeldahl have noted, the excitement of the pot is its very "outsider" quality, that it presents ideas, values, and issues that cannot be dealt with in the fine-arts establishment. Full membership in the fine arts would require the potter to give up many of the qualities that form the most intriguing aspect of the ceramics tradition. With a few exceptions, most potters work out of the decorative arts as their *base* and primary source of inspiration. As always, there are exceptions, and some nominal vessels, notably those of Arnold Zimmerman, have little to say about pottery and, given their scale (up to eight feet in height), reflect the artist's use of the vessel as an image for sculpture.

There is a growing trend toward examining the fine and decorative arts as equal but separate elements. The Museum of Modern Art's 1986 exhibition *Vienna 1900* is an excellent case in point, showing the period as a cultural entity that encompassed painting, sculpture, decorative arts, and architecture. Another example is the Art Museum of the Carnegie Institute, which now installs contemporary decorative arts and painting in the same halls. These developments, which are being emulated by other institutions, mean that the potter, while retaining his or her separateness, can look forward in the future to being integrated into major exhibitions and museums without having to kowtow to fine-arts formalism.[35] This ability to occupy the cusp between the fine and decorative arts will ultimately give the potter the greatest creative freedom and expressive potential.

In looking back over the past decade at the extraordinary progress of American ceramics, one cannot but wonder about the future of the medium.

The collector Fred Marer once referred to the activity of the historian as "predicting the past," which, even with all the facts at hand, is a perilous undertaking. Predicting the future is even more foolhardy. Yet it is always intriguing to peer over the wall of time and imagine what lies ahead. First, one perceives that the process of selection through the marketplace will continue and may become even more exclusive and restricted than it is today. As the collectors become more literate, they grow more sophisticated and demanding in their tastes. At the same time, rewards will increase for those whose level of achievement keeps them in the active arena.

For the ceramic sculptor the best scenario for the future might well be the dissolution of the "ceramic sculpture" movement and the integration of its best artists into the fine-arts mainstream. For the potter, a degree of aloofness and distance from the fine-arts embrace seems appropriate. This should not be seen as a gesture of dismissal, envy, or fear, but rather as one of independence and caution. If the trend of declining studio programs in the universities continues, the numbers in the ceramics movement (already radically lower than in the late seventies) will continue to diminish. This will cause new economic problems and solve some of the current ones. With fewer potters in the market, those who produce superior functional wares will be able to restore a once lucrative marketplace.

The major problem in this projection for American ceramics will be the young ceramist. Most of those who are today producing their mature work were supported during their formative periods by the educational institutions. Others survived by making objects for the more commercial "middle" market for crafts. Neither option is as open today, and thus the ceramist coming out of the art departments faces a tougher situation. He or she is usually too underdeveloped for the art market and has little chance of a teaching post. To some extent, attrition is healthy. American ceramics at the beginning of this decade had become bloated, with talentless ceramists being churned out year after year by over 450 graduate and postgraduate ceramics programs. So, after a period of oversupply, the current slimming program is healthy, but only to a point. The current generations that are surveyed in this book will carry ceramics into the twenty-first century with energy and literacy. Thirty years from now, however, the field may find itself losing continuity unless means can be found to bridge the present and the future for the young ceramist. Maintaining levels of achievement in American ceramics will always be the first priority of the goals for tomorrow, but this must now share its place on the agenda with a pedagogic imperative—making sure that there will be a new generation to whom the ceramic baton can be passed.

Arnold Zimmerman Five Ceramic Vessels, *1982. Stoneware, stains, height 72". Everson Museum of Art, Syracuse, New York. Gift of Lucia Beadel, Edward Beadel, Jr., and Lucia Wisenand in memory of Edward F. Beadel.*

NOTES

CHAPTER ONE 1876–89

1 Isaac Clarke, *Art and Industry* (Washington, D.C., Government Printing Office, 1885), 18–20.

2 See Carol Macht, *The Ladies God Bless 'Em* (Cincinnati: Cincinnati Art Museum, 1976), 7.

3 Among the students in the class were Mrs. William Dodd, Mrs. George Dominick, Miss Alice B. Holabird, Mrs. Charles Kebler, Mrs. Harriet Leonard, Mrs. A. B. Merriam, Miss Clara Chipman Newton, and Miss Julie Rice. These artists remained involved in china painting after the class was disbanded and were the founding members of the Cincinnati Pottery Club. See Mary Louise McLaughlin, "Miss McLaughlin Tells Her Own Story," *The Bulletin of the American Ceramic Society* 17 (May 1938), 218. The article is an extract from a paper read at the meeting of the Porcelain League, Cincinnati, Ohio, April 25, 1914.

4 The pioneer artist-potter Ernest Chaplet (1835–1909) developed the technique of *procès barbotine*, painting under a clear glaze with a liquid mixture of clay and oxides (pigments), in the 1860s while he was working for the *maître faïencier* Laurin of Bourg-la-Reine, France. A chance meeting with the artist Félix Bracquemond during the siege of Paris in 1872 led to Chaplet's being invited to join the Haviland Auteuil studio in Paris some years later. The studio, under the artistic direction of Bracquemond, provided an open, creative environment for various artists, painters, sculptors, and ceramists to work on the production of unique art wares. Chaplet introduced his *procès barbotine* to the studio and later succeeded Bracquemond as director. The works became known by the misnomer "Limoges faience" because of the sponsorship of the studio by Haviland of Limoges. See Jean d'Albis, "La Céramique impressioniste à l'atelier de Paris-Auteuil (1873–1885)," *Cahiers de la céramique* 41 (1968), 32–44, and *Ernest Chaplet* (Paris: La Presse de la Connaissance, 1976).

5 R. H. Soden Smith, *Reports on the Philadelphia International Exhibition of 1876* (London, 1877), 464. Smith was one of the few who reported favorably on American ceramics, commenting that "the self reliance, which is so marked a characteristic of the American, has strikingly come out in the progress of this industry." For further information on works shown at the exposition, see J. G. Stradling, "American Ceramics and the Philadelphia Centennial," *Antiques* (July 1976), 146–58. For an understanding of the conflicting decorative-arts influences and styles of the time, also see Alice C. Frelinghuysen, ed., *In Pursuit of Beauty: Americans and the Aesthetic Movement* (New York: The Metropolitan Museum of Art, 1986).

6 See McLaughlin (1938), 219.

7 Ibid.

8 Ibid. For an illustration of the wares described, see Macht (1976), 34.

9 Ibid.

10 Clara Chipman Newton, "The Porcelain League of Cincinnati," paper read at the Porcelain League Breakfast in honor of its twentieth birthday, January 10, 1914. The manuscript is lodged with the Historical and Philosophical Society of Ohio, Cincinnati; extracts are published in the *Bulletin of the American Ceramic Society* 18 (November 1939), 445.

11 See "War among Potters, T. J. Wheatley Secures a Patent on American Limoges," *Cincinnati Daily Gazette*, October 7, 1880. Nichols added that Wheatley "might as well get a patent for wood carving and that I might with better reason get out a patent on drawing dragons on vases." However, in 1893 the Nichols/McLaughlin rivalry flared up over an entry in the catalogue to the Cincinnati Room of the Woman's Building at the World's Columbian Exposition. The introduction credited McLaughlin with discovering the technique on which the Rookwood wares were based, and William Watts Taylor, the manager of Rookwood, demanded that the reference be removed. McLaughlin wrote to Nichols asking for clarification. Nichols replied, denying Rookwood's indebtedness to McLaughlin, a petty but not uncharacteristic move on Nichols's part that caused McLaughlin some anguish. In her Porcelain League address in 1914, McLaughlin bemoaned that she had been "credited with having done what I had never claimed to do [initiating the pottery-decorating craze] while the acknowledgement of what I had done was withheld" (Macht [1976], 64, and McLaughlin [1938], 219).

12 Clara Chipman Newton, "The Early Days of Rookwood," *The Bulletin of the American Ceramic Society* 18 (November 1939).

13 Kenneth Trapp, *Ode to Nature: Flowers and Landscapes of the Rookwood Pottery 1880–1940* (New York: Jordan-Volpe Gallery, 1980), 23. Trapp's essay is an informative examination of the stylistic concerns and influences of the Rookwood Pottery.

14 Newton (1939), 445. The comment refers to the location of the first pottery alongside the Ohio River. Nichols had chosen the site because she thought that clay could be brought in economically by barge. In fact, only one such delivery was arranged, and ironically the barge arrived when the water had fallen so low that the pottery was left high and dry. The cost of hauling the clay across the riverbed was as much as it would have been from the railway station. The siting was also alongside a railway and was appallingly dirty and unsuitable for a pottery. In 1892 Rookwood moved to spacious new premises on Mount Adams. The building still stands but was converted into a discothèque, with the bottle kilns serving as cubicles for a hamburger restaurant.

15 Japanese art played a strong role in Nichols's artistic development. Her introduction came through the gift in 1875 of "some little Japanese books of design," which were almost certainly Katsushika Hokusai's *Manga*. These prepared her for the beauty of the Japanese pottery exhibit at the Centennial, where, Nichols wrote, she "first felt a desire to have a place of my own where things could be made." In 1878 her husband, George Ward Nichols, an early enthusiast of the Orient, published *Pottery, How It Is Made, Its Shape and Decoration, Instructions for Painting on Porcelain and All Kinds of Pottery with Vitrifiable and Common Oil Colors* (New York: G. P. Putnam's Sons). The book includes six illustrations of suggested pottery designs by his wife taken almost directly from the *Manga*, which remained the primary source for Nichols's pottery creations. Her intensely personal art expression had a strong influence on the early decorators at Rookwood, especially Albert R. Valentien, and created a climate of acceptance for Oriental aesthetic ideals in the pottery. See Kenneth Trapp, "Japanese Influence in Early Rookwood Pottery," *Antiques* (January 1973), 193–97, and Kenneth Trapp, "Maria Longworth Storer: A Study of Her Bronze Objets d'Art in the Cincinnati Art Museum" (Master's thesis, Tulane University, 1972).

16 Fry adapted a mouth atomizer for the application of slips. This allowed the decorator greater freedom and resulted in the development of Standard Rookwood. Taylor was later to regret his advice that Fry patent the technique. She was granted her patent in 1889. Later, while on the staff of the

Lonhuda Pottery in Steubenville, Ohio, she made an attempt to deny Rookwood the use of the technique. The court ruled against Fry in 1898 on the grounds that it was simply the new application of an old tool. See Kenneth E. Smith, "Laura Anne Fry: Originator of Atomizing Process for Application of Underglaze Color," *The Bulletin of the American Ceramic Society* 17 (1938), 368–72.

17 See William Walton, "Charles Volkmar, Potter," *The International Studio* 36 (January 1909), lxxv–lxxx; and Mary G. Humphries, "Charles Volkmar," *The Art Amateur* (January 1883), 42–43.

CHAPTER TWO 1890–99

1 See Eileen Boris, *Art and Labor* (Philadelphia: Temple University Press, 1986), 32. Boris's study is an in-depth look at the impact of the Arts and Crafts Movement on modern American culture and clearly explains the manner in which the various societies were formed and organized.

2 The influence of Dutch ceramics has been little explored. The American ceramists were aware of the prophetic work taking place at Rozenburg Potters, The Hague. As early as 1900 in Zanesville, Ohio, J. B. Owens was producing wares that were apparently modeled on the lines of the Rozenburg Art Nouveau and given the inappropriate title "Henri Deux." The title was from the French Orion ware (with which the work had no technical or stylistic relationship) and was probably selected as a red herring to detract from the real source of the plagiarism. See Marion John Nelson, "Art Nouveau in American Ceramics," *The Art Quarterly* 26 (1963), 454; and Frederick Rhead, "Some Dutch Pottery," *The Artist* 24 (1899), 34–40, 64–73.

3 See Newton (1939), 446.

4 Frackelton's involvement with ceramics began in 1883, when she established the Frackelton China and Decorating Works in Milwaukee, Wisconsin, where her trained decorators produced from 1,500 to 2,000 pieces a week. She eventually turned to stoneware to take advantage of local clays. The use of salt-glazed decorative stoneware was rare during the Arts and Crafts period, and the only other pottery producing these kinds of wares was the Graham Pottery in Brooklyn, New York. Paul Evans, *Art Pottery in the United States* (New York: Charles Scribner's Sons, 1974), 105–8, 114–15. The work of Frackelton for the exposition is extensively reported by Richard G. Frackelton

in the *Clay-Worker* 21 (April 1894), 437–38.

5 Newcomb grew, much as had Rookwood, indirectly out of a local ceramic enterprise, the New Orleans Art Pottery. The small pottery, which catered to the needs of the local art league, was run by Joseph Meyer and George E. Ohr. William and Ellsworth Woodward, two artist-teachers, became associated with the venture, which was later taken over by the Art League Pottery Club. From this involvement, Ellsworth Woodward developed his interest in vocational training for women and formed the Newcomb Pottery, with William as its supervisor.

6 The pottery won medals at expositions in Paris in 1900, in Buffalo in 1901, Charleston in 1902, Saint Louis in 1904, Portland in 1905, Jamestown in 1907, Knoxville in 1913, and San Francisco in 1915. See Evans (1974), 185.

7 One of the noteworthy private collections was that of the Detroit connoisseur Charles Freer, who assembled one of the finest collections of Oriental ceramics in the West. The collection is now housed in the Freer Gallery, Washington, D.C.

8 Robertson did not create the design concept for Dedham. He devised the gray/white cracquelle glaze. The inspiration for the stenciled decoration came from the *Rabbit Plate* designed for the Dedham Pottery in 1891 by Joseph Lindon Smith, director of the Boston Museum of Fine Arts, and his wife, Alice.

9 The starting date of the Grueby Faience Company is generally given as 1897, but this was the year of incorporation; in fact, the pottery had already commenced production of architectural faience in 1894. In 1899 Grueby started to use the name Grueby Pottery to differentiate the artware production from tiles. See Martin Eidelberg, "The Ceramic Art of William H. Grueby," *The American Connoisseur* (September 1973), 47–54.

10 W. P. Jervis, *The Encyclopedia of Ceramics* (New York, 1902), 263.

11 See Gabriel Mourey, "The Potter's Art: With Especial Reference to the Work of Auguste Delaherche," *The Studio* 12 (1898), 112–18. Mary Chase Perry gives an account of Grueby's contact with Delaherche in "Grueby Potteries," *Keramik Studio* (1902), 250–53. Grueby wrote to Delaherche about purchasing some of his work and received a letter in reply with some ink sketches of

pots that Grueby found a trifle too expensive for his tastes. "Yet," claimed Perry, "[Grueby] is no more in Delaherche's debt than are all of us to one who has produced works of beauty which continue to be a stimulus and inspiration." They proved to be a particular inspiration to Perry as well and so her support of Grueby was partly a defensive act on her part. Some Grueby scholars, notably Robert Blasberg, discount the importance of Delaherche.

12 Robert Blasberg, *Grueby* (Syracuse, N.Y.: Everson Museum of Art, 1981), 7.

13 Ibid., 9. Blasberg provides an informative description of the process:

> The durable clay was formed into vessels by the following steps. Once the bearded potter had finished throwing the piece it was left to dry somewhat and then passed onto the modelling squad. The young women in the squad were graduates of area art schools and were proud of their skills. Their first attack on the damp piece was to incise a freehand outline of the specified relief, drawing lightly with a small applewood instrument. Next they would roll out some of the outlining fillets as though planning to build a delicate coil-method piece. Each fillet (about the size of a knitting needle) was then pressed into the vessel wall and worked in along with the inside edge to simulate the body of the form while being rounded up on the outer edge for maximum contrast to the background. Whether leaves or flowers, the relief elements were formed in much the same way. The tricky part of the technique was to start the wall clay and relief clay at the same degree of moistness and keep them that way during the modelling. If one became drier than its partner, the proper bond could not be effected and the relief would never become an integral part of the vessel structure. The girls were under no constraint to vary the design a little for "creative" effect. Uniformity facilitated ordering from the company catalogue.

14 Adelaide Alsop Robineau, "Mary Chase Perry," *Keramik Studio* 10 (1905), 217.

15 McLaughlin (1938), 219.

16 Mary Louise McLaughlin, "Losanti-

ware," *The Craftsman* 3 (December 1902), 187.

17   See Adelaide Alsop Robineau, "Royal Copenhagen Porcelain," *Keramic Studio* 3 (May 1901), 11, in which she wrote: "Europeans have thus far the monopoly of artistic porcelain, but there is no reason why it should be so, as we have in this country large deposits of kaolin and all materials necessary for the manufacture of the best porcelains. . . . There is among our decorators such a strong feeling that the time has come to give up the old styles of decoration and turn to more serious and thorough work, that undoubtedly the next generation will see the birth of artistic porcelain manufactories on this side of the Atlantic." This quote is of particular interest, as we shall discover in the next chapter, because it reveals Robineau's own hidden agenda.

18   See George E. Ohr, "Some Facts in the History of a Unique Personality," *Crockery and Glass Journal* 54 (December 1901), 123–25. All statements by Ohr that are otherwise unascribed are from this source.

19   Paul E. Cox, *Ceramic Age* 25 (April 1935), 140.

20   For a fuller statement of Ohr's aesthetic importance, see Garth Clark, "George E. Ohr," *Antiques* 78 (September 1985), and other writings on Ohr by the author.

21   See John Perreault, "Either Ohr," *The Village Voice*, March 5, 1985.

22   Taken from a critical lecture on the *Arts and Crafts Exhibition* reported in the *Buffalo Express*, April 21, 1900. Ohr's response appeared in *Crockery and Glass Journal* 53 (1901).

23   Quoted from Paul Evans, "Reflections of Frederick Hurten Rhead," *Pottery Collectors Newsletter* 9 (September/October 1980), 45.

24   Ohr (December 1901), 123–25.

25   Robert Blasberg, *George E. Ohr and His Biloxi Art Pottery* (Port Jervis, N.Y.: Carpenter, 1972), 21.

CHAPTER THREE 1900–09

1   See Herbert Peck, "Rookwood Pottery and Foreign Museum Collections," *The Connoisseur* 172 (September 1969), 43–49; and "Some New Designs and Methods in Rookwood and Grueby Faience," *The Paris Exhibition*, in *The Art Journal*, special extra number, June 1900, pt. 2 (London: Virtue, 1900), 60.

2   Oscar Lovell Triggs, *Chapters in the History of the Arts and Crafts Movement* (Chicago: Bohemian Guild of Arts and Crafts, 1902), 161.

3   For a review of the Paris exhibition, see *Glass and Pottery World* 11 (June 1903), 43. The Louisiana Purchase International Exposition is discussed in *Keramik Studio,* May 1905, 8.

4   Artus Van Briggle, quoted in Barbara M. Arnest, "Van Briggle, Several Perspectives," *Van Briggle Pottery: The Early Years* (Colorado Springs: Fine Arts Center, 1975), 13.

5   See Martin P. Eidelberg, "Tiffany Favrile Pottery: A New Study of a Few Known Facts," *The Connoisseur,* September 1968, 57–61.

6   In his study "Art Nouveau in American Ceramics," *The Art Quarterly* 26, no. 4 (1963), Marion John Nelson highlighted the prophecy of the Bennington Parian wares, but concluded that the pieces produced about 1850 were "too early" to be considered "proto–Art Nouveau." This seems to be an unduly rigid manner of looking at the work. The wares, particularly in the "cornfield" designs illustrated here, anticipate Art Nouveau to an extraordinary degree and are closer to the grammar of the style than are the much-vaunted earthenwares by Grainger and Company and the porcelains of the Royal Porcelain Works of Munich. The latter were exhibited in the 1851 *Great Exhibition* at the Crystal Palace in London and have been used by several historians as examples of the first stirrings of the Art Nouveau style. These wares are illustrated and discussed in S. Tschudi Madsen, *Sources of Art Nouveau* (Oslo: Aschehoug, 1956), and in Hugh Wakefield, "Ceramics," in *Late Nineteenth-Century Art: The Art, Architecture, and Applied Art of Pompon's Age,* ed. Hans Jurgen Hansen (New York: McGraw-Hill, 1972).

7   See Kirsten Hoving Keen, *American Art Pottery* (Wilmington: Delaware Art Museum, 1978), 31–32. Keen describes the style as being "essentially structural with the decoration rising in low relief" as opposed to European Art Nouveau, which is simplistically described as comprising "exuberant whiplash designs." The French—and to an extent the Belgian and Dutch—forms of Art Nouveau did employ the distinctive linear energy in their work. But the structural qualities that Keen identifies as American were equally popular in Europe, particularly in the German Jugendstil and Austrian Sezessionstil variants of the style.

In addition, the first style of Art Nouveau, the Franco-Belgian abstract-organic style of Hector Guimard and Henry van de Velde, was also primarily concerned with structural, or constructive, elements. Explorations in these areas occurred many years before their development in the United States.

8   William Burton, "Oriental Influence on Twentieth Century Pottery," *The Pottery Gazette* 44 (1905), 33.

9   Charles T. Harris, lessee of the local Celadon Terra Cotta Company, recommended Alfred, New York, as the site of a ceramic school. A bill founding the school was signed into law by Governor Theodore Roosevelt on April 12, 1900, providing $15,000 for the building and equipment and $5,000 for the first year's maintenance and operation. In June, when the cornerstone was laid, Binns ventured the following prediction: "I see the school thronging with busy workers . . . I hear the roar of kilns . . . see those who dream of graceful form and glowing colors realizing, by the work of the hands, the creations of the brain. I see technical and training schools arise . . . and their professors are men from Alfred." John Nelson Norwood, *Fifty Years of Ceramic Education* (Alfred, N.Y.: New York State College of Ceramics, 1950), 7.

10   The first school in the country, in Columbus, was that of Ohio State University, which was founded in 1894 under the direction of Edward Orton, Jr. A third was established at Rutgers University, New Brunswick, New Jersey, under C. W. Parmelee in 1902. Thereafter ceramic education expanded rapidly.

11   Quoted in Roger Ault, "Mary Chase Perry Stratton and Her Pewabic Pottery," *Great Lakes Informant* 1, no. 4 (n.d.), 6.

12   Frederick Rhead, "Adelaide Alsop Robineau—Maker of Porcelains," *The Potter,* February 1917, 88. Rhead saw this work during a visit to the Robineaus in 1909.

13   Adelaide Alsop Robineau, "Editorial," *Keramic Studio* 1, no. 1 (1899), 1.

14   See Martin P. Eidelberg, "Robineau's Early Design," in *Adelaide Alsop Robineau: Glory in Porcelain,* ed. Peg Weiss (Syracuse, N.Y.: Syracuse University Press, 1981), 43–92. Eidelberg's interrogation of Robineau's early work and its sources is fascinating reading and provides a model for scholarship of this kind.

15   Ibid., fig. 12.

16   Ibid.

17 "The National Arts Club Exhibit of Porcelain and Pottery at the Pan-American," *Keramic Studio* 3 (November 1901), 143.

18 See Susan Frackelton, "Organized Effort," *Keramic Studio* 3 (December 1901), 100–101.

19 See [Adelaide Alsop Robineau], "Copenhagen Porcelains—Bing and Grondahl," *Keramic Studio* 3 (July 1901), 60–61.

20 Samuel Robineau, "Adelaide Alsop Robineau," *Design,* April 1929, 202–3.

21 Ibid., 204.

22 Quoted in Rhead (1917), 87.

23 Thomas P. Bruhn, *American Decorative Tiles 1870–1930* (Storrs, Conn.: The William Benton Museum of Art, The University of Connecticut, 1979), 6. Bruhn provides a concise study of the development of the "art" tile in American ceramics and of its major participants. Also see Everett Townsend, "Development of the Tile Industry in the United States," *The Bulletin of the American Ceramic Society* 22 (May 1943), 126–52.

24 Edwin Atlee Barber, "Recent Advances in the Pottery Industry," *Popular Science Monthly* 40 (January 1892), 307.

25 For a description of Perry's achievements in this area, see both biographies here and the excellent essay by Thomas W. Brunk, "Pewabic Pottery," *Arts and Crafts in Detroit 1906–1976* (Detroit: The Detroit Institute of Arts, 1976), 141–53.

26 Mercer's estate, Fonthill, was acquired by the Bucks County Historical Society in 1969. The estate included three concrete buildings: his home; the museum that housed his Tools of the Nationmakers, a collection of over six thousand hand-tools; and the tileworks, which is operated as a living museum today. In addition, there are a vast number of papers, which have yet to be catalogued and assessed. Some pioneering work has been done on Mercer by the historian Cleota Gabriel Reed under grants from the Philosophical Society and the New York State Council on the Arts. Her study *The Arts and Crafts Ideal* (Syracuse, N.Y.: The Institute for Development of Evolutionary Architecture, 1978) traces the collaboration of architect and artists, involving Mercer, the glassmaker Keck, and the architect Ward Wellington. In late 1987 the University of Pennsylvania Press published a major book on Mercer by Reed.

CHAPTER FOUR 1910–19

1 Paul Evans, "Frederick Hurten Rhead, 'The University City Venture,' " in Weiss, ed. (1981). Evans assembled and edited the article from "Chats on Pottery," an ongoing weekly column that Rhead wrote in *Potters Herald* between 1931 and 1935. All unascribed quotes from Rhead on the University City Pottery are drawn from this source.

2 Lois Kohlenberger, "Ceramics at the People's University," *Ceramics Monthly* 24 (November 1976), 34. For a broader study of University City and its short, troubled history, see Sidney Morse, *The Siege of University City: The Dreyfus Case in America* (Saint Louis: University City Publishing, 1912).

3 Rhead (1917), 86–87.

4 See Martin P. Eidelberg, "Robineau's Early Designs," in Weiss, ed. (1981), 89.

5 See "La Ligue américaine de la femme," *Catalogue des porcelaines Robineau* (Saint Louis: University City Publishing, 1911). The catalogue accompanied Robineau's work to Turin and then to the showings in Paris.

6 See Anna W. Olmsted, "The Memorial Collection of Robineau Porcelains," *Design,* December 1931, 153.

7 For a detailed bibliography of Rhead's writings, see Sharon Dale, *Frederick Hurten Rhead: An English Potter in America* (Erie, Pa.: Erie Art Museum, 1986).

8 Charles Fergus Binns, "In Defense of Fire," *The Craftsman,* March 1903, 369–72.

9 Boris (1986), 189.

10 Martin P. Eidelberg, "The American Pottery Movement—A Critical Analysis," in *Transactions of the Ceramics Symposium 1979,* ed. Garth Clark (Los Angeles: Institute for Ceramic History, 1980), 32.

11 Ibid.

CHAPTER FIVE 1920–29

1 See John Coplans, *Abstract Expressionist Ceramics* (Irvine: University of California, 1966), 18.

2 Frank Lloyd Wright, "In the Cause of Architecture: The Meaning of Materials—The Kiln," *Architectural Record,* June 1928, 561.

3 See Arthur E. Baggs, "The Story of a Potter," *The Handicrafter* 1 (April/May 1929).

4 William I. Homer, "Carl Walters, Ceramic Sculptor," *Art in America* 44 (Fall 1956), 42–43.

5 William M. Milliken, "Ohio Ceramics," *Design,* November 1937, 17.

6 Ross Anderson, "Introductory Essays," in *Diversions of Keramos: American Clay Sculpture 1925–1950* (Syracuse, N.Y.: Everson Museum of Art, 1983), xv. This catalogue, by Anderson and Barbara Perry, the Everson's curator of ceramics, is a thoughtful examination of polychrome sculpture in the United States and includes essays on the life and work of Waylande Gregory, Vally Wieselthier, Viktor Schreckengost, Thelma Frazier Winter, Edris Eckhardt, Russell Barnett Aitken, Walter Sinz, and Carl Walters.

7 The Wiener Werkstätte was a design workshop founded in Vienna in 1903 by the architect Josef Hoffman and the painter-designer Koloman Moser. It rapidly became one of the most significant forces in modern design in Europe. At first, its pottery was produced by Wiener Keramik, a firm founded in 1905 by Michael Powolny and Bertholdt Löffler. Later the Wiener Werkstätte began to employ its own ceramists, and during the 1920s some of the finest ceramists in Austria—Gudrun Baudisch, Hertha Bucher, Matilde Flögel, Erna Kopriva, Dina Kuhn, Kitty Rix, Susi Singer, and Vally Wieselthier—worked with or designed for the firm.

8 Helen Appleton Read, "Metropolitan Museum Opens Current Art Season with Fine Display of Ceramics," *Brooklyn Daily Eagle,* October 14, 1928, 32. The review was later included in the American Federation of Arts, *Critical Comments on the International Exhibition of Ceramic Art* (New York: The American Federation of Arts, 1928).

9 See Vally Wieselthier, "Ceramics," *Design* 31 (November 1929), 101.

10 Quoted in Linda Steigleder, "Ceramics and Design," in *Henry Varnum Poor 1887–1970* (University Park, Pa.: Pennsylvania State University, 1983), 41. The catalogue is an excellent examination of Poor's career and deals with his pottery in considerable depth and with real insight.

11 Ibid., 40.

12 H. Philips, interview with H. V. Poor, 1964, reel-to-reel tape and transcript, Archives of American Art.

13 The American Designers' Gallery was

similar to the American Union of Decorative Artists (AUDA), which was incorporated in the same year. Both were, among other things, to provide marketing support for the artist and to negotiate contracts for work with industry. For further information, see Steigleder (1983); W. K. Storey, ''The Widening Scope of Decorative Art,'' *The New York Times*, March 31, 1929; and the catalogue *The American Designers* (New York: AUDA, 1929).

14   H. V. Poor to Senator William Benton, October 11, 1966, reel 925, frame 873, William Benton Papers, Archives of American Art.

CHAPTER SIX   1930–39

1   Quoted in Ault, ''Mary Chase Perry Stratton,'' 6.

2   The interest in clay as a final material was the result of a growing purism in sculpture concerning the aesthetic of materials. The greatest sin was considered to be to ''mix manners'' and to conceive a work in clay and then translate it into a large, carved piece. This insistence upon truth to materials—as well as the austerity of the times—encouraged artists to look upon fired clay as a final material for certain works. For a study of the sculptural aesthetic of this time, see Daniel Robbins, ''Statues to Sculpture: From the Nineties to the Thirties,'' in Tom Armstrong et al., *200 Years of American Sculpture* (n.p.: Godine in association with the Whitney Museum of American Art, 1976), 113–59.

3   Lincoln Kirstein, *Figures and Figurines by Elie Nadelman* (New York: Hewitt Gallery, 1958), unpaged.

4   David Bourdon, ''The Sleek, Witty and Elegant Art of Elie Nadelman,'' *Smithsonian*, February 1975, 90.

5   Ibid.

6   See Karal Ann Marling, ''New Deal Ceramics: The Cleveland Workshop,'' *Ceramics Monthly*, June 1977, 25–31.

7   See E. W. Watson, ''Waylande Gregory's Ceramic Art,'' *American Artist*, September 1944, 14.

8   Ibid.

9   See Ross Anderson and Barbara Perry, *Diversions of Keramos* (Syracuse, N.Y.: Everson Museum of Art, 1983), 14.

10   The nomenclature of the annual changed over the years. It was inaugurated as the Robineau Memorial Ceramic Exhibition and was held under this title until 1936, when it was titled the National Ceramic Exhibition, later becoming known as the Ceramic National. In addition, the name of the Syracuse Museum of Fine Arts was changed to the Everson Museum of Art in 1968, when the new I. M. Pei building was opened.

11   Anna Wetherill Olmsted, ''The Ceramic National Founded in Memory of Adelaide Alsop Robineau.'' Manuscript, Everson Museum of Art, Syracuse, N.Y., n.d.

12   Although there had been no exhibition in Europe specifically of ceramics, several potters had already had exposure through exhibitions such as the 1930 *Exhibition of American Industrial Arts* at the Röhsska Museum in Göteborg, Sweden, where five potters were featured. For comments on the reception of the American work, see extract of a letter from Gustav Munthe in Olmsted, ''The Ceramic National.''

13   ''The Art with the Inferiority Complex,'' *Fortune* 16 (December 1937), 114.

14   Baggs (1929), 6.

15   Otto Natzler, *Gertrud and Otto Natzler Ceramics* (Los Angeles: Los Angeles County Museum of Art, 1968). The text makes fascinating reading and provides unusually revealing insight into the aesthetic views of an artist.

16   Glen Lukens, ''The New Craftsman,'' *Design*, November 1937, 39.

17   Quoted in Roger Hollenbeck, ''Review,'' *The Bulletin of the American Ceramic Society*, April 1938, 194. The exhibition took place at the Los Angeles County Museum of Art and was arranged by Reginald Poland of the Fine Arts Gallery in San Diego, with Lukens as one of the judges. For additional comments, see ''California Ceramics,'' *Art Digest*, March 15, 1938, 16.

18   For a detailed study of the formative period of studio pottery in California, see Hazel Bray, *The Potter's Art in California: 1885–1955* (Oakland Museum, 1980).

CHAPTER SEVEN   1940–49

1   See Rosalind A. Krauss, ''Magician's Game: Decades of Transformation, 1930–1950,'' in Armstrong et al. (1976), 162.

2   For an appreciation of Schreckengost's work, see James Stubblebine and Martin Eidelberg, ''Viktor Schreckengost and the Cleveland School,'' *Craft Horizons*, June 1975, 34–35, 52–53.

3   Quoted in Elaine Levin, ''Pioneers of Contemporary American Ceramics: Maija Grotell, Herbert Sanders,'' *Ceramics Monthly*, November 1976, 50.

4   For an examination of the Cranbrook ceramic legacy under Grotell, see Martin P. Eidelberg, ''Ceramics,'' in *Design in America: The Cranbook Vision* (New York: Abrams, 1983), 213–35. For a survey of more recent achievement, see L. Dunn Parks, *Cranbrook Ceramics* (Bloomfield Hills, Mich.: Cranbrook Academy of Art, 1983).

5   Interview with Haile's widow, Marianne de Trey, Dartington Hall, Devon, England, summer 1976.

6   ''The Arts of Living,'' *Architectural Forum*, March 1949, 177.

7   Ibid.

8   For a discussion of Wood's early art career and her involvement with the Dada movement, see Francis Naumann, ''Drawings of Beatrice Wood,'' *Arts Magazine*, March 1983; also see Garth Clark and Francis Naumann, *Beatrice Wood: Retrospective* (Fullerton, Calif.: California State University, 1983).

9   Anaïs Nin, ''Beatrice Wood,'' *Artforum*, January 1965, 40.

CHAPTER EIGHT   1950–59

1   Daisetz Suzuki, *Zen and Japanese Culture* (New York: Pantheon Books, 1959), 23–24.

2   In writing about the Zen aesthetic, Alan Watts notes that André Malraux always speaks of the artist's conquering his material, ''as our explorers and scientists also speak of conquering mountains or conquering space. To Chinese or Japanese ears these are grotesque expressions. For when you climb it is as much the mountain as your own legs which lifts you upwards, and when you paint it is the brush, ink and paper which determine the result as much as your own hand.'' See Alan Watts, *The Way of Zen* (New York: Pantheon Books; London: Thames and Hudson, 1957), 174–75. This dualistic attitude that divides spirit from nature and materials is what separates Western aesthetic concepts from those of the East.

3   See Bernard Leach, ''American Impressions,'' *Craft Horizons*, Winter 1950. In response to Leach's comment that the American ceramist was without a taproot, Marguerite Wildenhain wrote in ''An Open Letter to Bernard Leach from Marguerite Wildenhain'' (*Craft Horizons* 13 [May/June

1953]) that, "it ought to be clear that American potters cannot possibly grow roots by implanting Sung pottery or by copying the way of life of the rural population of Japan. Conscious copying of the works of a culture unrelated to the mind and soul of our generation would only produce dubious makeshifts and turn our struggling potters into either dilettantes or pure fakes. As creative craftsmen, we reject the tendency to force our generation into a mold that does not belong to it."

4   See Bernard Leach, *Belief and Hope* (Saint Ives, Cornwall, England: Saint Ives Council, 1968), 4.

5   Sidney Cardozo, "Rosanjin," *Craft Horizons*, April 1972, 65. Rosanjin isolated himself from the rest of the "folk" potters. For instance, when designated by that eminent ceramic authority Koyama Fujio to receive the *ningen kokuho* award, Rosanjin flatly refused to accept it, thereby reinforcing his aloofness from the ceramic mainstream.

6   From the transcript of a lecture given April 10, 1954, at Mills College, Oakland, California, translated by Noriko Yamamoto. I express my thanks to Viola Frey and Charles Fiske for access to this document.

7   For a brief history, see Dave Depew, "The Archie Bray Foundation," *Ceramics Monthly*, May 1972, 18–23.

8   Voulkos discussed the short but important role of music in the development of a new aesthetic credo in his work in his keynote address at the National Council on Education for the Ceramic Arts Conference in Philadelphia, 1975.

9   Mac McCloud, "Otis Clay: 1956–1957," *Ceramic Arts* 1 (Spring 1983), 2.

10   See Coplans (1966), 8.

11   Ibid., 7.

12   Jim Melchert, "Origins of the Collection," *The Fred and Mary Marer Collection* (Claremont, Calif.: Scripps College, 1974), unpaged.

13   See Conrad Brown, "Peter Voulkos," *Craft Horizons*, October 1956, 12.

14   See Daniel-Henry Kahnweiler, *Picasso's Ceramics* (Hannover: Fackelträger, 1957), 17. Kahnweiler repeats a conversation in his office between Picasso and Henri Laurens in which Picasso commented, "You ought to go into ceramics. It is amazing. I made a head. . . . Well, you look at it from all angles and it is flat. Of course it is the painting that makes it flat." Picasso went

on to muse about the strangeness that painting a canvas gives depth and painting ceramics robs the object of depth.

15   Paul Soldner and Peter Voulkos, "West Coast Ceramics," *Craft Horizons* 26 (July 1966), 26.

16   Christopher Knight, "Otis Clay: A Revolution in the Tradition of Pottery," Los Angeles *Herald Examiner*, September 29, 1982. The exhibition took place at the Garth Clark Gallery, Los Angeles.

17   Coplans (1966), 16.

18   Martin Duberman, *Black Mountain: An Exploration in Community* (New York: E. P. Dutton, 1972), 344.

19   Ibid. For further insights into Black Mountain, see Mary Caroline Richards, "Black Mountain College, a Golden Seed," *Craft Horizons*, June 1977, 20–22, 70. Richards was one of the handful of students at Black Mountain who worked seriously in ceramics.

20   See Coplans (1966), 8.

CHAPTER NINE 1960–69

1   Rose Slivka, "The New Ceramic Presence," *Craft Horizons*, July/August 1961, 36.

2   Coplans (1966), 7.

3   Coplans, in an interview with the author, New York, spring 1976.

4   Harold Paris, "Sweet Land of Funk," *Art in America*, March/April 1967, 95.

5   Peter Selz, *Funk Art* (Berkeley: University of California, 1967), 5.

6   Salvador Dalí, "Objets Surréalistes," *La Surréalisme au service de la révolution* (December 1931), 16.

7   William Rubin, *Dada and Surrealist Art* (London: Thames and Hudson, 1969), 9.

8   Suzanne Foley, *A Decade of Ceramic Art, 1962–1972: From the Collection of Professor and Mrs. R. Joseph Monsen* (San Francisco: San Francisco Museum of Art, 1972), unpaged.

9   Quoted in Alfred Frankenstein, "The Ceramic Sculpture of Robert Arneson," *ARTnews*, January 1976, 48.

10   A letter from Arneson to Paul J. Smith of the Museum of Contemporary Crafts dealing with this event is reprinted in *Clayworks: Twenty Americans* (New York: Museum of Contemporary Crafts, 1971).

11   See Neal Benezra, *Robert Arneson—A Retrospective* (Des Moines, Iowa: Des Moines Art Center, 1986), 18.

12   Robert Arneson, quoted in Benezra (1986), 23.

13   Ibid.

14   For a review of the exhibition, see Joseph Pugliese, "Ceramics from Davis," *Craft Horizons* 26 (November/December 1966). The American Craft Council was then called the American Craftsmen's Council.

15   Dennis Adrian, "Robert Arneson's Feats of Clay," *Art in America* 64 (September 1974), 80.

16   See Alfred Frankenstein, "Of Bricks, Pop Bottles and a Better Mousetrap," *San Francisco Sunday Examiner and Chronicle*, October 6, 1974, 37.

17   Comment by Bailey to the author, Porta Costa, California, March 1976.

18   Cynthia Barlow, "Arts Review," *Saint Louis Globe Democrat*, September 19, 1965.

19   Paris (1967), 98.

20   Henry Hopkins, "Kenneth Price, Untitled Ceramic," *Artforum*, August 1963, 41.

21   Quoted in Susan Wechsler, *Low-Fire Ceramics* (New York: Watson-Guptill, 1981), 103.

22   See John Coplans, "Out of Clay: West Coast Ceramic Sculpture Emerges as a Strong Regional Trend," *Art in America*, December 1963, 40.

23   For an investigation of the role of china painting in this new aesthetic, see Richard Shaw, "Beyond the Barriers of Tradition," in *Overglaze Imagery* (Fullerton: Art Gallery, California State University, 1977), 157–60.

24   John Coplans, ed., *Roy Lichtenstein: Documentary Monograph in Modern Art* (New York: Praeger, 1972), 91.

25   Ellen H. Johnson, "The Lichtenstein Paradox," *Art and Artists*, January 1968, 15.

26   Alice Adams, "Exhibitions," *Craft Horizons*, September/October 1966, 42.

27   Most of the collection was given to the American Craft Museum and is now in its permanent collection. The exhibition opened at the National Collection of Fine Arts, Smithsonian Institution, in Washington, D.C., and then traveled nationally and internationally. A book of the same title, by Lee Nordness, was published by the Viking Press, New York, in 1970.

CHAPTER TEN 1970–79

1   Donna Nicholas, "The Ceramic Nationals at Syracuse," *Craft Horizons*, December 1972, 33.

2   Ibid., 31.

3   Evert Johnson, "Two Happenings at Southern Illinois University: 1) Clay Unfired," *Craft Horizons*, October 1970, 39.

4   Tobi Smith, "Clayworks in Progress," Los Angeles Institute of Contemporary Art *Journal*, November/December 1975, 38–47. The event, which was curated by Tobi Smith, included the work of George Geyer, Tom McMillan, Larry Shep, Roger Sweet, and Tom Colgrove.

5   See Everson Museum of Art, *New Works in Clay by Contemporary Painters and Sculptors* (Syracuse, N.Y.: Everson Museum of Art, 1976). The museum had originally intended to curate an exhibition of ceramic works by Picasso, Gauguin, Miró, and others, but found the exhibition too expensive. The "New Works" project replaced this original idea. This event was the second one of its kind in America. The first, which was initiated by *Art in America*, took place in 1963. Twelve artists, directed by the painter Cleve Gray and with the technical assistance of David Gil of Bennington Potters, Vermont, had produced a body of limited-edition ceramics. Those involved in the project were Louise Nevelson, Cleve Gray, Alexander Liberman, Milton Avery, Helen Frankenthaler, David Smith, James Metcalf, Ben Shahn, Jack Youngerman, Leonard Baskin, Seymour Lipton, and Richard Anuszkiewicz. See "Ceramics by Twelve Artists," *Art in America* 52 (December 1964), 27–41, and Richard Lafean, "Ceramics by Twelve Artists," *Craft Horizons* 25 (January 1965), 30–33, 48–49. In addition, the Clay Works Studio Workshop in New York, established by Susan Peterson for nonclay artists to explore clay with ceramists during three-week work sessions, was established as a pilot project in 1973. It was inspired by the collaborative format of June Wayne and the Tamarind Lithography Workshop; the original inspiration came from Rose Slivka, the editor of *Craft Horizons*, who took the concept of a collaborative workshop in clay to the National Endowment for the Arts in 1971 and helped guide its inception. Later a permanent and independent home for the Clay Studio was established in downtown New York, with a capable young "veteran" of the New Works project, James Walsh, as its director. Andrea DiNoto and Léopold Foulem are currently writing a complete study of the role of "visiting" painters and sculptors during this century that will be published in 1989 by Abbeville Press, New York.

6   Hilton Kramer, "Art: Sensual, Serene Sculpture," *The New York Times*, January 25, 1975.

7   Hilton Kramer, "Sculpture—From the Boring to the Brilliant," *The New York Times*, May 15, 1977.

8   Michael McTwigan, *Heroes and Clowns* (New York: Allan Frumkin Gallery, 1979), 11–13.

9   See Harvey L. Jones, *Stephen DeStaebler: Sculpture* (Oakland, Calif.: Oakland Museum, 1974), unpaginated catalogue.

10   Viola Frey, "Artist's Statement," in *Viewpoints: Ceramics 1977* (El Cajón, Calif.: Grossmont College Art Gallery, 1977).

11   For a more detailed examination of the link between Lévi-Strauss's notion of the *bricoleur* and the exploration of this theme in Frey's work, see Garth Clark, "Cracks in the Sidewalk: A Chronological Study of the Art and World of Viola Frey," in *Viola Frey: Retrospective* (Sacramento, Calif.: Crocker Museum, 1981).

12   Claude Lévi-Strauss, *The Savage Mind* (Chicago: The University of Chicago Press, 1962), 22.

13   Harold Rosenberg, "Reality Again," in *Super Realism: A Critical Anthology*, ed. Gregory Battcock (New York: E. P. Dutton, 1975), 139–40. The essay was first published in the *New Yorker* (February 5, 1972).

14   Kim Levin, "The Ersatz Object," *Arts Magazine*, February 1974.

15   See Lukman Glasgow, *Illusionistic Realism as Defined in Contemporary Ceramic Sculpture* (Laguna Beach, Calif.: Laguna Beach Museum of Art, 1977).

16   Thomas Albright, "The Dividing Line between Ceramics and Schlock," *San Francisco Chronicle*, August 21, 1979, 41.

17   Rose Slivka, *The Object as Poet* (Washington, D.C.: Renwick Gallery, National Collection of Fine Arts, Smithsonian Institution, 1977), 12.

18   Kenneth W. Jones, "Richard E. DeVore," *Philadelphia Arts Exchange* 1 (March/April 1977), 7.

19   Andy Nasisse, "The Ceramic Vessel as Metaphor," *New Art Examiner*, January 1976. The title was later taken for an exhibition at the Evanston [Illinois] Art Center in 1977.

20   See Edy de Wilde, "Preface," in *West Coast Ceramics* (Amsterdam: Stedelijk Museum, 1979), 1. Credit must be given to de Wilde's prescience if not to his scholarship. While American museums were ignoring the achievement of the West Coast potters, de Wilde was assembling a collection of masterpieces by Arneson, Voulkos, Notkin, Price, Nagle, Gilhooly, Shaw, and Brady that, for its period, has yet to be matched by any American institution.

21   See Ed Lebow, "Turner," *American Craft* 46 (June/July 1986), 67. The article is an excellent analysis of Turner's development.

22   Ibid.

23   George Woodman, "Ceramics Decoration and the Concept of Ceramics as a Decorative Art," in *Transactions of the Ceramics Symposium 1979*, ed. Garth Clark, (Los Angeles: Institute for Ceramic History, 1980), 107.

24   Discussion between the author and Price, November 21, 1979; the discussion revolved around Price's inclusion in the author's book *American Potters*.

25   See Suzanne Muchnic, "Curios from the Home Folk," *Los Angeles Times*, April 16, 1978, 96.

26   Joan Simon, "An Interview with Kenneth Price," *Art in America* 68 (January 1980), 32.

27   Judy Chicago, *The Dinner Party: A Symbol of Our Heritage* (New York: Doubleday, Anchor Books, 1979), 29.

28   Laurel Reuter, "The Dinner Party: A Personal Response," *The Shards Newsletter* 1, no. 2 (Winter 1980–81), 3.

29   Chicago (1979), 32.

30   Reuter (1980–81).

31   John Ashbery, "Feelin' Grueby," *The New York Times*, March 17, 1980, 56.

32   Donald B. Kuspit, "Elemental Realities," *Art in America*, January 1981, 79, 87.

33   The ICH briefly published the *Shards Newsletter* but functions primarily as a catalyst for the running of the International Ceramics Symposium, which was held at Syracuse University in 1979; at the Waldorf-Astoria, New York, in 1981; in Kansas City in 1983; in Toronto in 1985; and at the Victoria and Albert Museum, London, in 1986. The

symposium now has a permanent home at the Everson Museum of Art, where the event will be presented every three years.

34   The NCECA changed the focus of its conferences after its 1981 conference at San Jose examined the West Coast contribution to ceramics. Although technical panels and papers are still a major interest, the NCECA conferences have increasingly brought in serious scholars, commissioned presentations on history, published transactions of the conferences, and established a journal. The 1985 conference dealt with architectural ceramics; the 1987 conference, at the Everson Museum of Art, discussed the theme "Ceramics and the Art World," reflecting the new priorities.

35   See Clement Greenberg, "The Status of Clay," *The Shards Newsletter* 1, no. 2 (Winter 1980–81). Also published in *Transactions of the Ceramics Symposium 1979*, ed. Garth Clark (Los Angeles: Institute for Ceramic History, 1980).

CHAPTER ELEVEN   1980–the Present

1   The figurative style thrived on the West Coast largely because of Bay Area painters. During the fifties and sixties, the painters David Park, Richard Diebenkorn, Elmer Bischoff, and James Weeks dynamically combined the notion of abstraction and figuration, keeping the tradition of the figure vital long after it had been pronounced dead on the East Coast.

2   Letter from Dianne Feinstein to San Francisco Art Commission, December 4, 1981.

3   William Wilson, "S. F. Exhibit: Clay . . . And Now Moscone," *Los Angeles Times*, April 25, 1986, 86.

4   Hilton Kramer, "Sculpture—From Boring to Brilliant," *The New York Times*, May 15, 1977, D27.

5   Hilton Kramer, "Ceramic Sculpture and the Taste of California," *The New York Times*, December 20, 1981, 31.

6   Arneson, quoted in Susan Wechsler's "Views on the Figure," *American Ceramics* 3, no. 1 (1984): 23.

7   Kramer (1981).

8   Robert Hughes, "Molding the Human Clay," *Time*, January 18, 1982, 66.

9   See Jeff Kelley, "Re Clay," *Arts Magazine*, 56 (March 1982), 77–79; and John Perreault, "Fear of Clay," *Artforum* 21 (April 1982),

70–71.

10   Perreault (1982), 71.

11   See Beth Cofflet, "East Is East and West Is West: The Great Divide," *San Francisco Sunday Examiner and Chronicle*, April 4, 1982, 24–30. Cofflet's article is an indictment of East Coast snobbism. After reviewing the comments of Hilton Kramer, Robert Hughes, and Peter Schjeldahl, she criticizes their writings as a classic case of the territorial imperative, comparing them to the ring-tailed lemur, who, "when threatened by newcomers to his arena, does a handstand, raises his tail and squeezes a perineal gland located near its rear end to mark off its territory and warn off interlopers" (p. 25). She also quotes Kay Larson (art critic for *New York* magazine), who wrote that "California can claim half a dozen art ideas that are wholly its own but getting the East Coast to acknowledge them can be harder than originating them." See Kay Larson, "California Clay Rush," *New York*, January 11, 1982, 41.

12   Michael McTwigan, "A Portrait of Our Time," in *In the Eye of the Beholder: A Portrait of Our Time* (New Paltz, N.Y.: College Art Gallery, State University of New York, College at New Paltz, 1985), 17.

13   William Wilson, "The Art Galleries: Viola Frey," *Los Angeles Times*, March 28, 1986, 10.

14   Mark Shannon, "Michael Lucero: The Unnatural Science of Dreams," *American Ceramics* 5, no. 2 (1986), 33.

15   Matthew Kangas, "Rudy Autio," *American Ceramics* 3, no. 4 (1985), 65. In part, Kangas's attitude has to do with the fact that he is a highly partisan writer, promoting the cause of Seattle ceramic sculpture. Seattle has not produced any vessel makers of national consequence and this, no doubt, contributes to Kangas's unease with the notion of the pot as art.

16   John Perreault, "Feats of Clay," *Soho News*, March 5, 1980, 47.

17   Philip Rawson, "Keynote Address: Echoes Symposium," unpublished paper, 1983, 3.

18   Perreault (1982), 71.

19   Jeff Perrone, "Some Sherds on Pottery," in *Surface/Function/Shape: Selections from the Earl Millard Collection* (Edwardsville, Ill.: Southern Illinois University, 1985).

20   Ibid.

21   George Woodman, "Ceramic Decoration and the Concept of Ceramics as a Decorative Art," in *Transactions of the Ceramics Symposium 1979*, ed. Garth Clark, (Los Angeles: Institute for Ceramic History, 1980), 109.

22   For a description of the installation, see John Perreault, "A Pattern of Exchange," *Soho News*, March 9, 1982, 52.

23   Jeff Perrone, "Betty Woodman: A Working Analysis," in *The Ceramics of Betty Woodman* (Reading, Pa.: Freedman Gallery, 1986), 6.

24   John Russell, "Art: Household Objects Don Mysterious Guises," *The New York Times*, December 18, 1981, 23.

25   Roberta Smith, "Simple Pleasures," *The Village Voice*, December 16, 1981, 17.

26   Michael McTwigan, "Andrew Lord," *American Ceramics* 1, no. 2 (Spring 1982), 58.

27   Christopher Knight, "Lord of the Latter Day Impressionists," *Los Angeles Herald Examiner*, June 5, 1985, E5.

28   Ibid.

29   Ibid.

30   Rudy Autio, "About Drawing," *Studio Potter* 14, no. 1 (December 1985), 49.

31   Edward Lebow, "The Flesh Pots of Rudy Autio," *American Ceramics* 4, no. 1 (1985), 34.

32   Peter Schjeldahl, "The Smart Pot: Adrian Saxe and Post-Everything Ceramics," in *Adrian Saxe* (Kansas City, Mo.: University of Missouri Art Gallery, 1987).

33   Christopher Knight, "Artists' Vessels Sail on a Revolutionary Sea," *Los Angeles Herald Examiner*, November 10, 1985, E5.

34   Schjeldahl (1987).

35   For further discussion of this matter, see Garth Clark, "Comment," *American Craft* 46 (December 1985); and Lorne Falk, "Will Ceramics Secede from the Art World?" *New Art Examiner* 13 (May 1986).

CHRONOLOGY

Only major exhibitions have been included in this chronology. For a more definitive listing of ceramics exhibitions and a complete roster of the Ceramic Nationals, please see the appendix "Selected Exhibitions."

1876

Centennial Exposition, Philadelphia. The exhibition of Japanese pottery and French *barbotine* wares has a strong influence on the nascent ceramic-arts movement in America.

Pennsylvania Museum (renamed Philadelphia Museum of Art in 1938) is founded. Under the guidance of the ceramics historian and curator Edwin Atlee Barber, the museum is one of the first to develop a major collection of art pottery. A large part of the collection would later be deaccessioned.

1878

Mary Louise McLaughlin produces the first successful underglaze slip-painted ware.

1879

Formation of the Cincinnati [Ohio] Pottery Club.

McLaughlin receives an honorable mention for her wares at the Exposition Universelle, Paris.

1880

Maria Longworth Nichols (later Mrs. Bellamy Storer) founds the Rookwood Pottery in Cincinnati.

McLaughlin publishes her Cincinnati Limoges technique in the handbook *Pottery Decoration under the Glaze*.

1881

Rookwood School for Pottery Decoration opens in Cincinnati; closes in 1884.

1882

Oscar Wilde visits the Rookwood Pottery.

1883

Laura Anne Fry adapts the atomizer to apply colored slips to greenware.

1884

The Rookwood Pottery discovers the tiger's-eye glaze.

1887

Pennsylvania Museum and School of Industrial Art sponsors the *Pottery and Porcelain Exhibition*, Philadelphia. Rookwood wins two first prizes.

Kataro Shirayamadani joins the Rookwood Pottery.

Rookwood wins special mention at the twelfth Annual Exhibition of Painting on China, London.

1889

The Rookwood Pottery wins a gold medal at the Exposition Universelle, Paris. McLaughlin receives a silver medal for china painting.

1890

Organization of the Keramic Club of San Francisco.

1892

Susan Frackelton forms the National League of Mineral Painters.

Formation of the Chicago Ceramic Association.

Organization of the New York Society of Ceramic Arts.

1893

World's Columbian Exposition, Chicago. Rookwood receives the highest award in ceramics.

Publication of Edwin Atlee Barber's *Pottery and Porcelain of the United States*.

Ceramic Congress held in Chicago.

1894

Ohio State University, Columbus, opens the first school of ceramics in the United States; directed by Edward Orton, Jr.

1895

Establishment of the Newcomb Pottery in New Orleans.

First issue of *Ceramic Monthly*; last issue in 1900.

1897

William Grueby produces his first mat glazes. (Mat glazes had previously been produced on an experimental basis by the Chelsea Keramik Art Works.)

First Exhibition of Arts and Crafts in Boston sets off a popular interest in the Arts and Crafts Movement. Other exhibiting societies form throughout the United States.

1899

American Ceramic Society founded.

Publication of *Keramik Studio*, with Adelaide Alsop Robineau as the editor. It was renamed *Design–Keramik Studio* in 1924, and *Design* in 1930.

1900

Exposition Universelle, Paris; Rookwood, Newcomb, Dedham, and Grueby win honors.

New York School of Clayworking and Ceramics, Alfred University, Alfred, New York, founded, under the direction of Charles Fergus Binns.

1901

Pan-American Exposition, Buffalo, New York.

Artus Van Briggle commences commercial production in Colorado Springs, Colorado.

Publication of the first issue of the *Craftsman* by founder/editor Gustav Stickley.

1902

New Jersey School of Clayworking and Ceramics opens at Rutgers University, New Brunswick, New Jersey, under the direction of C. W. Parmelee.

1903

The Pewabic Pottery founded in Detroit.

1904

Louisiana Purchase International Exposition, Saint Louis, Missouri.

1906

Formation of the Detroit Society of Arts and Crafts.

Organization of the National Society of Craftsmen in New York; it is later merged with the New York Society of Ceramic Arts, by which name it becomes known.

1910

Formation of the School of Ceramic Art at the People's University in University City (a suburb of Saint Louis), Missouri; Taxile Doat is the first director.

The Newark Museum, Newark, New Jersey, under the direction of John Cotton Dana, holds its first exhibition of contemporary art pottery, *Modern American Pottery*. Newark's progressive approach to industrial design and decorative art strongly influences other institutions.

1911

Turin Exposition, Turin, Italy. The American Women's League wins the grand prize for fifty-five porcelains by Adelaide Alsop Robineau. The artist herself receives the Diploma della Benemerenza.

The Newark Museum begins its collection of contemporary ceramics.

1915

Panama-Pacific International Exposition, San Francisco.

1916

Frederick Rhead publishes the first issue of the *Potter*.

1917

Syracuse [New York] University confers the degree of doctor of ceramic sciences on Adelaide Alsop Robineau.

1918

First issue of *American Ceramic Society Journal*.

1922

First issue of the *Bulletin of the American Ceramic Society*, Columbus, Ohio.

First issue of *Ceramic Age*.

Henry Varnum Poor holds his first exhibition of ceramics at Montross Gallery, New York.

1924

Keramik Studio becomes *Design–Keramik Studio*.

1925

Exposition Internationale des Arts Décoratifs et Industriels Modernes, Paris.

1926

American Ceramic Society awards the first Charles Fergus Binns Award for "notable contribution to the advancement of ceramic art" to Marion L. Fosdick, a professor of ceramics at Alfred University.

1927

Annual Exhibition of Work by Cleveland Artists and Craftsmen (the "May Show") creates a new category, Ceramic Sculpture, and awards the first prize to Alexander Blazys.

1928

American Federation of the Arts holds the *International Exhibition of Ceramic Art* at the Metropolitan Museum of Art, New York.

1929

Adelaide Alsop Robineau dies; the Metropolitan Museum of Art, New York, holds a memorial exhibition of her work.

1932

First Robineau Memorial Ceramic Exhibition, at the Syracuse Museum of Fine Arts. In 1932 the entrants are limited to artists from New York State. In 1936 it is renamed the National Ceramic Exhibition and by 1947 is known as the Ceramic National. Held annually from 1932 to 1952, and biennially from 1952 to 1970, the National (the twenty-seventh) was cancelled in 1972. It was revived in 1987.

New York School of Clayworking and Ceramics is renamed New York State College of Ceramics.

The University of Southern California, Los Angeles, offers its first ceramics courses under Glen Lukens.

Waylande Gregory initiates a ceramics course at the Cranbrook Academy of Art, Bloomfield Hills, Michigan. Maija Grotell is appointed head of ceramics in 1938.

1933

Establishment of the federal Welfare Art Program of the Works Progress Administration. In 1935 Edris Eckhardt becomes director of the WAP's Ceramic Sculpture Division.

Scripps College, Claremont, California, offers its first ceramics course, under William Manker.

1934

Charles Fergus Binns dies.

1935

The Metropolitan Museum of Art, New York, holds a memorial exhibition of Binns's work.

California Pacific International Exposition, San Diego.

1936

Laura Andreson revives ceramics education at the University of California, Los Angeles. Pottery had been first offered as a course in 1920, under Olive Newcomb, and later discontinued.

1937

Contemporary American Ceramics exhibition tours Helsinki; Göteborg, Sweden; Copenhagen; and Stoke-on-Trent, England, and is then shown at the Whitney Museum of American Art, New York.

1938

Waylande Gregory creates *The Fountain of Atoms* for the New York World's Fair. The fountain consists of twelve figures, each weighing over a ton. He also creates *American Imports and Exports* for the General Motors Corporation.

First California Ceramics Exhibition, organized by William Manker, Glen Lukens, and Reginald Poland. Repeated in 1939.

1939

World's Fair, New York.

Golden Gate International Exposition, San Francisco.

Aileen Osborne Webb organizes the Handcraft League of Craftsmen, which merges with another organization to become the Handcraft Cooperative League of America. Renamed on several occasions, the latter is finally named the American Craft Council in 1979. The ACC would become the primary institution for the craft media, with a membership of over forty thousand craftspersons.

1941

First issue of *Craft Horizons* published by the Handcraft Cooperative League of America. The publication is renamed *American Craft* in 1979.

1945

William Manker establishes the Scripps College Annual Ceramic Exhibition. Continued to the present, by Rick Petterson and Paul Soldner, the exhibition is the longest continual ceramics annual in the United States.

F. Carlton Ball organizes the Association of San Francisco Potters.

1946

Wichita National Decorative Arts Competitive Exhibit is founded; closes in 1972 and is reinstituted in 1985.

1949

Robert Turner organizes a ceramics course at Black Mountain College, Asheville, North Carolina. The course closes in 1956.

1950

Bernard Leach tours the United States for four months and receives the Binns Medal from the American Ceramic Society.

First *Young Americans* exhibition at America House, New York, showing work by craftspersons under thirty years of age. From 1971 on it is held at the Museum of Contemporary Crafts, New York.

1951

Archie Bray Foundation, Helena, Montana, is founded, with Rudy Autio as the resident sculptor and Peter Voulkos as potter. Later directed by Ken Ferguson and David Shaner; the current director is Kurt Weiser. In 1984 the foundation expands and acquires the adjacent brickworks.

1952

Bernard Leach tours the United States with Shoji Hamada and Soetsu Yanagi. The tour is organized by Alix MacKenzie.

1953

International Ceramics Symposium, Black Mountain College, Asheville, North Carolina, with Bernard Leach, Shoji Hamada, Soetsu Yanagi, and Marguerite Wildenhain.

First issue of *Ceramics Monthly*.

1954

Peter Voulkos joins the Los Angeles County Art Institute (later known as the Otis Art Institute).

Rosanjin tours the United States; donates a collection of his work to the Museum of Modern Art, New York; and has an exhibition at the Grace Borgenicht Gallery, New York.

1955

International Ceramics Exposition, Cannes,

France; the gold medal is awarded to Peter Voulkos.

1956

American Craftsmen's Council (formerly the Handcraft Cooperative League of America and now the American Craft Council) establishes the Museum of Contemporary Crafts in New York. It is renamed the American Craft Museum in 1979.

1957

The Clay Art Center is founded in Port Chester, New York.

First National Craftsman's Conference, at Asilomar, California.

1958

World's Fair, Brussels.

1959

International Ceramics Exhibition, Ostend, Belgium; the United States wins the Grand Prix des Nations.

1961

Establishment of the Design Division of the Educational Council of the American Ceramic Society.

1962

Adventures in Art, Fine Arts Pavilion, Century 21 Exposition, Seattle.

1963

Works in Clay by Six Artists, San Francisco Art Institute.

Clay Today, University of Iowa, Iowa City.

1965

Art in America initiates the exhibition *Ceramics by Twelve Artists*, which is presented by the American Federation of Arts, New York.

1966

John Coplans organizes the exhibition *Abstract Expressionist Ceramics* at the University of California, Irvine.

National Council on Education for the Ceramic Arts (NCECA) is founded out of the Design Division of the American Ceramic Society.

1967

Peter Selz organizes the exhibition *Funk* at

the University of California, Berkeley.

First Annual Conference of the National Council on Education for the Ceramic Arts (NCECA), Michigan State University, East Lansing.

John Michael Kohler Arts Center, Sheboygan, Wisconsin, founds its arts and industry program, providing ceramists with four-week residencies at the Kohler ceramic works.

1968

Dada, Surrealism and Their Heritage, the Museum of Modern Art, New York; includes the work of Robert Arneson.

SuperMud, annual ceramics symposium, organized at Pennsylvania State University, University Park; last one held in 1978.

Syracuse Museum of Fine Arts, Syracuse, New York, is renamed Everson Museum of Art.

1969

Objects: USA, exhibition of the Johnson Wax collection; organized by Lee Nordness. Opens at the National Collection of Fine Arts, Smithsonian Institution, Washington, D.C.

1970

Ceramics 70 Plus Woven Forms is held in place of the traditional Ceramic National Exhibition, though later it is apparently interpreted as a Ceramic National.

1972

What is then viewed at the twenty-seventh Ceramic National Exhibition does not take place as a Ceramic National. When jurors Jeff Schlanger, Robert Turner, and Peter Voulkos reject 4,500 entries for this exhibition at the Everson Museum of Art, Syracuse, New York, a compromise exhibition—part invitational, part an assembly of past Ceramic National prize winners—is held. There is no catalogue. The National is revived in 1987.

Sharp-Focus Realism, Sidney Janis Gallery, New York; includes work of Marilyn Levine.

1973

Ceramics International '73, Alberta College of Art, Calgary, Alberta, Canada.

The Carborundum Company establishes the Ceramics Museum, Niagara Falls, New York. It is renamed the Crafts Museum in

1975 and closes in 1976.

Edith Wyle founds the Craft and Folk Art Museum in Los Angeles.

The National Endowment for the Arts establishes a Crafts Program within the Visual Arts Division and awards its first fellowships.

1974

Robert Arneson—Retrospective, Museum of Contemporary Art, Chicago, and San Francisco Museum of Art.

Hunter College, City University of New York, organizes Clayworks Studio Workshops as an artist-in-residence program.

1976

New Works in Clay by Contemporary Painters and Sculptors, Everson Museum of Arts, Syracuse, New York; exhibition and collaboration by Margie Hughto.

1977

First course in modern ceramic art history, Bennington College, Bennington, Vermont.

1978

Peter Voulkos: Retrospective opens at the San Francisco Museum of Modern Art and makes a short national tour that includes its organizer, the Museum of Contemporary Crafts, New York.

1979

Founding of the Institute for Ceramic History (ICH) by Garth Clark. The ICH holds the First International Ceramics Symposium at Syracuse University, New York; organized by Anne Mortimer.

A Century of Ceramics in the United States 1878–1978, Everson Museum of Art, Syracuse, New York. The exhibition travels for three years to, among other locations, the Smithsonian Institution's Renwick Gallery, National Collection of Fine Arts, Washington D.C., and Cooper-Hewitt Museum, New York.

American Crafts Council is renamed American Craft Council; its Museum of Contemporary Crafts becomes the American Craft Museum, and its publication *Craft Horizons* is retitled *American Craft*.

1980

First issue of *Craft International*; founding editor, Rose Slivka.

The National Council on Education for the Ceramic Arts publishes the first issue of the *NCECA Journal*.

1981

Symposium on Scholarship and Language in Craft Criticism, cosponsored by the National Endowment for the Arts and the National Endowment for the Humanities, Washington, D.C.

Second International Ceramics Symposium of the Institute for Ceramic History, the Waldorf-Astoria, New York. The theme of the symposium, organized by Mark Del Vecchio, is "Ceramics and Modernism: The Response of the Artist, Craftsman, Designer and Architect."

Ceramic Sculpture: Six Artists, Whitney Museum of American Art, New York, and San Francisco Museum of Modern Art, attracts hostile reviews from New York critics and provokes national dialogue.

Viola Frey: A Restrospective opens at the Crocker Art Museum, Sacramento, California; an abridged version travels to seven institutions through 1983.

1982

First issue of *American Ceramics*; Michael McTwigan is the founding editor.

A ceramic portrait of slain Mayor George Moscone, commissioned from Robert Arneson, is rejected by the City of San Francisco and causes a national furor.

NCECA: San Jose [California] '82 conference examines the role of the West Coast in American ceramics.

1983

Ceramic Echoes: Historical References in Contemporary Ceramic Art, the Nelson-Atkins Museum of Art, Kansas City, Missouri; presented by the Contemporary Art Society as part of the celebration of the museum's fiftieth anniversary.

The Contemporary Art Society, Kansas City, Missouri, organizes the Third International Ceramics Symposium of the Institute for Ceramic History; coordinated by Lennie Berkowitz.

West Coast Ceramics, at the Anderson Ranch, Aspen, Colorado, a historic week-long conference that brings together Peter Voulkos, Robert Arneson, Ron Nagle, Jerry Rothman, Richard Shaw, Marilyn Levine, Philip Cornelius, Michael and Magdalena

Frimkess, Viola Frey. Garth Clark and Patterson Sims serve as cochairs.

Rudy Autio Retrospective opens in Helena, Montana, prior to a national tour that ends at the American Craft Museum, New York.

1984

Ceramics and Architecture, NCECA Conference, Saint Louis.

1985

Fourth International Ceramics Symposium of the Institute for Ceramic History in Toronto, accompanied by fifty-five exhibits of ceramics, is organized by Anne Mortimer and Margaret Melchiori-Malouf.

American Potters Today, Victoria and Albert Museum, London. The Fifth International Ceramics Symposium of the ICH, organized by Garth Clark and John Huntingford, takes place at the Victoria and Albert Museum in connection with the exhibition. The symposium moves to the Everson Museum of Art, Syracuse, New York, as its permanent home.

Art/Culture/Future, ninth national conference of the American Craft Council, Oakland, California.

Robert Arneson: Retrospective, Des Moines Art Center, Des Moines, Iowa. The exhibition travels nationally to, among other places, the Hirshhorn Museum and Sculpture Garden, Smithsonian Institution, Washington, D.C.; and the Oakland Museum, Oakland, California.

American Craft Museum, New York, reopens in a new building, with the inaugural exhibition *Craft Today: Poetry of the Physical*.

The Everson Museum of Art, Syracuse, New York, opens the Syracuse China Center for the Study of American Ceramics.

New Art Forms Exposition, Navy Pier, Chicago.

1987

Art of Collecting Ceramics, symposium sponsored by *American Ceramics* at Equitable Center, New York.

Ceramics and the Art World, NCECA conference at the Everson Museum of Art, Syracuse, New York.

New Art Forms Exposition: 20th Century Decorative and Applied Arts, Navy Pier, Chicago.

SELECTED EXHIBITIONS

Several thousand exhibitions of American ceramics have taken place in public and private spaces within the last decade alone. This listing of exhibitions is by necessity, therefore, not exhaustive. Exhibitions have been listed if they generated significant publications and/or reviews, if they introduced aesthetic innovation, or if they were otherwise historically significant. International exhibitions have been included when American ceramics played an important role either through a large number of participating American artists or an American artist taking one of the major prizes. Multimedia exhibitions that meet the aforementioned criteria have also been included. Titles and dates of the Ceramic Nationals are given as they appear on the title pages of the exhibition's catalogues. When the titles on the covers of the catalogues do not correspond exactly to the wording on their title pages, both titles are indicated.

1876
Centennial Exposition, Philadelphia.

1879
Exposition Universelle, Paris.

1880
First Annual Reception and Exhibition of the Cincinnati Pottery Club, Frederick Dallas Pottery, Cincinnati.

1887
Pottery and Porcelain Exhibition, Pennsylvania Museum and School of Art, Philadelphia.

1889
Exposition Universelle, Paris.

1890
Tenth (and last) Annual Reception and Exhibition of the Cincinnati Pottery Club, Cincinnati.

1893
World's Columbian Exposition, Chicago.

1897
First Exhibition of Arts and Crafts, Representing the Application of Art to Industry . . . , Copley and Allston Halls, Boston.

1899
First Annual Exhibition of the Society of Arts and Crafts, Copley and Allston Halls, Boston.

1900
Exposition Universelle, Paris.

1901
Pan-American Exposition, Buffalo, New York.
Exposition Internationale de Céramique et Verrière, Saint Petersburg, Russia.
French Ceramic Art, Tiffany's, New York.

1903
Arts and Crafts Exhibitions, Syracuse Museum of Fine Arts (later known as the Everson Museum of Art), Syracuse, New York.

1904
Louisiana Purchase International Exposition, Saint Louis, Missouri.

1910
Modern American Pottery, The Newark Museum, Newark, New Jersey.

1911
Turin Exposition of Decorative Art, Turin, Italy.

1915
Clay Products of New Jersey at the Present Time, The Newark Museum, Newark, New Jersey.
Panama-Pacific International Exposition, Golden Gate Park, San Francisco.

1922
Exhibition of Decorated Pottery, Paintings and Drawings by H. Varnum Poor, Montross Gallery, New York.

1928
American Designers' Gallery Exposition, New York.
International Exhibition of Ceramic Art, The Metropolitan Museum of Art, New York.

1929
Adelaide Alsop Robineau Memorial Exhibition, The Metropolitan Museum of Art, New York.

1931
Exhibition of Contemporary American Ceramics, W. & J. Sloane and Company, New York.

1932
Murals by American Painters and Photographers, The Museum of Modern Art, New York.
Robineau Memorial Ceramic Exhibition, Syracuse Museum of Fine Arts, Syracuse, New York.

1933
Second Annual Robineau Memorial Ceramic Exhibition (National), Syracuse Museum of Fine Arts, Syracuse, New York.

1934
Third Annual Robineau Memorial Ceramic Exhibition (National), Syracuse Museum of Fine Arts, Syracuse, New York.

1935
California Pacific International Exposition, San Diego.
Charles Fergus Binns: Memorial Exhibition, The Metropolitan Museum of Art, New York.
Fourth Annual Robineau Memorial Ceramic National Exhibition (National), Syracuse Museum of Fine Arts, Syracuse, New York.

1936
Contemporary American Ceramics, Syracuse Museum of Fine Arts, Syracuse, New York, traveled to Scandinavia; England; and Whitney Museum of American Art, New York, in 1937.
The Fifth National Ceramic Exhibition (The Robineau Memorial), Syracuse Museum of Fine Arts, Syracuse, New York.

1937
The Sixth National Ceramic Exhibition (The Robineau Memorial), Syracuse Museum of Fine Arts, Syracuse, New York.

1938
First California Ceramics Exhibition, Los Angeles County Museum of Art.
The Seventh National Ceramic Exhibition, Syracuse Museum of Fine Arts, Syracuse, New York.

1939
Decorative Arts, Denver Art Museum.
Golden Gate International Exposition, San Francisco.
New York World's Fair.
Second California Ceramics Exhibition, Los Angeles County Museum of Art.

The Eighth Annual National Ceramic Exhibition, Syracuse Museum of Fine Arts, Syracuse, New York.

1940

Contemporary European and American Decorative Arts, The Toledo Museum of Art, Toledo, Ohio.

The Ninth Annual National Ceramic Exhibition, Syracuse Museum of Fine Arts, Syracuse, New York.

1941

Contemporary Ceramics of the Western Hemisphere: In Celebration of the Tenth Anniversary of the National Ceramic Exhibition, Syracuse Museum of Fine Arts, Syracuse, New York.

1943

America House Gallery—Inaugural Exhibition, America House, New York.

1944

Contemporary American Craft, The Baltimore Museum of Art.

First Scripps College Annual Ceramic Exhibition, Scripps College, Claremont, California.

1946

Maija Grotell/Natzler, The Art Institute of Chicago.

Eleventh National Ceramic Exhibition, Syracuse Museum of Fine Arts, Syracuse, New York.

Wildenhain/Longenecker/Natzler, University of Oregon Museum of Art, Eugene.

1947

Twelfth National Ceramic/Ceramic National Exhibition, Syracuse Museum of Fine Arts, Syracuse, New York.

1948

Modern Design and Craft, Los Angeles County Museum of Art.

Sam Haile Memorial Exhibition, Institute for Contemporary Art, Washington, D.C.

Thirteenth National Ceramic/Ceramic National Exhibition, Syracuse Museum of Fine Arts, Syracuse, New York.

1949

Fourteenth National Ceramic/Ceramic National Exhibition, Syracuse Museum of Fine Arts, Syracuse, New York.

1950

Bernard Leach, Institute for Contemporary Art, Washington, D.C.

First International Exhibition of Ceramic Art, National Collection of Fine Arts, Washington, D.C.

Fifteenth National Ceramic/Ceramic National Exhibition, Syracuse Museum of Fine Arts, Syracuse, New York.

Small Sculptures by Elie Nadelman, Edwin Hewitt Gallery, New York.

Young Americans, America House, New York.

1951

16th Ceramic National, Syracuse Museum of Fine Arts, Syracuse, New York.

Industrie und Handwerk USA, Stuttgart, Germany.

1952

Design for Use, USA, XXI Salon des Arts Ménagers, Grand Palais, Paris.

5000 Years of Art in Clay, Fine Arts Building, Los Angeles County Fair, Pomona, Calfornia.

17th Ceramic National, Syracuse Museum of Fine Arts, Syracuse, New York.

1953

Isamu Noguchi—Ceramics, Bijutsu Shuppan-Sha, Tokyo.

1954

18th Ceramic National, Syracuse Museum of Fine Arts, Syracuse, New York.

1955

California Design, Pasadena Art Museum, Pasadena, California.

International Ceramics Exposition, Cannes, France.

1956

19th Ceramic National, Syracuse Museum of Fine Arts, Syracuse, New York.

Peter Voulkos: Ceramics, Felix Landau Gallery, Los Angeles.

1957

Peter Voulkos, Museum of Contemporary Crafts, New York.

1958

XX Ceramic International, Syracuse Museum of Fine Arts, Syracuse, New York.

Figures and Figurines by Elie Nadelman, Edwin Hewitt Gallery, New York.

World's Fair, Brussels, Belgium.

1959

Amerikanische Keramik, Stuttgart, Germany.

First Paris Biennial, Musée National d'Art Moderne, Paris.

International Ceramics Exhibition, Ostend, Belgium.

Man and Clay, Wight Art Gallery, University of California, Los Angeles.

Peter Voulkos: Bronzes and Ceramics, Stuart-Primus Gallery, Los Angeles.

Peter Voulkos: Ceramic Sculpture and Paintings, Pasadena Art Museum, Pasadena, California.

1960

American Keramik, Antwerp, Belgium.

Ceramics and Sculpture by Robert Arneson, The Oakland Museum, Oakland, California.

Moderne Amerikansk Keramik, Copenhagen, Denmark.

Peter Voulkos: Ceramic Sculpture and Painting, The Museum of Modern Art, New York.

XXI Ceramic National, Syracuse Museum of Fine Arts, Syracuse, New York.

1961

Craft Forms from the Earth: 1000 Years of Pottery in America, Museum of Contemporary Crafts, New York.

1962

Amerikanische Keramik 1960/1962, Prague, Czechoslovakia.

Ceramics 1962, Paul Sargent Gallery, University of Illinois, Chicago.

Contemporary Craftsmen of the Far West, Museum of Contemporary Crafts, New York.

Robert Arneson: Ceramics, Drawings, and Collages, M. H. de Young Memorial Museum, San Francisco.

22nd Ceramic National Exhibition, Syracuse Museum of Fine Arts, Syracuse, New York.

Works in Clay by Six Artists, San Francisco Art Institute Galleries.

1963

Clay Today, University of Iowa, Iowa City.

1964

California Sculpture Today, Kaiser Center, Oakland, California.

Critters/Clayton Bailey, Museum of Contemporary Crafts, New York.

International Exhibition of Contemporary Ceramic Art, National Museum, Tokyo.

23rd Ceramic National Exhibition, Syracuse Museum of Fine Arts, Syracuse, New York.

1965

Ceramics by Twelve Artists, American Federation of Arts, New York.

New Ceramic Forms, Museum of Contemporary Crafts, New York.

Peter Voulkos: Sculpture, Los Angeles County Museum of Art.

1966

Abstract Expressionist Ceramics, Art Gallery, University of California, Irvine.

Ceramic Arts USA 1966, International Minerals and Chemical Corporation, Skokie, Illinois.

Ceramics from Davis, Museum West, American Craftsmen's Council, San Francisco

Ceramic Work of Gertrud and Otto Natzler, Los Angeles County Museum of Art.

John Mason—Ceramic Sculpture, Los Angeles County Museum of Art.

Roy Lichtenstein: Ceramics, Leo Castelli Gallery, New York.

Twenty American Studio Potters, Victoria and Albert Museum, London.

24th Ceramic National Exhibition, Syracuse Museum of Fine Arts, Syracuse, New York.

1967

Alexander Archipenko: A Memorial Exhibition, Wight Art Gallery, University of California, Los Angeles.

Ceramics USA, Art Academy, Spoleto, Italy.

Funk Art, University Art Museum, Berkeley, California.

Maija Grotell, Cranbrook Academy of Art Museum, Bloomfield Hills, Michigan.

Surrealist Paintings and Drawings of Sam Haile, City Art Gallery, Manchester, England.

1968

Dada, Surrealism and Their Heritage, The Museum of Modern Art, New York.

Dedham Pottery and the Earlier Robertson's Chelsea Potteries, Dedham Historical Society, Dedham, Massachusetts.

Gertrud and Otto Natzler Ceramics: Collection of Mrs. Leonard M. Sperry, Los Angeles County Museum of Art.

25th Ceramic National Exhibition, Everson Museum of Art, Syracuse, New York.

1969

Objects: USA, National Collection of Fine Arts, Washington, D.C.

25 Years of American Art in Clay, Art Gallery, Scripps College, Claremont, California.

1970

Ceramics 70 Plus Woven Forms (later appears to have been interpreted as twenty-sixth Ceramic National) Everson Museum of Art, Syracuse, New York.

Laura Andreson: A Retrospective, University of California, Los Angeles.

Unfired Clay, University Museum, Southern Illinois University, Carbondale.

1971

Ceramic Work of Gertrud and Otto Natzler: Retrospective 1940–1971, M. H. de Young Memorial Museum, San Francisco.

Clayworks: 20 Americans, Museum of Contemporary Crafts, New York.

Contemporary Ceramic Art: Canada, U.S.A., Mexico, Japan, National Museum of Modern Art, Tokyo.

Nut Pot or Art without Tears? The Art Center of the World, Davis, California.

Porcelains by Jack Earl, Museum of Contemporary Crafts, New York.

1972

Arts and Crafts Movement in America 1876– 1916, The Art Museum, Princeton University, Princeton, New Jersey.

Ceramic invitational (replaces twenty-seventh Ceramic National), Everson Museum of Art, Syracuse, New York.

Decade of Ceramic Art: 1962–1972, San Francisco Museum of Art.

George E. Ohr and His Biloxi Pottery, J. W. Carpenter, Port Jervis, New York.

International Ceramics 72, Victoria and Albert Museum, London.

Nut Art, University Art Gallery, California State University, Hayward.

1973

Beatrice Wood: A Retrospective, Phoenix Art Museum, Phoenix, Arizona.

Form and Fire: Natzler Ceramics 1939–1972, Renwick Gallery, National Collection of Fine Arts, Smithsonian Institution, Washington, D.C.

Ceramics International '73, Alberta College of Art, Alberta, Canada.

Richard Shaw/Robert Hudson: Works in Porcelain, San Francisco Museum of Art.

Thinking, Touching, Drinking Cup: International Exhibition, Nagoya, Japan.

1974

Baroque '74, Museum of Contemporary Crafts, New York.

California Ceramics and Glass 1974, The Oakland Museum, Oakland, California.

California Design, 1910, Pasadena Center, Pasadena, California.

Clay, Whitney Museum of American Art, Downtown Branch, New York.

Clay Images, California State University, Los Angeles.

Frans Wildenhain Retrospective, University Art Gallery, State University of New York, Binghamton.

Fred and Mary Marer Collection, Scripps College, Claremont, California.

In Praise of Hands, World Crafts Council, Ontario Science Center, Toronto.

John Mason: Ceramic Sculpture, Pasadena Museum of Art, Pasadena, California.

Robert Arneson—Retrospective, Museum of Contemporary Art, Chicago.

Stephen DeStaebler: Sculpture, The Oakland Museum, Oakland, California.

1975

Catalogue of Kaolithic Curiosities and Scientific Wonders, Wonders of the World Museum, Porta Costa, California.

Clayworks in Progress, Los Angeles Institute of Contemporary Art.

Craft Multiples, Renwick Gallery, National Collection of Fine Arts, Smithsonian Institution, Washington, D.C.

Exhibition of Master Potters, Fairtree Gallery, New York.

Frans Wildenhain, Rochester Institute of Technology, Rochester, New York.

Homage to the Bag, Museum of Contemporary Crafts, New York.

Jim Melchert, San Francisco Museum of Art.

1976

American Crafts 76: An Aesthetic View, Museum of Contemporary Art, Chicago.

Art Deco Environment, Everson Museum of Art, Syracuse, New York.

Clay: The Medium and the Method, University Art Museum, University of California, Santa Barbara.

Contemporary Clay: Ten Approaches, Hood Museum of Art, Dartmouth College, Hanover, New Hampshire.

David Gilhooly, Museum of Contemporary Art, Chicago.

The Ladies, God Bless 'Em: The Women's Art Movement in Cincinnati, Cincinnati Art Museum.

New Works in Clay by Contemporary Painters and Sculptors, Everson Museum of Art, Syracuse, New York.

The Object as Poet, Renwick Gallery, National Collection of Fine Arts, Smithsonian Institution, Washington, D.C.

Richard Shaw, Ed Blackburn, Tony Costanzo, Redd Ekks, John Roloff, Art Gallery, California State University, Fullerton.

Soup Tureens: 1976, Campbell Museum, Camden, New Jersey.

200 Years of American Sculpture, Whitney Museum of American Art, New York.

Viktor Schreckengost, Cleveland Institute of Art.

1977

Arts and Crafts in Detroit 1906–1976: The Movement, the Society, the School, The Detroit Institute of Arts.

Beaux-Arts Designer, Gallery of Fine Art, Ohio State University, Columbus.

Ceramic Conjunction 1977, Long Beach Museum of Art, Long Beach, California.

Ceramic Vessel as Metaphor, Evanston Art Center, Evanston, Illinois.

Civilizations, John Michael Kohler Arts Center, Sheboygan, Wisconsin.

Contemporary Ceramic Sculpture, William Hayes Ackland Art Center, University of North Carolina, Chapel Hill.

Educational Exhibit by Professor Clayton Bailey, California State University, Hayward.

Fiber, Metal and Clay, Slusser Gallery, University of Michigan, Ann Arbor.

Illusionistic Realism as Defined in Contemporary Ceramic Sculpture, Laguna Beach Museum of Art, Laguna Beach, California.

Karen Karnes: Works 1964–1977, Hadler/Rodriguez Gallery, New York.

Overglaze Imagery, Art Gallery, California State University, Fullerton.

Perceptions of the Spirit, Indianapolis Museum of Art.

Robert Arneson—Portraits, Allan Frumkin Gallery, New York.

Robert Hudson, The Goldie Paley Gallery, Moore College of Art, Philadelphia.

Roy Lichtenstein Ceramic Sculpture, University Art Gallery, California State University, Long Beach.

Ruth Duckworth, Exhibit A, Evanston, Illinois.

Study in Regional Taste, The May Show 1919–1975, Cleveland Museum of Art.

1978

American Art Pottery 1875–1930, Delaware Art Museum, Wilmington.

Arts and Crafts Ideal: The Ward House, Institute for the Development of Experimental Architecture, Syracuse, New York.

Biloxi Art Pottery of George E. Ohr, Mississippi State Historical Museum, Jackson.

Clay from Molds: Multiples, Altered Castings, Combinations, John Michael Kohler Arts Center, Sheboygan, Wisconsin.

Cowan Pottery Studio, Ohio Public Library, Rocky River.

Jerry Rothman: Bauhaus Baroque, Vanguard Gallery, Los Angeles.

Happy's Curios: Kenneth Price, Los Angeles County Museum of Art.

Mary Frank: Sculpture/Drawings/Prints, Neuberger Museum, State University of New York, Purchase.

New Works in Clay II, Joe and Emily Lowe Art Gallery, Syracuse University, Syracuse, New York.

Nine West Coast Clay Sculptors, Everson Museum of Art, Syracuse, New York.

Peter Voulkos: Retrospective, Museum of Contemporary Crafts, New York.

Ron Nagle: The Adaline Kent Award Exhibition, San Francisco Art Institute Galleries.

Young Americans: Clay/Glass, Museum of Contemporary Crafts, New York.

1979

American Decorative Tiles 1870–1930, The William Benton Museum of Art, The University of Connecticut, Storrs.

Another Side to Art: Ceramic Sculpture in the Northwest 1950–1979, Seattle Art Museum.

A Century of Ceramics in the United States 1878–1978, Everson Museum of Art, Syracuse, New York.

Contemporary Ceramics of Missouri: 1978–1979, Hendren Gallery, Lindenwood College, Saint Charles, Missouri.

The Dinner Party, San Francisco Museum of Modern Art.

Fulper Art Pottery: An Aesthetic Appreciation 1909–1929, Jordan-Volpe Gallery, New York.

Functional Forms in Clay: Four Decades, Henry Art Gallery, University of Washington, Seattle.

Harrison McIntosh: Studio Potter, Rex W. Wignall Museum, Chaffey, California.

Heroes and Clowns: Robert Arneson, Allan Frumkin Gallery, New York.

Jane Ford: Recent Work, Everson Museum of Art, Syracuse, New York.

Margie Hughto: Clay and Paper Works 1978–1979, Nina Freudenheim Gallery, Buffalo, New York.

Northern California Clay Routes: Sculpture Now, San Francisco Museum of Modern Art.

Robert Arneson: Self Portraits, The Goldie Paley Gallery, Moore College of Art, Philadelphia.

Ruth Duckworth/Claire Zeisler, The Goldie Paley Gallery, Moore College of Art, Philadelphia.

Studio Potter: A Question of Quality, Sun Valley Center for the Arts, Sun Valley, Idaho.

Unpainted Portrait: Contemporary Portraiture in Non-Traditional Media, John Michael Kohler Arts Center, Sheboygan, Wisconsin.

Viewpoint: Ceramics 1979, Grossmont College, El Cajon, California.

West Coast Ceramics, Stedelijk Museum, Amsterdam.

West Coast Clay Spectrum, Security Pacific Bank, Los Angeles.

1980

American Porcelain: New Expressions in an Ancient Art, Timber Press, Forest Grove, Oregon.

Betty Woodman: The Storm in a Teacup, Rochester Art Center, Rochester, Minnesota.

Contemporary American Potter: Recent Vessels, Gallery of Art, University of Northern Iowa, Cedar Falls, Iowa.

Contemporary Ceramics: A Response to Wedgwood, Museum of the Philadelphia Civic Center.

Continental Clay Connection, MacKenzie Art Gallery, University of Regina, Regina, Saskatchewan.

For the Tabletop, American Craft Museum, New York.

Marguerite Wildenhain: A Retrospective Exhibition of the Work of a Master Potter, Herbert F. Johnson Museum of Art, Cornell University, Ithaca, New York.

Ode to Nature: Flowers and Landscapes of Rookwood Pottery 1880–1940, Jordan-Volpe Gallery, New York.

Potters' Art in California: 1885–1955, The Oakland Museum, Oakland, California.

Robert L. Pfannebecker Collection, The Goldie Paley Gallery, Moore College of Art, Philadelphia.

Viewpoint Ceramics, 1980, Grossmont College, El Cajon, California.

1981

Centering on Contemporary Clay: American Ceramics from the Joan Mannheimer Collection, Museum of Art, University of Iowa, Iowa City.

Ceramic Sculpture: Six Artists, Whitney Museum of American Art, New York.

Clay Alternatives, Fisher Gallery, University of Southern California, Los Angeles.

Clay Figure, American Craft Museum, New York.

Grueby, Everson Museum of Art, Syracuse, New York.

KLEI, Netherlands Art Foundation, Amsterdam.

Made in L.A.: Contemporary Crafts 81, Craft and Folk Art Museum, Los Angeles.

Minnesota Pottery: A Potter's View, University Gallery, University of Minnesota, Minneapolis.

Painted Clay, John Michael Kohler Arts Center, Sheboygan, Wisconsin.

Richard DeVore, Exhibit A, Chicago.

Richard Shaw/Ceramic Sculpture, Braunstein Gallery, San Francisco.

Ritual and Function, Museum of Art, Rhode Island School of Design, Providence.

Robert Sperry, Erica Williams/Anne Johnson Gallery, Seattle.

Rudolf Staffel, Helen Drutt Gallery, Philadelphia.

Tea Pots USA, Southern Illinois University, Edwardsville.

The Vessel, Delahunty Gallery, Dallas.

Viola Frey: A Retrospective, Crocker Art Museum, Sacramento, California.

William Daley: Selected Works 1954–1982, Massachusetts College of Art, Boston.

1982

Ancient Inspirations—Contemporary Interpretations, Roberson Center for the Arts and Sciences, Binghamton, New York.

Art and/or Craft: USA & Japan, Kanazawa Museum of Art, Kanazawa, Japan.

Clay Bodies: Autio—DeStaebler—Frey, Maryland Institute, College of Art, Baltimore.

Figurative Clay Sculpture: Northern California, Quay Gallery, San Francisco.

Glen Lukens: Pioneer of the Vessel Aesthetic, Art Gallery, California State University, Los Angeles.

Laura Andreson: A Retrospective in Clay, Mingei International Museum of World Folk Art, San Diego, California.

Master Craftsmen, Jacksonville Art Museum, Jacksonville, Florida.

Michael and Magdelena Frimkess: A Retrospective View 1956–1981, Garth Clark Gallery, Los Angeles.

Otis Clay: The Revolutionary Years 1955–1965, Garth Clark Gallery, Los Angeles.

Pacific Currents/Ceramics 1982, San Jose Museum of Art, San Jose, California.

Production Lines: Art/Craft/Design, Philadelphia College of Art.

Thirty Years of Archie Bray Foundation Ceramics, Montana Historical Society, Helena.

1983

American Clay Artists '83, Clay Studio Gallery, Philadelphia.

Arts and Crafts in New York State, Tyler School of Art Gallery, Temple University, Philadelphia.

Beatrice Wood: Retrospective, Art Gallery, California State University, Fullerton.

Bernard Leach in America, Garth Clark Gallery, New York.

Ceramic Artists: Distinguished Alumni of Kansas City Art Institute, Kemper Gallery, Kansas City Art Institute, Kansas City, Missouri.

Ceramic Echoes: Historical References in Contemporary Ceramic Art, Nelson-Atkins Museum of Art, Kansas City, Missouri.

Cranbrook Ceramics 1950–1980, Cranbrook Academy of Art Museum, Bloomfield Hills, Michigan.

Design in America: The Cranbrook Vision 1925–1950, The Detroit Institute of Arts.

Diversions of Keramos: American Clay Sculpture 1925–1950, Everson Museum of Art, Syracuse, New York.

George E. Ohr, University of Mississippi, University.

Henry Varnum Poor 1887–1970, Museum of Art, Pennsylvania State University, University Park.

Mary Frank: Sculpture and Monotypes 1981/1982, Zabriskie Gallery, New York.

Orange County Clay, Laguna Beach Museum of Art, Laguna Beach, California.

Ornamentalism, Hudson River Museum, Yonkers, New York.

Raw Edge: Ceramics of the 80's, Hillwood Art Gallery, C. W. Post Center, Long Island University, Greenvale, New York.

The Red and the Black, Wheelwright Museum, Santa Fe, New Mexico.

Richard DeVore: 1972–1982, Milwaukee Art Museum.

Roberta B. Marks/Ethos, Barbara Gillman Gallery, Miami, Florida.

Rudy Autio Retrospective, School of Art, University of Montana, Missoula.

Soup, Soup, Beautiful Soup, Campbell Museum, Camden, New Jersey.

Viola Frey: Paintings/Sculpture/Drawings, Quay Gallery, San Francisco.

Who's Afraid of American Pottery?, Dienst voor Beeldende Kunst, 's-Hertogenbosch, the Netherlands.

1984

Art in Clay: 1950s to 1980s in Southern California, Los Angeles Municipal Art Gallery.

Ceci n'est pas le Surréalisme—California Idioms of Surrealism, Fisher Gallery, University of Southern California, Los Angeles.

Contemporary Ceramic Vessels: Two Los Angeles Collections, Baxter Art Gallery, California Institute of Technology, Pasadena.

Design in the Service of Tea, Cooper-Hewitt Museum, Smithsonian Institution, New York.

Directions in American Ceramics, Museum of Fine Arts, Boston.

Earth and Fire: The Marer Collection of Contemporary Ceramics, Montgomery Gallery, Pomona College, Claremont, California.

Elsa Rady: Porcelain, Janus Gallery, Los Angeles.

Frans Wildenhain, Memorial Art Gallery, University of Rochester, Rochester, New York.

George E. Ohr: Artworld Homage, Garth Clark Gallery, New York.

Henry Varnum Poor 1887–1970, Museum of Art, Pennsylvania State University, University Park.

Irvin Tepper, Newport Harbor Art Museum, Newport Beach, California.

It's All Part of the Clay: Viola Frey, The Goldie Paley Gallery, Moore College of Art, Philadelphia.

Multiplicity in Clay, Metal & Fiber, Art Gallery, Skidmore College, Saratoga Springs, New York.

Newark Collection of Art Pottery, The Newark Museum, Newark, New Jersey.

Newcomb Pottery: An Enterprise for Southern Women, 1895–1940, Smithsonian Traveling Exhibition Services, Washington, D.C.

Passionate Vision: Contemporary Ceramics from the Daniel Jacobs Collection, DeCordova and Dana Museum and Park, Lincoln, Massachusetts.

Potters and Prints, Sun Valley Center for the Arts, Sun Valley, Idaho.

Women in Clay: The Ongoing Tradition, Octagon Center for the Arts, Ames, Iowa.

1985

Architectural Ceramics: 8 Concepts, Gallery of Art, Washington University, Saint Louis.

Caroll & Hiroko Hansen Collection of Ceramic Art, Arvada Center for the Arts, Arvada, Colorado.

Chronicles: Historical References in Contemporary Art, Nora Eccles Harrison Museum of Art, Utah State University, Logan.

Contemporary American Ceramics—Twenty Artists, Newport Harbor Art Museum, Newport Beach, California.

High Style: Twentieth-Century American Design, Whitney Museum of American Art, New York.

In the Eye of the Beholder: A Portrait of Our Time, College Art Gallery, State University of New York, New Paltz.

Is Anybody Home? Esther Saks Gallery, Chicago.

Joyce Kozloff: Visionary Ornament, Art Gallery, Boston University Art Gallery.

Living Treasures of California, Crocker Art Museum, Sacramento, California.

Mark Burns—A Decade in Pennsylvania: 1975–1985, Society for Art in Craft, Verona, Pennsylvania.

Pacific Connections, Los Angeles Institute of Contemporary Art.

Richard Shaw: Illusionism in Clay 1971–1985, Braunstein Gallery, San Francisco.

Robert Arneson: A Retrospective, Des Moines Art Center, Des Moines, Iowa.

Robert Sperry: A Retrospective, Bellevue Art Museum, Bellevue, Washington.

Robert Turner: A Potter's Retrospective, Milwaukee Art Museum.

Surface/Function/Shape: Selections from the Earl Millard Collection, Southern Illinois University, Edwardsville.

Teapots: Sanford M. Besser Collection of Contemporary Teapots, Decorative Arts Museum, Arkansas Arts Center, Little Rock, Arkansas.

Thirteenth Chunichi International Exhibition of Ceramic Art, Nagoya, Japan.

1986

American Potters Today, Victoria and Albert Museum, London.

Andrew Lord: New Work, BlumHelman, New York.

Ceramics of Betty Woodman, Freedman Gallery, Albright College, Reading, Pennsylvania.

Contemporary Arts: An Expanding View, The Squibb Gallery, Princeton, New Jersey.

Craft Today: Poetry of the Physical, American Craft Museum, New York.

Daniel Rhodes: The California Years, Art Museum of Santa Cruz County, California.

Elders of the Tribe, Bernice Steinbaum Gallery, New York.

Esposizione Internationale D'Arte, La Biennale da Venezia, Venice, Italy.

Frederick Hurten Rhead: An English Potter in America, Erie Art Museum, Erie, Pennsylvania.

Graham Marks: New Works, Everson Museum of Art, Syracuse, New York.

International Contemporary Ceramics Salon, Garth Clark Gallery and Smith's Galleries, London.

Painted Volumes, The Chrysler Museum, Norfolk, Virginia.

Robert Arneson: Points of View, Pittsburgh Center for the Arts.

Robert Turner, Milwaukee Art Museum.

Useful Pottery, Pyramid Arts Center, Rochester, New York.

1987

Adrian Saxe, Art Gallery, University of Missouri, Kansas City.

American Ceramics Now: The 27th Ceramic National Exhibition, Everson Museum of Art, Syracuse, New York.

Art That Is Life, Museum of Fine Arts, Boston.

Contemporary Ceramics from the Smits Collection, Los Angeles County Museum of Art.

Drawn to the Surface, Pittsburgh Center for the Arts.

Eloquent Object, Philbrook Art Center, Tulsa, Oklahoma.

Figurative Clay '87, Southern Illinois University, Edwardsville.

From the Native Clay, Christie's, New York.

Functional Glamour: Utility in Contemporary American Ceramics, Museum het Kruithuis, 's-Hertogenbosch, the Netherlands.

Hispanic Art in America, Museum of Fine Arts, Houston.

Howard Kottler: Recent Clay Sculpture, Bellevue Art Museum, Bellevue, Washington.

What's New? American Ceramics since 1980: The Alfred and Mary Shands Collection, J.B. Speed Art Museum, Louisville, Kentucky.

Aebersold, Jane Ford (1941–). Born in San Angelo, Texas, Aebersold received her B.F.A. from Tulane University, New Orleans, in 1969 and her M.F.A. from Alfred University, Alfred, New York, in 1971. She now teaches at Bennington College in Bennington, Vermont.

Aebersold works with luster surfaces, in a sense continuing the studio pottery tradition begun by Mary Chase Perry. Aebersold's palette is, however, closer to that of the French ceramist Jacques Sicard, who worked for Weller at the beginning of the century. She has made both thrown and slab forms, although slabbed pots now predominate. After glazing her stoneware pots, Aebersold applies on-glaze lusters, which she then fumes in a muffle kiln. Louis Comfort Tiffany, whom Aebersold greatly admires, employed a similar technique of fuming his glass to obtain iridescent surfaces.

Aebersold does not approach her field merely from the point of view of a historicist. She is also strongly influenced by modern painting. She became interested in Helen Frankenthaler's work through the painter's close involvement with Bennington College. Aebersold is most fascinated, however, by the paintings of Mark Rothko, with their rich but brooding palette and luminous, saturated color. Writing about Aebersold's works in a review of an exhibition at the Meier, Breier, Weiss Gallery in San Francisco, Joanne Burstein noted: "The dramatic shifts of color across the forms and around the corners go beyond the lush, atmospheric coloration of Abstract Expressionist painting, as golden lavender dissolves into silver turquoise at no discernible point. At their most successful, they remind one of the dazzling negative retinal images of sunlight on white walls." (Burstein, 1983.)

Aebersold's most recent works show several shifts: she is introducing new "landscape forms" that provide a horizontal rather than a vertical format. In addition, the surfaces are changing; she is experimenting with china paints. Now thick, shimmering trails of seemingly wet gold trail over her surfaces, working as a spatial device to create a sense of foreground and background.

Aitken, Russell Barnett (1910–). One of the youngest artists to graduate (in 1931) from the ceramics program at the Cleveland School of Art, Aitken studied in 1931–32 under Professor Michael Powolny at the Kunstgewerbeschule in Vienna. Returning to the United States in 1933, Aitken set up a studio in Cleveland, moved briefly to White Sulphur Springs, West Virginia, and in 1935 opened a studio in New York. Aitken achieved early success during the 1930s, when he was a consistent prize winner in pottery and ceramic sculpture at the annual May Shows at the Cleveland Museum and was the recipient of several awards at the Ceramic Nationals. In addition, he exhibited at the Sloane, Ferargill, and Brownell-Lamberton galleries in New York City, as well as at the Neue Galerie in Vienna.

Aitken attracted considerable attention in 1935, when a piece entitled *Futility of a Well-Ordered Life* (the Museum of Modern Art, New York) was included in a Surrealist exhibition at the Walker Galleries, New York, and won a $1,000 award from the Carnegie Foundation. The work is a parody of the art of Salvador Dalí, whom Aitken had at first admired but later found tiresomely clownish. It includes elements from Dalí's iconography (lamb chops on the shoulders, watches for breasts), but is executed in the Viennese style. Aitken placed a vessel in the woman's abdomen, a motif of the Wiener Werkstätte potter Gudrun Baudisch.

After 1945 Aitken ceased sculpting and turned to other interests. In a discussion of the artist's work, Geoffrey Archbold described Aitken thus: "An incurable romantic given to numerous boyish extravagant and exotic ventures, he turns out a surprisingly large quantity of excellent work" (Archbold, 1934).

Andreson, Laura (1902–). Born in San Bernardino, California, Andreson studied at the University of California, Los Angeles, where she received her B.A. in 1932. The following year she began the M.A. program in painting at Columbia University, New York, graduating in 1936. While a student at Columbia, she taught during the summers at UCLA. At UCLA in 1934 Andreson introduced one of the pioneering pottery courses on the West Coast. When she heard that Carlton Ball had developed a wheel and excellent throwing skills, she sent a student to study with him. On her return, the student repeated these lessons to Andreson. Andreson first exhibited at the René Rosenthal Gallery in New York; in 1940 she had a one-person exhibition in Honolulu. In 1946 the Museum of Modern Art, New York, acquired an example of her work for its permanent collection.

An accidental reduction firing of her kiln in 1948, together with the discovery of stoneware clay deposits in northern California during the same year, led Andreson away from low-fire, gloss-glazed earthenware. She began to concentrate on developing a range of stoneware glazes and bodies, and in 1957 she started to work in porcelain as well.

Andreson retired from UCLA in 1970, but as professor emerita she has remained a vital force in the studio. She contends that her retirement from teaching marks the truly creative phase of her work; since her retirement she has participated in over sixty-eight invitational and one-person exhibitions. Her works blend the clean, simplified forms of the Scandinavian tradition with the sensitivity to color found in the pottery of Japan. Her selection of color and its vibrancy is drawn from many areas, including Andreson's still-clear memories of her youth in San Bernardino, "surrounded by orange orchards and the alpine glow of the mountains." In 1982 a major retrospective of her work was organized by Martha Longnecker at the Mingei International Museum of World Folk Art in La Jolla, California. The exhibition was accompanied by an elegant catalogue, with essays by Bernard Kester and commentary by Martha Longnecker. The catalogue contains a detailed listing of the many exhibitions in which Andreson has participated.

Archipenko, Alexander (1887–1964). Born in Kiev, Russia, Archipenko studied painting and sculpture at the Kiev Art School from 1902 to 1905. He later moved to Paris, where in 1908 he attended the Ecole des Beaux-Arts. Two years later he exhibited with the Cubists at the Salon des Artistes Indépendants and in 1911 at the Salon d'Automne. Archipenko immigrated to the United States in 1923, founding an art school in New York City. He played an active part in American art, both as a teacher and as an exhibiting artist. There were more than 118 one-man exhibitions of his work during his lifetime. In 1967 the UCLA Art Gallery organized a major posthumous, traveling retrospective of Archipenko's work, and more recently, in 1986, the Hirshhorn Museum and Sculpture Garden in Washington, D.C., held a major retrospective.

Archipenko worked frequently in polychrome terra-cotta, occasionally exhibiting at the Ceramic Nationals. In some pieces, he used clay as a cheap alternative to bronze, but in other works—notably *Walking Woman* (1937)—he exploited qualities of modeling, texture, and color that emphasized the material.

Arneson, Robert (1930–   ). Born in Benicia, California, Arneson studied at the College of Marin, Kentfield, California, from 1949 to 1951; at the California College of Arts and Crafts (Oakland), where he received the B.A. degree in 1954; and at Mills College (Oakland), where he was awarded the M.F.A. degree in 1958. Thereafter, Arneson taught at several schools, working from 1960 to 1962 as an assistant to Tony Prieto at Mills College and from 1962 to the present as head of the ceramics department at the University of California, Davis. Arneson has had numerous one-man exhibitions, including a major retrospective in 1974 at the Museum of Contemporary Art, Chicago, and at the San Francisco Museum of Art. A second retrospective opened in 1986 at the Des Moines Art Center and traveled to the Hirshhorn Museum and Sculpture Garden, Smithsonian Institution, in Washington, D.C., and to other venues. His work is included in numerous collections, including the San Francisco Museum of Modern Art; the Oakland Museum; the University Art Museum, University of California, Berkeley; the Whitney Museum of American Art, New York; the Guggenheim Museum, New York; the Philadelphia Museum of Art; the Stedelijk Museum, Amsterdam; and the Hirshhorn Museum.

Robert Arneson

Although Arneson had studied ceramics at the California College of Arts and Crafts, he says that it was during his period of teaching high-school students and showing them how to throw and handle clay that his real interest in the medium began to develop. By 1958 he had made sufficient progress in ceramics to join Prieto as a graduate student, making what he terms "slick bottles in the Mills tradition" (Mu-

seum of Contemporary Crafts, 1971). He won second prize at the 1958 Wichita National. At this stage, the work of Peter Voulkos began to influence him, and Arneson produced a body of more-or-less Abstract Expressionist ceramics, which Elena Natherby christened his "Mastodon droppings."

Arneson had already begun to move toward a more personal statement, when, in 1961, while demonstrating pottery techniques at the California State Fair alongside Tony Prieto and Wayne Taylor, he threw "a handsome, sturdy bottle about a quart size. He carefully sealed it with a clay bottlecap and then stamped it *No Return*. That's what it's really about, isn't it?" (Museum of Contemporary Crafts, 1971). The piece was first exhibited in 1962 at an exhibition at the M.H. de Young Memorial Museum, where the object stood alongside a group of conventional vessels. "As for the *No Deposit Bottle*," sniffed a writer for *Craft Horizons*, "if the purpose of including this in the exhibition was to irritate the reviewers, it did" (Meisel, 1964). In the years that followed, Arneson did more than irritate— he profoundly offended, dismayed, and delighted both the sculptural world and the world of the ceramic arts.

Since 1963 Arneson has worked on a series of explorations, the most extreme of which was his *John* series. This was the beginning of a dialogue on ceramics that in subsequent years dealt with a wide range of ceramic themes, from throwing lessons to the treasure-house associations of ninth-century Song celadons. Arneson described the toilet as the "ultimate ceramic," and above all, an object within the ceramic tradition that had no art heritage. The shock aspect of these pieces—which include penis handles, red clitoral drains, generous amounts of ceramic excrement, and various oozes and pustules—represented the ceramic equivalent of Duchamp's exhibitions of a urinal, *The Fountain*, in 1917, and was an equally calculated gesture. In ceramics the dismay at these objects was all the greater, as the material had been for so long identified with the timid decorative-art format; these objects created a major furor.

The works of the mid-1960s have less bite and deal with more comic themes than do the works of the early sixties: in *Toaster* (1965) a hand emerges from the appliance's innards; and in *Typewriter* (1965–66) red, lacquered fingernails substitute for keys. Arneson also produced food series, such as *Crisco* (1966). Soon after this body of work, he began to work on his seminal

Alice Street series, which dealt with his suburban home environment. This series is less dramatic than Arneson's early works and attracted little critical attention. Yet these works, with their modular format, have developed into one of Arneson's richest areas of investigation. They have freed him from the preciousness of an object-making tradition and brought his works fully into the realm of sculpture, allowing him to work in a monumental, mock-heroic style. Among the major works that have been created from this modular method of construction are *Mountain and Lake* (1975) and *Pool with Splash* (1977). Arneson also explored this method in some of his portraits, notably *Smorgi-Bob, the Cook* (1971), and in one of his masterpieces, *Fragments of Western Civilization* (1975).

His self-portraits and portraits of friends have developed into the most masterful of his many series of explorations. The first exhibition of his self-portraits took place in 1972 at the Hansen Fuller Gallery in San Francisco. In *Classical Exposure* (1972) the seditious, Dada quality of his early works remains, but with a new maturity—the humor is layered and underpinned with a satiric intelligence. Commenting on the works of Arneson at his retrospective in 1974, Dennis Adrian remarked that the work had taken on an increasingly complex, visionary, and even profound character: "His probing of the various implications of puns, both visual and verbal, and, more broadly, of metamorphosis, has brought Arneson into the area of metaphysical statement about the conditions and varieties of artistic processes and forms…the true foci of Arneson's interests are not easy gags or Funk conceits, but the consistently varied investigations of ambiguities in the materials, processes and rationales of artistic activity itself" (Adrian, 1974).

Since his first exhibition of self-portraits in 1972, Arneson has moved deeper and deeper into caricature—a realm that the art world has traditionally regarded with great ambivalence. Increasingly during the seventies, critics drew connections between the work of Arneson and that of two "legitimate" masters of caricature—F. X. Messerschmidt, who made self-portraits in the eighteenth century, and Honoré Daumier, who created small bronzes in the 1830s satirizing the deputies of Louis Philippe. While a good deal of Arneson's satire had previously been directed at the hermetic world of ceramics, during the seventies he began to fire barbs at larger cultural targets. In *George and Mona in the Baths of Coloma*

(1976), for example, two of the most famous faces—Mona Lisa and George Washington (the latter dressed in his finest banknote green)—share the waters. Through this piece Arneson expressed his cynicism about the art world—art, money, and fame—and his own ambivalent ambition to be a member of the club.

His exhibition *Heroes and Clowns,* held at the Alan Frumkin Gallery, New York, in 1979, brought a new sophistication to his work, with portraits of Elvis Presley, Rrose Sélavy (Duchamp's female alter ego), Vincent van Gogh, and Arneson's close friend, the painter William T. Wiley. The heroic aspect of Arneson's work began to appear in the larger-than-life scale of his works of the seventies and in his use of the traditional bust format—a format historically associated with nobility and the military. In part, the title of the exhibition was also autobiographical, for Arneson's image in the art world at large and within the narrower boundaries of the ceramics community was part hero, part clown. The heroism came from his courage in challenging the traditional notions of ceramics as a sculptural medium. On the other hand, the content of his work was frequently dismissed as childish clowning—the dilemma of the artist who uses humor as his primary vehicle and then asks the world to take him seriously.

The early 1980s saw a change in Arneson's work. His portraits of artists—particularly major works such as *Pablo Ruiz with Itch* and *A Likeness of Francis B.* (1981)—became more complex, more deeply rooted in the literature of art history, and, in a sense, more academic—further from the visceral Arneson of the sixties. Much like Duchamp, whose shadowy presence seldom seems far from Arneson's oeuvre, the artist had become an art critic, or at least a debunker of the heroic notion of the artist. Also at about this time Arneson's drawings began to come into their own. Always an inspired draftsman, Arneson now began to create magnificent drawings that in the past six years have come close to overtaking his achievement in ceramics.

In 1981 Arneson became embroiled in a public debate over his portrait of the slain mayor of San Francisco, George Moscone. This event, explained in detail in chapter 11, had a surprisingly profound impact on Arneson and was one of the reasons for a radical change in his subject matter. Arneson began to deal with nuclear weapons, an issue that concerned many artists at that time. After 1982 he began to explore this theme in works which lacked his usual hu-

mor. They are painful portraits of victims, mutants that were delivered by a nuclear age. While the artist denies that the move from comic-heroism to death has anything to do with his own personal battle with cancer, this must play a role in the new sense of mortality and vulnerability that has entered his work. The critic Donald Kuspit, however, argues that death, in a quieter, less dramatic form, has always been a part of Arneson's work:

No Deposit, No Return presents a discarded bottle—a negated form, fit only for art. And *Funk John* and *John with Art* (1964) are really about excrement, which is a form of death. Arneson's effort to sexualize objects, as in *Call Girl* and *Typewriter,* both 1966, creates life in dead objects. And the hand reaching out of *Toaster,* 1965, is like the hand of Lazarus as it reaches out of the tomb. *Smorgi-Bob, the Cook,* 1971, is a memorial to the abundance of life that is possible in the dead space of Art—about the contradiction in terms, the living death (death of living, living of death) which art is. With *Fragments of Western Civilization* and *Assassination of a Famous Nut Artist,* death became an explicit theme in Arneson's art—both the world's death and self's death. He was now openly on the way to the great tragic artist he has become. (Kuspit, 1986)

Autio, Rudy (1926–). Born in Butte, Montana, Autio was educated at the Aviation Machinist's Mate School, United States Navy (1943–44); and at Montana State University, Bozeman, where he studied ceramics with Frances Senska and graduated with a B.S. in 1950. In 1952 he received the M.F.A. from Washington State University, Pullman, after which Autio, together with Peter Voulkos, was resident artist at the Archie Bray Foundation (Helena, Montana) until 1956. During that period, he completed a number of architectural commissions, including a ten-foot-by-thirty-foot ceramic wall relief, *The Sermon on the Mount,* for the First Methodist Church in Great Falls, Montana. In 1957 Autio became assistant curator of the Montana Museum (Missoula), transferring shortly thereafter to the University of Montana, Missoula, where he was professor of ceramics and sculpture until his retirement.

Autio had originally been hired as a sculptor (Voulkos as the potter) by Archie Bray, but found himself attracted to the vessel form. In the 1960s Autio began to produce pots that were inspired by what was happening at Otis as well as by his own interest in Abstract Expressionism:

"The forms were concoctions of thrown and shaped cylinders and slabs. Pinched, folded, scored and creased, their clamorous surfaces showed that Autio's emotions were in his fingers. They worked feverishly to convey what he knew in his eyes. The volumes themselves seemed to squirm, anxious to find room and comfort for the awkward bulges in their developing anatomy" (Lebow, 1985).

The scarcely suppressed anthropomorphism gradually gave way to the fully figurative work on which Autio's reputation as an artist is now based. A landmark in this development is *Flesh Pot* (1963), which presides "over his relatively modest previous works like one of those gargantuan water tanks that inevitably command hilltops at the outskirts of small towns" (Lebow, 1985). But in this pot the form had not yet found its signature. The work is monumental but conventional. It was in his black-and-white *Double Lady Vessel,* exhibited at the Ceramic National in 1964, that the full expression of Autio's style emerged—the abstracted, vigorous drawing, and the sensual, somewhat fragmented structure of the forms. Another masterwork of this time is *Kewpie Doll* (1968), a large, hedonistic vessel, with its decadent surface of overglaze luster.

Autio's ceramics attracted little attention at the time outside the ceramics world. He turned to other sculptural materials—working in concrete and metal—and made relatively little clay during the 1970s. Ex-

Rudy Autio

hibitions such as *A Century of Ceramics in the United States 1878–1978* in 1979 and *The Contemporary American Potter* in 1980, helped to reintroduce the artist to collectors at a point in time when the art world had taken up the pluralist banner and was again interested in the figurative vessel. Autio's interest in ceramics was revived by the increased attention, and in 1980 he produced a significant body of work for an exhibition at Greenwich House in New York. This was followed by highly acclaimed, one-person exhibitions at Exhibit A in Chicago and in 1981 at Okun/Thomas in Saint Louis.

In 1981 Autio visited the Arabia factory in Helsinki, Finland, and stayed on as artist in residence. At Arabia he worked in porcelain, a simple undertaking within the support structure of a large factory. In 1982 he returned to the United States with a brighter palette and continued to work in porcelain. However, he found porcelain to be too temperamental a material for the large scale that he was developing in his work. Before returning to stoneware clays, however, he created some major porcelain pieces, notably his *Sacrifice of Iphigenia on Her Wedding Day* (1983), a large, complex lidded vessel in which the drawing takes on a three-dimensionality as horses' heads erupt from the surface of the pot, adding a sense of drama to the painted imagery.

The new pots have changed from their predecessors in the 1960s; the forms no longer encompass one figure but are now landscapes inhabited by legends, floating women, and animals. Instead of creating the form around the figure, Autio now fashions a ceramic "canvas" without a preconceived notion of what will be painted on the surface. Once the form is complete, he begins his "search for the figures," and the drawings begin to occupy "a dream space in which the most irrational urges of the psyche appear, transformed, in linear equivalents. Figures of people and animals romp and float in a directionless but enveloping atmosphere. Not up, not down, but around and around, their eroticism borne by the rich suggestiveness of a hollow clay device with a hole in the top" (Lebow, 1985).

In 1983 the University of Montana organized a retrospective of his work, which traveled to the American Craft Museum in New York. The retrospective provided an enticing glimpse of Autio's genius but was disappointing in terms of its installation, uneven selection of works, and poor catalogue. The true retrospective and evaluation of Autio's work have yet to arrive.

Bacerra, Ralph (1938–). Born in Orange County, California, Bacerra studied under Vivika Heino at the Chouinard Art Institute, Los Angeles, where he received his B.F.A. After teaching briefly at Chouinard, Bacerra left in 1961 for two years of military service. Heino also left Chouinard in the same year, for the Rhode Island School of Design, so when Bacerra returned to Los Angeles, in 1963, he became chairman of the Chouinard ceramics department. He proved to be an effective and passionate teacher, who had a strong influence on his students. Heino had taught a kind of technical fundamentalism at Chouinard and to some extent Bacerra continued this, insisting on regular and formal critique sessions with the students. At these sessions the students developed an appreciation for technique as an "edge," which if pushed far enough can provide tension, character, and content in the work. In many other schools at the time it was the vogue to approach the science of ceramics on a very informal level, but Bacerra also insisted on classes in glaze formulation.

The importance of Bacerra's teaching was not immediately apparent. The students at Chouinard were late bloomers. But by the late 1970s his students—Elsa Rady, Adrian Saxe, Mineo Mizuno, Peter Shire, and Don Pilcher—had risen to prominence. Most were linked by a distinctive finesse and richness in their handling of materials that became known colloquially as the "Chouinard school," even though in terms of content and vision, their work had little else in common.

In 1972 the ceramics department closed and Chouinard, renamed the California Institute of the Arts, moved to Valencia, on the outskirts of Los Angeles. Bacerra now divided his time between developing his own work and creating innovative technology for industry, in particular, creating special tiles with the thermal shock qualities necessary for induction heating in ceramic stove tops. By 1968 his work had begun to drift away from the functional, traditional look that the Chouinard students had inherited from Heino—creating organic forms with dry, brightly colored glazes and slick, gold-lustered mouths.

In 1975 Bacerra made an extraordinary series of "horses," inspired by a Tang horse and camel he had bought in the Far East. Bacerra eventually returned to the vessel format, but his horses signaled a new complexity in his surfaces and forms. The direction came from two primary sources: nature (he maintains a large hothouse of

orchids and other rare plants) and the decorated ceramics of Japan. He was particularly fascinated by Imari wares, as well as by Kutani pottery, Chinese polychromes, and Persian miniatures. Bacerra developed a complex surface system of repeating images, interlocking, overlapping, and combining them to create larger versions of the same image. He developed this partly from the example of W. C. Escher, the Dutch graphic artist, but also from similar traditions in Japanese decorative art, in particular in fabric design from 1650 to 1900. In turn, these fabric designs were the basis for the interlocking patterns in Imari and Kutani wares, as well as in Nabeshima wares (which Bacerra finds too cold and perfect).

In 1983 Bacerra temporarily set aside the vessel again to make a series of large wall pieces constructed out of interlocking tiles and using a bird motif. Sarah Bodine wrote about these works, which were exhibited at the Theo Portnoy Gallery in New York: "Bacerra has pulled his delicate porcelain casserole lids flat and made their decoration jump into three dimensions like a kind of child's pop-up toy. The rhythmic bird-form motifs are now enlarged into a pillowlike, sensuous, tangible relief. An aesthetic comparison with [Escher] is inevitable, although Bacerra's shapes and progressive relationships of form are less mechanical, less calculated, less resolved...like Cubist painting, this work contorts perceptual expectations" (Bodine, 1983).

Bacerra subsequently turned to a major series of works on the platter form and to the creation of elaborately painted boxes. The play with flat pattern has for the present been interrupted. Bacerra's plates now are host to an equally complex, illusory painting of floating boxes, cylinders, and triangles—moving from the surface into the conceptual volumes of "potter's space." Bacerra's contribution to American ceramics has yet to be fully explored or appreciated. This is due in part to the artist's intermittent production, but it is also due to his placement in a decorative-arts category with which the art world is only now coming to terms.

Baggs, Arthur Eugene (1886–1947). Baggs was living in Alfred, New York, in 1900 when New York State established the School of Ceramics at Alfred. He entered the school to study drawing and design, without any thought of becoming a potter, but "in the general course of things I made a few pots and got the bug which has been spreading its infection through my system ever since" (Baggs, 1929). Professor Charles Fergus

Binns sent Baggs to Marblehead, Massachusetts, for a summer job at the end of his sophomore year. In Marblehead Baggs assisted Dr. Herbert J. Hall in setting up a pottery department for occupational therapy at his sanitarium. By 1908 the Marblehead Pottery had developed into an independent, commercial venture with a weekly output of two hundred pieces, most designed by Baggs, with subtle, conventionalized decoration and mat glazes. For six years, Baggs taught elementary pottery and provided technical assistance for the Ethical Culture School of New York City, while studying at the Art Students League. In 1915 he purchased the Marblehead Pottery from Dr. Hall and continued to work there during the summers until the closing of the pottery in 1936. During the academic years from 1925 to 1928, Baggs worked as a glaze chemist for the Cowan Art Pottery Studio and taught at the Cleveland School of Art. In 1928 Baggs became professor of ceramic arts at Ohio State University, Columbus.

Baggs's work shows an obsession with glaze chemistry, ranging from his superbly bland, mat glazes for Marblehead to the Egyptian blue and Persian green glazes for

Arthur Baggs

Cowan. In the 1930s Baggs became interested in reviving the salt-glaze process, which, apart from isolated work such as that of Susan Frackelton in the 1890s, had been neglected as a decorative medium.

Baggs won many awards during his career, including the Ogden Armour Prize at the *Exhibition of Applied Art* in Chicago (1915); the medal of the Boston Society of Arts and Crafts (1925); the Charles F. Binns Medal at the American Ceramic Society (1928); and first prize for pottery at the May Show, Cleveland (1928). He was an active exhibitor at the Ceramic Nationals, winning first prize in 1933 and 1938 and a second prize in 1935. His *Cookie Jar,* which won the first prize at the Ceramic National in 1938, is considered his masterwork and one of the major pieces of the decade.

Bailey, Clayton (1939–). Born in Antigo, Wisconsin, Bailey received his M.A. from the University of Wisconsin in 1962, having studied under Harvey Littleton, Clyde Bert, and Toshiko Takaezu. After graduation, Bailey taught at various midwestern universities and became instructor of ceramics at the University of Wisconsin, Whitewater. After two semesters as a guest artist at the University of California in Davis, working alongside the painters Roy De Forest and Wayne Thiebaud and ceramist Robert Arneson, Bailey settled permanently in California, teaching at California State College, Hayward.

By the time of his move to California, Bailey had already established a reputation as an unconventional artist, exhibiting four-foot-long inflatable rubber grubs and "nose-pots" that were covered in tacky layers of latex "glaze." He had also had major one-man shows, including one in 1964 at the Museum of Contemporary Crafts, New York, and one at the Milwaukee Art Center in 1967. In the 1970s Bailey dealt with a series of themes in his work, ranging from pornography, the medical establishment, and primitive man of the "kaolithian" period, explored through his now-famous workshops and staged events. The latter masterfully exploited the ceramic-arts tendency toward a craft hypochondria—a neurotic search for new glazes and craft skills to cure imagined creative ills.

Bailey's work is the most truly Funk of the Bay Area artists and he is one of the few whose work still patently belongs to this genre. In 1976 he installed his works in a "penny arcade" installation in Porta Costa, California. Viewers paid a nominal entrance fee to see the Wonders of the World Museum, where Bailey maintained that his public could enjoy his works without the alienation of a museum or art gallery environment. The museum has now been

transferred to his home. In the past few years Bailey's ceramic output has slowed, replaced with an interest in metal and a fascination with robots.

Ball, F. Carlton (1911–). Born in Sutter Creek, California, Ball studied painting at the University of Southern California, Los Angeles, from 1931 to 1936. While a student at USC, Ball became interested in pottery through the classes offered by Glen Lukens. In 1936 Ball had the opportunity to teach pottery at the California College of Arts and Crafts (Oakland) and arrived with some hastily assembled glaze recipes from Lukens. Ceramics was an empiric craft on the West Coast and Ball admits that he had never "stacked a kiln or lit one, or mixed a glaze" until he taught his first pottery classes (Bray, 1980). Ball taught at Mills College (Oakland, California) from 1939 to 1950, also teaching craft skills through the war years in the United States Army Occupational Therapy Emergency Program. By the time he left Mills College, in 1950, its ceramics department had been transformed into one of the most active on the West Coast. In addition, the Mills Ceramic Guild had been formed to promote workshops and exhibitions. Ball later taught at the University of Wisconsin (1950–51); Southern Illinois University (1951–56); and the University of Puget Sound, Washington, from 1968 until his retirement, in 1977.

Concerned about the lack of educational material in the field, Ball has published numerous technical articles for *Ceramics Monthly* and other publications. He was one of the pioneers on the West Coast in the use of the wheel and directed much of his energy toward achieving proficiency in this area. He was particularly interested in the skills necessary to throw and assemble the very large vessel forms that are the most distinctive works in his oeuvre.

Bauer, Fred (1937–). Born in Memphis, Tennessee, Bauer studied at the Memphis Academy of Art, taking his B.F.A. in 1962, and in 1964 receiving his M.F.A. from the University of Washington. He worked at the Archie Bray Foundation in Helena, Montana, in 1964, and taught at the University of Wisconsin, Madison (1964–65); the Aztec Mountain School of Craft, Liberty, Maine (1967); the University of Michigan, Ann Arbor (1965–68); and the University of Washington, Seattle, until 1971. In 1966 he was the recipient of a Louis Comfort Tiffany Foundation Grant.

Fred Bauer

The mercurial Bauer achieved early notoriety as a ceramic artist in the Funk/Super-Object vein. Bauer's style, irreverence, and evident talent made him a romantic hero for the young ceramic artists of his day. He presented numerous workshops and gave elaborate slide presentations. Eventually the pressures of being artist-performer-guru were destructive, and Bauer abruptly left ceramics in 1972, seeking seclusion as a farmer in northern California. Despite the short period of his involvement, Bauer was a prolific producer, developing from a skilled, functional potter to an imaginative sculptor. His oeuvre from the latter part of the 1960s is the most interesting, with its phallic cameras, plates with pyramids of lustered peas, and six-foot-high Funk pumps.

Bengston, Billy Al (1934–). Born in Dodge City, Kansas, Bengston moved at an early age to California, where he attended the Manual Arts High School in Los Angeles. It was there that he first became involved in ceramics. After leaving high school, Bengston studied at Los Angeles City College from 1953 to 1956 and the Otis Art Institute in Los Angeles in 1956–57. He was part of the group of experimental artists around Peter Voulkos, working as a technical assistant at Otis and signing his works

"Moonstone." After leaving Otis, Bengston turned from pottery to painting. The rich, spontaneous surfaces of two genres of Japanese ceramics—raku and Oribe—strongly influenced his painting. He returned to ceramics in June 1975, when he was invited to participate, in the *New Works in Clay by Contemporary Painters and Sculptors* exhibition at the Everson Museum of Art. His works were produced with the assistance of the Syracuse China Corporation from designs (wax models and drawings) that he submitted for execution. These required several modifications before the final plaster molds were prepared by Don Foley for production in flintware. In this body of work, Bengston employed the iris motif by spraying glazes over a template. The iris, what he terms "dracula," is a favorite motif in Bengston's ceramic work and also appears in many of his paintings.

Bertoni, Christina (1945–). Born in Ann Arbor, Michigan, Bertoni studied at the University of Michigan, Ann Arbor, where she received her B.F.A. in 1967. She received her M.F.A. in 1976 from the Cranbrook Academy of Art, Bloomfield Hills, Michigan. She currently works in Pascoag, Rhode Island.

Bertoni's primary format is the vessel. During the eighties she has at times departed from this discipline to make relief wall sculpture. Her early works dealt with astrological themes. They also strongly emphasized the inside and outside of the vessel, which Bertoni manipulated with strong contrasts of black interiors and white exteriors. In her more recent work, Bertoni has approached the vessel with a more conceptual edge, writing legends on her works and creating simple yet evocative marks and signs on the surfaces of shallow shapes that evoke the sense of small moon craters rather than vessels in the cultural and functional sense. Bertoni describes her work as "a process of exploring a body of ideas and attempting to articulate them visually.... Bowls are vehicles for my speculations on the nature of such things as existence/non-existence, order/chaos, microcosm/macrocosm, space/matter" (Clark and Watson, 1986).

Binns, Charles Fergus (1857–1934). Born in Worcester, England, Charles Fergus Binns was the son of Richard William Binns, director of the Royal Worcester Porcelain Works. As a child the younger Binns attended the Cathedral King School, and at the age of fourteen he was apprenticed to his father at the porcelain works. Charles

Fergus Binns studied chemistry in Birmingham, England, after which he established a ceramics laboratory at the plant, which sought to bring the production at the factory under more scientific control. In 1897 Binns came to the United States to become principal of the Technical School of Sciences and Art in Trenton, New Jersey, and in 1900 he became the first director of the New York School of Clayworking and Ceramics (renamed the New York State College of Ceramics in 1932) at Alfred University. A year after joining Alfred, the university gave him the honorary degree of master of science in recognition of his work; and in 1925 it presented him with the degree of doctor of science.

Binns was one of the charter members of the American Ceramic Society, which was founded in 1899. He was elected trustee at the first meeting; the following year he was made vice-president and in 1901 president of the society. When Professor Edward Orton resigned as secretary in 1918, Binns accepted that office and acted as secretary of the society for four years. He was also a member of the English Ceramics Society and various art organizations, as well as a fellow of the Boston Society of Arts and Crafts. He was the author of numerous essays and technical papers that were published in the *Craftsman*, *Keramik Studio*, *Transactions*, and *Journal of the American Ceramic Society*, as well as other publications.

Charles Fergus Binns

He also wrote three books: *The Story of the Potter, The Potter's Craft,* and *Ceramic Technology.*

Binn's greatest contribution came in the field of ceramic education. Under his guidance, a generation of significant ceramics teachers emerged, including Arthur Baggs, Harold Nash, Myrtle French, Paul Cox, R. Guy Cowan, Ruth Canfield, and Charles Harder. Binns was a man of strong convictions—evident both in the standards he set for his work as an artist and in his dedication to the church. In 1923 Binns was ordained as a priest in the Protestant Episcopal Church. After his death a memorial exhibition of the superbly glazed stonewares for which he was famous was held in New York at the Metropolitan Museum of Art in 1935. A full account of Binns's contribution to education in American ceramics can be found in Melvin Bernstein's fascinating study *Art and Design at Alfred.*

Bogatay, Paul (1905–1972). Born in Ada, Ohio, Bogatay studied at the Cleveland School of Art under R. Guy Cowan and briefly under Arthur Baggs. Bogatay was later a graduate student under Baggs at Ohio State University (Columbus), where he himself became a ceramics instructor in the early 1930s, remaining there until 1971. Bogatay received two first prizes for his sculptural works at the Ceramic Nationals, and a $100 purchase prize in 1946. He was the recipient of a Tiffany Fellowship, and for three years he was a fellow of the Rockefeller Foundation. Apart from his interest in clay as a sculptural material, Bogatay was also strongly involved in industrial concerns and was an active member and officer of the American Ceramic Society.

Bohnert, Thom R. (1948–). Bohnert studied at Southern Illinois University, Edwardsville, from 1965 to 1969, when he received his B.A. He earned his M.F.A. in 1971 at the Cranbrook Academy of Art, Bloomfield Hills, Michigan, where he majored in ceramics and minored in printmaking and metalsmithing. Bohnert has exhibited extensively since 1966 and has received numerous scholarships and awards, including the National Endowment for the Arts' Craftsman Fellowship in 1978.

Bohnert has evolved a unique method of dealing with both volume and space. He creates polychrome assemblage vessels with wire and ceramics so that the "pot" becomes a series of lines and fragments suspended in space. In essence, Bohnert's work is an act of drawing in which the vessel becomes the subject. Writing on "linear order" (*Studio Potter,* 1985) Bohnert describes his involvement with drawing and how he attempts to translate the two-dimensional dynamic into form: "The 3-D form strives to obtain drawing elements: contours that define multiple interplay with volume and shape, a sensation of depth also communicated by the color of each line and fragmented plane."

Brady, Robert David (1946–). Born in Reno, Nevada, Brady studied with Viola Frey and Vernon Coykendall at the California College of Arts and Crafts in Oakland, receiving his B.F.A. in 1968; he received his M.F.A. in 1975 from the University of California at Davis. Brady taught for six months at the Appalachian Center for the Crafts in Smithville, Tennessee, and currently maintains a studio in Sacramento, where he teaches with Peter Vandenberge at California State University.

Brady's early exhibitions were distinguished by a random eclecticism; indeed, his 1978 exhibition of ceramics and paintings was so diverse and scattered that at least one critic described the event as a group exhibition. There was a particularly obvious debt in these works to both Viola Frey and to the Jasper Johns retrospective at the San Francisco Museum of Modern Art, which preceded Brady's one-person show.

The eighties have seen an impressive growth and sense of individuality and maturity in Brady's figurative sculpture. Today Brady ranks among the most original and provocative of the ceramic sculptors. He has moved back to the vessel forms that he first showed in 1975 and again in 1983 at the Braunstein Gallery, San Francisco. These large, hand-built vessels have gradually become less and less specific in their sense of being pots and are now simply hollow mounds with a strange biomorphic presence. But it is his figures and masks that dominate his ouevre. In 1982 he produced an inspired group of masks whose forms refer to African primitive art. The surfaces, however, are covered with an elegant series of black circles on white. Several of these masks were included in the exhibition *Modern Masks* at the Whitney Museum of American Art in 1984. Brady's figures have distinctive sticklike arms and legs, shriveled genitalia, and a somewhat tortured surface that speak of an inner pain and disquiet. Brady's contribution to American ceramic sculpture has yet to receive its full due and is at an ideal point for a mid-career survey.

Breschi, Karen (1941–). Born in Oakland, California, Breschi studied at the California College of Arts and Crafts, Oakland, where she received her B.F.A. in 1963. She continued her studies at San Francisco State College through 1965, and from 1968 to 1971 she studied at the San Francisco Art Institute, where she taught after graduating. Breschi had her first one-person show, *Dreams and Visions,* in 1972, at the University Art Gallery, Berkeley. Subsequently she has shown at the Braunstein Gallery, San Francisco.

Breschi creates fired-clay figurative sculptures, which she later paints and occasionally embellishes with other materials and found objects. These works involve macabre dream imagery in which animals dressed in clothes act out human dramas dealing with highly personal issues and an underlying feminist agenda. Her later work has involved a series of self-portraits and figures, such as *False Fronted Man* (1973). These have extended Breschi's investigation of the mask, a theme that she has explored extensively in her work. Over the past decade her output (and involvement with ceramics) has been sporadic.

Burns, Mark A. (1950–). Born in Springfield, Ohio, Burns received his B.F.A. in 1972 from the College of the Dayton Art Institute, Dayton, Ohio, with a major in ceramics. He took his M.F.A. in 1974 at the University of Washington, Seattle, under Howard Kottler and Patti Warashina. He has taught at the College of the Dayton Art Institute; the University of Washington; the Factory of Visual Arts, Seattle; the State University of New York, Oswego; the Philadelphia College of Art; and California State University, Chico.

Labeling Burns's work "Punk Art" is to oversimplify what are in fact intensely personal statements of the artist's search for identity. Burns employs bizarre, exotic, and sadomasochistic imagery in his immaculately crafted works. In 1977 he held a one-man exhibition of his works at the Drutt Gallery, Philadelphia, which incorporated a total painted environment. In 1984 he was commissioned by the Pennsylvania Academy of the Fine Arts to create an installation as an homage to the architect Frank Furness. The Society for Art in Craft, Verona, Pennsylvania, organized a mid-career survey of his work in 1986 entitled *Mark Burns—Decade in Philadelphia.*

Buzio, Lidya (1948–). Born in Montevideo, Uruguay, Buzio studied drawing and painting with Horacio Torres, J. Montes, and G. Fernandez (1964–66), and ceramics with José Collel in 1967. In 1972 she moved to the United States and set up a studio in New York City.

Buzio's art reflects many influences, but the formative one was undoubtedly that of Joaquin Torres-Garcia (1874–1949), the Uruguayan modernist painter. Although Torres-Garcia died a year after Buzio was born, her sister married his son Horacio. Lidya Buzio grew up surrounded by Torres-Garcia's art, and that of his sons and his followers. Her work is not, however, imitative of Torres-Garcia's. Indeed, Buzio's style is very personal and distinct. But what she has taken from the Uruguayan master is a particular sense of structure and geometry, which, since he was a Constructivist, was the central factor in his work.

Lidya Buzio

There is also a parallel in their response to New York City. When Torres-Garcia visited in 1920, he filled his sketchbook with cityscapes. Buzio, trained in the figurative traditions of Horacio Torres and José Collel, also found herself drifting toward the cityscape after her move to New York. In her case the fascination was with the roofs of SoHo and their strange Italianate quality. She began to transfer these to slab-built pots, burnishing the images onto the surface of the unfired vessel. Inspired by Renaissance frescos, she created a dry, slightly transparent surface with a delicate play of tonal values. Painted onto the tense, curving surfaces of her work, the space she creates is strangely illusory.

Ed Lebow wrote of the spatial issues in her work, commenting: "Buzio splices illusory space with real. She has a keen eye for the fundamental difference between working on flat and on three-dimensional ground. Unlike a flat surface, a volumetric one is not static. It moves through space, lending the image it carries the full effects of the hollows and swells. Since there are no true straight or flat lines Buzio cheats the eye by gently tilting the edges of buildings to give them a plumb appearance, or by toying with angles and curves to accentuate the volumes that the walls and lines seem to hold and describe" (Lebow, 1983).

The result of this surface distortion is a kind of visual "breathing" in which the eye moves from the real surface of the pot into the imaginary space it suggests in line and perspective, only to be drawn back by the slightest distraction to the burnished surface. Philip Rawson, the distinguished writer on aesthetic theory in ceramics, sees this as the consequence of a masterful use of what he terms "potter's space." In an unpublished address to the Kansas City Third International Ceramics Symposium in 1983, he spoke of potter's space as comprising not only one volume (the vessel) but a number of component volumes: "One of the most splendid uses of potter's space seems to me to be in Lidya Buzio's pots. The tension between the curved surfaces which subtend that independent potter's volume and the superficially banal perspectives of the cityscapes that she paints onto them seems to be what generates their extraordinary enigmatic atmosphere…. One volume-content flows into another to make a beautifully modulated content of space: something carvers or makers can never achieve, only potters."

Carhartt, Elaine (1951–). Born in 1951 in Grand Junction, Colorado, Carhartt studied at Colorado State University, Fort Collins, receiving her B.F.A. in 1975. The following year she moved to Pasadena, California, where she established a studio, and in 1980 received the prestigious New Talent Award of the Los Angeles County Museum of Art. Her work is figurative; it involves curious and disquieting figures that are at once saccharine in their charm and curiously untrustworthy, even threatening. The sweetness and charm of the work suggest something subterranean and uneasy. As the *Los Angeles Times* art critic Suzanne Muchnic comments, "Carhartt's work always had more going for it than charm…. New pieces seem to have acquired an in-

creasingly unsettling twist… What are we to make of a pig, a penguin and yes, a worm that stares up at us through human eyes?… their faces are masks as inscrutable as a sphinx" (Muchnic, 1985).

Carman, Nancy (1950–). Born in Tucson, Arizona, Carman studied at the University of California, Davis, receiving her B.A. in 1972, and at the University of Washington, Seattle, from which she graduated with a M.F.A. in 1976. In 1980 she received a Visual Artists Fellowship from the National Endowment for the Arts. Carman makes small figurative sculptures that are a blend of "poetic narratives and psychological drama that is very much autobiographical" (Bell, 1985).

Chicago, Judy (1939–). Born Judith Cohen in Chicago, she changed her name in 1970 to Judy Chicago to "divest myself of all names imposed upon me through male social dominance." Chicago received her B.A. from the Art Institute of Chicago in 1962 and her M.F.A. from the University of California in Los Angeles in 1964. She became a central figure in the feminist movement, founding (with Miriam Schapiro) the first feminist art program at Fresno State University and playing an important role in establishing the Woman's Building in Los Angeles. In 1975 Chicago published her autobiography *Through the Flower: My Struggle as a Woman Artist.*

Chicago's interest in ceramics began to develop on a trip along the Northwest Coast in 1972, when she stopped at an antiques shop and saw a porcelain plate that was china painted with "the most delectable roses." Chicago felt that the china painting medium had a great deal of expressive potential and began to study china painting in the hobbyist circuit. Soon Chicago realized that china painting was very much a woman's art form in the twentieth century and that in addition to the painterly quality of the technique, it had close historic and symbolic ties to the women's movement.

In 1975 she established and obtained funding for a major project, *The Dinner Party,* which involved four hundred women volunteers in the painting of the thirty-nine large dinner plates and tiles and in the embroidering of the fabric runners that were the focus of the piece. *The Dinner Party* was first shown at the San Francisco Museum of Modern Art, and then traveled throughout the United States and Europe. The exhibition attracted widely differing reviews. It was hailed by feminist critics such as Lucy Lippard, but damned by others, particularly and predictably by male critics. The exhibition did have its flaws, in particular the accompanying book/catalogue, *The Dinner Party: A Symbol of Our Heritage,* by Judy Chicago. John Richardson's article in the *New York Review of Books* in 1980 is a particularly interesting examination of the *Dinner Party* saga. As Richardson states, the event came into its own less as an art piece than as a political event: *''The Dinner Party* deserves to be taken seriously as agit-prop of remarkable potential.... It has served as a sorely needed rallying point in women's ongoing war of independence.... And, not least, it has given the women who worked on [the project] a gratifying sense of communal fulfillment that has been an inspiration to women's groups all over the country'' (Richardson, 1980).

Cornelius, Philip (1934–   ). Born in San Bernardino, California, Cornelius discovered art in the Army Services Library. After his return from army duty he studied at San Jose State University, where he received his B.A. in 1960, and at the Claremont Graduate School, receiving his M.F.A. in 1965. He is a professor at Pasadena City College and maintains a studio in Pasadena, California. Cornelius received two major Visual Artists Fellowships from the National Endowment for the Arts, in 1981 and 1984.

While in San Jose Cornelius studied with Herbert Sanders, from whom he learned about glaze chemistry. At the Claremont Graduate School, where he studied with Paul Soldner, he began to explore the aesthetic energy of ceramics. His early work consisted of large stoneware vessels, often lidded, with hard-edged, architectonic shapes decorated with various patterns and the recurring motif of the salamander.

In 1970 Cornelius accidentally stumbled onto a technique that was to introduce a totally original field of exploration and to become his central focus for the next seventeen years:

> While Cornelius was making some large platters, a thin slab of residue stoneware came loose from the platter bat. This intriguing sheet of clay demanded investigation, so he cut open his paper coffee cup and, using it as a template, constructed an identical cup from the paper thin stoneware. To prove to himself that nothing so fragile could survive a firing, he included it in the next kiln load. Amazingly it held together and the first "thinware" was completed. Over the years Cornelius developed these pieces into more complex forms, finally

settling on the teapot—the most complex of utilitarian ceramic forms. (Burstein, 1982)

This breakthrough in Cornelius's work highlights the way in which many ceramists innovate—through the complex technology of the medium. Except for a few ceramists who use the most rudimentary of processes, technique remains a central and often a creative core. Parallel to his interest in thinware, Cornelius was exploring charcoal firing, attempting to achieve the same expressionistic effects in a modern gas kiln as the Japanese potters were achieving with traditional village kilns. He visited Japan in 1977. At first the charcoal effects were explored on heavy stoneware pieces, but then Cornelius decided to combine this effect with his thinware (which he was now making in porcelain). Surprisingly, even though the mortality rate was high, a large number of the thinwares survived the charcoal firing, and the results on the surface were stunningly dramatic and powerful. In these teapots—with their slab structures derived loosely from World War I tanks and later from aircraft—Cornelius has made a unique and rich contribution to American ceramics, extending the traditions with which he has been nourished.

Cowan, R. Guy (1884–1957). Born in East Liverpool, Ohio, to a family that had been in the pottery industry for generations, Cowan was one of the first graduates of the New York School of Clayworking and Ceramics, where he studied under Charles Fergus Binns. In 1913 he opened his own pottery in Cleveland, scoring his first public success in 1917, when he was awarded the first prize for pottery at the Art Institute of Chicago.

After World War I Cowan moved his pottery to Rocky River, a suburb of Cleveland, and changed the company name from Cleveland Tile and Pottery Company to Cowan Pottery Studio. There he concentrated on molded, limited-edition ceramics, winning many awards, including the Logan Medal for Beauty in Design (Chicago, 1924). He also worked with a white porcelain clay, designing most of the figurative and vessel pieces himself until 1927, when Paul Manship, Waylande Gregory, A. Drexler Jacobsen, and Thelma Frazier began to design limited-edition works for the pottery. With the addition of Arthur Eugene Baggs to the staff between 1925 and 1928, Cowan's glazes also improved in variety and quality. Cowan's ceramics, particularly the figurines,

R. Guy Cowan

were popular, and the company was reincorporated with $100,000 capital. Still, the studio was unable to survive the Depression and in 1931 went into receivership.

Cowan moved to Syracuse, New York, and became the art director for the Onondaga Pottery Company, producers of Syracuse china. In Syracuse he became one of the guiding figures in the Ceramic Nationals. A fitting memorial to his achievement now exists in the Cowan Pottery Museum at the Rocky River Public Library, which has a collection of over eight hundred works and comprehensive archives of catalogues and correspondence. The collection is based mainly on the John Brodbeck collection, which the library purchased in December 1976.

Currier, Anne C. (1950–   ). Born in Louisville, Kentucky, Currier studied at the Art Institute of Chicago, where she received her B.F.A. in 1972, and at the University of Washington, Seattle, where she received her M.F.A. in 1974. She has received several awards, including a Visual Artists Fellowship from the National Endowment for the Arts in 1986. Currier currently teaches at the New York State College of Ceramics at Alfred University, Alfred, New York.

Currier is one of the few artists to graduate from the University of Washington's ceramics program who has not followed a figurative style. Instead, her interests have focused on minimal, hard-edged forms, at first black-and-white vessels that echoed the stylization of Art Deco. However, she soon moved away from the vessel and has concentrated on sculptural forms, influenced by such sculptors as Sol LeWitt. Her latest works are a rhythmic exploration of volumetric elements in a tightly linear format.

Cushing, Val Murat (1931–). Born in Rochester, New York, Cushing received his education at the New York College of Ceramics at Alfred University, Alfred, New York, taking his B.F.A. in 1952 and his M.F.A. in 1956. He later taught at the University of Illinois, Champaign-Urbana, and was the director of the Alfred University summer school course in pottery from 1957 to 1965. He is now a professor of pottery at Alfred University and is an active participant in the ceramic arts. Cushing was chairman of the Standards Committee of the New York State Craftsmen and from 1962 to 1966 chairman of the Technical Committee of the National Council for Education in the Ceramic Arts. His work has been extensively exhibited in major group and one-man shows, and he was recently awarded the Binns Medal of the American Ceramic Society. In recent years Cushing's work has revolved around the exploration of a "roll-top," lidded jar, with the formal climax of the vessel arriving through the tall, spirelike handles of his lids.

Daley, William (1925–). Born in Hastings-on-Hudson, New York, Bill Daley studied at the Massachusetts College of Art in Boston and at Columbia University Teachers College, New York, receiving his M.Ed. in 1951. He has taught in Iowa, New York, New Mexico, and since 1966 at the Philadelphia College of Art, where he heads the ceramics department. Daley has developed a distinctive architectonic form, creating large, press-molded, stoneware vessels. In addition, he has considerable experience in architectural ceramics. He has created murals, both in bronze and ceramic, for the Atlantic Richfield Corporation, the South African Airlines office in New York, and a work entitled *Symbolic Screen* for the IBM Pavilion at the Seattle Century 21 Exposition in 1962.

His early vessels grew out of an interest in Shang bells, with their ellipsoidal cross sections and scooped rims. Gradually other influences altered his vessels. The forms evolved slowly, always retaining the common theme of a play between inner and outer

William Daley

space. An important turning point for his work came in 1972, when as a guest lecturer in New Mexico, Daley was introduced to Anasazi cliff dwellings and to collections of early Pueblo pottery. The black-and-white painted Mimbres pots particularly fascinated Daley, because they spoke to his own obsession with negative and positive space. When he returned to the East he attempted to translate the abstract designs from Pueblo pottery into three-dimensional forms: "the steps and zigzags were marvelous building structures when three-dimensional, recapitulating earlier play with modules, bumps and patterns—from pummelled clay surfaces to Iowa tractor treads and worm gears" (McTwigan, 1983).

In order to increase the exploration of the inner/outer space, Daley began to work on multiple "exits" and "entrances" that lead the eye in and out of the vessel: "attempting to use the edge to control the sense of open and closed, sometimes outside segments had larger negative sections to suggest they might be inside a greater space" (Clark, *American Potters*, 1981). In the catalogue *Who's Afraid of American Pottery?* (Clark et al., 1983), Michael McTwigan likened the complexity of geometry in Daley's pots to Islamic ornament (a subject that fascinates Daley). McTwigan quotes Henri Foçillon's explanation of the tesselation systems in Islamic ornament: " 'a sort of fever seems to goad on and to multiply the shapes; some mysterious genius of complication interlocks, enfolds, disorganizes and reorganizes the entire laby-

rinth...whether they be read as voids or solids, as vertical aexesor diagonals, each one or both withholds the secret and exposes the reality of an immense number of possibilities.' "

Daly, Matthew A. (1860–1937). Born in Cincinnati, Daly counted among his boyhood companions Artus Van Briggle and Ernst Blumenshein, the magazine illustrator. Daly was one of the first decorators to join the Rookwood Pottery, where he remained for twenty years. He left Rookwood to become the art director of the United States Playing Card Company, a post he held for thirty years. Daly was a charter member and president of the Cincinnati Art Club, as well as a member of the American Artists' Professional League.

Delisle, Roseline (1952–). Born in Quebec, Canada, Delisle studied at the Collège du Vieux Montreal in 1975. Coming to the United States in 1978, she established a studio in Venice, California, and soon attracted attention for her small porcelain vessels with their precise black-and-white decoration. Some of her vessels are lidded, with complex, turned finials. In 1985 Delisle received a commission from the J. Paul Getty Center for the History of Art and the Humanities in Santa Monica, California, to make vases for the entrance area. This pushed her into increasing the scale of her work considerably. Her works, still with their mat black decoration on a white porcelain body, have taken on a new monumentality.

DeStaebler, Stephen (1933–). Born in Saint Louis, Missouri, DeStaebler studied with Ben Shahn and Robert Motherwell at Black Mountain College in 1951. He subsequently traveled to Europe, where he concentrated on making stained-glass windows. In 1954 he received his B.A. degree, with high honors, in religion from Princeton University. He served in Germany with the United States Army from 1954 to 1955. In 1957 he worked at the Union Settlement House, East Harlem, New York, and studied ceramics with Ka-Kwong Hui at the Brooklyn Museum School. He later moved to southern California, where he taught history and art at the Chadwick School in Rolling Hills. In 1958 he studied ceramics with Peter Voulkos and took his M.A. in art history at the University of California, Berkeley. Since 1967 he has been associate professor of sculpture at San Francisco State University. DeStaebler is an active sculptor,

Stephen DeStaebler

exhibiting in major group shows since 1962 and carrying out commissions for the Newman Center Chapel, the University Art Museum, Berkeley, and the Bay Area Rapid Transit Station at Concord, as well as for private residences. In 1974 he had a major one-man show at the Oakland Museum.

DeStaebler works on a large scale (his freestanding sculptures are eight to nine feet in height) and draws his inspiration from the terrain and landscapes, particularly of the West. Insofar as there is direct symbolism in his work, he draws strongly from the gestation of earth and rock. Nature, not cultural references, is the major source in his works. Writing about DeStaebler in the 1974 catalogue of his one-man exhibition at the Oakland Museum, Harvey L. Jones remarked that the power and appeal of DeStaebler's sculpture derives in a large part from his attitude toward the clay:

He has learned by long experience to recognize the intrinsic character and beauty of the medium and, more important, to respect its natural limitations. DeStaebler responds to the peculiar qualities which clay possesses: its plasticity when wet, its fragility when dry, its tendency to warp, crack, and slump during the drying and firing processes. He equates the obvious but frequently overlooked fact that clay is earth. He has developed a vocabulary of earth forces: gravity and pressure, eruption and erosion, shearing and breaking. By yielding to clay and discovering what it wants to do, he has evolved a unique art form. Since 1982 DeStaebler has been working

in bronze as well as clay. The bronzes are constructed from the shards of previous clay pieces that were technically unsuccessful. This has enabled DeStaebler to extend the figure in directions that were "antithetical to clay's structural properties." Writing of his work in *American Ceramics* (1984), Joanne Burstein comments, "Above all, the tactile surfaces of his work strike an emotional chord, not an analytic one, as we see the whole destroyed and reassembled with honor.... These are the dichotomies of reverence in an age without religion."

DeVore, Richard E. (1933–). Born in Toledo, Ohio, DeVore was educated at the University of Toledo, where he received his B.Ed. in 1955; and at the Cranbrook Academy of Art, Bloomfield Hills, Michigan, where he studied under Maija Grotell and received an M.F.A. in 1957. In 1966 Grotell chose DeVore as her successor to head the ceramics department, a position he held until 1978, when he joined the faculty of the University of Colorado at Fort Collins.

During the 1960s DeVore's work explored a range of interests, from brightly colored vessels to lustered male torsos preciously contained in framed glass boxes. Since 1970 this eclecticism has been replaced with an intense, sharply focused investigation of the vessel format. His works reveal a virtuoso handling of the dynamics of the potter's aesthetic, presenting a refined and tensely controlled treatment of line, volume, entrapped and displaced space, tactilism, and color. This process of distillation to achieve the essence of these qualities is understandably a highly conscious and intellectual pursuit. While the cerebral quality of DeVore's work is certainly evident—and potent in its power and attraction—the vessels never lapse into an academic format.

One of the dominant features of DeVore's vessels is the lip or rim area, which, as the final act of making, establishes and orders the compositional priorities in the eye of the viewer. Although the forms seem a mixture of the biomorphic and the anthropomorphic, the rims, frequently offset by points or protuberances, allude to a geometric logic that is the foundation of DeVore's compositional style. His aesthetic Achilles' heel is the foot of the vessel. In common with his teacher Grotell, he often seems to render the foot awkwardly and without convincingly integrating it with the rest of the form. This is most noticeable in DeVore's "torso" forms. But on his bowls (particularly what Gerald Nordland terms his "deep"

bowls), works that are arguably his toughest and finest work, the foot disappears under the vessel and the bowls simply float in space. These bowls, with their small interior cavities, create some of the most complex geometries of his works and the most layered sense of metaphor: "A bowl may begin one way and then as the artist changes the cross section of the cylinder, the piece takes on a new posture.... With an undulating of the outer wall DeVore can gain a new impression suggesting a slumping motive, as if a pressure were operating negatively beyond the centrifugal and gravitational forces required for its forming" (Nordland, 1983).

In dealing with the sensual anthropomorphism of the work, Andy Nasisse refers to DeVore's pots as androgynous, combining the male, or dark principle, with a contrasting, light-giving female principle:

The open bowl form is receptive, which embodies the female principle. The various heights allow a versatility of presentation, some related more to the male principle.... The female quality of light as opposed to male darkness is inherent in DeVore's use of color. Often the interior surface has a mottled use of color which appears to give off its own light. The surface is always mat but never flat. Even in pieces seemingly all black there is a subtle combination of deep hued color which appears gradually. DeVore's particular genius and paradox is his ability to create an object of almost seductive beauty and serenity, which at the same time is invested with an extremely turbulent level of spatial reality. (Nasisse, 1976)

Diederich, Hunt (1884–1953). Born in Hungary, Diederich studied in Paris, in Rome, and at the Pennsylvania Academy of the Fine Arts in Philadelphia. Diederich worked primarily in bronze, specializing in animals and figures for monuments and fountains and winning several awards, including the gold medal from the Architectural League. He produced his ceramics in the mid-1920s, painting individual pieces as well as designing for mass production. His works were included in the *International Exhibition of Ceramic Art* at the Metropolitan Museum of Art in 1928. Diederich's ceramics, although produced for a limited period, exhibit both superb draftsmanship and an ability to employ the translucency of his glazes to achieve a sense of depth.

Dillingham, James Richard (1952–). Born in Lake Forest, Illinois, Rick Dillingham studied at the California College of Arts and Crafts, Oakland, and at the University of New Mexico, Albuquerque, where he received his B.F.A. in 1974. In 1979 he received his M.F.A. from the Claremont Graduate School, Claremont, California. Dillingham received Visual Artists Fellowships from the National Endowment for the Arts in 1977 and 1982. He maintains a studio in Santa Fe, New Mexico. Apart from his work as an artist, Dillingham has interested himself in a broad range of activities. He is a dealer in historic American Indian pottery and Navajo textiles. He has also written on American Indian pottery and curated a number of exhibitions—the most recent being *The Red and the Black,* a 1983 retrospective of the Santa Clara potter Margaret Tafoya at the Wheelwright Museum in Santa Fe.

Dillingham's pottery reflects his knowledge of and interest in American prehistoric Indian pottery. The pots are not imitative in any sense, although they draw from forms that are generic to most so-called primitive pottery. Dillingham became intrigued by the notion of the vessel as an assembly of shards when he was restoring pots at the Museum of New Mexico, Laboratory of Anthropology, in Santa Fe. Dillingham's pots are not simply broken and reassembled. The breaks are carefully controlled and "drawn" into the pot before firing. Apart from setting up a different context and mood for his work, the act of reassembling the pot from a number of pieces allows Dillingham a variety of discrete elements on which to paint. Each shard is treated separately and painted with line and pattern out of a palette that is a mixture of bright, primary colors and earthy hues. Some shards are painted with a flat color or covered in gold and silver leaf. When they are reassembled, there is a compositional unity and complexity that places Dillingham's surface painting among the most complex and sophisticated work of this type in contemporary ceramics.

Doat, Taxile (1851–1938). Born in Albi, France, Doat was a student at the Ecole des Arts Décoratifs, Limoges, France, and the Ecole des Beaux-Arts, Paris, and also studied with the sculptor Augustin Dumont. In 1879 Doat joined the Sèvres Manufactory as a sculptor, modeler, and decorator. He became a specialist in *pâte-sur-pâte,* a technique of painting porcelain slips in light relief against contrasting ground, using the translucency to give qualities of light and shade. Doat became one of the leading ceramists in France, winning gold medals for

his porcelains at Antwerp in 1885, Barcelona in 1888, and at the Exposition Universelle in Paris in 1889. In 1898 he established his own studio in Sèvres at 47, rue Brancas. Doat was in contact with the American publisher of *Keramik Studio,* Samuel Robineau, and with Robineau's wife, Adelaide, by 1903. The Robineaus first published a series of Doat's articles on high-fire ceramics in *Keramik Studio* and in 1905 published them together as a book, *Grand Feu Ceramics.* It was the first handbook of its kind to be published in English and had a strong impact on the ceramics community in the United States.

Doat came to the United States in 1909 at the invitation of Edward G. Lewis, founder of the American Women's League, and the People's University in University City near Saint Louis, Missouri. The purpose of the trip was to have a "conference with the League's architects in order that the erection of one of the most perfectly designed and equipped art potteries in the world might be immediately begun." Doat was appointed director of the University City Pottery, where he assembled a distinguished faculty, including Adelaide Robineau, Frederick Rhead, Katherine E. Cherry (a local china painter), and two of his European associates—Eugène Labarrière, foreman of a pottery in the suburbs of Paris, and Emile Diffloth, former art director of the Boch Frères Pottery, La Louvière, Belgium. The first firing of the kiln took place in April 1910, and although the American Women's League foundered in 1911, Doat reorganized the pottery and continued it

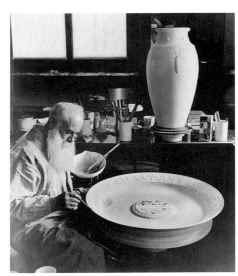

Taxile Doat

until early 1915, when he returned permanently to France.

While in the United States, Doat sold his collection of almost two hundred pieces to the league for $7,000. Herbert Rhead described the group as "without exception…one of the finest groups of the work of one potter in existence" (Weiss, 1981). It was a meticulous selection of his works, showing each and every change in his style and technique. The collection was later housed in the Saint Louis Art Museum. In 1945 the collection was deaccessioned by the museum and only eighteen pieces were retained.

Duckworth, Ruth (1919–). Born in Hamburg, Germany, Duckworth moved to England in 1936. While in Germany, she, as a Jew, was not allowed to enter any art school. Not long after World War II, she filed a "loss of education" claim against the German government and bought her first kiln with the money she received. In England she studied at the Liverpool School of Art from 1936 to 1940. Duckworth worked as a sculptor, learning to carve stone and even earning a living for a while carving tombstones. She began to see and admire pots; she remembers attending a Red Rose Guild exhibition in London, where she saw a very large pot: "I don't know who made it…I know I wanted to put my arms around it and hug it" (Duckworth and Westphal, 1977).

Around 1955 she began to do some simple clay sculpture, and at the suggestion of the potter Lucie Rie she returned to school to learn about glazing. After a short period at the Hammersmith School of Art, which she found too doctrinaire, requiring that "a pot must have a foot, a middle, a lip," she moved to the Central School of Arts and Crafts in London (1956–58). It was there that her work began to develop, and by 1960 she was teaching at the Central School. In 1964 she moved to Chicago to assume a teaching position at the University of Chicago, accepting the offer because she was "curious to see the United States and Mexico and to find out why people made those ugly pots I saw so often in *Craft Horizons*" (Duckworth, 1977). She is now a resident of Chicago, where she has her studio.

Duckworth's involvement with ceramics covers a wide spectrum. Her early work ranged from small, delicate, highly secretive porcelain forms of an organic nature to large, roughly textured weed pots in stoneware. She later created massive stoneware murals, freestanding sculptural forms, vessels, and delicate porcelain forms reminiscent of her earlier work. Recently she has returned to small-scale porcelain vessels, an area where her sensibility is most powerfully expressed, and, paradoxically, where she seems to provide most effortlessly an illusion of monumentality. The pots are created in groups of three to four, with delicate, flat "keys" inserted into the form.

Duckworth has been one of the strongest influences on the liberalization of ceramics in the United Kingdom and has been a successful teacher and artist in the United States. She has participated in several one-woman and many group exhibitions, and has produced several architectural commissions, including *Earth, Water and Sky* (1968) at the Laboratory for Geophysical Sciences, the University of Chicago; *Clouds over Lake Michigan* (1976), a 240-square-foot mural for the Dresner Bank in the Chicago Board of Trade building; *The Creation* (1983) for Congregation Beth Israel, Hammond, Indiana; and a mural in 1984 for the State of Illinois Building in Chicago.

Earl, Jack (1934–). Born in Unipolis, Ohio, Earl took his B.A. at Bluffton College, Ohio, in 1956, returning to school in 1964 to take an M.A. at Ohio State University in Columbus. From 1963 to 1972 he taught at the Toledo [Ohio] Museum of Art, where the magnificent collection of ceramics—early Meissen figures, Kandler dinner services, faience sculptures of the Della Robbia family, and other works—had a strong impact on his work and his perfectionist craftsmanship.

Initially there was little evidence of aesthetic vision in Earl's work; he first made a populist style of pottery that was distinctly commercial, then turned to Japanese pottery for inspiration. But by the time of his one-man show at the Museum of Contemporary Crafts in New York in 1971, a unique style had emerged. One of the centerpieces of the exhibition was a dog in slippers that was a disarmingly realistic portrait of an actual animal, including the trickle of ooze from the dog's eyes. Although inspired by the eighteenth-century porcelains of Europe, the style was anything but imitative of this tradition. Also, for this work a distinctive, long title had emerged, giving the work a strange shamanistic/folk context:

Dogs are nice and make wonderful companions I've been told, and most people get dogs when they are young and cute and so much fun to play with, not thinking about how long a dog can live. You got to train them when they are young too, of course a kid can't train a dog right. I wouldn't take a grown dog who had a previous owner, cause you can never tell what you are getting, even though some of them look real good and lay still for you. You can't change a used dog's bad habits either and they stink, dogs all smell the same. The best dog has a greedy streak and will howl and drool and paw until they get what they want and I like old dogs best because they just lay around and don't bother you so much any more.

Increasingly this mood of narrative has defined Earl's works, recently resulting in complex, delicately painted landscapes and portraits that appear to have magically become three-dimensional. With the move from porcelain to painted earthenware, the sense of figurative ceramic traditions has been severed. But the personal chord remains the same; "Turning a penetrating eye outward at people and places and events around him, Jack Earl succeeds in making viewers look inward and reconsider their relationship with reality" (R. H. Cohen, 1985). In 1985 Earl's biography, *Jack Earl: The Genesis and Triumphant Survival of an Underground Ohio Artist*, written by Lee Nordness, was published.

Eckhardt, Edris (1907–). Born in Cleveland, Eckhardt studied at the Cleveland School of Art, where she was awarded a scholarship and remained for five years, graduating in 1932. In her last year at the

Edris Eckhardt

school, she participated in a collaborative ceramics program created by three institutions: the Cleveland School of Art, the Cleveland Museum of Art, and the Cowan Pottery. After leaving the school, she set up her own studio and became involved with glaze chemistry.

In 1933–34 Eckhardt participated in a pilot program of the Public Works of Art Project (PWAP), which operated for five months and provided a number of specific assignments for individual artists. Through this program she conceived the idea of producing small-scale sculptures for use in children's library programs. These were based on *Alice in Wonderland*, the Mother Goose stories, and W. H. Hudson's *Green Mansions*, then popular with adolescent readers. Her *Alice in Wonderland* series was particularly successful; a piece from this series was acquired by Queen Elizabeth II for her private collection.

In 1935, when the WPA-FAP began local operation, Eckhardt was made director of the Cleveland department of ceramic sculpture. She held this position until the program, which later passed into state control, was finally discontinued, in 1941. Eckhardt continued to work in the ceramic medium, producing one of her major pieces, *Painted Mask*, which she exhibited in Cleveland at the May Show in 1947.

In 1953 Eckhardt began to work in glass and rediscovered the technique of fusing gold leaf between sheets of glass—producing the first-known examples of gold glass in almost two thousand years. The original technique had been perfected by the Egyptians, who used it in glass vessels and jewelry. Eckhardt has since developed her technique into multiple laminations of sheet glass, using layers of enamels, foils, and other materials to add depth to the surfaces.

Eckhardt has been the recipient of several awards for her research and was a Guggenheim Fellow in 1956 and again in 1959. She has also received a Louis Comfort Tiffany Fellowship for her work in stained glass. Eckhardt is an active exhibitor throughout the country in both one-woman and group shows and is recognized as one of the pioneering glass artists.

Elozua, Raymon (1947–). Born in Germany, Elozua came to the United States in 1951. He studied at the University of Chicago, originally intending to be a lawyer. But in his third year as a political-science major, Elozua was attracted to the work of Ruth Duckworth, who was a member of the university's art faculty. Elozua was so drawn both to Duckworth as a teacher and to clay as a material that he dropped out of all his classes and spent six months in the clay studios. He recalls: "Ruth Duckworth had a special attitude and sensibility that was really refreshing. She taught you how to think about what you were doing" (Wechsler, 1982).

In 1969 Elozua moved to New York and worked on set construction at Juilliard but found the theater world too precarious financially. In 1974 he bought a kiln and five hundred pounds of clay, and by 1975 he had been accepted for the Rhinebeck Craft Fair, where he exhibited small bowls and porcelain sculptures. In the eighties his sculptural instincts led him to produce complex, moody miniature "landscapes" of abandoned mining buildings, decaying amusement parks, and decrepit sawmills and billboards. This work was rendered in a detailed, realist style. In a sense it was a continuation of his work at Juilliard, where he always made small models of the stage sets. Elozua says, "What I have really done is remove the proscenium. I look at the work as maybe shadow boxes without the box" (Wechsler, 1982).

Around 1983 Elozua began to explore a new content in his work. Derived from his earlier series of billboards, these works have a sharpened political edge. In fact, it is so sharp that Ivan Karp, after first approving the work for an exhibition at the O.K. Harris Gallery, abruptly changed his mind and at the last minute refused to exhibit the works. Writing about the shift in emphasis, Akiko Busch commented: "If Elozua first considered the machinery of the American Dream, he now considers its operators. His new work looks at the blue-collar workers who fought World War II and returned to make good in the post-war manufacturing boom; at the millworkers and steelworkers whose labors have been rewarded by the erosion of American industry, who bought the American Dream, and watched it fall flat" (Akiko Busch, 1987). The portraits are somber, built up of small shardlike pieces of clay assembled on large panels. The shards make up images of eagles, helmeted G.I.s, fighter pilots, and the Statue of Liberty, mixing symbols of patriotism with an overall mood of decay and disillusionment. Still working with the shard, Elozua has also begun to explore the still life, dealing with the notion of fragmentation and reassembly.

Kenneth Ferguson

Ferguson, Kenneth (1938–). Born in Elwood, Indiana, Ken Ferguson studied at the American Academy of Art (summer school), Chicago; at the Carnegie Institute of Technology, Pittsburgh, where he received his B.F.A., in 1952; and at Alfred University, Alfred, New York, where he was awarded an M.F.A. in 1954. He has taught at various institutions, including the Carnegie Institute; Alfred University; and the Archie Bray Foundation, Helena, Montana. From the early 1960s through the present, he has headed the ceramics department of the Kansas City [Missouri] Art Institute. Under Ferguson's guidance KCAI has become one of the most important undergraduate ceramics schools in the country. His students from the 1970s now dominate the leading edge in American ceramics—John and Andrea Gill, Richard Notkin, Chris Gustin, Irv Tepper, Akio Takamori, Arnie Zimmerman, Chris Staley, Kurt Weiser, and others.

Ferguson has been a strong influence as a functional potter; his work is distinguished by a sensuality of form and surface. In summing up his personal view of his art, Ferguson comments: "I enjoy the versatility. For this reason I work with functional and nonfunctional forms—stoneware, salt firing, raku, porcelain and low temperature, thrown forms and handbuilding, and castware. I reflect the fine arts traditional craft and the need to make things. I try to be honest with myself and honest with clay" (Nordness, 1970).

In the 1980s his work has taken a strong step forward, to become more sculptural and more personally subjective than his earlier work, which was more involved with utility. In a review in the *Los Angeles Times* of a 1986 exhibition of Ferguson's pots, the critic Colin Gardner wrote:

There is an urgent Dionysiac vitality about Kenneth Ferguson's pots and platters that injects his basically utilitarian works with a strangely animalistic eroticism. The veteran ceramist mines the muscular fluid decoration of Japanese oribe pottery as well as the 17th-century tradition of Staffordshire "Adam and Eve" iconography to create an idiosyncratic hybrid that is at once graceful, voluptuous and slightly clumsy, much like the contours of a Rubens nude. Ferguson's favourite form is a lidded jar, in this case a small smoke-stack-like piece, whose gun-metal metallic glazes, protuberant lines and patinaed surface suggest aging industrial architecture rather than a decorous household object. The platters and baskets are slightly more genteel, particularly those in white clay with ethereal blue glazes. Yet their deeply etched motifs (mermaids, Adam and Eve, bounding rabbits) express a barely restrained bawdiness, as if the malleable clay were metamorphosing into human flesh, ripe for kneading and probing. (Gardner, 1986)

Frackelton, Susan Stuart Goodrich (1848–1932). The daughter of a brickmaker, Frackelton established the Frackelton China and Decorating Works in Milwaukee in 1883. She employed decorators, and within a short time the factory's weekly production of objects ranged from 1,500 to 2,000 pieces. In 1885 she published *Trial by Fire*, which rapidly became the bible of the china painters. In addition, in 1892 she organized the National League of Mineral Painters, whose membership included Adelaide Robineau and Mary Chase Perry, and in 1894 she patented "Frackelton's Dry Colors." Frackelton exhibited salt-glazed wares at the World's Columbian Exposition in Chicago in 1893. She later moved on to what were termed delftwares—blue, underglaze-decorated wares—which she exhibited at the 1900 Exposition Universelle in Paris. Frackelton ceased potting at the beginning of the twentieth century and moved to Chicago, where she was an active lecturer until her death in 1932.

Edwin Atlee Barber paid $500 for her famed *Olive Jar* (1893), which he purchased for the collection of the Pennsylvania Museum. The major collection of her work is

Susan Frackelton

in the State Historical Society, Madison, Wisconsin; most of this collection was donated by her daughter, Susan Frackelton.

Frank, Mary (1933–). Born in London, England, Frank was the only child of Eleanore Lockspeiser, a painter, and Edward Lockspeiser, a musicologist and critic. She immigrated to the United States in 1940, and at the age of seventeen worked for a short period in the studio of the sculptor Alfred van Loen and studied modern dance with Martha Graham. Following her marriage to the Swiss photographer Robert Frank, she studied drawing with Max Beckmann at the American Art School in Holland, and after 1951 studied drawing with Hans Hofmann at his Eighth Street School in New York.

Although she never formally studied sculpture, Frank was attracted to this medium. Her early works were small, wooden figures influenced by Giacometti, Egyptian art, and the work of Henry Moore. Inspired by Reuben Nakian's ceramic wall plaques and Margaret Israel's ceramic sculpture, Frank began to work in wet clay; since 1969 most of her works have been produced in stoneware. The first major exhibition of these works took place at the Zabriskie Gallery, New York, receiving an enthusiastic notice from Hilton Kramer, who called her works "marvels of poetic invention...the very process of the ceramic medium seems to have released the requisite spontaneity" (Kramer, 1970). Three years later, Frank

produced her first larger-than-life figures, demonstrating maturity in the handling of her material and great originality, showing only a slight debt to the strong, early inspiration of Nakian.

Since the early seventies, Frank's work has grown rapidly in stature, has been charged with erotic energy, and has consistently explored myth and metamorphosis. Hayden Herrera, the guest curator of Frank's one-woman exhibition in 1978 at the Neuberger Museum, State University of New York, Purchase, wrote evocatively of the artist's having "created a strange, Arcadian world populated by nudes, earth goddesses, forest spirits, Nereids and winged nymphs in flowing gowns. In this world the human figure is at home in nature. There is no hint of the romantic artist's insatiable yearning to connect with nature; figures *are* nature, embodying all time. All this without a glimmer of romantic nostalgia; although her sculpture is full of poetic whimsy, it is too urgent and earthy ever to be sentimental or sweet" (Herrera, 1978).

Frankenthaler, Helen (1928–). Born in New York City, Frankenthaler received her art education at Bennington College, Vermont. Her work has been widely exhibited, including a one-woman retrospective at the Whitney Museum of American Art in 1969. Her paintings are clear, simple forms with irregular boundaries that avoid the familiar and the geometric. She is particularly known for her technique of stain painting, in which she washes colors onto unprimed canvas.

In 1964–65 Frankenthaler participated in the *Art in America* project *Ceramics by Twelve Artists*, producing a limited number of plates that echoed the transparency of color on her canvases. Ten years later, in November 1975, she worked at the Clay Institute in Syracuse on the Everson Museum of Art's project *New Works in Clay by Contemporary Painters and Sculptors*. Frankenthaler approached the project with caution and afterward wrote: "The idea of working in clay has never really appealed to me; in all ways it is too fragile and my fantasy-scale of what I wanted to do sculpturally seemed to go way beyond the possibilities of wet earth. But the project called me— much in the same way I had made metal sculpture, a ceramic tile wall and a series of 71 ceramic tiles" (Hughto, 1976). In working on her pieces, Frankenthaler was not interested in using drawings or models or running tests, but wished to stress the immediacy of her contact with the medium: "From the beginning I wanted nothing to

resemble arts-and-crafts, ashtrays, abstract lamp bases, etc. The point was sculpture out of clay in my terms" (Hughto, 1976).

Frazier, Bernard ("Poco") (1906–1976). Born on a cattle ranch near Athol, Kansas, Frazier received his first artistic training at Kansas Wesleyan University in Salinas in 1924. He then enrolled in the newly created school of design at the University of Kansas, Lawrence. Upon graduation in 1929, he traveled to Chicago to work as an apprentice to the sculptors Lorado Taft and Fred Torrey, studying there intermittently at the National Academy of Art, the Chicago School of Sculpture, and the Art Institute of Chicago, as well as briefly at Moholy-Nagy's New School, an offshoot of the Bauhaus. Returning to Kansas in the mid-1930s, he was awarded a grant in 1938 by the Andrew Carnegie Foundation to serve as sculptor in residence at the University of Kansas, remaining there to establish the first regular department of sculpture. During the next three decades, his local reputation grew and he was continually involved in the fulfillment of important commissions. Two of his major ceramic works—*Untamed* (1948) and *Prairie Combat* (1940)—are in the permanent collection of the Everson Museum of Art, Syracuse, New York.

Frey, Viola (1933–). Born in Lodi, California, Frey studied at the California College of Arts and Crafts, Oakland, receiving her B.F.A. in 1956. While a student she studied painting under Richard Diebenkorn and took an elective course in ceramics under Vernon Coykendall and Charles Fiske. She received her M.F.A. in 1958 from Tulane University in New Orleans, where she studied under Katherine Choy. After graduating, she joined Choy's newly founded cooperative, the Clay Art Center, in Port Chester, New York, and took a bookkeeping job at the Museum of Modern Art in New York. In 1960 she returned to the Bay Area, where she began to exhibit actively. In 1965 Frey joined the California College of Arts and Crafts (CCAC) faculty in a part-time capacity while maintaining a full-time job at Macy's, Oakland. In 1970 she turned to full-time teaching, working in the ceramics department, as well as teaching a course on color in the CCAC painting department. Frey still teaches at the CCAC in the ceramics department.

Frey's early work was involved with the Bay Area's fashionable interest in Japanese and Chinese ceramics during the 1950s.

For a time she made only pots, but gradually she returned to her figurative concerns. In the 1960s her work became more iconographic. Influenced by Robert Arneson's toilets and trophies, she turned to everyday objects for her subjects. On weekends she haunted the giant flea market at Alameda and developed a large collection of dime-store figurines and other industrially made decorative ceramics, which the artist felt had "a frozen presence far beyond their value. They become images from childhood, memories enlarged and scary. Amongst these artifacts are little animals—dogs, cats, roosters, birds—and their attendant human. I decided to make them big—take them out of the crib and off the coffee tables, make them myths of childhood. I altered their poster colors using overglazes to give them alertness and vividness, and to unfreeze them" (Chicago et al., 1977).

Frey's interest in overglaze painting grew out of her color-light studies at the CCAC. She sees this involvement in two phases: the first, trying to match effects achieved in painting—spray effects for clouds and the modulation of colors to add activity and depth to the surface of the object. In the second phase she used china painting to manipulate the surface of forms. By painting light and shadow, she was able to establish auxiliary forms upon the base structure.

By 1970 her work had grown in complexity, scale, and volume. She was now beginning to develop a name as a ceramist, and her exhibitions sold very well. Frey was at a crucial point in her personal development, and it distressed her to see pieces leave the studio so rapidly, before she could live with and learn from them. As a result, in the mid-seventies she withdrew from all public exhibiting and began to work at a furious pace, filling her five-storied home from ground floor to attic with her works. Several series of works emerged between then and 1981: detailed, china-painted tableaux with the look of incomplete "paint by numbers" projects that explored the chiaroscuro of light and shade in its most subtle modulations; the *Desert Toys*—ominous, brutal-looking pieces with raw surfaces and a sense of menace; large assemblages of cast ceramic bric-a-brac that Frey called her "bricolages" after Claude Lévi-Strauss's notion of the junkman, or *bricoleur*, as an artist; paintings and life-size ceramic figures that began to develop in scale and abstraction.

In 1979 she returned briefly to the public arena in the exhibition *A Century of Ceramics in the United States*, her first major national exhibition platform. But she kept out of the commercial circuit until after her acclaimed retrospective in 1981, which opened at the Crocker Art Museum in Sacramento and then traveled to seven other institutions. Since then Frey has had an active exhibit record, including a one-person exhibition at the Whitney Museum of American Art in 1984.

Her oeuvre of the early eighties has been dominated by an interest in the figure; the life-size portraits of family and self from the late seventies have now become massive figures that stand up to eleven feet in height. Yet, despite their scale, they remain tied to the notion of the figurine. In a brochure for Frey's exhibition at the Whitney, the curator, Patterson Sims, described the figures as "immobile sentinels…they engage the viewer in an unequal dialogue. Intimidatingly aggressive they glower at their human counterparts, turning the viewer into the figurine. Grown-up and fantastic versions of Frey's beloved bric-a-brac, they amplify her dictum that 'figurines function in order to make acceptable those things our culture finds unacceptable.' Frey's huge figures …reveal the average, kitsch, and the stereotype as mirrors of American cultural values" (Clark and Sims, 1984).

About late 1985–86 Frey's tall, clothed figures began to take on an awkward quality, straining to cope more with their complex concerns of engineering and gravity than with content. But the earlier inventiveness returned through a generation of smaller figures, which has returned the tableaux to Frey's work and the sense of what Lévi-Strauss termed "deviousness." The larger figures have now shed their clothes and become recumbent, strangely fascinating vulgarizations of the classical nude.

The strongest link of her present work to the Frey of the seventies can be seen in her platters. Plates bring Frey back to the uncomplicated play with ideas and forms; "they are created in a limited time. It can take several weeks to create a figure but I can do several plates in an afternoon. They explore whatever the time allows" (Clark and Sims, 1984). In these pieces the *bricoleur* still reigns supreme, encrusting the surfaces with a relief of cast objects, glazed with the lavalike lines of Egyptian paste and viscous, bright glaze. They are the sculpture of a major American sculptor entering her creative prime.

Frimkess, Michael (1937–), and Magdalena Suarez Frimkess (1929–). Born in Los Angeles, Michael Frimkess entered the Otis Art Institute at the age of fifteen to study sculpture. He was one of Otis's youngest students and one of the last to join the ceramics course under Peter Voulkos, a decision he made after a peyote trip, during which he had the vision of throwing a pot. At nineteen Frimkess moved to Italy, where he worked in a ceramics factory in the south. He returned to Los Angeles in 1958 and spent some time at the Berkeley "pot shop" at the University of California. In 1963 he moved to New York, where some of his work was shown at the Allan Stone Gallery. When he delivered his work, Frimkess found the gallery crammed with the china-painted works of Robert Arneson: "I was shocked.... They took my breath away, it was like seeing one aspect of myself. I could have done that if I had the opportunity. But I had been wax finishing Malvina Hoffman's bronzes at the Italian Bronze Foundry in Queens" (Clark and Frimkess, 1982).

Michael Frimkess

Frimkess later worked at a commercial pottery in Pennsylvania, where he replaced an Italian potter who had been using a technique of throwing hard clay without water. Frimkess learned this technique and began studying the ancient Greek ceramics in the Metropolitan Museum of Art, deciding that they had probably been thrown by this method. He returned to Venice, California, where he established a studio.

Since the late sixties the central focus on Frimkess's work has become the throwing of hard clay without water. His forms have distinct cultural references, such as the Greek amphora and the Chinese ginger jar. These he decorates with bright, overglaze patterns. Some consist of purely decorative motifs, and others employ complex, comicbook illustrations that deal with his experiences of being a member of "the last Jewish family left in Boyle Heights," where he grew up with Japanese, Chicano, and black children. The objects he has created have symbolically become ethnic melting pots, wherein all racial differences and discrimination can be dissolved.

From 1966 to the early seventies there was an extraordinary outpouring of vessels from Frimkess's studio. Jazz musicians played riffs on Kang Xi vases, and cyclists pedaled across volute kraters (*Ecology Krater II*, 1976). Labels for the fictional firm Gilbey's and Benson appeared on panathenaic amphorae, and in *Covered Jar* (1968) Uncle Sam, with rape on his mind, pursues third-world maidens across ginger jars, while various godheads and superheroes look on.

These works represent a major departure in style from his earlier pieces, which dealt with iconographic assemblages in mixed media and with bronze television-set sculptures, such as *Hooker* (1962). The vessel remains the main Frimkess format: "Today's pottery continues as ever, an art form. Wheel throwers remain philosophers, humanitarians, and men of conscience, aware of their time's mission, ever on a par with the greatest sculptors, perfectionist painters, writers and musicians. Due to throwing's freedom-giving limitations, it is still one of the finest roads towards self improvement" (Frimkess, 1966). During the past two decades illness has greatly reduced Frimkess's output and particularly limited his drawing.

In addition to the independent works of Michael Frimkess are the many important pieces on which he and his wife, Magdalena Suarez, have collaborated. She had studied painting at the Escuela Artis Plastica in Caracas, Venezuela, showing a great facility for draftsmanship. She interrupted her studies in 1947, when she was married, and did not return to them until 1954, when she took classes at the Catholic University of Chile in Santiago. Magdalena came to the United States on a scholarship to study at the Clay Art Center in Port Chester, New York. There she met Michael Frimkess. Several years later they married and began to collaborate in their work. In some ways her work is similar to Michael's in that she uses a mixture of national styles, her most distinctive being a blending of Mayan and Hispano-Moresque. Unlike her husband, however, she makes no attempt at philosophical statements in her work. She achieves these mixes intuitively: "I only care what my work looks like, whether it works compositionally, whether the color is right…I am indifferent to what it means" (Clark and Frimkess, 1982).

Fry, Laura Anne (1857–1943). Born in Indiana, Fry was the daughter of a noted wood-carver, William Henry Fry. She studied wood carving, china painting, sculpture, and drawing at the Cincinnati School of Design from 1872 to 1876. She continued her studies in Trenton, New Jersey (the American equivalent of Stoke-on-Trent, Britain's industrial center for ceramics), and then in France and England. In 1881 she joined the decorating team at the Rookwood Pottery, where she worked in the style of Hanna Barlow (an artist from Doulton's Lambeth Art Studio), incising decoration and rubbing in cobalt oxide.

In July 1883 Fry introduced the technique of applying slips to greenware with an atomizer—the first use of the "spray gun" in American ceramics. She was granted a patent for the technique in 1889. Fry became professor of industrial art at Purdue University, Lafayette, Indiana, in 1891, but a year later she returned to Ohio, joining the Lonhuda Pottery in Steubenville. There she attempted to restrain Rookwood from using her atomizer technique, but the courts ruled against her in a judgment delivered by Judge William Howard Taft in 1898.

Fry returned to her teaching post at Purdue after finding the public interest in the women's decorative-art movement to be sharply on the wane. She remained at Purdue until 1922. Fry was one of the leading figures in the Cincinnati women's art movement; her innovation in pottery decoration was directly responsible for the "Standard Rookwood" style. Upset by the failure of her patent claim, however, Fry refused to give any of her works to the Cincinnati Art Museum and instead donated a substantial collection of her wares to the Saint Louis Art Museum in 1911.

Fulper, William H. (1872–1928). Born in New Jersey, Fulper came from a family that had operated a pottery since 1805. The importance of the pottery in the production of art ware was slight until late in 1909, when the Fulper Pottery Company first introduced the Vasekraft line at their plant in Flemington, New Jersey. The body used in these wares was made from a natural New Jersey clay and was fired at a high temperature alongside the pottery's commercial ware. The superb range of luster crystalline, mat, and high-gloss glazes attracted considerable attention—but the most prestigious glaze was the so-called *famille rose* developed by William Fulper. Fulper effectively capitalized upon the interest in Chinese pottery in his Ashes of Rose glaze, selling individual works for as much as $125. The Fulper was one of the few "regenerative" art potteries of post-1910, selling well at a time when most other art potteries were in decline. Fulper Vasekraft won the gold medal of honor at the Panama-Pacific International Exposition in 1915. Fulper shared a stand with Gustav Stickley, and the vases were shown on Stickley's furniture.

One year after Fulper's death in 1928, the Flemington plant was destroyed by fire and with it all the pottery's records. Production was transferred to the new plant in Trenton, New Jersey. In 1930 the pottery was acquired by J. Martin Stangl, formerly the superintendent of the pottery's technical division. Despite their frequent and often heated differences of opinion, Stangl had risen to become Fulper's right-hand man in the pottery. In 1955 the corporate title was formally changed to the Stangl Pottery Company.

A collection of major works of Fulper art ware was given to the Philadelphia Museum of Art in 1911. Other important collections are at the Newark Museum and New Jersey State Museum, Trenton. In 1979 an exhibition organized by Robert Blasberg for the Jordan-Volpe Gallery in New York brought a new wave of interest in collecting Fulper wares and, for a while, some overoptimistic speculation as to the financial value of the wares.

Gilhooly, David (1943–). Born in Auburn, California, Gilhooly received his B.A. from the University of California, Davis, in 1965 and his M.A. in 1967. He has taught at San Jose State University, California; Canada's University of Saskatchewan, Regina, and York University, Toronto; and the University of California, Davis (1975–76).

Gilhooly's early work was based on a satirical play on animal motifs, such as his *Elephant Ottoman* (1966). Between 1968 and 1984, he worked prolifically on a body of work that is almost without parallel in the ceramic arts. Each year has seen the production of several hundred frog objects of one kind or another. In a detailed discussion of "the Gilhooly mythology," Dale Mc-Conathy remarked: "These pieces, dispersed almost as soon as they are made and never shown in the full context of their creation, comprise a sort of archaeology in reverse—the random deposits of the artifacts of Gilhooly's frog world.... A cast, disturbing, deeply dark *speculum mundi*...the depth of that mirror further clouded by an uneasiness about just what the correspondences are—the sort of troubled ambivalence found in lists that mark off the boundaries of what is human and non-human" (McConathy, 1975).

Like other Funk artists of the ceramic genre, Gilhooly gives his work titles that add significance beyond identification: they are clues to the artist's intent and at the same time give substance to the object. In the uneven plethora of works produced by Gilhooly are several masterworks, notably *Miscegenation* (1974), *Cosmic Egg* (1975), *Tantric Frog Buddha* (1975), and the series of portraits *Frog Victoria* and *Mao Tse Toad*.

Through the 1970s Gilhooly was without doubt the most exhibited ceramic artist in the United States and has to date had over thirty one-man exhibitions, including a major retrospective in 1976 at the Museum of Contemporary Art, Chicago. However, this period of massive production, of everything from large-scale sculpture to the "donut stores" that he would set up outside his exhibitions to sell ceramic "food," began to slow down as interest in his particular vision waned. The critical response to his work in the 1981 exhibition *Ceramic Sculpture: Six Artists* at the Whitney Museum of American Art was poor. He has since altered his work considerably and is currently working in plastics. His peculiar frog vision of life remains, nevertheless, an important part of the Funk movement in American ceramics.

Gill, Elizabeth Andrea (1948–   ). Born in Newark, New Jersey, Andrea Gray studied at the Rhode Island School of Design, from which she received her B.F.A. in 1971. She then studied for a year and a half, in 1972–73, at the Kansas City Art Institute and received her M.F.A. in 1974 from the New York State College of Ceramics at Alfred University. She is currently an associate professor at Alfred University, where she teaches with her husband, John Gill.

Andrea Gill has developed a distinctly and highly decorative style of work. Some of her vessels are simply painted with pattern while others, notably the "madonna" vases, employ figurative imagery. In the eighties she has increasingly explored the figurative form, influenced by pottery made by the Wiener Werkstätte ceramists of the twenties, in particular Vally Wieselthier, Susi Singer, and Gudrun Baudisch.

Writing about Gill's work in the exhibition catalogue *Who's Afraid of American Pottery?* (Clark et al., 1983), Susan Wechsler remarked on the emphasis of the decorative over content:

> Many artists who employ the figure to confront personal, psychological, or narrative issues might criticize these figures as complacent or facile. But that would be to lose sight of Gill's intentions. Regardless of her figurative interests, the artist's primary purpose is to make *decorative* pots; they remain foremost a vehicle for the skillful painting she employs to pattern her pieces. But, however decorative the work, it manages to successfully challenge our perceptions about pottery concepts.

Gill, John Patrick (1949–   ). Born in Renton, Washington, Gill studied pottery at the Cornish School of Art, Seattle, first with a traditional potter, Thorne Edwards, and later with Patti Warashina and Irvin Tepper. In 1971 he studied with Ken Ferguson at the Kansas City Art Institute, receiving his B.A. in 1973 and his M.F.A. in 1975 from the New York State College of Ceramics at Alfred University. He married his fellow student Andrea Gray in 1975 and subsequently taught at the Rhode Island School of Design (1975–77), Colorado State University in Fort Collins (1977–78), and Kent State University (1979–84). He is currently associate professor at the New York State College of Ceramics at Alfred University.

Gill's visual vocabulary was essentially formed during his undergraduate studies in Kansas City. What Gill appreciated at KCAI was the sympathetic atmosphere regarding historical ceramics. Gill had already acquired an affection for early English porcelains and creamwares. "At KCAI," he remembers, "there were two main factions: one group was trying to break with the past and make 'art'; the other sought to define, analyze and extend the historical traditions of potmaking" (Carr, 1984). In particular, he gravitated to Persian ceramics, with their rich-hued palette and complex form structures. Gill was also influenced by painting, in particular by Arthur Dove's work and by Giorgio Morandi's tense exploration of negative and positive space.

Gill's forms fall into three distinct categories: the house pot, which he has been making since his student years; pitchers and teapots; and last, an organic "muscle" pot that turns the surface of the pot into a rubbery, biomorphic composition that is part Surrealist and part Cubist. But it is the ewer that Gill has made his own, and his eccentric forms are masterful plays with structure, juxtaposition, color, and function. The ewers combine references to the elegance of the Persian wine ewers, with suggestions of mechanical parts in his oversized funnels, some with corkscrew twists—all energetically combined into curiously weighted vessels. They do resemble birds, as some writers have pointed out, but are perhaps closer to the oddly shaped dodo than the heron, their concern not being flight but rather coming to terms with gravity and volume.

John Glick

Glick, John Parker (1938–   ). Born in Detroit, Glick received his B.F.A. from Wayne State University, Detroit, in 1960 and his M.F.A. in 1962 from the Cranbrook Academy of Art, Bloomfield Hills, Michigan. After two years in the United States Army, he set up the Plum Tree Pottery in Farmington, Michigan, producing hand-thrown, functional wares. Over the years Glick has developed a unique and distinctive style of decoration, drawing on the surface of forms with glaze and slips. His work is strongly influenced by his interest in Japanese pottery, but at the same time it is reminiscent of the early Abstract Expressionist works of such artists as Mark Tobey.

Unlike many potters in the United States who rely upon the state-fair system to market their work, Glick has over the years built up a dedicated following. More than two-thirds of the pots produced at his pottery are sold from his own showroom. During the 1970s he concentrated on commissions for dinnerware, which he produced on an individual, personalized basis. Despite his heavy work schedule, Glick sets aside time to participate in the broader, educational responsibilities of his art. He provides tours through the pottery for schoolchildren, teachers, and craft groups, and he has lectured and given workshops extensively throughout the United States. Glick is one of a select cadre of functional potters whose example and free sharing of information have contributed to the rising standard of production pottery in the United States.

González, Arthur (1954–).

Born in Sacramento, California, González attended the American River College in Sacramento for two years, then transferred to California State University, Sacramento, where he received his B.A. in painting in 1977 and M.A. in painting in 1979. He then studied with Arneson and Manuel Neri at the University of California, Davis, receiving an M.F.A. in clay sculpture in 1981.

González was at first attracted to photorealist art, but after leaving American River College he sought out a more expressive and personal style. This he began to define through a number of sources: Lucas Samaras's collages, Ellsworth Kelly's Minimalism, and the ceramics of Robert Brady and Arneson. Brady in particular became González's mentor, introducing him to a broader study of art. González began to exhibit actively in 1981, and his series of impressive exhibitions at the Deborah Sharpe Gallery in New York brought his talents to the attention of the sculpture world.

González's sculpture is not free*standing*. His sculptures begin at the waist or chest and emerge from the wall, where they are suspended. They are not, however, part of the tradition of relief sculpture. The emerging figures are fully three-dimensional. One can see in these works an amalgam of his early interest in realism and Minimalism.

As William Zimmer comments, "The pronounced ellipse across the front of the figure *Time Traveller* (1984) is a sort of homage to Minimalism, especially González avers, to Carl Andre and Ellsworth Kelly. 'That's the real craft,' González says of the Minimalists, 'those pieces which are about how little we can show and still bring about one-hundred percent perception. To make it count, it has to be done with impeccable craftsmanship' " (Zimmer, 1985).

Gregory, Waylande DeSantis (1905–1971).

Born in Baxter Springs, Kansas, Gregory took art classes at the State Manual Training Normal School (Pittsburgh) from sixth grade through high school. He later studied at the Kansas State Teacher's College, Emporia; and at the Kansas City Art Institute. Gregory was an unusually precocious and energetic student and while still in his teens was invited by Lorado Taft to work in residence at the Art Institute of Chicago. He became involved in ceramics through a job with the Midland Terra Cotta Company in nearby Cicero. At the age of twenty, Gregory received a major commission to design and execute several decorative interiors for the Hotel President in Kansas City. In 1928 he accompanied Lorado Taft to Italy, where he studied for some time in Florence. During his early career Gregory worked in both bronze and ceramics; the latter gradually became his major medium. One of his last major works in bronze was a sculpture for the University of Chicago chapel, which he completed in May 1928.

Later that year Gregory left the studio that he had shared in Chicago for several years with Lorado Taft and joined the Cowan Art Pottery Studio in Rocky River, a suburb of Cleveland. Gregory created many of Cowan's most successful major works of 1929, including *Diana and Two Fawns*, which was produced in a limited edition of one hundred and won the first prize at the Cleveland Museum of Art's May Show in 1929; *Marguerite, at Her Lessons* (1929); and *Burlesque Dancer* (1929–30). After leaving the Cowan Pottery in 1932, he worked briefly as artist in residence at the Cranbrook Academy of Art, Bloomfield Hills, Michigan. He also taught at Cooper Union in New York before moving to Bound Brook, New Jersey, where he set up his studio.

Gregory made an arrangement with Atlantic Terra Cotta Company in Perth Amboy, New Jersey, to set up a workshop in the

Waylande Gregory

plant, where he would have access to the factory's giant kilns. One of the first monumental pieces, *The Swimmer* (1936), was selected for the annual sculpture show at the Whitney Museum of American Art. In 1938 he completed two mammoth commissions, *American Imports and Exports* for General Motors and *The Fountain of Atoms*, comprising twelve ceramic figures, each weighing over a ton. This was exhibited at the 1939 World's Fair in New York. In order to produce these pieces, Gregory developed a unique building technique that he described as "inner modelling." The later works by Gregory show the strong influence of Paul Manship, who produced some designs for the Cowan Pottery in the last two years of its operation and may have also been involved earlier.

In 1940, after Gregory had completed a commission for the Municipal Center in Washington, D.C., his career, which had until then taken place in the glare of national publicity, quite suddenly began to decline. He received no further commissions of any consequence. His one-person exhibitions did not produce many sales, partly because he tended to set prices two to three times that of his contemporaries. To support himself he began to manufacture limited-edition figurines, plates, candlesticks, and ashtrays to sell to stores such as Sloane's,

Hammacher Schlemmer, Georg Jensen, and Gump's. In 1956 he became the guest for a children's TV program, "Ding Dong School," in which he told and illustrated stories. He also gave art lessons at his home. Then, in 1962, he was involved in a disastrous attempt to set up a visual-arts center in Massachusetts near Ted Shawn's Jacob's Pillow Dance Center. The proposed center ran into problems with its sponsors, the Farmer family, and the project ended with the murder of Mrs. Farmer by her husband.

Gregory returned to New Jersey, where he worked in metal and in plastic foam. But he retained his special love of ceramics: "Earthen sculpture was the magnificent solution for me, nature's generous way, her invitation to destiny.... Nature's voice seemed so much nearer in the formless clay, so abundant on every hand, awaiting the command of release from chaos" (Watson, 1944). In 1983 the Everson Museum of Art, in cooperation with the trustees of the Gregory estate, included thirty-six sculptures by the artist in the exhibition *Diversions of Keramos: American Clay Sculpture 1925–1950*, the first extensive showing of the artist's sculpture in over thirty years.

Grotell, Maija (1899–1973). Born in a village outside Helsinki, Finland, Maija Grotell studied at the School of Industrial Art in Helsinki, taking courses in painting, design, and sculpture. She also did six years of postgraduate work in pottery under Alfred William Finch, one of Europe's finest pioneer artist-potters. In 1927 she came to the United States and taught at the Henry Street Settlement House in New York. From 1936 to 1938 she was an instructor of pottery in the School of Ceramic Engineering at Rutgers University, New Brunswick, New Jersey. In 1938, at the invitation of a fellow Finn, Eliel Saarinen, she joined the faculty at the Cranbrook Academy of Art in Bloomfield Hills, Michigan, where she headed the ceramics department until 1966.

In the beginning, her position at Cranbrook was not very glamorous; she had only a small stipend and few serious students. But Grotell was a dedicated and inspirational teacher and soon expanded the importance of the ceramics department. Unfortunately this was at the expense of her own production as an artist. As a teacher she avoided directing her students too closely, saying that "good potters must develop their own approach. I am against influence" (Hakanson, 1960). When she was critical, she was cautious and often oblique.

Maija Grotell

In "Pioneers of the Vessel Aesthetic" (1980), Elaine Levin recorded an interview with one of Grotell's students, Rhoda Lopez. Lopez recalled that Grotell once examined her pots and said that though the pots were nice, she did not like them. After pondering the problem for a few days, she returned to Lopez with a few newspaper cuttings about her own work and explained her unhappiness with the pots: "We are so different, you and I. I am a heavy person. These newspaper articles call my work 'stolid'—my work *is* heavy. You are thin, nervous, quick and energetic. Your vases remind me of tall skinny ladies wearing high-heeled shoes. The ware does not seem stable to me." John Glick, one of her students, said that above all Grotell taught her students to love "the search" in making pots. "She prized inquiry alone, above all...and hell was rained on anyone who believed otherwise."

During her career, Grotell received twenty-five major awards, including a diploma from the 1929 International Exposition in Barcelona, and six awards from the Ceramic Nationals in Syracuse. She was also a recipient of the Binns Medal of the American Ceramic Society in 1961. She established Cranbrook as a major center for ceramic art education, even though the actual number of her students was modest. Her graduates, such as Richard DeVore (who replaced her at Cranbrook), Toshiko Takaezu, John Glick, Susanne Stephenson, and Jeff Schlanger, have had a strong influence on contemporary ceramics.

Grueby, William H. (1867–1925). At the age of fifteen, Grueby was apprenticed to the Low Art Tile Works, Chelsea, Massachusetts, where he remained for about ten years. In 1892, with Eugene R. Atwood, he formed his own company, Atwood and Grueby, which was associated with a larger company, Fiske, Coleman and Company. In 1893 Grueby went to the World's Columbian Exposition in Chicago to manage the exhibition of tiles from Fiske, Coleman and Company. It was there that he became acquainted with the *grès flamme* of Chaplet and Delaherche, two pioneering French artist-potters. Delaherche had a particularly strong influence on Grueby's work; this relationship is discussed in chapter 2.

In 1894 Grueby opened his own firm, Grueby Faience Company, in Boston. He exhibited in February 1895 at the annual exhibition of the Architectural League, New York; at that stage he was primarily concerned with architectural faience, emphasizing historical style. In 1897 the company was formally incorporated and reorganized. From that year on, having discovered the mat glazes for which he was to become famous, Grueby began to produce art pottery. Between 1898 and 1902 the forms were designed by George Prentiss Kendrick. Thereafter the designs, while similar to the early ones by Kendrick, were the work of Addison B. Le Boutiller, a French architect.

Grueby's wares won considerable acclaim, including one silver and two gold medals at the Exposition Universelle in Paris in 1900; the Grand Prix at the Pan-American Exposition in Buffalo, New York, in 1901; a gold medal at Saint Petersburg, Russia, in 1901; the Grand Prix at Turin, Italy, in 1902; and the Grand Prix at the Louisiana Purchase International Exposition, Saint Louis, in 1904.

In spite of its success, the company experienced financial problems, and in 1908 Grueby ceded the presidency of Grueby Faience to Augustus A. Carpenter of Chicago, who brought new capital. But a year later the company was declared bankrupt and went into receivership. Undaunted, Grueby opened another company in the same year, Grueby Faience and Tile Company, continuing at the same factory. The production of wares continued at the Grueby Pottery (a marketing division formed in 1898), although there, too, operations were affected by financial pressures. The production of wares appears to have ceased about 1909–11. In 1913 the company suffered a devastating fire, from which it never fully recovered. Just before the fire Grueby had staked most of the capital available to him to install thermostatically controlled fur-

Christopher Gustin

naces. Grueby survived further crises until 1919, when C. Pardee Works of Perth Amboy, New Jersey, acquired the firm. Grueby died six years later. His death went largely unnoticed, except for a cursory obituary in the *Bulletin of the American Ceramic Society*.

Gustin, Christopher (1952–   ). Born in Los Angeles, Gustin studied biology and sociology at the University of California, Irvine. In 1970, intrigued by John Mason's activities at the university's clay studio, Gustin took an elective class in ceramics. After traveling through Europe and later working for a ceramics manufacturer in Pasadena, California, Gustin attended the Kansas City Art Institute, from which he received his B.F.A. in 1975. At the institute he was part of a particularly gifted class that included John and Andrea Gill, Arnie Zimmerman, Akio Takamori, Stan Welsh, and others. He joined many of the KCAI students at the New York State College of Ceramics, Alfred University, from which he received his M.F.A. in 1977. In 1984 Gustin began to work for the Program in Artisanry at Boston University. In 1986 the program moved to the Swain School of Design in New Bedford, Massachusetts, where Gustin continues to teach as professor of ceramics.

While at Alfred, Gustin was particularly influenced by Kylliki Salmenhaara, a visiting artist from Helsinki, Finland. Gustin says that she "profoundly influenced ideas concerning the figure in my pots. Her critiques were not with words, but through body movement and gesture. Explaining its stance and volume through caricature, Kylliki would pantomime each form. If a pot was dumpy she would walk low to the ground, waddle and quack like a duck. If a pot was light and graceful she would throw her head high, arch her back and become like a bird in flight" (Gustin, 1982).

Gustin was also influenced by the work of Robert Turner, particularly by Turner's palette of mat glazes. In common with Turner, Gustin likes to work with a limited number of glazes, controlling the texture of the surfaces through sandblasting. The anthropomorphic quality of his work has continued to grow over the years. Although in most cases the reference to the figure is extremely abstracted, the asymmetrical vessels speak strongly of sexuality in their voluptuous, rounded forms and through the phallic imagery employed in the spouts of the pitchers. In addition to using the form in a highly plastic manner, Gustin "draws" on the surface with a mixture of

line and soft, rounded, relief elements. The pots, with their structure of nesting volumes, are among the most radical and abstract investigations into potter's space.

Hafner, Dorothy (1952–   ). Born in Woodbridge, Connecticut, Hafner received her B.S. from Skidmore College in Saratoga Springs, New York, in 1974. After graduation she worked for the New York State Craftsmen as production manager for the International Craft Film Festival and in 1976 for the Museum of Contemporary Crafts, New York, directing its international department. Hafner was an artist in residence at Artpark, Lewiston, New York, in 1977 and 1978. In 1979 she set up a studio, Art for Dining, in New York City, where she designs porcelain tablewares that are then handpainted by a team of decorators. In a sense Hafner is functioning as a latter-day Clarice Cliff, the popular ceramic designer active in Britain before World War II. Cliff was a designer with an exuberant sense of the decorative who eventually employed a small army of decorators (over two hundred) to paint her wares. Hafner's operation is much smaller. Unlike Cliff, who produced wares for the general market, Hafner directs her work toward the market's upper end. Hafner has sold her dinnerware at Neiman-Marcus and at other department stores. She has also created exclusive designs for Tiffany in New York, and since 1982 has designed for Rosenthal in Germany, for which she received the Westerwald Industrial Design Award. In 1983 she received the Certificate of Honor from Women in Design, Ross, California. Hafner also makes one-of-a-kind works, centering on the soup tureen as her primary form. Her work is distinguished by a fresh and inventive use of pattern, color, and line.

Haile, Thomas Samuel ("Sam") (1908–1948). Born in London, England, Haile worked as a shipping clerk, taking night classes in art at the Clapham School of Art. In 1931 he won a scholarship to study painting at the Royal College of Art. The professors in painting objected to his Surrealist tendencies, so he transferred to ceramics, under William Staite Murray. Haile taught full time at the Leicester College of Art in 1935 and later shared a pottery studio with Margueret Rey at Raynes Park. In 1937 he held his first one-man exhibition of ceramics at the Brygos Gallery in London.

Haile moved to the United States in 1939, accompanied by his wife, Marianne de Trey. He was by then a member of the Surrealist circle. For a time he lived by doing a number of odd jobs. Then Charles Harder arranged for him to teach at Alfred University, where he himself taught ceramics; Haile was ostensibly at Alfred as a student to satisfy immigration restrictions. In 1942–43 Haile taught at the University of Michigan, Ann Arbor, and presented a paper, "English and American Ceramic Design Problems," before the American Ceramic Society in 1942.

Haile joined the United States Army in 1944 and then transferred to the British army. In 1947 he set up a new pottery in Shinner's Bridge, Dartington Hall, Devonshire, England, but was killed in an automobile accident the following year. Memorial exhibitions were held at the Southampton Art Gallery, England, in 1948; at the Institute of Contemporary Arts, Washington, D.C., in 1948; and at the Crafts Centre, London, in 1951.

Harder, Charles M. (1889–1959). Born in Birmingham, Alabama, Harder attended Texas A & M University for one year (1919) as a student member of the United States Army Training Corps. After graduating from the Art Institute of Chicago in 1925, he taught at Peabody High School in Pittsburgh, Pennsylvania. Harder joined the staff of the New York State College of Ceramics at Alfred, New York, as an instructor in 1927 and became assistant professor in 1931. While teaching, he continued his own studies under Charles Fergus Binns, and received his B.S. degree in ceramics in 1935. Harder spent the next year doing postgraduate studies at the Art Institute of Chicago and surveying the curricular

Charles M. Harder

administration of other art schools. He returned to Alfred in 1936 as a professor of ceramic art and reorganized the curriculum to conform to New York State's requirements for industrial and professional design. Harder was named acting head of the design department in 1938 and head in 1944.

Harder received many prizes and honors during his career. Among the most treasured of these was the gold medal from the International Exposition in Paris in 1937. In the following year, he was awarded the Binns Medal of the American Ceramic Society. Harder had joined the society in 1928 and was made a fellow in 1947. He held all the offices of its Design Division and was a member of the Ceramic Education Council. Melvin Bernstein's recently published study, *Art and Design at Alfred*, provides a detailed account of Harder's impact as an educator.

Heino, Otto (1915–). Born in East Hampton, Connecticut, Heino became involved in ceramics in the late 1940s, when he returned from duty with the United States Air Force in England. He studied ceramics under the GI Bill at the League of New Hampshire Arts and Crafts, Concord. In 1950 he married Vivika Timeriasieff, his teacher, and two years later they moved to California. Together the couple established a pottery on Hoover Street in Los Angeles. Otto worked almost full time as a potter while Vivika taught in various schools in California and elsewhere. The couple now operates a pottery in Ojai, California, producing a range of architectural, functional, and decorative wares. The Heinos have received numerous awards for their work; in 1978 Otto received the gold medal from the sixth Biennale Internationale de Céramique d'Art, Vallauris, France.

Heino, Vivika Timeriasieff (1909–). Born in Caledonia, New York, Heino studied at New York State College of Ceramics, Alfred, New York, receiving her M.A. in 1944, and at the California School of Fine Arts. In the late 1940s she taught ceramics for the League of New Hampshire Arts and Crafts in Concord, where she met Otto Heino, who was studying ceramics. They were married in 1950 and moved two years later to California. In 1952 Vivika Heino relieved Glen Lukens, head of the ceramics department of the University of Southern California, while he was on sabbatical and remained there for three years. In 1955 she was invited by the Chouinard Art Institute in Los Angeles to reorganize its ceramics department, and

she remained there for eight years. In 1963 she taught at the Rhode Island School of Design in Providence, reopening the Heinos' New Hampshire home and studio in Hopkinton in 1965. They later returned to California, acquiring the house built by Beatrice Wood in Ojai, a small community nestled in the mountains northwest of Los Angeles. There Vivika Heino operates a pottery together with her husband, producing work for architectural commissions as well as

Wayne Higby

decorative and functional vessels. The work of the Heinos has won several awards, including a silver medal from the *International Ceramics Exhibition* in Ostend, Belgium, in 1959.

Higby, Wayne (1943–). Born in Colorado Springs, Higby was educated at the University of Colorado, Boulder (switching from law to art), where he received a B.A. in painting and art education in 1968. He then took his M.F.A. in 1968 with John Stephenson and Fred Bauer at the University of Michigan, Ann Arbor. From 1968 to 1973 Higby taught at the University of Nebraska, Omaha; Scripps College, Claremont, California; and at the Rhode Island School of Design, Providence. In 1973 he was appointed associate professor of ceramics at the New York State College of Ceramics, Alfred, and is now professor of ceramics.

Higby's inventive use of raku and landscape imagery was a welcome and necessary break from the aesthetic of the "Alfred vessel," which had been constantly reinforced by the tradition of employing Alfred graduates. Higby uses his vessels as a three-dimensional canvas on which valleys, lakes, and canyons appear. In some works the image is used in an illusionary manner that blends the vessel's interior and exterior. Higby defines his works (and indeed all vessels made with artistic intent) as objects "that present the formal essence of a pot exaggerated to reveal a personal artistic vision uninhibited by pragmatic issues of function" (Higby, 1986).

Higby uses only two forms—a high, oval bowl and a nest of lidded vessels. The forms are emphatically pots but deliberately without direct cultural or historic reference. Higby sees his work as dealing with the symbolic nature of the vessel. Speaking of his work in a recent article, Higby commented on both its visual schema and its aesthetic content:

I like to think that there's an equal tension of balance between the three-dimensional form and the drawn illusion of projecting and receding space. It's a balancing [act]. I think of [my] pot as a figure. People ask why there aren't any people in my landscapes, but the pot itself is a figure, a personification of a kind of human condition, a series of polarities: the pot is me. As the bowl radiates outward, it becomes a metaphor for human consciousness and our strange existence in space. The bowl form has that potential resonance; it can deal with finite space and infinite, illusory space-things that also exist in our psyches." (Klemperer, "Higby," 1985)

Over the past fifteen years Higby has refined his forms and surface imagery within a narrow palette and range of forms. The growth has been directed horizontally, with subtle nuances and shifts, rather than with any vertical movement. In the 1980s his energies have increasingly been directed toward the ceramics field at large. He has become an active writer on ceramics and has served on the boards and committees of many organizations, including the Haystack Mountain School of Crafts, the Gallery Association of New York State, the National Endowment for the Arts, and the New York State Council on the Arts. Higby's works have been widely exhibited, and in 1973 he was given a one-man show at the Museum of Contemporary Crafts in New York.

Holcomb, Jan (1945–). Born in Washington, D.C., Holcomb attended the University of Michigan, Ann Arbor, where he received a B.A. in history in 1968 and a B.F.A. in painting and ceramics in 1975. In 1977 he received his M.A. in ceramics from California State University, Sacramento. He has taught ceramics at the Rhode Island School of Design since 1978 and maintains a studio in Pascoag, Rhode Island. Holcomb's sculpture deals with the landscape in the Surrealist sense as a metaphor for the subconscious. Alienation and loneliness are recurring themes but are presented with objective distance. There is no self-pity or even latent anger in the work—just a perceptive and gentle observation of the human condition.

The influences active on Holcomb's art are diverse, ranging from Disney cartoons and political caricaturists to Max Ernst and Funk artists Robert Arneson and Jim Nutt. Holcomb places the greatest emphasis in his work on the face, giving it a stylized quality with a touch of the grotesque. He says that his work "always starts with the face, because that is really the focus of the psychological and emotional energy and information. The figure is like an appendage of the face" (Wechsler, 1984). Holcomb's landscapes were originally produced as tableaux but now they are mainly wall sculptures, modeled in relief with very carefully detailed painting on the surface. "My work is very controlled," says Holcomb; "The handling of the imagery is neatly done. I really enjoy taking all the care to clean them up and make them nice.... [But] the figures are really not nice, and there's the contrast between their attractiveness and the emotional states that is not attractive. Some of the figures are darker than others, some characters have to do with darker issues, like mortality. Some are defensive characters, with emotions of fear or trying to fend people off. Sometimes it's exterior forces that are creating anxiety. Whether overt or subtle, it's sort of an existential plight" (Wechsler, 1984).

Hudson, Robert (1938–). Born in Salt Lake City, Hudson studied at the San Francisco Art Institute, where he received his B.F.A. in 1962 and an M.F.A. in 1963. Hudson is known for his exploratory use of color in his distinctive polychrome metal sculpture and for his fastidious craftsmanship. In 1972–73 he produced a body of ceramic works in conjunction with Richard Shaw. Although they shared molds and techniques, they worked individually, sharing inspiration and knowledge. Writing of these works, Peter Schjeldahl commented:

Even in California's twenty-year history of avant-garde clayworks I wonder how many pieces, judged by the standard of Hudson and Shaw, seem primarily or even necessarily to be ceramic objects rather than extensions into the medium of generalized art intentions. The achievement of Hudson and Shaw was to perceive the limitation of the ceramic object as a thing of, if not domestic function, domestic scale and feeling and to realize within that limitation a maximum creative freedom. There is a kind of dreamlike abstract logic to these works, a blend of nonchalance and inevitability that can be best understood, I believe, in terms of a radical coming to grips with the medium. (*Robert Hudson*, 1977)

Hughto, Margie (1944–). Born in Endicott, New York, Hughto studied at the State University of New York at Buffalo, where she received her B.S. in art education, with minors in ceramics and painting, in 1966. She later studied at the Cranbrook Academy of Art in Bloomfield Hills, Michigan, and received an M.F.A. in ceramics in 1971. Both before and after graduating from Cranbrook, Hughto taught at public high schools in Michigan and New York State. In 1971 she joined the faculty of Syracuse University, Syracuse, New York, where she has been a full-time ceramics instructor since 1974.

In 1975 Hughto became project director and curator for the exhibition *New Works in Clay by Contemporary Painters and Sculptors*, producing a ninety-six-page catalogue that documented the project and the exhibition. The project brought together ten major figures in the fine arts to work during a concentrated period on the production of a body of ceramic sculpture. The project was a considerable success. With funds from the Ford Foundation, Syracuse University established its Clay Institute, which occupies the full top floor of the old Consolidated Can Company building. Since 1976 several of the artists who participated in the original project, including Anthony Caro and Friedel Dzubas, have returned to work with Hughto. There have also been new artists: Kenneth Noland, Mary Frank, Stephen DeStaebler, and others. Hughto was responsible for initiating and co-curating the exhibition *A Century of Ceramics in the United States 1878–1978*, which was accompanied by the first edition of this book.

Hughto has continued an important tradition at Syracuse University of dedicated women artists who support the ceramics field at large. Much like the editor-artist Adelaide Alsop Robineau and the author-sculptor Ruth Randall, both of whom are from Syracuse, Hughto has developed her own work into one of the more original statements in contemporary ceramics today. She has also contributed richly toward the broad needs of the art through her directing of the Clay Institute and, until 1981, as adjunct curator of ceramics at the Everson Museum of Art, Syracuse. Hughto curated *Nine West Coast Clay Sculptors: 1978*, the first major exhibition on the East Coast to look specifically at the importance of the West Coast in the post–World War II development of ceramic art. She organized an exhibition, *New Works II*, in 1979 and then in 1980, *New Works III*, the last of the *New Works* series.

In the eighties Hughto has concentrated mainly on large-scale ceramic commissions for IBM, the Buffalo Mass Transit System, and other corporations and institutions. She has organized a model studio in Syracuse for these labor-intensive projects, while continuing to hold one-person exhibitions, including her 1980 exhibition at the André Emmerich Gallery in New York. Her interest in paper, which began through her collaboration with Kenneth Noland, has continued through the years and is as important as her work in clay. In her clay work the abstracted image of the fan has been replaced with a series that deals with floral subject matter, but again abstractly rendered in roughly textured, high-relief wall pieces.

Hui, Ka-Kwong (1922–). Born in Hong Kong, Hui attended Kong Jung Art School in Canton, China, and the Shanghai School of Fine Arts in Shanghai. Before coming to the United States in 1948, he was apprenticed to Cheng Ho, a sculptor. He worked with the Wildenhains at Pond Farm in California and then went to Alfred University, where he received both his B.F.A. and M.F.A. from the New York State College of Ceramics. After obtaining his degrees, Hui taught at the Brooklyn Museum Art School and at Douglass College, Rutgers University, New Brunswick, New Jersey. In 1964–65 Roy Lichtenstein invited Hui to be his technical collaborator in a series of cup sculptures and ceramic mannequin heads that were later exhibited at the Leo Castelli Gallery in New York. Although Hui was not working in the Pop idiom as such, there was a strong affinity between his work—

the flat, bright color of his forms—and Lichtenstein's. Hui continues to work in the style of his early works.

Irvine, Sadie (1887–1970). A graduate of the Sophie Newcomb Memorial College for Women, New Orleans, Irvine was one of the best-known decorators of the Newcomb Pottery's mat-glazed pottery after the arrival of Paul Cox in 1910. Little firm biographical information is available on Irvine. In her correspondence with Robert Blasberg (Blasberg, 1971), she was vague about dates, giving the year that she joined the pottery as "between 1910 and 1912." She was the originator of one of the pottery's most popular designs, the live oak, an honor that she later claimed to regret. The beautiful moss-draped oak trees appealed to the buying public, "but nothing is less suited to the tall graceful vases—no way to convey the true character of the tree—and oh how boring it was to use the same motif over and over again." She presented one of these vases to Sarah Bernhardt "on one of her many farewell tours" (Blasberg, 1971). Irvine remained at Newcomb and taught there until 1952. In later years her creative activities were directed toward watercolors and block prints.

Karnes, Karen (1920–). Born in New York City, Karnes studied at Brooklyn College,

New York, in 1946 and at the New York State College for Ceramics at Alfred University, Alfred, New York, from 1951 to 1952. In 1952 Karnes and her husband David Weinrib became potters in residence at Black Mountain College in Asheville, North Carolina. Karnes and Weinrib set up their own pottery at Stony Point, New York, in 1954. Karnes was later divorced but remained at Stony Point and established herself as one of the leading functional potters in the United States. Her works are distinctive for their sturdy, powerful forms and their superbly textured salt-glazing. Karnes has received many awards and honors, including the Tiffany Fellowship in 1958; awards from the Everson Museum's Ceramic Nationals in 1950 and 1958; a silver medal at the thirteenth Triennale de Milano, Italy. In 1976 she was made a member of the Academy of Fellows of the American Craft Council and received a fellowship from the National Endowment for the Arts. In 1980 she was made a fellow of the National Council on Education in the Ceramic Arts.

In the late seventies her work began to take on a dual identity. She continued to make inexpensive utilitarian pottery, but also made one-of-a-kind pots. An important exhibition in this development took place at the Hadler/Rodriquez Gallery in New York in 1977. Writing of the work in the exhibition catalogue, Judith Schwartz com-

Karen Karnes

mented, "In an age of plastic icons, throwaway bottles, consumable values and mercurial fashions, it is comforting to know that there are those amongst us who, in independent, peaceful, and disciplined ways, create works which are, at once, practical, timeless and beautiful, and, in so doing, enrich us all" (Schwartz, 1977).

In 1979 Karnes moved to Vermont, where she currently maintains a studio in Morgan. The move resulted in important developments in her work. She began to change her forms and turned from salt-glazing to a new wood-fired palette, producing a superb range of new glazes with deep, singing blue surfaces and a more austere palette of black and gray-brown. The eighties is an exciting period of innovation and experiment for an acknowledged master in the field.

Kottler, Howard (1930–). Born in Cleveland, Kottler studied at Ohio State University, Columbus, receiving his B.A. in 1952, an M.A. in 1956, and a Ph.D. in 1964. He also received an M.F.A. from the Cranbrook Academy of Art, Bloomfield Hills, Michigan, in 1957. He taught first at Ohio State University, from 1961 to 1964, and then from 1964 to the present at the University of Washington, Seattle. He received a Fulbright grant in 1957 and a National Endowment for the Arts fellowship in 1975.

Kottler's early works are traditional stoneware, both functional objects and chunky, expressionist weed pots. An interest in surface imagery and china painting, which he developed in the late 1960s, led Kottler toward a new form of expression. This he explored in two directions: first, a successful series of Art Deco vessels, such as *Playmate Pot* (1969), *Mondo Reflecto* (1967), and *Bunny Hop Pot* (1970); second, and running parallel to this series, was his plate series, a limited-edition presentation of commercial plates and decals. The "content" of the work was based on Kottler's interference with the known images that he used on his decals and the lavish packaging and presentation of the works. Kottler's *The Old Bag Next Door Is Nuts* (1976) was first exhibited in *Illusionistic Realism as Defined in Contemporary Ceramic Sculpture* at the Laguna Beach [California] Museum of Art in 1977. When the piece was subsequently illustrated in *Ceramics Monthly*, it caused a furor. A reader discovered that the house used in the piece was produced from a commercial mold, and her outrage resulted in a long, ongoing correspondence between the left and right wings of ceramic sculpture.

During the 1970s Kottler emerged strongly as what can only be termed a "supermannerist," displaying a slick comedy of manners and a style that employs the visual sleight of hand of trompe l'oeil painting. Kottler freely acknowledges the lack of content or depth in his work, and in an exhibition catalogue he made the following statement:

> Most of my work in ceramic sculpture involves the use of camouflage coupled with the relationship between non-related images. I like the perfection of industrial techniques and commercial ceramic ware. I am lazy, I use images already available—casting is simpler and faster than modelling. I purchase molded pieces already cast, use prepared glazes and junked ceramic objects; in fact, I seldom touch clay. I use other people's molds, other people's ideas and other people make my ceramic decals. I just assemble the parts. The resulting work ranges from the bad to the interesting with an occasional hot piece. (Laguna Beach Museum of Art, 1967)

Kottler has been one of the most influential teachers in the ceramic-sculpture movement. A generation of innovative, successful artists has emerged from this school: Jacqueline Rice, David Furman, Anne Currier, Mark Burns, Michael Lucero, and many others. Kottler used to exhibit extensively; by 1978 he had been included in over 250 group and one-man exhibitions in the United States. He withdrew from the exhibition circuit from 1981 until 1987, when he returned with his first major exhibition in nearly ten years, organized by LeMar Harrington at the Bellevue Art Museum, Bellevue, Washington. In the new works he uses a stylized Cubist/Art Deco format and frequently covers the clay surfaces with contact paper that creates a *faux* surface in imitation of wood or marble.

Kozloff, Joyce (1942–). Born in Somerville, New York, Kozloff attended the Carnegie Institute of Technology and received her B.F.A. in 1964. In 1967 she received her M.F.A. from Columbia University, New York. In the mid-seventies, Kozloff had become increasingly interested in decorative issues, co-founding the Pattern and Decoration movement (P&D). She began to work with fabric and tiles, the latter exploration inspired by her second trip to the Alhambra, the fourteenth-century Moorish palace in Granada, Spain. Islamic and Mexican folk art became the two strongest forces in her work; the influence of both can be seen in some of her major tile and mosaic installations: *New England Decorative Arts* (1979–85, Harvard Square Subway Station, Cambridge, Massachusetts), *Bay Area Victorian, Bay Area Deco, Bay Area Funk* (1982–83, San Francisco International Airport), *Topkapi Pullman* (1985, Suburban Train Station, Philadelphia), and *Untitled* (1983–84, Humbolt Hospital Subway Station, Buffalo, New York).

As Kozloff points out, her choice of the so-called minor arts as her focus has a social agenda: "More cultural history is contained in the minor arts than anywhere else, because so many people participated in them, and these artisans didn't have to be so 'important.' My work is about that anonymous craft work that is around, but people don't see. I want to say, 'Take a look' " (Johnston, 1986).

Kraus, Anne (1956–). Born in Short Hills, New Jersey, Kraus studied painting at the University of Pennsylvania, Philadelphia. Following her graduation in 1978, she lived and worked as a painter in New York. In 1982, for purely recreational reasons, she took a ceramics course at the Greenwich House Pottery. She became so intrigued by the medium that she went back to school, receiving her M.F.A. from the New York State College of Ceramics at Alfred University, Alfred, New York, in 1984. She maintains a studio in Short Hills.

Kraus is one of the few contemporary ceramists working with narrative and language. She paints scenes and includes either brief legends, such as "PATIENCE" and "AMBITION," or else more complex writings, which expound on issues of coming to terms with life, with alienation and rejection. The potent use of simple but poetic phrases and the gentle, illustrative style project the contradiction of tenderness and hurt that one finds in the paintings of Neil Jenney. However, unlike Jenney, there is no attempt to deal with social macrocosms—instead, Kraus is most intrigued by microcosms in human relationships.

She is strongly influenced by early porcelains, in particular by those of Meissen and Sèvres, as well as by the delightfully vulgar and overly eclectic Prussian porcelains of the nineteenth century. As far as the issue of function is concerned, her orientation is toward the palace rather than the cottage for she has commented that "to make a teacup, one can make a cottage of a cup or one can make it into a palace. Something that is simple, brown and inexpensive is not more functional than a palace effort with all its complexities, brilliant notes and financial expense. Both are homes, both are items used for morning coffee or tea." Kraus uses the domesticity of the cup, albeit quite elaborate in form and surface, to lull the viewer into a tactile and intimate contact with the work. Only then does the viewer come into contact with legends and statements that are lightly printed on the pieces, giving clues to the intensely revealing and often chillingly painful emotions that the vessels contain.

Her works elicit a variety of responses. Writing about her work at her one-person exhibition at the Garth Clark Gallery in Los Angeles, the *Los Angeles Times* critic Colin Gardner saw the pots as

> stages for lovelorn, anxious scenarios and texts, where Edward Gorey–like figures pine for lost loves or revive their spirits with sudden inspirations seemingly conjured from Samuel Smiles's "Self Help" Manual. Kraus creates an hermetic overly precious world that evokes a repressive Victorianism, where taking tea or arranging flowers in a vase become ritualistic escapes from the rather barren torment of brooding loneliness and despair. Form thus perfectly complements content. (Gardner, 1986)

Finally, Gardner found the content "suffocating" and trapping the artist in too personal a vision. On the other hand, Patricia Mallarcher, writing for the *New York Times* in 1986 on the occasion of Kraus's one-person exhibition at the Newark Museum, saw the work as being "without a dull interval" and seeming to offer points of entry for a larger significance: a connection with universal yearnings and fears, as well as the tensions of relationships…metaphorical journeys with moments of hesitation and decision."

Lawton, James Barnard (1954–). Born in Fairborn, Ohio, Lawton attended Florida State University, Tallahassee, where he received his B.S. in 1976. He obtained his M.F.A. in 1980 from Louisiana State University, Baton Rouge. Lawton received Visual Artists Fellowships from the National Endowment for the Arts in 1984 and 1986. He has taught at various universities and art schools in the United States, including Louisiana State University, Baton Rouge; the New York State College of Ceramics at Alfred University, Alfred, New York; and the Penland School of Crafts, Penland, North Carolina.

Lawton works with the raku technique but produces works of a complexity and graphic clarity that are unusual in the medium. His forms are particularly distinctive, dealing mainly with the notion of movement and distortion. In some works this sense of movement is combined with the image of a toppling table, a falling cup, or spilling liquid. The artist comments that his intention is to use imagery that will "orient the pot to its 'household' [i.e., casual] surroundings; in a sense to give context to the form" ("James Lawton," 1984). His work with the teapot form is of particular distinction: he creates a rubbery yet elegant form with a powerful, dominant spout that thrusts out of the pot. Lawton maintains a studio in Bluffton, South Carolina.

Levine, Marilyn (1935–). Levine was born in Medicine Hat, Alberta, Canada, and studied at the University of Alberta, Edmonton, where she received her B.Sc. in chemistry in 1957 and M.Sc. in 1959. Thereafter she studied at the School of Art, University of Regina, Regina, Saskatchewan. In 1970 she received her M.A. from the University of California, Berkeley, and in the following year her M.F.A. in sculpture. Since graduating she has taught in both Canada and the United States and has exhibited extensively. Her work has employed a material transformation, giving clay the appearance of leather and producing various satchels, suitcases, and other objects. These objects are related to the super-

Marilyn Levine

realist school but at the same time lack many characteristics of this genre. Instead they proclaim a pure kind of objecthood, in which the material becomes the content. Also, the artist sees another aspect that is an important element of her work: "An acquaintance of mine, Marc Treib, described pretty neatly the two types of impact man has on the world, *intent* and *trace*. He defines intent as man acting consciously. This would include design, building and purposeful action. *Trace* on the other hand is the accumulation of marks left by the realization of man's intent, such as trampled grass, grease spots and dirt. In *trace* we find richness, a humanity often omitted in *intent*" (Foote, 1972). It is the ability of leather to accumulate the history of man's traces that has so fascinated Levine and kept her single-mindedly pursuing this trompe l'oeil odyssey for the past fifteen years.

Lichtenstein, Roy (1923–). Born in New York City, Lichtenstein studied under Reginald Marsh at the Art Students League. Lichtenstein attended Ohio State University, Columbus, from 1940 to 1949, interrupted by his service in the United States Army from 1943 to 1945. He received his B.F.A. from Ohio State University in 1949. Thereafter, he taught at Ohio State University and at the State University of New York, Oswego, and in 1960 he became assistant professor at Rutgers University, New Brunswick, New Jersey. In 1964 he resigned from the Rutgers faculty to devote himself full-time to painting and began his maquettes for the ceramic "heads."

From November 20 to December 11, 1965, after a year-long collaboration with Ka-Kwong Hui, Lichtenstein exhibited his ceramic sculptures at the Leo Castelli Gallery, New York. These works had a strong influence on the development of a Super-Object/Pop idiom in ceramics. No Pop ceramics produced thereafter managed to match this body of work in its clarity of purpose and sculptural/pictorial power. The works have been extensively exhibited and illustrated. In 1977 the Art Galleries of California State University at Long Beach organized a major exhibition of Lichtenstein's ceramic sculpture. In 1985 Lichtenstein added to his ceramic oeuvre by designing a limited-edition tea service that was produced by the Rosenthal Porcelain Works in Germany.

Little, Ken D. (1947–). Born in Canyon, Texas, Little received his B.F.A. from the Texas Technical University, Lubbock, and his M.F.A. in 1972 from the University of Utah, Salt Lake City. Little has taught extensively, and from 1972 to 1979 was on the faculty of the University of Montana, Missoula. Between 1971 and 1977 he was the recipient of several research grants, including the Research Advisory Council grant for ceramic and mixed-media sculpture (1975–76), and "Spaces, an Artist-Teacher Exploration" (1976–77). Little has been actively involved in his field, and from 1975 to 1977 was director-at-large for the National Council on Education for the Ceramic Arts. Since 1980 his work has taken him away from ceramics, although the material is sometimes used in his multimedia sculpture. While no longer a central player in the ceramics world, he has left behind a strong influence as an innovative sculptor and passionate teacher.

Lord, Andrew (1950–　). Born in Rochdale, England, Lord studied at the Rochdale School of Art from 1966 to 1968 and studied ceramics at the Central School of Art in London until 1971. After leaving school he moved to Rotterdam and later to Amsterdam, where he exhibited at Art and Project, a highly respected and innovative gallery. While in Holland he developed a fascination with delftwares; in a letter to the author in 1975 he explained his fascination with the wares:

> I didn't always draw from highly evolved ceramics (by that I think you mean technically so) and I never found Delft pretentiously grand. I love its simplicity and humanity, its wobbles and domesticity. And its imagery. The Dutch potter in the 17th century was totally at one with his world and his work. He was an articulate voice of his culture, and thus his work had wings. And that is the essence of the Delft pot. Or a Meissen pot. Or an Egyptian pot. They really meant it. Of course I am not a 17th century Dutchman.... And it is the difference in those positions which is interesting and explains much of what I am doing.

In 1981 Lord had his first exhibition in the United States, at the BlumHelman gallery in New York. The show was received with great enthusiasm by New York critics but somewhat cynically by the ceramics world. Lord has subsequently set up residence and his studio in New York City.

Lord's work has grown strongly during his six years of exhibiting in the United States. The work plays with sophisticated notions of geometry, of still life, and of appropriation from modern painters—ranging from Cézanne to Picasso and Braque. In Lord's art the pot exists more as a motif in a quasi-pictorial plane that has somehow been rendered in three dimensions rather than as a "pot" in the traditional view. The beauty of each individual vessel is less significant than the contextual milieu in which they are presented. In the same manner, when one views a pot in a still-life painting one is not concerned with whether the pot is aesthetically valid in its own right, but rather with its contribution as an element within the total picture.

Lord's pots cannot sever all signs of having once been joined to the umbilical cord of the pottery tradition. They remain tied to the notion of the vessel, and with that, to the association of functioning within the rituals of daily life. As Christopher Knight explains, "Lord's vessels don't look like the ordinary domestic variety you'd find around the house; but they do look completely normal, authentic and 'real' nonetheless. There is a pronounced sense of familarity imbedded within them while in a completely contradictory manner you feel as if you are seeing them for the first time" (Knight, 1986).

Loughran, Patrick (1948–　). Born in Bethlehem, Pennsylvania, Loughran received his B.A. in 1970 from Columbia University, New York, majoring in political science, and his M.A. in 1975, also from Columbia, in sculpture and crafts. Loughran works in earthenware to exploit the common, folk-art associations of the medium. His decoration is free, inventive, and expressive. Speaking to Susan Wechsler of his art in the exhibition catalogue *Functional Glamour: Utility in Contemporary American Ceramics*, he comments: "Producing functional pottery is part of my everyday professional life, and I get pleasure making it. It's got to be somewhat humorous, somewhat sexy, somewhat tentative, a little bit ugly and a little bit conformist too. I still feel there's lots of room for poetry on work that's made to be used" (Clark et al., 1987)

Lucero, Michael (1953–　). Born in Tracy, California, Lucero received his B.A. in 1975 from Humboldt State University, Arcata, California, and his M.F.A. in 1978 from the University of Washington, Seattle. He was awarded a Visual Artists Fellowship from the National Endowment for the Arts in 1979. Lucero moved to New York City after receiving his M.F.A. and currently maintains a studio there.

Lucero was a precocious talent, and his first "mature" works began to appear before he completed his graduate studies. These were tall, hanging figures made up of hundreds of small shards that were wired to armatures made from wire mesh and, later, pipes. The figures bristled with an "aura" of telephone wires. At first the heads on these figures were pots, a gesture loaded with reference and wit. In a narrow sense it pointed back to traditions out of which Lucero had evolved, but the metaphor also had a broader, more universal implication.

In 1981–82 the head began to merge more strongly in his works, and the body, in its more literal form, began to disappear as Lucero began work on his totem series. Each totem comprised seven heads and was deliberately about the height of a human form. In 1984 the first "dreamers" emerged. The head had now increased in scale and complexity. These large forms had become brightly painted dreamscape/landscapes in which the subconscious was released. Apart from the sense of violence implicit in the frequent appearance of the volcano in his works, these environments were not hostile—they were in a sense reassuring and affirmative statements made out of a youthful sense of confidence.

But hardly had this exploration begun to take form than a new body of works emerged. The head, which had been the central focus, was suddenly absent. The landscapes remained, but this time were painted on huge insects and animals. Quite suddenly the content had shifted. The landscapes that seemed so appealing in his "dreamers" seemed distinctly threatening when juxtaposed against a giant beetle or termite. Also, some of the landscapes had changed, cluttered and clogged with unidentifiable objects, and the sense of light and color had shifted. In these new works we are seeing the dark side of Lucero and a rejection of the somewhat decorative edge of his early work. As Mark Shannon comments about these new works, "Though still inviting and attractive, there is an unmistakable air of the grotesque about many of these figures. Aesthetic desire, the shape of one's relation with the world, have taken an unsettling turn. On one hand the work continues to celebrate the natural world; on the other, it seems to be witnessing its death" (Shannon, 1986).

Lukens, Glen (1887–1967). Born in Cowgill, Missouri, Lukens and his family later moved farther west in search of better farmlands. Starting in 1921 Glen Lukens studied agriculture at Oregon State University, but he was destined to use earth in a manner different from that of his father. Toward the end of his course, Lukens became interested in art and moved to Chicago, where he studied ceramics at the Art Institute of Chicago under Myrtle French. His conversion of a sewing machine into a potter's wheel came to the attention of the Surgeon General, who invited Lukens to run a pottery program to help rehabilitate the wounded of World War I. He subsequently moved to California, in about 1924, and taught crafts on the secondary-school level.

During the first stage of his career, Lukens was obsessed with a small, 3,000-year-old Egyptian pottery figure that he had seen in the Walker Art Center in Minneapolis. Lukens, like many potters of this time, was haunted by the figure's startlingly beautiful, bright-blue glaze. By 1931, while teaching ceramics at the high school in Fullerton, California, he had managed to produce a blue that approximated the vibrancy of the Egyptian glaze. He exhibited ceramic beads in this color in the Golden Gate Exposition of 1931 in San Francisco.

Lukens had earlier begun to explore simple, raw materials, creating raw alkaline glazes from materials gathered from the

Glen Lukens

Mojave Desert and Death Valley. The superb, dense glazes have rich and unusual colors. Unlike most of his contemporaries, Lukens was not obsessed with Oriental glazes, although his work was known for the range and drama of the craquelle effects. Lukens was conversant with the wheel, but he did not use it in the forming of his work, only to trim and shape the works later on. His forms were made in simple, slump molds, the traditional method of some Mexican folk pottery. He chose this technique because of its simplicity, saying it was "the earth speaking." Once the piece was leather-hard, Lukens would place the pot on the wheel and trim the surface with a metal tool, sometimes allowing it to dry further, and then retrim the outside of the pot to achieve a rough-textured surface—a technique known as "chattering."

In the late 1930s, Lukens entered his most productive period as an artist, winning awards at the Ceramic Nationals and representing the West Coast at the 1937 Paris Exposition Universelle. After World War II, ceramics remained his main interest, but less as a personal art form than as an educational activity.

Lukens played a major role in getting the ceramics movement on its feet on the West Coast and was an important teacher. For thirty years, beginning in the early 1930s, he was professor of ceramics at the University of Southern California, Los Angeles. Beatrice Wood, Vivika Heino, and F. Carlton Ball were among his students. As a teacher he projected a contagious humanity and a gift for communicating his sensitivity to his students. He would frequently remind them of what had been his personal credo as a ceramic artist: "The new in art is incredibly old and the old is still vastly new" (Lukens, 1937).

In 1945 Lukens took a leave of absence from USC and became involved with pottery training in Haiti. His activity there lasted into the 1950s, under the aegis of various sponsors, including UNESCO. The purpose was to set up a folk-pottery industry to create ceramic vessels that could replace the traditional gourds. The gourds, which the Haitians used for water, were unhygienic and caused severe health problems.

Upon his return to California in 1952, Lukens found that a revolution had taken place. The world of earthenware clays and bright, low-fire glazes had now been taken over by stoneware and its "brown bread" palette. Troubled by arthritis, he now concentrated more on glass. Lukens received an honorary doctorate in the ceramic sci-

ences from his alma mater, Oregon State University; the Charles Fergus Binns Medal in 1949; and, in 1951, L'Ordre National Honneur et Mérite, from the government of Haiti. A long-overdue retrospective of Lukens's pottery and glass was organized in 1982 by the Art Gallery, California State University, Los Angeles. The exhibition, curated by Elaine Levin, was also shown at the American Craft Museum in New York. Otto Natzler, who had met Lukens in 1938, recalled his first impressions of him: "He was what you call today, a natural—going by instinct toward what he believed was right, very convincing and very much in love with the medium...he could talk about it in an interesting way without being sophisticated—you really felt his joy" (Levin, 1976).

Lukens's most productive period of work was from 1935 to 1945. However, he was never a prolific potter, and very little of his pottery seems to have survived. There are no public collections of any consequence, although some museums do have single works or small collections. The Everson Museum of Art, Syracuse, New York, has a masterpiece, a large terra-cotta platter with a "trickle-glazed" rim of "Death Valley blue"; and the Newark Museum has a superb yellow bowl with a particularly fine crackle glaze. The few pieces that remain give a clear sense of Lukens's honest, no-nonsense artistic credo. Speaking before the Design Division of the American Ceramic Society in 1942, he said:

When a person works with raw materials of the earth, when he selects the ingredients of a clay mix, and when he studies the heating power of natural gas and helps to build his own kiln, he follows the immemorial pattern of primitive man in making all the gestures of creation, and the cheap desire to imitate some other artist's style and manner gradually gives way to more honest creative methods as he toils over the raw materials of his craft. (Bray, 1980)

Lysohir, Marilyn (1950–). Born in Sharon, Pennsylvania, Lysohir received her B.A. from Ohio Northern University, Ada, in 1972 and her M.F.A. from Washington State University, Pullman, in 1979. She makes extremely complex, large-scale ceramic sculptures. Her early work dealt with the figure. In *BAMS* (1980), which comprised eleven, three-quarter-sized women Marines on a platform of tiles, the pieces were fired with colored *terra-sigillata* surfaces that provided her work with a smooth, warm, mat surface. In 1985 she created another major work, entitled *Bad Manners,* which was the centerpiece of her exhibition at the Asher/Faure gallery in Los Angeles. The work consisted of a six-foot-long dining-room table, heaped with food and attended by four "figures," which were compellingly surrealist, with the clothes of the diners in human form but sans the bodies.

Lysohir's most ambitious work to date is *The Dark Side of Dazzle* (1986), exhibited at Asher/Faure. This work and its accompanying drawings deal with an anti-war theme. The piece is a ceramic and wood battleship, twenty-four feet in length, that took nine months to construct. The focus of the piece was not the horror of war but, more disturbingly, its seductive qualities. The battleship was covered in a camouflage pattern of charming pastel hues. A group of chairs was placed alongside the battleship, and viewers sat and listened to a continuous recording of war stories told by veterans. Writing about the exhibition, the *Los Angeles Times* critic Suzanne Muchnic stated that Lysohir's sculpture wins her a place in figurative ceramic sculpture alongside Viola Frey and Elaine Carhartt, but that her work has strange vectors. Despite the "clear position on the infiltration of military aggression [Lysohir] walks a precarious line between decoration and politics" (Muchnic, 1986). Lysohir's fascination with the military (derived in part from her mother's being in the Marine Corps during World War II) and her tender, decorative edge do make strange bedfellows. At the same time, however, this gives the work a curious resonance that is distinctly and powerfully subversive.

Maberry, Phillip (1951–). Born in Stanford, Texas, Maberry studied at East Texas State University in Commerce, Texas, receiving his B.A. in 1975. Maberry approached ceramics from a highly decorative point of view, at first creating superb slip-cast porcelain bowls. He also makes furniture and has undertaken multimedia installations and interiors, such as his room-sized piece *Paradise Fountain* at the 1983 Whitney Biennial and his installation of a bathroom for the Holly Solomon Gallery in New York. Maberry's most recent works deal with the vessel in a more intense manner. The forms are thrown and assembled with complex handles that appear to float languidly alongside his forms. There is a direct, almost expressionist quality to his current use of clay that contrasts markedly with his early and more detached use of

porcelain. In part, this is the result of a growing interest in Mexican folk pottery, which has merged with his early fetish for the style of the 1950s.

McClain (McCloud), Malcolm (1933–). Mac McClain studied painting and sculpture in France, New York City, Mexico, and California. He received his B.A. from Pomona College, Claremont, California, in 1956 and studied ceramics at Scripps College, Claremont, as well as with Peter Voulkos at the Los Angeles County Art Institute (later known as the Otis Art Institute). McClain's involvement with ceramics was strongly intellectual, dealing with carefully conceived compositions of form, and also showed a constructivist tendency. Although his activity was brief, he made an important contribution to the energies at Otis. In the 1960s he ceased working in ceramics and became a poet. Nonetheless he has retained his involvement in ceramics throughout as a teacher and as an active critic of the medium. He has also recently begun to make ceramics again.

MacDonald, William Purcel (1865–1931). Born in Cincinnati, MacDonald studied at the Graduate School of Design at the University of Cincinnati, joining the Rookwood Pottery in 1882. He spent his entire life working at Rookwood and became one of its most accomplished decorators. Following the departure of Valentien in 1898, MacDonald took over the direction of the decorating department and later was responsible for the running of an architectural department at Rookwood. MacDonald was a member of the Duveneck Society, Cincinnati Art Club, and MacDowell Society.

Warren MacKenzie

McIntosh, Harrison (1914–). Born in Vallejo, California, McIntosh studied under Glen Lukens at the University of Southern California in 1940. In 1947, after his wartime service, McIntosh served an informal apprenticeship with Albert and Louisa King at their Lotus and Acanthus Pottery Studios, "[where] he entered a world of celadon on porcelain and transmutations in reduction firing by the single fire 'Grand Feu' method" (Clark and Bray, 1979). McIntosh then studied with Rick Petterson at the Claremont Graduate School from 1949 to 1952 and worked with Marguerite Wildenhain at the Pond Farm workshop in California in 1953. McIntosh taught at the Otis Art Institute with Peter Voulkos in 1954.

It is characteristic of McIntosh's strength of purpose that he could appreciate the energies of the Otis group without losing his own emerging style. To this day Voulkos is the potter he most admires. In stylistic terms McIntosh is closest to the Europeans who settled in the United States during the 1920s and 1930s—Maija Grotell, Gertrud and Otto Natzler, and Marguerite Wildenhain. McIntosh has built upon the refinement of their work with a commitment to a highly technical quality and a precise, clear sense of decoration. He has worked as a professional studio potter since the mid-fifties, supplementing his sales with designs of ceramic and glass wares (together with his wife, Marguerite) for the Japanese company Mikasa and for other factories.

MacKenzie, Alix (1922–1962). In 1946 MacKenzie graduated from the Art Institute of Chicago. In 1952 she was responsible for organizing the tour through the United States of Bernard Leach, Shoji Hamada, and Soetsu Yanagi, an event that left an indelible imprint on American ceramics. Together with her husband, Warren MacKenzie, she spent two years during the mid-1950s as an apprentice to Bernard Leach at the Leach Pottery, Saint Ives, England. Later she established a workshop with her husband at Stillwater, Minnesota, working on the production of functional, wheel-thrown, reduction-fired wares.

MacKenzie, Warren (1924–). MacKenzie graduated from the Art Institute of Chicago in 1947, and together with his wife, Alix, spent two years in the 1950s as an apprentice at the studio of Bernard Leach, Saint Ives, England. Until his recent retirement, MacKenzie was professor of art at the University of Minnesota. As the éminence grise of utilitarian pottery, he has taught and lectured extensively throughout the country.

He has been one of the major forces in the United States in establishing the aesthetic-philosophical credo of the functional potter, based on his affinities with the Anglo-Oriental beliefs of Leach. MacKenzie's pottery, produced at his own workshop in Stillwater, Minnesota, is wheel-thrown and fired in a reduction kiln. The low cost of his works reflects MacKenzie's desire that they be objects of utility rather than mantelpiece ornaments. In a statement made some years back, MacKenzie outlined the basis of his belief:

A pot must be made with an immediacy, without unlimited change being possible, which is unique in the visual arts. For this reason each piece, in a sense, becomes a sketch or variation of an idea which may develop over hours, days, or months and requires up to several hundred pieces to come to full development. One pot suggests another, proportions are altered, curves are filled out or made more angular, a different termination or beginning of a line is tried—not searching for the perfect pot but exploring and making statements with the language at hand. From thousands of pots produced some few may sing. The others are sound steppingstones to these high points and can also communicate between the artist and the user. ("Ceramics: Double Issue," 1958)

MacKenzie's pots are simple, traditional wares, but they contain a sense of importance. The best of them are among the finest "straight" pots being made in the United States today.

MacKenzie and his students—Wayne Branum, Tim Crane, Randy Johnston, Jeff Oestreich, Mark Pharis, and others—are collectively known as the "Mingeisota." The term, at once satiric and reverential, is drawn from the state in which the potters work, Minnesota, and the Mingei—a folkart movement established by Soetsu Yanagi in Japan. For some time the Mingeisota was the last outpost of Leachian fundamentalism in American pottery. However, this has now altered, with many of the group, notably Pharis, making works that are less and less concerned with utility. In addition, the group found the legacy of MacKenzie's utopian pricing to be unrealistic and, in fact, a real hardship. But MacKenzie has steadfastly retained his ideals and his dislike of cerebral "art" pots and the world they occupy. In a catalogue essay, MacKenzie quoted Soetsu Yanagi and gave a clear statement of his values: "To

Graham Marks

'see' is to go direct to the core; to know the facts about an object of beauty is to go around the periphery. Intellectual discrimination is less essential to an understanding of beauty than the power of intuition that precedes it" (MacKenzie, 1981).

McLaughlin, Mary Louise (1847–1939). Born in Cincinnati to a prominent family, McLaughlin took an early interest in the arts and studied privately until 1873. In that year she joined the Cincinnati School of Design, where in 1874 she was introduced to china painting. In 1876 she exhibited in the Centennial Exposition in Philadelphia, and the following year she graduated from the Cincinnati School of Design. She later

Roberta B. Marks

returned to her alma mater to do life drawing with Frank Duveneck, "the only teacher who had any influence on my artistic development" (McLaughlin, 1938). In 1878 McLaughlin produced her first technically successful Limoges faience, at the Patrick L. Coultry Pottery, exhibiting the wares in Cincinnati and New York and at the 1879 Paris Exposition Universelle, where she received an honorable mention.

In 1879 McLaughlin founded and became president of the Cincinnati Pottery Club. It was there that she made her famous *Ali Baba Vase*, which she exhibited at the first annual exhibition of the club, in 1880. In 1883, when the club was evicted from the Rookwood Pottery, McLaughlin turned to on-glaze decoration and decorative metalwork. In 1889 she received a silver medal at the Exposition Universelle for her china painting and metallic effects. She returned to ceramics in 1895, working first in inlaid earthenware and then in porcelain. At the 1900 Exposition Universelle, she was awarded a silver medal for her metalwork, and a bronze medal at the Buffalo exposition in 1901 for her once-fired porcelains.

McLaughlin gave up her work in ceramics in 1914 and turned to writing, celebrating her eighty-eighth birthday by publishing a book on the great military battles. More than any other figure during her time, McLaughlin was responsible for initiating the aesthetic that art pottery was to follow for three decades, and for setting standards of professionalism for a pioneer studio pottery movement.

McVey, Leza Marie Sullivan (1907–). Born in Cleveland, McVey studied at the Cleveland Institute of Art (1927–32). In 1932 she married the sculptor William McVey. From 1935 to 1944 she worked in Texas as a ceramist: in Houston, 1935–37; Austin, 1939–42; San Antonio, 1943–44. She studied at the Colorado Springs Fine Art Center in 1943–44, returning briefly to Austin. Then, in 1947, she moved with her husband to the Cranbrook Academy of Art in Bloomfield Hills, Michigan. In 1948 she taught a summer school course for Maija Grotell and continued to teach at the school until 1953, when she moved to Cleveland, establishing a studio in nearby Pepper Pike. After 1955 her production of work began to slow down, and her last major exhibition was a one-person show at the Cleveland Institute of Art in 1965. McVey's pots were among the most innovative and original of her time. She disliked the symmetry of wheel-thrown pottery and instead produced assertive, asymmetrical forms with intriguing stoppers that formally closed the strong organic forms. McVey's work is a significant contribution to the history of American ceramics and one that needs to be more fully addressed.

Makins, James D. (1946–). Born in Johnstown, Pennsylvania, Makins studied at the Philadelphia College of Art, where he received his B.F.A. in 1968, and at the Cranbrook Academy of Art, Bloomfield Hills, Michigan, under Richard DeVore, receiving his M.F.A. in 1973. Makins currently maintains a studio in New York City. He has received Visual Artists Fellowships from the National Endowment for the Arts in 1976 and 1980 and in 1986 received a fellowship of the New York Foundation for the Arts. Makins works with functional forms, making extremely pure porcelain forms that are without decoration (and sometimes without glaze). They are distinguished by their delicate, thin walls and an undulating texture of rhythmic throwing rings. Makins has made an important contribution to the functional traditions of the contemporary potter while at the same time retaining the tension of a committed and objectively passionate artist.

Marks, Graham (1951–). Born in New York City, Marks studied at the Philadelphia College of Art under William Daley, receiving his B.F.A. in 1971, and at the New York State College of Ceramics, Alfred University, Alfred, New York, receiving his M.F.A. in 1974. He currently heads the ceramics department at the Cranbrook Academy of Art in Bloomfield Hills, Michigan. Marks's earliest works revealed a fascination with a single-form motif—a large, podlike form that was at once unspecific and yet redolent of memory traces, resembling some vast broken clay vessel, a prehistoric egg, or, as Wayne Higby writes, "the petrified remains of a Mesozoic tropical fruit" (Licka and Higby, 1986). In early forms the colors and surfaces of his works were bright and optimistic—sparkling orange slips and thick, glossy Mediterranean-blue glazes. As the work has progressed, Marks has retained his form, but the surfaces have shifted radically. In his last exhibition, at the Everson Museum of Art in 1986, the forms now began to deal with decayed surfaces, with textures of industrial waste, and with the erosion of time. Apart from the metaphoric context of the surfaces, they also suggest that the artist is reaching a point of departure

in his work, the exhausting of what has been a long and narrowly focused examination of a particular form.

Marks, Roberta B. (1936–). Born in Savannah, Georgia, Marks studied at the University of Florida, Gainesville; University of Miami, Coral Gables, Florida; Metropolitan Museum of Art, New York; Art Center, Miami, Florida; and Penland School of Crafts, Penland, North Carolina. She has been a visiting artist at numerous schools throughout the United States, and her work has been extensively exhibited in group and one-person exhibitions. In her work, she exploits primitive firing techniques, including pit, sawdust, raku, and dung firings—using the action of the fire to create the interest and patination on the surface. In the 1980s she began to paint on the pots with acrylic, transferring the same information onto her pots that she was exploring on her canvases and works on paper. In 1982 she set up a studio in Key West, Florida, where she also began to make sculpture—wooden boxes in the spirit of Joseph Cornell. After 1986 she again began to work with sawdust firing and moved away from the acrylic-painted vessels.

Martinez, Maria (1884–1981). Born in San Ildefonso Pueblo, New Mexico, Martinez first made polychrome pottery in 1897, painting with red clays and a black pigment from wild spinach called *guaco*. Later she and her husband, Julian Martinez, were asked to re-create shapes from pottery shards found in the Frijoles Canyon. They experimented and soon discovered the technique of the burnished pottery, with its silver-black sheen. Julian and Maria rapidly became famous for their skillfully executed wares, and were invited to demonstrate at all the major world's fairs up until World War II. After Julian's death in 1943, Maria continued to work on her own and with members of her family, including her son Popovi, until her own death. Her traditional style of pottery continued to be produced by Santana Martinez, her daughter-in-law, and by other members of her family at the pueblo. In her book about the artist, Susan Peterson wrote:

> In these gleaming black pots scattered on the ground, part of the life of this pueblo is represented: the Indian way, singular devotion to their own artistic roots, and the naturally flowing repetitive work that lets them relate directly to their own methods. These are true

John Mason

craftsmen. Maria's contribution has been to revive and build on the black pottery technique of the ancient pueblo people. Other Indian women in other pueblos have become part of a similar lineage, with their own methods. But Maria's personality and her love for people and ability to relate to them carried her name and craft out into the Anglo world. At the same time she became a standard held high for her own people. (Peterson, 1977)

Maria Martinez was feted at the White House by four presidents, received two honorary doctorates, and was chosen to lay the cornerstone for New York City's Rockefeller Center. She was also the subject of an excellent book by Peterson, *The Living Tradition of Maria Martinez*, and in 1978 of a retrospective exhibition at the Renwick Gallery, Smithsonian Institution, Washington, D.C.

Mason, John (1927–). Born in Madrid, Nebraska, Mason spent much of his youth in Nevada. He was educated at the Chouinard Art Institute in Los Angeles, where he worked under Susan Peterson, and at the Otis Art Institute (then the Los Angeles County Art Institute) under Peter Voulkos. He subsequently taught at Pomona College, Claremont, California; the University of California, Irvine and Berkeley; the Otis Art Institute; and, from 1974 to 1985, Hunter College, New York. He currently maintains a studio in Los Angeles.

Mason's early involvement with ceramics was through pottery, and for some time he also designed dinnerware for industry at

Franciscan China. In 1957 he began a search for a more sculptural application of ceramics and produced his first monumental wall pieces. Arguably the finest of these and the one closest to Abstract Expressionist paintings is *The Blue Wall* (1959), for which Mason employed a technique analogous to the manner in which Jackson Pollock painted some of his early Abstract Expressionist canvases. Mason has continued his involvement with architectural ceramics, and has permanently installed several of his works: *The Blue Wall* at the now-defunct Ferus Gallery, Los Angeles; a work at the Tischman Building in Los Angeles; and works in several private homes. The development of the wall pieces continued through the mid-1960s, when Mason began to create massive, freestanding walls composed of modular panels, a "structuring device necessitated by the size of the kiln" (Haskell, 1974). But the modularity extends beyond pure structural requirements and is the distinguishing factor even in the smaller, vessel-oriented works, where the even pacing of interior volumes was not determined by technical restraints but by an aesthetic empathy for modular composition.

His freestanding ceramic sculptures follow the same progress as the walls, from an expressionist handling of the material to a cool, formalist statement. His work in this genre culminated in 1966 with an exhibition at the Los Angeles County Museum of Art, of monolithic primary forms up to six feet in height, with bright monochrome glazes. These works were intended to function within the Minimalist school established earlier in the decade by such artists as Tony Smith, Robert Morris, Carl Andre, and others. But despite the careful planning by Mason, which included the construction of a collapsible tubular system to withdraw the air evenly from within his forms and thus minimize any cracking or warpage, the character of the clay emerges forcibly, and the surfaces of the forms are covered in a rich wash of expressive, streaked glaze, while the form itself is fissured with cracks.

More successful during this period was Mason's construction of slab-built totems, an exploration that he had begun in the early 1960s and continued to the end of the decade. *Vertical Sculpture* (1962) is one of the masterpieces of this exploration and one of the most important works to be exhibited in the Whitney Museum's 1981 exhibition *Ceramic Sculpture: Six Artists*. Despite the success of this series, however, Mason had grown increasingly unhappy with the manipulation of clay and had earlier voiced his reservations about the medium:

Today's stigma is deeply rooted in our ceramic form. Timidity of spirit, coupled with little real conviction, has resulted in a ceramic form synonymous with hobbyists, dilettantes and three-dimensional cartoonists. The self-conscious reaction of this association has been fastidious, technical execution of craft in an effort to attain professional status. Unfortunately, individuals following this trend have too often sacrificed inner experience, techniques, and standards of good taste. It can only follow that content must suffer. This professionalism has produced a ceramic form empty in content and lacking in vitality, as demonstrated by the examples seen in our stores, exhibitions and architectural commissions. ("Ceramics: Double Issue," 1958)

In 1971–72 Mason began to work with fire bricks, the material from which kilns are constructed. In fact, the kiln itself proved to be the inspiration for his first piece, involving an arch form, fitted together so that the piece was structurally supported by the tensions and pressure of its own weight. In 1972 he began to work on a series of floor pieces in fire brick, culminating in 1978 with his *Installations from the Hudson River* series, a project funded by the National Endowment for the Arts, which involved the creation of a series of works at major museums across the United States. This enabled Mason to deal with the modularity, systemization, and formalistic concerns that have always underpinned his aesthetic vision. Mason's work in fire brick belongs only by association to ceramics and is no more "ceramic sculpture" than are the earlier brick installations by Andre. It was a means of escaping the craft-intensive milieu of ceramics and allowed Mason to concentrate on the conceptual implications of his installations, an investigation that tended to be somewhat dry and academic.

Mason's major contribution to the field was made between 1958 and 1969, when he produced some of the finest abstract sculptural works in clay. In the eighties he made a surprising volte-face and returned to the vessel, a format that he had earlier seen as being somewhat banal as a vehicle for high art. The new pieces have the kind of surface intelligence that we have seen in all of Mason's art. They are not pots so much as they are coldly analytic inquiries about the pot as architecture, beautifully glazed in a nostalgic and decorative style of the 1950s that is reminiscent of *Scandinavia modern*.

Mayeri, Beverly (1940–). Born in New York City, Mayeri received a B.A. in zoology in 1967 from the University of California, Berkeley, with the intention of becoming a marine biologist. She had painted since 1960 and was attracted to ceramics, and began to work in the ceramics studio of the Sausalito Art Center. In 1974 she was inspired by an exhibition of work by Karen Breschi and decided to return to school, entering San Francisco State University in that year. There she studied with Breschi and Stephen DeStaebler and received her M.A. in sculpture in 1976. She maintains a studio in Sausalito, California.

Mayeri's sculpture is surrealist at heart but explores form with a greater refinement of image and surface than is usual in ceramic sculpture. She is primarily interested in clay for its modeling possibilities, but neither leaves the clay exposed nor uses any ceramic materials on the surface. Each piece is meticulously painted in acrylics. Her images have gradually evolved from superrealist portraiture into curious elongations of the figure and the head. In early works the elongation was achieved in part by slicing the works into strips and repositioning the object with gaps between each section. In the newer works, however, the elongation has taken on a sensual Modigliani-esque sensibility. The focus in her work is the eyes, peering out with a contradictory mixture of intensity and vulnerability, and the mouth.

Mayeri's pieces are layered with personal meanings and symbols. In *Under Scrutiny* (1985) Mayeri sees the textured skin and elongated arms and face as being "baboon-like and primitive: "This related to the part of our cerebral nature that keeps us from enjoying our basic animal qualities.... The figure is also about vulnerability, exposure and personal armor" (Mayeri, 1986). The scale of Mayeri's works has constantly increased, with her 1987 figures "standing" over six feet in height. In contrast to these monumental works, Mayeri has continued to work on masks, which have become smaller in scale as the figures and heads have become larger, creating a strong, eerie presence that is quite disproportionate to their size. Mayeri has received numerous awards for her sculpture and in 1982 was a recipient of a Visual Artists Fellowship from the National Endowment for the Arts.

Melchert, James ("Jim") (1930–). Born in New Bremen, Ohio, Melchert studied at Princeton University, receiving a B.A. in

1952, and at the University of Chicago, where he received his M.F.A. in 1957. In 1958 he moved to California and studied with Peter Voulkos at the University of California, Berkeley, receiving his M.A. in 1961.

Melchert's early works involved the vessel format. At first he dealt with the clay in an Abstract Expressionist mode, but from 1960 he produced carefully considered forms, such as his *Legpot I* (1962), a combination of stoneware, lead, and cloth inlay. Influenced by the manner in which the arm on a broken Greek torso would abruptly terminate in a cross section, Melchert revealed in *Legpot I* his impatience with "the conventions that seemed to tyrannize potters, the vertical, bilaterally symmetrical structure of a vessel and the unquestioning acceptance of a single material" (Nordness, 1970). In developing the form, he was influenced by primitive art, in which he had been impressed by the frequent juxtaposition of incongruous shapes without transition.

As a teacher at the San Francisco Art Institute, Melchert came under the influence of fellow artists at the institute, such as William Wiley, William Geis, and Robert Hudson, in whose work content took precedence over form. As a result, Melchert moved away from the earthy rusticity of stoneware and toward the use of low-fire, brightly colored glazes on whiteware. He began to treat the surfaces of his works with painted and relief images of pyramids, Mickey Mouse ears, fragments of words, benday dots, and motifs that challenged the traditional relationships of surface and volume.

In 1974, the Hansen Fuller Gallery, San Francisco, held a one-man exhibition of Melchert's *Ghostwares*, works that had been inspired by a single line spoken by one of the sisters in Ingmar Bergman's movie *The Silence*: "Tread carefully among the ghosts of the past." These pieces constituted a series of masks with blind, skeletal faces on boxes or plates surrounded by fragmented visual codes. This series was followed in 1967 by the *Games* series, consisting of molded and at times identifiable objects placed on a grid or on a rectangular base. These works, so reminiscent of the assemblages of Alberto Giacometti in the 1930s, excluded the expressive qualities of the medium in favor of a more intensely intellectual statement.

The last object series by Melchert was inspired by Raymond Queneau's book *Exercises in Style*, which retold an inconsequential story in one hundred literary styles. Using the lower-case *a*, he began to create

a series of sculptures made from various materials, with the title as the all-important key to the content of the form: *Precious a* (a small glazed and lustered piece mounted on a plinth), *Pre-a* (comprising twenty pounds of unfired clay), and *a Made Forty Pounds Lighter* (a form from which handfuls of clay had been roughly gouged from the surface before firing). The most interesting of the three exhibitions of this body of work was the installation at the San Francisco Art Institute in February 1970. The works were presented on a large grid taped to the floor, providing a continuation of the visual vocabulary that Melchert first established with the *Games* series.

In 1972 Melchert took clay into the conceptual realm in the happening titled *Changes*. Based on the drying processes of clay, the event took place at a friend's studio in Amsterdam. Melchert moved away from ceramics to an audiovisual projection of images. He then became director of the Visual Arts Division of the National Endowment for the Arts in Washington, D.C., presiding over one of the most tempestuous attempts to deal with the art/craft divide. After his return to Berkeley in 1980, he again worked with ceramics, creating large tile paintings. In his sixteen-odd years in ceramics, Melchert has been a strong influence, deemphasizing the romantic preconceptions of the medium and providing a model for its probing, intelligent sculptural application.

Mercer, Henry Chapman (1856–1930). Born in Doylestown, Pennsylvania, Mercer was brought up as a Quaker. Although trained as a lawyer, he became an archaeologist on the staff of the University Museum in Philadelphia, where he achieved some prominence for his unconventional scholarship. Mercer became involved in ceramics as an outgrowth of his interest in American pioneer handcraft tools and his discovery that the Pennsylvania German pottery tradition was almost extinct. At the Bucks County Historical Society he initiated a project to revive an eighteenth-century Pennsylvania German pottery in upper Bucks County, collaborating with Mr. Herstine, a craftsman-potter. Although the few pieces Mercer managed to produce were disappointing, he was intrigued with the medium.

In 1898 Mercer founded the Moravian Tile Works in Doylestown, named after the Moravian cast-iron stove plates that inspired his first tile designs. Mercer was responsible for all the tile designs, ensuring that the

tiles reflected the handmade production methods and the celebrated qualities of the local red clay. Mercer was a confirmed eclectic and drew his tile designs from many sources. One of the richest sources of models came through his friend Sir Charles Hercules Read of the British Museum. Read not only permitted Mercer to make impressions of and reproduce medieval English floor tiles in the museum's collection, he also gave him access to large and valuable collections of drawings and tracings of ancient tiles from ruined English abbeys and priories. From Professor Hans Bausch of the Germanic Museum in Nuremberg, Mercer obtained designs of eighteenth-century German tiles.

Between 1910 and 1912, after the original pottery had burned to the ground, Mercer designed and supervised the building of a larger structure, of reinforced concrete. The new pottery was one of only three reinforced-concrete buildings in the country at that time; another was the concrete home that Mercer himself had previously built. Between 1914 and 1916 he constructed his third concrete building, a museum to house his collection of over six thousand hand tools, which he named "Tools of the Nation Makers."

Mercer saw art and craft as interwoven, and he was as creative in technical matters as he was in terms of art. In particular, he was interested in what he termed the "literary side of craft," the making of narrative tile panels: "While I understand [narrative] has been said to 'contaminate' painting, this story telling has been my primary impulse.... I agree with them that the design must be an aesthetic success in color, pat-

Henry Chapman Mercer

tern, conventionalism, balance, etc., and further that it may be a success without any meaning at all. But if tiles could not tell a story, inspire, or teach nobody, and only serve to produce aesthetic thrills, I would have stopped making them long ago" (Reed, 1979).

In 1904 Mercer was awarded the grand prize for his tiles at the Louisiana Purchase International Exposition in Saint Louis and went on to win many more awards and honors. Mercer's tiles became sought after and were used in a variety of public buildings, including Grauman's Chinese Theater in Hollywood, California; the Casino at Monte Carlo, Monaco; the Isabella Stewart Gardner Museum in Boston; the Museum of Fine Arts in Boston; the now-demolished Traymore Hotel in Atlantic City, New Jersey; the library of Bryn Mawr College in Pennsylvania; and the state capitol building in Harrisburg, Pennsylvania.

Mercer's decision to create innovative machines to assist in the making of tiles lowered labor costs and was the factor that enabled the Moravian Tile Works to survive and prosper, when, in Mercer's words, "most of our artistic rivals are in the Sheriff's hands—Grueby of Boston included, whose watermelon enamel was setting the world on fire about 1900" (Reed, 1979). The pottery continued after Mercer's death, in 1930, for another twenty-four years, under the direction of Mercer's friend, foreman, and heir, Frank King Swain. It was during these years that the pottery began to have financial difficulties, and it closed when Swain died, in 1954. The Bucks County Historical Society has operated the tile works since 1969 as a living museum. Mercer's pottery and buildings are a memorial to one of the most complex and remarkable figures of the American Arts and Crafts Movement, a man who worked toward the single goal of "the acquisition and dissemination of knowledge concerning the arts and crafts fundamental to the development of a civilized society" (Fox, 1973).

Meyer, Joseph Fortune (1848–1931). Born in France, Meyer immigrated with his family to the United States, where he settled in Biloxi, Mississippi. After his marriage, Meyer operated a pottery, producing simple wares from local clay. In 1886 he became the first potter at the New Orleans Art Pottery Company, where he was soon joined for a brief period by George E. Ohr. In April 1896 Meyer joined the Newcomb Pottery, a unique experiment by Sophie Newcomb Memorial College (the women's

division of Tulane University in New Orleans) that provided a professional ceramic environment for the students to study the art of pottery decoration. He remained the main thrower at the pottery until 1925. Sadie Irvine, one of the best known of the Newcomb designers, wrote of Meyer: "He was truly a master craftsman and his failing vision did not seem too great a handicap. His strong, sensitive fingers drew up the clay as though it rose of itself. It was a joy to watch him. We had a constant flow of visitors from all over the world for whom Mr. Meyer would wordlessly perform" (Blasberg, "Sadie Irvine Letters," 1971).

Moonelis, Judy (1953–). Born in Jackson Heights, Queens, New York, Judy Moonelis received her B.F.A. in 1975 from the Tyler School of Art, Temple University, Philadelphia, and her M.F.A. in 1978 from the New York State College of Ceramics, Alfred University, Alfred, New York. She has already received many awards and honors, including two Visual Artists Fellowships from the National Endowment for the Arts (1980, 1986); the Reeb Memorial Award for Sculpture from the Albright-Knox Art Gallery, Buffalo, New York; and a fellowship in 1985 from the New York Foundation for the Arts. Moonelis is one of a small group of successful ceramic sculptors who is not a product of the San Francisco–Davis–Seattle axis. She has attracted intense interest in her work and has been included in over thirty-seven exhibitions in the eighties alone.

Her work touches a contemporary nerve that has expressed itself in New York City's East Village art scene. The work is deliberately crudely drawn, raw, and energetic. Moonelis plays with the figure and the face in large pieces that stand up to six feet in height. Her works do not work continuously in the round; rather, they consist of two distinct "flat" sides. In early works this proved to be a problem, because one side carried what was obviously the primary image while the other seemed to be simply a structure to keep the work upright, rather than a statement in its own right. Moonelis has gradually altered this imbalance. In *Untitled* (1986), for example, there are two complete but different images. The clay and surfaces are masterfully handled, although the final feeling is not always one of clay. The sculpture at times has the appearance of fiercely carved and stained wood and, at other times, of huge chunks of congealed oil paint.

Nadelman, Elie (1882–1946). Born in Warsaw, Poland, where he studied briefly, Elie Nadelman served in the Russian army before moving to Paris. There, in 1905, he decided to devote his energies to sculpture, becoming known to the Parisian avant-garde, including the Steins, Apollinaire, Brancusi, and Picasso. In 1915, with the assistance of Helena Rubinstein, Nadelman came to New York, where he was well established by 1920.

After 1929 the Depression brought hardships; Nadelman lost his studio and refused to exhibit or sell his works. In the 1930s he began to work with clay, having previously used papier-mâché, metaloplastic, and bronze as his major materials. In 1912–13, just prior to his move to the United States, Nadelman had produced some superb, large terra-cottas. He became interested in ceramics again during the thirties, through Mrs. Voorhees and Miss La Prince at the Inwood Potteries in Inwood Park, New York. He later set up his own kiln and produced a body of figurative forms, using glazes that he had devised himself between 1933 and 1935. Apart from this body of work, there is a second body of ceramics by Nadelman, which was produced posthumously at the Inwood Potteries by Julius Gargani, who had been Nadelman's assistant during his limited involvement with ceramics in the 1930s. These terra-cottas were from the small plaster figures made by Nadelman in his last ten years. "There is no doubt that Nadelman intended these figures to be cast in baked earth. He preserved many fragments of Tanagrine and Myrrhine figures...his library was filled with catalogues of antique clay figures" (Hewitt, 1950).

Nagle, Ron (1939–). Born in San Francisco, Nagle received his art education and a B.A. from San Francisco State College. Between 1961 and 1978, he taught sporadically at the San Francisco Art Institute; the University of California, Berkeley; the California College of Arts and Crafts, Oakland; and several other schools. He currently teaches at Mills College in Oakland, California.

Nagle's early work reflects his contact with Peter Voulkos and shows a decorative interpretation of Abstract Expressionism. Henry Takemoto introduced Nagle to Japanese wares. Nagle became particularly infatuated with the eighteenth-century wares of the Momoyama period, with their rich but muted color and thick, sensual glazing.

Throughout his career Nagle has used the vessel as his format, concentrating since

1968 on the cup form. From his expressive, energetic works of the early 1960s, Nagle went on to explore the potential of china painting and photo decals. In 1968 he had an exhibition at the Dilexi Gallery, San Francisco, showing the first of his now-familiar china-painted cup forms, with their high stylization; intense, pulsating china-painted color; and molded form. In addition to creating the cups, Nagle produced an environment for his objects in the form of custom-designed wood and plastic boxes. These works were "in a sense not...*cup[s]*: but instead *about cups*" (Nordness, 1970).

The Dilexi exhibition was his last major showing for seven years, during which time Nagle concentrated on his parallel interest in pop music and developed something of a reputation as an underground figure in the ceramic arts. He returned to ceramics in 1975 with a dazzling exhibition at the Quay Ceramics Gallery, San Francisco, showing twelve low-fire cup forms. These were meticulously slip-cast and multifired up to twenty times to achieve the saturation and depth of color that he required from the china-painted surfaces. The complex painting and forms of these works contrast with the flat, solid color of his earlier cups. The increasing sophistication of Nagle's works culminated with his exhibiting at the San Francisco Art Institute in 1978 as a recipient of the Adaline Kent Award; his forms had returned to something of the informality of his earliest works.

A strong emphasis in Nagle's pieces is frontality; he places the accent on the defining lip and foot of the cup, abstracting the form to the point where it consists of a bottomless cylinder. Nagle's primary concern is silhouette, not volume: "I'm concerned with the graphic profile of these pieces.... I always go back to Morandi.... I am going to make pottery that has that loose kind of feel that he has when he draws pottery...that tough and tender look the Japanese wares have, too" (Brown, 1978).

Nagle's work shows strong and continuing reference to that of Kenneth Price, who has similarly used the cup as a format in his work. Nagle has referred to his ceramics as being of the "precious asshole school" (Felton, 1978), dealing with a painterly sense of abstraction with occasional literal, visual punning, as with his *Frank Lloyd Wright Cup* (in the shape of the Guggenheim Museum). But the keys to Nagle's aesthetics come from two words: *tasteful* and *style,* terms that recur frequently in his own discussion of his work. Speaking of his dual careers as ceramist and song-

writer/producer, Nagle remarked, "I carry lyrics and color chips in the same bag. My music and art have similarities: they're both emotional, warm and romantic; they're abstract and semi-slick; they both have flash and style, but I am also shooting for content" (Brown, 1978).

At the exhibitions of his works at the Charles Cowles Gallery in New York during the 1980s, Nagle has retained the cup form, although its "residual handle" has become progressively more and more abstracted. In his works from 1983 the handle is a relief element emerging from the side of his square "cups." In 1985, following Price's lead, he turned to organic forms, as in *Blue Waltz,* where the cups begin to resemble jewel-colored crustacea whose spiraling structures curl into small, tense "residual" handles.

Nakian, Reuben (1897–1986). Born in College Point, Queens, New York, Nakian began to study art at the age of thirteen, when he moved with his family to New Jersey. He worked in advertising for several years and studied at the Independent Art School and at the Beaux-Arts Institute of Design in New York City. He was apprenticed to Paul Manship in 1916 and shared a studio with Manship's assistant, Gaston Lachaise, from 1920 to 1923. From 1922 to 1928, Nakian was supported by the Whitney Studio Club. His first one-man show was held in 1926.

Nakian frequently produced stylized animal sculptures in terra-cotta. Toward the end of the 1940s, he began two series of terra-cotta, incised-relief plaques and works that exploited more fully the three-dimensional potential of the material. Both series were based on erotic themes from classical mythology. This new body of work was first shown in 1949 at a one-man exhibition at the Egan Gallery in New York. Although Nakian moved on to metal, plaster, and other materials, he continued to make works in clay, from time to time both producing his tablets and drawing onto vases that were thrown for him.

Natzler, Gertrud Amon (1908–1971), and **Otto (1908–   ).** Born in Vienna, Otto Natzler and Gertrud Amon met in 1933 and began a collaboration in ceramics. Gertrud had previously studied at the Handelsakademie and worked (unhappily) as a secretary until 1938. Otto graduated from the Lehranstalt für Textilindustrie in Vienna in 1927, and until 1933 worked as a designer of textiles. Apart from a short period of study with Franz Iskra in 1934, they were primarily

Gertrud and Otto Natzler

self-taught in ceramics, setting up their first studio in 1935. Neither responded to the ornate work of the Wiener Werkstätte ceramists such as Vally Wieselthier, Gudrun Baudisch, and Susi Singer—instead they developed a more purist and classical style. Their work involved the use of clean, sharply outlined classical forms to which was applied Otto's remarkable decorative glazes. Superficially their work was similar to the work of another ceramist active in Vienna at the time, Lucie Rie. Neither Rie nor the Natzlers, however, were aware of the other at the time.

The Natzlers agreed upon a division of talent, Gertrud throwing the forms and Otto devising the glazes. Both became masters of their speciality, with Gertrud emerging as one of the most sensitive and refined throwers of her era. In 1937 they were featured in an exhibition at the Galerie Wurthle and achieved their first major success, winning the silver medal at the Paris International Exposition. In the following year, they moved to the United States, finally settling in Los Angeles in 1939. For the first three years the Natzlers had to give ceramic instruction to earn income until they could establish a market for their work. In 1939 the Natzlers won first prize at the Ceramic National in Syracuse and rapidly established themselves as leading figures in American ceramic art. They drew international attention for their mastery of glaze technology—particularly their definitive work with the so-called volcanic or crater glazes. Gertrud was for a while one of the only potters in southern California who made her pots entirely on the wheel.

The Natzlers have received numerous awards, both in the United States and Europe. Their work is represented in more than thirty-five museums, including the Metropolitan Museum of Art, New York; the Museum of Modern Art, New York; the Art Institute of Chicago; the Philadelphia Museum of Art; and the Los Angeles County Museum of Art. In addition, they have been the subject of seven major museum exhibitions, including several retrospectives. In 1976, five years after Gertrud's death, Otto began to make slab constructions, which he showed in 1977 at the Craft and Folk Art Museum in Los Angeles. He has since exhibited actively in Washington, Los Angeles, and New York.

Nelson, Arthur ("Art") (1942–). Born in Denver, Nelson studied at the University of Colorado, Boulder, where he received his B.A. in 1964, and at the California College of Arts and Crafts (CCAC), Oakland, receiving his M.F.A. in 1969. In the same year he began to teach at the CCAC, where he now holds the position of associate professor of art.

Nelson has worked through several styles, from brightly colored Funk ceramics to a superrealist phase during which he made monumental key chains up to six feet in length. Over the past seven years he has divided his energies between making vessels and working with sculptural form made up of china paste over heat-resistant metal grids. Nelson's pots are thrown, double-walled vessels. At one stage several of these vessels were asembled in brightly colored stacking "totems"—a playful Pop constructivism. Writing about his work, the art historian Charles Fiske comments, "Rhythm, repetition and development of movement have always been dominant in Nelson's work.... The elements brighten the sober geometry of the vessel by making the surface a light catching shadow, casting activity within the structure of the vessel itself" ("Art Nelson," 1981). In addition to maintaining an active program of exhibitions and teaching, Nelson is also one of several artists who is active in the art/industry program at Kohler Industries in Sheboygan, Wisconsin, where he has been designing bathroom fixtures.

Neri, Manuel (1931–). Born in Sanger, California, Manuel Neri studied at the University of California, Berkeley (1951–52); the California College of Arts and Crafts, Oakland (1952–57); and the California School of Fine Arts, San Francisco (1957–59). Neri had his first one-man show in 1957, at 6 Gallery, San Francisco, and has since emerged as a major American sculptor. While studying at the California College of Arts and Crafts, he became involved in ceramics, producing his distinctive "loop" sculptures. These arch forms, with their bright glazes, were prophetic works in the medium, and up to the mid-1960s had a strong influence on ceramic sculpture on the West Coast. In recent years Neri has moved to marble and plaster as his primary materials.

Nevelson, Louise (1900–). Born in Kiev, Russia, by 1905 Louise Nevelson had immigrated with her family to America and settled in Rockland, Maine. In 1920 she married and moved to New York, attending the Art Students League in 1929–30. She continued her studies with Hans Hofmann in Munich in 1931 and also worked as an assistant to the muralist Diego Rivera. She has since become established as one of the foremost sculptors in the United States and has been the subject of major retrospectives, in 1967, 1969–70, and 1975.

Nevelson's major involvement with ceramics was during the 1940s, when she used the material to explore a series of Cubist-Constructivist figural structures. Her most important work of this series is *Moving—Static—Moving Figures* (1945), a group of eighteen terra-cottas now in the collection of the Whitney Museum of American Art. Other pieces from this period are in the collection of the Hirshhorn Museum and Sculpture Garden, Smithsonian Institution, Washington, D.C.

Nevelson was one of the participants in 1964 in *Art in America*'s project *Ceramics by Twelve Artists*. Writing of her accomplishments, Richard Lafean comments, "She has embraced clay as a medium for a particular expression and retains high quality when she presents the solidity of the slab, the imprint on plastic clay, and the burnishing of vitreous slip into the clay surface, exposing areas of the body. Louise Nevelson's work is the most professional presentation in the exhibit" (Lafean, 1965).

Newton, Clara Chipman (1848–1936). Born in Delphos, Ohio, Newton moved to Cincinnati in 1852. She was a classmate of Maria Longworth Nichols and studied at the Cincinnati School of Design from 1873 to 1874. Newton decorated china for the Centennial Exposition and the *Cincinnati Loan Exhibition* in 1878. In 1879 she was elected secretary of the Cincinnati Pottery Club and then, in 1881, of the Rookwood Pottery, where she functioned as general factotum and decorator as well as an instructor at the Rookwood School for Pottery Decoration. She left the pottery in 1884 as a result of her unhappiness over the eviction of the Pottery Club. Thereafter, she maintained her own studio in downtown Cincinnati and taught at the Thane Miller School. She was actively involved in a number of ceramics and crafts groups, her last appointment being secretary of the Crafters, beginning in 1911.

Nichols, Maria Longworth (1849–1932). Born in Cincinnati, Nichols was the daughter of a wealthy family, with a tradition of supporting the arts. Her father, Joseph Longworth, was the major contributor to the founding of the Cincinnati Art Museum. Maria Longworth married Colonel George Ward Nichols at age nineteen. Her first success in the arts came when she suggested the May Festival of Music, which was held for the first time in 1873, subsidized largely by Longworth money.

In 1875 Maria Longworth Nichols developed an interest in china painting and the ceramic arts. After seeing the exhibition of Japanese pottery at the 1876 Centennial her interest intensified. In 1879 she worked at the Frederick Dallas Pottery. The following year, with Joseph Bailey, Jr., she set up her own pottery, Rookwood, named after her father's Grandin Road estate. In 1883, having set the project in motion, she handed over the management of the pottery to William Watts Taylor, who became general manager.

In 1886, after the death of Colonel Nichols, she married Bellamy Storer. She continued her involvement in the arts, returning to study painting at the Cincinnati Art Academy under Thomas Noble. She worked in metal and occasionally returned to pottery, exhibiting wares at the 1893 World's Columbian Exposition and at the 1900 Exposition Universelle, where she received a gold medal for her pottery and metalwork. Her style of work can only be described as an awkward *japonisme* with oddly proportioned painted elements on ungainly forms, the result being less decorative than they are perversely sexual. The Storers settled in Paris after Bellamy Storer's brief diplomatic career as ambassador to Spain and to Austria-Hungary was brought to an early end by his wife's "indiscretion and naïve interference in the affairs of church and state" (Trapp, 1972). Mrs. Storer died in Paris at the age of eighty-three.

Noguchi, Isamu (1904–). Born in Los Angeles to a Japanese poet father and an American writer-teacher mother, Noguchi spent his childhood in Japan. He moved back to America in 1918 to become a student at the Interlaken School in Indiana. Noguchi was apprenticed to Gutzon Borglum for a short period in 1922. Afterward he moved to New York City, where in 1924 he studied sculpture under Onorio Ruotolo at the Leonardo da Vinci Art School. In 1927–28 Noguchi won a Guggenheim Fellowship to study in Paris, where he met Alexander Calder and became studio assistant to Constantin Brancusi. From 1930 to 1932 Noguchi made a series of ceramic sculptures in Japan, influenced strongly by Haniwa figures and Bizen and Shigaraki wares. During the early 1950s, he returned to Japan and produced an even larger body of ceramic sculptures, encouraged and befriended by Rosanjin. Writing of his works, Shuzo Takiguchi commented:

> Here in Japan he is seemingly devouring the Japanese clay, firing in the traditional kilns Karatsu, Shigaraki, Seto and Bizen; he has become a potter…this is an exhibition of pottery. Nevertheless Noguchi is firing his pottery as sculpture, or, at least they are being fired in a manner that captivates the fancy of the sculptor. Of course, in the Western world there is a tradition of terracotta sculptures and from there in springboard fashion Noguchi has jumped right into the world of Japanese pottery, which naturally accounts for his preserving the raw texture of the clay in the firing. He finds rightful justification in the primitive Haniwa sculptures; no modern potter shall deny the sculptural position of the Haniwa. The Haniwa is ultimately united with the ancient earthenwares and pottery; Noguchi's aim is the revivification of this primitive relationship. Moreover, he seeks in his pottery the possibility of the various idioms of modern sculpture. The adaptation of the characteristic spatial volumes caused by the hollowness of pottery, consequently, has been appropriately expressed in all his works. (*Hasegawa, S., et al.*, 1953)

The first exhibition of these works in the United States took place at the Stable Gallery, New York, in 1954.

Notkin, Richard (1948–). Born in Chicago, Notkin studied at the Kansas City Art Institute, where he received a B.F.A., and at the University of California, Davis, receiving his M.F.A. in 1973. He currently works in Myrtle Creek, Oregon. From the outset Notkin has been intrigued by the surprising

monumentality of the miniature. Kurt Weiser, director of the Archie Bray Foundation, recalls that the first time he met Notkin as a fellow student at the Kansas City Art Institute, Notkin was using a hypodermic syringe to inject slip into the mold of a tiny insect. That image of the artist at work is a potent one, for it sets Notkin apart from his contemporaries, revealing the priority he sets in terms of scale. Notkin's work involves meticulous craftsmanship and a passionate commitment to detail. These aesthetic priorities in his work could produce fussy and shallow objects were it not for the strong social and political agenda that underpins his work.

Notkin is a concerned and vociferous follower of political theater, although the political edge has not always been evident in his work. Often it was stated subtly in early tableaux that dealt with the ecological issues evoked by the use of assemblages of consumer waste and by the frequent use of the garbage can as a potent metaphor. In *Demons of the Intellect (Professing to Be Wise They Became Fools)* (1979–80), Notkin aimed a cartoonish barb at political leadership. The use of the skulls in this piece connects it to a series of works that employed this image. In their penetrating study of Notkin's art, Michael Dunas and Sarah Bodine explain the significance of the skull:

> The human skull [is] Notkin's attempt to identify a symbol for individual conscience using a universally recognized image. For Notkin, the skull represents human uniqueness—his ability to think. But Notkin manipulates the skull for his own ends, portraying it as an empty container—one devoid of brains, spirit, or life, an airhead, a numbskull. Formally the skulls are seductive. These perfect specimens, with their sensuous porcelain surfaces and meticulous detailing exude a permanence, a lack of decay. . . . The skull, this empty-headed everyman, reinforces Notkin's condemnation of society for accepting the *status quo* and shrinking from responsibility. (Dunas and Bodine, 1987)

But the political statements became more specific and ideologically clear in works such as *Universal Hostage Crisis* (1981) and *Contraceptive and Munitions* (1981), where Notkin began to dwell on the gamesmanship and dangerous instability of international politics with his miniature chessboards becoming metaphors for strategic policy-making.

In 1980 he began to work with pre-Columbian ceramics as a device to use the cultural images of a past society to reflect certain realities within our own. This led him early in the eighties to his *Yixing* series,

which has become a significant and unique body of work. Yixing teapots were first produced in the late Ming period, toward the end of the sixteenth century. These teapots were made from a refined stoneware clay and were unglazed, relying upon the exquisite clay bodies for their surface appeal. The colors range from a purplish-brown clay through light beiges, reddish-browns, and black. The wares were considered too coarse for the imperial court, but they did attract the attention and collaboration of Ming and Qing dynasty scholars and artists. This collaboration between scholar and craftsman was rare in Chinese society and gave the wares an art status and intellectual edge that intrigued Notkin.

Notkin is particularly interested in the symbolism that the works employed; a peach form indicated longevity, a Buddha's hand citron meant good luck, and a pomegranate teapot with handles and feet made up of carefully molded nuts symbolized numerous offspring. Notkin set out to play a game of style with the Yixing teapot, retaining its elegance of style and fetishist detailing and craft, but replacing the symbolism of the Ming dynasty with the dynastic symbols of our own time. None of these symbols/images is more potent than that of nuclear cooling towers—suggesting power and energy on the one hand and pollution and death on the other—one of the great follies of twentieth-century leadership. In 1982 Notkin was inspired to produce his double-cooling tower series. Politically he was motivated by the near miss of Three Mile Island reactor break-

Richard Notkin

down and formally by a seventeenth-century Yixing teapot consisting of two cubes. The meaningfulness of this image became clear in 1986 with the Chernobyl incident, when the deadly consequence of a nuclear mishap was dramatically demonstrated.

Other forms in Notkin's play with the teapot are strangely at odds with his acerbic political edge. In some works, such as his "curbside teapots," one finds a strangely nostalgic quality in this microcosmic urban landscape. The introduction of an emaciated dog into his 1986 curbside teapots should function as a metaphor for the urban homeless, but they end up being charming in a manner that the artist does not intend— that is, "cute." This sentimentality is certainly removed from his latest teapots, which take the heart as an image for the vessel. The heart teapots, in common with all of Notkin's works, are molded. But the basic form is an original work, modeled by hand. Notkin does not cast from existing objects, insisting that the forms be entirely his own.

The heart teapots have disturbing precise detail, showing fatty tissues and ventricular arteries that emerge to form handles and spouts. The result is a disturbingly painful image. Even though the teapot is patently made of clay, its modeling is detailed enough to suggest reality and therefore a sense of some violence having been done to this crucial and vulnerable human organ. Just as the skull symbolized the intellect, so the heart conjures up notions of compassion ("have a heart" or "heartfelt"). Then, by title and treatment, the teapot is connected to events in which that compassion is noticeably absent, as in *Sharpesville* (1986), where a black, stoneware teapot is covered with beautifully detailed rose thorns—the title relating the work to the 1961 riots and killing of black demonstrators in South Africa.

Notkin's achievement is turning the teapot into an eloquent means of dealing with heroic, political issues, and is a reminder not to undervalue the potential of the potter to deal with such matters. As Dunas and Bodine comment, "In the Lilliputian theatre of the miniature, where scale is the allegory of power, Notkin shares the spotlight most notably with [Jack] Earl. Where Earl's populist homilies undress contemporary conceits, Notkin's cautionary tales expose [their social consequences. As Swift views the human body] for his critique of the political body, Notkin uses the table top to narrate the complexity and magnitude of society's actions" (Dunas and Bodine, 1987).

Oestreich, Jeffrey N. (1947–). Born in Saint Paul, Minnesota, Jeff Oestreich studied with Warren MacKenzie at the University of Minnesota, Minneapolis, from 1967 to 1968 and attended Bemidji State University, Minnesota, where he received his B.A. in 1969. From 1969 to 1971 he was one of the last potters to apprentice with Bernard Leach at Saint Ives, England. The experience of working at the Leach Pottery left an indelible mark on Oestreich's vocabulary as a potter and set boundaries on his art. But Oestreich finds these boundaries to be "liberating, not confining," providing him with the sense of being part of a pottery "family." He has the unique ability to follow a tradition while at the same time expanding its boundaries. Despite their clearly inherited style, Oestreich's works have also achieved a contemporary statement and presence. Indeed, Oestreich has achieved a remarkable balance between contemporary and personal style and the continuation of the Leach tradition. He still employs all the formal elements and even techniques for which Leach was known. His limited palette of eight glazes is also mainly from Leach.

In his early works, Oestreich employed a Hamada-style brushwork on his pots; he has found his interest is primarily in form and now decorates only occasionally. Rhythm and repetition are crucial to Oestreich, who calls this discipline "the strongest element a potter has to work with." Oestreich's functional pots (vases, teapots, platters, bowls) are among the most classical and elegant vessels being made in the United States today. In common with the work of fellow "Mingeisota" potters, including Mark Pharis, Randy Johnson, and others, that of Oestreich is evidence of the growing vitality and strength of the "functionalists" in contemporary pottery. Oestreich now works from a pottery he established on a small farm near Taylor's Falls, Minnesota.

Ohr, George Edgar (1857–1918). Born in Biloxi, Mississippi, the son of German immigrant parents, Ohr ran away from home at an early age, working at a ship chandler's store in New Orleans. In the years that followed, he worked variously as an apprentice in a file cutter's shop, in a tinker's shop, and again in a ship's store. In 1879 a family friend, Joseph Fortune Meyer, offered Ohr the opportunity to apprentice as a potter at a wage of $10 a month. Ohr accepted and worked for Meyer until 1881, acquiring the rudimentary skills of his craft.

Ohr then left on a two-year, sixteen-state tour of the nation's potteries, returning to Biloxi in 1883 to set up his own workshop with $26.80 in capital. Later Ohr worked again with Meyer at the New Orleans Pottery Company, and possibly also worked at the Crescent City Pottery. He supposedly worked at the Newcomb Pottery for a brief period about 1898. It is claimed that he was dismissed because he was an unsuitable influence on refined young ladies, but no evidence exists to prove this contention. There is also an indication that Ohr collaborated with Susan Frackelton, but no knowledge of how this association came about. Ohr's pottery burned down in 1894, and a new, bizarre, pagodalike building replaced it, becoming one of the landmarks of Biloxi and even included on the souvenir porcelain plates made for the city in Europe.

The fire appears to have been a turning point for Ohr, igniting in the artist a radicalism that was to peak shortly after 1900. From this point on Ohr began to make lyrical, paper-thin, twisted pots with sinuous, curving handles, which are arguably the most important ceramics of the era. In 1904 Ohr's father died, leaving his son with a comfortable inheritance. In about 1906 George Ohr stopped his work as a potter and later joined his son in a Cadillac dealership.

Ohr's work was the most prophetic of his day. Robert Blasberg accurately observes that Ohr was an aesthetic loner, who had little impact on his own time but instead "did a less common thing by anticipating much of the innovation in ours" (Blasberg, 1972). Apart from his gestural play with

George E. Ohr

George Ohr at the Cotton States and International Exposition, Atlanta, 1895

the material, Ohr was also involved in an expression that, had the pieces been produced in the last twenty years, would certainly be labeled Funk. He produced erotic-humorous objects, such as his vagina money boxes and pornographic buttons.

He was also the father of the "verbal visual" in American ceramics, playing as freely with words as with clay. His attitude toward the relationship between title and object is indicated in a poster at one of his fair appearances: "Acts are fruit, words are leaves." An example of this application can be found in the naming of his many children. Their first names were also their initials, so the large Ohr brood went through life with the legacy of names such as Leo, Lio, Zio, Oto, Clo, Ojo, and Geo. In his ceramic work, Ohr used titles frequently and also inscribed some of his wares with long, rambling letters—one of which was addressed to the Smithsonian Institution. The Smithsonian has one of the more interesting works in this genre, a pair of top hats. The first is titled *Nine O'Clock in the Evening* (c. 1900) and is pristine and elegant, while the other, *Three O'Clock in the Morning* (c. 1900), is disheveled and crumpled. They anticipate the cartoon-strip Pop imagery in American clay of the 1960s and 1970s and are based on the same principles as Robert Arneson's *Sinking Cup* sequence (1972) and other objects that deal with the passage of time, and with banal imagery.

Ohr received some recognition in his day, with awards from the Pan American Exposition of 1901 and the Louisiana Purchase International Exposition in 1904. But generally he remained misunderstood by peers who were involved in much more academic approaches to the ceramic medium. However, he did find notoriety as a Southern "character" and even inspired a novel entitled *The Wonderful Wheel*, by Mary Tracy Early (New York: Century Company, 1896), about a "queer old potter with strange flashing black eyes, and a black moustache so long that he draped it over his ears when he worked...making queerly shaped jugs and vases, and mugs which poured water out where you were not expecting it" (also see Hecht, 1982).

Ohr's true recognition has come, as he anticipated, from later generations. He has become actively sought after, and his collectors read like a who's who of art and craft collecting and the contemporary arts world. There have been two small museum exhibitions of his work, and in 1983 the first show of his pots in New York, entitled *George E. Ohr: An Artworld Homage*, with works loaned from the collections of Irving Blum, Charles Cowles, Jasper Johns, and others, took place at the Garth Clark Gallery. Writing of this exhibition in the *Village Voice*, the critic John Perreault stated: "The show is only a tease, but what a tease: look at each vessel, carefully, sensing how it would feel to move the clay in these ways; look at

each vessel as a sculpture occupying space and time; look at each vessel as a painting. We see all these things simultaneously, along with the wit, handles stuck here and there, the elegant accidents, the crush and twist. George Ohr is a great artist" (Perreault, 1983).

But the most tender homage to Ohr came from Jasper Johns, in his 1983 exhibition at the Leo Castelli Gallery in New York. With what John Russell, senior art critic for the *New York Times*, termed "a touching fidelity," Johns painted images of the Ohr pots from his own collection into his paintings. A more mercenary tribute to Ohr's growing fame and reputation as an artist (and one which arguably would have given Ohr the greatest amusement) comes from the fact that his pots are now being forged. At first only bisque pots by Ohr, with a contemporary glaze, were appearing in this market, but recently forgers have begun to create (with limited success) the forms as well, *caveat emptor.*

Owen, Ben (1904–1983). Born in North Carolina, Owen was taught pottery by his father on their farm in northern Moore County. Owen was hired in 1922 by Jacques and Juliana Busbee to throw pots in their Jugtown Pottery in Seagrove, North Carolina. The Busbees wanted to revitalize the southern folk pottery and arranged to sell Jugtown wares in New York. They took Owen on trips to museums in New York, Washington, D.C., and New Orleans to study Korean and Persian pottery. The Jugtown Pottery became known for its so-called Jugtown-blue glaze, and Owen began to merge Oriental ceramic into southern tradition.

In 1959, after nearly forty years with Jugtown, Owen opened his own pottery and ran it until 1972, when ill health forced him to close it. The large amount of unfired and bisqued wares that had been left on the shelves was finally fired in 1981 by his son Ben, Jr., and by his thirteen-year-old grandson Ben III.

Perry, Mary Chase (1867–1961). Born in Hancock, Michigan, Perry studied briefly with the Bohemian painter Frans Bischoff, a particular favorite of the china-painting movement, who taught classes in Detroit. In search of a more formal understanding of art, Perry studied at the Cincinnati School of Design between 1887 and 1889. Among her fellow students were Maria Longworth Nichols and the Japanese artist Kataro Shirayamadani. After a brief return to Detroit, where she attended classes at the museum school, Perry moved to Asheville, North Carolina. There she joined her parents, opening a small china-painting studio where she gave instruction and sold wares. In 1893 she returned to Detroit and opened a china-painting studio on West Adams Street, where she and two partners gave lessons. By chance she discovered that her neighbour, Horace J. Caulkins (1850–1923), had invented a portable, kerosene-burning kiln for use with dental porcelains. Perry persuaded him to convert the kiln for use by china painters; the ingenious product was named the Revelation kiln and soon became a standard for American ceramists. Perry traveled around the country demonstrating the new kiln as well as the application of different effects and enamels, such as the "floating enamels," "raised paste," "dry dusting," and the other tricks of the china-painting trade.

In 1903, somewhat exhausted by her travels and commercial endeavors, Perry decided to return to the role of artist. Taking the same route as her close friend Adelaide Alsop Robineau, she ceased overglaze decoration and opened the Pewabic Pottery with Caulkins. She converted a stable into a primitive pottery studio, employed Joseph Herrick, a thrower from the pottery town of Zarburg in Alsace-Lorraine, and began to make work. Her first pieces were somewhat imitative of Grueby and received a lot of criticism. The first major order was for 132 pieces of pottery from the firm of

Mary Chase Perry

Burley & Company in Chicago and was soon followed by several other orders. The art connoisseur Charles Lang Freer was an enthusiastic supporter of the pottery.

The wares Perry exhibited at the 1904 Louisiana Purchase International Exposition in Saint Louis showed the strong influence of the French potter Auguste Delaherche as well as of the Art Nouveau movement. Perry continued to have her forms thrown for her and concentrated on glaze chemistry. In 1909 she removed from the kiln "a tiny piece, not more than three inches in height"; it had an astonishing glow that came from its iridescent glaze. She was greatly excited by this "fragile bit of pottery whose surface catches the light and reflects it in opalescent, shimmering tints that defy naming, slipping and melting into other tones, now paling, now deepening with every movement of the little vase" (*Highlights of Pewabic Pottery, 1977*). Perry had arrived at the glaze by empirical process. It immediately became a popular success, firmly establishing Perry's reputation as a studio potter.

Much of her creative energy, however, went into the architectural commissions that were to become the mainstay and, arguably, the most creative element of the pottery. Among her commissions were those for Saint Paul's Cathedral, Detroit (1908); Rice Institute, Houston (1913); the National Shrine of the Immaculate Conception, Washington, D.C. (1923–31); and the Detroit Institute of Arts (1927). As a result of the demand for her tiles, Perry was one of the few ceramists to become wealthy from her craft. Changes in architectural design did away with murals to a great extent, but the pottery remained active under Perry's guidance until her death, in 1961, at the age of ninety-four. The pottery continued operations under the direction of Mrs. Ella Peters until 1965, when it was given to Michigan State University, East Lansing, which now maintains it as a museum and runs it as an independent, nonprofit organization.

Perry received several awards in her career, including the Binns Medal in 1947. A number of her works are in public collections, one of the most significant being the group of carefully selected pieces given by Charles Freer to the Detroit Institute of Arts.

Pharis, Mark (1947–). Born in Minneapolis, Pharis studied at the University of Minnesota under the supervision of Curt Hoard and Warren MacKenzie. He currently maintains a studio in Houston, Minnesota, and teaches at the University of Minnesota in Minneapolis. In 1977, 1980, and 1986 he

was a recipient of a Visual Artists Fellowship from the National Endowment for the Arts.

Pharis is one of the most radical potters to emerge from the so-called Mingeisota school around MacKenzie. Pharis is not attracted to the symmetry of thrown wares but prefers to work with slab-built forms while still retaining a traditionalist's respect for both utility and humility in pottery. Over the years he has moved away from utilitarianism as a practical and domestic concern, although conceptually he remains tied to functional forms. Over the past few years he has focused on a relatively small number of forms—the vase, the teapot, and the saucepot. His pure, Minimalist explorations are among the most important examinations of the functional/art edge in contemporary pottery.

Poor, Henry Varnum (1888–1971). Born in Chapman, Kansas, Poor grew up on the prairie. He studied economics and art at Stanford University, Palo Alto, California, and later enrolled at the Slade School of Art in London. While studying there he was strongly influenced by Roger Fry's *First Impressionist Exhibition* at the Grafton Gallery in 1910, which gave a startled English audience their first taste of Cubism. This inspired Poor's move to Paris, where he studied at the Académie Julian.

On his return to the United States in 1912, Poor taught at Stanford and at the Mark Hopkins Art Institute, San Francisco. In 1922 his first exhibition of ceramics was held at the Montross Gallery in New York. He joined the American Designers' cooperative as a founding member in 1928, designing bathrooms and furniture. Until 1933 he devoted himself mainly to ceramics, establishing a national reputation and winning a number of awards, including the Architectural League's gold medal of honor and the Binns Medal of the American Ceramic Society in 1942. In the late twenties he received a number of commissions, and in 1932 a commission from Donald Deskey to create four ceramic lamps and a number of vases for Radio City Music Hall. The lamps were stolen during the gala opening and the vases disappeared shortly afterward.

In 1958 Poor published *A Book of Pottery: From Mud to Immortality*, a book on the art and craft of the potter. The British *doyen* of the pottery world, Bernard Leach, was impressed enough with the book to write Poor a letter:

During my odd moments for several days past I have been reading and looking at your book with delight. I have known

Henry Varnum Poor

your name for perhaps 30 years.... Now we are both getting old. We both draw and write besides making pots.... I feel we have much in common. You say so many things which I have deeply felt and have expressed, in some cases, with perhaps a different accent.... I look at your pots in this book, recognize a difference in temperament, background, and motivation, but still find *life* which as you write somewhere is the real test. (Steigleder, 1983)

Poor's métier was the plate. The finest of his work was done in this format and that of the open bowl. Poor also made vases and pitchers, which were very well painted but whose forms generally lacked the distinction of his plates and bowls. Despite many invitations from institutions such as New York University, Poor never taught. Ceramics became for him an increasingly private, intensely personal art form. He was "fiercely protective of his time and energy," doing all the arduous work himself, even refusing to take on assistants or apprentices.

Poor continued to make pots until virtually the day before his death. His studio at Crow House, in Rockland County, New York (which he began to build in 1920), remains very much as it was the day that he set down his brushes for the last time. On the morning that he died, December 8, 1971, "his kiln was filled with plates, goblets and wine decanters.... Fired by his good friend Alfred Rossin, these were the last works of an artist who for fifty years remained disdainful of fashion but ever excited by the lively forms and images he could achieve by using the resources of the earth around him" (Steigleder, 1983).

Price, Kenneth (1935–). Born in Los Angeles, Price studied at the Chouinard Art Institute in 1953–54 and at the University of Southern California, where he received a B.F.A. in 1956. In 1957–58 he was one of the central participants in the experiment taking place at the Otis Art Institute under the loose but inspired leadership of Peter Voulkos. Seeking new ideas, Price went to the New York State College of Ceramics at Alfred University, Alfred, New York, where he received his M.F.A. in 1959. He returned to Los Angeles the following year for a one-man show at the Ferus Gallery. As part of the Ferus stable, he shared concerns for craftsmanship, finish, and color with Ed Ruscha and Craig Kauffman. From Robert Irwin and Ed Kienholz he developed an interest in certain environmental aspects of art.

At this point, he broke from his earlier format of the pot and began to develop a personal sculptural style, employing brightly painted and glazed surfaces on biomorphic "egg" forms that extended the vision of the Surrealist sculptures of Brancusi, Arp, and Miró. Speaking of Price's "egg" forms at the 4th International Ceramics Symposium in Toronto in 1986, Edward Lebow said that these "protoplasmic shapes floated out of Miró, Matta, Ernst, and Arp, passed through Gorky and landed on the surfaces of Price's ovoid forms" (Lebow, 1987). It was an adventurous use of color in sculpture at a time when the polychrome metal movement on the West Coast was still in its infancy. The works were well received. Writing of these forms in *Art International*, John Coplans referred to Sartre's remark that "Color is man smiling, modelling, man is in tears," when he wrote: "Price's work invokes to a remarkable degree a strange interplay between the joyful and the ominous. His color is physically brilliant, almost gaudy: these colors are set off against an imagery which is dark, murky, very elementary, and primordial—it is the last in the world that one would think to use this coloration with. It is this upsetting quality, the hard, bright, finite finishes against the vague, dark, elemental imagery that makes Price's sculpture so striking" (Coplans, 1964).

From these sexually associative forms, Price moved on to an exploration of the cup as format. In such works as *California Snail Cup* (1967), he dealt with the cup theme through drawings and lithographs. According to Lebow, "His cups presented a nuisance for those art writers who had embraced the artistry of those eggs.... They weren't sure what to do with these pots."

Far from being a "hobby," Price's cups have consistently proved to be the more powerful and important of his works. The most sophisticated of his cup themes were produced between 1972 and 1974, when he created a series of constructivist cup assemblages. These forms dealt with a series of concerns: Price's distinctive play with flat, bright color; the tease between two and three dimensions; and the dialogue between fine and decorative art that flowed from the use of what was identified as functional forms. The constructivist cups also reflect the ambiance of Taos, New Mexico, his home from 1972 to 1980. In many ways the squat cups, with their play of light and shade, mimic the shapes of the traditional adobe houses in Taos, particularly in the late afternoon when the sun causes strong, angular shadows and dramatic contrasts of light and shade.

The works are complex, witty, and sculpturally involving. Spatially they refer to the Futurist-sculpture theory of Umberto Boccioni. Boccioni demanded that the sculptor do more than simply present the volume of an object; he should also capture the space that surrounds it. This Price achieved by placing small, geometric forms around his cups as boundaries to their spatial presence. Writing of Price's work in 1976, the critic Mary King wrote that what Price brought off with these cups was taking the practical object—cup—and transforming it through "a great visual sophistication, and a dizzying shift of spatial gears. Like a ball in an enclosed court the spectator bounces off ideas of the humble cup into the rarefied sophistication of Frank Stella

Kenneth Price

reincarnated in 3-D, with persistent changes of scale wherein the curiously shaped container becomes an architectural monument, the bright fragment of an Art Deco dream'' (King, 1976).

Running parallel to this body of work was a major project that Price had intended to have culminate in the creation of a huge curio shop. These ''curios'' were strongly influenced by the ''airport'' art of New Mexico and were eventually assembled into a smaller but immaculately presented exhibition *Happy's Curios*, at the Los Angeles County Museum of Art in 1978. The exhibition comprised mainly groups of painted ceramic forms—some produced with a stylistic reference to folk pottery—that were assembled in custom-made, wooden shelving units. The exhibition, with its radiance and lush coloring, was a strong statement on decorative art, and, in a sense, on painting as well. The reference to certain pieces, such as the *Shrine Assemblages*, was more directly related to cultural archetypes. For the rest, however, the works dealt, as the art of Price has always done, with broad and major concerns in fine art today.

The complexity of Price's style and issues cannot easily be condensed into a short biography. One of the most succinct summaries of his work comes from a single paragraph in a review in *Art in America* by Phyllis Derfner:

> Price is surely one of the most intelligent of contemporary American artists, and his intelligence is complete—it includes wit. He has discarded the idea that art can or should be a single-minded pursuit of a single quality or set of qualities. His selection from a grab-bag of stylistic possibilities that are very recent but just old enough to be quoted from has been assembled with an elegance so perfectly poised it seems incapable of slipping except, perhaps, into hilarity of the most exalted kind. (Derfner, 1975)

During the eighties Price has continued to make works that are about pottery, whether these be his pornographic pot series or his very much abstracted lidded vessels, such as *Gomo* (1985). He was one of the few artists to receive consistent praise in the Whitney Museum's 1981 exhibition *Ceramic Sculpture: Six Artists*. Hilton Kramer, then art critic for the *New York Times,* wrote of Price, singling out his cups from 1972–74 for particular commendation, ''dazzling in color and brilliantly resourceful in their formal invention.... They remind me of some of Frank Stella's wall reliefs, and I would

not be surprised to learn that Mr. Stella had studied them with profit.... [Price's cups] handle the problem of color in sculpture with an authority that few of Mr. Price's contemporaries have equalled'' (Kramer, 1981).

Prieto, Antonio (1912–1967). Born in Valdepeñas, Spain, Prieto came to the United States with his family in 1916. In 1940 he moved to San Francisco from Chico, California, taking adult education classes at the California School of Fine Arts in painting, sculpture, and ceramics. After World War II he completed his studies at the New York State College of Ceramics at Alfred University, Alfred, New York, and in 1946 began to teach at the California College of Arts and Crafts in Oakland. F. Carlton Ball had established the Mills Ceramic Guild based at nearby Mills College. A close cooperation developed between Prieto at the CCAC and Ball at Mills, and they shared their resources, creating a lively and competitive climate.

In 1950 Prieto succeeded Ball at Mills and established an aggressive ceramic-arts program that attracted many talented students, including Robert Arneson. In 1952 Prieto traveled to England to represent the United States at the First Conference of Potters and Weavers, at Dartington Hall. In 1955 he won the silver medal at the International Ceramics Exhibition in Cannes. The following year he was inducted as the first craftsman trustee on the board of what is now the American Craft Council. In 1964 he received a Fulbright Fellowship and was on his way to establishing a national and international reputation when he died, in 1967. Prieto's work was influenced by ceramic tradition but it also expressed a dominant interest in European modern art, in particular the works of Miró and Max Ernst. After his death a memorial collection of ceramic art was established at Mills College. Prieto is another of those American ceramists (such as McVey and others) whose works have been somewhat overlooked and deserve a reappraisal.

Rady, Elsa (1943–). Born in New York City, Rady studied under Ralph Bacerra and Vivika Heino at the Chouinard Art Institute from 1962 to 1966. Rady received a Visual Artists Fellowship from the National Endowment for the Arts and a collaborative grant (with Laddie John Dill) in 1983. Rady works with porcelain in a distinctive style,

with even, glazed surfaces; a tense, bowl form; and a lip that is cut into various Art Deco–inspired stepped shapes. In some cases these are assembled in groups of two or three on a granite slab—what the artist terms ''conjugations.'' She maintains a studio in Venice, California.

Randall, Theodore (''Ted'') (1914–1985). Born in Indianapolis, Randall studied at Yale University, receiving his B.F.A. in 1938. He worked as a sculptor in New York until 1942. After serving in the United States Army (1942–45) he returned to school, receiving his M.F.A. from the New York State College of Ceramics at Alfred University, Alfred, New York, in 1949. His was the third Randall generation to be involved in ceramics; in 1884 his grandfather Theodore founded the *Clay-Worker*, which was continued by the Randall family. Until 1955 Ted Randall operated the Randall Pottery, beginning his dual career as artist-teacher at Alfred in 1951. In 1958 he assumed the mantle of Charles Harder and became the new head of the Division of Art and Design at Alfred, taking the school through its most difficult period of transition into its current status of offering a full fine-arts program. Randall was president of the National Association of Schools of Art and Design and a founding father of the National Council on Education for the Ceramic Arts (NCECA). His dedication to teaching resulted in a small output of work until his retirement, when he became a more prolific producer and his work took on a new sense of presence. He received many awards in his lifetime, including the International Ceramic Symposium Award in 1983. In 1987 the NCECA organized a memorial exhibition, *Ted Randall (1914–1985)—A Retrospective*, at the Lowe Art Gallery, Syracuse University. Melvin Bernstein's *Art and Design in Alfred* is recommended for a full discussion of Randall's role as an educator.

Rauschenberg, Robert (1925–). Milton Ernest (later Robert) Rauschenberg was born in Port Arthur, Texas. His first formal art training was in 1946 on the GI Bill at the Kansas City Art Institute, Missouri. In the following year he left for Paris, where he studied at the Académie Julian, a favorite of American artists. In 1948–49 he studied under Josef Albers at Black Mountain College in North Carolina. Rauschenberg subsequently became known as a controversial, inventive figure in the arts and also as a political activist. He promoted several social and political causes for the artist, including royalty legislation and an artist-support system, "Change, Incorporated."

Rauschenberg's involvement with clay came in 1972 during a three-month stay at Graphicstudio, the University of South Florida, Tampa, where he created a suite of five pieces in clay related in imagery to his *Made in Tampa* prints suite. They reflect a superrealist approach to the medium and are among the most successful ceramics in this style. Each of the five pieces was produced in a limited edition under the supervision of Allen Eaker and Julio Juristo.

In 1983 Rauschenberg showed his second body of ceramic works at Leo Castelli's Greene Street gallery in SoHo, New York. The works were created in 1982 on large tile panels at the Otsuka-Ohmi factory in Japan. The title of the series of works, *Recreational Clay-Works*, reflects their playful and witty quality. For instance, in *Pneumonia Lisa*, Mona Lisa's hands and face are superimposed over Botticelli's *Venus*. In other works Rauschenberg created more complex structures, with trompe l'oeil ceramic bamboo, chains, and hinges. Robert Hughes wrote in *Time* that the new work, "a hybrid of traditional and new technologies, look[s] both archaic and slick" (Hughes, 1982). In *Art in America* the work was acclaimed as "the most luscious painting Rauschenberg has done in years...there is a productive contradiction between the clunkiness of the material and the thin translucent surface in which the images seem to float, free here from the conventional Rauschenberg grid" (Marasso, 1983).

Rhead, Frederick Hurten (1880–1942). Born in Hanley, Staffordshire, England, Rhead followed six generations of potters in his family, becoming art director of the Waddle Art Pottery, Hanley, before he was twenty years of age. In 1902 he moved to the United States, where he worked with William P. Jervis at Vance/Avon. He joined the S. A. Weller Pottery as a designer in 1904 but soon left to become art director of the Roseville Pottery, Zanesville, Ohio, for which he produced some interesting designs. In 1908 he rejoined Jervis, this time at the Jervis Pottery on Long Island, and in 1910 Rhead became an instructor in pottery at the University City Pottery near Saint Louis. The following year he joined the Arequipa Pottery in Marin County, California, as a ceramics instructor. Inspired by the success

of Dr. H. J. Hall's Marblehead Pottery in Massachusetts, Dr. Philip King Brown had organized Arequipa to train young women with tuberculosis.

Late in 1913 Rhead moved to southern California, where he opened the Rhead Pottery in Santa Barbara. There he experimented with glazes, managing to produce the Chinese black-mirror glaze after fifteen years of research. While in Santa Barbara Rhead attempted to publish a magazine, the *Potter*. The first issue came out in December 1916 and the third and final issue in February 1917. The magazine was excellently produced and included articles from some of the leading artists and historians of the day. Rhead used the magazine to give vent to his personal opinions. His singular independence as a critic is well illustrated in his comments regarding Adelaide Alsop Robineau's *Scarab Vase*. While everyone else hailed it as a masterpiece, Rhead called this work "a monstrosity" (Rhead, 1916). In 1917 he closed his pottery and returned to the Midwest, joining the American Encaustic Tiling Company of Zanesville as research director.

From 1927 until his death, he was art director of the Homer Laughlin China Company, Newark, West Virginia. At Homer Laughlin, Rhead scored one of the great successes of his career, the creation of Fiesta ware. The pottery was modeled somewhat directly on the bright monochrome wares that were being produced in southern California by potteries such as Bauer. These wares were in turn a modernist response to the colorful Mexican folk pottery. Developed in 1935 and introduced to the market in 1936 at the Pittsburgh Pottery and Glass Fair, Fiesta became an immediate and popular success. Although Rhead acknowledged his debt to the California monochromes, he saw Fiesta as being different in many ways. Certainly it was a much more refined work than the cruder West Coast wares. Rhead also introduced the concept of mixing and matching the five colors of the ware in a single service.

The success of Fiesta symbolizes Rhead's talents. He was not an inventive or original potter. His artworks and designs were derived, almost to the point of plagiarism, from preexisting work. But as with Fiesta, he could refine and restyle his original inspiration with great flair and intelligence.

Rhead won a gold medal at the San Francisco Panama-Pacific International Exposition in 1915 and the Charles F. Binns Medal of the American Ceramic Society in 1934. In 1920 he organized the Art Division

of the American Ceramic Society and served as its chairman from 1920 to 1925; he held a similar position in the United States Pottery Association. In 1986 the Erie Art Museum, Erie, Pennsylvania, organized a detailed survey of Rhead's pottery, *Frederick Hurten Rhead: An English Potter in America*, accompanied by a fully illustrated catalogue in which Sharon Dale provides an objective, scholarly assessment of his art and influence.

Rhodes, Daniel (1911–). Born in Fort Dodge, Iowa, Rhodes studied at the Art Institute of Chicago, Art Students League in New York, and New York State College of Ceramics at Alfred University, Alfred, New York, where he was the first graduate student to study under Charles Harder and Sam Haile. In 1947 Harder invited Rhodes to teach at Alfred, where he remained until his retirement in 1973. Rhodes currently lives in Davenport, California, where he maintains a studio.

Rhodes has worked both as a potter and as a sculptor, bringing technical innovation to the field with the large sculptural forms that he exhibited in 1967 at the Museum of Contemporary Crafts, New York. These tall forms were created (and survived the firing) through the use of fiberglass fabric, which provided both a textural quality and strength for tall structures. Although Rhodes remains an active, exhibiting artist (a traveling exhibition of recent works entitled *Daniel Rhodes: The California Years* was organized in 1986 by the Art Museum of Santa Cruz), his most important contribution is as an educator. His books, *Clay and Glazes for the Potter* (1957), *Stoneware and Porcelain* (1959), *Kilns* (1968), and *Pottery Form* (1976) are indispensable teaching aids and have been used to educate three generations of ceramists.

Rice, Jacqueline Ione (1941–). Born in Orange, California, Rice studied at the University of Washington, Seattle, under Howard Kottler, Robert Sperry, and Fred Bauer, receiving her B.A. in 1968 and her M.F.A. in 1970. She has taught at the Kansas City Art Institute (1971–73) and the University of Michigan, Ann Arbor (1973–77), and since 1977 has been head of the ceramics program at the Rhode Island School of Design, where from 1985 to 1986 she was also acting dean of the fine-arts department. Rice's influence as an educator in the eighties has been substantial, as has been her involvement in innovatory tableware designs.

Her early work dealt with sculptural form overlaid with a strong sense of the decorative. Her vocabulary involved the layering or weaving of elements of color and pattern into complex structures. This style of work proved to be equally expressive in other materials, and Rice has worked in wood and paper (and continues to produce paper collages).

In the early eighties she began to involve herself more with functional form, partly the result of having to teach throwing. In 1984 this interest was further developed through a trip through Italy on a Mellon grant to study indigenous pottery. Her growing interest in decorative wares led her to design tablewares for Grazia, a maiolica factory in Deruta, Italy. Rice also makes handmade tablewares that, in a more literal sense, continue to explore her interest in layering—presenting sets of plates stacked in a lidded ceramic "box." The sense of composition and surface decoration evolves and expands as each plate is removed from the box.

Rippon, Tom (1954–   ). Born in Sacramento, California, Rippon received his M.F.A. in 1973 from the Art Institute of Chicago but was largely self-taught in terms of ceramics. He has taught at the University of California, Davis (1973–74), Art Institute of Chicago (1977–79), and Appalachian Center for the Crafts in Smithville, Tennessee. In 1974 he received a Visual Artists Fellowship from the National Endowment for the Arts. Rippon works in porcelain, and his style derives from the Chicago Funk school of painters such as Jim Nutt. Rippon's sculpture is linear rather than volumetric. He draws with thin defining "lines" of colored porcelain, creating figures and objects in a surrealist setting. Recently he has exchanged his early palette of bright colors and mother-of-pearl lusters for a more limited range of white, gray, and black, producing witty, graphic, and effective homages to the landscapes of the Italian modernist Giorgio de Chirico.

Robertson, Hugh Cornwall (1844–1908). Born in Wolviston, Durham County, England, Robertson moved with his family from Edinburgh to New Jersey in 1853. The family resettled in East Boston, Massachusetts, where the father, James Robertson, and Nathaniel Plympton formed the Plympton and Robertson Pottery. In 1866 Alexander, one of James Robertson's sons, established an independent art pottery in Chelsea,

Massachusetts. The following year Hugh Robertson joined his brother's firm, which they amalgamated with their father's pottery in 1872, changing the name of the firm to Chelsea Keramik Art Works. After his father's death and his brother's move to California, Hugh became the master potter.

The Victorian pastiche of the early art wares slowly gave way to Hugh Robertson's infatuation with the Orient. In particular, he became involved in the search for the *sang de boeuf*, or oxblood, glaze, which was achieved through the reduction of copper. He first accomplished this in 1885 and finally perfected it in 1888, but at such cost to his health and fortunes that he often laconically alluded to it as "Robertson's blood." Another of his achievements was the discovery in 1886 of a gray-white Oriental crackle glaze, which later became the distinguishing feature of the Dedham Pottery.

Robertson was now so obsessed with his glaze chemistry that he neglected the company's finances and general management. In 1889 Robertson, "at the height of his creativity, exhausted and probably poisoned from the lead in his own glazes, unable to buy another day's fuel for the fire, closed the doors of Chelsea Keramik Art Works" (Hecht, 1987). In 1891 a group of influential Bostonians provided the capital to reestablish the pottery as the Chelsea Pottery; in 1893 the name was changed to Dedham Pottery. The pottery was known for its distinctive craquelle wares, with their blue stencil decorations. Robertson received honors for this work at the Exposition Universelle in Paris in 1900, the Saint Louis Louisiana Purchase International Exposition in 1904, and the Panama-Pacific International Exposition in San Francisco in 1915. Following Robertson's death, his son William assumed management of the Dedham works until 1929. The Dedham Pottery finally closed its doors in 1943, when it was faced with a shortage of skilled labor and with escalating costs of production. The era of the Robertson family's involvement with ceramics came to an end on September 19, 1943, when the contents of the pottery and its museum were dispersed at a clearance sale at Gimbels department store, where the works were offered at half price on an "easy payment plan" (Hecht, 1987).

Robineau, Adelaide Alsop (1865–1929). Born in Middletown, Connecticut, Adelaide Alsop took an early interest in painting, intent upon earning an independent living. She was attracted to china painting, and although largely self-taught, soon became

a prominent decorator and a member of the National League of Mineral Painters. She taught for a short time at Saint Mary's in Minnesota and then studied in New York with William Merritt Chase. She exhibited watercolors at the annual exhibitions of the National Academy in New York and painted miniatures on ivory. In 1899 she married Samuel Robineau. In the same year, with an associate, George H. Clark, the Robineaus established the periodical *Keramik Studio*, which Adelaide Robineau edited until her death. In 1901 she and Samuel moved to Syracuse, New York, where they built their home and studio, Four Winds. Robineau began to show an interest in moving from china painting to studio pottery as early as 1900, inspired by Danish porcelains—first Royal Copenhagen and then the more sculptural works of Bing & Grondahl. She made her first pot in 1901 at the studio of Charles Volkmar, from whom she apparently took lessons. Robineau was also influenced by the French ceramist Taxile Doat, although perhaps more encouraged technically by the French ceramist's knowledge than she was influenced by his aesthetics.

Adelaide Alsop Robineau

Robineau gave up china painting and turned full time to the making of fine porcelains in 1903. In 1910 she joined the faculty of the University City Pottery under Taxile Doat, but resigned her post in 1911. That year she received the first acknowledgment of her work, when a group of fifty-five porcelains was declared, with a grand rhetorical flourish, "the best porcelain in the world" at the Turin Exposition. The American Women's League from University City,

Saint Louis, submitted the works and received the grand prize, while Robineau was given the Diploma della Benemerenza (the grand prize could not be awarded to an individual).

One of the fifty-five pieces was the *Scarab Vase* (1910), which had been commissioned by Edward Lewis for the American Women's League. According to Samuel Robineau the piece emerged from its first firing with bad cracks in the base. Robineau then spent hours filling the cracks with ground porcelain. She then glazed the pot, and it emerged from its glaze firings with no sign of the original cracks at all. Sensing the instability of Lewis's Women's League, Samuel Robineau had been careful to secure a mortgage on the *Scarab Vase,* and when the league collapsed in 1911, he was able to retrieve this and other masterworks (discussed further in chapter 4).

In 1911 Adelaide Robineau was invited to exhibit at both the Paris Salon and Paris's Musée des Arts Décoratifs. Medals and prizes were given to her by the Art Institute of Chicago and the societies of Arts and Crafts in Boston and Detroit. In 1915 her porcelains won another Grand Prix at the Panama-Pacific International Exposition in San Francisco. Two years later Syracuse University conferred on her an honorary doctorate of the ceramic sciences. In 1920 she joined the faculty of Syracuse University, remaining there until 1928. Following her death, the Metropolitan Museum of Art, New York, held a memorial exhibition of her works as a tribute to the skill with which she "wrought the paste into forms of beauty, sometimes austerely massive, sometimes exquisitely fragile and graceful...in the difficult arts of fire" (The Metropolitan Museum of Art, 1929).

There is a postscript that must be added to Robineau's biography, acknowledging the enormous contribution that her dedicated husband, Samuel Edouard Robineau, made to her career. Samuel was her adviser; he was also responsible for the delicate and temperamental firing of the kiln, for some of the research and creation of glazes, and for assisting his wife in many other ways throughout her career. He was a canny investor, which allowed him to dedicate his life to Robineau's art, clearing from her path any impediments that stood in the way of her creating her art. Upon her death, Samuel Robineau wrote a touching memorial to her genius: "Clay and glazes were the raw materials which kindled in her imagination the vision of form and color so related and integrated that their subtlety of relationship could capture and hold fast the sensations aroused in her dreams. These were the elements which lured her on to the inevitable struggle of capturing and imprisoning the essence of her emotion, that she might evoke it in others" (Robineau, 1929).

Roloff, John (1947–). Born in Portland, Oregon, Roloff received his B.A. from the University of California, Davis, in 1970 and his M.A. from California State University, Humboldt, in 1973. He received Visual Artists Fellowships from the National Endowment for the Arts in 1977 and 1980 and a Guggenheim Fellowship in 1983. Roloff maintains a studio in Oakland and teaches at Mills College.

His use of the ship as a central theme in his formal sculpture reflects his interest in the sea. In 1974 he produced his *Exile* series, a group of white ceramic ships caught in reeds or beached on some stretch of sand. The boat became a metaphor for searching into the unknown and at first drew on narrative associations.

Since 1980 he has been exploring large outdoor installation pieces as well. Inspiration for his installation pieces came in part from a visit to Hawaii and Roloff's response to the transformation of the lush landscape by volcanic action. What he created were large ships up to thirty-two feet in length. These were created from a ceramic fiber blanket shaped over a simple welded metal structure. The night firings of these structures, with six gas burners and two 500-gallon tanks of high-pressure propane, were watched by an audience of artists, students, and others from the sponsoring university. These "performances" are part of an ongoing search by Roloff for a dialogue with materials and geological process. Also, in his reference to the kiln and other ceramic associations, Roloff is keenly aware of tradition and its pitfalls, "developing one's own attitude toward the material that encompasses history, perspective, and an open-ended idea. There's a fine line between reverence and irreverence toward the material. Tradition can dictate its use in a certain way, or the artist may discover the material's malleability allows going in many directions" (Levin, 1986). At least one of the directions that Roloff has chosen has been keeping alive the fires of conceptual and process art in ceramics.

Rothman, Jerry (1933–). Born in Brooklyn, New York, Rothman studied at Los Angeles City College (1953–55) and at the Art Center School, Los Angeles, where he took his B.A. in 1956. From 1956 to 1958

Jerry Rothman

and again in 1960–61, he studied at the Otis Art Institute, Los Angeles, majoring in ceramics and sculpture and earning his M.F.A. In 1957 he exhibited with Paul Soldner and John Mason at the Ferus Gallery, Los Angeles. Rothman's large, constructivist clay assemblages on steel rods show an early avante-garde view of ceramics. He has received many prizes and awards, including the purchase prize for ceramic sculpture in 1962 at the seventeenth National Decorative Arts Competitive Exhibit in Wichita, Kansas; the Louis Comfort Tiffany Award in 1963; and sculpture awards at the Ceramic Nationals in 1964, 1968, and 1969. In 1976 he had a one-man exhibition of large ceramic sculptures at the Oakland Museum, Oakland, California.

Rothman's aesthetic credo is largely based on the belief that there is no such thing as intrinsic beauty in any given material, contending that the intrinsic qualities of a material are simply those that the artist can see and extract. Therefore, much of his technical development has been directed toward ending what he calls "the limitations of clay." He created a shrink-free clay that has allowed him to produce sculptures of up to twenty feet in height. Another innovation was Rothman's combining high-fire metals with his sculptural pieces. This allows him to build long cantilevered armatures with internal metal rods. Ordinarily these extensions would collapse in the kiln, but the inclusion of the metal elements gives them the strength to survive the firings.

In addition to working sculpturally, Rothman has also consistently produced ceramic vessels. Of these, his series *Sky Pots,* commenced late in the 1950s, is among the major achievements in vessel making of the sixties. He returned to the vessel in 1976 with a group of tureens exhibited in Campbell's *Soup Tureen* show, developing a style that Rothman teasingly refers to as "Bauhaus Baroque," a combination of formal composition and sensual, expressionist elements. This exhibition set Rothman off on one of his most fertile periods of experiment; he continued to work with the tureen format until 1982–83. Rothman's tureens relate to the elaborate tureens of the eighteenth century and are, at least by Rothman's standards, "traditional." These monumental, sculptural works have, however, greatly advanced the notion of the tureen as a format, adhering to a practical, utilitarian role, albeit in a more elaborate and ceremonial context. Rothman's seven years of producing these elegantly sensual works must be seen, as his *Sky Pots* were in the sixties, as seminal explorations of the vessel aesthetic.

Since 1983 Rothman has returned to forms and figurative images that are reminiscent of his sculpture between 1963 and 1976. The theme of Leda and the swan dominates these large, articulated vessels. These works are, in a sense, much more "difficult" than his tureen series, merging several elements of style into a single piece and using the dry, sandy textures and colors of his sculptural works. Rothman remains one of the few unrepentant mavericks in American ceramics. He enjoys the role of provocateur, is uneasy with his work when it appears to "fit" within current art concerns, is somewhat disdainful of success, and is constantly taking what seem to the viewer to be oblique and sudden turns from stylish, abstracted objects to mawkish and disturbing, figurative imagery.

Rubin, Mel (1948–   ). Born in Philadelphia, Rubin received his B.F.A. from the Tyler School of Art, Temple University, Philadelphia, and his M.F.A. from the same institution in 1972. Beginning in that year he exhibited in a number of group shows, but his major exposure and recognition came after 1981, the year of his one-person ex-

hibition, *Architectural Attitudes,* at the Jan Baum Gallery in Los Angeles. Rubin creates relief sculpture from painted ceramic and wood, playing alternately with the flattening and deepening of perspectives. There is a

Judith Salomon

touch of the nostalgic in his work that recalls the lonely city streets of Edward Hopper, portrayed with a rare affection for the architectural vernacular.

Salomon, Judith (1952–   ). Born in Providence, Salomon studied at the Penland School of Crafts, Penland, North Carolina (1974–75); the School for American Craftsmen, Rochester, New York, where she received her B.F.A. in 1975; and the New York State College of Ceramics at Alfred University, Alfred, New York, from which she earned her M.F.A. in 1977. Salomon is an associate professor at the Cleveland Institute of Art. She has developed a distinctive expression through hand-built vessels that are geometric assemblages with brightly colored, low-fire glazes on the surface. Her constructivist sensibility is tempered with a refined and elegant eye for proportion and composition.

Saxe, Adrian (1943–   ). Born in Glendale, California, Saxe studied with Ralph Bacerra from 1965 to 1969 at the Chouinard Art Institute in Los Angeles. In 1974 Saxe received his B.F.A. from the California Institute of the Arts (Chouinard's subsequent name), Valencia, California. In 1971–72, while still an undergraduate, he was also an instructor of art at California State University, Long Beach, where he taught special courses in ceramics for seniors and grad-

uate-level ceramics majors. From 1973 to the present he has headed the ceramics department at the University of California, Los Angeles, where he is currently an associate professor of art. Saxe has received numerous awards and research grants, including a Visual Artists Fellowship from the National Endowment for the Arts in 1986 and the United States/France Exchange Fellowship of the United States Information Agency and the Government of France. In addition, in 1983 Saxe was the first artist to be selected by the Mitterand government to work at the Atelier Expérimental de Recherche et de Création at the Manufacture Nationale de Sèvres in Paris.

In his early work Saxe set out to explore sculptural forms but found himself drawn to the vessel and the qualities of porcelain clay. This in turn led to an interest in the eclectic inventiveness of eighteenth-century court porcelains. The emergence of the antelope, which was to become the leitmotif in his work, came through a period of research for a commission of two jardinieres for the Huntington Gallery in San Marino, California. In his research Saxe was drawn to the use of the ram and other hunting animals in eighteenth- and nineteenth-century English silver. During the seventies he began to employ the antelope as a formal and naturalistic climax to large, lidded vessels. The antelope created a contrast to the rest of the form, which was rooted in man's history and culture. Furthermore, the delicacy and evident fragility of the modeled antelope caused a dysfunction in its role as the handle to the lid. As the artist explained,

> By changing its scale and making it very prominent, one is directed to its apparent function as handle. Yet by making it difficult to use as a lifting device, one is denying the way in which the animal has been used in pottery before (conventionalizing the form so that it *could* function as a handle). One begins to think about what a handle is, what it means, and what it means to be denied this function. So one appraises the vessel's function in the manner it was intended; it is concerned with aesthetic ritual—didactic and visual rather than [utilitarian]. (Clark, "Adrian Saxe," 1982)

In his earlier work the content was primarily decorative, but as the work moved into the eighties, a tough, witty sense of inquiry began to appear. The technical tour de force did not lessen with the introduction of a greater intellectual edge. Indeed, Saxe now began to push his craft even further over the edge of sobriety. Delicate, small clouds float on stilts about the surface of his pieces; porcelain and stoneware are fired together; and forms are wrapped in veils of luster.

Some have found the overwhelming craft too distracting. Calling Saxe a "modern-day Fabergé," Ed Forde argued against the technical edge: "Maintaining critical distance while feasting on precious surfaces and perfect detailing, as in the exquisite miniature antelope, is difficult.... The work is too rich, obsessed with technical virtuosity and the fetish of quality" (Forde, 1983). But the critic Jeff Perrone warns the viewer not to mistake Saxe's facility for being facile: "This work is, on one level, spectacular craft...nothing is offhanded: the skillful performance becomes a content, a most difficult subject, and not a mere means to the end of content" (Perrone, 1984).

It is the ability to merge beauty and tension that makes Saxe's work so provocative. Peter Schjeldahl, writing in the catalogue for Saxe's 1987 exhibition at the Art Gallery, University of Missouri, Kansas City, warns that understanding of this quality should not be rushed:

His jarring juxtapositions—abstract pots topped with antelopes or "brass knuckles," rock-like forms and ornate geometries like shotgun weddings of Nature and Culture—are vulnerable to being taken with defensive superficiality, a comfortable sense of *getting the joke.* They *are* jokes (witticisms, to be exact) but their elements are not neutralized by the release of humor. It took me a while to get this about Saxe. I was disconcerted by the crudity of the non sequiturs, funny in a way that made me forget to laugh. Then gradually I learned to focus on the parts individually, letting the troubled whole take care of itself. My reward was, and is, a sense of poised and inexhaustible complexity. It entails a conviction of the utter specificity of each element—what it specifically is, what specific class of thing it signifies—and a visceral sensation of how much each fights for autonomy. A Saxe disjuncture is like a war in which both sides win, which isn't to say it's not violent. Facture and color key each form way, way up, making the balance excruciatingly risky. (Schjeldahl, 1987)

Scheier, Edwin (1910–   ), and **Mary Goldsmith (1910–   )**. Born in New York City, Edwin Scheier studied for two years at the New York School of Industrial Arts. He spent the summer months as a merchant seaman, an occupation that gave him his love for the art of tattooing, a skill in which

he later became adept and which had a strong influence on his work in pottery. After a period of time working for the Federal Art Project, he became the field supervisor of crafts for the southern states. In 1935 he met and married Mary Goldsmith. The couple resigned their jobs as art supervisors and traveled throughout the United States with a puppet show. In Norris, Tennessee, they met Hewitt Wilson, who suggested that they work in clay, a suggestion that they soon took up.

The Scheiers set up their first pottery in Glade Spring, Virginia, after accidentally discovering the superb quality of the local red clay. They achieved early success and exhibited pieces made during the first year in the *Contemporary Industrial Arts Exhibition* at the Metropolitan Museum of Art, New York. In 1938, at the invitation of the League of New Hampshire Arts and Crafts, they assumed teaching positions in ceramics at the University of New Hampshire. Their exhibit of nine pieces later won first prize at the *Western Hemisphere Exhibition* in Syracuse, New York, in 1941. In 1945 the Scheiers were part of Operation Bootstrap, training Puerto Ricans in ceramic techniques. They remained at the University of New Hampshire until 1950, and on their retirement moved to Oaxaca, Mexico, where they continued to operate their pottery until their return to the United States. The couple now live near Phoenix and continue to operate a pottery.

Schreckengost, Viktor (1906–   ). Born in Sebring, Ohio, the son of a potter, Schreckengost studied at the Cleveland School of Art from 1924 to 1929. In 1929–30 he did his postgraduate study at the Kunstgewerbeschule, Vienna, where he studied ceramics and sculpture under Michael Powolny. Returning to Cleveland, he accepted a post on the faculty of the Cleveland School of Art (renamed the Cleveland Art Institute) and at the same time became a designer and assistant to R. Guy Cowan, of the Cowan Pottery Studio. While working at the Cowan Pottery, Schreckengost produced a set of twenty punch bowls commissioned by Eleanor Roosevelt for a party at the governor's mansion in Albany, New York. The bowls were produced in a sgraffito technique, using a bright blue slip. The superb designs were an assemblage of words and images: skyscrapers, cruise ships, and words such as "stop," "go," and "café," interspersed with effervescent bubbles and stars. The commercial version of the pieces that was later produced became

highly popular during the closing period of the Cowan Pottery Studio.

After the Cowan Pottery's closing in 1931, Schreckengost divided his time between producing individual ceramic sculptures and working as a designer for several ceramic firms in the United States. In 1933 he reorganized the production of the American Limoges Ceramics Company (Sebring, Ohio), which had been running at less than thirty percent of its production. Schreckengost's sleek, unadorned sculptural-style dinnerware proved to be extremely popular, and within a year the company had to expand production in order to meet the demand for these wares. This move toward an Art Moderne style was soon followed by that of the other potteries in the United States. Schreckengost later developed similar designs for the Sebring Pottery, Leigh Potters (Alliance, Ohio), and Salem China (Salem, Ohio). Throughout this period Schreckengost was an active exhibitor in the May Shows at the Cleveland Museum of Art and at the Ceramic Nationals.

After World War II Schreckengost directed his interests mainly toward industrial design. He became chairman of the industrial-design department at the Cleveland Art Institute and for a time was the art director and designer of the Murray Ohio Company, Cleveland, manufacturer of children's toys. In addition, he has also retained an active involvement with ceramics. In the early 1950s, he developed a new style of working by carving vessels out of dry chunks of clay. He also worked on numerous architectural commissions, including a major series of terra-cottas for the bird tower and the pachyderm building at the Cleveland Zoo. Schreckengost's contribution to architectural ceramics was acknowledged in 1958, when he received the gold medal of the American Institute of Architects.

Schreckengost has received over fifty awards for his work in sculpture, ceramics, and painting, including nine special awards for outstanding excellence from the Cleveland Museum of Art; first prize for sculpture (1938) at the sixth Ceramic National; the IBM Sculpture Award (1951); first prize for sculpture from the New York Architectural League (1954); the Philadelphia Museum of Art Award of Merit (1938); the Butler Institute of American Art Sculpture Award (1948); the Grumbacher Award (1955); and the Charles Fergus Binns Medal of the American Ceramic Society for Outstanding Contribution to the Ceramic Field (1939).

Schreckengost is a past president of the American Ceramic Society and remains one of the most active and significant figures in the activities of the Art and Design Division of this organization. He recently made a gift of a substantial number of his works from 1930 to 1950 to the Renwick Gallery, National Museum of American Art, Washington D.C.

Shaner, David (1934–). Born in Pottstown, Pennsylvania, Shaner took his M.F.A. in ceramic design at Alfred University, Alfred, New York, in 1959. From 1959 to 1963 he was assistant professor of art, University of Illinois, Champaign-Urbana; and from 1963 to 1970 he was the resident potter and director of the Archie Bray Foundation, Helena, Montana. Since 1970 he has run his pottery near Big Fork, Montana, on a full-time basis, producing mainly functional wares. Shaner's work, distinguished by its sturdy reductivist forms, has been exhibited widely in over 150 regional, national, and international juried and invitational exhibitions since 1960. Shaner has received several awards, including the Louis Comfort Tiffany Scholarship in 1963 and the National Endowment for the Arts Craftsman Fellowship in 1973 and 1978.

Shaw, Richard (1941–). Born in Hollywood, California, Shaw studied at the Orange Coast College, Costa Mesa, California, from 1961 to 1963 and received his B.F.A. from the San Francisco Art Institute in 1965. In 1965 he studied at the New York State College of Ceramics at Alfred University, Alfred, New York, and earned his M.F.A. from the University of California, Davis, in 1968. He had his first one-person exhibition in 1967, at the San Francisco Art Institute, and has since had twenty-eight one-person exhibitions and has participated in over ninety group exhibitions. In 1970 he received a fellowship from the National Endowment for the Arts and in 1973 received a project grant to study the four-color silkscreening of ceramic decals.

Shaw has been the most influential figure in the development of a Super-Object school in the Bay Area; his influence on the younger generation of ceramic artists also extends throughout the country. Shaw's works are a continuation of the concerns that first appeared among the Surrealist object-makers during the 1930s. However, his work avoids the unease of objects such as the *Fur-Lined Cup* (1936) by Meret Oppenheim and *Lobster Telephone* (1936) by Salvador Dalí. Instead, his style follows the lead indicated by the gentle, sensual, and poetic assem-

blages of Miró that deal with scatological combinations of elements, from stuffed birds to wooden legs. In addition, in works such as his early series of ceramic couches from 1966–67, there is a strong reflection of the graphic, illustrative style of René Magritte.

In his later works, however, Shaw has begun to deal less with the illustrative concerns of Surrealism. This was particularly apparent at his exhibition with Robert Hudson at the San Francisco Museum of Modern Art in 1973, where birds, deer hooves, decoy ducks, twigs, and branches were assembled into what we identify as functional objects—teapots, teacups, and bowls. In these works, Shaw appeared to be more concerned with the technical seduction of trompe l'oeil surfaces than with content.

While these objects deal with metamorphosis, they do so without employing the shock tactic of the Dada object-makers. Nonetheless, several reviewers have linked Shaw's work to this early object-making expression. A particular example is the review of the exhibition by Mary Fuller McChesney (1973), who attempted to apply the words of the early Dadaist Tristan Tzara to the works of Shaw. In so doing, McChesney misunderstood both the essence of Dada and that of Shaw's works. Whereas Dada was concerned with the conceptual and contextual relevance of the object, Shaw's investigation has been primarily iconographic and unashamedly decorative.

Shaw's works deal with a long tradition in ceramics of trompe l'oeil that dates back to pre-dynastic Egypt and proceeds through late Ming Yixing wares and the tin-glazed eighteenth-century pottery of Niderviller and others. Similarly, the nineteenth-century American realist painters John F. Peto, John Haberle, and William Harnett have been an important and direct source of information. Some of the finest of Shaw's works have been his platters, which are less technocratic than his larger works and allow for subtle and ambiguous relationships between material and image—real and illusionary. About 1981 he began to experiment with figurative forms, and a new dimension was added to his work. The work now seems more sculptural, less decorative. The figures are created, much as in earlier works, from throwaways of a consumer culture. "Dilapidated objects which seem gleaned from trash heaps are resurrected as awkwardly parading anthropomorphic images. This art exalts the most mundane of objects…and as Richard Shaw demonstrates, is a 'way to make pottery' " (Pugliese, 1985).

Sheerer, Mary Given (1865–1954). Born in Covington, Kentucky, Sheerer spent her youth in New Orleans. She won a scholarship to study at the Cincinnati Art Institute under Frank Duveneck and attended his classes in still life. In 1894 she joined the Sophie Newcomb Memorial College School of Art in New Orleans, where she eventually became professor of ceramics and drawing, a position that she retained until 1931. A pottery established at the college was run along professional lines, and the work of students was sold when it reached a sufficient quality. Sheerer was responsible for the selection of all objects for sale and so was largely responsible for the aesthetic direction and initial success of the pottery, which reached its peak in 1915, when it received the grand prize at the Panama-Pacific International Exposition. Writing of the pottery's dual role, Sheerer commented:

> The fact of its being under the support of a college would make it possible to aim for only the truest and the best, and so it would not be forced to consider too closely the tastes of the public, but to follow honestly and sincerely its own principles. To this end it was decided that the decorator should be given full rein to this fancy…it was also decreed that no two pieces should be alike and that each should be fresh—inspired by the form demands of that particular vase or cup. The whole thing was to be a Southern product, made of Southern clays, by Southern artists, decorated with Southern subjects. There were possibilities in it. And so with these hopes and fears the Newcomb Pottery was given birth. (Sheerer, 1899)

Although the interest in the art-pottery movement diminished rapidly after World War I, the work of the Newcomb Pottery remained popular. Its works were not seen in terms of a mainstream aesthetic but rather as a nostalgic holdover. Sadie Irvine remarked that critics frequently used the term *Victorian* in describing its wares. In 1910 Paul Ernest Cox took responsibility for the technical operation of the pottery. In her excellent study of the Newcomb Pottery, Jessie Poesch comments that Newcomb was anything but the feminist nirvana that some writers have portrayed: "Women were fit to be designers but men would remain in charge of the technical and physical side of production" (Poesch, 1984). As Sheerer learned more and more about the technical aspects of her medium, Cox and Newcomb's potter, Joseph Meyer, resented her growing knowledge and took pleasure in thwarting her progress.

Sheerer gave up her interest in china painting and turned to an active, broader role in the ceramic arts. From 1924 to 1927 she was chairman of the Art Division of the American Ceramic Society and was made a fellow in 1931. In 1925 she was honored by being elected a delegate on the Hoover Commission to the Exposition Internationale des Arts Décoratifs et Industriels Modernes in Paris. Sheerer retired from her post at the Newcomb College School of Art in June 1931 and settled in Cincinnati.

Shirayamadani, Kataro (1865–1948). Born in Kanazawa, Japan, Shirayamadani came to the United States as part of a traveling Japanese village. In May 1887 he was invited to join the decorating staff of the Rookwood Pottery. While continuing to work at the pottery, he studied at the Cincinnati Art Academy and soon became one of the finest artists on the staff of Rookwood. Except for ten years in Japan, from 1915 to 1925, he remained at Rookwood until his death. Shirayamadani is credited with developing the electrodeposit method of surfacing ceramics with metal, and with designing many of the standard shapes used at Rookwood.

Shire, Peter (1947–). Born in Los Angeles, Shire attended the Chouinard Art Institute in Los Angeles, receiving his B.F.A. in 1970. Shire is very much a part of the Los Angeles art scene and has participated in a wide range of the city's cultural events, from designing sets for the Hollywood Bowl to working on the design team for the 23rd Olympiad. He was also an early member of the Milan-based Memphis design group. Shire first attracted attention for his colorful ceramics and held a series of highly successful exhibitions with the Janus Gallery in Los Angeles. The works are strongly influenced by constructivist notions of form and color, although more directed toward a playful and decorative interpretation than observing the minimal purity of his inspiration. In 1985 Shire ceased working in ceramics as his primary medium and now focuses on furniture and large, metal sculptural fabrications.

Sicard, Jacques (1865–1923). Born in France, Sicard came to the United States in 1901 after a long association with the pottery of Clement Massier of Golfe Juan in France. The pottery, established in 1881 in a small town close to Cannes, originally produced lusterwares—the result of Massier's inspiration from the Hispano-Moresque pots that

he had seen in Italian collections. Massier eventually produced an iridescent glaze for which his pottery became renowned. In the United States Sicard worked for Samuel A. Weller, one of the most commercially successful of the American art potteries. Together with his assistant Henri Gellie, Sicard produced individual works that were known as Sicardo wares or Sicardo-Weller. He worked on fluid, simple forms, decorating them with floral and other motifs, achieving an exciting tonal range from purple, red, and rich pink to peacock blue. Sicard returned to France in 1907, but Weller continued to offer the Sicardo wares for sale until after 1912. There is a sizable collection of Sicard's work at the Zanesville [Ohio] Art Center Museum. The Cooper-Hewitt Museum in New York also has a group of major works by Sicard.

Silver, Anna (1935–). Born in Flint, Michigan, Silver studied at the Léger Atelier in Paris in 1950, and upon her return to Los Angeles, with the painter John Altoon at his La Cienega Boulevard studio. She also took classes at the University of California, Los Angeles, and at the Otis Art Institute. She currently maintains a studio in Los Angeles.

Silver has been exhibiting her ceramics since 1977. Her work has a bias toward surface. Forms are simple and stylized from classical sources. The underglaze and overglaze painting on the pots is extremely sophisticated and fully exploits the vitality of her brightly colored palette: "The palette is appropriately unserious although not frivolous: swipes of turquoise through a deep celadon or lustered gray and lavender, and the forms themselves [are] well proportioned with a grace of Silver's own devising, conventional and yet speaking of tradition" (Chambers, 1985).

Singer, Susi (1895–1949). Born in Austria, Singer studied at the Kunstgewerbeschule, Vienna, under Professor Michael Powolny. She produced ceramics for the Wiener Werkstätte and also produced independent pieces in her own studio, which she established in 1925 at Grünbach. Singer rapidly established herself as one of the leading European ceramic artists, exhibiting at the 1925 Exposition Internationale in Paris and winning several awards at later world's fairs, including a first prize in London (1934), a second prize in Brussels (1935), and a first prize at the Arts et Techniques Exposition in Paris (1937). In the late 1930s, she moved to the United States, making her home in Pasadena, California. A Scripps College

research grant from the Fine Arts Foundation in 1946 permitted Singer to expand her experiments with American slips and glazes. A collection of over thirty ceramic figures created under this grant is in the permanent collection of the Scripps College Museum, Claremont, California.

Soldner, Paul (1921–). Born in Summerfield, Illinois, Soldner studied at Bluffton College, Ohio, where he received his B.A. While taking his master's degree at the University of Colorado, Boulder, he became interested in pottery through Katie Horseman, a visiting lecturer and head of ceramics at the Edinburgh College of Art in Scotland. In 1954 Soldner decided to become a potter and enrolled at the Los Angeles County Art Institute (later renamed the Otis Art Institute), becoming Peter Voulkos's first student in the newly established ceramics department. At Otis Soldner produced exploratory works such as his monumental floor pots, which were later to inspire Voulkos's now distinctive *Stack* pot series.

In 1960, in response to a request to provide a pottery demonstration for students at a crafts fair, Soldner decided to experiment with the raku firing technique. Using Bernard Leach's *A Potter's Book* as a guide, he set up a simple kiln and improvised a few lead-based glazes. The results were disappointing; the clay body did not respond well to the quick, harsh raku glaze firing and the glazes were shiny, brightly colored, and too vulgar for Soldner's taste. Soldner persevered after his initially disappointing results. He first produced tea bowls but soon rejected this form as being without context in a Western culture, and concentrated on vase forms. Soldner adopted the

Paul Soldner

raku technique as his major medium of expression and through his frequent workshops across the country was responsible for establishing raku as one of the major areas of art expression in American ceramics. American raku derives from a sixteenth-century tradition in Japan of creating tea bowls for the Zen tea ceremonies.

Soldner was an influential teacher both as the head of ceramics at Scripps College in Claremont, California, and through his numerous visiting lectureships and workshops around the country. He acknowledges that raku has grown away from the Oriental tradition and has become a strongly American art form. He believes that if the technique is to become more than an amusing parlor trick, the same demands for depth and sensitivity that are required of the Oriental raku artist are essential for their Western counterparts:

> In the spirit of raku, there is the necessity to embrace the element of surprise. There can be no fear of losing what was once planned and there must be an urge to grow along with the discovery of the unknown. In the spirit of raku: make no demands, expect nothing, follow no absolute plan, be secure in change, learn to accept another solution and, finally, prefer to gamble on your own intuition. Raku offers us deep understanding of those qualities in pottery which are of a more spiritual nature, of pots by men willing to create objects that have meaning as well as function. (Soldner, 1973)

Sperry, Robert (1927–). Born in Bushnell, Illinois, Sperry received his B.A. from the University of Saskatchewan in 1950, his B.F.A. from the Art Institute of Chicago in 1953, and his M.F.A. from the University of Washington, Seattle, in 1955. Although Sperry had first studied as a painter, his interests drew him toward pottery, where (in common with several of his contemporaries at the time) he combined an interest in Abstract Expressionist painting with that of Japanese pottery. In 1963 he visited Japan and produced a film, *The Village Potters of Onda*. Sperry soon became an important influence in the Pacific Northwest, teaching at the University of Washington, Seattle. His importance has been eclipsed until recently by the more theatrical sculptural work being done in the area.

The breakthrough came in 1979, when Sperry, inspired by a small Alberto Burri exhibition that he saw in Rome, began to move away from his decorative vessels, with their polychromatic luster painting, and turned to the sober (but by no means limiting) use of white slip on a black ground.

Working on industrially made mullite kiln shelves, Sperry was now liberated in terms of scale. *Untitled #625* (1985) comprises 176 tiles and is thirty feet long. Sperry has worked on several public art projects. *Untitled #625* was installed in the King County Building in Seattle, and other murals have been produced for IBM in Atlanta and the Chubb Insurance Headquarters in New Jersey. Sperry's tiles and plates reflect his continuing interest in Abstract Expressionism, as well as in the processes and qualities of his medium. In addition, his works seem indebted to the "white writing" in Mark Tobey's calligraphic paintings. Lastly, there is a lingering sense of Robert Motherwell's stark black-and-white compositions.

But these influences have not resulted in a dated or imitative aesthetic. Sperry's new works are among the most innovative and convincing in ceramics today. He is one of the few ceramists in the eighties to bring a regenerative energy to the use of an abstract vocabulary in the medium, outpacing earlier leaders in the field such as John Mason.

The dry, white, cracked surfaces occasionally resemble dried-up salt pans but these are static works. Sperry is at his best when evoking movement and energy, either creating furious spirals in his platters or the stark spurts and eruptions of his larger murals. As Matthew Kangas wrote in a catalogue essay for an exhibition held in 1981 at the Williams/Johnson Gallery, Seattle, "By enlarging the size of his work once again and expanding the breadth of his gesture, [Sperry] may be proving that, more than anything else, modern American painting of the 1950's was a reflection—not a creation—of an anxious and dynamic sensibility still present in American society" (Kangas, 1981). Sperry's work has continued to grow impressively, and he may yet emerge as the least regional and most profound ceramic talent from the Pacific Northwest.

Staffel, Rudolph ("Rudi") (1911–). Born in San Antonio, Staffel studied under various artists, including Hans Hofmann in New York and the Spanish painter José Arpa. In 1931 Staffel studied at the Art Institute of Chicago under Louis Ripman and Laura Van Papelladam. Six years later Staffel was invited to teach ceramics at the Arts and Crafts Club of New Orleans. In addition to teaching there, he also worked on a part-time basis with Paul Cox, who established a sophisticated production pottery in New Orleans for the manufacture of strawberry-canning pots for the Louisiana

Rudolph Staffel

jam industry. Staffel was to learn a great deal from Cox about the traditions and history of ceramic art. In 1940 Staffel joined the Tyler School of Art, Temple University, Philadelphia, where he taught until his retirement in 1978.

The breakthrough in Staffel's art came in the 1950s, when he was invited to produce a set of dinnerware in porcelain. Up until that point he had felt that porcelain was alien to the craft tradition. He experimented with slip decorating and, fascinated by the translucency of the material, began to work toward a combination of form and material that would actually transmit light. Staffel worked with highly volatile, porcelaneous clay bodies and enjoyed the considerable risk element inherent in the medium. This is apparent from his comment: "The best body that I have ever worked with is the body that I know nothing about or very little about" (Winokur and Winokur, 1977). Staffel relates his work to the push-pull of the Hofmann mode of expression, emphasizing that one is not aware of the push until one sees the pull. Working on this basis, he builds and throws his vessels—known as "light gatherers"—in order to create different intensities of opacity in his forms. He is fond of incising the porcelain to reveal the light through the thin layer of clay. In other vessels he builds his forms out of a number of small clay slabs of different thinnesses and colors. The 1970s saw the most fertile growth of this unique expression in the medium, establishing Staffel as one of the most original vessel makers in American ceramics.

Staley, Christopher P. (1954–). Staley received his B.F.A. in 1977 from Wittenberg University, in Springfield, Ohio. He was taken on as a special student at the Kansas City Art Institute in 1977–78, and in 1980 received his M.F.A. from the New York State College of Ceramics at Alfred University, Alfred, New York. In 1986 he was the recipient of a Visual Artists Fellowship from the National Endowment for the Arts. He currently teaches at the University of Kansas, Wichita. Writing of his work, the *Los Angeles Times* critic Suzanne Muchnic comments, "Chris Staley is marvelously adept at transforming traditional ceramic forms into organic abstractions. Fluid sweeps of clay and soft-colored glazes turn a teapot, large plates and covered jars into lyrical landscapes that use clay's plasticity gracefully" (Muchnic, 1985).

Susanne G. Stephenson

Stephenson, Susanne G. (1935–). Born in Canton, Ohio, Stephenson studied at Carnegie-Mellon University, Pittsburgh, and graduated in 1959 with an M.F.A. from the Cranbrook Academy of Art, Bloomfield Hills, Michigan. Stephenson's work involves an ongoing investigation of the vessel form. Her studies took her to Japan in 1962–63, where she explored ash glazes in wood-fired kilns. More recently, in 1973, she studied luster glazes in Spain. She taught at the University of Michigan in 1960–61 and has been professor of art at Eastern Michigan University, Ypsilanti, since 1963. She has exhibited extensively since 1963 and has held several one-person exhibitions. In 1985 she received the prestigious Michigan Foundation of the Arts Award. Stephenson maintains a studio in Ann Arbor, Michigan.

Despite her studies in Japan and Spain, of historical ceramics, Stephenson's work has increasingly dealt with nature and has revealed very little of the cultural history of the vessel or a history of art (although Abstract Expressionist painting is the root of her style). Writing of her work, Kristin McKenna, art critic for the *Los Angeles Times,* commented, "Stephenson's exuberantly crude vessels have a yeasty, organic stink.... [She] not only allows the raw earthiness intrinsic to clay to remain to the fore, she enhances it by slathering her roughly formed vessels with explosive passages of color. It's an approach to clay that Ken Russell would no doubt approve of: tactile, sensual and just a tad bombastic" (McKenna, 1987).

Takaezu, Toshiko (1929–). Born in Pepeekeo, Hawaii, Takaezu studied at the Honolulu School of Art and under Maija Grotell at the Cranbrook Academy of Art, Bloomfield Hills, Michigan. Takaezu acknowledges a strong debt to Grotell's influence as a perceptive critic and teacher: "Maija didn't say very much, and what she didn't say was as important as what she did say, once you realized that she was thoroughly aware of everything that you did." Takaezu has taught at the Cranbrook Academy; University of Michigan, Ann Arbor; Haystack Mountain School of Crafts, Liberty, Maine; Penland School of Crafts in North Carolina; and on a part-time basis in the Creative Arts Program at Princeton University. In 1968 she decided to give up full-time teaching in order to concentrate on her studio work, establishing a home and studio in Quakertown, New Jersey.

Takaezu's inspiration comes from a blending of East and West: "'Delicately asymmetrical forms reminiscent of a Zen tradition are balanced and vitalized by the application of abstract and lyrical 'color clouds' that recall the floor and sky of Hawaii. For Toshiko the creative process is not a hurried affair: the works remain 'non-finito'—continually presenting new possibilities to be explored until finally placed in the kiln" (Nordness, 1970). Takaezu has been involved for several years in the exploration of sound and ceramics, placing pebbles of clay in her closed-form pots and in the bases of chalices before firing. When the pot is moved, the pebbles emit sounds ranging from the most subtle rustling to clear, bell-like tones. Although her use of color, in both her plaques and her serene bulbous forms, is strongly inspired by Abstract Expressionist painting, her work frequently suggests an ongoing play with landscape.

The strongest distinguishing characteristic in Takaezu's work is the privacy of her forms. Except for the earlier plates, they all deal with closure. Sometimes the vestigial mouths of her pots, which are usually barely discernible, disappear altogether. In a planned multimedia installation, Takaezu even considered a setting where the lighting diminished as one approached a pot and then increased as one retreated: "That is how I feel about human relationships, not that they close up exactly, although I have thought of making a pot with a suspended lid which closed as you come near it" (Hurley, 1979).

In 1983 Takaezu created the *Ceramic Forest* for an award exhibition at the Trout Gallery of Dickinson College, Carlisle, Pennsylvania. This comprised a group of thirteen pieces, each about sixty-six inches in height. Ann Tsubota in her review of the exhibition wrote of the installation, "Each cylinder has its own unique form and glaze treatment. The pieces create a violent age of strong shapes thrust into the earth. Half buried unexploded bombs come to mind. Or perhaps a postnuclear war landscape. The imagery is provocative, uneasy, awkward. One applauds the risks in this body of work" (Tsubota, 1984).

Takamori, Akio (1950–). Born in Nobeoka, Miyazaki, Japan, Takamori studied at the Musashino Art College in Tokyo from 1969 to 1971. From 1972 to 1974 he apprenticed with Oita, a master folk potter working on traditional utilitarian pottery, Koishawara ware, in Fukuoka. Takamori later studied with Ken Ferguson at the Kansas City Art Institute, receiving his B.F.A. in 1976 and his M.F.A. from the New York State College of Ceramics, Alfred University, Alfred, New York, in 1978. His work was included in the 1977 *Young Americans: Clay* exhibition at the Museum of Contemporary Crafts in New York and has since been exhibited extensively in the United States as well as in Japan. Takamori maintains a studio in Helena, Montana.

Takamori worked sculpturally during his time at Kansas City and Alfred but after leaving school returned to the vessel form and began to work innovatively with its structure. His sources are bicultural and complex. Takamori remembers being fascinated as a child by a book on Western art that he found in his father's library. An illustration of Pieter Brueghel's painting *The Fall of Icarus* awoke in him a fascination with the surrealism of mythology. Takamori was also equally interested in Japanese art, particularly in the traditional woodblock prints. The work of a contemporary print-maker, Shiko Munakato, crystallized his sense of forming a vessel out of the inter-twined figures of a man and a woman. In particular, Takamori recalls that one crucial print of an old man making love to his young wife inspired him to make his sexual, envelope-shaped vessels.

Takamori was attracted to the envelope format because of its graphic possibilities, its ability to liberate the rim as an element of drawing, and, lastly, because it gave the "space" between his foreground and back-ground figures distinctly emotional, erotic, and psychological overtones. A precedent for Takamori's style of work exists in erotic, pre-Columbian pottery and in China in the *mukozuke* dishes—the Kosometsuke export wares made in late Ming China for the Japanese tea ceremony market. The *muko-zuke* dishes were created in the silhouette shapes of horses, birds, squirrels, and fish, with graphic, fresh drawing in cobalt blue. But nowhere in the history of pottery has the idea been taken so far, both in terms of the eccentricity of the rim and in the complexity of content.

The volumes of his pot are generally narrow, oval enclosures, but Takamori de-velops a sense of depth on his surfaces by using foreshortening and other perspectival techniques. What keeps coming through is the content—mainly Takamori's mixture of fascination and ambivalence with the sexual. Writing in *American Ceramics,* Andy Nasisse explains the complexity of the vessels:

> The container forms have an explorative searching quality in the way the inside space is enclosed by dynamic human and animal figures caught in the act of embracing, bonding, seducing, nursing, exposing, violating, fighting and loving each other. Often there is a gallery of small heads (our social conscience) which appear to look on...at forbidden acts implied by clever juxtapositions of private parts and personal pleasure. Through Takamori's erotic vocabulary of oppo-sitions, transformations from one thing to another occur; a horse becomes a vo-luptuous female, Christ becomes a cross, the mother becomes a child, a fish has the breasts of a woman, the woman changes into a man. (Nasisse, 1986)

Even though his figures freely sport their genitals, their gender is nonetheless left somewhat ambiguous. By leaving hair off the heads of his figures Takamori gives the faces the soft, androgynous appearance of the Persian miniature. He is able to deal with sexuality so effectively because he

treats it matter-of-factly. There is no intention to shock or dismay. Takamori talks of sexual issues with an ingenuous openness, re-vealing it as the ordinary, baffling, and es-sential force that it is—totally oblivious to the taboos that still surround this issue in our culture. This attitude came, in part, from Takamori's early years in Nobeoka, where his father, a skin specialist, ran a clinic for venereal disease in the city's red-light district. For some, this experience could have been warping, but for Takamori it produced a kind of leveling, a nonjudg-mental acceptance of sexuality without, at the same time, clarifying its mysteries and conflicts.

In a review of an exhibition of Takamori's work at the Garth Clark Gallery in New York in June 1986, Helen Giambruni un-derscored the psychological content in Tak-amori's art: "If on the one hand Takamori celebrates the power of female sexuality, he also keeps a certain psychological distance from his subjects, and there is an under-current of black humor in his work. He is keenly aware of the wayward impulses, the duplicity and blind destructiveness that ac-company the erotic drive. Takamori's work grows steadily more powerful and psycho-logically complex. It seems to me he is only beginning to hit his stride" (Giambruni, 1986).

Henry Takemoto

Takemoto, Henry (1930–). Born in Ho-nolulu, Takemoto studied at the University of Hawaii, where he received his B.A. in 1957, and graduated with an M.F.A. from the Otis Art Institute, Los Angeles, in 1959. Takemoto has taught at the San Francisco Art Institute; Montana State University, Missoula; Scripps College, Claremont, California; and the Claremont College

Graduate School. His work during the 1950s, with its dynamic use of organic form and calligraphic and lively decoration, was among the finest work of the so-called Ab-stract Expressionist school that revolved around Peter Voulkos at the Otis Art Insti-tute. Takemoto proved to be a considerable influence at the time and an inspiration for many artists, including Ron Nagle. In the early 1960s, Takemoto abruptly turned from art to design, working thereafter as a de-signer for Interpace Corporation and the Wedgwood Pottery. In 1983 he returned to ceramics education and taught first at the Otis Art Institute and then at California State University, Los Angeles. Despite the brevity of his involvement, Takemoto's ce-ramics—from his immense pots on metal stands to his large wall murals—are among the most important work from the Otis group.

Tepper, Irvin (1947–). Born in Saint Louis, Tepper studied at the Kansas City Art In-stitute, where he received his B.F.A. in 1969, and at the University of Washington, Seattle, receiving his M.F.A. in 1971. The artist cur-rently maintains a studio in New York City. In Seattle Tepper's interest in ceramics be-came less and less traditional, turning eventually towards photography as the me-dium for his conceptually based art. In 1971 he became part of the San Francisco con-ceptual-art movement, working in video, performance, and photography. His return to ceramics was prompted by his drawing *Idea Drawing for a Flawed Cup* (1975). The cup (purloined from the University of Washington during Tepper's graduate-stu-dent days) had always fascinated him. "It was the standard Syracuse china coffee cup. However, it had a crooked handle. I was excited about this cup because it had an imperfection. It was a machine-made product and it was not perfect" (Schimmel, 1984). It took nearly two years after the drawing before the first molded cup emerged. The cups were paper-thin, cracked, translucent, and seemingly ancient. Tepper made photographs of some of the best cups, most of which were named spe-cifically for the collector who was to receive them. In addition, the cups became the subject matter for some handsome prints, in which, as with his drawings, he explores narrative through diaristic notations. Tep-per's work is of considerable interest because he approaches ceramics with an objectivity and conceptual distance that are rare in this field. The cup format continues in his work and has taken on a radically increased scale, but it is no longer his central focus.

Tiffany, Louis Comfort (1848–1933). Born in New York City, Tiffany was the son of the founder of the jewelers Tiffany and Company. The younger Tiffany studied painting with George Inness in 1866 and exhibited at the Philadelphia Centennial Exposition in 1876. In that year he began to work in glass, producing his first ornamental stained-glass window. In 1879 Louis C. Tiffany & Company, Associated Artists, was founded in New York along the lines of Morris & Company in London. The collaboration of artists was short-lived, however, and by the mid-1880s Tiffany was working on his own with a team of craftsmen. By 1894 he had patented his famous Favrile glass and had established himself as the major figure of the American Arts and Crafts Movement. The commercial phase of Tiffany's operation began in 1902, with the formation of Tiffany Studios. Tiffany Studios continued through the crash of 1929 and finally went into receivership in 1932.

Tiffany's involvement with ceramics appears to have begun about 1898 (Eidelberg, 1968). In that year, he began experimenting at his factory in Corona, Long Island, proceeding with great secrecy until 1902, when rumors of Tiffany's new interest began to circulate in New York. The wares he developed were first shown publicly in 1904, at the Louisiana Purchase International Exposition in Saint Louis, where three Favrile vases with the "old ivory" glazes were shown as part of the Tiffany Studios display. In 1905 these went on display at an exhibition of the New York Keramik Society, but it was only in the latter part of that year that the pottery was made available for sale at the new building of Tiffany and Company at Fifth Avenue and Fifty-seventh Street.

In addition to producing wares, Tiffany also advanced interest in the ceramic arts by exhibiting the works of leading American ceramists, such as Adelaide Alsop Robineau. In 1901 he held a major exhibition of French artist-potters that included Auguste Delaherche, Pierre-Adrienne Dalpayrat, Taxile Doat, and Alexander Bigot. By 1914 it was apparent that Tiffany's interest in ceramics, never a successful venture commercially, was beginning to wane. The production of the wares continued, however, until 1919. Tiffany's pottery was little appreciated in his day—never receiving the recognition of his sumptuous work in glass. Yet, in restrospect, the Favrile pottery now emerges as being one of the finest achievements of American art pottery.

Turner, Robert (1913–). Born in Port Washington, New York, Turner received his B.A. from Swarthmore College, Swarthmore, Pennsylvania, in 1936. Thereafter, he studied painting for five years at the Pennsylvania Academy of the Fine Arts, Philadelphia, and the Barnes Foundation, Merion, Pennsylvania. Turner spent several years in Europe, painting and studying at public museums on a scholarship from the Pennsylvania Academy. Unsatisfied with the medium of painting, he turned to pottery. In 1946 he entered the New York State College of Ceramics at Alfred University, Alfred, New York, and worked there until 1949.

After leaving Alfred, Turner was invited to establish a pottery studio at Black Mountain College in North Carolina. He remained there until 1951; in the following year he moved to Alfred Station, New York, where he set up a pottery studio. From then until his retirement from teaching, Turner divided his time between his work and his teaching commitments at Alfred University. He now lives in Alfred and in Santa Fe, New Mexico, although he still makes most of his pottery in his studio at Alfred.

Except for a short period during his student years, Turner has worked only in stoneware. He admits an early debt to Sam Haile, Alex Giampietro, and others who worked at Alfred during the 1940s, when the problems of working in stoneware—finding suitable stoneware bodies and glazes and, above all, learning the disciplines of reduction firing—were still being explored. Turner's early works were never imitative, however, and from the outset he exhibited a clarity of style and identity in his work. Through the years, he has dealt with a very limited vocabulary of forms, constantly sophisticating and synthesizing these vessel formats.

In speaking of his work, Turner states that he has not consciously tried to keep his pottery simple:

It seems to come out that way when I succeed in making the most complete statement that I am capable of. Since almost all of my pots leave the shop soon after they are made, I do not feel bound by what I have done previously, and in each style of work I find myself searching for new solutions to new problems. In most of my works I have tried to keep within the limitation of what the material will do quite naturally—to be true to its reality. (Rhodes, 1957)

Following a visit to Africa in 1971–72, Turner was strongly influenced by the example of traditional Nigerian pottery. Works such as *Niger I* (1974) pay homage to the forms, decoration, and ceremonial vigor of the African potter's art. At this time Voulkos also influenced Turner, enabling him to deal with form in a more expressive manner. There was not, however, a sudden change in either the style or content of Turner's vessels. Furthermore, Turner still drew, as he did in his earliest works, from nature—especially the desert and the seashore. Turner likens his drawings on the vessel surfaces to the tidal traces left on the beach—drawing on the clay only what the clay accepts.

Perhaps the most distinctive quality in Turner's refined stoneware is the sense of what could be termed "inner volume." In common with the finest thrown forms of the past, the swelling sense of the pot seems to grow from the volume contained within it rather than from a hard and conscious forming of the vessel from without. Turner is the doyen of the traditionalists; his forms are an acknowledgment of an art of limitations, seeking an essence through repetition and interpretation of an existing form vocabulary that one can parallel to that of a sensitive classical musician, providing a reminder of the purest notes of the pottery aesthetic.

In 1985 the Milwaukee Art Museum organized *Robert Turner: A Potter's Retrospective*, an exhibition that traveled through 1987. The exhibition presented Turner as something of a revolutionary, whose work radically altered in the late 1960s. It underscored this point by including only one piece from his busy years in the fifties as a functional potter.

Turner is presented as a potter without a past, particularly a utilitarian past," complained Ed Lebow (Lebow, 1986). In stressing the work of the seventies and eighties, the exhibition missed the gentle, probing, inquiring continuity that links all of his pots, whether utilitarian or contemplative. He has a distinctive style that has constantly grown but never changed—minimalist, refined, and imbued with a spiritual gravity that is rare in the decorative arts.

Valentien, Albert R. (1862–1925). Born in Cincinnati, Valentine (later changed to Valentien) studied at the Cincinnati Art Academy under T. S. Noble and Frank Duveneck. He later taught underglaze pottery decoration at Thomas J. Wheatley's pottery at 23 Hunt Street. In 1881 he joined the Rookwood Pottery as its first full-time decorator, became head of the decorating department, and remained there until 1903. In 1907 Valentien and his wife, Anna Marie Bookprinter, moved to San Diego, California. There they established the Valentien Pottery. The move was prompted by a commission from Ellen Scripps to do nature studies of all the California wildflowers. The commission influenced the choice of decorative motifs at the Valentien Pottery. These motifs were produced both as painted decoration by Albert and in relief-modeled forms by Anna Valentien.

Valentien, Anna Marie Bookprinter (1862–1947). Born in Cincinnati, Anna Marie Bookprinter (anglicized from Buchdrücker) studied at the Cincinnati Art Academy from 1884 to 1898. She joined Rookwood in 1884 and remained there until 1905. In 1887 she married Rookwood's first decorator, Albert R. Valentien. Together they traveled to France, where Anna studied under Auguste Rodin, Jean-Antoine Injalbert, and Antoine Bourdelle. On her return to Cincinnati, she attempted to interest Rookwood in a sculptural style, but only a few pieces of the kind were produced. In 1907 she moved to San Diego, where she and her husband set up the Valentien Pottery.

Van Briggle, Artus (1869–1904). Born in Felicity, Ohio, Van Briggle was encouraged to be an artist by his ambitious parents, who enjoyed the family's claim to descent from the sixteenth-century Netherlandish painter Pieter Brueghel. Van Briggle studied at the Cincinnati Art Academy with Frank Duveneck from 1886. To pay for his studies, he began in the same year to work on a part-time basis at Karl Langenbeck's Avon Pottery in Cincinnati. He became a decorator at the Rookwood Pottery in 1887 (Hecht, 1987). From 1893 to 1896, supported by a scholarship of $605.10 from Rookwood, he studied painting with Jean Paul Laurens and Benjamin Constant at the Académie Julian in Paris, and clay modeling at the Beaux-Arts academy. Upon his return to the Rookwood Pottery in 1896, Van Briggle began to experiment with mat glazes and achieved his first success in 1898, making a prototype for what was later to become his *Lorelei* vase, one of his finest and most famous works.

His interest in Art Nouveau and in a greater sense of movement in decoration and form was apparent during this period and had an impact on those with whom he worked. His interest in *style moderne* can be seen in the vase he created for the 1900

Exposition Universelle, where he carved and painted a full frontal view of a dancing woman with swirling veils that wrap around the pot in a slightly frozen application of the curvilinear movement of Art Nouveau.

In 1899, before this vase was exhibited in Paris, Van Briggle resigned from Rookwood because of his worsening tuberculosis. In search of a better climate, he moved to Colorado Springs, Colorado. While living with the family of Asaheal Sutton, he began to conduct experiments, using the local clays and raw materials. He fired these at Colorado College with the assistance of Professor William H. Strieby. In 1901 he opened the Van Briggle Pottery Company at 650 North Nevada Avenue, Colorado Springs, and in December of that year the first exhibition of three hundred pieces took place. The company was formally incorporated a year later and achieved early success. His twenty-four-piece entry to the Paris Salon of 1903 was accepted in its entirety and was awarded two gold, one silver, and twelve bronze medals. In 1904 Van Briggle was at the Louisiana Purchase International Exposition in Saint Louis and won two gold, one silver, and two bronze medals. Only a ruling preventing the awarding of the *Grand Prix* to first-time exhibitors prevented him from receiving this honor as well. Van Briggle died while the exposition in Saint Louis was in progress, and his exhibition cases were draped in mourning black.

Van Briggle's work during the short period from 1901 to 1904 represents the finest achievement of American Art Nouveau. In particular, pieces such as *Toast Cup*, *Despondency*, and *Lorelei* are significant works of the Arts and Crafts period, as were later pieces with conventionalized leaf and flower motifs. The use of dense, mat monochrome glazes emphasized Van Briggle's distinct massing of volume in his form and the tense edge of the defining line. The pottery was continued after his death by his wife, Anne Lawrence Gregory Van Briggle, who managed it until 1913. In 1920 the pottery was reorganized and began to mass-produce art wares. Some of the original Van Briggle designs are still in production, although with steadily decreasing quality they have lost the grace and linear tension of the originals.

Vandenberge, Peter (1935–). Born in the Hague, Netherlands, Vandenberge studied at California State University, Sacramento, where he received his B.A. in 1959, and at the University of California, Davis, receiving an M.A. in 1963. Since 1973 he has taught

at California State University, Sacramento. In 1981 he was the recipient of a Visual Artists Fellowship from the National Endowment for the Arts. He has exhibited widely but sporadically since the mid-1960s. His earliest work comprised stoneware vessels with the traditional speckled glazes. However, he soon turned to figurative imagery and has become one of the more intriguing talents in West Coast figurative sculpture. European art has influenced his figures, from the Léger-like quality of *The Bird Watcher* (1981) to his more stylized figures, in which the head is elongated, creating a curious sensuality reminiscent of Modigliani's attenuated portraits.

Charles Volkmar

Volkmar, Charles (1841–1914). Born in Baltimore, Volkmar was the son of a German portrait painter and restorer. While in his teens, Volkmar studied under Antoine-Louis Barye at the Jardin des Plantes in Paris. He spent nearly fifteen years in France, with only a brief return to the United States, "for the purpose of voting for the second term of Lincoln" (Walton, 1909). Upon his return to Paris he took over a studio just vacated by a fellow American, Will J. Low, and began to work in ceramics. He made his first appearance at the Paris Salon in 1875 and became a regular exhibitor of paintings, etchings, and pottery. He was one of a group of young painters, including Jean-Charles Cazin, Hermanus Anker, and Léon Couturière, who had become involved in ceramics. Eugène Carrière, who later became a famous painter, invited Volkmar to set up a kiln in partnership with him. Instead, Volkmar worked in Paris with the faiencier Theodore Deck, from whom he learned the *procès barbotine* underglaze slip-painting technique.

He returned to the United States and set up kilns at Greenpoint, Long Island, in 1879; Tremont, New York, in 1882; Menlo Park, New Jersey, in 1888; and Metuchen, New Jersey, in 1902. He played an important role in the development of ceramics on the Eastern seaboard, although his impact was more that of a teacher than of an artist. He gave classes at the Salmagundi Club in New York City and at his various potteries. He was also associated with Edwin Atlee Barber's School of Industrial Art in Philadelphia. His work was continued by his son Leon, who worked in his father's later style of simple Oriental forms and monochrome glazes. Two of Charles Volkmar's best-known students were Adelaide Alsop Robineau and Jeannie Rice; the latter founded the Durant Kilns in New York, together with Leon, in 1910.

Voulkos, Peter (1924–). Born in Bozeman, Montana, Voulkos was the son of recent immigrants from Greece. He worked as an apprentice molder in an Oregon iron foundry before entering Montana State University, Bozeman, in 1946 to study painting on the GI Bill. In his last year at Montana State his interest turned to pottery; he studied with Frances Senska, and he showed an exceptional facility for the medium. In 1949 Voulkos won the Potters As-

Peter Voulkos

sociation Prize at the Ceramic National in Syracuse for his pots, with their distinctive wax-resist decoration. Although these early works were highly decorative, Voulkos has retained a respect for them and was upset when these vases were converted into lamps. As Rudy Autio explains, "It is singularly disturbing to him when others fail to see the simple decorative purpose of pottery" (Slivka, 1978).

In 1950 Voulkos enrolled in a graduate program in ceramics at the California College of Arts and Crafts, Oakland, receiving an M.F.A. in 1952. (His graduate thesis was on the lidded jar.) In 1952 he joined his friend Rudy Autio as the first resident potter at the newly established Archie Bray Foundation in Helena, Montana (Autio was the resident sculptor). There he met Bernard Leach, Shoji Hamada (who impressed Voulkos immensely), and the craft philosopher and founder of the Mingei movement, Soetsu Yanagi.

Voulkos was still making conventional functional pottery at this time. In 1953 came the event that began the process of change and radicalism in his work. He spent three weeks teaching at Black Mountain College in Asheville, North Carolina, where he met Josef Albers, John Cage, Merce Cunningham, and other members of an emerging American avant-garde. During the same year he also visited New York at the invitation of the poet-potter M. C. Richards and met several of the leading Abstract Expressionists. This was the turning point for Voulkos. He returned to Helena with a new sense of ambition and was, in the words of Autio, "never the same again" (Slivka, 1978). There was, however, no immediate change in his work. It was not until 1955–56 that his work began to exhibit what are now his signature qualities.

In 1954 Voulkos moved to Los Angeles to become the chairman of a newly established ceramics department at the Los Angeles County Art Institute (later renamed the Otis Art Institute). The institute's conservative director, Millard Sheets, was later to regret his appointment of Voulkos as he and Voulkos began to clash on issues of aesthetic freedom. When Voulkos joined Otis he was very interested in the ceramics of Picasso and Miró, and for a time his Abstract Expressionist interests became secondary. Voulkos soon assembled a remarkable group of students: Paul Soldner, Jerry Rothman, Kenneth Price, Billy Al Bengston, Michael Frimkess, Malcolm McClain (McCloud), John Mason, Henry Takemoto, and others.

After 1955 a new direction developed in Voulkos's work. In that year Voulkos received the gold medal at the International Ceramics Exposition, Cannes, France—becoming the first American to capture this honor. This was the last exhibition of Voulkos's "straight" pots. An exhibition of Fritz Wotruba's sculpture at the Los Angeles County Museum of Art had inspired a new sense of structure and composition in his pots and later in his assembled sculptures.

Voulkos's work became more and more ambitious. The Los Angeles art dealer Felix Landau began to exhibit his work, attracting the attention and praise of his peers in painting and sculpture. By 1958 the relationship with Sheets had deteriorated considerably. Sheets accused Voulkos of adopting an "ivory tower mentality" and argued that pottery should remain modest and traditional. Voulkos countered by starting an exhibition space with his students that they entitled "The Ivory Tower." An exhibition of pots that included one by Billy Al Bengston with the words "Fuck You" sgraffitoed on the surface particularly enraged Sheets, but Voulkos defended his student's freedom of expression. Finally, in May 1959, when Voulkos charred the ceiling of the new building during a firing, Sheets dismissed him.

In June of that year the art and design departments of the University of California, Berkeley, appointed Voulkos assistant professor of ceramics (in 1976 he became a full professor in the Department of Art). Here a new group of students—James Melchert, Ron Nagle, Stephen DeStaebler, and others—assembled. The artist Vaea became Voulkos's technical assistant and an unsung hero in his career—a constant supportive presence over the past twenty-six years. In 1959 Voulkos won the Rodin Prize for sculpture at the First Paris Biennale, Musée National d'Art Moderne, Paris. His career as a sculptor seemed poised for international success.

The following year Voulkos was given a one-person exhibition at the Museum of Modern Art in New York. The exhibition was organized by Peter Selz, then curator of painting and sculpture, as part of a *New Talent* series. Six paintings and six large ceramic sculptures were shown. Except for Dore Ashton, who wrote about the exhibition in the *New York Times* and in *Craft Horizons*, the critics ignored the exhibition. According to Slivka, the reason for the poor response to the exhibition was that "New York was snobbish about the modesty of the material." But it could also have been that without his work in the pottery format, Voulkos was not being seen in the proper perspective.

By 1961 Voulkos's attention had begun to focus on bronze sculpture and, as the decade progressed, he worked less and less in ceramics. He did, however, produce three extraordinary pottery exhibitions. The first was a series of bottles exhibited at the Primus-Stuart Gallery in 1961, and the second was a group of masterfully slashed, cracked, and painted ceramics at the Hansen-Fuller Gallery in San Francisco in 1964. Third, there was an exhibition of black pots and plates in 1968 at the Quay Gallery, San Francisco (the works were made in 1967). Jim Melchert wrote about this exhibition for *Craft Horizons:* "The group is composed of the most haptic pottery I've seen in a long time; it wouldn't surprise me if the work was made in the dark. The glazes, mostly dull black, function as a skin that registers the activity of the body underneath. As the major forms swell and shift, the surface tension is kept taut, interrupted here and there by slashes and perforations.... To me the beauties of the group are the plates. They seem the most transparent and consequently the toughest. The conception is so individual and dependent upon him, that each pot works as a complete system in itself. It's not pottery that anyone else could take further" (Melchert, 1968).

Encouraged by Arnoldo Pomodoro,

Voulkos visited Italy in 1967 and met a number of artists, including Alberto Burri and Lucio Fontana. Both artists had an impact on Voulkos, but Fontana's was particularly strong. Fontana, the first Abstract Expressionist in post–World War II ceramics, had been cutting through vessel forms and drawing on plates with punctures and slashes (much as he did on his canvases) for some seventeen years, producing what he termed his *concetto spaziale.* Although Voulkos had already been using the same set of drawing techniques before his trip to Italy, he now began to use them with a refinement and classical sense of composition that was much closer to the conventions and style of Fontana.

In 1972 Voulkos began a slow return to ceramics as his primary medium, working on an edition of two hundred plates that were thrown for him. On the surface of these he incised a vocabulary of lines and punctured holes and small imbedded porcelain pellets. The plates were originally created for a multiples project initiated by Lee Nordness. Later in the decade Voulkos expanded this series, throwing the plates himself. The plates now became larger and more muscular, with much of the visual attention centered on the rim. This now became a deep, plastic collar around the pots, surrounding a drawing of geometric and surprisingly classical composition. Voulkos fired the plates in a gas kiln with

a commercial glaze that produced an ersatz wood-fired look. In the 1980s, however, Voulkos began to fire his plates in the traditional Japanese Anagama wood-fired kilns. In some ways he was returning to a traditional stance and exploring the techniques of the Bizen, Seto, and Shigaraki potters. These traditions had influenced him earlier in his career, but now his references to this work were more direct and literal.

Voulkos has continued to explore the plate and the stack pot, introducing a new form—the so-called ice bucket. But his output has been erratic. In 1986 he returned to bronze, casting his vessel forms and achieving an extraordinary patina on his works. Over the past ten years Voulkos has been honored by numerous organizations, has received many fellowships from the National Endowment for the Arts, and has been appointed to the Academy of Fellows of the American Craft Council. In 1978 the Museum of Contemporary Crafts, New York, organized a traveling retrospective of his work, which was accompanied by a book by Rose Slivka.

Voulkos's contribution to the development of pottery as an art form is complex. While many artists have participated in America's liberation of ceramic art, it was unquestionably Voulkos who took the leadership role through the fifties and sixties. He is one of only a handful of American potters who have achieved international status. For many he personifies the post-1950s spirit in the medium. He reached and influenced tens of thousands of young potters through his workshop tours of the United States and his demonstrations at SuperMud and other conferences. He gave the young potters the confidence to break the rules, to work as artists, and to search for inner vision. Voulkos's work has also been influential in a broader sense, having an impact on painters such as Robert Irwin and the sculptors Manuel Neri, Robert Hudson, Robert Arneson, and others.

Walters, Carl (1883–1955). Born in Fort Madison, Iowa, Walters took his first art class at the Minneapolis School of Art, where he remained as a student from 1905 to 1907. He continued his education as a painter under Robert Henri at the Chase School in New York from 1908 to 1911. Following his marriage in 1912, he established himself as an artist in Portland, Oregon. Exhibiting continually from 1913 to 1919, he was considered one of the most promising young

Left to right: *Soetsu Yanagi, Bernard Leach, Rudy Autio, Peter Voulkos, and Shoji Hamada.*

painters of the Northwest. Walters decided to return to New York in 1919, and it was there that his first experiments in ceramics took place. He spent almost two years in the development of the Egyptian blue glaze, the obsession of most of the potters of his day. He set up his first workshop in Cornish, New Hampshire, in 1921, moving in the summer of 1922 to Woodstock, New York, where he fired his earliest pieces of ceramic sculpture. In 1924 he showed at the Whitney Studio Club, New York, in an exhibition from which the Whitney Museum of American Art, New York, later acquired *The Stallion*. Walters's works have also been included in other leading American collections, including the Metropolitan Museum of Art, Art Institute of Chicago, Minneapolis Institute of Arts, Detroit Institute of Arts, and Museum of Modern Art in New York. He was a Guggenheim Fellow in 1936 and 1937.

In looking at Walters's work, one finds the comment by R. Guy Cowan that "he paints his sculpture like plates" to be highly instructive. William Homer points out that Walters never forgot that his pieces were *decorated* clay: "Walters made an array of figures that were confident and unspoiled. For his animals he relied on the lively gesture, the gentle torsion and the overall stance to communicate; textural copying and literal details were not necessary in conveying the inner meaning of these creatures. Instead, the surface was made into an abstract pattern which usually covered the entire piece. Feathers, scales, and fur were transformed into rosettes, hatching or stripes" (Homer, 1956). Walter's concern with surface came from his roots in painting. He had developed a close and lasting friendship with a group of New York painters, most of whom belonged to the so-called Ashcan school. He taught ceramics for the first time only in his later years, establishing a ceramics department at the Norton School of Art in West Palm Beach, Florida. Following Walters's death, in 1955 a memorial exhibition of his ceramic sculptures was presented by the Museum of Art of Ogunquit, Maine.

Warashina, Patti (1939–). Born in Spokane, Washington, Warashina studied at the University of Washington, Seattle, where she received her B.F.A. in 1962 and her M.F.A. in 1964. Since 1970 she has taught at the University of Washington with Howard Kottler, establishing one of the most successful ceramic-sculpture programs on the West Coast. She received a Visual Artists Fellowship from the National Endowment for the Arts in 1975 and a Seattle Arts Commission Award in 1985 to produce a complex mural for the Seattle Opera House.

Her early work reflected an interest in simple, functional pottery, with painted surfaces that reflected an interest in the calligraphic style of Klee, Gorky, and Miró. In addition, she enjoyed the same qualities that appeared in the spirited slip decoration by the Japanese potter Kanjiro Kawai. In 1965 Warashina and her first husband, Fred Bauer (she later divorced Bauer and married Robert Sperry), began to use china paints and acrylic paint in their work—a direction that had begun about three years earlier at the San Francisco Art Institute under the "leadership" of James Melchert and Ron Nagle. In the late sixties Warashina produced a series of brightly colored, lustered, Pop art pieces, such as *Ketchup Kiss* (1969) and *Moon Dog Dream* (1969).

In the seventies she started her altar series, ostensibly to honor women, but rather she presented them as a being "sacrificed" to domesticity and traditional role playing, as in *Wear and Tear* (1976). This body of work established and perhaps overemphasized Warashina's role as a feminist artist. Although this is an important part of her work, it does not overwhelm all other issues, as it does in, say, the work of Judy Chicago. In 1979 Warashina's small, white Barbie doll figurines began to make their appearance and have now overrun her work. Frozen, mute, and strangely impersonal—they inhabit surreal landscapes, acting out rituals, wrestling with steam irons or octopus automobiles. "As a child," says Warashina, "I collected dolls, dreams, fantasies. An an 'adult' I still collect dolls, dreams, fantasies and feel lucky that work involves translating these collective observations from my psyche into a tangible form" (Chicago, Clark, and Shaw, 1977).

In *Who Said I Couldn't Fly* (1979), Warashina was influenced by reading Erica Jong's *Fear of Flying*, connecting the notion of flight to the creation of a nest and the fecund associations of eggs and reproduction. What has held all her work together has been a consistent interest in Surrealism: "I want my work to be dreamlike. I want to deal with reality, but take it back and forth between a real and dreamlike state. [My imagery] may or may not make sense to anybody else, it has to make sense to me. I don't want a juxtaposition of anything with anything else. Back in the sixties Richard Shaw and Robert Hudson made a series of pieces in which they threw together sticks, ducks—anything at random. I don't do that. I feel more akin to Magritte. Look at his selection of objects—the grouping doesn't make sense in a rational way, but it does in terms of feeling" (Klemperer, 1983). Warashina's flinty feminist edge and clear vision as a woman and an artist has brought a welcome sense of political issues to a medium that is too frequently obsessed with whimsy and the one-liner.

David Weinrib

Weinrib, David (1924–). Educated in New York City schools, Weinrib took an art course at Brooklyn College and studied painting, sculpture, and pottery at Alfred University, Alfred, New York. He also studied painting in the classic manner at the Accademia, Florence, Italy. With his wife, Karen Karnes, he was potter in residence at Black Mountain College from 1952 to 1954. In 1954 they joined friends in an incorporated community of artists established on one hundred wooded acres at Stony Point, New York.

At first Weinrib assembled his forms from thrown and slabbed elements. In 1958 he invented a slabbing machine, and from then on he did away with all throwing and built all of his forms out of slabs. In 1958 he also extended his studio, working in both clay and metal, and later also in plaster sculpture. Weinrib rapidly established a reputation as an internationally known sculptor and ceased working in ceramics until 1980, when he revived his interest in the medium, both making and teaching ceramics.

Valerie ("Vally") Wieselthier

Wieselthier, Valerie ("Vally") (1895–1945).
Born in Austria, Wieselthier studied at the Kunstgewerbeschule under Professor Michael Powolny from 1914 to 1920. Thereafter she worked closely with the Wiener Werkstätte (then under the artistic direction of Dagobert Peche) and established herself as one of the leading ceramic artists in Europe. In 1928 her work was exhibited in the United States at the *International Exhibition of Ceramic Art*, which opened at the Metropolitan Museum of Art in New York and later toured to several museums throughout the country. In 1929 she decided to settle in the United States, joining the Contempora Group in New York (a collaborative and gallery with artists that included Rockwell Kent, Paul Poiret, and others), as well as designing for the Sebring Pottery in Ohio. She established a studio in New York, where she produced large ceramic sculptures and gave lessons. An energetic, impressive, and regal woman, she was an influential figure in the early development of ceramic sculpture in the United States, even though the work produced in the United States (much like that of her compatriot Susi Singer) did not match the standard of her work in Vienna.

Wildenhain, Frans (1905–1980). Born in Leipzig, Germany, Wildenhain attended the Bauhaus (1924–25), where he first studied

with Paul Klee and later specialized in pottery under *Formmeister* Gerhard Marcks and the potter Max Krehan. Remembering his brief stay at the Bauhaus, Wildenhain wrote some fifty years later, "It was somehow too much at once, I am a slow learner. The seed fell and since [that] time it has grown. The result is me—still growing" (Norton, 1985). After the closing of the pottery workshop at Dornburg, following the move of the Bauhaus to Dessau, Wildenhain went to the State School of Applied Art at Halle-Saale, where he received his master of crafts degree in 1929; in the following year he married Marguerite Friedlander, a fellow student at the Bauhaus. Later he headed the pottery department at the Folkwang workshops in Essen-Ruhr and then taught at the State School of Applied Art at Halle-Saale. In 1933 Marguerite and he went to Holland, where they established a workshop together at Putten. In 1941 he moved to Amsterdam, coming to the United States in 1947 by way of England. He briefly joined his wife at the Pond Farm workshop in Guerneville, California, but the couple divorced in 1955. From 1950 until his retirement in 1975, he was an instructor of pottery and sculpture of the School for American Craftsmen at the Rochester Institute for Technology, Rochester, New York.

Both his art and his pedagogic style of teaching reflected his formative Bauhaus training. But in his pots he changed focus from his early designerly works to developing a fecund, sculptural, and biomorphic style. His passion was directed toward capturing the essence of nature in his work; he remarked, "Nature reveals to me the real and the abstract. The one doesn't exist without the other. The emerging result is an object expressing what is going on in my mind" (Norton, 1985). However, no matter how sculptural his work became, he adhered to the vessel format and it remained a lifelong obsession. Wildenhain was awarded a Guggenheim Fellowship in 1958 for his creative work in relating ceramics and architecture. In 1975 he became a fellow in the Collegium of Craftsmen of the American Craft Council. In 1984 a memorial exhibition of his work was held at the University of Rochester.

Wildenhain, Marguerite (1896–1985).
Marguerite Friedlander was born in Lyon, France, of German and English parents, and was educated in France, England, and Germany. Her early art training was in sculpture at the School of Fine and Applied

Arts in Berlin. Later she worked as a designer of porcelain at the factory in Thuringia, and in 1919 she went as an apprentice in pottery to the Bauhaus in Weimar, where she studied with Max Krehan and the sculptor Gerhard Marcks. In 1926, after six years at the Bauhaus, she became the head of the ceramics department at the Municipal School for Arts and Crafts in Halle-Saale. With the rise of National Socialism in 1933, she moved to Holland, where she and her husband, Frans Wildenhain, operated a workshop in Putten. While in Germany, Wildenhain had produced several designs for the Royal Berlin Porcelain Manufactory. She continued this activity in Holland, producing designs for mass production at the Regout Porcelain Factory in Maastricht, Holland, and winning a second prize for her designs at the international exhibition *Arts et Techniques* in Paris in 1937. Just before the Nazi invasion of Holland, she immigrated to the United States and taught for two years at the California College of Arts and Crafts in Oakland. In 1942 she started her own workshop at Pond Farm in Guerneville, California, where she lived until her death. At Pond Farm, Wildenhain directed a popular summer school that attracted students from as far away as China and India.

Wildenhain was a strong influence on the functional school of ceramics, having written three books and published numerous articles. In the fifties she turned her back on the "cold Abstraction of the Bauhaus" and no longer designed for industry. She insisted on a stern craft ethic: "I have formerly made many models for mass production. Today, though, I feel it is increasingly important again to stress the values of the way of life of a craftsman, to try and educate towards a basic understanding of the essence of a life dedicated to an idea that is not based on success and money, but on human independence and dignity" ("Ceramics: Double Issue," 1958).

In her own work she turned from the minimalism of her pre-fifties work to a highly sentimental style of drawing and decoration taken from the example of folk art. In 1984 a major retrospective was organized by the Herbert F. Johnson Museum of Art, Cornell University, Ithaca, New York. The exhibition traveled to the Oakland Museum, California, and the Mint Museum of Art, Charlotte, North Carolina. Wildenhain was the recipient of many honors, including the Charles Fergus Binns Award from the American Ceramic Society in 1958.

Wood, Beatrice (1893–). Born in San Francisco, Wood studied in Paris during her late teens. Studying art briefly at the Académie Julian, she was soon attracted to the stage and transferred her studies to the Comédie Française. Upon her return to the United States in 1914, Wood joined the French Repertory Theater in New York. While visiting the French composer Edgar Varèse in a New York hospital in 1916, she was introduced to Marcel Duchamp. She soon became an intimate friend of the painter and a member of his recherché cultural clique, which included Francis Picabia, Man Ray, Albert Gleizes, Walt Kuhn, and others. As a contributor to Duchamp's avant-garde magazines, *Rogue* and the *Blindman*, she produced drawings and shared editorial space with such luminaries of the day as Gertrude Stein.

Encouraged by Duchamp, Wood began to draw. One of her entries for the 1917 *Exhibition of the Society of Independent Artists* in New York, *Un peu d'eau dans du savon*, was a drawing of a female nude with a bar of soap placed strategically on the figure. Duchamp suggested that instead of painting the bar of soap as she had planned, that she attach an actual bar of Vignola soap to the painting. What caused the painting to become the succès de scandale of the exhibition was her error in titling the piece. Instead of being translated as "A little soap in some water," it read as "A little water in some soap." The piece attracted pages of angry critical attention. (For a more detailed examination of Wood's early career and drawings, see Clark and Naumann, 1983.)

Beatrice Wood

Wood's interest in ceramics was aroused in 1933, when she purchased a set of six luster plates. She wanted to produce a matching teapot, and it was suggested that she make one at the pottery classes of the Hollywood High School. About 1938 she studied with Glen Lukens at the University of Southern California, and in 1940 with the Austrian potters Gertrud and Otto Natzler. She remembers being "the most interested student in [Lukens's] class and certainly the least gifted—I was not a born craftsman. Many with natural talent do not have to struggle, they ride on easy talent and never soar. But I worked and worked, obsessed with learning" (Clark, "Beatrice Wood," 1983). Since then, Wood has developed a personal and uniquely expressive art form with her lusterwares. Her sense of theater is still vividly alive in these works, with their exotic palette of colors and unconventional form.

Wood's home for nearly forty years has been Ojai, California. She recently moved to a new home and studio, built on the land of the Happy Valley School of the Theosophical Society, with which she has been associated since its foundation in 1946 by Aldous Huxley, Krishnamurti, and Annie Besant. The 1970s and 1980s have proved to be Wood's most productive decades for her ceramic art. The year 1978 saw three concurrent exhibitions of her work, at the Everson Museum of Art, Syracuse, New York; the Hadler Galleries, New York; and the Philadelphia Museum of Art.

In 1983 the Art Galleries of California State University at Fullerton organized a large retrospective of the artist's sixty-six years of activity as an artist. The exhibition was later toured nationally by the Garth Clark Gallery. Writing about the exhibition, Christopher Knight commented that the biographical nature of the exhibition created an awkward dichotomy: "The show is trying to direct our attention towards the artist, while the art is busy directing its attention towards us.... In the end it is the art—specifically the post-1950 luster glaze pottery—that wins the battle. These humble-but-dazzling ceramics are extraordinary props for a theater of life" (Knight, 1983).

Shortly after the opening of the retrospective, the author organized the Blindman's Ball to honor Wood on the occasion of her ninetieth birthday, for the benefit of the Los Angeles Children's Cancer Hospital. The Ball was a re-creation of a Dada event that Wood, Duchamp, and Francis Picabia had organized in New York in 1917 to raise funds for the *Blindman* magazine.

In 1985 Wood published her autobiography, *I Shock Myself*. Interviewed shortly thereafter, Wood explained her philosophy of life at the age of ninety-three: "The Japanese have these little—what do you call them?—Yes, haiku. This is mine. The first sentence is, 'Now,' which I firmly believe in. Everything's in the present. The second sentence is, 'Shit,' because nothing really matters. The third sentence is, 'I do not know.' That's the whole philosophy" (Stanley, 1983).

In 1986 one of Wood's figurative pieces, *The Naugty* [sic] *Snake* (1972) was selected for the Venice Biennale and was shown in a section entitled "Reconciliation of Opposites," together with the work of Arp, Ernst, Breton, Miró, Kandinsky, and others—and received excellent reviews. The figures are an important and highly personal part of Wood's oeuvre. In a 1985 exhibition of her figures, the *Los Angeles Times* critic Suzanne Muchnic wrote of the playfully erotic content: "She doesn't always spell out debauchery, she just sets out the players and lets us expect the worst of them. A middle-aged gent with a moustache and top hat sits stiffly on a chair holding a prim little blond girl on his lap in *Innocence Is Not Enough*. He doesn't touch her or even ogle her but we know he is a lecher" (Muchnic, May 17, 1985).

Wood has received numerous honors in the past few years. She was given the Ceramics Symposium Award of the Institute for Ceramic History in 1983 and the outstanding-achievement award of the Women's Caucus for Art in 1987, the year she was made a fellow of both the National Council on Education for the Ceramic Arts and the American Craft Council.

Typically, Wood celebrated her ninety-fourth birthday by changing technologies, replacing her electric kiln with a new, state-of-the-art gas kiln. With greater control of the reduction process, Wood is beginning to reproduce some of the complex glaze surfaces of her classic pots from the fifties. Now, however, the forms have become more complex and more evolved, comprising several assembled elements, with multiple handles. In her work, Wood accepts no rules or theories. The freedom and constant movement of her work reflect the aesthetic credo that she learned from Marcel Duchamp, who told her, "Never do the commonplace, rules are fatal to the progress of art" (Bryan, 1970).

Woodman, Elizabeth ("Betty") Abrahams (1930–). Born in Norwalk, Connecticut, Woodman studied at the School for American Craftsmen (then at Alfred University, Alfred, New York) from 1948 to 1950, majoring in pottery. As soon as she completed her studies, she set up her own studio on a production basis and has been self-supporting since then. From 1957 to 1973 she taught at and administered the City of Boulder [Colorado] Recreation Pottery Program, which has now evolved into a major course, with its own building, 350 adult and child students, and a teaching staff of eight. As one of the oldest, largest, and most successful programs of its kind, the course has become something of a model, and Woodman has frequently consulted with directors of pottery programs in other cities. In 1976 she joined the Fine Arts Department of the University of Colorado, Boulder, where she is now an associate professor. Woodman has been the recipient of several awards, including Visual Artists Fellowships from the National Endowment for the Arts in 1980 and 1986 and selection as a visiting artist at the Manufacture Nationale de Sèvres in 1985.

Since 1951, Woodman has lived and worked in Italy nearly every year for varying periods of time, ranging from two to twelve months. She maintains a summer studio in Antella, outside Florence. This constant cultural counterplay between the United States and Europe shows strongly in her work, particularly in that of the last ten years. In these works the forms and surface sensitivities, although explored with the dash and adventure associated with the more lively elements of American ceramics, strongly reflect the Mediterranean ceramic tradition and ambience. Writing of Woodman's work in *Craft Horizons,* fellow potter Richard DeVore comments; "Raucously juxtaposing apparent disparate elements is an approach we have not witnessed since Oribeware. Yet Woodman is the only ceramist I know (other than Peter Voulkos with certain works) who so convincingly presents this idea with such a satisfyingly ordered chaos. Her pieces combine surface-piercing manipulation of planes and a clear record of the shaping process" (DeVore, 1978).

Woodman's expansion of the pottery tradition began to take clearer shape in the mid-seventies, as she worked less and less in the purely utilitarian realm. She also

Betty Woodman

began to take responsibility for the decoration of her pieces (something that she had previously done in collaboration with her husband, the painter George Woodman). In 1980 she established a studio in New York City, and through her collaborations with Joyce Kozloff (1981) and Cynthia Carlson (1982), she began to be identified with the Pattern and Decoration movement in American art.

Woodman based her early reputation on being a production potter, a maker of utilitarian ware. Over the years function has become less of an issue in the literal sense, but it has remained a potent symbolic factor in her work. Even today many pieces are named for a specific purpose: *Summer Caffé Latte Tray and Pitchers, Double Pitcher Bun Basket, Turkish Water Tray.* Although her work has expanded to include installations, monoprints, and other activities beyond the realm of the single vessel, the primary language of the pottery remains central to her art: "Rather than trying to blur or obliterate the line between sculpture and pottery as many do, I am concerned with producing pots that make a significant reference to the vernacular of pottery" (Woodman, 1980).

An important aspect of her work is its play with history. Woodman appropriates (to use the patois of postmodernism) from many sources—Tang, Minoan, Oribe, Etruscan, Iznik, and even from the high-style porcelains of Sèvres. In his formal analysis of Woodman's aesthetic, Jeff Per-

rone examines this "grafting" of history on her work: "One must take another attitude toward the material of ceramics when describing Woodman's art. It's not just clay and glaze. It is not simply those raw materials processed by throwing, rolling, extruding, and firing. The material is history itself, a material body of shapes, forms, decoration—in a word, everything that signifies *Style*" (Perrone, 1986).

Wyman, William (1922–1980). Born in Boston, Wyman received his education at the Massachusetts College of Art and at Columbia University, New York. Since 1953 Wyman was a professional potter and sculptor and operated the Herring Run Pottery in East Weymouth, Massachusetts, where he created individually crafted functional and nonfunctional stoneware objects. Wyman taught at Drake University, Des Moines; the University of Maryland, College Park; the Massachusetts College of Art, Boston; and the De Cordova and Dana Museum and Park, Lincoln, Massachusetts.

Wyman was particularly noted for his inventive use of slab-built vessels. His pots became canvases for sgraffitoed surfaces with cartoons, poems, and catch phrases. At first the poetry was related to contemporary jazz and to other popular expressions, and then slowly it evolved into expressions of political and deeply introspective personal philosophies. In 1965 Wyman worked in Honduras on a project sponsored by the Agency for International Development, with the idea of fostering native potteries. On his way home he visited the ruins of Copán, a ceremonial center of the Mayan religion. This visit was to have a profound effect on his work from 1977 to 1979, when he made his last and most distinguished group of works, the *Temple* series. Relating Wyman's work to Stonehenge, Copán, and Chartres Cathedral, all of which were direct sources for Wyman's miniature, white-earthenware temples, Susan J. Montgomery wrote, in 1985: "The designers and builders of all three places were able to realign human experience...all was planned to disorient worshippers from the everyday world to another level of emotional, intuitive, and perhaps uncertain experience. These are not places for people to feel 'at home.' They are intended to disrupt normality and inspire a sense of otherworldliness.... Wyman's temples are unsettling and disconcerting in a similar way."

Youngblood, Daisy (1945–). Born in Asheville, North Carolina, Youngblood studied at the Virginia Commonwealth University, 1963–67. She currently maintains a studio in Minneapolis. Youngblood's sculpture deals with the figure but in a manner very different from that of the West Coast ceramist. There is no humor or decorativeness in her approach. The clay is used simply, directly, and powerfully. Writing of her work in a catalogue essay for the exhibition *In the Eye of the Beholder,* Michael McTwigan comments, "Her sculpted figures tell real stories, not metaphorical ones, and her message hits home. But despite its immediacy, Youngblood's raw, primitive yet realistic style is timeless, the voice she speaks with is as old as the mummies of ancient Egypt. Her figures are stripped down, withered, sometimes prostrate or bound up with rope. What we see in their fallen state, however, is the still-glowing ember of the human spirit" (McTwigan, 1985).

Zimmerman, Arnold (1954–). Born in Poughkeepsie, New York, Zimmerman studied at the Kansas City Art Institute, where he received his B.F.A. in 1977, and at the New York State College of Ceramics at Alfred University, where he received his M.F.A. in 1979. Zimmerman received a Visual Artists Fellowship from the National Endowment for the Arts in 1980 and a Connecticut Commission on the Arts Grant in 1981. He maintains a studio in Brooklyn, New York.

From the outset Zimmerman has been interested in scale and has made large works, with a sense of urgency and immediacy in his surface painting. His strongest influences came from architecture (particularly the Romanesque cathedrals of north-central Italy). His scale and approach to the vessel are similarly architectonic. His forms rapidly grew into large scale: "Larger than life-size, the pots stand seven to nine feet when finished. They weigh roughly a thousand pounds, and are constructed of three-to-five-inch-thick walls of coarse stoneware clay. When they bulge, they bulge a foot. Where they twist they almost become disjointed. Where they are carved the relief is cut deep. They ask to be felt, pushed on, leaned against. In short, their physical character asserts itself so boldly that the viewer feels an equally physical response" (Priest, 1983). The works have a massive, awkward presence—part of their monumentality derives from their scale and part from the context of taking the domestic form of the pot and projecting it into an architectural realm. In this manner Zimmerman's works share the same sculptural device as Claes Oldenburg's giant Pop sculpture, playing with a huge increase in scale for objects that are generally small and domestic in content. However, in recent work Zimmerman has moved away from the pot and is now building giant arches that weigh over two tons, moving the work into a less ambiguous sculptural arena.

—. *China Painting: Manual . . . for Decoration of Hard Porcelain.*
—. *The China Painters' Handbook: The Practical Series.*
Meyer, Fred. *Sculpture in Ceramics.*
Natzler, Otto. "The Natzler Glazes."
Nelson, G. *Ceramics: A Potter's Handbook.*
Nichols, George Ward. *Pottery . . . Instructions for Painting.*
Poor, Henry Varnum. *A Book of Pottery: From Mud to Immortality.*
Randall, Ruth Hunie. *Ceramic Sculpture.*
Rhead, Frederick H. *Studio Pottery.*
—. "Planning and Operating a Studio Pottery."
—. "What the Industries Want from the Ceramic Artist."
Rhodes, Daniel. *Clay and Glazes for the Potter.*
—. *Stoneware and Porcelain: The Art of High-Fired Pottery.*
—. *Kilns: Design, Construction and Operation.*
—. "The Potter and His Kiln."
Riegger, Harold Eaton. *Raku: Art and Technique.*
—. *Primitive Pottery.*
—. Sanders, Herbert H. *Glazes for Special Effects.*
Sheerer, Mary G. "The Development . . . Decorative Processes at Newcomb."
Smith, Kenneth E. "Laura Anne Fry . . . Atomizing Process."
"Some New Designs and Methods in Rookwood and Grueby Faience," *The Paris Exhibition.*
Speight, Charlotte. *Hands in Clay.*
—. *Images in Clay Sculpture.*
Stratton, Mary Chase Perry. *Ceramic Processes.*
Volkmar, Charles. "Hints on Underglaze."
Wechsler, Susan. *Low-Fire Ceramics: A New Direction in American Clay.*
Wildenhain, Marguerite. *Pottery: Form and Expression.*

ARTISTS

AEBERSOLD, JANE FORD

Burstein, Joanne. "Jane Ford Aebersold."
Sandy, Stephen. *Jane Ford: Recent Work.*
—. "Ceramics and the Art of Jane Ford."

AITKEN, RUSSELL BARNETT

Anderson, Ross, and Barbara Perry. *Diversions of Keramos.*
Archbold, G. "Ceramic Sculpture of Russell Aitken."
"Russell Barnett Aitken."

ANDRESON, LAURA

Kester, Bernard. "Laura Andreson."
—. *Laura Andreson: A Retrospective in Clay.*
Levin, Elaine. "Pioneers . . . Laura Andreson."
Petterson, Richard B. "Timeless . . . Porcelains of Laura Andreson."
Rico, Diana. "Laura Andreson."

ARCHIPENKO, ALEXANDER

University of California, Los Angeles. *Alexander Archipenko.*

ARNESON, ROBERT

Adrian, Dennis. "Robert Arneson's Feats of Clay."
Albright, Thomas. "San Francisco: Mickey Mouse and Memorabilia."
—. "In Memoriam, In Storage."
—. *Art in the San Francisco Bay Area, 1945–1980.*
Armstrong, Lois, "Los Angeles: Roy Forest and Robert Arneson."
Arneson, Robert. *My Head in Ceramics.*
Baker, Kenneth. "Arneson Takes on Nuclear Threat."
Ball, Fred. "Arneson."
Ballatore, Sandy. "The California Clay Rush."
Benezra, Neal. *Robert Arneson: A Retrospective.*
Bismanis, Maija, and Ric Gomez. *The Continental Clay Connection.*
Brown, Christopher. "Arneson—From Comic Books to Self-Portrait."
Coffelt, Beth. *Robert Arneson: Self-Portraits.*
Coplans, John. "Out of Clay: West Coast Ceramic Sculpture."
Cummings, Paul. *Robert Arneson: Points of View.*
Fineberg, Jonathan. "Robert Arneson: Pablo Ruiz with Itch."
Foley, Suzanne, and Richard Marshall. *Ceramic Sculpture.*
—, and Stephen Prokopoff. *Robert Arneson.*
Frankenstein, Alfred. "Of Bricks, Pop Bottles. . . ."
—. "The Ceramic Sculpture of Robert Arneson."
Glueck, Grace. "Art People: A Partner to His Kiln."
—. "Art: The Clay Figure at the Craft Museum."
Hopkins, Henry T. *50 West Coast Artists.*
Hughes, Robert. "Molding the Human Clay."
Jones, Mady. *Figurative Clay Sculpture: Northern California.*
Judd, Donald. "Robert Arneson."
Kelley, Jeff. "Re Clay."
Knute, Stiles. "Robert Arneson."
Kramer, Hilton. "Sculpture—From Boring to Brilliant."
—. "Ceramic Sculpture and the Taste of California."
Kuspit, Donald B. "Arneson's Outrage."
—. "Robert Arneson's Sense of Self."
Larson, Kay. "California Clay Rush."
Last, Martin. "Robert Arneson."
McTwigan, Michael. *Heroes and Clowns: Robert Arneson.*
—. *In the Eye of the Beholder: A Portrait of Our Time.*
Malcolm, J. "On and Off the Avenue: About the House."
Meisel, Alan R. "Robert Arneson."
Museum of Contemporary Crafts. *Clayworks.*
"New York Reviews: Robert Arneson."
Paris, Harold. "Sweet Land of Funk."
Perreault, John. "Robert Arneson."
Perrone, Jeff. "Robert Arneson."
Polley, Elisabeth M. "Robert Arneson."
Prokopoff, Stephen, and Suzanne Foley. *Robert Arneson—Retrospective.*
Pugliese, Joseph. "Ceramics from Davis."
Raynor, Vivian. "Art: Ceramic Caricatures by Robert Arneson."
Schjeldahl, Peter. "Robert Arneson."
Schwartz, Judith S. *Contemporary American Ceramic Sculpture.*
Selz, Peter. *Funk Art.*
Slivka, Rose. "The New Ceramic Presence."
—. *West Coast Ceramics.*
Stone, D. J. "Robert Arneson."
Wilson, William. "San Francisco Exhibit: Clay . . . and Now Moscone."
—. "Arneson the Artist."
Zack, David. "Funk Art."
—. "California Myth Making."
—. "The Ceramics of Robert Arneson."
—. "Nut Art in Quake Time."
—. "California Myth Makers."
—. *Nut Pot or Art without Tears?*

AUTIO, RUDY

Autio, Lela, and Rudy Autio. "Peter H. Voulkos."
Autio, Rudy. "About Drawing."
Clark, Garth, and Sanford S. Shaman. *The Contemporary American Potter.*
Depew, Dave. "The Archie Bray Foundation."
Fairbanks, Jonathan, and K. W. Moffett. *Directions in American Ceramics.*
Harrington, LaMar. "Letter from Seattle—Rudy Autio."
Kangas, Matthew. "Massive Narrations."
—. *Rudy Autio Retrospective.*
—. "Rudy Autio."
Lang, Ron. *Clay Bodies. Autio—DeStaebler—Frey.*

CUSHING, VAL

Bodine, Sarah. "Val Cushing."
Clark, Garth, and Sanford S. Shaman. *The Contemporary American Potter.*
Lebow, Edward. "Val Cushing."

DALEY, WILLIAM

Ashton, Dore, et al. *Multiplicity in Clay, Metal & Fiber.*
Clark, Garth, and Sanford S. Shaman. *The Contemporary American Potter.*
—, et al. *Who's Afraid of American Pottery?*
Daley, William. "On Drawing."
McTwigan, Michael. "The Duality in Clay: William Daley."
Parry, William. *William Daley: Selected Works 1954–1982.*

DELISLE, ROSELINE

Garth Clark, et al. *Pacific Connections.*

DeSTAEBLER, STEPHEN

Ashton, Dore. *Modern American Sculpture.*
Burstein, Joanne. "Stephen DeStaebler."
Clark, Garth. *New Works in Clay II.*
Dillenberger, Jane. *Perceptions of the Spirit.*
Edwards, Sharon. "A Conversation with Stephen DeStaebler."
Jones, Harvey L. *Stephen DeStaebler: Sculpture.*
Lang, Ron. *Clay Bodies: Autio—DeStaebler—Frey.*
Levin, Elaine. "Stephen DeStaebler."
Meisel, Alan R. "Heavy Clay by Stephen DeStaebler."

DeVORE, RICHARD

Abatt, Corinne. "Ceramic Artist Makes a Forceful Statement."
Artner, Alan G. "Vessels Brimming with Excellence."
Clark, Garth, et al. *Who's Afraid of American Pottery?*
Colby, Joy H. "Sculpture by Another Name."
DeVore, Richard. "Ceramics of Betty Woodman."
Donohoe, Victoria. "Major Ceramic Artist."
Jones, Kenneth W. "Richard E. DeVore."
Kalamazoo Institute of Arts. *Contemporary Ceramics.*
Kline, Katy. "Pots, Paintings: A Common Thread."
Koplos, Janet. "Richard DeVore."
Mehring, Howard. "Richard DeVore" (1977).
—. "Richard DeVore" (1978).
Miro, Marsha. "What Makes Art out of a Pottery Bowl?"
Nasisse, Andy. "The Ceramic Vessel as Metaphor."

Nordland, Gerald. *Richard DeVore.*
—. *Richard DeVore: 1972–1982.*
"A Potter Called DeVore."
Rubenfeld, Florence. "Pottery of Richard DeVore."

DILLINGHAM, RICK

Bell, David. "Rick Dillingham: Works in Clay."
Curtis, Phil. "Artists Find Mystery in Pottery."
Huntington, Richard. "Pots Echo Distant Times."
Kane, Sid. "Patchwork Pots."
Zwinger, S. "Rick Dillingham."

DOAT, TAXILE

Belot, Leon. *Taxile Doat Céramiste.*
Evans, Paul F. "American Art Porcelain: University City Pottery."
Jervis, William P. "Taxile Doat."
Kohlenberger, Lois H. "Ceramics at the People's University."
Sargent, Irene. "Taxile Doat."
Verneuil, M. D. "Taxile Doat."
Weiss, Peg, ed. *Adelaide Alsop Robineau.*

DUCKWORTH, RUTH

Artner, Alan G. "Duckworth: Shaped by Honor."
Duckworth, Ruth, and Alice Westphal. *Ruth Duckworth.*
McTwigan, Michael. *Ruth Duckworth/Claire Zeisler.*
Westphal, Alice. "The Ceramics of Ruth Duckworth."

EARL, JACK

Ballatore, Sandy. *Viewpoint Ceramics, 1980.*
Cohen, Karl F. *Porcelains by Jack Earl.*
Cohen, Ronny H. "Jack Earl."
Klassen, John. "A Conversation with Jack Earl."
Nordness, Lee. "Jack Earl."
—. *Jack Earl.*

ECKHARDT, EDRIS

Barrie, Dennis. "Edris Eckhardt Interviewed."
Eckhardt, Edris. "WPA Ceramics."
Marling, Karal Ann. *Federal Art in Cleveland 1933–1943.*
—. "New Deal Ceramics: The Cleveland Workshop."

ELOZUA, RAYMON

Busch, Akiko. "Decorated Tiles."
Wechsler, Susan. *Raymon Elozua.*

FERGUSON, KENNETH

Clark, Garth, and Sanford S. Shaman. *The Contemporary American Potter.*
Depew, Dave. "The Archie Bray Foundation."
Ferguson, Kenneth. "Starting at the Ears."
Gardner, Colin. "Reviews: Ferguson and Kraus."
Lang, Ron. "NCECA/SuperMud Conference."
Melcher, Victoria Kirsch. "Tradition and Vitality."
Rubin, Michael G. "Kenneth Ferguson."
Sewalt, Charlotte. "An Interview with Ken Ferguson."

FRACKELTON, SUSAN

Frackelton, Richard G. "Susan Frackelton."
Frackelton, Susan S. *Tried by Fire: A Work on China Painting.*
—. "Organized Effort."
—. "Our American Potteries."
—. "Rookwood Pottery."
Stover, Frances. "Susan Goodrich Frackelton and the China Painters."
Weedon, George A. *Susan S. Frackelton.*

FRANK, MARY

Ashton, Dore. "Perceiving the Clay Figure."
"Ceramics by Twelve Artists."
Clark, Garth. *New Works in Clay II.*
Henry, Gerrit. "The Clay Landscapes of Mary Frank."
Herrera, Hayden. *Mary Frank: Sculpture/ Drawings/ Prints.*
—. "Myth and Metamorphosis: Mary Frank."
—. *Mary Frank: Sculpture and Monotypes 1981–1982.*
Hughto, Margie. *New Works in Clay.*
Kramer, Hilton. "The Sculpture of Mary Frank."
—. "Art: Sensual, Serene Sculpture."
Lafean, Richard. "Ceramics by Twelve Artists."
Mellow, James R. "About Woman as a Sexual Being."
—. "Mary Frank Explores Women's Erotic Fantasies."
"Museum Clay at Everson."
Sawin, Martica. "The Sculpture of Mary Frank."

FRANKENTHALER, HELEN

"Ceramics by Twelve Artists."
Hughto, Margie. *New Works in Clay.*
Lafean, Richard. "Ceramics by Twelve Artists."
"Museum Clay at Everson."

Whitney Museum of American Art. *Sculptures and Drawings of Elie Nadelman.*

NAGLE, RON

Brody, Harvey. *The Book of Low-Fire Ceramics.*
Brown, Sylvia. "The Tough and Tender . . . Wares."
Clark, Garth, et al. *Pacific Connections.*
Coplans, John. *Abstract Expressionist Ceramics.*
Felton, David. "Nagle among the Termites."
Haverstadt, Hal. "Ron Nagle in Rock and Glass."
McDonald, Robert. "New Work by Ron Nagle."
McTwigan, Michael. "Ron Nagle."
Nordness, Lee. *Objects: USA.*
Slivka, Rose. *West Coast Ceramics.*
Wechsler, Susan. "Ron Nagle: An Interview."

NAKIAN, REUBEN

Armstrong, Tom, et al. *200 Years of American Sculpture.*
Nakian, Reuben. "Apprentice to the Gods."

NATZLER, GERTRUD and OTTO

Andreson, Laura. "The Natzlers."
Bray, Hazel. *The Potter's Art in California: 1885–1955.*
Henderson, R. "Gertrud and Otto Natzler."
Levin, Elaine. "An Interview with Otto Natzler."
Los Angeles County Museum of Art. *Ceramic Work of . . . Natzler.*
Natzler, Otto. "The Natzler Glazes."
—. *Natzler Ceramics: Collection of Mrs. Leonard M. Sperry.*
Penny, Janice. "The Natzlers, Masters of Ceramic Art."
Renwick Gallery. *Form and Fire: Natzler Ceramics 1930–1972.*
Rubenfeld, Florence. "Otto Natzler: Solo."

NELSON, ART

"Art Nelson."
Fiske, Charles. "Art Nelson."

NERI, MANUEL

Coplans, John. *Abstract Expressionist Ceramics.*
Selz, Peter. *Funk Art.*

NEVELSON, LOUISE

Armstrong, Tom, et al. *200 Years of American Sculpture.*
"Ceramics by Twelve Artists."

Lafean, Richard. "Ceramics by Twelve Artists."

NEWCOMB POTTERY

Blasberg, Robert W. "Newcomb Pottery."
—. "The Sadie Irvine Letters."
Cox, Paul E. "Newcomb Pottery Active in New Orleans."
Evans, Paul F. "Newcomb Pottery Decorators."
Hutson, Ethel. "Newcomb Pottery . . . Experiment in Applied Art."
Poesch, Jessie. *Newcomb Pottery.* Schiffer Publishing.
—. *Newcomb Pottery.* Smithsonian Traveling Exhibition.
Sheerer, Mary G. "Newcomb Pottery."
—. "The Development of the Decorative Processes at Newcomb."
Smith, Kenneth E. "The Origin, Development . . . of Newcomb Pottery."
—. "Ceramics at Newcomb College."

NEWTON, CLARA CHIPMAN

Newton, Clara Chipman. "Early Days at Rookwood Pottery."
Trapp, Kenneth R. "Japanese Influence in Early Rookwood Pottery."

NICHOLS, MARIA LONGWORTH

Macht, Carol, and Kenneth Trapp. *The Ladies, God Bless 'Em.*
Newton, Clara Chipman. "Early Days at Rookwood Pottery."
Peck, Herbert. "The Amateur Antecedents of Rookwood Pottery."
—. *The Book of Rookwood Pottery.*
Storer, Maria Longworth (Nichols). *Cincinnati Musical Festivals.*
Trapp, Kenneth R. "Maria Longworth Storer . . . Her Bronze Objets d'Art."
—. "Japanese Influence in Early Rookwood Pottery."

NOGUCHI, ISAMU

Hasegawa, S., et al. *Isamu Noguchi: Ceramics.*

NOTKIN, RICHARD

Bodine, Sarah, and Michael Dunas. "The Precarious Scale of Justice."
Chronicles: Historical References in Contemporary Art.
Cromwell-Lacy, Sherry, ed. *Ceramic Artists.*
Eder, Lynn. "Richard Notkin."
Lang, Ron. "NCECA/Super Mud Conference."
Slivka, Rose. *West Coast Ceramics.*

OESTREICH, JEFF

Murphy, Terri. "Jeff Oestreich: Potter."
Oestreich, Jeff. "Some Thoughts on Studio Pottery."

OHR, GEORGE E.

Blasberg, Robert W. *George E. Ohr and His Biloxi Art Pottery.*
Clark, Garth. *The Biloxi Art Pottery of George E. Ohr.*
—. "George E. Ohr—Clay Prophet."
—. "Ohr/Robineau: A Study in Polarities."
—. "George E. Ohr: Avant-Garde Volumes."
—. *George E. Ohr.*
—. "George E. Ohr," *American Ceramics.*
—. "George E. Ohr," *Antiques.*
Cox, Paul E. "Potteries of the Gulf Coast."
Dietz, Ulysses G. *The Newark Collection of Art Pottery.*
Evans, Paul F. "Reflections of Frederick Hurten Rhead."
Hecht, Eugene. "An Ohr Primer: Part I."
—. "An Ohr Primer: Part II."
—. "An Ohr Primer: Part III—The Artist and the Bad Guys."
—. "An Ohr Primer: Part IV."
Kaplan, Wendy, ed. *The Art That Is Life.*
King, William A. "Ceramic Art at the Pan-American Exhibition."
Ohr, George E. "Some Facts in the History of a Unique Personality."
Perreault, John. "Either Ohr."
Reif, Rita. "Rediscovering a Potter."

PERRY, MARY CHASE

Ault, R. "Mary Chase Perry Stratton and Her Pewabic Pottery."
Bleicher, Fred, et al. *Pewabic Pottery: An Official History.*
Brunk, Thomas W. "Pewabic Pottery."
—. *Pewabic Pottery: Marks and Labels.*
—. "The Pewabic Pottery."
Flu, E. B. "The Pewabic Pottery at Detroit."
Hegarty, M. "Selected . . . Pewabic Pottery by M. C. Stratton."
Nelson, Marion John. "Art Nouveau in American Ceramics."
Pear, Lillian Myers. *The Pewabic Pottery.*
Perry, Mary Chase. "Decorative Pottery of Cincinnati."
—. "The Work of Cincinnati Women in Decorated Pottery."
—. "Grueby Potteries" (1900).
—. "Grueby Potteries" (1902).
Plumb, Helen. "The Pewabic Pottery."
Robineau, Adelaide A. "Mary Chase Perry—the Potter."

—. "Ceramics at the Paris Exposition."
Robineau, Samuel. "The Robineau Porcelains."
—. "Adelaide Alsop Robineau."
"Syracuse Gets Robineau Memorial Group."
Weiss, Peg, ed. *Adelaide Alsop Robineau: Glory in Porcelain.*
Wise, E. B. "Adelaide Alsop Robineau—American Ceramist."

ROLOFF, JOHN

Burstein, Joanne. "The Travels of John Roloff."
Foley, Suzanne. *Richard Shaw . . . John Roloff.*
Levin, Elaine. "John Roloff."

ROOKWOOD POTTERY

Bopp, H. F. "Art and Science in the Development of Rookwood Pottery."
Boulden, Jane L. "Rookwood."
Frackelton, Susan S. "Rookwood Pottery."
Hasselle, Bob. "Rookwood: An American Art Pottery."
Kinsley, Rose. "Rookwood Pottery."
Kircher, Edwin J., et al. *Rookwood . . . 1880–1929.*
Peck, Herbert. "Rookwood Pottery and Foreign Museum Collections."
—. "Some Early Collections of Rookwood Pottery."
Peck, Margaret. *Catalog of Rookwood Art Pottery Shapes.*
"Some New Designs and Methods in Rookwood and Grueby Faience," *The Paris Exhibition.*
Storer, Maria Longworth (Nichols). *History of the Cincinnati Musical Festivals and of the Rookwood Pottery.*
Taylor, William Watts. "The Rookwood Pottery."
Trapp, Kenneth R. *Ode to Nature . . . Rookwood Pottery 1880–1940.*
—. "The Japanese Influence on Rookwood Pottery."
Valentine, John. "Rookwood Pottery."
Yaeger, D. "Rookwood, Pioneer American Art Pottery."

ROTHMAN, JERRY

Ballatore, Sandy. *Viewpoint Ceramics, 1980.*
Clark, Garth. *Jerry Rothman: Bauhaus Baroque.*
—. *Orange County Clay.*
—, and Sanford S. Shaman. *The Contemporary American Potter.*
Dempsey, Bruce H. *Master Craftsmen.*
Glasgow, Lukman. "Jerry Rothman."
"Jerry Rothman."
Melchert, Jim, and Paul Soldner. *The Fred and Mary Marer Collection.*

Olson, J. Bennett. "Exhibitions: Soldner, Mason, Rothman."
Slivka, Rose. "The New Ceramic Presence."
Victoria and Albert Museum. *20 American Studio Potters.*

SAXE, ADRIAN

Bettleheim, Judith. "Pacific Connections."
Clark, Garth. "Adrian Saxe: An Interview."
—, et al. *Pacific Connections.*
Forde, Ed. "Exhibitions: Adrian Saxe."
Knight, Christopher. "Artist's Vessels Sail on a Revolutionary Sea."
Perrone, Jeff. "Porcelain and Pop."
—, and Peter Schjeldahl. *Adrian Saxe.*
Schjeldahl, Peter. "The Smart Pot: Adrian Saxe."

SCHEIER, EDWIN and MARY

Horn, Richard. *Fifties Style: Then and Now.*
Levin, Elaine. "Pioneers . . . Edwin and Mary Scheier."
Randall, Ruth Hunie. "Ceramics by Edwin and Mary Scheier."
—. "Potter Looks at Scheier Pottery."

SCHRECKENGOST, VIKTOR

Grafly, Dorothy. "Viktor Schreckengost."
Hoffman, J., et al. *A Study in Regional Taste.*
McCullough, Joseph, and Joseph Schmeckebier. *Viktor Schreckengost.*
Milliken, William M. "Ohio Ceramics."
"New Designs for Mass Production . . . by V. Schreckengost."
Perry, Barbara. "The Figure Emerges."
Stubblebine, James, and Martin P. Eidelberg. "Viktor Schreckengost."
"Viktor Schreckengost."

SHANER, DAVID

Clark, Larry. "David Shaner."
Rhodes, Daniel. "David Shaner."

SHAW, RICHARD

Albright, Thomas. "San Francisco: Star Streaks."
Barcellana, M. "Shaw Sculpture."
Brody, Harvey. *The Book of Low-Fire Ceramics.*
Butterfield, Jan. *Richard Shaw/Ceramic Sculpture.*
Chicago, Judy, et al. *Overglaze Imagery.*
Foley, Suzanne. *Richard Shaw/Robert Hudson: Works in Porcelain.*
—. *Richard Shaw, Ed Blackburn.*
—, and Richard Marshall. *Ceramic Sculpture.*
Glueck, Grace. "Art: The Clay Figure at the Craft Museum."
Hopkins, Henry T. *50 West Coast Artists.*

Hughes, Robert. "Molding the Human Clay."
Jones, Mady. *Figurative Clay Sculpture: Northern California.*
Kelley, Jeff. "Re Clay."
—. *Potters and Prints.*
—. "Potters and Prints."
Kramer, Hilton. "Ceramic Sculpture and the Taste of California."
Larson, Kay. "California Clay Rush."
McChesney, Mary Fuller. "Porcelain by Richard Shaw and Robert Hudson."
Pugliese, Joseph. "Ceramics from Davis."
—. *Richard Shaw: Illusionism in Clay 1971–1985.*
Schjeldahl, Peter. "California Goes to Pot."
Slivka, Rose. *The Object as Poet.*
—. *West Coast Ceramics.*
—. "Richard Shaw at Frumkin."

SHEERER, MARY G.

Ormond, Suzanne, and Mary E. Irvine. *Louisiana's Art Nouveau.*
Poesch, Jessie. *Newcomb Pottery.*
Sheerer, Mary G. "Newcomb Pottery."
—. "The Development of the Decorative Processes at Newcomb."
—, and Paul E. Cox. "Newcomb Pottery."
Smith, Kenneth E. "Ceramics at Newcomb College."

SHIRAYAMADANI, KATARO

Trapp, Kenneth R. "Japanese Influence in Early Rookwood Pottery."

SHIRE, PETER

Maines, Penny, ed. *Art in Clay.*

SICARD, JACQUES

Henzke, Lucille. "Weller's Sicardo."

SILVER, ANNA

Chambers, Karen. "Anna Silver."

SINGER, SUSI

Bielheimer, Ruth. "Viennese Ceramic Artist Becomes Pasadenan."
Levin, Elaine. "Vally Wieselthier/Susi Singer."
Neuwirth, Waltraud. *Wiener Keramik.*

SOLDNER, PAUL

Ballatore, Sandy. *Viewpoint Ceramics, 1980.*
Dunham, Judith. "Paul Soldner."
Levin, Elaine. "Portfolio: Paul Soldner."
Melchert, Jim, and Paul Soldner. *The Fred and Mary Marer Collection.*

Levin, Elaine. "Peter Voulkos: A Retrospective, 1949–1978."
—. "Portfolio: Peter Voulkos."
Los Angeles County Museum of Art. *Peter Voulkos: Sculpture.*
McCloud, Mac. "Otis Clay: 1956–1957."
Melchert, Jim. "Peter Voulkos: A Return to Pottery."
—, and Paul Soldner. *The Fred and Mary Marer Collection.*
Muchnic, Suzanne. "Reviews: Chris Staley/ Beatrice Wood."
The Museum of Modern Art, New York. *Peter Voulkos.*
Perreault, John. "Fear of Clay."
Phillips, Lisa, ed. *High Styles.*
Schjeldahl, Peter. "California Goes to Pot."
Senska, Frances. "Pottery in a Brickyard."
Slivka, Rose. "Peter Voulkos at Bonnier's."
—. "The New Ceramic Presence."
—. The New Clay Drawings of Peter Voulkos."
—. *Peter Voulkos: A Dialogue with Clay.*
Soldner, Paul E., and Peter Voulkos. "Ceramics West Coast."
Victoria and Albert Museum. *20 American Studio Potters.*
Wilson, William. "S.F. Exhibit: Clay . . . And Now Moscone."

WALTERS, CARL

Anderson, Ross, and Barbara Perry. *The Diversions of Keramos.*
Brace, E. "Carl Walters."
Hegarty, M. "Caterpillar by Carl Walters."
Homer, William I. "Carl Walters, Ceramic Sculpture."
Perry, Barbara. "The Figure . . . American Clay Sculpture 1925–1950."

WARASHINA, PATTI

Ashton, Dore. "Perceiving the Clay Figure."
Chicago, Judy, et al. *Overglaze Imagery.*
Dempsey, Bruce H. *Master Craftsmen.*
Harrington, LaMar. *Ceramics of the Pacific Northwest.*
Klemperer, Louise. "Surreal or So Real?"

WEINRIB, DAVID

Duberman, Martin. *Black Mountain: An Exploration in Community.*
Harris, Mary Emma. *The Arts and Black Mountain College.*
Richards, M. C. "Black Mountain College: A Golden Seed."

WIESELTHIER, VALERIE ("VALLY")

Levin, Elaine. "Vally Wieselthier/Susi Singer."
Neuwirth, Waltraud. *Wiener Keramik.*

WILDENHAIN, FRANS

Norton, Deborah. "Frans Wildenhain."
Richards, M. C. "Frans Wildenhain."
Rochester Institute of Technology. *Frans Wildenhain.*

WILDENHAIN, MARGUERITE

Bray, Hazel. *The Potter's Art in California: 1885–1955.*
"Ceramics: Double Issue."
Horn, Richard. *Fifties Style: Then and Now.*
Petterson, Richard B. "Marguerite Wildenhain."
Press, Nancy, and Terry F. A. Weihs. *Marguerite Wildenhain: A Retrospective.*
Prothro, Hunt. "Sustained Presence: Marguerite Wildenhain."
Wildenhain, Marguerite. "Pottery as a Creative Craft."
—. "An Open Letter to Bernard Leach from Marguerite Wildenhain."
—. *Pottery: Form and Expression.*
—. *Invisible Core: A Potter's Life and Thoughts.*

WOOD, BEATRICE

"Beatrice Wood's Ceramics."
Bryan, Robert. "The Ceramics of Beatrice Wood."
—. "The Art of Ceramic Light—Beatrice Wood."
—. "Beatrice Wood."
—, and Francis M. Naumann. *Beatrice Wood: Retrospective.*
"Ceramics by B. Wood."
Clark, Garth. "Beatrice Wood Luster: The Art of Ceramic Light."
Danisch, Jim, and Richard Handley. "Beatrice Wood."
Frankel, Robert H. *Beatrice Wood: A Retrospective.*
Freudenheim, Betty. "Lusterware Shown by California Potter."
Hapwood, E. R. "All the Cataclysms: . . . the Life of Beatrice Wood."
Hare, Denise. "The Lustrous Life of Beatrice Wood."
Horn, Richard. *Fifties Style: Then and Now.*
Knight, Christopher. "Portrait of a Bohemian Artist."

Muchnic, Suzanne. "Reviews: Chris Staley/ Beatrice Wood."
Naumann, Francis. "Drawings of Beatrice Wood."
Nin, Anaïs. "Beatrice Wood."
Speigel, Janet. "A Dinner with Mama to the Dadas."
Steinbaum, Bernice. *Elders of the Tribe.*
Wood, Beatrice. *I Shock Myself.*

WOODMAN, BETTY

Clark, Garth. *Betty Woodman: The Storm in a Teacup.*
—, et al. *Who's Afraid of American Pottery?*
—; Gert Staal; et al. *Functional Glamour.*
DeVore, Richard. "Ceramics of Betty Woodman."
Fairbanks, Jonathan, and K. W. Moffett. *Directions in American Ceramics.*
Falk, Lorne. "The Omaha Brickworks."
Frank, Peter. "Joyce Kozloff and Betty Woodman: A Collaboration."
Jensen, Robert. "Architectural Ceramics: Eight Concepts."
Kansas City Art Institute. *Eight Independent Production Potters.*
Lang, Ron. "NCECA/SuperMud Conference."
McTwigan, Michael. "An Interior Exchanged."
Perreault, John. "Fear of Clay."
—. "Pattern of Exchange."
Perrone, Jeff. *The Ceramics of Betty Woodman.*
Phillips, Lisa, ed. *High Styles.*
Rubin, Michael G. *Architectural Ceramics: 8 Concepts.*
Woodman, Betty, and George Woodman. "Ceramists' Odyssey . . . Italy."
Woodman, George. "Ceramic Decoration."

WYMAN, WILLIAM

Horowitz, Israel. "William Wyman: The Rebel in the Conservative."
Montgomery, S. J. "William Wyman."
Victoria and Albert Museum. *20 American Studio Potters.*

YOUNGBLOOD, DAISY

Henry, Gerrit. "Daisy Youngblood at Barbara Gladstone."
Indiana, Gary. "Framing Creatures."
McTwigan, Michael. *In the Eye of the Beholder.*
Silverthorne, Jeanne. "Daisy Youngblood."

ZIMMERMAN, ARNOLD

Priest, Ellen. "Arnold Zimmerman."
Wechsler, Susan. *The Raw Edge.*

Abatt, Corinne. "Ceramic Artist Makes A Forceful Statement," *Birmingham Eccentric* (September 15, 1977).

Adrian, Dennis. "Robert Arneson's Feats of Clay," *Art in America* 62 (September 1974).

"Akio Takamori," *Ceramics Monthly* 31 (September 1983).

Albright, Thomas. "Zappy Artists in Richmond," *San Francisco Chronicle* (February 8, 1973).
—. "Grisly Experiments in the Medical Arts." *San Francisco Chronicle* (November 11, 1975).
—. "San Francisco: Mickey Mouse and Memorabilia," *ARTnews* 75 (March 1976).
—. "Digging in for the Magic," *San Francisco Chronicle* (May 6, 1976).
—. "Peter Voulkos, What Do You Call Yourself?" *ARTnews* 77 (October 1978).
—. "San Francisco: Star Streaks," *ARTnews* 78 (April 1979).
—. "The Dividing Line between Ceramics and Schlock," *San Francisco Chronicle* (August 21, 1979).
—. "Mythmaker Art—Humor and Fantasy," *San Francisco Chronicle* (August 8, 1981).
—. "In Memoriam, In Storage," *ARTnews* 81 (February 1982).
—. *Art in the San Francisco Bay Area, 1945–1980: An Illustrated History.* Berkeley: University of California Press, 1985.

Alcauz, Marie de. *Ceci n'est pas le Surréalisme—California Idioms of Surrealism.* Los Angeles: Fisher Gallery, University of Southern California, 1984.

Alexander, Donald E. *Roseville Pottery for Collectors.* Richmond, Ind.: Privately published, 1970.

Alloway, Lawrence. "Roy Lichtenstein's Period Style," *Arts* 42 (January 1967).

The American Federation of Arts. *Critical Comments on the International Exhibition of Ceramic Art.* New York: The American Federation of Arts, 1928.
—. *International Exhibition of Ceramic Art.* New York: The Metropolitan Museum of Art, 1928.

Anderson, Ross, and Barbara Perry. *The Diversions of Keramos: American Clay Sculpture 1925–1950.* Syracuse, N.Y.: Everson Museum of Art, 1983.

Anderson, Timothy J., et al. *California Design, 1910.* Pasadena, Calif.: Pasadena Center, 1974.

Andrea, Christopher. "Interview: Jim Melchert and His Games," *Christian Science Monitor* (January 10, 1969).

Andreson, Laura. "The Natzlers," *California Arts and Architecture* 58 (July 1941).

Archbold, G. "Ceramic Sculpture of Russell Aitken," *Design* 36 (December 1934).

Armstrong, Lois. "Los Angeles: Roy Forest and Robert Arneson," *ARTnews* 68 (October 1969).

Armstrong, Tom, et al. *200 Years of American Sculpture.* N.p.: Godine in association with the Whitney Museum of American Art, 1976.

Arneson, Robert. *My Head in Ceramics.* Davis, Calif.: Privately published, 1972.

Arnest, Barbara M. *Van Briggle Pottery: The Early Years.* Colorado Springs, Colo.: Colorado Springs Fine Arts Center, 1975.

"Art Nelson," *Ceramics Monthly* 29 (June 1981).

"The Art with the Inferiority Complex," *Fortune* 16 (December 1937).

Artner, Alan G. "Ceramics: From Craft to Class," *Chicago Tribune* (February 8, 1976).
—. "Duckworth: Shaped by Honor," *Chicago Tribune* (June 10, 1977).
—. "Vessels Brimming with Excellence: Richard DeVore's Powerful Pottery," *Chicago Tribune* (May 1, 1983).

"Arts of Living," *Architectural Forum* 90 (March 1949).

Ashbery, John. "Feelin' Grueby," *New York* (March 17, 1980).

Ashton, Dore. "Exhibitions: Peter Voulkos," *Craft Horizons* 20 (April 1960).
—. *Modern American Sculpture.* New York: Harry N. Abrams, 1967.
—. "New York Commentary," *Studio International* 178 (1969).
—. "Perceiving the Clay Figure," *American Craft* 41 (April 1981).
—, et al. *Multiplicity in Clay, Metal & Fiber.* Saratoga Springs, N.Y.: Department of Art, Skidmore College, 1984.

Auer, James. "Collector: Karen Johnson Keland," *American Craft* 42 (April 1982).

Ault, R. "Mary Chase Perry Stratton and Her Pewabic Pottery," *Great Lakes Informant* (n.d.).

Autio, Lela, and Rudy Autio. "Peter H. Voulkos," *Montana Institute of Arts Quarterly* (Fall 1954).

Autio, Rudy. "About Drawing," *Studio Potter* 14 (December 1985).

Avery, C. L. "Memorial Exhibition of the Work of Charles F. Binns," *The Metropolitan Museum of Art Bulletin* 30 (May 1935).

Axel, Jan, and Karen McCready. *Porcelain: Traditions and New Visions.* New York: Watson-Guptill, 1981.

Bacher, H. R. "Problems of the Present-Day Art Pottery," *The Bulletin of the American Ceramic Society* 17 (August 1938).

Backlin, Hedy. "Collaboration: Artist and Architect," *Craft Horizons* 32 (May 1962).

Baggs, Arthur E. "The Story of a Potter," *Handicrafter* 1 (April 1929).

Bailey, Clayton. *Catalogue of Kaolithic Curiosities and Scientific Wonders.* Porta Costa, Calif.: Wonders of the World Museum, 1975.

Baker, Kenneth. "Arneson Takes on Nuclear Threat," *San Francisco Chronicle* (November 9, 1985).

Ball, F. Carlton. *Decorating Pottery with Clay, Slip and Glaze.* Columbus, Ohio: Professional Publications, 1967.
—. "Autobiographical Notes: Part 1," *Ceramics Monthly* 29 (March 1981).
—. "Autobiographical Notes: Part 2," *Ceramics Monthly* 29 (April 1981).
—, and Janice Lovoos. *Making Pottery without a Wheel: Texture and Form in Clay.* New York: Reinhold, 1967.

Ball, Fred. "Arneson," *Craft Horizons* 34 (February 1974).

Ballatore, Sandy. "The California Clay Rush," *Art in America* 64 (July 1976).
—. *Viewpoint Ceramics, 1980.* El Cajon, Calif.: Grossmont College, 1983.

Barber, Edwin Atlee. "Recent Advances in the Pottery Industry," *Popular Science Monthly* 40 (January 1892).
—. *Catalogue of American Potteries and Porcelain.* Philadelphia: Pennsylvania Museum, 1893.

—. *Pottery and Porcelain of the United States: Marks of American Potters.* New York: J. P. Putnam's Sons, 1893.

—. "Cincinnati Women Art Workers," *Art Interchange* 36 (February 1896).

—. *Marks of American Potters.* Philadelphia: Patterson and White Company, 1904.

Barbero, Kathleen Hill. "Portfolio: Cowan Pottery," *Ceramics Monthly* 33 (October 1985).

Barcellana, M. "Shaw Sculpture," *Ceramics Monthly* 24 (March 1976).

Barlow, Cynthia. "Arts Review," *Saint Louis Globe* (September 19, 1965).

Barnard, Rob. "Interview with Garth Clark," *New Art Examiner* 13 (September 1985).

Barnes, Benjamin H. *The Moravian Pottery: Memories of Forty-Six Years.* Doylestown, Pa.: Bucks County Historical Society, 1970.

Baro, Gene. "Roy Lichtenstein: Technique and Style," *Art International* 12 (November 1968).

Barrie, Dennis. "Edris Echardt Interviewed," *Link* 12, no. 3. (1978).

Battcock, Gregory, *Super Realism: A Critical Anthology.* New York: Dutton Paperbacks, 1975.

Beardsley, John, Jane Livingston, and Octavio Paz. *Hispanic Art in the United States: Thirty Contemporary Painters and Sculptors.* Houston: Museum of Fine Arts, 1987.

"Beatrice Wood's Ceramics," *Arts and Architecture* 64 (1947).

Bell, David. "Rick Dillingham: Works in Clay," *Artlines* 2 (November 1981).

Bell, Michael S. *Nancy Carman.* Philadelphia: Helen Drutt Gallery, 1985.

Bellevue Art Museum. *Howard Kottler: Recent Clay Sculpture.* Bellevue, Wash.: Bellevue Art Museum, 1987.

Belloli, Jay, ed. *Contemporary Ceramic Vessels: Two Los Angeles Collections.* Pasadena, Calif.: Baxter Art Gallery, California Institute of Technology, 1984.

Belot, Leon. *Taxile Doat Céramiste.* Sèvres, France, 1909.

Benezra, Neal. *Robert Arneson: A Retrospective.* Des Moines, Iowa: Des Moines Art Center, 1985.

Benjamin, Marcus. "The American Art Pottery," *Glass and Pottery World* 15 (February 1907).

Bernstein, Melvin H. "To Think for Industry and the A.C.S.," in *Transactions of the Ceramics Symposium 1979,* ed. Garth Clark. Los Angeles: Institute for Ceramic History, 1980.

—. *Art and Design at Alfred: Chronicle of a Ceramics College.* Philadelphia: Associated University Presses, 1986.

—, and Val Cushing. *Ted Randall (1914–1985): A Retrospective.* Syracuse, N.Y.: Lowe Art Gallery, Syracuse University, 1987.

Bettleheim, Judith. "Pacific Connections," *American Crafts* 46 (April 1986).

—, and Jay Kvapil, eds. *NCECA: San Jose 1982.* Alfred, N.Y.: National Council on Education for the Ceramic Arts, 1982.

Bevlin, M. E. *Design Through Discovery.* New York: Holt, Rinehart and Winston, 1967.

Bielheimer, Ruth. "Prominent Viennese Ceramic Artist Becomes Pasadenan," *Star News* (December 1939).

Binns, Charles Fergus. *Notes on the History and Manufacture of Pottery and Porcelain.* London: Newton, 1894.

—. *Ceramic Technology.* London: Scott, Greenwood, 1898.

—. *The Story of the Potter.* London: G. Newnes, 1898.

—. "In Defense of Fire," *The Craftsman* (March 1903).

—. *The Potter's Craft.* London: Constable, 1910.

—. "Pottery in America," *American Magazine of Art* 7 (February 1916).

—, et al. *Manual of Ceramic Calculations.* Columbus, Ohio, 1900.

Bismanis, Maija, and Ric Gomez. *The Continental Clay Connection.* Regina, Sask.: MacKenzie Art Gallery, University of Regina, 1980.

Blackall, C.H. "The Grueby Faience," *Brick Builder* 7 (August 1898).

Blasberg, Robert W. "Newcomb Pottery," *Antiques* 94 (July 1968).

—. "Reform Art for a Reform Era," *Craft Horizons* 30 (October 1970).

—. "Moravian Tile: Fairy Tales in Colored Clay," *Spinning Wheel* 27 (June 1971).

—. "Grueby Art Pottery," *Antiques* 100 (August 1971).

—. "The Sadie Irvine Letters," *Antiques* 100 (August 1971).

—. *George E. Ohr and His Biloxi Art Pottery.* Port Jervis, N.Y.: J. W. Carpenter, 1972.

—. "Twenty Years of Fulper," *Antiques* 29 (October 1973).

—. *Grueby.* Syracuse, N.Y.: Everson Museum of Art, 1981.

—, and Carol L. Bohdan. *Fulper Art Pottery: An Aesthetic Appreciation, 1909–1929.* New York: Jordan-Volpe Gallery, 1979.

Bleicher, Fred, et al. *Pewabic Pottery: An Official History.* Ann Arbor, Mich.: Arts Ceramica, 1977.

Bodine, Sarah. "Mocking the Strongman Image: The Vessels of Christopher Gustin," *American Ceramics* 1, no. 2 (1982).

—. "Val Cushing," *American Ceramics* 1, no. 3 (1982).

—. "Ralph Bacerra," *American Ceramics* 2, no. 3 (1983).

—, and Michael Dunas. "The Precarious Scale of Justice: Richard Notkin's Precious Protest," *American Ceramics* 5, no. 3 (1987).

—, and Gerry Williams. *Studio Pottery Book.* Warner, N.H.: Daniel Clark Books, 1978.

Bogatay, P. "There's Madness in Method," *Design* 50 (June 1948).

Bogue, Dorothy McGray. *The Van Briggle Story.* Colorado Springs, Colo.: Century One Press, 1976.

Bohnert, Thom. "Linear Order," *Studio Potter* 14 (December 1985).

Bopp, H. F. "Art and Science in the Development of Rookwood Pottery," *The Bulletin of the American Ceramic Society* 15 (1936).

Boris, Eileen. *Art and Labor.* Philadelphia: Temple University Press, 1986.

Boulden, Jane L. "Rookwood," *Art Interchange* 46 (June 1901).

Bourdon, David. "The Sleek, Witty and Elegant Art of Elie Nadelman," *Smithsonian* (February 1975).

Bowdoin, W. G. "The Grueby Pottery," *Art Interchange* 45 (December 1900).

Bower, Gary. "Clayton Bailey," *Craft Horizons* 28 (January 1968).

Brace, E. "Carl Walters," *Creative Art* 10 (June 1932).

Brawer, Katherine. "Don Reitz and Bruce Breckenridge," *Ceramics Monthly* 19 (March 1971).

Bray, Hazel. *California Ceramics and Glass 1974.* Oakland, Calif.: The Oakland Museum, 1974.

—. *The Potter's Art in California: 1885–1955.* Oakland, Calif.: The Oakland Museum, 1980.

—, and Garth Clark. *Harrison McIntosh: Studio Potter.* Chaffey, Calif.: Rex W. Wignall Museum, 1979.

Breck, Joseph. *Adelaide Alsop Robineau.* New York: The Metropolitan Museum of Art, 1929.

Breckenridge, Bruce M. *Critters/Clayton Bailey.* New York: Museum of Contemporary Crafts, 1964.

—. "The Object: Still Life," *Craft Horizons* 25–26 (September 1965).

Brinker, Lea J. "Women's Role in the Development of Art in 19th-Century Cincinnati." Master's thesis, University of Cincinnati, 1970.

Britton, Allison. "American Ceramics Today," *Ceramics* 1 (May 1986).

Brodbeck, John. "Cowan Pottery," *Spinning Wheel* 29 (March 1973).

Brody, Harvey. *The Book of Low-Fire Ceramics.* New York: Holt, Rinehart and Winston, 1979.

Broner, R. "Exhibitions," *Craft Horizons* 27 (January 1967).

Brown, Christopher. "Bob Arneson—From Comic Books to Self-Portrait," *Artweek* 7 (October 16, 1976).

—. "Karen Breschi's Fantasies," *Artweek* (March 18, 1978).

Brown, Conrad. "Peter Voulkos," *Craft Horizons* 16 (October 1956).

—. "Toshiko Takaezu," *Craft Horizons* 19–20 (March 1959).

Brown, Sylvia. "The Tough and Tender Look of Ron Nagle's Wares," in *Ron Nagle: Adaline Kent Award Exhibition.* San Francisco: San Francisco Art Institute, 1978.

Bruhn, Thomas P. *American Decorative Tiles 1870–1930.* Storrs, Conn.: The William Benton Museum of Art, The University of Connecticut, 1979.

Brunk, Thomas W. "Pewabic Pottery," in *Arts and Crafts in Detroit 1906–1976.* Detroit: The Detroit Institute of Arts, 1976.

—. Pewabic Pottery: Marks and Labels. Detroit: Historical Indian Village Press, 1978.

—. "The Pewabic Pottery," in *Transactions of the Ceramics Symposium 1979,* ed. Garth Clark. Los Angeles: Institute for Ceramic History, 1980.

Brunner, Astrid. "Edges in Thought, in History, in Clay," *Arts Atlantic* 25 (Spring 1986).

Brunsman, Sue. "The European Origins of Early Cincinnati Art Pottery 1870–1900." Master's thesis, University of Cincinnati, 1973.

Bryan, Robert. "The Ceramics of Beatrice Wood," *Craft Horizons* 30 (April 1970).

Burstein, Joanne. "Michael and Magdalena Frimkess," *American Ceramics* 1, no. 4 (1982).

—. "Philip Cornelius: The Container Continuum," *American Ceramics* 1, no. 4 (1982).

—. "The Travels of John Roloff," *American Ceramics* 2, no. 3 (1983).

—. "Jane Ford Aebersold," *American Ceramics* 2, no. 1 (1983).

—. "Stephen DeStaebler," *American Ceramics* 3, no. 1 (1984).

—. "Robert Turner," *American Ceramics* 3, no. 4 (1985).

Burton, William. "Oriental Influence on 20th-Century Pottery," *The Pottery Gazette* 44 (1985).

Busch, Akiko. "Decorated Tiles: A Medium to Conjure With," *Metropolis* (April 1983).

—. "Raymon Elozua," *American Ceramics* 5, no. 3 (1987).

Butterfield, Jan. *Richard Shaw/Ceramic Sculpture.* San Francisco: Braunstein Gallery, 1981.

—. *Viola Frey: Paintings/Sculpture/Drawings.* San Francisco: Quay Gallery, 1983.

Buxton, Virginia Hillway. *Roseville Pottery for Love or Money.* Nashville, Tenn.: Tymbre Hill, 1977.

Buzio, Lidya. "Ceramic Cityscapes," *Studio Potter* 11 (1983).

—. "Line and Rhythm," *Studio Potter* 14 (December 1985).

"California Ceramics," *Art Digest* 12 (March 15, 1938).

"California Crafts and Craftsmen," *Craft Horizons* 16 (September 1956).

California State University, Hayward. *An Educational Exhibit by Professor Clayton Bailey.* Hayward, Calif.: California State University, 1977.

California State University, Los Angeles. *Clay Images.* Los Angeles: California State University, 1974.

Calkins, Donald H. "Cowan Pottery," *Antique Dealer Weekly* (November 30, 1977).

—. "Cowan Returns Home," *American Art Pottery* (March 1978).

Canavier, Elean Karina. "Kohler Conference: Art Industry Alliance," *Ceramics Monthly* 21 (November 1973).

Canfield, Ruth, "The Pottery of Vally Wieselthier," *Design* 31 (October 1979).

Cardozo, Sidney. "Rosanjin," *Craft Horizons* 31 (April 1972).

Carlson, Prudence, et al. *Tit for Tat Lin.* New York: Alternative Museum, 1984.

Carr, Carolyn. "Andrea Gill/John Gill," *American Craft* 43 (December 1983).

Cary, Elisabeth L., et al. *Critical Comments on the International Exhibition of Ceramic Art.* New York: The American Federation of the Arts, 1928.

"Ceramics by B. Wood," *Arts and Architecture* 63 (January 1946).

"Ceramics by Poor at the Rehn Galleries," *Art Digest* 22 (December 15, 1947).

"Ceramics by Twelve Artists," *Art in America* 52 (December 1964).

"Ceramics: Double Issue," *Design Quarterly* 42–43 (1958).

"Ceramics East Coast," *Craft Horizons* 26 (June 1966).

Chalke, John. "The Ceramic Identity Scandal of the 70s," *Ceramics Monthly* 28 (December 1980).

Chambers, Karen. "Anna Silver," *Craft International* (April 1985).

Chamberlain, Marcia, et al. *NCECA: San Jose '82.* San Jose, CA: National Council on Education for the Ceramic Arts, 1982.

"Charles M. Harder," *The Bulletin of the American Ceramic Society* 38 (November 1959).

Chicago, Judy. "World of the China Painter," *Ceramics Monthly* 26 (May 1978).

—. *The Dinner Party: A Symbol of Our Heritage.* New York: Doubleday, Anchor Press, 1979.

—, et al. *Overglaze Imagery.* Fullerton, Calif.: Art Gallery, California State University, 1977.

Chronicles: Historical References in Contemporary Art. Logan, Utah: Nora Eccles Harrison Museum of Art, Utah State University, 1985.

Cincinnati Historical Society. *Articles on Art and Artists in Cincinnati.* Cincinnati: Cincinnati Historical Society, 1967.

Clark, Edna Maria. *Ohio Art and Artists.* Richmond, Va.: Garrett and Massie, 1932.

Clark, Garth. "The Ceramic Canvas," in *Overglaze Imagery.* Fullerton, Calif.: Art Gallery, California State University, 1977.
—. "Comment," *Ceramics Monthly* 25 (October 1977).
—. *The Biloxi Art Pottery of George E. Ohr.* Jackson, Miss.: Mississippi State Historical Museum, 1978.
—, ed. *Ceramic Art: Comment and Review 1882–1978.* New York: Dutton Paperbacks, 1978.
—. "George E. Ohr—Clay Prophet," *Craft Horizons* 38 (October 1978).
—. *Jerry Rothman: Bauhaus Baroque.* Claremont, Calif.: Ceramic Arts Library, 1978.
—. *New Works in Clay II.* Syracuse, N.Y.: Joe and Emily Lowe Art Gallery, Syracuse University, 1978.
—. "Sam Haile 1909–1948: A Memorial," *Studio Potter* 7, no. 1 (1978).
—. *A Century of Ceramics in the United States 1878–1978.* New York: E. P. Dutton, 1979.
—. "From the Potter's Wheel: An American Art," *Antiques World* 1 (September 1979).
—. *Viewpoint: Ceramics 1979.* El Cajon, Calif.: Grossmont College, 1979.
—. "Beauty in Balance: Two Vases by Adelaide Alsop Robineau," *Antiques World* 2 (February 1980).
—. *Betty Woodman: The Storm in a Teacup.* Rochester, Minn.: Rochester Art Center, 1980.
—. "Ohr/Robineau: A Study in Polarities," in *Transactions of the Ceramics Symposium 1979,* ed. Garth Clark. Los Angeles: Institute for Ceramic History, 1980.
—, ed. *Transactions of the Ceramics Symposium 1979.* Los Angeles: Institute for Ceramic History, 1980.
—. *American Potters: The Work of Twenty Modern Masters.* New York: Watson-Guptill, 1981.
—. "Ceramic Criticism at the Waldorf," *World Crafts Council Newsletter* (August 1981).
—. "Ceramic Vanguard and the West," in *That Awesome Space.* Salt Lake City: Westwater Press, 1981.
—. *Rudolf Staffel.* Philadelphia: Helen Drutt Gallery, 1981.
—. *Viola Frey: Retrospective.* Sacramento, Calif.: Crocker Art Museum, 1981.
—. "Adrian Saxe: An Interview," *American Ceramics* 1, no. 4 (1982).
—. "Ceramic Art: Redefinition," *American Ceramics* 1, no. 1 (1982).

—, ed. *Ceramics and Modernism: Response of the Artist, Designer, Craftsman and Architect.* Los Angeles: Institute for Ceramic History, 1982.
—. *Production Lines: Art/Craft/Design.* Philadelphia: Philadelphia College of Art, 1982.
—. "The Art of Ceramic Light—Beatrice Wood," *Ceramic Arts* 1, no. 1 (1983).
—. "Beatrice Wood," *American Craft* 43, no. 4 (1983).
—. "Beatrice Wood Luster: The Art of Ceramic Light." *Helicon Nine* 8 (1983).
—, ed. *Ceramic Echoes: Historical References in Contemporary Ceramic Art.* Kansas City, Mo.: Nelson-Atkins Museum of Art, 1983.
—. *George E. Ohr.* University, Miss.: University of Mississippi, 1983.
—. "George E. Ohr: Avant-Garde Volumes," *Studio Potter* 12 (December 1983).
—. *Orange County Clay.* Laguna Beach, Calif.: Laguna Beach Museum of Art, 1983.
—. "Leach in America: The 1950s," *Ceramic Arts* 1, no. 2 (1984).
—. "Comment," *American Craft* 46 (December 1985).
—. "George E. Ohr," *American Ceramics* 4, no. 4 (1985).
—. "George E. Ohr," *Antiques* 78 (September 1985).
—. "The Pictorialization of the Vessel: American Ceramics," *Crafts* 80 (May 1986).
—, and Michael Frimkess. *Michael and Magdalena Frimkess: A Retrospective View 1956–1981.* Los Angeles: Garth Clark Gallery, 1982.
—, and Francis M. Naumann. *Beatrice Wood: Retrospective.* Fullerton, Calif.: Art Gallery, California State University, 1983.
—, and Sanford S. Shaman. *The Contemporary American Potter: Recent Vessels.* Cedar Falls, Iowa: Art Gallery, University of Northern Iowa, 1980.
—, and Patterson Sims. *It's All Part of the Clay: Viola Frey.* Philadelphia: Moore College of Art, 1984.
—, and Oliver Watson. *American Potters Today.* London: Victoria and Albert Museum, 1986.
—, et al. *Roberta D. Marks/Ethos.* Miami, Fla.: Roberta Marks, 1983.
—, et al. *Who's Afraid of American Pottery?* 's-Hertogenbosch, the Netherlands: Dienst voor Beeldende Kunst, 1983.
—, et al. *Pacific Connections.* Los Angeles: Los Angeles Institute of Contemporary Art, 1985.

—, Gert Staal; et al. *Functional Glamour: Utility in Contemporary American Ceramics.* 's-Hertogenbosch, the Netherlands: Museum het Kruithuis, 1987.

Clark, Larry. "David Shaner," *Craft Horizons* 35 (June 1978).

Clark, Robert Judson, ed. *The Arts and Crafts Movement in America 1876–1916.* Princeton, N.J.: The Art Museum, Princeton University, 1972.
—, et al. *Design in America: The Cranbrook Vision 1925–1950.* New York: Abrams, 1983.

Clark, Susan. "Intelligence Tempers Collages, Pottery," *Buffalo News* (March 29, 1978).

Clarke, Isaac. *Art and Industry.* Washington, D.C.: Government Printing Office, 1885.

Cobb, James. "Philip Maberry," *American Ceramics* 3, no. 3 (1984).

Cochran, Malcolm. *Contemporary Clay: Ten Approaches.* Hanover, N.H.: Dartmouth College, 1976.

Coffelt, Beth. *Robert Arneson: Self-Portraits.* Philadelphia: Moore College of Art, 1979.
—. "East Is East and West Is West: The Great Divide," *San Francisco Sunday Chronicle* (April 4, 1982).

Cohen, Karl F. *Porcelains by Jack Earl.* New York: Museum of Contemporary Crafts, 1971.

Cohen, Ronny H. "Clay at the Whitney," *American Craft* 42 (February 1982).
—. "Jack Earl," *American Craft* 45 (August 1985).

Colby, Joy H. "Sculpture by Another Name," *Detroit News* (January 22, 1978).

Colgate, Beatrice, "Dorothea O'Hara," *Darien Review* (November 22, 1955).

Collier, Ralph, and Helen Drutt, *Soup Tureens: 1976.* Camden, N.J. Campbell Museum, 1976.

Coplans, John. "Sculpture in California: The Clay Movement," *Artforum* 2 (August 1963).
—. "Out of Clay: West Coast Ceramic Sculpture Emerges as Strong Regional Trend," *Art in America* 51 (December 1963).
—. "The Sculpture of Kenneth Price," *Art International* 8 (March 20, 1964).
—. "Redemption through Ceramics," *ARTnews* 64 (1965).
—. *Abstract Expressionist Ceramics.* Irvine, Calif.: Art Gallery, University of Cali-

fornia, 1966.

—, ed. *Roy Lichtenstein: Documentary Monograph of Modern Art.* New York: Praeger, 1972.

Cowan Pottery Museum. *Cowan Pottery Studio.* Rocky River, Ohio: Ohio Public Library, 1978.

Cowan, R. G. "Fine Art of Ceramics," *Design* 38 (October 1937).

Cox, David. "Utah," *Craft Horizons* 38 (February 1976).

Cox, George. *Pottery for Artists, Craftsmen and Teachers.* New York: Macmillan, 1914.

Cox, Paul E. "Newcomb Pottery Active in New Orleans," *The Bulletin of the American Ceramic Society* 13 (May 1934).

—. "Potteries of the Gulf Coast," *Ceramic Age* 3 (April 1935).

Cox, Warren E. *The Book of Pottery and Porcelain.* New York: Crown, 1944.

Cranbrook Academy of Art. *Maija Grotell.* Bloomfield Hills, Mich.: Cranbrook Art Museum, 1967.

"Cranbrook 12: Portfolio," *Ceramics Monthly* 24 (June 1976).

Cromwell-Lacy, Sherry, ed. *Ceramic Artists: Distinguished Alumni of Kansas City Art Institute.* Kansas City, Mo.: Kemper Gallery, Kansas City Art Institute, 1983.

Cullinan, Helen. "Clay Set in Wheels of Genius," *Cleveland Plain Dealer* (March 14, 1976).

Cummings, Paul. *Robert Arneson: Points of View.* Pittsburgh: Pittsburgh Center for the Arts, 1986.

Curtis, Phil. "Artist Finds Mystery in Pottery," *Albuquerque Journal* (February 23, 1986).

Curtis, Tom. "University of Southern California Offers New Ceramic Courses," *The Bulletin of the American Ceramic Society* 26 (November 1934).

Dale, Sharon. "An Englishman in America: Frederick Hurten Rhead," *American Ceramics* 5, no. 2 (1986).

—. *Frederick Hurten Rhead: An English Potter in America.* Erie, Pa.: Erie Art Museum, 1986.

Daley, William. "Celebration of Clay: 100 Years of American Ceramics at the Everson Museum," *American Craft* 39 (August 1979.)

—. "On Drawing," *American Ceramics* 1, no. 1 (1982).

"Daniel Rhodes: Pottery and the Person," *Ceramics Monthly* 25 (January 1977).

Danisch, Jim, and Richard Handley. "Beatrice Wood," *Ceramics Monthly* 31 (April 1983).

Darling, Sharon S. *Chicago Ceramics and Glass: An Illustrated History, 1871–1933.* Chicago: Chicago Historical Society, 1980.

Dault, Gary M. "With David Gilhooly in the Frog World," *Artscanada* 29 (1972).

Davis, Douglas. "Crock Art," *Newsweek* 78 (July 5, 1971).

Davis, Elrick B. "Ceramic Sculpture Is City's Unique Industry," *Cleveland Press* (July 26, 1928).

Dean, Patty. *Teapots: Sanford M. Besser Collection of Contemporary Teapots.* Little Rock, Ark.: Decorative Arts Museum, Arkansas Arts Center, 1985.

Delius, Jean. "25th Ceramic National," *Craft Horizons* 29 (January 1969)

Dempsey, Bruce H. *Master Craftsmen.* Jacksonville, Fla.: Jacksonville Art Museum, 1982.

Depew, Dave. "The Archie Bray Foundation," *Ceramics Monthly* 20 (May 1972).

Derfner, Phyllis. "New York Letter," *Art International* 19 (April 1975).
—. "Kenneth Price at Willard," *Art in America* 63 (May 1975).

DeTrey, Marianne. "Sam Haile," *Studio Potter* 7, no. 1 (1978).

The Detroit Institute of Arts. *Arts and Crafts in Detroit 1906–1976: The Movement, the Society, the School.* Detroit: The Detroit Institute of Arts, 1976.

DeVore, Richard. "Ceramics of Betty Woodman," *Craft Horizons* 38 (February 1978).

De Vries, Jan. "Exhibitions," *Craft Horizons* 36 (July 1976).

Dibble, Gladys Gage. "Adventurous Experiment," *Christian Science Monitor* (July 1952).

Dickson, Harold E., and Richard Porter. *Henry Varnum Poor 1887–1970.* University Park, Pa.: Museum of Art, Pennsylvania State University, 1983.

Dickson, Joanne A. "John Mason at the Hudson River Museum," *Art in America* 67 (January 1979).

Dietz, Ulysses G. *The Newark Collection of Art Pottery.* Newark, N.J.: The Newark Museum, 1984.

Digby, George Wingfield. *The Work of the Modern Potter in England.* London: John Murray, 1952.

Dillenberger, Jane, and John Dillenberger. *Perceptions of the Spirit.* Indianapolis, Ind.: Indianapolis Museum of Art, 1977.

Dillingham, Rick. *The Vessel.* Dallas: Delahunty Gallery, 1981.

Doat, Taxile. *Grand Feu Ceramics.* Syracuse, N.Y.: Keramik Studio Publishing Co., 1905.
—. *History of American Ceramics: The Studio Potter.* Dubuque, Iowa: Kendall/Hunt, 1978.

Donohoe, Victoria. "Major Ceramic Artist Keeps Things Fundamental," *Philadelphia Inquirer* (December 30, 1976).

Dormer, Peter. *The New Ceramics.* London: Thames and Hudson, 1986.

Drutt, Helen, ed. *Robert L. Pfannebecker Collection.* Philadelphia: Moore College of Art, 1980.
—. *Soup, Soup, Beautiful Soup.* Camden, N.J.: Campbell Museum, 1983.
—. *American Clay Artists '83.* Philadelphia: Clay Studio Gallery, 1983.
—, and Wayne Higby. *Contemporary Arts: An Expanding View.* Princeton, N.J.: The Squibb Gallery, 1986.

Drutt, Matthew. "Graham Marks," *Ceramics Monthly* 32 (June 1984).

Duberman, Martin. *Black Mountain: An Exploration in Community.* New York: E. P. Dutton, 1972.

Duckworth, Ruth, and Alice Westphal. *Ruth Duckworth.* Evanston, Ill.: Exhibit A, 1977.

Dunham, Judith. "Ceramic Bricolage: The Protean Art of Viola Frey," *American Craft* 41 (August 1981).
—. "Paul Soldner," *American Craft* 42 (October 1982).

Earley, George W. "New 'Kaolithic Age' Discoveries in California," *Info Journal* 5 (September 1976).

Eckhardt, Edris. "WPA Ceramics," in *Transactions of the Ceramic Symposium 1979,* ed. Garth Clark. Los Angeles: Institute for Ceramic History, 1980.

Eder, Lynn. "Richard Notkin," *Ceramics Monthly* 30 (November 1982).

Edwards, Sharon. "A Conversation with Stephen DeStaebler," *Ceramics Monthly* 29 (April 1981).

Eidelberg, Martin P. "Tiffany Favrile Pottery," *The Connoisseur* 169 (September 1968).

—. "Art Pottery," in *The Arts and Crafts Movement in America 1878 to 1916.* Princeton, N.J.: Princeton University Press, 1972.

—. "The Ceramic Art of William H. Grueby," *The American Connoisseur* 184 (September 1973).

—. "The American Art Pottery Movement," in *Transactions of the Ceramics Symposium 1979,* ed. Garth Clark. Los Angeles: Institute for Ceramic History, 1980.

—. "Apotheosis of the Toiler," *American Craft* 41 (December 1981).

—, ed. *From the Native Clay.* New York: American Ceramic Art Society, 1987.

Elliot, Charles W. *Pottery and Porcelain: From Early Times Down to the Philadelphia Exposition.* New York: Appleton, 1878.

Elliot, Maude Howe, ed. *Art and Handicrafts in the Women's Building, World's Columbian Exposition.* New York and Paris: Guptill, 1893.

Emerson, Gertrude. "Marblehead Pottery," *Craftsman* 29 (March 1916).

Emery, Olivia H. *Craftsman Lifestyle: The Gentle Revolution.* Pasadena, Calif.: Design Publications, 1977.

Evans, Meryle, and Lorna Sass. *For the Tabletop.* New York: American Craft Museum, 1980.

Evans, Paul F. "American Art Porcelain: the Work of the University City Pottery," *Spinning Wheel* 27 (December 1971).

—. *Art Pottery of The United States: An Encyclopedia of Producers and Their Marks.* New York: Charles Scribner's Sons, 1974.

—. "Newcomb Pottery Decorators," *Spinning Wheel* 30 (April 1974).

—. "Art Pottery in California: An American Era in Microcosm," in *Transactions of the Ceramics Symposium 1979,* ed. Garth Clark. Los Angeles: Institute for Ceramic History, 1980.

—. "Reflections of Frederick Hurten Rhead," *Pottery Collectors Newsletter* 9 (September 1980).

Everson Museum of Art. *Animal Kingdom in American Art.* Syracuse, N.Y.: Everson Museum of Art, 1978.

Fairbanks, Jonathan, and K.W. Moffett. *Directions in American Ceramics.* Boston: Museum of Fine Arts, 1984.

Falk, Lorne. "The Omaha Brickworks," *American Ceramics* 2 (August 1983).

—. "Will Ceramics Secede from the Art World?" *New Art Examiner* 13 (May 1986).

"Fantasy at Kohler," *Craft Horizons* 34 (December 1974).

Felton, David. "Nagle among the Termites," *Rolling Stone* (August 24, 1978).

Ferguson, Kenneth. "Starting at the Ears," *Studio Potter* 14 (December 1985).

Fields, Mary D. "Portfolio: Jugtown Pottery," *Ceramics Monthly* 31 (March 1983).

Fineberg, Jonathan. "Robert Arneson: Pablo Ruiz with Itch," *Harvard Magazine* (January 1984).

Finkel, Marylin. "Susanne Stephenson," *Craft Horizons* 38 (January 1978).

Fischer, Hal. "The Art of Peter Voulkos," *Artforum* 17 (November 1978).

Fiske, Charles. "Art Nelson," *American Ceramics* 2, no. 1 (1983).

Fitzgibbon, John. "Sacramento!" *Art in America* 59 (December 1971).

Flu, E. B. "The Pewabic Pottery at Detroit," *Ceramic Age* (January 1927).

Foley, Suzanne. *A Decade of Ceramic Art: 1962–1972.* San Francisco: San Francisco Museum of Art, 1972.

—. *Richard Shaw/Robert Hudson: Works in Porcelain.* San Francisco: San Francisco Museum of Art, 1973.

—. *Jim Melchert.* San Francisco: San Francisco Museum of Art, 1975.

—. *Richard Shaw, Ed Blackburn, Tony Costanzo, Redd Ekks, John Roloff.* Fullerton, Calif.: Art Gallery. California State University, 1976.

—. "The Ceramic Phenomenon: The Bay Area," in *Transactions of the Ceramics Symposium 1979,* ed. Garth Clark. Los Angeles: Institute for Ceramic History, 1980.

—, and Richard Marshall. *Ceramic Sculpture: Six Artists.* New York: Whitney Museum of American Art, 1981.

—, and Stephen Prokopoff. *Robert Arneson—Retrospective.* Chicago: Museum of Contemporary Art, 1974.

—, and Sherri Warner. *Pacific Currents/Ceramics 1982.* San Jose, Calif.: San Jose Museum of Art, 1982.

Foote, Nancy. "The Photo Realists," *Art in America* 60 (November 1972).

Forde, Ed. "Exhibitions: Adrian Saxe," *American Ceramics* 2 (June 1983).

Fosdick, Marion L. "Modelled Treatment of Pottery," *American Ceramic Society Journal* 9 (1926).

Foster, Edith D. "William A. Robertson, Master Potter," *International Studio* 51 (November 1913).

—. "Dedham Pottery," *House Beautiful* 36 (August 1914).

Fox, Claire G. "Henry Chapman Mercer: Tilemaker, Collector, and Builder Extraordinary," *Antiques* 104 (October 1973).

Frackelton, Richard G. "Susan Frackelton," *The Clay-Worker* 21 (April 21, 1894).

Frackelton, Susan S. *Tried by Fire: A Work on China Painting.* New York: Appleton, 1886.

—. "Organized Effort," *Keramik Studio* 3 (December 1901).

—. "Our American Potteries," *Sketch Book* 5 (October 1905).

—. "Rookwood Pottery," *Sketch Book* 5 (1906).

Frank, Peter. "Joyce Kozloff and Betty Woodman: A Collaboration," *ArtXpress* (May 1981).

Frankel, Robert H. *Beatrice Wood: A Retrospective.* Phoenix: Phoenix Art Museum, 1973.

Frankenstein, Alfred. "Of Bricks, Pop Bottles and a Better Mousetrap," *San Francisco Sunday Examiner and Chronicle* (October 6, 1974).

—. "The Ceramic Sculpture of Robert Arneson," *ARTnews* 75 (January 1976).

—. "Voulkos Gave Creative Precedence to Clay," *San Francisco Chronicle* (February 26, 1978).

Frazier, T. "The Art of Ceramic Sculpture," *American Artist* 5 (November 1941).

French, Myrtle. "Modern Pottery Class: School of the Art Institute of Chicago," *Design* 26 (May 1924).

—. "Freeing the Creative Power of the Individual," *Design* 29 (April 1927).

Freudenheim, Betty. "Lusterware Shown by California Potter," *The New York Times* (October 3, 1985).

—. "Voulkos's Ceramic Pots: Total Involvement in Clay," *The New York Times* (April 17, 1986).

Freylinghuysen, Alice C., ed. *In Pursuit of Beauty: America and the Aesthetic Movement.* New York: The Metropolitan Museum of Art, 1986.

Friedrich, Maria. *A Passionate Vision: Contemporary Ceramics from the Daniel Jacobs Collection.* Lincoln, Mass.: DeCordova and Dana Museum and Park, 1984.

Frimkess, Michael. "The Importance of Being Classical," *Craft Horizons* 26 (March 1986).

Fryatt, F. E. "Pottery in the United States," *Harper's New Monthly Magazine* 62 (February 1881).

Gabriel, Cleota. *See* Reed, Cleota Gabriel.

Galloway, George D. "The Van Briggle Pottery," *Brush and Pencil* 9 (October 1901).

Gardner, Colin. "Reviews: Ferguson and Kraus," *Los Angeles Times* (March 21, 1986).

Gaunt, W. "Design in Pottery: The Position of the Artist," *Commercial Art* 18 (February 1935).

Giambruni, Helen. "Abstract Expressionist Ceramics," *Craft Horizons* 36 (November 1966).
—. "Exhibitions: John Mason," *Craft Horizons* 37 (January 1967).
—. "Reviews: Akio Takamori," *Craft International* (April 1986).

Glasgow, Lukman. *Illusionistic Realism as Defined in Contemporary Ceramic Sculpture.* Laguna Beach, Calif.: Laguna Beach Museum of Art, 1977.
—. "Jerry Rothman," *Ceramics Monthly* 29 (September 1981).

Glenn, Constance W. *Roy Lichtenstein Ceramic Sculpture.* Long Beach, Calif.; University Art Museum, California State University, 1977.

Glick, John. "Renewal," *Studio Potter* 12 (December 1983).

Glueck, Grace. "Art People: A Partner to His Kiln," *The New York Times* (May 15, 1981).
—. "Art: The Clay Figure at the Craft Museum," *The New York Times* (February 20, 1981).

Goodheart, John. "Don Pilcher," *Craft Horizons* 32 (1972).

Grafly, Dorothy. "Viktor Schreckengost," *American Artist* 13 (May 1949).

Gray, Walter Elsworth. "Latter-day Developments in American Pottery," *Brush and Pencil* 10 (January 1902).

Greenberg, Clement. "The Status of Clay," in *Transactions of the Ceramics Symposium 1979*, ed. Garth Clark. Los Angeles: Institute for Ceramic History, 1980.

Gregory, W. "Ceramic Sculpture," *Design* 43 (December 1941).

Gronborg, Erik. "The New Generation of Ceramic Artists," *Craft Horizons* 29 (January 1969).
—. *Viewpoint: Ceramics 1977.* El Cajon, Calif.: Grossmont College, 1977.

Gustin, Chris. "A Potter's Journey," *Ceramics Monthly* 30 (December 1982).

"H. V. Poor," *Art Digest* 22 (December 1947).

Haile, T. S. "English and American Ceramic Design Problems," *The Bulletin of the American Ceramic Society* 21 (1942).

Hakanson, Joy. "A Visit with Maija Grotell," *Detroit News* (August 28, 1960).

Hall, Alice C. "Cincinnati Faience," *Potter's American Monthly* 15 (August 1980).

Hall, Herbert J. "Marblehead Pottery," *Keramik Studio* 10 (June 1908).

Hamilton, David. *Architectural Ceramics.* London: Thames and Hudson, 1978.

Hapwood, E.R. "All the Cataclysms: A Brief Survey of the Life of Beatrice Wood," *Arts Magazine* 52 (1977).

Harder, Charles M. "Functional Design," *The Bulletin of the American Ceramic Society* 21 (August 15, 1942).
—. "A Message to Ceramic Designers," *Ceramic Industry* (June 1945).

Hardranft, Ann. "Everson Offers Varied Shows," *Syracuse Herald Journal American* (May 28, 1972).

Hare, Denise. "The Lustrous Life of Beatrice Wood," *Craft Horizons* 38 (June 1978).

Harrington, LaMar. "Letter from Seattle—Rudy Autio," *Craft Horizons* 23 (June 1963).
—. *Ceramics of the Pacific Northwest.* Seattle, Wash.: University of Washington Press, 1979.

Harris, Mary Emma, *The Arts and Black Mountain College.* Cambridge, Mass.: MIT Press, 1987.

Hasegawa, S., et al. *Isamu Noguchi.* Tokyo: Bijutsu Shuppan-Sha, 1953.

Haskell, Barbara. *John Mason: Ceramic Sculpture.* Pasadena, Calif.: Pasadena Museum of Modern Art, 1974.

Hasselle, Bob. "Rookwood: An American Art Pottery," *Ceramics Monthly* 26 (June 1978).

Haverstadt, Hal. "Ron Nagle in Rock and Glass," *Craft Horizons* 31 (June 1971).

Hawes, Lloyd E. "Hugh Cornwall Robertson and the Chelsea Period," *Antiques* 89 (March 1966).
—. *The Dedham Pottery and the Earlier Robertson's Chelsea Potteries.* Dedham, Mass.: Dedham Historical Society, 1968.

Haworth, Dale K., and Karen F. Beall. "Holding the Center: Warren MacKenzie and the Core of Vesselmaking," *American Ceramics* 3, no. 4 (1985).

Hayward Art Gallery. *Nut Art.* Hayward, Calif.: California State University, 1972.

Hecht, Eugene. "An Ohr Primer: Part I," *American Art Pottery* 67 (December 1981).
—. "An Ohr Primer: Part II," *American Art Pottery* 73 (June 1982).
—. "An Ohr Primer: Part III—The Artist and the Bad Guys," *American Art Pottery* 93 (February 1984).
—. "An Ohr Primer: Part IV," *American Art Pottery* 97 (June 1984).
—. "Artus Van Briggle: The Formative Years," *Arts and Crafts Quarterly* 1 (January 1987).
—. "The East Coast Robertsons," *Ceramics Monthly* 35 (February 1987).

Hegarty, M. "Selected Pieces from Pewabic Pottery by M. C. Stratton," *The Detroit Institute of Arts Bulletin* 26, no. 3 (1947).
—. "Caterpillar by Carl Walters," *The Detroit Institute of Arts Bulletin* 27, no. 3 (1948).

Henderson, R. "Gertrud and Otto Natzler," *Design* 49 (January 1948).

"Henry Varnum Poor 1887–1970," *Craft Horizons* 31 (April 1971).

Henry, Gerrit. "The Clay Landscapes of Mary Frank," *Craft Horizons* 49 (December 1971).
—. "Daisy Youngblood at Barbara Gladstone," *Art in America* 72 (April 1984).

Henzke, Lucille. "Weller's Sicardo," *Spinning Wheel* 25 (September 1969).
—. *American Art Pottery.* Camden, N.J.: Nelson, 1970.

Hepburn, Tony. "American Ceramics 1970," *Ceramic Review* 7 (1970).
—. "The Role of Ceramics in Sculpture—Directions," in *Transactions of the Ceramic Symposium 1979*, ed. Garth Clark. Los Angeles: Institute for Ceramic History, 1980.
—. "On Taking Risks: Decline of the Avant-Garde," *American Ceramics* 1, no. 2 (1982).
—. "Art Press Review: Ceramics," *New Art Examiner* 13 (September 1985).

Herman, Lloyd E. *American Porcelain: New Expressions in an Ancient Art.* Forest Grove, Ore.: Timber Press, 1980.

Herrera, Hayden. *Mary Frank: Sculpture/ Drawings/Prints.* Purchase, N.Y.: Neuberger Museum, State University of New York, 1978.

—. "Myth and Metamorphosis: Mary Frank," *Artscanada* 35 (April 1978).

—. *Mary Frank: Sculpture and Monotypes 1981/1982.* New York: Zabriskie Gallery, 1982.

Hewitt, Edwin. *Small Sculptures by Elie Nadelman.* New York: Edwin Hewitt Gallery, 1950.

Higby, Wayne. "The Vessel Is Like a Pot," *American Ceramics* 3, no. 4 (1985).

—. "Drawing as Intelligence," *Studio Potter* 14, no. 1 (December 1985).

—. "The Vessel: Denying Function," *Ceramics Monthly* 34 (December 1986).

—, and Graham Marks. *Useful Pottery.* Rochester, N.Y.: Pyramid Arts Center, 1986.

High-Fire Porcelains: Adelaide Alsop Robineau, Potter. San Francisco: Panama-Pacific International Exposition, 1915.

"Hirschhorn Collection," *Ceramics Monthly* 23 (May 1975).

Hobbs, Louise. *Contemporary Ceramic Sculpture.* Chapel Hill, N.C.: William Hayes Ackland Art Center, University of North Carolina, 1977.

Hoffman, J., et al. *A Study in Regional Taste: The May Show 1919–1975.* Cleveland: Cleveland Art Institute, 1977.

Hoffman, Marilyn. "Each Piece Should Come from the Potter's Hand, Says Robert Sperry," *Christian Science Monitor* (July 15, 1964).

—. "Collecting the Crafts," *American Craft* 43 (February 1983).

Homer, William I. "Carl Walters, Ceramic Sculpture," *Art in America* 44 (1956).

Hopkins, Henry T. "Kenneth Price, Untitled Ceramic," *Artforum* 2 (August 1963).

—. *50 West Coast Artists.* San Francisco: Chronicle Books, 1981.

Horn, Richard. *Fifties Style: Then and Now.* New York: Beech Tree Press, 1985.

Horowitz, Israel. "William Wyman: The Rebel in the Conservative," *Craft Horizons* (October 1970).

Hughes, Robert. "Molding the Human Clay," *Time* (January 18, 1982).

—. "The Arcadian as Utopian," *Time* (January 24, 1983).

Hughto, Margie. *New Works in Clay by Contemporary Painters and Sculptors.* Syracuse, N.Y.: Everson Museum of Art, 1976.

Hull, William. "Some Notes on Early Robineau Porcelains," *Everson Museum of Art Bulletin* 22 (1960).

Huntington, Richard. "Pots Echo Distant Times," *Buffalo Courier Express* (April 25, 1980).

Hurley, Joseph. "Excellence: Toshiko Takaezu," *American Craft* 39 (October 1979).

Hutson, Ethel. "Newcomb Pottery, A Successful Experiment in Applied Art," *The Clay Worker* 45 (1906).

Indiana, Gary. "Framing Creatures," *The Village Voice* (May 7, 1985).

Isaacs, W. F. "Paul Bonifas, Potter from Switzerland," *Design* 49 (September 1947).

Iwabuchi, Junko. "Peter Voulkos in Japan," *Ceramics Monthly* 31 (September 1983).

Jaffe-Friede and Straus Galleries. *Contemporary Clay—Ten Approaches.* Hanover, N.H.: Dartmouth College Press, 1976.

"James Lawton," *Ceramics Monthly* 32 (May 1984).

Jarmusch, Ann. "...From Mesas through Canyons to the Sea and Back," *American Craft* 41 (April 1981).

Jense, Robert, and Patricia Conway. *Ornamentalism: The New Decorativeness in Architecture and Design.* New York: Clarkson N. Potter, 1982.

Jensen, Robert. "Architectural Ceramics: Eight Concepts," *American Craft* 45 (June 1985).

"Jerry Rothman," *Ceramics Monthly* 26 (November 1976).

Jervis, William P. *The Encyclopedia of Ceramics.* New York: 1902.

—. "Taxile Doat," *Keramik Studio* 4 (June 1902).

"John and Ruby Glick," *Ceramics Monthly* 23 (January 1975).

Johnson, Evert. "Two Happenings at Southern Illinois University: 1) Clay Unfired," *Craft Horizons* 30 (October 1970).

Johnson, Philip. *Machine Art.* New York: The Museum of Modern Art, 1934.

Johnston, Ellen H. "The Lichtenstein Paradox," *Art and Artists* (January 1966).

Johnston, Patricia A. *Joyce Kozloff: Visionary Ornament.* Boston: Art Gallery, Boston University, 1986.

Johnston, R. H. *Frans Wildenhain.* New York: Rochester Institute of Technology, 1975.

Jones, Harvey L. *Stephen DeStaebler: Sculpture.* Oakland, Calif.: The Oakland Museum, 1974.

Jones, Kenneth W. "Richard E. DeVore," *Philadelphia Arts Exchange* 1 (March 1977).

Jones, Mady. *Figurative Clay Sculpture: Northern California.* San Francisco: Quay Gallery, 1982.

—. "Six at the Whitney: Kudos to Come," *American Ceramics* 1, no. 1 (1982).

Judd, Donald. "Robert Arneson," *Arts Magazine* 39 (January 1965).

Kalamazoo Institute of Arts. *Contemporary Ceramics: The Artist's Viewpoint.* Kalamazoo, Mich.: Kalamazoo Institute of Arts, 1977.

Kane, Sid. "Patchwork Pots," *American Craft* 41 (October 1981).

Kangas, Matthew. "Massive Narrations," *American Craft* 40 (October 1980).

—. *Robert Sperry.* Seattle: Erica Williams/ Anne Johnson Gallery, 1981.

—. "Towards a Bicameral Aesthetic of Clay," *American Ceramics* 1, no. 1 (1982).

—. *Rudy Autio Retrospective.* Missoula, Mont., School of Art, University of Montana, 1983.

—. "Tablets of Earth," *American Ceramics* 2, no. 3 (1983).

—. "Rudy Autio," *American Ceramics* 3, no. 4 (1985).

—. "Robert Sperry: Planetary Clay," *American Craft* 41 (December 1986).

Kansas City Art Institute. *Eight Independent Production Potters.* Kansas City, Mo.: Kansas City Art Institute, 1976.

Kaplan, Wendy, ed. *The Art That Is Life.* Boston: Museum of Fine Arts, 1987.

Keen, Kirsten Hoving. *American Art Pottery 1875–1930.* Wilmington, Del.: Delaware Art Museum, 1978.

—. "Art Pottery in Context," in *Transactions of the Ceramics Symposium 1979,* ed. Garth Clark. New York: Institute for Ceramic History, 1980.

Kelder, Diane. "Made in Graphicstudio," *Art in America* 61 (1973).

Keller, Martha. "Susanne Stephenson," *Ceramics Monthly* 30, no. 6 (1982).

Kelley, Jeff. "John Mason," *Arts Magazine* 55 (September 1980).
—. "Re Clay," *Arts Magazine* 56 (March 1982).
—. "In Search of a Transparent Art: John Mason," *American Ceramics* 2, no. 1 (1983).
—. *Potters and Prints.* Sun Valley, Idaho: Sun Valley Center for the Arts, 1984.
—. "Viola Frey," *American Ceramics* 3, no. 1 (1984).
—. "Potters and Prints," *American Ceramics* 4, no. 1 (1985).

Kester, Bernard. "Laura Andreson," *Craft Horizons* 30 (December 1970).
—. "Los Angeles," *Craft Horizons* 36 (December 1976).
—. *Laura Andreson: A Retrospective in Clay.* San Diego, Calif.: Mingei International Museum of World Folk Art, 1982.
—, and S. Peterson. "Exhibitions," *Craft Horizons* 27 (November, 1967).

Keynes, Helen Johnson. "The Pottery of Glen Lukens," *Christian Science Monitor* (April 23, 1940).

King, Mary. "Ceramics Exhibit by Kenneth Price," *St. Louis Post-Dispatch* (October 3, 1976).

King, William A. "Ceramic Art at the Pan American Exhibition," *Crockery and Glass Journal* 53 (May 30, 1901).

Kinsley, Rose. "Rookwood Pottery," *Art Journal* 23 (1897).

Kircher, Edwin J., et al. *Rookwood: Its Golden Era of Art Pottery 1880–1929.* Cincinnati: Rookwood Golden Era, 1969.

Kirstein, Lincoln. *Figures and Figurines by Elie Nadelman.* New York: Edwin Hewitt Gallery, 1958.
—. *Elie Nadelman.* New York: The Eakins Press, 1973.

Klassen, John. "A Conversation with Jack Earl," *Ceramics Monthly* 29 (October 1981).

Klemperer, Louise. "Critical Dimensions: How Shall We Judge?" *American Ceramics* 1, no. 3 (1982).
—. "Wayne Higby," *American Ceramics* 3, no. 4 (1985).
—. "Surreal or So Real?" *American Ceramics* 4, no. 2 (1985).

Kline, Katy. "Pots, Paintings: A Common Thread," *Buffalo* [N.Y.] *Courier Express* (April 1978).

Knight, Christopher. "Otis Clay: A Revolution in the Tradition of Pottery," *Los Angeles Herald Examiner* (September 29, 1982).
—. "Portrait of a Bohemian Artist: Beatrice Wood's Stylish Devices," *Los Angeles Herald Examiner* (February 23, 1983).
—. "Lord of the Latter Day Impressionists," *Los Angeles Herald Examiner* (June 9, 1985).
—. *Andrew Lord: New Work.* New York: BlumHelman, 1986.
—. "Artist's Vessels Sail on a Revolutionary Sea," *Los Angeles Herald Examiner* (November 10, 1986).

Knute, Stiles. "Robert Arneson," *Artforum* 3 (November 1964).

Koch, Robert. "The Pottery of Artus Van Briggle," *Art in America* 52 (June 1964).

Kohl, Joyce. *Clay Alternatives.* Los Angeles: Fisher Gallery, University of Southern California, 1981.

Kohlenberger, Lois H. "Ceramics at the People's University," *Ceramics Monthly* 24 (November 1976).

Koplos, Janet. "Paint on Clay," *American Craft* 41 (June 1981).
—. "Alterations: The Ceramics of Susanne Stephenson," *American Craft* 42 (December 1982).
—. "Exhibitions: Thom Bonhert," *American Ceramics* 2, no. 2 (1983).
—. "Richard DeVore," *Art Papers* 8 (March 1984).

Kovel, Ralph, and Terry Kovel. *Kovel's Collectors Guide to American Art Pottery.* New York: Crown, 1974.

Kramer, Hilton. "The Sculpture of Mary Frank: Poetical, Metaphorical, Interior . . . ," *The New York Times* (February 22, 1970).
—. "For Nadelman, There Is No Lost Grandeur," *The New York Times* (March 17, 1974).
—. "Art: Sensual, Serene Sculpture," *The New York Times* (January 25, 1975).
—. "Sculpture—From Boring to Brilliant," *The New York Times* (May 15, 1977).
—. "Ceramic Sculpture and the Taste of California," *The New York Times* (December 20, 1983).

Krauss, Rosalind. "John Mason and Post-Modernist Sculpture," *Art in America* 67 (May 1979).

Kuspit, Donald B. "Elemental Realities," *Art in America* 69 (January 1981).

—. "Arneson's Outrage," *Art in America* 73 (May 1985).
—. "Robert Arneson's Sense of Self: Squirming in Procrustean Place," *American Craft* 46 (October 1986).

Lafean, Richard. "Ceramics by Twelve Artists," *Craft Horizons* 25 (January 1965).

Lang, Ron. "NCECA/Super Mud Conference," *Ceramics Monthly* 27 (June 1979).
—. *Clay Bodies: Autio—DeStaebler—Frey.* Baltimore: Maryland Institute, College of Art, 1982.

Langston, Linda Frank. *Northern California Clay Routes: Sculpture Now.* San Francisco: San Francisco Museum of Modern Art, 1979.

Larson, Kay. "California Clay Rush," *New York* (January 11, 1982).

Last, Martin. "Robert Arneson," *ARTnews* 68 (December 1969).

Lawson, Donna. "The Constant Cup," *Craft Horizons* 30 (December 1970).

Layton, Peter. "Kenneth Price Cups at Kasmin until 8 February," *Studio International* 179 (February 1970).

Leach, Bernard. *A Potter's Book.* London: Faber & Faber, 1940.

—. "American Impressions," *Craft Horizons* 10 (Winter 1950).

Lebow, Edward. "Val Cushing," *American Ceramics* 1, no. 3 (1982).
—. "Lidya Buzio: Duple Rhythms," *Ceramic Arts* 1, no. 1 (1982).
—. "Lidya Buzio in Perspective," *American Ceramics* 2, no. 2 (1983).
—. "The Flesh Pots of Rudy Autio," *American Graphics* 4, no. 1 (1985).
—. "Robert Turner," *American Ceramics* 46, no. 3 (June 1986).
—. "Ken Price," *Fusion* 10, no. 2 (1987).

Leonard, Ann B. "Pottery and Porcelain at the Paris Exposition," *Keramik Studio* 2 (August 1900).

Levin, Elaine. "Pioneers of Contemporary American Ceramics: Charles Binns, Adelaide Robineau," *Ceramics Monthly* 23 (November 1975).
—. "Pioneers of Contemporary American Ceramics: Arthur Baggs, Glen Lukens," *Ceramics Monthly* 24 (January 1976).
—. "Pioneers of Contemporary American Ceramics: Laura Andreson, Edwin and Mary Scheier," *Ceramics Monthly* 24 (May 1976).

—. "Pioneers of Contemporary American Ceramics: Maija Grotell, Herbert Sanders," *Ceramics Monthly* 24 (November 1976).

—. "Ralph Bacerra," *Ceramics Monthly* 25 (April 1977).

—. "Otto and Vivika Heino," *Ceramics Monthly* 25 (October 1977).

—. "Peter Voulkos: A Retrospective, 1949–1978," *Artweek* (March 18, 1978).

—. "Portfolio: Peter Voulkos," *Ceramics Monthly* 26 (June 1978).

—. "Judy Chicago: The Dinner Party," *Ceramics Monthly* 27 (June 1979).

—. "Portfolio: Paul Soldner," *Ceramics Monthly* 27 (June 1979).

—. *West Coast Clay Spectrum.* Los Angeles: Security Pacific Bank, 1979.

—. "Pioneers of the Vessel Aesthetic: Glen Lukens and Maija Grotell," in *Transactions of the Ceramics Symposium 1979,* ed. Garth Clark. Los Angeles: Institute for Ceramic History, 1980.

—. "Stephen DeStaebler," *Ceramics Monthly* 29 (April 1981).

—. "Maija Grotell," *American Ceramics* 1, no. 1 (1982).

—. "Glen Lukens: Pioneer of the Vessel Aesthetic," *American Ceramics* 1, no. 2 (1982).

—. *Glen Lukens: Pioneer of the Vessel Aesthetic.* Los Angeles: Art Gallery, California State University, 1982.

—. "Glen Lukens," *Ceramics Monthly* 30 (May 1982).

—. "An Interview with Otto Natzler," *Ceramics Monthly* 30 (June 1982).

—. "Mary Louise McLaughlin and the Cincinnati Art Pottery Movement," *American Craft* 42 (December 1982).

—. *Frans Wildenhain.* Rochester, N.Y.: Memorial Art Gallery, University of Rochester, 1984.

—. *The Caroll & Hiroko Hansen Collection of Ceramic Art.* Arvada, Colo.: Arvada Center for the Arts, 1985.

—. "John Roloff," *Ceramics Monthly* (June 1986).

—. "Vally Wieselthier/Susi Singer," *American Craft* 46 (December 1986).

Levin, Kim. "The Ersatz Object," *Arts Magazine* 49 (February 1974).

"Leza McVey," *Ceramics Monthly* 2 (June 1953).

Licka, C. E. "A Primafacie Clay Sampler: A Case for Popular Ceramics, Part I," *Currant* 1 (August 1975).

—, and Wayne Higby. *Graham Marks: New Works.* Syracuse, N.Y.: Everson Museum of Art, 1986.

Ligue Américaine de la Femme. *Catalogue des Porcelaines Robineau.* Saint Louis: University City Publishing, 1911.

Lipofsky, Marvin. "Young Americans: Clay/Glass," *Craft Horizons* 38 (June 1978).

Lippard, Lucy R. "The Dinner Party," *Art in America* 68 (April 1980).

—. "Battle Cries," *The Village Voice* (December 4, 1984).

Long Beach Museum of Art. *Ceramic Conjunction 1977.* Long Beach, Calif.: Long Beach Museum of Art, 1977.

Los Angeles County Museum of Art. *Peter Voulkos: Sculpture.* Los Angeles: Los Angeles County Museum of Art, 1965.

—. *The Ceramic Work of Gertrud and Otto Natzler.* Los Angeles: Los Angeles County Museum of Art, 1966.

Lovoos, Janice. "F. Carlton Ball, Master Potter," *Ceramics Monthly* 13 (September 1965).

Low, J. G., and J. F. Low. *Illustrated Catalogue of Art Tiles.* Chelsea, Mass.: Low Art Tile Works, 1884.

Loyau, Maggy. "Harrison McIntosh," *Cahiers de la Céramique* 56 (1974).

Lucie-Smith, Edward. *Craft Today: Poetry of the Physical.* New York: American Craft Museum, 1986.

Ludwig, Coy. *Arts and Crafts in New York State.* Philadelphia: Tyler School of Art Gallery, Temple University 1983.

Lukens, Glen. "Ceramic Art at the University of Southern California," *Design* 38 (November 1937).

—. "The New Craftsman," *Design* 38 (November 1937).

—. "Potters and Defense," *Los Angeles Times Home Magazine* (June 11, 1943).

McChesney, Mary Fuller. "Porcelain by Richard Shaw and Robert Hudson," *Craft Horizons* 33 (October 1973).

—. "Michael Frimkess and the Cultured Pot," *Craft Horizons* 33 (December 1973).

McCloud, Mac. "Glen Lukens: Pioneer Ceramist," *American Craft* 42 (June 1982).

—. "Otis Clay: 1956–1957," *Ceramics Arts* 1, no. 1 (1983).

—. "Elsa Rady: Porcelain Vessels," *American Ceramics* 3, no. 4 (1985).

—. "Harrison McIntosh," *American Craft* 45 (April 1985).

—. "Ralph Bacerra," *American Craft* 47 (June 1987).

—, and Fred Marer. *Earth and Fire: The Marer Collection of Contemporary Ceramics.* Claremont, Calif.: Galleries of the Claremont Colleges, 1984.

McConathy, Dale. "David Gilhooly's Mythanthropy: From the Slime to the Ridiculous," *Artscanada* 32 (June 1975).

McCready, Karen. *Contemporary American Ceramics—Twenty Artists.* Newport Beach, Calif.: Newport Harbor Art Museum, 1985.

McCullough, Joseph, and Joseph Schmeckebier. *Viktor Schreckengost.* Cleveland: Cleveland Institute of Art, 1976.

McDonald, Robert. "New Work by Ron Nagle," *Artweek* (November 22, 1975).

—. "Daniel Rhodes," *American Craft* 46 (February 1986).

Macht, Carol, and Kenneth Trapp. *The Ladies, God Bless 'em: The Women's Art Movement in Cincinnati.* Cincinnati: Cincinnati Art Museum, 1976.

McGill, Douglas C. "Artworks Enhance Elegance of Region's Restored Train Stations," *The New York Times* (June 14, 1984).

McIntosh, Catherine. "Harrison McIntosh: Studio Potter," *Ceramics Monthly* 27 (October 1979).

McKenna, Kristine. "Wilshire Center," *Los Angeles Times* (April 24, 1986).

MacKenzie, Warren. "Minnesota Pottery: A Potter's View," *Ceramics Monthly* 29 (May 1981).

—. *Minnesota Pottery: A Potter's View.* Minneapolis: Art Gallery, University of Minnesota, 1981.

—. "Comment: The Vessel," *Ceramics Monthly* 35 (February 1986).

McKinley, D. "24th Ceramic National," *Craft Horizons* 36 (December 1966).

McKinnell, J., and Abner Jonas. *Clay Today.* Iowa City, Iowa: University of Iowa, 1963.

McLaughlin, Mary Louise. *Suggestions to China Painters.* Cincinnati: Clarke, 1883.

—. *China Painting: Manual for the Amateur in the Decoration of Hard Porcelain.* Cincinnati: Clarke, 1897.

—. "Losantiware," *The Craftsman* 3 (December 1902).

—. *The China Painters' Handbook: The Practical Series.* Cincinnati: n.p., 1917.

—. "Paper Read at the Meeting of the Porcelain League, April 24, 1914...," *The Bulletin of the American Ceramic Society* 17 (May 1938).

MacSwiggan, Amelia E. "The Marblehead Pottery," *Spinning Wheel* 26 (March 1972).

McTwigan, Michael. *Heroes and Clowns: Robert Arneson.* New York: Allan Frumkin Gallery, 1979.

—. *Ruth Duckworth/Claire Zeisler.* Philadelphia: Moore College of Art, 1979.

—. "Duality in Clay: William Daley," *American Craft* (December 1980).

—. "Figurative Ceramic Sculpture," in *Transactions of the Ceramics Symposium 1979,* ed. Garth Clark. Los Angeles: Institute for Ceramic History, 1980.

—. "First Things First," *American Ceramics* 1, no. 1 (1982).

—. "The Fruitful Mysteries of Graham Marks," *American Ceramics* 1, no. 2 (1982).

—. "An Interior Exchanged: Cynthia Carlson and Betty Woodman in Collaboration," *Arts Magazine* 57 (May 1982).

—. "Andrew Lord," *American Ceramics* 1, no. 3 (1982).

—. "Modernism and Ceramics Today: An Overview," in *Ceramics and Modernism....* Los Angeles: Garth Clark Gallery, 1982.

—. "Ron Nagle," *American Ceramics* 2, no. 4 (1984).

—. "A Handful of Beauty, a Hint of Beast," *American Ceramics* 3, no. 4 (1985).

—. *In the Eye of the Beholder: A Portrait of Our Time.* New Paltz, N.Y.: College Art Gallery, State University of New York, 1985.

Madsen, S. Tshudi. *Sources of Art Nouveau.* Oslo: H. A. Aschehoug, 1956.

Maines, Penny, ed. *Art in Clay: 1950s to 1980s in Southern California.* Los Angeles: Los Angeles Municipal Art Gallery, 1984.

Malarcher, Patricia. "Storytelling in Clay and Fabric," *The New York Times* (June 1, 1986).

Malcolm, J. "On and Off the Avenue: About the House," *The New Yorker* (September 4, 1971).

Mannel, E. "Pacific Coast Ceramic-Sculpture and Pottery Exhibition: Sixth Annual...," *Design* 49 (October 1947).

Marasso, Lizbeth. "Robert Rauschenberg at Castelli and Sonnabend," *Art in America* 71 (April 1983).

Marks, Graham. "Open Letter to the *New York Times*," *Shards Newsletter* 1, no. 1 (1980).

Marling, Karal Ann. *Federal Art in Cleveland 1933–1943.* Cleveland: Cleveland Public Library, 1976.

—. "New Deal Ceramics: The Cleveland Workshop," *Ceramics Monthly* 25 (June 1977).

"Mary Louise McLaughlin: Originator of Plastic Slip Underglaze Painting...," *The Bulletin of the American Ceramic Society* 17 (May 1938).

Matthews, J.M. "Ostend: International Show of Ceramics Today," *Craft Horizons* 19 (September 1959).

Mayeri, Beverly. "Ceramic Portraiture," *Ceramics Monthly* 31 (December 1983).

—. "Expressive Realism," *Ceramics Monthly* 34 (April 1986).

Mehring, Howard. "Richard DeVore," *Washington Review* (December 1977).

—. "Richard DeVore," *Washington Review* (January 1978).

Meisel, Alan R. "Robert Arneson," *Craft Horizons* 24 (September 1964).

—. "Heavy Clay by Stephen DeStaebler," *Craft Horizons* 35 (February 1975).

Melcher, Victoria Kirsch. "Tradition and Vitality: The Ceramics of Ken Ferguson," *American Craft* 39 (December 1979).

Melchert, Jim. "Peter Voulkos: A Return to Pottery," *Craft Horizons* 28 (September 1968).

—. "Fred Marer and the Clay People," *Craft Horizons* 34 (June 1974).

—, and Paul Soldner. *The Fred and Mary Marer Collection.* Claremont, Calif.: Scripps College, 1974.

Mellow, James R. "About Woman as a Sexual Being," *The New York Times* (April 22, 1973).

—. "Mary Frank Explores Women's Erotic Fantasies," *The New York Times* (January 19, 1975).

The Metropolitan Museum of Art, New York. *A Memorial Exhibition of Porcelain and Stoneware by Adelaide Alsop Robineau.* New York: The Metropolitan Museum of Art, 1929.

Meyer, Fred. *Sculpture in Ceramics.* New York: Watson-Guptill, 1971.

Milliken, William M. "Modern Ceramics and the Museum," *The Bulletin of the American Ceramic Society* 16 (November 1935).

—. "Ohio Ceramics," *Design* 38 (November 1937).

Miro, Marsha. "What Makes Art out of a Pottery Bowl?" *Detroit Free Press* (January 22, 1978).

"Modern Ceramics, 1934 Century of Progress Exhibition," *Design* 36 (June 1934).

Montgomery, S. J. "William Wyman," *American Ceramics* 4, no. 3 (1985).

Morgan, Robert C. "Reconstructing with Shards," *American Ceramics* 2, no. 1 (1983).

Morse, Barbara White. "Low Art Tiles," *Spinning Wheel* 25 (March 1969).

Morse Sidney. *The Siege of University City: The Dreyfus Case in America.* Saint Louis: University City Publishing, 1912.

Mosley Linda. *Contemporary Ceramics of Missouri: 1978–1979.* Charles, Mo.: Hendren Gallery, Lindenwood College, 1979.

Mourey, Gabriel. "The Potter's Art with Especial Reference to the Work of Auguste Delaherche," *The Studio* 12 (1898).

Mowry, L. "Ceramic Guild at Mills," *Design* 48 (December 1946).

Muchnic, Suzanne. "Curios from the Home Folk," *Los Angeles Times* (April 16, 1978).

—. "Reviews: Chris Staley/Beatrice Wood," *Los Angeles Times* (May 17, 1985).

—. The Art Galleries: Elaine Carhartt," *Los Angeles Times* (November 29, 1985).

—. "Reviews: Lysohir," *Los Angeles Times* (July 15, 1986).

Murphy, Terri. "Jeff Oestreich: Potter," *Ceramics Monthly* 29 (September 1986).

"Museum Clay at Everson," *Craft Horizons* 36 (April 1976).

Museum of Contemporary Art, Chicago. *David Gilhooly.* Chicago: Museum of Contemporary Art, 1976.

Museum of Contemporary Crafts, New York. *Craft Forms from the Earth: 1000 Years of Pottery in America.* New York: Museum of Contemporary Crafts, 1961.

—. *Clayworks: 20 Americans.* New York: Museum of Contemporary Crafts, 1971.

—. *Baroque '74.* New York: Museum of Contemporary Crafts. 1974.

—. *Young Americans: Clay/Glass.* New York: American Craft Council, 1978.

The Museum of Modern Art, New York. *Peter Voulkos.* New York: The Museum of Modern Art, 1960.

Nakamura, Kimpei. *Art and/or Craft: USA & Japan.* Kanazawa, Japan: n.p., 1982.

Nakian, Reuben. "Apprentice to the Gods," *Studio Potter* 14 (December 1985).

Nasisse, Andy. "The Ceramic Vessel as Metaphor," *New Art Examiner* (January 1976).

—. "The Battleground of Eros: Akio Takamori," *American Ceramics* 5, no.1 (1986).

"National Arts Club Exhibition of Porcelain and Pottery at the Pan American," *Keramik Studio* 3 (November 1901).

Natzler, Otto. "The Natzler Glazes," *Craft Horizons* 24 (July 1964).

—. *Gertrud and Otto Natzler Ceramics: Collection of Mrs. Leonard M. Sperry.* Los Angeles: Los Angeles County Museum of Art, 1968.

Naumann, Francis. "Drawings of Beatrice Wood," *Arts Magazine* (March 1983).

Nelson, G. *Ceramics: A Potter's Handbook.* New York: Holt, Rinehart & Winston, 1977.

Nelson, Marion John. "Art Nouveau in American Ceramics," *The Art Quarterly* 26, no. 4 (1963).

—. "Indigenous Characteristics in American Art Pottery," *Antiques* 89 (June 1966).

Neuwirth, Waltraud. *Wiener Keramik.* Brunswick, W. Germany: Klinkhardt & Bierman, 1975.

"New Designs for Mass Production: Four Sets of Tableware...by V. Schreckengost," *Design* 37 (November 1935).

"New York Reviews: Robert Arneson," *ARTnews* 74 (April 1975).

Newton, Clara Chipman. "The Early Days of Rookwood Pottery," *The Bulletin of the American Ceramic Society* 18 (November 1939).

—. "The Cincinnati Pottery Club," *The Bulletin of the American Ceramic Society* 19 (September 1940).

Nicholas, Donna. "The Ceramic Nationals at Syracuse," *Craft Horizons* 32 (December 1972).

Nichols, George Ward. *Pottery, How It Is Made...: Instructions for Painting on Porcelain and Pottery....* New York: G. P. Putnam's Sons, 1878.

Nin, Anaïs. "Beatrice Wood," *Artforum* (January 1965).

Nina Freudenheim Gallery. *Margie Hughto: Clay and Paper Works 1978–1979.* Buffalo, N.Y.: Nina Freudenheim Gallery, 1979.

Nordland, Gerald. "John Mason," *Craft Horizons* 20 (May 1960).

—. *Richard DeVore.* Chicago: Exhibit A, 1981.

—. *Richard DeVore: 1972–1982.* Milwaukee: Milwaukee Art Museum, 1983.

Nordness, Lee. *Objects: USA.* New York: The Viking Press, 1970.

—. "Jack Earl," *American Ceramics* 4, no. 1 (1985).

—. *Jack Earl—The Genesis and Triumphant Survival of an Underground Ohio Artist.* Racine, Wis.: Perimeter Press, 1985.

Nordstrom, Sherry C. "Getting Their Hands In," *Syracuse Guide* (February 1978).

Normark, Don. "Ceramics and Robert Sperry," *Craft Horizons* 22 (January 1962).

Norton, Deborah. "Frans Wildenhain," *American Ceramics* 4, no. 2 (1985).

Norwood, John Nelson. *Fifty Years of Ceramic Education at State College of Ceramics, Alfred.* Alfred, N.Y.: Alfred University, 1950.

Nos, Gnosis. "Stay with Your Numbers: A Story about Robert Brady," *American Ceramics* 4, no. 2 (1985).

—. "Crossing the Boundaries of Intimacy," *American Ceramics* 5, no. 2 (1986).

Oestreich, Jeff. "Some Thoughts on Studio Pottery," *Ceramics Monthly* 31 (October 1983).

Ohio State University. *Beaux-Arts Designer.* Columbus, Ohio: Ohio State University, 1977.

Ohr, George E. "Some Facts in the History of a Unique Personality," *Crockery and Glass Journal* 54 (December 1901).

Okazaki, Arthur. "Marilyn Lysohir," *American Ceramics* 4, no. 1 (1985).

Olmsted, Anna Wetherill. "The Ceramic National Founded in Memory of Adelaide Alsop Robineau." Manuscript, Everson Museum of Art, Syracuse, N.Y., n.d.

—. "The Memorial Collection of Robineau Porcelains," *Design* 33 (1931).

—. "First Annual Robineau Memorial Ceramic Exhibition," *Design* 34 (June 1932).

—. *Contemporary American Ceramics.* Syracuse, N.Y.: Syracuse Museum of Fine Arts, 1937.

—. "American Ceramic Sculpture to the Fore," *American Artist* 11 (January 1947).

Olson, J. Bennett. "Exhibitions: Soldner, Mason, Rothman," *Craft Horizons* 17 (September 1957).

Ormond, Suzanne, and Mary E. Irvine. *Louisiana's Art Nouveau: The Crafts of the Newcomb Style.* Gretna, La.: Pelican Publishing, 1976.

Paris, Harold. "Sweet Land of Funk," *Art in America* 30 (March 1967).

Parks, Dennis. "Paul Soldner," *Craft Horizons* 36 (January 1976).

Parks, Linda Dunne. *Cranbrook Ceramics 1950–1980.* Bloomfield Hills, Mich.: Cranbrook Academy of Art, 1983.

Parry, William. *William Daley: Selected Works 1954–1982.* Boston: Massachusetts College of Art, 1981.

Pear, Lillian Myers. *The Pewabic Pottery: A History of Its Products and People.* Des Moines: Wallace-Homestead Book Co., 1976.

Peck, Herbert. "The Amateur Antecedents of Rookwood Pottery," *Cincinnati Historical Society Bulletin* 26 (October 1968).

—. *The Book of Rookwood Pottery.* New York: Crown, 1968.

—. "Rookwood Pottery and Foreign Museum Collections," *American Connoisseur* 178 (September 1969).

—. "Some Early Collections of Rookwood Pottery," *Auction* (September 1969).

Peck, Margaret. *Catalog of Rookwood Art Pottery Shapes.* New York: Kingston, 1971.

Peeler, Richard. "Clay," *Craft Horizons* 34 (December 1974).

Penny, Janice. "The Natzlers, Masters of Ceramic Art," *American Artist* 14 (March 1950).

Perreault, John. "Robert Arneson," *Soho News* (March 6, 1974).

—. "This Price Is Right," *Soho News* (October 8, 1980).

—. "No Reservations," *Soho News* (October 22, 1980).

—. "Clay Feats," *Soho News* (March 5, 1980).

—. "Pattern of Exchange," *Soho News* (March 9, 1982).

—. "Fear of Clay," *Artforum* 21 (April 1982).

—. "Either Ohr," *The Village Voice* (March 5, 1985).

Perrone, Jeff. "Robert Arneson," *Artforum* 16 (September 1977).

—. "Porcelain and Pop," *Arts Magazine* 58 (March 1984).

—. "Some Sherds on Ceramics," in *Surface/Function/Shapes: Selections from the Earl Millard Collection.* Edwardsville, Ill.: Southern Illinois University, 1985.

—. *The Ceramics of Betty Woodman.* Reading, Pa.: Freedman Gallery, Albright College, 1986.

—, and Peter Schjeldahl. *Adrian Saxe.* Kansas City, Mo.: Art Gallery, University of Missouri, 1987.

Perry, Barbara. "The Figure Emerges: American Clay Sculpture 1925–1950," *American Ceramics* 3, no. 1 (1984).

—. *American Ceramics Now: The Twenty-Seventh Ceramic National.* Syracuse, N.Y.: Everson Museum of Art, 1987.

Perry, Mary Chase. "Decorative Pottery of Cincinnati," *Harper's New Monthly Magazine* 62 (April 1881).

—. "The Work of Cincinnati Women in Decorated Pottery," in *Art and Handicraft...Woman's Building...Chicago,* Chicago: n.p., 1894.

—. "Grueby Potteries," *Keramik Studio* 2 (1900).

—. "Grueby Potteries," *Keramik Studio* 4 (1902).

Peterson, Susan. "Antonio Prieto 1912–1967," *Craft Horizons* 27 (July 1967).

—. "Glen Lukens 1887–1967," *Craft Horizons* 28 (March 1968).

—. "Wayne Higby," *Craft Horizons* 33 (June 1973).

—. "The Ceramics of Marilyn Levine," *Craft Horizons* 37 (February 1977).

—. *The Living Traditions of Maria Martinez.* Tokyo: Kodansha International, 1977.

Petterson, Richard B. *Ceramic Art in America.* Columbus, Ohio: Professional Publications, 1969.

—. "Marguerite Wildenhain," *Ceramics Monthly* 25 (March 1977).

—. "Timeless Vessels: The Porcelains of Laura Andreson," *American Craft* 42 (August 1982).

Phillips, Lisa, ed. *High Styles: Twentieth-Century American Design.* New York: Whitney Museum of American Art, 1985.

Pierre, Jose. "Funk Art," *L'Oeil* 190 (October 1970).

Pile, John. "High Styles," *American Craft* 45 (December 1985).

Pincus, Robert L. "Reviews: John and Andrea Gill," *Los Angeles Times* (July 8, 1986).

Plagens, Peter. *Sunshine Muse.* New York: Praeger, 1974.

Plumb, Helen. "The Pewabic Pottery," *Art and Progress* 2 (January 1911).

Poesch, Jessie. *Newcomb Pottery: An Enterprise for Southern Women, 1895–1940.* Exton, Pa.: Schiffer Publishing, 1984.

—. *Newcomb Pottery: An Enterprise for Southern Women, 1895–1940.* Washington, D.C.: Smithsonian Traveling Exhibition Services, 1984.

Polley, Elizabeth M. "Robert Arneson," *Artforum* 2 (January 1964).

Pomeroy, Ralph. "Breschi and the Beasts," *Art and Artists* 7 (November 1973).

Poor, Henry Varnum. "Ceramic Exhibition," *Baltimore Museum News* 12 (November 1948).

—. *Twentieth Ceramic International.* Syracuse, N.Y.: Syracuse Museum of Fine Arts, 1958.

—. *A Book of Pottery: From Mud to Immortality.* Englewood Cliffs, N.J.: Prentice-Hall, 1958.

"Pots and Pans by Students of Lukens at the University of Southern California," *Magazine of Art* 36 (November 1943).

"A Potter Called DeVore," *Cranbrook Magazine* (September 1972).

"Pottery of Sam Haile," *Architectural Forum* 90 (March 1949).

Preaud, Tamara, and Serge Gauthier. *Ceramics of the 20th Century.* New York: Rizzoli, 1982.

Press, Nancy, and Terry F. A. Weihs. *Marguerite Wildenhain: A Retrospective Exhibition of the Work of a Master Potter.* Ithaca, N.Y.: Herbert F. Johnson Museum of Art, Cornell University 1980.

Priest, Ellen. "Arnold Zimmerman," *American Ceramics* 2, no. 3 (1983).

"Professor Charles F. Binns," *Design* 36 (January 1935).

Prokopoff, Stephen, and Suzanne Foley. *Robert Arneson—Retrospective.* Chicago: Museum of Contemporary Art, 1974.

Prothro, Hunt. "Sustained Presence: Marguerite Wildenhain," *American Craft* 40 (August 1986).

Pugliese, Joseph. "Ceramics from Davis," *Craft Horizons* 26 (November/December 1966).

—. "The Decade," *Craft Horizons* 35 (February 1975).

—. *Richard Shaw: Illusionism in Clay 1971–1985.* San Francisco: Braunstein Gallery, 1985.

Purviance, Louise. *Weller Art Pottery in Color.* Des Moines: Wallace-Homestead Book Co., 1971.

—, et al. *Roseville Art Pottery in Color.* Des Moines: Wallace-Homestead Book Co., 1968.

Pyron, Bernard. "From Pottery to Amateur Science: Clayton Bailey's Digs." Manuscript, Institute for Ceramic History, Los Angeles, n.d.

—. "The Tao and Dada of Recent American Ceramic Art," *Artforum* (March 1984).

Randall, Ruth Hunie. "Ceramics by Edwin and Mary Scheier," *Rhode Island School of Design Bulletin* 4 (January 1946).

—. "Potter Looks at Scheier Pottery," *Design* 47 (January 1946).

—. *Ceramic Sculpture.* New York: Watson-Guptill, 1948.

Raven, Arlene, and Susan Rennie. "Interview with Judy Chicago," *Chrysalis* 1, no. 4 (1978).

Rawson, Jonathan A., Jr. "Recent American Pottery," *House Beautiful* 31 (April 1912).

Rawson, Philip. *Ceramics: The Appreciation of the Arts,* 2nd ed. Philadelphia: University of Pennsylvania Press, 1984.

—. "Ceramic Echoes," *Ceramic Arts* 1, no. 2 (1984).

—. "The Vessel as Center," *American Ceramics* 3, no. 4 (1985).

Raynor, Vivian. "Art: Ceramics Caricatures by Robert Arneson," *The New York Times* (May 8, 1981).

Read, Helen Appleton. "Metropolitan Museum Opens Current Season with Fine Display of Ceramics," *Brooklyn Daily Eagle* (October 14, 1928).

Reed, Cleota Gabriel. *The Arts and Crafts Ideal: The Ward House.* Syracuse, N.Y., Institute for the Development of Evolutionary Architecture, 1978.

—. "Henry Chapman Mercer and the Moravian Pottery," in *Transactions of the Ceramics Symposium 1979,* ed. Garth Clark. Los Angeles: Institute for Ceramic History, 1980.

—. "Henry Chapman Mercer: Moravian Pottery and Tileworks," *American Ceramics* 4, no. 3 (1985).

—. *Henry Chapman Mercer and the Moravian Pottery and Tile Works.* Philadelphia: University of Pennsylvania Press, 1987.

Reeve, John. "Warren MacKenzie and the Straight Pot," *Craft Horizons* 36 (June 1976).

Reif, Rita. "American Art Pottery—A Craft Tradition," *The New York Times* (March 26, 1978).

—. "Rediscovering a Potter," *The New York Times* (February 24, 1985).

Renwick Gallery, National Collection of Fine Arts, *Form and Fire: Natzler Ceramics 1938–1972*. Washington, D.C.: Smithsonian Institution Press, 1973.

—. *Crafts-Multiples*. Washington, D.C.: Smithsonian Institution Press, 1975.

Reuter, Laurel. "The Dinner Party: A Personal Response," *Shards Newsletter* 1, no. 2 (1980).

Rhead, Frederick H. "Some Dutch Pottery," *The Artist* 24 (January 1899).

—. "America as a Ceramic Art Center," *Fine Arts Journal* 23 (April 1910).

—. *Studio Pottery*. University City, Mo.: People's University Press, 1910.

—. "Planning and Operating a Studio Pottery," *The Potter* 1 (1917).

—. "Adelaide Alsop Robineau—Maker of Porcelains," *The Potter* (February 1917).

—. "What the Industries Want from the Ceramic Artist," *The Bulletin of the American Ceramic Society* 5 (1925).

—. "Advances in Decorative Arts as Applied to Ceramics," *Pottery, Glass and Brass Salesman* 62 (1930).

—. "Dinnerware Style and Decoration," *Crockery and Glass Journal* 118 (1936).

Rhodes, Daniel. *Clay and Glazes for the Potter*. Philadelphia: Chilton, 1957.

—. "Robert Turner," *Craft Horizons* 17 (May 1957).

—. *Stoneware and Porcelain: The Art of High-Fired Pottery*. Philadelphia: Chilton, 1959.

—. *Kilns: Design, Construction and Operation*. Philadelphia: Chilton, 1968.

—. "The Potter and His Kiln," *Craft Horizons* 28 (March 1969).

—. *Tamba Pottery: The Timeless Art of a Japanese Village*. Tokyo: Kodansha International, 1970.

—. *Pottery Form*. Radnor, Pa.: Chilton, 1976.

—. "David Shaner," *American Craft* 43 (February 1983).

Richards, Agnes Gertrude. "Important Exhibition of American Ceramics," *Fine Arts Journal* 33 (1915).

Richards, Charles R. "The International Ceramic Exhibition," *Creative Art* 3 (1928).

Richards, M. C. "Dan Rhodes," *Craft Horizons* 18 (September 1958).

—. "Frans Wildenhain," *Craft Horizons* 35 (February 1975).

—. "Black Mountain College: A Golden Seed," *Craft Horizons* 37 (June 1977).

Richardson, Brenda. "California Ceramics," *Art in America* 51 (May 1969).

Rico, Diana. "Laura Andreson," *American Ceramics* 3, no. 2 (1984).

Riegger, Harold Eaton. *Raku: Art and Technique*. New York: Van Nostrand Reinhold, 1970.

—. *Primitive Pottery*. New York: Van Nostrand Reinhold, 1972.

Ripley, L. A. "When Mantle Fell on New Dean of Artists," *Cincinnati Times-Star* (December 4, 1933).

Robbins, Carl. "Cowan of Cleveland, Follower of an Ancient Craft," *Cleveland Bystander* (September 7, 1929).

"Robert Rauschenberg Ceramics," *Ceramics Monthly* 31 (May 1983).

Robertson, Seonaid. "Karen Karnes," *Ceramic Review* (March 1978).

Robineau, Adelaide A. "Editorial," *Keramik Studio* 1, no. 1 (1899).

—. "Mary Chase Perry—the Potter," *Keramik Studio* 6, no. 10 (1905).

—. "Ceramics at the Paris Exposition" [a series of ten articles], *Design* 27–28 (December 1925).

Robineau, Samuel. "The Robineau Porcelains," *Keramik Studio* 12 (1911).

—. "Adelaide Alsop Robineau," *Design* 30 (April 1929).

Rochester Institute of Technology. *Frans Wildenhain*. Rochester, N.Y.: Rochester Institute of Technology, 1975.

Romberg, Jim, ed. *The Studio Potter: A Question of Quality*. Sun Valley, Idaho: Sun Valley Center for the Arts, 1979.

Rose, Muriel. *Artist Potters in England*. London: Faber & Faber, 1955.

Rosenberg, Harold. "Reality Again," in *Super Realism*, ed. Gregory Battcock. New York: Dutton Paperbacks, 1975.

Rubenfeld, Florence. *Paint on Clay*. Sheboygan, Wis.: John Michael Kohler Arts Center, 1981.

—. "Otto Natzler: Solo," *American Craft* 42 (February 1982).

—. "Pottery of Richard DeVore," *American Craft* 43 (August 1983).

Rubin, Michael G. "Paul Soldner," *American Ceramics* 1, no. 4 (1982).

—. "Kenneth Ferguson," *American Ceramics* 2, no. 3 (1983).

—. *Architectural Ceramics: 8 Concepts*. Saint Louis: Gallery of Art, Washington University, 1985.

Ruff, Dale. "Clay Roots and Routes," *American Ceramics* 1, no. 3 (1982).

Ruge, Clara. "Amerikanische Keramik," *Dekorative Kunst* (January 1906).

—. "American Ceramics—A Brief Review of Progress," *International Studio* 28 (March 1906).

"Russell Barnett Aitken," *Milwaukee Art Institute Bulletin* 10 (February 1936).

Russell, Arthur. "Grueby Pottery," *House Beautiful* 5 (December 1898).

Russell, John. "Art: Household Objects Don Mysterious Disguises," *The New York Times* (December 18, 1981).

—. "Andrew Lord," *The New York Times* (April 20, 1984).

Sachs, Sid. "Rudolf Staffel: Past and Present," *American Ceramics* 1, no. 1 (1982).

—. "Mark Burns: Saints and Sinners," *American Ceramics* 3, no. 1 (1984).

Sanders, Herbert H. *Glazes for Special Effects*. New York: Watson-Guptill, 1974.

—, and K. Tomimoto. *The World of Japanese Ceramics: Historical and Modern Techniques*. Tokyo: Kodansha International, 1967.

Sandy, Stephen. *Jane Ford: Recent Work*. Syracuse, N.Y.: Everson Museum of Art, 1979.

—. "Ceramics and the Art of Jane Ford," *Bennington Review* (January 1980).

Sargent, Irene. "Potters and Their Products," *Craftsmen* 4 (August 1903).

—. "Chinese Pots and Modern Faience," *Craftsman* 4 (September 1903).

—. "Taxile Doat," *Keramik Studio* 8 (December 1906).

Saunier, Charles. "Poteries de la Cie Grueby," *L'Art Décoratif* (August 1901).

Sawin, Martica. "The Sculpture of Mary Frank," *Arts Magazine* 51 (March 1977).

Scherma, George W. "R. Guy Cowan and His Associates," in *Transactions of the Ceramics Symposium 1979*, ed. Garth Clark. Los Angeles: Institute for Ceramic History, 1980.

Schimmel, Paul. "Conversation Pieces: The Cups of Irv Tepper," *American Ceramics* 3, no. 2 (1984).

—. *Irv Tepper.* Newport Beach, Calif.: Newport Harbor Art Museum, 1984.

Schjeldahl, Peter. "Robert Arneson," *ARTnews* 65 (June 1966).

—. "The Playful Improvisations of West Coast Ceramic Art," *The New York Times* (June 9, 1974).

—. *Robert Hudson.* Philadelphia: Moore College of Art Galleries, 1977.

—. "Ken Price: Los Angeles County Museum," *Artforum* 17 (November 1978).

—. "California Goes to Pot," *The Village Voice* (December 23, 1981).

—. "The Smart Pot: Adrian Saxe and Post-Everything Ceramics," in *Adrian Saxe.* Kansas City, Mo.: Gallery of Art, University of Missouri, 1987.

Schlanger, Jeff. "Ceramics and Pop—Roy Lichtenstein,"*Craft Horizons* 26 (January 1966).

—. "Roy Lichtenstein," *Craft Horizons* 26 (March 1966).

—. "Ceramics and Photography," *Craft Horizons* 27 (January 1967).

—. "Maija Grotell," *Craft Horizons* 29 (November 1969).

Schmidt, James Ropiequet. *Figurative Clay '87.* Edwardsville, Ill.: Southern Illinois University, 1987.

Schneider, Norris F. *Zanesville Art Pottery.* Zanesville, Ohio: Zanesville Art Pottery, 1963.

Schwartz, Fred R. "Exhibitions," *Craft Horizons* 28 (January 1968).

Schwartz, Judith S. "Tureens. Soup's In," *Craft Horizons* 36 (April 1976).

—. *Karen Karnes: Works 1964–1977.* New York: Hadler/Rodriquez Gallery, 1977.

—. *Contemporary American Ceramic Sculpture: Satire in Selected Works of Robert Arneson, David Gilhooly, and Howard Kottler.* Ann Arbor, Mich.: University Microfilm International, 1983.

—. "Directions/Clay," *American Craft* 44 (August 1984).

Schwartz, M. D., and R. A. Wolfe. *A History of American Art Porcelain.* New York: Renaissance Editions, 1967.

Scripps College. *Second Bi-Annual Ceramic Exhibition.* Claremont, Calif.: Scripps College, 1947.

Selz, Peter. *Funk Art.* Berkeley, Calif.: University Art Museum, University of California, 1967.

Senska, Frances. "Rudy Autio," *Montana Institute of the Arts Quarterly* (Spring 1954).

—. "Pottery in a Brickyard," *American Craft* 42 (February 1982).

Sewalt, Charlotte. "An Interview with Ken Ferguson," *Ceramics Monthly* 26 (February 1978).

Sewter, A. C. "T. S. Haile, Potter and Painter," *Apollo* 44 (December 1946).

—. *The Surrealist Paintings and Drawings of Sam Haile.* Manchester, England: City Art Gallery, 1967.

Shadbolt, Doris. "The Transparency of Clay," *Ceramics Monthly* 34 (February 1986).

Shafer, Tom. "John Glick," *Ceramics Monthly* 20 (September 1972).

Shannon, Mark. "Michael Lucero: The Unnatural Science of Dreams," *American Ceramics* 5, no. 2 (1986).

Shapiro, H. Y. "I Love You Bob Turner," *Craft Horizons* 32 (August 1972).

Shaw, Richard. "Beyond the Barriers of Tradition," in *Overglaze Imagery.* Fullerton, Calif.: Art Gallery, California State University, 1977.

Sheerer, Mary G. "Newcomb Pottery," *Keramik Studio* 1 (1899).

—. "The Development of the Decorative Processes at Newcomb," *American Ceramic Society Journal* 7 (August 1924).

—, and Paul E. Cox. "Newcomb Pottery," *American Ceramic Society Journal* 1 (August 1918).

Shuebrook, R. "Regina Funk," *Art and Artists* 38 (August 1973).

Silver, Jonathan. "Elie Nadelman: A Single Notion of Style," *ARTnews* 74 (November 1975).

Silverthorne, Jeanne. "Daisy Youngblood," *Artforum* (April 1984).

Simon, Joan. "An Interview with Ken Price," *Art in America* 68 (January 1980).

Sims, Patterson. "Viola Frey at the Whitney," *Ceramics Monthly* 32 (November 1984).

Siple, Ella S. "The International Exhibition of Ceramic Art," *American Magazine of Art* 19 (1928).

Slivka, Rose. "Peter Voulkos at Bonnier's," *Craft Horizons* 19 (April 1957).

—. "The New Ceramic Presence," *Craft Horizons* 21 (July/August 1961).

—. "Laugh-In in Clay," *Craft Horizons* 31 (October 1971).

—. "The New Clay Drawings of Peter Voulkos," *Craft Horizons* 34 (October 1974).

—. *The Object as Poet.* Washington, D.C.: Smithsonian Institution Press, 1977.

—. *Peter Voulkos: A Dialogue with Clay.* Greenwich, Conn.: New York Graphic Society, 1978.

—. *West Coast Ceramics.* Amsterdam: Stedelijk Museum, 1979.

—. "Richard Shaw at Frumkin," *Art in America* 69 (February 1981).

Sloane, W. J. "American Ceramics," *ARTnews* 30 (November 14, 1931).

Smith, Dido. "Karen Karnes," *Craft Horizons* 18, no. 3 (May 1958).

Smith, Gary. *Daniel Rhodes: The California Years.* Santa Cruz, Calif.: Art Museum of Santa Cruz County, 1986.

Smith, Kenneth E. "Laura Anne Fry: Originator of Atomizing Process for... Underglaze Color," *The Bulletin of the American Ceramic Society* 17 (1938).

—. "The Origin, Development and Present Status of Newcomb Pottery," *The Bulletin of the American Ceramic Society* 17 (1938).

—. "Ceramics at Newcomb College," *Design* 46 (December 1944).

Smith, R. H. Soden. *Reports on the Philadelphia International Exhibition of 1876.* London, 1877.

Smith, Roberta. "Simple Pleasures," *The Village Voice* (December 16, 1981).

Smith, Tobi. "Clayworks in Progress," Los Angeles Institute of Contemporary Art *Journal* (November 1975).

Smith, Walter, and Joseph M. Wilson. *The Masterpieces of the Centennial International Exposition.* Philadelphia: Gebbie & Barrie, 1876.

Society for Art in Craft. *Mark Burns—A Decade in Pennsylvania: 1975–1985.* Verona, Pa.: Society for Art in Craft, 1985.

Soldner, Paul E. "Raku as I Know It," *Ceramic Review* (April 1973).

—. "The Personal Mark," *Studio Potter* 14 (December 1985).

—, and Peter Voulkos. "Ceramics West Coast," *Craft Horizons* 26 (July 1966).

"Some New Designs and Methods in Rookwood and Grueby Faience," *The Paris Exhibition,* in *The Art Journal,* special extra number (June 1900, pt. 2). London: H. Virtue, 1900.

Speed Art Museum. *What's New? American Ceramics Since 1980: The Alfred and Mary Shands Collection.* Louisville, Ky.: J. B. Speed Art Museum, 1987.

Speight, Charlotte. *Hands in Clay.* Sherman Oaks, Calif.: Alfred Publishing Company, 1979.

—. *Images in Clay Sculpture: Historical and Contemporary Techniques.* New York: Harper & Row, 1983.

Sperry, Robert. "Recording the Gesture," *Studio Potter* 14 (December 1985).

Spiegel, Janet. "A Dinner with Mama to the Dadas," *Los Angeles Times* (September 25, 1983).

Steigleder, Linda. *Checklist of Marks and Supplementary Information: A Century of Ceramics in the United States.* Syracuse, N.Y.: Everson Museum of Art, 1979.

—. "Henry Varnum Poor: The Effect of the Hudson River Valley," *Studio Potter* 12 (December 1983).

—. "Ceramics and Design," in *Henry Varnum Poor 1887–1970,* by Harold E. Dickson and Richard Porter. University Park, Pa.: Museum of Art, Pennsylvania State University, 1983.

—. "Henry Varnum Poor 1887–1970," *American Craft* 44 (February 1984).

Steinbaum, Bernice. *Elders of the Tribe.* New York: Bernice Steinbaum Gallery, 1986.

Stevens, Mark. "Guess Who's Coming to Dinner," *Newsweek* (April 2, 1979).

Stewart, Lewis W. "Breaking the Bone Barrier," *Pacific Sun* (November 1975).

Stiles, Helen E. *Pottery in the United States.* New York: E. P. Dutton, 1941.

Stone, D. J. "Robert Arneson," *Arts Magazine* 39 (January 1965).

"Stoneware Vases of Charles Fergus Binns," *The Bulletin of the American Ceramic Society* 15 (July 1935).

Storer, Maria Longworth (Nichols). *History of the Cincinnati Musical Festivals and of the Rookwood Pottery.* Paris: Herbert Clark, Printer, 1919.

Storey, W. K. "The Widening Scope of Decorative Art," *The New York Times* (March 31, 1929).

Stover, Frances. "Susan Goodrich Frackelton and the China Painters," *Historical Messenger...Milwaukee County Historical Society* (March 1954).

Stradling, J. G. "American Ceramics and the Philadelphia Centennial," *Antiques* (July 1976).

Stratton, Mary Chase Perry. "Inventory of the Parker Collection." Manuscript, *Pewabic Pottery Archives* 21 (December 1937).

—. *Ceramic Processes.* Ann Arbor, Mich.: Edwards, 1941.

—. "Pewabic Records," *American Ceramic Society Bulletin* 25 (October 15, 1946).

Strong, Susan R. "The Searching Flame: Charles Fergus Binns," *American Ceramics* 1, no. 3 (1982).

—. *History of American Ceramics: An Annotated Bibliography.* Metuchen, N.J.: Scarecrow Press, 1983.

Stubblebine, James, and Martin P. Eidelberg. "Viktor Schreckengost and the Cleveland School," *Craft Horizons* 35 (June 1975).

Sturgis, Russell. "American Potters," *Scribners Magazine* 32 (1902).

—. "American Pottery, Second Paper," *Scribners Magazine* 33 (January 1903).

Supensky, Tom. "Exhibitions," *Craft Horizons* 35 (June 1975).

Swain, F. K. "Moravian Pottery and Tile Works Founded by H. C. Mercer, Doylestown, Pa.," *Antiques* 24 (November 1933).

Swan, Mabel M. "The Dedham Pottery," *Antiques* 10 (August 1926).

"Syracuse Gets Robineau Memorial Group." *Art Digest* 5 (January 15, 1931).

Syracuse Museum of Fine Arts. *Contemporary Ceramics of the Western Hemisphere.* Syracuse, N.Y.: Syracuse Museum of Fine Arts, 1941.

"T. S. Haile, Ceramist," *Craft Horizons* 9 (June 1949).

Taft, Lisa Factor. *Herman Carl Mueller: Architectural Ceramics, the Arts and Crafts Movement.* Trenton, N.J.: New Jersey State Museum, 1979.

Tanenhaus, Ruth Amdur. *Homage to the Bag.* New York: Museum of Contemporary Crafts, 1975.

Tarshis, Jerome. "Playing Around," *ARTnews* 73 (December 1974).

Taylor, William Watts. "The Rookwood Pottery," *Faenza* 3 (1915).

Tipton, Barbara. "A Century of Ceramics in the United States," *Ceramics Monthly* 27 (October 1979).

Trapp, Kenneth R. "Maria Longworth Storer...Her Bronze Objets d'Art in the Cincinnati Art Museum." Master's thesis, Tulane University, 1972.

—. "Japanese Influence in Early Rookwood Pottery," *Antiques* 103 (January 1973).

—. *Ode to Nature: Flowers and Landscapes of Rookwood Pottery 1880–1940.* New York: Jordan-Volpe Gallery, 1980.

—. "The Japanese Influence on Rookwood Pottery," in *Transactions of the Ceramics Symposium 1979,* ed. Garth Clark. Los Angeles: Institute for the History of Ceramics, 1980.

Traux, H. A. "Daniel Rhodes...Contemporary American Studio Ceramics." Ph.D. dissertation, Columbia University, 1969.

[Treacy, Eleanor.] "The Art with the Inferiority Complex," *Fortune* 16 (December 1937).

Triggs, Oscar Lovell. *Chapters in the History of the Arts and Crafts Movement.* New York: Benjamin Blom, 1971.

Troy, Jack. "Don Reitz," *Craft Horizons* 34 (October 1974).

—. "May Pots Survive Their Writers," *American Ceramics* 4, no. 2 (1985).

Tsubota, Anne. "Toshiko Takaezu," *American Ceramics* 2, no. 4 (1984).

Tuchman, Maurice. *Happy's Curios: Kenneth Price.* Los Angeles: Los Angeles County Museum of Art, 1978.

Tunis, Roslyn. *Ancient Inspirations—Contemporary Interpretations.* Binghamton, N.Y.: Roberson Center for the Arts and Sciences, 1982.

Tvrdik, Valerie. *The Unpainted Portrait: Contemporary Portraiture in Non-Traditional Media.* Sheboygan, Wis.: John Michael Kohler Art Center, 1979.

University of California, Los Angeles. *Alexander Archipenko: A Memorial Exhibition.* Los Angeles: University Art Galleries, 1967.

University of California, Santa Barbara. *Clay: The Medium and the Method.* Santa Barbara, Calif.: University Art Galleries, University of California, 1976.

University of Michigan, Slusser Gallery. *Fiber, Metal and Clay.* Ann Arbor, Michigan: Slusser Gallery, University of Michigan, 1977.

Untracht, Oppi. "Architectonics in Clay," *Craft Horizons* 16 (January 1956).

Valentine, John. "Rookwood Pottery," *House Beautiful* 4 (September 1898).

Van Burkom, Frans. *KLEI.* Amsterdam: Netherlands Art Foundation, 1981.

Verneuil, M. D. "Taxile Doat," *Art et décoration* (September 1904).

Victoria and Albert Museum. *20 American Studio Potters.* London: Victoria and Albert Museum, 1966.

—. *International Ceramics 72*. London: Victoria and Albert Museum, 1972.

"Viktor Schreckengost," *The Studio* 1 (1933).

Volkmar, Charles. "Hints on Underglaze," *Keramik Studio* 1 (May 1899).

Volpe, Todd M., and Robert W. Blasberg. "Fulper Art Pottery: Amazing Glazes," *American Art and Antiques* (July 1978).

Voorhees, John. "Discipline Leads to Quality in Sperry Exhibition," *Seattle Times* (December 4, 1969).

Walton, William. "Charles Volkmar, Potter," *International Studio* 36 (January 1909).

"War among Potters, T. J. Wheatley Secures a Patent on American Limoges," *Cincinnati Daily Gazette* (October 7, 1880).

Watson, E.W. "Waylande Gregory's Ceramic Art: Interview," *American Artist* 8 (September 1944).

Wechsler, Susan. *Low-Fire Ceramics: A New Direction in American Clay*. New York: Watson-Guptill, 1981.
—. "Ron Nagle: An Interview," *American Ceramics* 1, no. 1 (1982).
—. "Raymon Elozua," *American Ceramics* 1, no. 3 (1982).
—. *The Raw Edge: Ceramics of the 80's*. Greenvale, N.Y.: C.W. Post Center, Long Island University, 1983.
—. "Celestial Bodies—Christina Bertoni," *American Ceramics* 2, no. 2 (1983).
—. "Views on the Figure," *American Ceramics* 3, no. 1 (1984).
—. *Is Anybody Home?* Chicago: Esther Saks Gallery, 1985.

Weedon, George A. *Susan S. Frackelton & the American Arts and Crafts Movement*. Milwaukee, Wis.: Box Press, 1975.

Weidner, Ruth Irwin. "The Early Literature of Ceramics," *American Ceramics* 1, no. 4 (1982).
—. *American Ceramics before 1930: A Bibliography*. Westport, Conn.: 1982.

Weinrich, Peter H. *Bibliographic Guide to Books on Ceramics*. Toronto: Canadian Craft Council, 1976.

Weiss, Peg. *The Art Deco Environment*. Syracuse, N.Y.: Everson Museum of Art, 1976.
—. "Bernard Frazier: American Sculptor of the Plains," *Everson Museum of Art Bulletin* (March 1978).
—, ed. *Adelaide Alsop Robineau: Glory in Porcelain*. Syracuse, N.Y.: Syracuse University Press, 1981.

Wenger, Lesley. "Viola Frey," *Currant* 1 (August 1975).
—. "Special Un-Scientific Supplement," *Currant* 1 (October 1975).

Westerbeck, Colin. "Louis Sullivan's Clay Gardens," *Artforum* 25 (February 1987).

Westphal, Alice. "The Ceramics of Ruth Duckworth," *Craft Horizons* 37 (August 1977).
—. *The Ceramic Vessel as Metaphor*. Evanston, Ill.: Evanston Art Center, 1977.

Westphal, Kenneth, and Gerald Nordland. *Robert Turner*. Milwaukee, Wis.: Milwaukee Art Museum, 1986.

Whiting, Margaret C. "Charles Volkmar's Crown Point Pottery," *House Beautiful* 8 (October 1900).

Whitney Museum of American Art. *Sculptures and Drawings of Elie Nadelman 1882–1946*. New York: Whitney Museum of American Art, 1975.

Wieselthier, Vally. "Ceramics," *Design* 31 (November 1929).

Wildenhain, Marguerite. "Pottery as a Creative Craft," *Craft Horizons* 10, no. 2 (1950).
—. "An Open Letter to Bernard Leach from Marguerite Wildenhain," *Craft Horizons* 13 (May/June 1953).
—. *Pottery: Form and Expression*. New York: American Craftsmen's Council and Reinhold Corp., 1959.
—. *Invisible Core: A Potter's Life and Thoughts*. Palo Alto, Calif.: Pacific Books, 1973.

Williams, Gerry. "The Role of the Traditional Potter in Contemporary Society," in *Transactions of the Ceramics Symposium 1979*, ed. Garth Clark. Los Angeles: Institute for the History of Ceramics, 1980.

Wilson, Bess M. "Ceramist at University of Southern California Trains Instructors in Haiti," *Los Angeles Times* (October 28, 1946).

Wilson, William. "The Art Galleries: Viola Frey," *Los Angeles Times* (March 28, 1986).
—. "S.F. Exhibit: Clay...And Now Moscone," *Los Angeles Times* (April 25, 1986).
—. "Arneson the Artist," *Los Angeles Times* (January 25, 1987).

Winokur, P. "Wayne Higby," *Craft Horizons* 36 (August 1976).
—, and Robert Winokur. "The Light of Rudolph Staffel," *Crafts Horizons* 37 (April 1977).

Wise, E. B. "Adelaide Alsop Robineau—American Ceramist," *American Magazine of Art* (December 1929).

Wood, Beatrice. *I Shock Myself*. Ojai, Calif.: Dillingham Press, 1985.

Woodman, Betty, and George Woodman. "Ceramists' Odyssey of Clay: Italy," *Craft Horizons* 30 (June 1970).

Woodman, George. "Ceramic Decoration and the Concept of Ceramics as a Decorative Art," in *Transactions of the Ceramics Symposium 1979*, ed. Garth Clark. Los Angeles: Institute for the History of Ceramics, 1980.
—. "Ceramic Decoration and the Concept of Ceramics as a Decorative Art," *American Ceramics* 1, no. 1 (1982).
—. "Why (Not) Ceramics?" *New Art Examiner* 13 (September 1985).

Wortz, Melinda. *Elsa Rady: Porcelain*. Los Angeles: Elsa Rady, 1984.

Wright, Frank Lloyd. "In the Cause of Architecture: The Meaning of Materials—the Kiln," *Architectural Record* 63 (June 1928).

Yaeger. D. "Rookwood, Pioneer American Art Pottery," *American Collector* 12 (July 1943).

Young, Jenny. *The Ceramic Art: The History and Manufacture of Pottery and Porcelain*. New York: Harper, 1878.

Zack, David. "Funk Art," *Art and Artists* 2 (April 1967).
—. "California Myth Making," *Art and Artists* 4, no. 4 (July 1969).
—. "San Francisco," *ARTnews* 68 (September 1969).
—. "The Ceramics of Robert Arneson," *Craft Horizons* 30 (February 1970).
—. "Nut Art in Quake Time," *ARTnews* 69 (March 1970).
—. "California Myth Makers," *Art and Artists* 4 (March 1970).
—. "Saga of Clayton Bailey: Beyond Criticism and the Nose-Pot Aesthetic," *Arts in Society* 7 (April 1970).
—. *Nut Pot or Art Without Tears?* Davis, Calif.: The Art Center of the World, 1971.
—. "An Authentik and Historikal Discourse on the Phenomenon of Mail Art," *Art in America* 61 (January 1973).

Zimmer, William. "New Figure on the Horizon," *American Ceramics* 1, no. 1 (1982).
—. "Arthur Gonzalez: Of Melodramas, Movie Stars and Modern Times," *American Ceramics* 4, no. 1 (1985).

Zwinger, S. "Rick Dillingham," *American Ceramics* 3, no. 1 (1984).

PHOTOGRAPHY
CREDITS